Philosophy and the Contemporary World

The Mercersburg Theology Study Series
Volume 11

The Mercersburg Theology Study Series presents attractive, readable, scholarly modern editions of the key writings of the nineteenth-century theological movement led by Philip Schaff and John Nevin. It aims to introduce the academic community and the broader public more fully to Mercersburg's unique blend of American and European, and Reformed and Catholic theology.

Founding Editor
W. Bradford Littlejohn

Series Editors
Lee C. Barrett
David W. Layman

Published Volumes

1. *The Mystical Presence and the Doctrine of the Reformed Church on the Lord's Supper*
Edited by Linden J. DeBie

2. *Coena Mystica: Debating Reformed Eucharistic Theology*
Edited by Linden J. DeBie

3. *The Development of the Church*
Edited by David R. Bains and Theodore Louis Trost

4. *The Incarnate Word: Selected Writings on Christology*
Edited by William B. Evans

5. *One, Holy, Catholic, and Apostolic: John Nevin's Writings on Ecclesiology (1844–1849): Tome One*
Edited by Sam Hamstra Jr.

6. *Born of Water and the Spirit: Essays on the Sacraments and Christian Formation*
Edited by David W. Layman

7. *One, Holy, Catholic, and Apostolic: John Nevin's Writings on Ecclesiology (1851–1858): Tome Two*
Edited by Sam Hamstra Jr.

8. *The Early Creeds: The Mercersburg Theologians Appropriate the Creedal Heritage*
Edited by Charles Yrigoyen and Lee C. Barrett

9. *Christocentric Reformed Theology in Nineteenth-Century America: Key Writings of Emanuel Gerhart*
Edited by Annette G. Aubert

10. *The Heidelberg Catechism: The Mercersburg Understanding of the German Reformed Tradition*
Edited by Lee C. Barrett

Philosophy and the Contemporary World

Mercersburg, Culture, and the Church

By
JOHN WILLIAMSON NEVIN

Edited by
Adam S. Borneman and Patrick Carey

General Editor
David W. Layman

Foreword by
David R. Bains

WIPF & STOCK · Eugene, Oregon

PHILOSOPHY AND THE CONTEMPORARY WORLD
Mercersburg, Culture, and the Church

Mercersburg Theology Study Series 11

Copyright © 2024 Wipf and Stock Publishers. All rights reserved. Except for brief quotations in critical publications or reviews, no part of this book may be reproduced in any manner without prior written permission from the publisher. Write: Permissions, Wipf and Stock Publishers, 199 W. 8th Ave., Suite 3, Eugene, OR 97401.

Wipf & Stock
An Imprint of Wipf and Stock Publishers
199 W. 8th Ave., Suite 3
Eugene, OR 97401

www.wipfandstock.com

PAPERBACK ISBN: 978-1-6667-6271-6
HARDCOVER ISBN: 978-1-6667-6272-3
EBOOK ISBN: 978-1-6667-6273-0

01/04/24

Contents

Foreword by David R. Bains | vii
Editorial Approach and Acknowledgments | xi
Contributors | xv
Abbreviations | xvii

Part 1: Culture, Philosophy, Ethics, Anthropology
Edited by Adam S. Borneman

General Introduction, Part 1 | 3

Document 1: "The Year 1848" | 18
   Editor's Introduction
   The Year 1848 | 22

Document 2: *Human Freedom and a Plea for Philosophy* | 49
   Editor's Introduction
   Human Freedom | 54
   A Plea for Philosophy | 75

Document 3: "The Moral Order of Sex" | 95
   Editor's Introduction
   The Moral Order of Sex | 98

Document 4: "The Wonderful Nature of Man" | 120
   Editor's Introduction
   The Wonderful Nature of Man | 123

Document 5: "Our Relations To Germany" | 138
   Editor's Introduction
   Our Relations to Germany | 141

Document 6: "The Church Year" | 147
   Editor's Introduction
   The Church Year | 150

Part 2: The Church Question and Supernaturalism
Edited by Patrick Carey

General Introduction, Part 2 | 169

Document 7: "Brownson's Quarterly Review" | 193
    Editor's Introduction
    Brownson's Quarterly Review | 198

Document 8: "Brownson's Review Again" | 244
    Editor's Introduction
    Brownson's Review Again | 248

Document 9: "The Anglican Crisis" | 265
    Editor's Introduction
    The Anglican Crisis | 269

Document 10: "Evangelical Radicalism" | 307
    Editor's Introduction
    Evangelical Radicalism | 310

Document 11: "Man's True Destiny" | 315
    Editor's Introduction
    Man's True Destiny | 320

Document 12: "Natural and Supernatural" | 346
    Editor's Introduction
    Natural And Supernatural | 350

Bibliography | 377
Index | 395

Foreword

John Williamson Nevin is perhaps best known for his early works against "new measures" revivalism (*The Anxious Bench* [1843]) and advancing a more sacramental understanding of the Lord's supper (*The Mystical Presence* [1846]). Even so, in the pages of *The Mercersburg Review* (founded in 1849) he addressed many developments in church and culture, always from the distinctive perspective of the Mercersburg Theology grounded in the philosophical idealism, organic development, and communal unity.

In this eleventh volume of the Mercersburg Theological Study Series, Adam Borneman and Patrick Carey present twelve essays Nevin published between 1849 and 1867. At the time of the first, Nevin was still living in Mercersburg, Pennsylvania, and serving on the faculty of the Theological Seminary of the German Reformed Church and as president of Marshall College. By 1854 he had overseen the college's move to Lancaster where it had merged with Franklin College, and had resigned both of his positions. He moved from Mercersburg, first to Carlisle and then later closer to Lancaster.

Amid these moves his concerns about rationalism and sectarianism and his orientation to idealism and organic unity remained constant. The six essays in Part 1 are edited by Adam Borneman, author of a study of the social and political dimensions of Nevin's theology of the incarnation. They address the revolutions of 1848, responsible democratic engagement, gender roles, the relation of the theology of an immigrant church to that of its homeland, and the growing popularity of the church year. The six essays in Part 2 are edited by Patrick Carey, a distinguished historian of nineteenth-century American Catholicism, particularly the career of Orestes Brownson. In these essays Nevin considered the nature and constitution of the church, which his contemporaries called simply "the church question." Here he engages at length with two of his most notable contemporaries in American theology, Orestes Brownson and Horace Bushnell, as well as with Baptist polity and the Oxford Movement in Anglicanism. Ecclesiology is a pervasive subject of this volume. So too is philosophical reflection on the essential nature and destiny of humans, which for Nevin rests beyond the natural in the supernatural. A fundamental theme throughout is the organic unity of the natural and the supernatural, as the world is redeemed through the incarnation of

FOREWORD

Christ. In Part 2, the reader can follow how Nevin compares and contrasts this version of supernaturalism with alternative versions in contemporary American Christianity.

Introducing the Mercersburg theology in *Theology in America: Christian Thought from the Age of the Puritans to the Civil War*, E. Brooks Holifield explained that Nevin, Philip Schaff, and their allies positioned their theology "against many of the assumptions that other American theologians took for granted."[1] Many of these essays display this *contra mundum* spirit, but this is not because Nevin was an anti-worldly sectarian. Far from it! Instead it is because of Nevin's emphasis on the organic unity of Christians, the human race, and the process of history. Nevin's emphasis is displayed when he observes in the first essay that the revolutions of 1848 are "the product truly of the inmost life of history itself, the result of an organic process which has been going forward for centuries in the very heart of the world's civilization."[2]

A key point that distinguished Nevin and his Mercersburg colleagues from their American contemporaries was their dissent from the regnant Common Sense Realism, individualism, and simple biblicism. As someone who is sympathetic to Nevin's approach and who has taught for over two decades at a university founded by and governed by Baptists (from which Borneman graduated), I find the distinction Nevin drew clearest in "Evangelical Radicalism."[3] In this review of a Baptist church manual by William Crowell, Nevin wrote in a characteristically frank polemical style that lacked the empathetic engagement appropriate for ecumenism. Yet, he helpfully demarcates how his understanding of the church as supernatural, organic, and a means of grace differs from a common American Protestant one that views churches as the creations of Christians. In Nevin's day this common approach to the church was demonstrated not only by Baptists, but by many other denominations. In our day, it is exhibited by a very large number of nondenominational churches.

Nevin's two essays engaging with Brownson form a substantial part of this volume. As Carey observes in his review of the Crowell text, Nevin emphasized the objective nature of the church; in his engagement with Brownson, he emphasized the subjective more. Compared to most of his contemporaries' Catholicism in either its Roman or Anglican forms, Nevin saw the church as a dynamic, historical entity. It was less an institution whose purity needed to be maintained or restored, than an ever-evolving historical stream.[4] Nevin also faulted both Brownson and his many Protestant interlocutors for their strict rationalism. The Common Sense Realism that dominated American Protestant thought in Nevin's day was not materially different

---

1. Holifield, *Theology in America*, 467.

2. "The Year 1848," below, 28.

3. General Editor's note: this essay was overlooked in its original planning of the series, but I regard it as a minor classic of Nevin's oeuvre. I am grateful that Dr. Carey was willing to include it in his sequence of essays. His presentation adds significantly to the value of this volume.

4. For Nevin's colleague Philip Schaff's early treatment of these themes see Bains and Trost, "Philip Schaff: The Flow of Church History," 416–28; and MTSS 3.

in approach from that of the Roman Catholic Brownson and his bishop John Bernard Fitzpatrick. Nevin's combination of idealism and a developmental understanding of the church contributed to his distinctive contribution to American theology. The publication of these essays, with Carey's detailed introductions and footnotes, are essential to interpreting this important interaction in nineteenth-century American theology.

The Connecticut Congregationalist Horace Bushnell was closer to Nevin in many aspects. Holifield describes Bushnell as one of "the founders of American theological liberalism."[5] Nevin approached his *Nature and The Supernatural, as together constitute the One System of God* appreciatively but still noted his fundamental disagreements. He praised Bushnell for making the "the person of Christ" the center of his argument for the supernatural, but found that Bushnell insufficiently credited the transformational importance of the incarnation, "the coming down of God into the world." Nevin's view of the unity of nature and the supernatural is more organic than Bushnell's. Thus, he also finds Bushnell's ecclesiology insufficient since Bushnell keeps to the typical New England understanding of the church which is not far from that which Nevin soundly rejects in his review of Crowell's church manual.

Nevin rather poetically expresses the union of the natural and the supernatural in his essay on the church year. In the annual celebration of the seasonally linked religious festivals Nevin saw "the whole constitution and course of nature" glorified and "sublimated into a new and higher sense."[6] Of course, not all of Nevin's historical assertions should be relied upon today, nor does he consider the inversion of his links between festivals and seasons in the Southern Hemisphere. Yet, his discussion in this essay shows the power that the traditional, but always evolving, structures of historic Christianity had in his thought as well as the way he knew church, nature, and culture to be intertwined.

In their introductions and annotations, editors Borneman and Carey ground Nevin's writings in his culture and church experience and draw the connections with the many other writings now published in the Mercersburg Theological Study Series. They also show how later theologians have engaged his ideas. This enables philosophers, historians, and theologians to engage more surely with his profound reflections as they consider their implications for their own day.

    David R. Bains
    Professor
    Department of Biblical & Religious Studies
    Howard College of Arts and Sciences
    Samford University

---

5. Holifield, *Theology in America*, 452.
6. See below, 158–59.

Editorial Approach and Acknowledgments

The purpose of this series is to reprint the key writings of the Mercersburg theologians in a way that is both fully faithful to the original and yet easily accessible to non-specialist modern readers. These twin goals, often in conflict, have determined our editorial approach throughout. We have sought to do justice to both by being very hesitant to make any alterations to the original, but being very free with additions to the original in the form of annotations.

We have decided to leave spelling, capitalization, and emphasis exactly as in the original, except in cases of clear typographical errors, which have been corrected, usually without notation. The entirety of the text has been re-typeset and re-formatted to render it as clear and accessible as possible; pagination, of course, has accordingly been changed. Original section headings have been retained; in articles which lacked any section headings in the original, we have added headings of our own in brackets. We have taken a few liberties in altering punctuation—primarily comma usage, which is occasionally quite idiosyncratic and awkward in the original texts, but also other punctuation conventions which are nonstandard and potentially confusing today. We have also adopted standard modern conventions such as the italicization of book titles and foreign-language words. One major change in the present volume: the publisher has asked the editors to no longer replicate "small caps." So we have replaced that convention with italics. When the "small caps" seem significant, this has been noted in the footnotes. Another of Nevin's idiosyncrasies needs to be noted: portmanteau words (e.g., "everyday," "cannot," "textbook"), or terms that we hyphenate (e.g., "so-called," "well-informed"), were regularly spelled as separate words: e.g., "every day," "can not," "so called." These have not been changed.

Original footnotes are retained, though for ease of typesetting, they have been subsumed within the series of numbered footnotes which includes the annotations we have added to this edition. Our own annotations and additions, which comprise the majority of the footnotes, are wholly enclosed in brackets, whether that be within a footnote that was original, or around an entire footnote when it is one that we have added.

Source citations in the original have been retained in their original form, but where necessary, we have provided expanded citation information in brackets or numerated footnotes, and have sought to direct the reader toward modern editions of these works, where they exist. Where citations are lacking in the original, we have tried as much as possible to provide them in our footnotes.

In the annotations we have added (generally in the footnotes, though very occasionally in the form of brackets in the body text), we have attempted to be comprehensive without becoming cumbersome. In addition to offering citations for works referenced in the original, these additions fall under four further headings:

1. Translation
2. Unfamiliar terms and historical figures
3. Additional source material
4. Commentary

We have attempted to be comprehensive in providing translations of any untranslated foreign-language quotations in these works, and have wherever possible made use of existing translations in standard modern editions, to which the reader is referred.

Additional annotations serve to elucidate any unfamiliar words, concepts, or (especially) historical figures to which the authors refer, and where applicable, to provide references to sources where the reader may pursue further information (for these additional sources, only abbreviated citations are provided in the footnotes; for full bibliographical information, see the bibliography).

With ten volumes of the **Mercersburg Theology Study Series** published, most of the significant Mercersburg texts are now in "**MTSS**" editions. Where available, references will be made to those editions in the form "MTSS [volume number]." Scholars who need original bibliographical data on a text can consult the relevant volume. It is the firm belief of the editors that the MTSS series should in the future be considered the standard scholarly edition of the texts of the Mercersburg tradition.

Accordingly, we have sought to shed light on the issues under discussion. Although most commentary on the texts has been reserved for the general introductions and introductions to individual documents, further brief commentary on specific points of importance has occasionally been provided in footnotes to facilitate understanding of the significance of the arguments. We hope that our practice throughout will help bring these remarkable texts to life again for a new century, while also allowing the authors to be heard in their own authentic voices.

Acknowledgments

Volume Editors

I have found the process of studying, interpreting, and commenting on this volume's primary sources to be stimulating and enlightening, an experience made possible by David Layman and his encouraging me to re-engage with this multiyear project. I am deeply grateful for his invitation and for his incredibly gracious support and oversight every step of the way. Brad Littlejohn issued the initial invitation in 2010 for me to participate in this project, and I would be remiss not to thank him for doing so as this volume comes to fruition. I am also grateful to my incredible colleagues at The Ministry Collaborative, who always provide extraordinary flexibility for any members of our team to pursue projects and efforts beyond the typical scope of our work. My profoundly supportive wife and children continue to tolerate my taking on too many additional projects and interests, none of which would be possible without their steadfast love and encouragement. To the many other friends and colleagues who have proven such valuable conversation partners over the years in the areas of theology, church history, philosophy, and culture, know that traces of your insights are woven throughout this volume, and that I am truly grateful for your constructive engagement and support.
—Adam S. Borneman

I want to thank Marquette University Library and in particular the interlibrary loan librarians for their assistance in locating sources for this project. But most of all, I am grateful to David Layman for his expert editorial advice and suggestions for improving the texts that I have prepared for this volume. A number of my own graduate students over the years have been drawn to John Williamson Nevin's theology and have continued to examine his works after graduating. I have been influenced by their books on Nevin in my own work on this current project.
—Patrick Carey

General Editor

It has been this editor's task to help guide the development of these volumes for the past seven years, after his own editorship of volume 6 (*Born of Water and the Spirit*). Although the founding editor, Brad Littlejohn, has moved on to other interests, his editorial philosophy (stated in the above comments) continues to guide the series editors' endeavors. My fellow series editor, Lee Barrett, Stager Professor of Theology at Lancaster Theological Seminary (now under the umbrella of Moravian University) connects the enterprise to the institution that maintains the Mercersburg vision, and provides invaluable advice and encouragement. I am continually grateful that Prof. Barrett walks with me as we journey to the completion of the series. The Mercersburg

Society, presided over by the Rt. Reverend Nathan D. Baxter, provides a haven to discuss the continuing relevance of the issues raised in this Study Series. This series continues only because of the Society's financial support.

David R. Bains's foreword is a lucid overview of the essays and their biographical background, displaying their common themes and concerns. The editors of this volume, Adam Borneman and Patrick Carey, collaborated with remarkable skill and swiftness, and made the formation of this volume an immense pleasure. I have been privileged to work with two experienced scholars who have already displayed their erudition and accomplishments in Mercersburg studies specifically, as well as the wide field of theological research. Dr. Carey took time out of a well-deserved retirement to bring his lifetime of immersion in the life and writings of Orestes Brownson to this first-time complete presentation of Nevin's dialogue with Brownson.

Lancaster Theological Seminary and the Archives of the Evangelical and Reformed Historical Society (both in Lancaster, Pennsylvania) are the essential repositories of texts relevant to Mercersburg; Google Books and Internet Archive (archive.org) together comprise a world-class research library accessible and searchable from one's desktop. (Google's interface is easier to interact with; while Internet Archive includes more recent literature which can be digitally "checked out," and fills some crucial gaps found in the former.) A reader who wants to research the documents cited in the voluminous footnotes can in most cases read them in one of these two repositories.

Contributors

Adam S. Borneman is a Presbyterian Church (U.S.A.) pastor and independent scholar based in Atlanta, Georgia, where he currently serves as Program Director with The Ministry Collaborative. He earned his M.Div. and Th.M. from Gordon-Conwell Theological Seminary in 2009. He is the author of *Church, Sacrament, and American Democracy: The Social and Political Dimensions of John Williamson Nevin's Theology of Incarnation*.

Patrick Carey is Emeritus professor of theology at Marquette University, former chair of Marquette's Department of Theology, a past president of the American Catholic Historical Association, and author or editor of over twenty books and numerous articles on American Catholic life and thought.

David W. Layman earned his Ph.D. in Religion from Temple University in 1994. Since then, he has been a lecturer in religious studies, philosophy, and humanities at schools in south-central Pennsylvania. He is editor for volume 6 of the Mercersburg Theology Study Series, *Born of Water and the Spirit: Essays on the Sacraments and Christian Formation*, and has served as a General Editor of the Series since Volume 5.

Abbreviations

BQR   *Brownson Quarterly Review* (1844—)
MR   *Mercersburg Review* (1849–52, 1857–78; 1853–56: *Mercersburg Quarterly Review*)
MTSS Mercersburg Theology Study Series. Edited by W. Bradford Littlejohn (2012–17), Lee Barrett (2017–), and David W. Layman (2017–). Eugene, OR: Wipf & Stock, 2012–.

Part 1

Culture, Philosophy, Ethics, Anthropology

Edited by Adam S. Borneman

General Introduction, Part 1

I remain convinced that John Williamson Nevin is one of the most undervalued theological voices in American history. This is not only the case in the historiographic sense, as his life, career, and publications help us to more fully grasp the crucial, nation-shaping forces of nineteenth century American Christianity, but also in the way he can serve as a vital, ongoing conversation partner for our current discourse about church, culture, humanity, and creation. Nevin's relevance in this respect has only increased, in my estimation, as both ecclesial and civic institutions experience dramatic shifts, and as the culture critically re-examines religion, faith, and spirituality at fundamental levels. These shifts are concurrent with my evolving interest in Nevin's work. For many years I was primarily drawn to Nevin's attempt to integrate a "high" church sacramental theology within uniquely American expressions of the Reformed tradition and in opposition to nineteenth-century revivalism. This integration was perhaps always a hill too tall to climb for Nevin, facing the powerful headwinds of individualism and Common Sense Realism in the American religious impulse. I remain drawn to Nevin in that respect, but what now strikes me as most significant about Nevin's work is far broader in scope, penetrating the complex phenomena of Christianity and culture as we venture into the second quarter of the twenty-first century. To adequately orient readers to the foundational structures of thought that lie under the specific documents in this volume, I want to first suggest that those structures of thought present valuable points of intersection and overlap with modern theological and inter-disciplinary discourse.

At a fundamental level, Nevin joins others who offer an alternative hermeneutic to our culture's frequently reductionist, binary approaches to epistemology, theology, culture, politics, and beyond. The presumed poles of individual and community, subjectivist expression and naive scientific objectivity, idealism and materialism, are all challenged and constructively critiqued by Nevin's dialectical,[1] romanticist vision of

---

1. "Dialectic" is complex term with a long history. In the case of Nevin, it's important to grasp its use and advancement during the nineteenth century by Hegelian schools of thought. Hegel, influenced by Johann Gottlieb Fichte, developed an idealistic dialectic to model the relationship of nature and history. In this scheme, each stage of historical process is the product of contradictions inherent or implicit in the preceding stage. Nevin modified this model into a more distinctly theological vision

the cosmos, which for Nevin finds its true end and meaning in Jesus Christ, God Incarnate. To this end, Nevin launched a campaign against materialism, religious skepticism, and individualism, offering instead a theological idealism that insists upon the ideal over the material, the accessible reality and objectivity of the spiritual, and an integrated wholeness over individuality.[2] Viewed in this light, one begins to see Nevin as a more vital conversation partner in the modern era. Some of these partners include massively influential theologians of the twentieth century. DiPuccio has noted, for example, Nevin's points of intersection with Karl Barth:

> For Mercersburg, as for Barth, Christ is the foundational, epistemic norm for all theology and knowledge. Reason and experience are meaningful only insofar as they find their center in Christ. . . . [T]he Incarnation provides the context by which we interpret not only *our* world, but all of reality as well. It is the cosmic metanarrative in which all other narratives must find their place.[3]

In that same vein, William B. Evans has with great insight pointed out Nevin's points of intersection with T. F. Torrance:

> [B]oth are philosophical realists who consistently oppose dualistic and disjunctive modes of thought. . . . We see in Nevin a vigorous impulse toward unity and integration rather than disjunction, toward the a priori and ideal over against the a posteriori and empirical, and toward the general over the particular. In the critical realism of Torrance as well we find a powerful drive for integration.[4]

While exploring aspects of Nevin's theological anthropology and ethics, I've been struck by how this impulse toward unity and integration in Nevin's work lends itself to a model of faith formation that avoids the pitfalls of what George Lindbeck famously dichotomized as "experiential-expressivist" and "cognitive-propositional" models of faith.[5] Nevin's explicit rejection of seeing faith as either "downloading" information or unconstrained emotionalism continues to provide a valuable, highly relevant critique of religion in our modern age.

Beyond these more obvious instances, Nevin's potential conversation partners in today's theological milieu range broadly, from the likes of Robert Jenson to Marilynne

---

of God and history, finding its culmination in the Incarnation. One may also find in Nevin the well-known tripartite dialectic of thesis, antithesis, synthesis. The notion appears to have been formally developed by Heinrich Moritz Chalybäus, *Historical Development of Speculative Philosophy*, 366–67. Hegel discusses the "whole movement" of "the *actual*," but warns against reducing the "*triadic form*" to a "lifeless schema" in the Preface to *Phenomenology of Spirit*, 27, 29, emphases original. Michael Fox cautions against the "unfortunate caricature" of the dialectic (*Accessible Hegel*, 43, 52).

2. For an extensive treatment, see DiPuccio, "Dynamic Realism."

3. DiPuccio, *Interior,* 197–98, emphasis original. To use Bruce McCormack's description of Barth's theology, we may likewise describe Nevin's as a "critically realistic dialectical theology."

4. William Evans, "Twin Sons," 158.

5. Lindbeck, *Nature of Doctrine*.

Robinson, from John Milbank to Sarah Coakley, from the modern mysticism of Richard Rohr to liberation and black theology traditions.[6] I don't mean to naively suggest like-mindedness between Nevin and anyone who advances a decisively participationist or dialectical theology; indeed Nevin would have profound disagreements with the individuals and traditions I list here. But as modern theological discourse continues to wrestle with matters of human freedom, the nature of historical development, the integrity of creation, and the theological dynamics of socio-economic and political phenomena, the exclusion of Nevin's voice is a glaring omission.

Moreover, Nevin's broad-sweeping theological analysis ought not be confined to discourse among theologians. Nevin's career-long insistence that the movement of the world history, the natural world, humanity, and even the cosmos itself is an organic process that finds its final consummation in the divine, sets the stage for what is in my view a far more open-handed, dialectical, collaborative inquiry into theology and culture, one that is hospitable to voices from a broader array of disciplines that seek to critique ideologically entrenched and binary approaches to complex phenomena in our world. One such voice is Willie Jennings, who pleas "for a conversation between those deeply involved in the formation of space and those concerned with identity formation—urban planners, ecologists, scientists, real estate brokers, developers joined in conversation with theologians, ethicists, literary and postcolonial theorists, sociologists, anthropologists, and historians."[7] Throughout his published works, not least in those works included in this volume, Nevin lends himself to the sort of collaborative inquiry Jennings describes, frequently addressing and attempting to synthesize the world of science, culture, and anthropology with his theological project, and vice versa. From the Lancaster commencement address of 1867, for example, Nevin proclaims,

> Here is to be issued and adjudicated practically the old arch-controversy, between the rights of man, as they are called, and the duties of man. Here are

---

6. Jenson's configuration of the Incarnation's relationship to history is particularly intriguing on this front: Robert Jenson, *Systematic Theology, Volume 1*, 125–44. Marilynne Robinson's ongoing critique of postmodern atheism vis-à-vis science, religion, and consciousness provides potentially fruitful points of discussion, especially in *Absence of Mind*. On Nevin's possible points of intersection with John Milbank and the Radical Orthodoxy movement, see Borneman, *Church*, 134–48. Milbank attempts to advance a participationist metaphysic that echoes Nevin in some respects. I would also include in that discussion Julie Canlis and her recovery of participationist language in the Calvinist tradition. See especially Canlis, "Calvin, Osiander and Participation." Sarah Coakley's project of distilling the language of participation, human freedom, and human desire from the church fathers nicely aligns with a number of Nevin's essays: Coakley, *God, Sexuality*, 1–32. Nevin's idealism provides important points of constructive, critical engagement with the type of universalism Richard Rohr has advanced in numerous publications, especially Richard Rohr, *The Universal Christ*. Possible points of intersection between Nevin and black and liberation theology traditions include Willie Jennings (discussed later); Barbara Holmes gives a theological vision of wholeness and unity in *Race and the Cosmos*; see James Evans's accounts of history, hope, freedom, and the incarnation in *We Have Been Believers*, 165–82.

7. Jennings, *Christian Imagination*, 293–94.

to be met, and answered in some way, the tremendous politico-economical and social problems . . . . Here are to be shown, in the end, we must believe, the mightiest achievements of science, the greatest wonders of art, the most stupendous victories in the service of commerce and trade. Above all in interest for us, here must be settled the great ecclesiastical issues, with which the whole Christian world is wrestling at the present time, and which are felt by thousands everywhere to involve nothing less than the question of life or death for the universal cause of Christianity itself.[8]

This broad-sweeping way of viewing and interpreting the relationship of God's life and the life of the world in all its complex natural, social, and economic phenomena is captured in numerous texts throughout Nevin's career. The open lines of inquiry and frameworks of critique exhibited by Nevin are especially evident in the texts in this volume of Nevin's works. To better understand these documents, and to see more clearly Nevin as an ongoing conversation partner, we need to wade into the deeper waters of Nevin's theological reading of history, historical development, anthropology, and ethics. For Nevin, history is indeed God's history, and thus all national, world, and ecclesial events have to be interpreted as such.[9] Accordingly it will be helpful for readers of the following essays to be oriented to the philosophical movements of Nevin's context, the historical phenomena that accompanied those philosophical movements, Nevin's departure from such movements, and the theology of history and humanity that he believed was central for his project as a whole. We'll address each of these in turn.

America's Dominant Philosophical Orientation

I've noted above the extraordinary headwinds that Nevin and his Mercersburg colleagues faced when it came to advancing even their most basic theological and ecclesial convictions. These headwinds can be summarized by a few key historical phenomena and their philosophical foundations.

The complex historical progression of ecclesial division and invention, renegotiating denominational identities, and finding new forms of union throughout American Protestantism was in many respects unprecedented and quite distinct. Though likewise highly contentious within their various establishmentarian settings, European evangelical counterparts did not exhibit the same patterns. The new democratic republic in America appeared to offer opportunities for meaningful participation in society despite the waning of long-held establishmentarian institutions. This milieu was the catalyst for a smorgasbord of new religious expressions that not only energetically dissented from the ecclesial institutions that held to a more traditional liturgy,

---

8. Nevin, "Commencement Address," 496; also in Appel, *Life*, 643.

9. The first clear statement of this belief is perhaps in Nevin, *The Church*, MTSS 5:148. Note 15 gives the probable intellectual genealogy: F. H. W. Schelling to Philip Schaff to Nevin.

polity, and "high" sacramentology, but also expressed a growing distaste for any institutions held by the elite of society. The development of voluntary organizations and para-church ministry initiatives would ultimately be made possible by these severe cultural upheavals within American Christianity.[10]

Underlying this radical restructuring of social, political, and religious life of the antebellum era were several crucial ideological movements and seismic philosophical shifts. The extensive involvement of Protestants in the nation's life during this period was deeply rooted in these changes, reinforcing them along the way.[11] Firstly, republicanism emerged as a compelling and assumed vision of a liberated society, fundamentally reshaping how governments and their interconnectedness with the populace were perceived. This new understanding emphasized mixed-constitutional and democratic principles, prompting Americans to reassess their societal roles and the nature of social relationships. Secondly, albeit more subtly, the infiltration of Scottish philosophy introduced a brand of commonsense moral reasoning that challenged traditional notions of human perception and consciousness.[12]

Thirdly, social activism and the concept of a "benevolent empire" were fueled by a newfound confidence in moral causes and their relevance to broader social agendas. These developments were largely influenced by Enlightenment rationalism, which claimed the ability to explain cause-and-effect relationships in the real world. As American Protestants engaged with the cultural landscape of these philosophical shifts and the emerging American society, they utilized, internalized, and accelerated many key elements of republicanism, commonsense moral reasoning, and activism, all of which had profound effects on ecclesiology and Christian identity.

The degree to which American Protestantism played a vital role in these developments is perhaps mostly simply captured by the fact that historians have come to apply "revivalism"—originally a phenomenon within Anglo-American Christianity—to refer to all aspects of antebellum society, including its politics, economy, and religious practices. In one such study, sociologist George Thomas concludes that "revivalism was primarily an acceptance of the new order that both legitimated and was legitimated by the individuated market and the new myth of rational individualism. It comprehensively worked individualism into a unified cosmic order of things,

---

10. See Noll, *America's God*, 174–75.

11. For the following, Noll, *America's God*, 209–10, is especially helpful.

12. Founded by Scottish philosopher Thomas Reid, largely in opposition to Descartes's "Theory of Ideas," Common Sense Realism emphasized everyone's innate ability to perceive and interpret ideas and objects, and asserted that every individual has basic experiences that provide certainty of "self," real objects, and basic moral, ethical, and religious truths. "If there are certain principles, as I think there are, which the constitution of our nature leads us to believe, and which we are under a necessity to take for granted in the common concerns of life, without being able to give a reason for them— these are what we call the principles of common sense; and what is manifestly contrary to them, is what we call absurd." Reid, *Inquiry into the Human Mind*, 33; quoted in *The Cambridge Companion to Thomas Reid*, 85.

from family relations to individual action to national growth."[13] The combination of individualism and commonsense moral reasoning fostered a conviction that the pious lives of the converted would inevitably produce public acts of kindness, first with interpersonal relationships and then spreading to the most fundamental institutions of society. Notably, these initiatives were equally successful in inspiring secularists to make comparable efforts. Numerous voluntarist organizations took the initiative to pursue social and political transformation as a result of the new democratic feeling that was spreading across the nation. This development will be further described in the introduction to "The Year 1848," document 1 below.

These fundamental shifts in republicanism, moral reasoning, activism, and the rise of a free-market religious orientation spread democratization at an ever-accelerating pace in nineteenth-century America.[14] Conventional understandings of human identity and social existence came under scrutiny, both explicitly and implicitly, from multiple flanks of American life. The identity of Americans as defined by their allegiance to authority or adherence to a universal, unchanging law, especially one of transcendent origin, was rapidly losing relevance.

Given this post-revolutionary milieu, it is no wonder that "common sense" became a more overtly embraced concept. By insisting on the individual's inherent capacity to perceive the world as it truly is, thus reinforcing protest against totalitarianism and elitism, Common Sense Realism resonated deeply with emerging democratic ideology. It originated in Scottish philosophers Thomas Reid and Dugald Stewart (thus also known as *Scottish* Realism) and was subsequently advanced with great success in America by prominent figures like John Witherspoon.[15] This philosophical approach not only underpinned the intellectual assumptions of Americans throughout the latter half of the antebellum era, it was actively taught in most American colleges. As George Marsden puts it, despite the influx of various competing philosophies brought about by immigration and industrialization during the antebellum period, "Common Sense Realism remained unquestionably *the* American philosophy."[16] These prevailing individualist worldviews combined subjectivist expression with enlightenment objectivity and supported a view of reality that prioritized the finite and the particular. This philosophical stance, known as nominalism, entered American thought through the influence of John Locke. It posited a perspective of reality in which individuality takes precedence and all relationships are viewed as the outcome of individual consent, that is, through "social contract" (which Nevin criticized as a "monstrous fallacy").[17]

---

13. Thomas, *Revivalism and Cultural Change*, 162.
14. For a wide-ranging study of anti-elitism in religious institutions, see Hatch, *Democratization*.
15. James C. Livingston, *Enlightenment and the Nineteenth Century*, 303.
16. Marsden, *Fundamentalism and American Culture*, 14, emphasis original.
17. Nevin, "Philosophy of History," as noted by DiPuccio, *Interior Sense*, 170.

Nevin's Philosophical Divergence: History as Theology?

In contrast, Nevin advanced an idealist ontology that posits the primacy of the ideal and the universal in shaping reality, rather than the finite and the actual. He was influenced by the German idealism of Johann Fichte, F. W. J. Schelling, and of course Georg Wilhelm Friedrich Hegel.[18] In his famous *Science of Logic*, Hegel argued that reality cannot be grounded in the finite alone, as the finite is determined and dependent on other finite qualities. On the other hand, "spiritual" entities like God and morality require no further qualification and are not reliant on concrete existence.[19] Nevin's indebtedness to these streams of Hegelian thought are especially evident in his broader dialectical hermeneutic of thesis-antithesis-synthesis, not least in the case of historical process.[20] Throughout the Nevin corpus, there is a recurring sentiment that earlier forms of thought are incorporated and elevated by newer and "higher" concepts without being completely negated. Indeed these "former" or "lower" concepts are vital and necessary for the process. Nevin's hierarchical framework may appropriately be understood in terms of an *analogia entis*. Traditionally understood, the "analogy of being" constitutes an ontological continuum in which lower and higher orders of existence have an innate attraction for one another. In Nevin's hierarchy, as DiPuccio explains, "The lower orders adumbrate and anticipate the higher, while at the same time the higher orders take up and assimilate the lower just as an organism incorporates material from its environment. . . . The lower is thus made to transcend itself through the action of a higher power, thus fulfilling the created purpose or design of each class."[21] A key example of how this framework played out in Nevin's thinking—one that proved controversial throughout his career—emphasized that the contributions of Roman Catholicism should not be outright discarded but rather retained so that they might temper or correct the excesses of revivalist Protestantism. Nevin envisioned the ultimate fulfillment of Christianity when "the life of Catholicism" would merge as a valuable and balancing force into the Protestant stream, while

---

18. For excellent accounts of these influences, see DeBie, *Speculative Theology*, and William Evans, *Companion*. Students of Immanuel Kant, Johann Gottlieb Fichte and Friedrich Wilhelm Joseph Schelling are crucial figures in the development of German idealism and influential for Nevin's thought. Fichte is most famously known for his concept of the self, which he conceived as the starting point for all knowledge and experience. He argued that the self is the origin of all knowledge and that the self is free and autonomous. Schelling established and advanced a system of transcendental idealism in which he argued that the mind and the world are interconnected and that the mind can access the basic, organic unity of the world through the intellect. See Beiser, *German Idealism*; Guyer and Horstmann, "Idealism."

19. Hegel, *Science of Logic*, 66 (finite things), 128 (God).

20. Note the comments in the first footnote in this essay. This hermeneutic is commonly expressed in the Hegelian term *aufheben* [trans. "sublation"]. See Schaff's definition in *What is Church History?*, MTSS 3:289. For what follows, DiPuccio, *Interior Sense*, is an invaluable resource.

21. DiPuccio, *Interior Sense*, 36. This is exemplified in Nevin, "Bread of Life," MTSS 6:218–44.

still acknowledging the preeminence of Protestantism in most matters of doctrine, ecclesiology, and church polity.[22]

Nevin's modified idealism, one that was decidedly theological in its inquiry and arguments, drew upon the key insights of Hegel but departed where necessary. Nevin believed that Hegel and his followers lacked a genuine understanding of human sin and the necessity for a free human response to the divine. In other words, he felt that a more comprehensive theological framework was needed, specifically one centered in the Incarnation. As Holifield explains, "It was this [idealist] philosophical vision that enabled Nevin to view the Incarnation as an event that occurred in one divine-human person, recast the principle of human nature in which all people shared, and began to actualize the new ideal possibilities by drawing individuals into the working of its law."[23]

Nevin's departure from Hegel is most notably seen in his encounter with the influential work of Augustus Neander. After reading Neander's *General History of the Christian Religion and Church*,[24] Nevin significantly reconsidered the nature of historical development and its implications. It was a crucial turn in his thought and career, marking his abandonment of the Puritan subjectivist approach to theology that he had been taught at Princeton. He recalled:

> Before my acquaintance with Neander, it seems to me, now looking back upon my life, this sense of the historical was something which I could hardly be said to have even begun to possess at all. Since then it has come to condition all my views of life. I do not mean to say that it became all at once of such force for me through Neander's teachings. It was an idea or sentiment which grew, and took upon it full form, only in the course of following years; but to him I owe it first of all that any such idea began to dawn upon my mind. He first gave me the feeling in some measure, of what history means for the life of man everywhere, and most of all in the ruling central sphere of religion.[25]

The influence of Neander can be seen in a number of Nevin's most influential works. Published in 1843, *The Anxious Bench* (enlarged in 1844), specifically examined how the revivalist Puritanism of the past was transmitted into the nineteenth century, giving rise to individualism and a low-church ecclesiology.[26] This work primarily served as a rejection of Charles Finney's "New Measures," which had recently been promoted by a visiting preacher in a local German Reformed congregation in Mercersburg. However, the work had a broader landscape in view, as Nevin reflected rather explicitly on his growing disillusionment with the growing populist tendencies within the

---

22. Wallace, "History and Sacrament," 187.

23. Holifield, *Theology in America*, 477.

24. Neander, *Allgemeine Geschichte der christlichen Religion und Kirche* (1825). See Nevin, *My Own Life*, 140, for Nevin's ambiguous memory of the influence of Neander.

25. Nevin, *My Own Life*, 143–44; also in Appel, *Life*, 83.

26. *The Anxious Bench*, 2nd ed. (Chambersburg, Pa: M. Kieffer & Co., 1844). Reprinted in Nevin, *One, Holy, Catholic, and Apostolic: Tome 1*, MTSS 5:27–103.

German Reformed Church and American Protestantism in general. In his critique of Puritanism's and revivalism's evolutions, Nevin was already emphasizing history as a vital component of theological reflection. So also, in 1846, Nevin published his magnum opus, *The Mystical Presence*, which advances its key arguments primarily by historical analysis and the implications of ongoing historical dialectic.[27]

Nevin was not alone in this mode of inquiry and divergence from more common schools of thought. In 1846, Nevin's colleague Phillip Schaff published *What is Church History?* in which he provided an overview of various schools of thought and methodologies in the study of church history.[28] Like Nevin's works throughout the 1840s and beyond, Schaff exhibited Mercersburg's indebtedness to the mediating theologians and a modified Hegelian idealism, positing that the church's eschatological "idea," while already completely realized in Christ in one aspect, requires a more concrete, temporal manifestation. "Church and History altogether, since the introduction of Christianity, are so closely united, that respect and love towards the first, may be said to be essentially the same with a proper sense of what is comprised in the other."[29] Indeed, one may reasonably conclude that Schaff is the key conduit for Schelling's influence on Nevin's understanding of history and historical development.[30]

In the inaugural issue of *The Mercersburg Review* in 1849, Nevin penned a two-part article titled "The Sect System."[31] This article specifically targeted John Winebrenner's *History of All the Religious Denominations in the United States*, a compilation of articles written by authors from 53 denominations.[32] Nevin viewed Winebrenner as the epitome of a free-market, entrepreneurial Christian, and a significant contributor to the "sect plague," a term used to describe the rise of divisive religious factions.[33] This historical sketch shows us that the Mercersburg critique of antebellum society focused especially on its historical dimension. Nevin's and Schaff's fundamental argument was that the prevailing sectarian inclination within American Protestantism was not only rooted in faulty theological trends and cultural shifts, but was also a result of not taking seriously the context, phenomena, and possible implications of that history for grasping God's providence in the post-revolutionary America.

For readers to more thoroughly engage this particular MTSS volume of Nevin's writing, it's important to note how Nevin's view of historical development insists that

---

27. Nevin, *The Mystical Presence*, MTSS 1. See Nevin's translator's introduction to Schaff's *Principle of Protestantism*, MTSS 3:4, as well as Stell, general introduction to *Retrieving Catholicity in American Protestantism*, MTSS 12 (forthcoming, Wipf & Stock) for the historical dialectic in *Mystical Presence*.

28. Schaff, *What is Church History?*, MTSS 3:234–316.

29. Schaff, *What is Church History?*, MTSS 3:237. See Larson, "Philip Schaff's Idea."

30. See above, note 9.

31. Nevin, "The Sect System," MTSS 5:238–71.

32. Winebrenner, *History*. Winebrenner had either left or been removed from the pastorate of a German Reformed church, and founded the Church of God. See Nevin, *Anxious Bench*, MTSS 5:82; also the editor's introduction to Nevin, "The Sect System," MTSS 5:235–37.

33. On these themes, see also Hatch, *Democratization*.

one take seriously both the abstract and concrete, the theoretical and the practical outworking of historical process. With this lens, one begins to see more clearly, for example, how essays such as "The Year 1848" and "Wonderful Nature of Man" fit together within Nevin's broader project. Were Nevin to simply propose a theory of history or a theory of mankind without delving into the concrete realities of his antebellum world, he would abandon his commitments to the type of dialectic that guides his understanding of God's work in the world and the end for which it aims.

Nevin's historical situating of the Civil War bears out this dynamic. The nation as whole, and especially its most evangelical, optimistic, postmillennial[34] traditions, experienced a catastrophic and traumatic loss of optimism and idealism, due to the war as well as the subsequent violence and racial terror of the Reconstruction Era. It is not a stretch to suggest that these phenomena resulted in a widespread abandonment of hope in the "benevolent empire" and the identity of being a shining city on a hill. But this is precisely where Nevin's dialectical understanding of historical development enabled him to embrace the unpredictable events of history without losing hope in God's plan for both the nation and the world. In 1867, Nevin thought the Civil War revealed the United States's earlier stage of development, described as an "embryonic existence." Despite the transformative changes brought about by the war, Nevin expressed that, in a deeply meaningful way, the nation had experienced a rebirth; "it may be said that a nation has been born in a day" as a testament to this profound transformation.

> All that may have been new or great, or full of interest, in the previous history of the country: its discovery more than three centuries ago; its colonies and colonial times; its war of independence; the foundation and adoption of its constitution; and whatever has been of account in the enlargement of its resources or in the development of its powers since; all is found at last, I say, gathering itself up into the grandeur of this last crisis, and showing itself to have been significant only as it has served to prepare the way for its advent.[35]

Schaff echoed this interpretation: his belief that history was unfolding organically and dialectically prompted him to deduce that, despite the "streams of noble blood" and the many "sacrifices" of the government and the people, God would continue to guide events to an ultimate resolution. "The country," he romanticized, "has passed through the fiery trial and has now entered into the maturity of manly strength and self-sufficiency."[36]

It's fitting at this juncture to note Charles Hodge, not only because Hodge's contrasting view of history illustrates a more commonly held view of the time, but also

---

34. "Postmillennialism" posits that the millennium will be the culmination of human improvement, *after* which Christ will return. It will be the natural result of the church's activity, not a supernatural act of divine intervention.

35. Nevin, "Commencement Address," 489; also in Appel, *Life*, 638.

36. Schaff, *Der Bürgerkrieg*, 16, 17; trans., Noll, "'Both . . . Pray to the Same God,'" 16n20.

because it serves in part as the backdrop to "Relations to Germany" in this MTSS volume. Nevin's deeply rooted disagreements with Hodge and the Princeton school of theology about the nature of history, theology, ecclesiology, and their interconnections, are foundational for reading the texts that express Nevin's idealist hermeneutic and how it guides his discernment of the unfolding of history.

The contrasting assumptions of Princeton and Mercersburg were in some respects rather obvious.[37] Hodge explicitly formulated his view of historical development to oppose Nevin's "theory of the organic development of the Church.... With them the universe is the self-manifestation and evolution of the absolute Spirit."[38] Hodge balked at a dialectical interpretation of history and the nuances and intricacies of historical phenomena because he adhered to an objectivist examination of the past. While acknowledging that the meaning and implications of events and words could change across different contexts, he occasionally fell into a trap, as Nevin accused him, of "lumping the authorities" to fit his own historiographical biases, molding their content to align with the outcomes most suitable for his theological commitments and broader modes of inquiry.[39]

This divergence from and ongoing engagement with Hodge—with respect to, but not limited to a theology of history—should be noted when reading Nevin's "Relations to Germany." Having spent significant time in Germany himself, Hodge appreciated that not every German thinker who espoused seemingly pantheistic ideas was to be dismissed outright. But he was concerned that the diversity in their "modes of thought and expression" could influence not only their conscious adherents but also the language and thought patterns of the wider public. Thus when Hodge perceived threatening German ideas taking root in American soil, he fought back.[40] One of the German notions that Hodge explicitly rejects sounds like a page taken from Nevin's himself. Hodge warned that the German theological perspective held (contrary to his own conviction) that "Christianity is not a form of doctrine objectively revealed in the Scriptures. Christian theology is not the knowledge, or systematic exhibition of what the Bible teaches. It is the interpretation of this inner life."[41]

Alternatively, Nevin and his Mercersburg colleagues approached historical inquiry, less as detached observation of events in pursuit of objective reality, than as

---

37. For this account of Hodge's critique of Mercersburg historiography, I am especially indebted to Wallace, "History and Sacrament."

38. Hodge, *Systematic Theology*, 1:118. It should be noted that Hodge initially critiqued Schaff's, not Nevin's, version of this theory.

39. Nevin, "Doctrine of the Reformed Church," MTSS 1:227. See Wallace, "History and Sacrament," 183.

40. Wallace, "History and Sacrament," 184.

41. Hodge, *Systematic Theology* 1:119. Cited in Wallace, "History and Sacrament," 185. Hodge did not deny that religion was a "life." However, it was *also* a doctrine. Hodge, "What is Christianity," 119 (quoted in Layman, "Sources of Nevin's Piety," 10). For an interpretation of Nevin's rootage in Princeton theology, and his eventual separation from it, see Layman, "Sources."

a kaleidoscopic lens through which events could be—indeed must be—more comprehensively interpreted and drawn upon for discerning God's unfolding providence. Through this lens, all historical occurrences find their primary purpose in the unfolding principle of Christ's life, a principle that has been infused into human nature and holds the promise of reconciling all things. In "Natural and Supernatural," Nevin asserts,

> All History again must come to its proper unity in Christ, if he be indeed what he is made to be in the Gospel. Here, as in the constitution of Nature, God must have a plan in harmony with itself throughout; and this plan cannot possibly go aside from his main thought and purpose in the government of the world. It must centre in the Incarnation.[42]

Nevin views the Incarnation as the crucial event of history, the event by which God reconciles all history, raising it into the higher order of existence for which it was designed.

> The ethical world, the movement of humanity, the world of history as it may be called, begins and ends in Him; it is not chaotic, the sport of blind chance or iron fate; Christ is in it, causing all its powers and forces to converge throughout to what shall be found to be at last the world's last sense in the finished work of redemption.[43]

Situating Nevin's Theological Anthropology and Ethics

Central in this continuum from the world's natural state to the life of God Incarnate is the moral life of humanity.

> According to the first chapter of Genesis, the world is an organic whole which completes itself in man, and humanity is regarded throughout as a single grand fact, which is brought to pass, not at once, but in the way of history, unfolding always more and more its true interior sense, and reaching onward towards its final consummation.[44]

Humanity, made in God's image, bears a unique position: on one hand, it possesses an organic relation to the lower, natural, created order; on the other, since a person can be redeemed, he or she is a being that manifests God's reconciling, redemptive character. This vital role is fulfilled to the degree that humanity finds its true identity in union with the divine. By virtue of this process, the lower, organic sphere of social and political existence is reconciled unto God, and the fragmented elements of society

---

42. Nevin, "Natural and Supernatural," 192. See document 12 below.
43. Nevin, *Vindication of the Revised Liturgy*, 58; repr. Yrigoyen and Bricker, *Catholic and Reformed*, 368.
44. Nevin, "New Creation in Christ," MTSS 4:39–40.

are incorporated into the divine, objective whole. The visible locus of this whole is the church, which, by way of the ministry of word and sacrament, binds together the disparate remnants of the fallen, splintered creation. Therefore, the natural world *becomes* a moral, intelligent world *through* humanity. It reaches its fulfillment as it is linked with the divine through the second person of the Trinity.[45] "The organization of the world, as a system of nature comes to its completion in his person[.]" "Man is himself . . . the end of nature, the point where its whole process reaches its ultimate destination."[46] Nevin continues:

> [W]hat is in this way continually proclaimed by the general constitution of the world, finds its full echo in the moral nature of man himself. Whatever relation his intelligence and will may bear to the present world as such, they carry in their very constitution, at the same time, no less distinctly, a necessary reference also to something beyond this world, to a higher economy.[47]

Humanity thus retains its integrity as the climax of God's creative act, of which the Incarnation is the supreme expression.

One of the more intriguing elements of Nevin's anthropological and ethical analysis is how he applies his dialectical framework to humanity's "one versus many" dynamic, one which had (and has) deep resonance with the American democratic experiment, but which his theological peers shied away from. In Nevin's view, both the individual and the broader, generic structures of humanity have their necessary roles in historical development and societal flourishing, and they must be studied alongside one another if either is to be properly situated. "The idea of man," he writes in "The Moral Order of Sex," "in order that it may become actual, must resolve itself into an innumerable multitude of individual lives" who are to find their perfection in the "whole" constitution of mankind.[48] This formulation is especially palpable in "Party Spirit," an early (1839) lecture in which Nevin argues that our tendency to neglect the "general life" of humanity results in fragmentation and sectarianism, qualities which are contrary to the kingdom of God.

> The social principle, which binds men together in large as well as small platoons, enters vitally into the constitution of human nature, without which individual men would be mere atoms, and man would no longer be man or the common unity of races, nations, tribes, and individuals. Without contact and communion with other spirits like himself, he would have no development worthy of his nature, and no history that constantly leads him from one grade of perfection to another. There is a common mind belonging to each age and to every country, to every province and class of society, which surrounds men

---

45. Nevin, "Christianity and Humanity," 469.
46. Nevin, "Man's True Destiny," 4, 6.
47. Nevin, "Man's True Destiny," 7; see document 11 below, 321, 322–23.
48. See below, 101.

as an atmosphere and in the end forms the character of the individual and the community.[49]

Nevin was convinced that the natural order's redemption included the restoration and triumph of this "social principle," by which all individuals could more fully share in the general life of humanity, even the general life of creation. It is a principle that equally applies to all social, religious, and political realms, holding moreover that each realm be united to the objective, supernatural whole for which it was designed. It is to insist on "wholeness" rather than "allness."[50] Nevin thus rejected the "change the individual, change the world" philosophy of revivalism. While he would agree that both need to be redeemed, he would also insist upon a tight organic relationship between the two which necessitates a structural or societal approach. Redemption or "salvation" includes the individual, the family, and the state, a process which occurs through, by, and in the church.

> But to understand fully the inner mission of Christianity . . . we must look beyond the merely individual life as such to the moral organization of society, in which alone it can ever be found real and complete. Pure naked individuality in the case of man is an abstraction, for which there is no place whatever in the concrete human world. The single man is what he is always, only in virtue of the social life in which he is comprehended, and of which he is a part.[51]

Nevin's view of humanity and humanity's unique, providential role in historical development is a *sine qua non* component of his hermeneutics as a whole, and one that figures prominently in this MTSS volume. It's especially important for interpreting texts such as "The Moral Order of Sex," "Wonderful Nature of Man," and "Human Freedom." For Nevin, the history of humankind is not just a history of the natural order; it is a history which takes into account humanity's role in redemptive salvation history and the scope of its reach. Again, in "Catholicism":

> Art, science, commerce, politics, for instance, as they enter essentially into the idea of man, must all come within the range of this mission; . . . . It is full as needful for the complete and final triumph of the Gospel among men, that it should subdue the arts, music, painting, sculpture, poetry, . . . [and] fill them with its spirit . . . .[52]

These words bring us back to where we began, as we consider how Nevin is attempting to utilize his organic, dialectical idealism to draw together multiple facets of humanity and society with hopes that they might find harmony and redemption

---

49. Nevin, "Party Spirit," in Appel, *Life*, 118.

50. This distinction begins (at the latest) in Nevin, *Anxious Bench*, MTSS 5:90–97. He first used the terminology eight months later in "Catholic Unity," MTSS 5:118–19. Also see the following citations from "Catholicism," MTSS 7.

51. Nevin, "Catholicism," MTSS 7:18.

52. Nevin, "Catholicism," MTSS 7:20.

in the Incarnate one, Jesus Christ. It is an approach that for Nevin retains both deep theological commitments as well as a generous interpretive posture toward how the process of God's providence might be worked out. It rejects propositionalist dogmatism, naïve objectivity, material dualisms, and tenuous subjectivism, and it warrants our careful consideration for ongoing theological inquiry.

My aim here has been to simultaneously orient readers to the documents to Part 1 of this volume while implicitly making the case that the hermeneutical threads of Nevin's thought in this volume demonstrate why he remains a vital conversation partner for our time. The warring modernist epistemological and theological traditions seem to be hermetically sealed cells that jostle and press against each with no escape and no means of interaction. This perpetual cultural affray has proven inadequate. We need all the expressions of a more organic, idealist, even romanticist version of reality we can recover for this age. Nevin fits the bill. Particularly in reading the essays that follow, one gets the sense that Nevin himself is processing his own thinking[53] about the dynamics of reality itself in terms of God's providential orchestration of history and all that comes to bear on it, somehow finding its resolution in the eschatological Incarnate one, Jesus Christ. It's a fascinating intellectual journey he takes us on if we're willing to join him. Even where one finds themselves disagreeing with his arguments or conclusions, readers will be struck by the careful attentiveness and thoroughness of Nevin's basic commitments and his willingness to take them as far as he can.

---

53. These essays extend from Nevin's peak productivity at Mercersburg, in collaboration with Schaff, to a period when he is arguably disenchanted with Schaff's confidence in the historical development theory. For an introduction to the latter period, see William Evans, *Companion*, 84–85, 114–17, and the sources cited there. More details, as well as a discussion about this interpretation, can be found in the forthcoming setting of Nevin's essays on the church fathers: Nevin, *Retrieving Catholicity in American Protestantism*, MTSS 12.

Document 1

"The Year 1848"

Editor's Introduction

"The year 1848" is a uniquely instructive essay in the Nevin corpus for at least three reasons: its place along the trajectory of Nevin's increasingly polemical and voluminous writing career, its context of the remarkable turmoil in both Europe and the growing political crisis in the United States, and the way in which it draws together Nevin's broad understanding of historical development with very particular, concrete circumstances.

"The Year 1848" was published in early 1849, a time when Nevin held a tremendous amount of personal and professional responsibility. All eight of his children were born between 1836 and 1846, at which time Nevin had numerous teaching, administrative, and ministerial responsibilities. And yet Nevin found time and energy to write at an impressive rate, composing his magisterial *The Mystical Presence*[1] in 1846, and two years later, his most forceful assault upon American sectarianism, *Antichrist, or the Spirit of Sect and Schism*.[2] Nevin had become increasingly disillusioned with the populist impulse within American popular religion and the German Reformed Church in particular. This sentiment would be woven throughout much of his future work as well, notably in the first issue of *The Mercersburg Review* (1849), in which Nevin wrote his two-part article, "The Sect System." It was directed towards John Winebrenner's *History of All Religious Denominations in the United States* (1848), a compilation of articles written by authors from fifty-three denominations. Winebrenner, who had already been the object of Nevin's criticism five years earlier in *The Anxious Bench*, represented for Nevin the epitome of the free-market, entrepreneurial Christian, and a major source of the "sect plague."[3] Also in 1848, the Alumni Association of Marshall

---

1. See MTSS 1.
2. MTSS 5:165–232.
3. The essay addressed in particular the nineteenth-century manifestation of revivalist Puritanism, focusing on its "low" ecclesiology and individualism. It was primarily designed to be a refutation of

Document 1: "The Year 1848"

College sponsored *The Mercersburg Review* (a new periodical), that would be published quarterly as an outlet for Nevin, Schaff, and other similarly aligned colleagues. Nevin, of course became the primary contributor for some years to come. For the first 6 years of the review, he was responsible for nearly half of the journal's content, writing approximately 300 pages a year, from 1849 to 1853.

The broader historical, international context was likewise rather remarkable and is crucial for understanding not only "The Year 1848," but Nevin's thought and literary output during the era. The European Revolutions of 1848 (also known as Springtime of the Peoples or the Springtime of Nations), a series of social and political crises across Europe that started in 1848, were raging. These uprisings, though frequently short in duration, were widespread, and included different countries, including France, Germany, Poland, Italy, Denmark, and the Austrian empire. A steadily growing distrust of the institution of the monarchy was largely the culprit, a distrust which had reached a boiling point due to food shortages, labor crises, and general economic collapse in some cases. All of this was augmented by rapidly growing demand for democracy and relief from oppression and economic neglect. Revolutionary factions shared a fundamental desire to remove the existing monarchical structures and create independent nation-states. In all, over 50 countries were affected, but with little coordination or cooperation among their respective leaders or revolutionaries. Thousands lost their lives.[4]

The revolutions foreshadowed the more extensive conflicts of democracy and nation-building that would occur on both sides of the Atlantic. Nevin understood this dynamic: "The convulsions in Europe are made still more significant and impressive, when we consider in connection with them the course of events on this side of the Atlantic."[5] Although the 1848 Revolutions failed to generate significant American interest in intervention, they did influence the United States in other ways. Several, varied expressions of support for the more radical factions of Europe emerged. Americans took to the streets, donning revolutionary cockades and hosting banquets to demonstrate solidarity with the European rebels. Protestant ministers, particularly after Pius IX's removal from the Vatican, preached that the end of Catholicism and the start of a new era could be on the horizon. Meanwhile, veterans of the Mexican war and recent Irish and German immigrants banded together to form volunteer groups and raise funds and weapons to aid in Europe's liberation. Supporters of different reform movements, such as urban labor organizations, women's rights, and especially antislavery activists, recognized that reforms were gaining momentum

---

Charles Finney's "new measures," which had been recently promoted by a visiting preacher in a local German Reformed congregation in Mercersburg. *Anxious Bench*, MTSS 5:26–103; see also Borneman, *Church*, 65.

4. See Merriman, *History of Modern Europe*; Evans and von Strandmann, eds., *The Revolutions in Europe*.

5. "The Year 1848," 20.

across the Atlantic, leveraging them to advocate for similar changes in the United States.[6] After the 1848 Revolutions failed, many Americans believed that the United States was inherently more stable, a confidence that was short-lived, as the Civil War (1861–65) would prove more devastating than the European conflicts in almost every way imaginable.

A key event which Nevin explicitly mentions at points throughout the essay, the Mexican-American War, lasted from 1846 to 1848. It followed the 1845 American annexation of Texas, which was highly controversial because Mexico still considered Texas its territory, and the addition of Texas as a slave state upset the balance of power between Northern free states and Southern slave states. It is one of countless examples of how significant events of the era were rarely disconnected from the growing sectionalism and divides over the politics, economics, morality, and theological justifications of slavery. In 1846, Northern representatives in the U.S. House of Representatives passed the Wilmot Proviso, which aimed to prevent slavery in territory captured from Mexico. Southern Senators blocked its passage in the U.S. Senate, increasing tensions between the North and South. The Massachusetts legislature also passed a resolution in 1847 declaring the Mexican-American War unconstitutional and being waged for "the triple object of extending slavery, of strengthening the slave power, and of obtaining control of the free states."[7]

At the start of 1848, Americans were still basking in their triumphs in the Mexican war. Nevin celebrated the U.S. victory in Mexico as a means of acquiring new U.S. territory and enabling greater communal autonomy and freedom, and in this way demonstrated his Democratic tendencies. He also expressed support for immigration by suggesting that the era of "nativism" was ending. Yet, for Nevin, the key issue was not the political divides, but whether an America that valued democracy could find a balance between human freedom and submission to God's authority.

According to Nevin, certain nations emerge at various intervals throughout history as representatives, with the purpose of guiding other nations towards a more elevated mode of existence, culminating in an existence beyond history—the new creation. Nevin saw the tumultuous political environment of the pre-Civil War era in the United States as a time of searching for a novel synthesis that would establish America's unique position in global history. Later, he wrote,

> These spiritual and moral forces, now deeply at work everywhere in our modern civilization, no less, I say, than the more outward powers before spoken of, are tending with accumulating strength toward the introduction of a new order of life for the world at large, a new era altogether in the world's social and political history; and in doing so, it is plain that they are throwing themselves

---

6. See Curti, "Impact of the Revolutions;" Reynolds, *European Revolutions*.
7. McPherson, *Battle Cry of Freedom*, 51, see further 56–73.

Document 1: "The Year 1848"

more and more, with united volume, into the onward, moving destiny of our vast American Republic.[8]

This view was for Nevin a natural outworking of his modified Hegelian hermeneutic.[9]

Instead of disregarding the failures of other nations, the goal for Nevin was to integrate both the successes and failures of human history into the greater whole of God's providential plan. As a "theatre for the world," America must seek to raise the pitfalls and accidents of history into a more sacred existence.[10] Nevin envisioned America as a model of freedom towards which all nations could strive, rather than a nationalist or sectarian enclave. He believed that America's role was to elevate human existence into a higher order, with the goal of incorporating the life of the world into herself. Nevin saw America as the latest synthesis of world history, a means for other nations to reinterpret their aspirations in light of the American story, which ideally expressed the freedom available to humanity through Christ. "It has been plain for a long time past," he explains, "that the character and state of the world at large were likely to be powerfully affected in the end, by the progress of society in America."[11]

For Nevin, "The Year 1848" is a means of theologically integrating actual history into an idealist ontology that culminates in Christ and his church. Woven throughout the essay is the crucial conviction that the importance of recent events in both Europe and America is not solely in their individual phenomena, but in the relation between the two. If we believe that God guides history, then it is likely that the developments in both regions are part of a larger, unified plan that serves a universal purpose. Thus, we cannot fully understand the course of events in the old and new worlds without considering their relationship to each other, and indeed their relationship to God's providence in Christ. This dynamic is all in anticipation of the church taking on a "new form." The Church's present tumult and disorder, outwardly manifest especially in its sectarianism, is a necessary feature of this organic, dialectical movement toward that new form. In hope, Nevin held that the church would emerge in a new catholicity, wholeness, unity, and visibility.

---

8. Nevin, "Lancaster Commencement Address," in Appel, *Life and Work*, 641.

9. While Hegel's philosophy provided the basis for a progressive and dialectical view of history, the mediating school's ideas placed greater emphasis on themes of organic unity and development. See p. 22n3 for more details.

10. Borneman, *Church*, 50.

11. "The Year 1848," 20.

The Year 1848.[1]

Wonderful, and long to be remembered, has been the year 1848, now thrown into our rear. The outward end of much that is past, and the beginning, outwardly, of in great deal, that is to come. A year of revolution and change; of uncertainty, anxiety, and alarm; answering to the prophetic imagery of "signs in the sun, and in the moon, and in the stars;"[2] the powers of heaven shaken, and the order of the world thrown violently out of course. A year of mystery for the nations; involving a deep burden, which the whole civilized earth is concerned to hear and understand. Who shall pretend to fathom its sense? Who shall tell the mighty secret, that lies hid within its sybil leaves?

It is not for any age or period, fully to understand itself. While events are passing, they cannot, for the most part, be fairly seen in their true proportions and relations. The part of history, which it is always most difficult to interpret, is that which is in the process of immediate actual evolution. The present throws light upon the past; while its own sense again, so far as it is in any measure original and new, can find its clear and sufficient commentary at last only in the life of the unborn future.[3] We are in a much better position now, to comprehend the age of the Reformation, than were the men who themselves lived and acted in its stirring drama. We are better able than they were, to perceive the general force and bearing of the movement as a whole,

---

1. [*MR* 1 (January 1849) 10–43. A thorough study of the background to this essay has just been published in DeBie, *John Williamson Nevin*, 232–37.]

2. [Luke 21:25.]

3. [It's helpful for the reader to possess at least a basic understanding of Nevin's view of history and historical development for interpreting this essay and Nevin's theological project as a whole. In view here is especially the dialectical idealism employed with respect to future and past, outward and inward life of a nation, the parts and the whole, the particular and the universal. While Hegel had provided the foundations for a dialectical and progressive view of history, the mediating school, supplied analyses that situated more prominently themes of organic unity and development. The influence of thinkers such as Johann Fichte, F.W.J. Schelling, Frederick Rauch, Isaac Dorner and August Neander is prominent. The Church—and indeed the history of the Church—played a crucial role in this scheme. This constituted one of the key departures from Hegel, as Nevin and the Mercersburg school prioritized the history of the visible church and the union of Christ and his people, principally via the incarnation. See Borneman, *Church*, 65; DeBie, *Speculative Theology*, 51–56; Nevin, "Historical Development"; Schaff, *What is Church History?*, MTSS 3:287–316.]

to separate the merely accidental and transient from the necessary and constant, to reduce the tumultuating show of seemingly chaotic elements to system and reason. We are not overwhelmed and hurried along, as they were, by the wild tossing torrent of what was taking place at the time; but are permitted rather, as it were from some lofty height of observation afar off, to survey with full leisure, in a calm objective way, the entire tract of revolution, in its connections, both with the period going before and the period which has followed since. There are those, indeed, who do pretend still to exhaust the meaning of such an age, by looking into it under a purely separate view; as though history had no life of its own, extending forward perpetually from generation to generation, as the growth of a divine thought; but were made up of confused parcels only, each carrying its significance mainly in its own facts, and requiring no light besides, for its proper interpretation. But this is to insult philosophy and religion, in one breath. No man can possibly have any true knowledge of the sixteenth century, who sees not in it the product of forces long before at work in the bosom of the Catholic Church; and whose estimate of its meaning, at the same time, is not made to embrace also in one and the same view its historical consequences, as they lie exposed to observation now in the lapse of subsequent time. The history of Protestantism thus far, is the revelation of what lay hid, originally, in the great fact of the Reformation. So in the case of our own age. It can never be fully understood by itself, but only as it shall be seen hereafter, when its past and future connections are brought into view together, and made to explain the whole in its interior sense and design. Now we see through a glass darkly.[4]

[The Movement of History]

Still, we see enough, to make us profoundly solemn and thoughtful. So much has become clear for all thinking men, that the age in which we live, is not one of the merely common sort. History moves not with continuously equable stream towards its appointed end. Its progress rather, is by vast cycloids or stages, each fulfilling a certain problem within itself, and accomplishing its course under a regular given form, only to open the way finally for the general process to go forward again in a new way under some similar form. It goes, as we are accustomed, indeed, ordinarily to speak of it, by eras and epochs. There is a difference then, of course, between one age and another as regards significance, according to the place they occupy in the order of the world's life. So long as this life continues to move in a direction already fully settled, carrying out and completing simply the sense of some tendency established in the time which has gone before, it may be expected to proceed with comparative regularity and quiet, and there will be nothing special or extraordinary in the age, to which it belongs. Not so, however, where two great eras come together, (*contact of ages*, 1 Cor. x. 11) the old

---

4. [1 Cor 13:12.]

having finished its circuit, and a new one being at hand to take its place. Such going out and coming in are never accomplished, without more or less of commotion and struggle. The breaking up of the old, however gradually it may be brought to pass, involves necessarily a certain degree of violence and agitation; while the introduction of the new carries with it unavoidably also, the sense of exciting revolution. The age, within which such change falls, must ever, of course, be one of more than ordinary prominence on the field of history. It will stand out to view, through all succeeding time, as the revelation of a new epoch in the life of the world, and it will be attended, while it passes, with the consciousness of some such mighty birth, more or less clear, in the pangs and throes with which it is accomplished. So, we say, our own particular age is felt by all, who exercise any sort of earnest reflection, to be in this way of far more than common significance. Predictions and prophecies, for a long time past, as we are told, have been looking towards it as a period of eventful crisis, and change. A very general presentiment of such world historical revolution, as something close at hand, has gained ground in our own day far and wide, even among those who exercise but little speculation on this subject, but are of such temperament only, as to sympathize actively with the general life that surrounds them, and carries them in its bosom.

Such wide-spread bodings that grow out of no clear ratiocination or reflection, but spring forth spontaneously from the inmost life, as it were, of the world itself, are always entitled to consideration and respect. They come not without reason; and they have been found, in fact, to attend all grand turning points in the progress of earth's history. In the case before us, moreover, they are seconded and backed by the most cool and far-reaching calculations of reason. The men who think most, and who, by their position, are best qualified to think to some purpose, are those precisely who, of all others, participate most decidedly, we may say, in the general impression of which we now speak. It is felt that the lines and tendencies of history have been gradually working, for more than two centuries past, towards a common issue, which has now been reached; and in which they have gathered themselves into a sort of universal *knot*, that admits no further progress under the same form. The knot must be dissolved, whether with violence or without it, so as to make room for onward movement again, under some new and different form. One era is passing away, and another is on the eve of taking its place. Our age is emphatically the period of transition, in which the extremities of both are made to touch and meet. Such, at least, has become a very widely prevalent opinion; and we see no good reason for casting upon it any sort of doubt or discredit. The whole course of events rather, seems to be lending confirmation to it every year. Especially has this been the case with the developments of the year, *annus mirabilis*[5] we may well style it, which has just been conducted to its close.

It would seem to form, in some sense, the very hinge of the vast and mighty world epoch, which is supposed to be taking place; not the beginning of its revolution, of course, and much less in any view its end; but a sort of central revelation in the midst

5. [Trans. "wonderful year," or "marvelous year."]

Document 1: The Year 1848.

of the movement, suddenly disclosing the awful reality of its power, and determining in an outward way the absolute necessity of its going forward to its appointed consummation. In this respect, there has been no year like it, at least since the period of the Reformation. The world may be said, within the last twelve months, to have passed the Rubicon of a revolution,[6] that is destined to turn all its fortunes into a new channel for centuries to come. History is brought to occupy the summit level of a whole vast continent of time, from which slope in opposite directions, behind and before, the retreating past and far prospective future, as two broad tracts of life, which might seem to have no bond in common, save the everlasting mountain barriers that fling them asunder. Whatever of uncertainty might have attended the opinion before, now at least, it may be confidently assumed, and boldly affirmed that old things are passing away, and that all things are becoming new. A true crisis has been reached, in the revelations of the past year. The plot thickens; events crowd, with ever accumulating momentum, towards their appointed end; a thousand signs conspire to show that the funeral pile is already lighted, where from the ashes of a dying era another is prepared to take its wondrous birth, more bright and full of promise than any which has gone before. So much of significance, awful and vast, is comprehended in the history of the year now registered as 1848.

The idea of such a grand crisis or revolution, in the world's history, as we have now mentioned, implies two forms of action unitedly at work for its accomplishment. There must be, in one direction, the violent breaking up of what is old and ready to pass away, in the order of life as it has stood before; and there must be, at the same time, in another direction, the working of an inward nisus[7] and an outward providence jointly, towards the new form of existence, in which the process is required to become finally complete. On one side, the spirit is compelled to forsake the house of its former habitation as no longer suited to its wants; while on the other, it is carried forth, by inward longings, and outward beckonings, after the still unknown future, to which it is thus forced to look for help. In other words, the preparation that serves to usher in a new era, is at once negative and positive; not negative simply, and not positive only, but both these in union; the old making room by its own dissolution for the birth of the new, and the new foreshadowed and prefigured in the womb of the old.

---

6. [The Rubicon of course refers to the river in northern Italy famously crossed by Julius Caesar in 49 BCE. It has since become an idiom for an act of war or crossing a point of no return.]

7. [Nevin uses "nisus" multiple times in the essays in this volume. *Oxford English Dictionary* defines it as "Effort, endeavour; (now) *esp.* impulse, tendency." OED Online, "Nisus, n." Notably, Webster, *American Dictionary*, 557, has no entry for it.]

PART 1: CULTURE, PHILOSOPHY, ETHICS, ANTHROPOLOGY

[The Revolutions of 1848]

See, on the one hand, the late political revolutions in Europe.[8] When, in any age before, has the world beheld such a succession of broad and mighty changes, compressed into the compass of a single year! It is still as it were but the other day, since the nations were electrified by the tidings of the revolution in France. It seemed to be an event large enough of itself, to occupy the attention and speculation of mankind for years. And yet, how completely has it been shorn of its stupendous singularity, by the earthquake shocks that have since rapidly followed in its train. Italy, Austria, Prussia, in a measure, we may say, all Germany, have been suddenly seized with the same spirit of commotion, and change; agitation has succeeded agitation, in all the great centres of political life; the pillars of the social system have been made to tremble, if not absolutely to give way, in almost every direction. Never before was the aspect of the civilized world so altered, within so short a time. It has been hard to keep pace with the movement, even in imagination and thought. Astonishment itself has been paralysed, by the overwhelming vastness of what has taken place; and we are apt to think of it still as a sort of dream or dioramic show, something which has come and gone in the way of inward vision, rather than as an actual part of the world's outward waking history. It costs an effort of reflection, only to see and feel where the nations now stand, as compared with their posture on the first of January, 1843.

And yet it were a false view of the case entirely, to conceive of it, for this reason, as a mere passing accident, that is to be followed with no deep lasting effect upon the course of history. Sudden and violent as it may seem, it is the product of forces and tendencies, which have been steadily working towards this result for whole centuries past. In this respect, it is fully analogous with the general moral explosion that startled the slumbers of Europe, at the opening of the sixteenth century. The causes, which produced the Reformation, had been in powerful operation for a long period before, gradually, but surely, preparing the way for what was to follow. The political, commercial, social, and religious relations of the world, all pressed towards this result, as the necessary outlet of their force, and only proper and sufficient expression of their sense.

Earnest men saw, and felt long before, that a great and mighty crisis was drawing nigh. So, too, it has been evident enough for men of this sort, and, in the way of dark presentiment, we may say, it has been vaguely felt also by the popular mind, for a long time past, that some such crisis as that, to which we now have come, was preparing to break over men's heads. Ideas, principles, tendencies, and powers, have been deep at work in the whole structure of society, which could not fail finally, to reach this very issue, by springing the bands with which they were held, and demanding new forms of existence more adequate to the scope of their action.

---

8. [See introduction to this essay; also see Dowe, *Europe in 1848*.]

DOCUMENT 1: THE YEAR 1848.

It is all important here, to distinguish properly between two widely different sides of history, the merely human namely, and the divine. It is carried forward in one view by the free action of particular men, or classes of men, ruled, more or less, always by private purposes and aims; while in another, it obeys altogether the action of a deeper, universal, and objective law, representing at every point the mind and plan of God.[9] It amounts to nothing then, against the historical significance of the late revolutions in Europe, as now asserted, that the motives, and principles, and personal character, of those who have been most forward in bringing them to pass, may not commend themselves to our confidence, and respect. It is not by any such measure, that we can ever try truly the interior sense and weight of history as a whole. (Isaiah x. 5–7; John xi. 49–52; Acts ii. 22–23.)

With one of the boldest, and best, writers of our time, we are well persuaded that the very worst elements have been at work, and are at work still, in the whirlwind, which has been let loose in the old world.[10] We see in it, not the true law of reason and right at all, as the animating soul of the movement, but, on the contrary, the spirit predominantly of human wickedness and passion. It is not possible to justify it, at the bar of Christianity. It is not to be marvelled at, that many good men in Germany should look upon it with dismay, as the coming, emphatically, of Antichrist, or the letting loose of Satan in the last days.[11] Unprincipled radicalism, in no sympathy whatever with the mind of Jesus Christ, but inwardly full rather of diabolical hostility to all truth and righteousness, might seem to be the main force immediately concerned in what is going forward. The whole theory of revolution here, whatever may be said of the right of such violent change in other cases, is such as cannot for a moment bear examination. It goes on the assumption that a full reconstruction of society may be forcibly introduced at any time, when it is found practicable to bring it to pass. The right of revolution, is taken to be the right in full of any man, or set of men, to upset existing institutions from the bottom, to the best of their ability. "The claim comes fully up to the spirit of the word. It is the period of *revolution*, of *rolling over and over*; and this right of revolution or rolling over, has no place or principle at which it can consistently stop."[12] That even the *Christian* world on this side of the Atlantic, should

9. [The idea that history is the revelation of the mind of God probably came from Schaff, who learned it from F. H. W. Schelling (1773–1854). Penzel, *German Education of Christian Scholar Philip Schaff*, 117–18. See the statement in Schaff, *Principle of Protestantism*, MTSS 3:167.]

10. See an admirable tract entitled, *The Revolutionary Spirit, a Discourse*, by Taylor Lewis, Esq., New York, 1848 [Tayler Lewis, *The Revolutionary Spirit: A Discourse . . .* (New York: C. W. Benedict, 1848); the version cited below will be: "The Revolutionary Spirit," *The Biblical Repository and Classical Review*, Third Series 16 (October 1848) 670–98)].

11. [In other writings, Nevin frequently describes the Antichrist as stemming from sectarianism, Gnosticism, and streams of rationalism that he believes inherently promote such tendencies toward division. It's reasonable to suppose that this framework is in view in the current essay, as Nevin often describes these phenomena in historical terms, through the lens of his modified Hegelianism. See Nevin, *Antichrist*, MTSS 5:165–232.]

12. [Lewis, "The Revolutionary Spirit," 675, Lewis's emphases.]

be so ready and forward lo clap its hands, in joyful exultation, over the revolution in Paris, and other similar explosions, without the least regard to right or wrong in the case, as though the simple work of destruction were in and of itself something good and desirable, is, to say the least, a melancholy exemplification of human weakness.[13]

[The Divine Thought in the Flow of History]

But, after all this admission, we are bound, at the same time, reverently to acknowledge, as well as diligently to study, the presence of a deeper divine law in the whole movement, by which it is to be regarded as a sacred necessity in the progress of our general human history—a necessity also, intimately and vitally allied with the triumphant resolution, finally, of the great problem of Christianity itself. It is not enough, to resolve it pragmatically into all manner of bad motives and springs of action, on the part of the men concerned in it; we must see in it also the all-wise and infinitely glorious providence of God. Is it true that a sparrow may not fall to the ground without his notice and will?[14] How then should cities and nations be thus thrown into commotion, and thrones tumbled into the dust, apart from his eye and hand? But the providence of God involves necessarily the idea of counsel, connexion and plan. This in the end is the true sense of history, the evolution of a divine thought or purpose in the onward flow of human actions and events. In such view accordingly, we say, that sudden and abrupt as the late European revolutions may seem, they have not come by accident, and are not to be regarded as the product of mere momentary passion and caprice. No mob could hurry a whole nation into revolution, if the necessity of revolution were not already at hand historically in the constitution of the nation itself. It is only in such case the throat of a volcano, which seeks vent uncontrollably in this way. The stunning sound of this European explosion is but the outburst of pent up forces, whose action has been powerfully struggling towards this very issue for a long time past. The rumbling premonitions of its approach, for such as had an ear to hear, might be distinctly perceived many years ago. In one sense, the principles and tendencies which have led to it, may be said to have been at work since the epoch of the Reformation. It is no accident, no work of merely human hands, but the product truly of the inmost life of history itself, the result of an organic process which has been going forward for centuries in the very heart of the world's civilization.[15]

---

13. [See especially his criticisms of the enthusiasm for Hungarian revolutionary Kossuth in "Man's True Destiny," document 11 below. Also see "Early Christianity," 51–2n; repr. Yrigoyen and Bricker, *Catholic and Reformed*, 308–8.]

14. [Matt 10:29.]

15. [Generally referred to as the Wars of the Reformation or The European Wars of Religion, the bloody conflicts that characterized the aftermath of the Protestant Reformation of the sixteenth century are well documented even if highly debated by historians. Following the schism between the Roman Catholic church and Luther's followers, several additional conflicts emerged. Typically noted by historians are The German Peasants' War (1524–26) in the Holy Roman Empire, the Tudor conquest

Document 1: The Year 1848.

Thus springing from the life of the past, it carries in itself necessarily the deepest significance also for the future. Whatever of wrong on the part of men the movement may involve, it is not to be imagined that this is to be corrected by the simple negation or setting aside hereafter of what has now taken place. This is no merely outward and superficial change, of such nature that the course of the world can be expected to fall back from it again, in the way of wholesome reaction, to its old established channel. Clearly, it is a grand historical fact, that is destined to remain of force in all coming time. It is idle and vain to dream of so vast and startling a step as this, being recalled and taken back, and made to become as though it had never occurred, in the onward march of the world's life. Europe can never be again, politically, the same Europe, which it has been previously to the year 1848. Even if the old order of things might seem to be restored outwardly, the inward life would not be the same. But it is not to be presumed that any such outward restoration itself, can take place. It is the disproportion of the old forms to the reigning spirit, which has at length caused their strength to give way, and no power or art can avail to reinstate them again in their ancient authority. This is a point, which deserves to be well understood and considered. The nations of Europe have been borne forward, during the past year, to new ground. A vast and mighty change has taken place in their whole constitution and posture; a change, involving a new order of political existence, and so, of course, a new period of history, for each of them separately, and for all of them collectively; a change which must affect, sooner or later, every sphere of their existence, the momentous solemnity of whose consequences no political wisdom can now measure or foretell; a change, from the power of which, in this form, there can be no recovery or retreat. Well may a thoughtful mind be filled with awe, as it looks out on the great and mighty sea of providence, here opened to its gaze, and ask to what unknown shore its waves and billows lead.

For the case will not allow us to feel, that the change has come to an end. Our faith in God rather, and in history, as God's work, requires us to be fully persuaded that it has only begun. It were no better than atheistic impiety, to conceive of the powers of history as working into the hands of the revolutionary spirit, now rampant in Europe, *for its own sake*. This, we have seen already, to be prevailingly radical, infidel, and ungodly, the very power of Antichrist, as it might seem, himself. As such it is doomed, of course, in due time, to pass away. Such salvation and help then, as the age needs, is to be reached, not by falling back to what is past, but by pressing forward towards something better, which is still to come. So far as there is hope in these overturnings, it is not, assuredly, in the overturnings themselves (Luke xxi, 25–26) but only in the sign they show of a new and better period at hand in the future (v. 29–31). It is thus we may trust, that He, whose way is in the deep, who maketh the clouds his

---

of Ireland (1529–1603) the Savoyard–Waldensian wars (1655–90), the Nine Years' War (1688–97) and the War of the Spanish Succession (1701–14). See MacCulloch, *Reformation: Europe's House Divided*; Eire, *Reformations: The Early Modern World*.]

chariot and walketh on the wings of the wind, is leading the world forward, "with a mighty hand and an out stretched arm, and with great terribleness, and with signs and with wonders,"[16] to a state of such spiritual freedom and prosperity as it has never yet known. The commotion and revolution now at work, are only the beginning of the end—the first convulsive shudder produced by the crisis which is passing. Other like spasms may be expected to follow. It is not without reason that some look for a general war in Europe, which shall turn throughout on the issue now joined between monarchy and republicanism, the principle of established authority on the one side, and the principle of subjective freedom on the other.[17] "The present revolutionary period," it has been well said, "is in many respects *sui generis*. It is not so much resistance, even alleged resistance, to actual oppression, either foreign or domestic, as a war for abstract rights."[18] Here precisely lies its profound and terrible significance. It is this consideration, above all others, which clothes with portentous solemnity the memory of the year just fled. Here, however, comes into view also, the true encouragement it offers to the eye of faith. In proportion as we see and feel the greatness of the crisis which has come, are we prepared to hail from beyond it the glorious instauration it may be expected to usher in hereafter.

[The Significance of 1848 for America]

The convulsions in Europe are made still more significant and impressive, when we consider in connection with them the course of events on this side of the Atlantic. Every attentive observer must see, that the relative importance of our own country, as comprehended in the general system of the civilized world, has been greatly advanced during the past year. It has been plain for a long time past, that the character and state of the world at large were likely to be powerfully affected in the end, by the progress of society in America. But no adequate sense of the truth has existed heretofore, either in Europe or among ourselves. It is wonderful indeed, how slow the European world has been, for the most part, to acknowledge the prospective bearing of our American life on the course of universal history. Even well informed scholars, only a few years since, were ready to laugh at the suggestion of anything like a problem for the whole world, comprised in what has been going forward in these ends of the earth. And we have ourselves shared so far in this feeling, as to have at least no very full confidence in the originality and independence of our separate mission. With all our self-glorification, we have been prone to lean on foreign authority, as if not entirely sure of our own stability and strength. The whole course of events, however, within the past year, has served powerfully to bring in a new sentiment on both sides. The vast significance of

---

16. [Ps 104:3; Deut 26:8.]

17. [For more on Nevin's view of Republicanism, nationalism, and other antebellum political movements, see Borneman, *Church*; Wentz, "John Williamson Nevin and American Nationalism."]

18. [Lewis, "The Revolutionary Spirit," 675.]

Document 1: The Year 1848.

America has been made to loom into view, on the other side of the Atlantic, as never before. As the foundations of society are found to give way in the old world, men's minds are turned with increased attention and interest towards the new. In various ways, the unsettled state of Europe, involving as it does the failure of so much that has been trusted as permanently secure, is rapidly turning the scale of comparative promise and hope against itself, and in favor of our youthful republic. The rate of exchange, to speak in commercial phrase, has been suddenly reversed, by the terrible shock now given to all moral and political institutions in the trans-atlantic world; and both our credit and capital are made to rise, with the depreciation of so much spiritual property abroad. It has so happened besides, that the movement of history on our own side of the ocean, just at this juncture, has been such as wonderfully to justify and encourage such transfer of credit to our account. Never before has our country seemed to stand on so firm and solid a basis, as just at the present time. Never before have our institutions presented the same title to reverence and respect. Never before probably has the nation at large had the same sense of its greatness, the same consciousness of an independent world-embracing mission. The last year has done more than all years past, we may say, to emancipate the national spirit, politically and morally, from all foreign thraldom, in the way of true inward self-knowledge and self-possession. With this memorable year only, and not sooner, the American Republic might seem to have closed in full and forever the period of its minority.

It is not necessary to dwell in detail on the great and stirring events, which have passed in our history within the last three or four years, all resulting in the new posture which has now been settled and fixed in our territorial limits. Questions have come up, relating to Texas, to Oregon, to Mexico, that seemed to threaten in different ways the very existence of the Republic, filling the minds of sober men with apprehension, and seeming to turn into mockery all our dreams of enduring prosperity.[19] The wisest statesmen have felt, that the experiment of our government was called, in these circumstances, to pass through a crisis more trying, in some respects, than any which it had ever been subjected to before. It seemed not unreasonable to fear, that the vortex of excitement and agitation into which the nation was so suddenly drawn, and from which it had no power apparently, to make its escape, would end in desperate revolution, overturning our old established state, and carrying our destiny in some new direction. Had it been divinely foretold in 1845, that the revolutionary spirit was to be let loose as it has been since among the nations, without mention of the field it should traverse, the most sagacious politicians, probably, would have been ready to locate, at least its central catastrophe, in America rather than Europe. It must have been felt, at all events, that no such general convulsion could well take place in Europe, without communicating itself by sympathy and contagion to the predisposition which seemed to be already at hand, on all sides, for the same thing in this country. And yet it has

---

19. [Referring to the Mexican-American War, the Annexation of Texas, and the Oregon Boundary Dispute.]

not been so. Texas has taken her place quietly, in the circle of confederate States. The Oregon boundary has been peacefully settled. The Mexican war has been conducted through a series of brilliant victories, that have filled the whole world with admiration, to a triumphant well consolidated peace. While the European world seemed to be meditating only the proper time and way for interfering with our affairs, all its energies and thoughts have been suddenly called into requisition, by the universal crash which has fallen upon it, like thunder out of a clear sky, at home. In the very midst of this vast and fearful commotion, we have been enabled to bring our own troubles, as a nation, to the happy termination just mentioned, and to take our position, with calm dignity, on the same political ground we occupied before. The nation has resumed its ancient course, only with a field of action vastly more broad and free; and might seem, to have gathered fresh confidence and strength from its difficulties, coming out of them more recruited than exhausted, like a strong man girded for the race. It has indeed accomplished a change, that may be counted fairly parallel in a magnificent meaning with the change that has taken place in Europe, and that will be found to have just as much to do in the end, no doubt, with the world-historical epoch which has been reached at this time; but under what different aspect and form! We might seem authorised, by the contrast, to compare the epoch itself with the mystic cloud at the Red Sea, which was all darkness, we are told, on one side, and on the other full of light.[20] Its significance, in this view, may justify us in styling it emphatically, the American epoch.

It is hardly necessary to say that our sense of the vast significance of the crisis, through which the nation has lately passed, is not conditioned at all by any opinion we may entertain of the right and justice of the measures by which it has been accomplished. With the political morality of the Mexican war, we have here nothing to do whatever; just as little as we found it proper to take our measure of history, in the case of the late revolutions in Europe, from any particular estimate of the actors immediately concerned in bringing them to pass. In this case, as in that, we must distinguish between what is human in history, and what is properly universal and divine. The first may be worthy of all reprobation, where we are still bound to adore the presence of the second. It is with the second only, the interior objective life of history, its true and proper world-sense, that we are concerned at all in our present contemplation.

Certain it is, in this view, that the great events which have occurred in our history of late, are just as full of significance for a thoughtful mind, as has now been represented. It is not easy, adequately, to express, how much is involved in the movement which has taken place, or in the general result which has been reached by its means. It has served to test the capabilities of the nation, and to make the world sensible of its resources and powers, beyond any other ordeal through which it has passed. The experiment of our republican institutions has been placed by it on a far more sure footing, than ever before. Much that seemed problematical has been settled and made

20. [Exod 14:19–20.]

Document 1: The Year 1848.

sure. The mere fact of its being able to come so triumphantly through such a crisis, in the midst of so many disturbing forces at work on all sides, is an argument of utility and strength in the nation beyond any which has been exhibited before. The sudden expansion of its territory, is only in keeping with the development of its inward greatness; the moral holding equal step with the physical; the genius of the country, especially as set in contrast with the revolutionary spirit across the Atlantic, towering to an independent height, which is answerable, fairly, to the gigantic measure of its new bounds. Never before was it so respectable in the eyes of the world, never so sure of its own strength at home.

[The Election of 1848[21]]

The sense of what has now been said in a general way, seems to have impressed itself strongly on many persons, in connection particularly with the occasion of our late Presidential election. Coming, as this did, on the heels of the Mexican war, with all the new relations and exciting prospects which have grown out of it, after a most earnest political campaign, and in full face of the tumultuating agitations of the European world, it might have been apprehended that such an issue joined at this time between the two great parties of our country, would bring into jeopardy at least the interests of order and peace in every direction. These considerations could not fail, at all events, to place in strong relief the significance of the experiment and example the nation was called thus to present before the eyes of the civilized world; and when this took place under the most triumphantly successful form, it is not strange that the spectacle should have produced a feeling of moral sublimity, and a sentiment of faith in the destiny of the republic, such as no occasion of a like sort in its history ever wrought before. No more impressive commentary can well be imagined, on the spirit of our institutions; no more emphatic answer to all scepticism or scorn, as exercised at their expense. The whole world beside has no such spectacle to show; the very possibility of it can hardly be imagined in any land but our own. The following statement of the case by one of our secular papers, well deserves here to be repeated and kept in mind.

> Only consider it. In the short space of less than twelve hours, the dynasty of a great nation was to be changed. Four millions of people, representing the opinions, and the will, of nearly twenty millions, were, by a simultaneous act, to decide for themselves, amid all their own diversities of sentiment, to what hands they would commit the direction of their country's mighty energies. It must be a wonder to the millions of lookers-on, who are not imbued with republican influences, that the contest was decided so speedily, so quietly, with such an utter

---

21. [The election of November 7, 1848 pitted the Whig Zachary Taylor—a hero in the Mexican-American War—against Democrat Lewis Cass. See the description of the issues and dynamics in Howe, *What Hath God Wrought*, 827–36. Howe mentions that this was "the first modern presidential election" since it was "the first time all the states chose their electors on the same day" (832).]

absence of unreasoning passion; in fact, it may be said to have been governed solely by the inspiration of pure reason. Imagine the attempt of a people living under a monarchy, to change, we will not say the principle of their government, but merely the dynasty, the human instruments representing or embodying that principle. Such attempts have been made in various countries, and with various success. And everywhere the struggle has been protracted, furious, anarchical, destructive; bringing into action the wildest and most ungovernable impulses of human nature, and filling the land with misery and desolation. Here, under the benign influence and inspiration of republicanism, through the wholesome sway of matured republican habits, not only was the great work accomplished between the rising and the setting of the sun, but so calmly, in such perfect order, that no uninstructed observer could be aware that it was in progress. The usual avocations, amusements, and enjoyments of every-day life were pursued without a visible interruption. All the marts of business were in their accustomed activity; carriages, public and private, went up and down the streets, as is their wont; fair women thronged the fashionable side-walks, gay in apparel, graceful in movement, giving themselves up to the pleasure or more serious purpose of the hour, as if utterly unconscious of the great political crisis ripening around them—of which, indeed, there was nothing to remind them. Not that the magnitude of the crisis was not appreciated; not that the thousands and tens of thousands practically engaged in it were careless or indifferent as to the result; but simply because their sense of its importance was regulated and controlled by a corresponding perception of the dignity and beauty of good citizenship, which demands, first, the observance of order and decorum in all great public acts, and, second, a cheerful and hopeful acquiescence in every determination of the people's will, lawfully manifested in due and proper form by a majority of the people.[22]

[The Relationship of America and Europe]

The significance of what has taken place latterly on both sides of the Atlantic, lies not so much in the European or American movement separately considered, as in the relation which the one may be seen evidently to carry towards the other. It is not possible, if God be indeed at the helm of history, that the course of things in the old and new worlds should not be comprehended, in some way, in a common plan, and have regard thus to a single universal end; and it might reasonably be supposed, that in proportion as the elements and powers at work in each direction should acquire force, and seem ready to precipitate themselves in their last result, the reality of this correspondence and the general form and bearing of it also, would rise more and more into view. Accordingly, it is just here, in fact, that the earnest and contemplative student

---

22. ["The Election," repr. in *Western Literary Messenger* 11 no. 4 (December 1848) 190–91.]

Document 1: The Year 1848.

finds most to fix his attention and engage his admiration. The simultaneousness of the two series of developments, which have burst so suddenly and with such apparently independent process, on the world's astounded sense, here and in Europe, may be said to show, beyond all else perhaps, the solemn meaning of the age. On one side, we have the breaking up of old institutions and forms, in which has been comprehended for centuries, the central power of the world's civilization; as though this order of life had now finished its course, and the time were at last come for it to be taken out of the way, in order to make room for another stadium under some higher and better form. On the other side, we behold suddenly springing into new importance and promise, after long years of comparatively silent preparation, what might seem to be here, in America, the very asylum that is needed, and the best theatre that could be found, for the accomplishment of so great a metempsychosis in the flow of universal history. All indications on either side, point negatively or positively, precisely in this way. It is, in the first place, the spirit of America, or if we choose so to call it, the genius of Protestantism, itself, as it has come to identify itself with our American institutions, that forms, however blindly and darkly, the propelling force in the revolutions of Europe. They carry in themselves, under all their whirlwind violence, the force of a deep hidden sympathy and affinity, on the part of the old world, with the political tendency which has come to such successful experiment in the new. This is well understood by European statesmen and princes generally. The bent and effort of all these agitations and throes, is not in any way towards what has been hitherto the life of Europe, as such, but only and altogether towards the new form which life is found to be assuming in America. This itself speaks volumes in relation to the general nature of the crisis to which the world has now come. Then, along with this, we have the arms of America opening on all sides—her territory suddenly adapting itself to the emergency—to welcome into her bosom the emigration, if need be, of entire nations.[23] With such

---

23. It requires some effort of consideration, to have any tolerable conception at all of the territorial increase of our country latterly, and the field it now opens for the diffusion of our national life. Take the following statement, from the late Presidential Message.

"Within less than four years, the annexation of Texas to the Union, has been consummated; all conflicting title to the Oregon Territory, south of the forty-ninth degree of north latitude, being all that was insisted on by any of my predecessors, has been adjusted; and New Mexico and Upper California have been acquired by treaty. The area of these several territories, according to a report carefully prepared by the Commissioner of the General Land Office from the most authentic information in his possession, and which is herewith transmitted, contains 1,193,061 square miles, or 763,559,040 acres; while the area of the remaining 29 States, and the territory not yet organized into States, east of the Rocky Mountains, contains 2,590,513 square miles, or 1,318,126,058 acres. These estimates show that the territories recently acquired, and over which exclusive jurisdiction and dominion have been extended, constitute a country more than half as large as all that which was held by the United States before their acquisition. If Oregon he excluded from the estimate, there will still remain within the limits of Texas, New Mexico, and California, 851,598 square miles, or 545,012,720 acres; being an addition equal to more than one-third of all the territory owned by the United States before their acquisition: and, including Oregon, nearly as great an extent of territory, as the whole of Europe, Russia only excepted. The Mississippi, so lately the frontier of our country, is now only its centre. With the addition of the late acquisitions, the U. S. are now estimated to be nearly as large as the whole of

opportunity and invitation, co-operate all sorts of difficulty and distress abroad, to make the emigration such as the world has never before beheld. Nay, the very experiments which are made in Europe itself to satisfy the struggling tendency of the age, seem likely, for a time at least, to turn attention only the more powerfully, through their own disastrous issue, to the shores of America, as presenting the only field which is fairly open for its own order of life. Especially is such likely to be the result, when the failure of such experiments comes to be placed in broad contrast with the self-conservative vitality, by which this life at home, and upon its own soil, is carried so triumphantly through its complicated trials; showing itself equal to all emergencies, maintaining its identity through all changes, and absorbing into its own constitution, with overwhelming assimilation, all elements and tendencies, however uncongenial before with its own nature, or incongruous among themselves. It would seem as if God were plainly showing, by this very relation, the true sense of what is taking place; and that nothing can meet the necessities of the time, but such a new period of history as requires for its development, the winding up in full of that which has gone before, and with it the shifting entirely of theatre and scene to make room for its transaction. Should the course of things in Europe continue to be, for any length of time, as little auspicious as it has been thus far, it is quite possible that this reflection alone may become in the end a more powerful stimulus to emigration than all other causes now at work in this direction. Altogether, with the increase of inducement here, and constraining force at home, and easy communication between, the transplanting process which has now commenced, may easily enough assume hereafter, and that too, in a comparatively short time, such a form as hardly any imagination yet has ventured to dream. The world may yet see, in new form, another *Voelkerwanderung*,[24] that shall be cognised hereafter as parallel, in the history of Christianity and civilization, with that which overturned, in the fifth century, the old Roman life, to make room, through such chaos, for the new creation which has since risen in its place.

We wish to be rightly understood. When we read in the present state of the world, the approach of a new historical period, whose character and course are to be determined prevailingly by the new order of life which reigns in America, we are not so foolish as to conceive of this under the form of a simple triumph of our national spirit, as it now stands, over the social and political institutions of the old world; as

Europe." [Polk, "Fourth Annual Message," in *A Compilation of the Messages*, 4:633–34.]

California and New Mexico, alone, surpass in extent the whole original thirteen United States, by an excess which is equal to more than three times all New England. Adding Texas and the Santa Fe country, the new territory, without Oregon, is about equal to the *whole* territory *east* of the Mississippi, from the British provinces, to the Gulf of Mexico; or to the united territories of England, Scotland, Wales, and Ireland, France, Spain, Portugal, Italy, Prussia, Switzerland, Holland, Belgium and Denmark. If inhabited as densely as Massachusetts, it would sustain 78,000,000 of inhabitants, or four times as many as the present population of the whole United States; or if as densely as England, it would sustain 232,000,000—nearly one quarter of the present population of the globe.

24. [Trans., "wandering of the peoples," a reference to the barbarian invasions of Europe that ended the western Roman Empire.]

Document 1: The Year 1848.

though all had been wrong on this last side, and all on the first side were wise, and right and good; so that the controversy between them must be considered a contest purely of light and darkness, the cause of God and human happiness arrayed in broad and open antagonism to the cause of Satan and human wickedness. To hear some persons talk, one might suppose the history of the world to have been without sense or reason, until men came to exercise some little intelligence here lately, in America. The social organization of Europe, as it has existed since the Reformation itself, even in Protestant countries, is regarded as a system of unmitigated abominations, which it is only strange the human mind should have been willing to endure for so long a time. In the vocabulary of this wholesale school, monarchy and tyranny are identical terms, while republicanism is only another word for freedom. The full civilization and proper happiness of the world, are supposed to demand the prostration of all monarchical institutions, as a corruption and abuse. Kings are to be hated, as usurpers of a power which has never been given to them of God. It is by a righteous retribution, accordingly, that, in the providence of God, they are now driven from their thrones, or made to sit upon them with fear and trembling. The salvation of the world turns upon its coming in this way to a just sense of its inborn rights and capabilities; and we may trust accordingly, that God is interposing at this time, in the revolutionary spirit of the age, to bring the whole civilized world into the true liberty of nations, as we have it here happily exemplified, under the most perfect form, in these United States. How far this way of thinking prevails, need not be said. We own, however, no sympathy with it whatever. As already intimated, the revolutionary spirit, as now at work in Europe, is entitled to no sort of confidence or respect. In its own constitution, it is from beneath rather than from above; and the work accordingly, which it is pretending to accomplish, may not be expected to stand. Its significance is not so much in itself, as in the yet undeveloped life towards which transitionally it points and leads. This lies in the direction which the course of history has already begun to take in America, and may be expected to come to its central revelation finally, by means of the theatre here opened for its use. But we have no right to assume, in such case, that the ulterior life of the world, as it is to be reached in this way, will be simply our American state of society, as it now stands, substituted by universal exchange for every other political order; as though we had long since fallen on the perfect idea of both Church and State, and the rest of the world now were required only to throw away all its previous thoughts and habits, and come to our position. This would be a most weak and extravagant imagination. Of one thing we may be very sure. If America be indeed destined to introduce a new order of life for the world, and to open the way for a new period of universal history, it will not be by standing over against the whole previous life of the world, as something false and bad.[25] History in any case, goes forward, not by the mere negation and exclusion of what is thrown into the rear, but by such a setting aside of this as serves, at the same time, to save its interior substance and sense under a higher

25. [On Nevin's view of America's historical role, see Wentz, *John Williamson Nevin*, 97–111.]

form.[26] So, in the case before us, the problem to be accomplished is not, simply, the triumph of one existing order of life over another, in an outward way. It is not America wrestling with the world, as Hercules overcame the serpent in his cradle;[27] but it is the world itself rather, wrestling in its own inmost constitution, through the medium of American influence, towards a general and common end, which may be said to embrace the sense of its whole history for centuries past.

Nothing can well be more out of character here, than the sophomorical style of self-glorification with which we are assailed, in certain quarters, on this subject. It betrays always a narrow vulgarity of mind, which is as far as possible remote from the true genius of the dispensation, whose advent it affects to trumpet in this Pharisaic way. It is the exclusiveness of Chinese vanity, which dreams itself in possession already of the "celestial empire," and can only commiserate or despise the barbarian world that lies beyond; but which, for this very reason, is itself doomed to perpetual imprisonment in the treadmill of its own miserable pedantry and conceit.[28] If America be called to mediate and bring about a new historical period for the world, as so many signs seem to show, she must be the very opposite of China; not walling out the life of the world in its other forms, but making room for it rather, and offering it hearty welcome in her broad and capacious bosom. She must be willing to receive and learn from all sides, as well as to communicate and teach. She must feel, not that she is the world herself, but that she is fast becoming the theatre on which the central power of the world's history is to be displayed. In proportion, precisely, as this comes to be more and more the case, she must cease more and more to appear as an isolated interest; the substance of all previous history will be found pouring itself into the open channel of her life; and only in this way will she be prepared, more and more, with proper inward qualification on her own part, to become the organ of a new universal life for the nations. The activity of the old world, for the last three hundred years, has not been without purpose; and the results of it are not now to be set aside as null and void. Nor is it necessary, by any means, to suppose that the nations of Europe have yet completed their part in the great drama; or that they are to save their importance, only by at once confessing their whole past life to have been a lie, and consenting to take a fresh start politically, in the footsteps of the American republic. The case calls for no such wild extravagant supposition. Europe is not to be set aside as a grand failure. The true wealth of her past life will be

---

26. [A restatement of the Hegelian dialectic.]

27. [Referring to the Roman myth (originally Greek) in which Zeus had been unfaithful to Hera and she decided to murder his illegitimate child birthed by Queen Alcmena. Hera sent two serpents to the sleeping baby, Hercules, who defeated them. Nevin may also have in mind the famous 1788 painting by Sir Joshua Reynolds depicting the scene.]

28. ["Celestial Empire" is a phrase commonly used in the nineteenth and early twentieth centuries in reference to China. It is a western translation of the Chinese term "Tianchao;" meaning "Empire of Heaven." It is principally derived from Chinese folk religion in which the emperor of China was seen as the "Son of Heaven," further advancing notions of Chinese nationalism and Imperial supremacy during those eras.]

Document 1: The Year 1848.

carried forward to the new state, in which her institutions are to be finally perfected in their own form, by means of this crisis; only to become thus more valuable, by growing accumulation, always for the service of the world at large.

[The Historical Significance of America]

The historical significance of America thus far, lies mainly in this, that the substance of its life, as it is to be hereafter, is *not* yet fixed, but in the process only of general formation; under such conditions and relations as are needed to bring it finally to a character of universal wholeness and completeness, beyond all the world is found to have produced before. We cannot speak of our American nationality as a settled and given fact, in the same way that we may speak of the nationality of England or France. The nation is ruled indeed by its own independent genius, and carries in itself a certain inward law or type, that may be expected to determine permanently the leading form of its history. But all is still in a process of growth; and the circumstances of the country make it impossible to bind this process to any outward lines or limits. Even if the idea might have been entertained in any quarter heretofore, that some certain form of thought and life had acquired the right of stamping the country forever with its own image and superstition, to the exclusion of all besides, every such conception is in a fair way of being effectually exploded by the course of things at the present time. No pent up Utica[29] of this sort, which might have been tempted before to make itself the measure of the whole world, can well fail to be put out of countenance now, by the continental size of our territory, and the rolling tide of emigration, with which it is coming to be so rapidly occupied and filled from the other side of the Atlantic. The day for "Nativism," in all its forms, is fast drawing to an end.[30] Whether for weal or for woe, the life of Europe is to be poured in upon our shores without restraint or stint, till it shall cause the ancient blood of the land to become in quantity a mere nothing in comparison. God is fast showing, by the stupendous course of his providence, that this American continent was designed from the start, not for the use of a single race, but for the world at large. Here room has been provided, with all the outward necessary conditions, for the organization of a new order of life, that may be as broad and universal as the soil it shall cover; and now the material out of which it is to be formed, the elements that are needed for such world embracing constitution, are made to flow together from every side, for the purpose of being wrought into a new nationality which shall at last adequately represent the whole. What will be the form precisely

---

29. [A cliché attributed to "Jonathan Mitchell Sewell, a New Hampshire poet, as an epilogue to Addison's play of Cato, . . . in 1788." The relevant lines read: "'Rise, then, my countrymen, for fight prepare, / . . . / No pent-up Utica contracts our powers, / But the whole boundless continent is ours!'" (The vastness of the new continent is being compared to the confines of the Tunisian city of Utica.) "'No Pent-up Utica,'" *The Living Age* 71, no. 908 (October 26, 1861) 156.]

30. [See Billington, *Protestant Crusade*, for a study of anti-Catholic nativism.]

in which this nationality shall become complete, the historical substance in which it shall come finally to proper harmony and consistence within itself, in art, manners, literature, science and religion, it is impossible now, of course, to foresee or predict. We know only, that the social and moral character of America is not yet settled, and that the greatness of the country and its true promise, are comprehended in this fact. Its inward history is quite as young as its outward history; having but just passed, as it were, the stage of childhood, in its onward progress to mature life. It has been emphatically styled the land of the future; and so it is in truth. Its true significance, since the days of Columbus, has lain in its relations to coming time; and with all the actual importance now belonging to it, the full measure of its greatness is still comprehended in what it is soon to become, rather than what it has become already. All signs unite to show that a new order of world history is at hand, and that the way is to be prepared for it centrally in America. Here a theatre is already secured, sufficiently broad for the process; the conditions required for it are showing themselves to be more and more at hand; the elements to be used in it, are wonderfully brought together from all sides; while all the indications of God's providence are conspiring towards the grand result, in which it is to become complete.

It were a most arrogant presumption, contrary to all history and all true philosophy alike, to suppose that the new historical period required by the world, is to proceed from the life of this country, just as it now stands, in an outward mechanical way. The country offers simply the necessary basis and room, for the elaboration of what is wanted, a properly universal spirit, in which the contradictions of the past shall be made to pass away. All particularism is excluded from the process, by its very conception. It must involve the reciprocal action of manifold tendencies and powers. The result must be, not abstract Americanism over against the rest of the world, but such an incorporation of the true substance of history from all sides into the American character, as may fairly and fully qualify it to become the type of the world's life universally. It is not enough that the outward material of the nation be gathered from all lands; it must take up into its inward constitution also, what is of worth in the mind and heart of all lands; so as to be, not merely a mixture of the several reigning nationalities, but an inward reproduction of their true sense under a new organic and universal form. How much remains still to be accomplished for this purpose, in our literature and culture generally, it is not necessary to say. But the forces are already powerfully at work, whose vastly accumulated strength may be expected to prove fully sufficient in due time, for the accomplishment of so great an end; while the palpable destiny of the nation, in the view now under consideration, forms in itself, at the same time, a certain guaranty that it will not fail to be reached.

Document 1: The Year 1848.

[Prospects for the Future]

Did our limits allow, it might be interesting to notice in detail, some of the more striking indications or signs, in the form of single scattered facts, which go to confirm the general anticipation now presented. It lies in any just conception of the world, as the evolution of a divine plan, that every great change in its history, must be preceded by a certain amount of preparation in its whole system, revealing itself in many new facts, apparently unconnected, which serve, in different measure, to foreshadow what is coming. A number of such facts are known to have led the way for the great epoch of the Reformation. Among them may be mentioned, the fall of Constantinople, the invention of printing, the discovery of America, the revival of classical learning, and various changes to which the social and political systems of Europe had come in the process of their own action. These and other facts, were of force, not on the ground simply of any direct bearing they may have exercised on the event of the Reformation itself, but much more as their ultimate necessity and sense may be said to have lain far forward in the new period which was to follow. Their *significance* was in the future; and in such a future as the world could not then rightly comprehend. And in the same way, precisely, we may read the advent of the great period now in prospect, in many most significant facts of the present time, the full power and meaning of which, look plainly beyond the whole constitution of the world, as it now stands.

Here belong the wonderful discoveries and inventions of the age generally, which have been following each other for some time in such form as never before, and whose action is already undermining the existing order of things, quietly but surely, at so many different points. We are apt to lose sight of the broad difference that is coming to exist more and more in this way, between our own circumstances outwardly considered, and those in which the world has stood in former times; and we seldom appreciate properly the bearing of such change on the structure of society or the progress of history. It needs no great reflection, however, to see that this cause alone is carrying the world forward, with uncontrollable necessity, to a social and political state, in which our present modes of existence are likely to become as fully antiquated before long, as are to us now the social relations and forms of the period before the Reformation. The cause is one, moreover, which may be expected to grow continually upon itself, and to multiply its own powers indefinitely. The rate of improvement is accelerated by its own progress; every new invention but paves the way for another; and the first effects of the change also, in each case, are no adequate measure at all of the long train of results to follow. Only think of what has been already wrought by the agency of steam; and yet how small a part of its mission, in all probability, has it yet accomplished? The mastery of mind over matter, has been amazingly advanced within the present century. The resources and powers of nature have been brought into subjection and made subservient to the purposes of civilization in a way which it would have been madness to dream of in former times. Especially worthy of note is the conquest gained more and more over time and space; by which the different parts of the world are brought continually nearer together, and made to verge from all sides towards the idea of a truly universal life. Mountains fall, seas shrink, rough places are made plain, and crooked places straight, in preparation as it might seem, for the most free intercourse and union among the nations.[31] The ends of the earth are contracted, and its most retired and inaccessible regions are laid bare and open. Old barriers and divisions are fast falling away. With the entire change of relations which is coming upon it in this way, the world as it has been is plainly ready to vanish away; and it is equally plain that its history hereafter must show such a character of consolidation and universality as it has never known before.[32]

And it needs no very active imagination certainly, to see in these conquests over nature and time and space, a peculiar prophetic bearing on the mission of this country, as manifestly ordained of Heaven to lead the way in the new order of things which is thus at hand. The processes of improvement and culture, are thus made answerable to the vast scale of our resources and opportunities. The work of years is accomplished in as many days. The multiplication of wealth and power goes forward as by magic. Cities and states spring up like the creations of romance. And still this vast growth of the nation brings with it no unwieldiness or want of strength. On the contrary, with its increasing volume, it is becoming always only more and more compact. It is more present with itself in all its parts now, than it was at the time of the Revolution; and there is good reason to believe that, when its population shall reach from the Atlantic to the Pacific, the bond that holds it together will be still more close and sure than it is at the present time. Space and distance are more and more annihilated as they are brought into the way; and the horizon of the country falls in dynamically upon its centre, in proportion as it recedes from it, in the way of outward vision, on every side.

Who can estimate prospectively the bearings of the *Electric Telegraph* on the course of coming history?[33] It is sufficient of itself, in time, to change the entire order of the world's life. Shall we dream of it as an accident only, in the economy of providence? Or are we not bound rather to see in it a prophetic intimation of what is near at hand in God's plan, a new historical period, namely, in which full room shall be found for its widest use? Does it not point to such concentration and universalness in the coming civilization of the world, as men have had no conception of in ages past? Its main significance undoubtedly lies, not in the present, but in the future. Like the art of printing, it carries unborn revolutions in its womb. Those silent posts and wires mean

---

31. [Images drawn from Isa 40:4.]

32. [Later in life, Nevin becomes less enthusiastic about the potential of technology: "The Spiritual World," 517–19; "Once for All," 124.]

33. [Mass use of electrical telegraphs was for Nevin a new phenomenon. Used from the 1840s until the late twentieth century, electrical telegraphs were the first electrical telecommunications system that allowed people to communicate text messages more efficiently than physical transportation.]

Document 1: The Year 1848.

more than all the thunder of Napoleon's artillery. A thousand mobs of Paris or Berlin, are but as the drop of the bucket, or the small dust of the balance, in comparison.

One other American improvement, still only in theory, but destined, soon, we may trust, to pass into magnificent effect, deserves to fix for a moment, our most earnest attention. It is *Whitney's* project of a *railroad,* to span the entire continent, from Lake Michigan to the shores of the Pacific.[34] We hardly know how to trust ourselves in speaking of this vast and stupendous design. Thought is confounded, and the very imagination itself is made to stagger, in looking down the long vista of results which it opens to our gaze, more like the tales of the Arabian Nights, than the sober realities of experience as it now stands. And yet the whole thing lies as much within the range of plain rational calculation, as any Yankee economist could desire. The practicability of the measure is clear for all who choose to make it a subject of examination. It is equally clear, that all providential signs are urging at this time towards its accomplishment. The sense of our late acquisition of territory, can be made complete in no other way. Oregon and California can be held for the nation, only by this road. Thus the true significance of America for the world, would seem to hang upon its construction. Let no one say that this is making too much of the merely outward and physical, for human history. The outward and physical, here, are the force of mind itself, yoking nature to its chariot wheels. Who that knows anything of history, can be ignorant of the power which has been exercised upon it in all ages, by the course of commerce? A new channel opened for trade, has ever been sufficient to throw the kaleidoscope of nations into new form. Kingdoms rise and fall with the change of mercantile routes and marts. Tyre, Alexandria, Palmyra, Venice, what a lesson do they not read on this subject! But of all levers that have ever been applied in such way to the course of civilization, none can be named as fairly parallel with this railroad to the Pacific. Its consequences must be boundless for the entire globe. By no possibility can the world after its accomplishment continue to be the same. Europe and Asia must join hands across the American continent. We will be in truth the centre of the world, and not simply its centre in an outward view, but the great beating heart we may say of humanity itself, through which shall circulate the life blood of its nations, and that shall serve as a common bond to gather them all into one vast brotherhood of interest and love. New York will be brought within twenty-five days travel of China. The commerce of the whole earth will fall under our command and control. We shall become thus a thoroughfare for the world, and its treasures will be laid at our feet. At the same time, in thus connecting continents and oceans, we shall bind our own republic together with such a bond as we can have under no other form. This bridge of nations will form also the arch of the American union, and the world's weight always passing over it will serve only to

---

34. [Asa Whitney (1797–1872) was one of the earliest ardent promoters of an American transcontinental railroad, publishing *A Project for a Railroad to the Pacific* in 1849. Whitney's vision came to pass through the work of Theodore Judah who was instrumental in the opening of the Union Pacific in 1869.]

render it continually more solid and firm. It is utterly impossible to calculate at present the immense results that must flow from the accomplishment of this single work, for America and for the earth at large. All social and political relations, art, literature, science and religion, in one word, the universal course of history must be brought by means of it to assume an entirely new form.[35]

While Europe and Asia are in the way thus of coming together in the bonds of a new commerce mediated by America, it is most interesting to see the door opening apparently for a similar junction of our American life with the dark continent of Africa. Liberia is still an infant experiment; but the proportions of a Hercules already begin to show themselves in its limbs.—The experiment has proceeded so far, that prejudice itself is forced to look upon it with respect, as carrying in itself now every guaranty that could well be asked of an ultimate success, whose measure shall equal or perhaps transcend the largest calculations of its friends. It is no chimerical dream at present, to look forward to the day as by no means remote, when a flourishing and powerful nation, politically sprung from the American republic, and in close, active correspondence with its life, shall be found spreading far and wide along the shores of Africa, and carrying the blessings of civilization and religion towards its benighted interior. The results of this for Africa itself and for the world, it is not necessary that we should here pretend to foretell. Every one may see that they must be immense. What is mainly interesting, however, and worthy of note, is the concomitance in which this prospect stands with the signs of coming vast revolution in the entire order of the world's life on other continents, and the way in which it conspires with these signs from every side, to indicate prophetically the central relation of America to the period of universal history which is to follow. The world is fast coming together from the four ends of heaven;[36] it is urged from all sides towards a new system of existence, under such a character of consolidated universality as it has never yet known; and it would seem plain that the organic law by which all this is to be reached, is to proceed from the United States mainly, as the land through which, in God's plan, all the nations of the earth are to be blessed. In such view it is that we feel ourselves authorised to speak of the present crisis as emphatically the *American Epoch*.[37]

It has become an established maxim in the philosophy of history that the culture of the human race moves with the course of the sun, from east to west. "*Westward* the star of empire takes its way."[38] Art, literature, science, politics, philosophy and religion started in Asia, and their inward development from the beginning has been

---

35. [This way of situating art, science, and literature within the historical dialectic shows up throughout Nevin's corpus. E. g., Nevin, "Commencement Address: July 25, 1867," 496; Nevin, "Catholicism," MTSS 7:20; these two examples are also in Appel, *Life*, 643–44; 380.]

36. [Possible reference to Mark 13:27; Rev 7:1.]

37. ["*American Epoch*" is in "small caps" in the original.]

38. [George Berkeley wrote this in 1726 as "Westward the course of empire takes its sway" (quoted in Ellis, *After the Revolution*, 6). Nevin used a pervasive adaptation.]

accomplished by means of a corresponding outward emigration ever since towards the setting sun. Now they are in the process apparently of entering upon a new stadium on this side of the Atlantic; which, by analogy, may be expected to be more complete than any which has gone before. But, with the completion of our American civilization, the circuit of the globe will be fulfilled, and the end brought round once more to the beginning. Will the old movement then be gone over again under a higher form? Hardly. The world will be brought so together as to leave no room farther for the idea of any such successional cycle. All betokens rather the abrogation of this law, as one that shall have finished its necessary course, by making room for the integration of all stages of the world's life ultimately into the conception of its proper *manhood*, as this is to be revealed in the new universalized culture, towards which so many signs are pointing and so many powers struggling at the present time. But we venture here on no farther speculation.

Let no one think, however, that we make too much of the outward progress of the age, in inferring from it the approach of a new order also of culture and civilization. We know very well that the triumph of mind over matter is not of itself an advance in morality and religion; that a supreme devotion to material interests is at war with the higher ends of the spirit; that there may be a titanic mastery over nature, which is at last in league only with the powers of hell against the law of heaven. But we know too, that this is not the true constitution of our life. Man is formed to rule the world in the image of God and for God's glory. The great problem of morality is to be fulfilled by the complete subjugation of nature to its high behests. The last sense then of all outward improvements in the state of the world, lies necessarily in their final subserviency to its moral culture. It is not possible thus, with any faith in God, to look upon the signs of revolution with which we are now surrounded, as either without meaning altogether for man's spiritual history, or as significant only of coming evil. It is not by accident, surely, that so many new powers and resources are coming to be developed at this time, or that the outward relations of the world are so rapidly passing into new shape. All these things belong to a divine plan; and this, in the nature of the case, has regard to the highest end of humanity as comprehended in the religion of Jesus Christ. The victory of Christianity will be no Vandal barbarism,[39] exercised at the cost of all outward civilization; but the free and willing homage rather of all art and science at its feet. However adverse then, under any particular aspect, the present course of things may seem to be to spiritual Christianity, we are bound to see in it notwithstanding, not negatively only, but positively also, a glorious preparation for such a reign of the Spirit as has not yet been known. Indeed, there is no alternative here for Christianity, but conquest or defeat. It must keep pace with the onward movement of the world—a movement that cannot be put back; or else stand openly exposed, as impotent altogether for the accomplishment of its own mission. The accelerated, concentrated, consolidated action of the world's outward life, must lead in some way to a corresponding

39. [The Vandals were a Germanic tribe who sacked Rome in 455 CE.]

energy in its moral organization. Otherwise it must perish titanically, through the wanton exercise of its heaven-climbing powers. How all is to come to pass, it may be hard for us now to see; but in the end, the physical or merely natural maturity of our race, will bring along with it also a parallel ripeness in its spiritual constitution. Such a new order of things as we see to be at hand, is at once the argument and guaranty of a new advance to be made in universal civilization.

[Final Considerations: The Future of the Church]

As our article is already too long, we conclude with some general reflections, rapidly and briefly thrown together, in the way of hint merely, and stimulus for farther thought to such as know how to think.

1. There is a woe pronounced in the Bible, on those (Isaiah, iv. 12) that "regard not the work of the Lord, neither consider the operation of his hands." And surely it must be taken as the mark of an irreligious and brutish mind, at this time, not to be affected by the tokens of God's presence with which we are surrounded, or not to be roused by them to some earnest and profound thought. For the judgments of God are not merely to be gazed at with passive animal stupefaction. They are instinct with the light of reason, and are so many challenges to the exercise, first of faith, and then of manly, vigorous speculation. It is a poor thing, to be so immersed in material interests and forms, as to have no eye for the far more magnificent realities of the spirit. It is a sad business to be so occupied with the mere outward sound and show of history, as to have no sense for the divinity it enshrines within. To believe in God truly, one must see him in nature and history; and this implies an earnest apprehension of both, as full of infinite wisdom and love. To look upon history as chaos, without form and void, is such a sin against faith, as it were to banish in thought all order and reason out of nature in the same way.[40] And yet to this it comes at last, where men either deny openly and at once the idea of a universal plan and process in the course of the world's life, or at least deride all endeavors to understand it, as idle, if not presumptuous mysticism. From all such rationalistic *frivolousness* of the common understanding, deliver us, good Lord!

2. One great cause of such unbelief is found in the general selfishness of our nature, which prompts us to subordinate the general and universal to our own petty

---

40. [And yet it appears that Nevin himself eventually embraced the view that history was—at least to a degree—chaotic. David Layman detects the beginning of this shift at the end of "Cyprian." Apparently, he was unable to find a theory of "development" that allowed him to appropriate Cyprian's theology, and so he "snapped 'For development as such, in any shape, we care not a fig'" (Nevin et al., *Born of Water*, MTSS 6:132, quoting "Cyprian," 562 note). Twenty years later Nevin proposed replacing "development" with "historical movement," i.e., it would appear, simple change ("Reply to 'An Anglican Catholic,'" 421). For a discussion of this shift, see Evans, *Companion*, 84–85; a contrasting interpretation is presented in Stell, general introduction to *Retrieving Catholicity*, MTSS 12 (forthcoming).]

particularities. We are bound accordingly, in the case before us, to widen our thinking and interest, as much as possible, into some correspondence with the universal character of the crisis to which the world appears to have come. One great advantage of such a crisis is, that it naturally tends to produce this spiritual enlargement. Our constitution is such that universal interests are fitted to move us more deeply than any that are merely private, lying as they do indeed more intimately near the proper foundation of our life. It behooves us then to make room for their action in our souls. and not to shut it out by the stubborn egotism of our thoughts. We must not dream of bringing the course of universal history into subserviency to *our* particular interests and aims as such, as though God were concerned, in all the revolutions of the age, only to play into our hands, and were pleading the cause of American politics, American opinions, &c., as such, against all the rest of the world. In religion, for instance, we have no right to assume that all the truth of universal Christianity is gathered up into our particular sect or system, Methodism, Puritanism, or any other like narrow interest, and that all variant systems, past or present, are to the same extent false, needing simply to be perfected by an unreserved translocation over to *our* ecclesiastical camp. All such pedantry is ridiculous, and directly at war at the same time with the true sense and meaning of the age. The first condition, we may say, for understanding or fulfilling our duty is, that it should be fully laid aside. So in the case of literature, science, and philosophy in general.

3. As the present course of things invites to wide and comprehensive thinking, so it is also eminently suited to confound and put to shame all narrow theories and schemes. Mere insular traditions must give way; not only such as belong to the old world, Germany, France, England, &c., but those also which have already begun to assert their tough life in the new. The idea that the form of existence which is to rule the world hereafter, is at hand here, as a given fact, in some corner or section of America, under this or that phase of thought and life, however it may have been able to keep itself in countenance heretofore, is in a fair way now of being effectually put to rest. Outward formulas, hereditary notions, mechanical stereotype rules of any sort whatever, will not answer for the time that is now at hand. Only living intellect and waking will, may be expected to carry with them any force.

4. And still the revolution which is coming will not be radical, in such a way as to break with past history. In bursting the bonds of particular forms and traditions, it will yet seek to incorporate into itself the sense of the universal past. This is implied by the way in which it is coming to pass. All particularism is excluded for the very purpose of securing for it a universal character; and the powers of the world's life are made to flow together in its service, from every quarter. Not as an abrupt rupture with the previous civilization of Europe, but only as the true historical continuation of it under a higher and more world embracing form, will it be entitled at all to confidence and respect. Radicalism may mix itself with the course of history—is doing so at this time largely in Europe; just as blind traditionalism may mix with it also in a different

direction. These two, indeed, are apt to be coupled closely together, and strangely enough involve at bottom very much the same falsehood. But history itself is neither radical nor traditional. It always moves away from the past, and still at the same time, never leaves it behind.

5. In the midst of the general revolution which is coming, the *Church* will be brought to assume a new form. The year 1848, has done more to shake the outward organization of the Church, than any year before or since the time of the Reformation. Romanism is made to tremble in the very heart of its own empire. Its ancient pillars seem ready to give way. The Church of the Reformation, on the continent of Europe, is threatened with universal dilapidation. It must pass through a process of reconstruction, in order that it may at all continue to stand. Just now the pressure of political interests weighs down the question of the Church. But it will come forward in due time, with overwhelming interest. Nor can the posture of the Church in this country, be considered by any means as settled and complete. Our sect system is not the normal form of Christianity. No intelligent man is willing to stand forward openly in its defence, under any such view. In some way, sooner or later, it must come to an end. The *Church of the Future* cannot be the same in this respect with the Church of the Present.

6. In what form the Church will surmount finally her present trials, in the new period which appears to be at hand, we may not venture now of course to predict. The tendencies of the age seem on first view, it must be confessed, unfavorable to the idea of any outward catholic organization. But this is not at once to be taken for granted. What we see may be only the negative side of a process, whose ultimate sense is very different. One thing is clear. The way is opening for an universal consolidation in the general life of the world, far beyond all that has been seen in previous ages; and this of course must embrace Christianity and the Church as well as other interests. Is it to be supposed that the Church, in these circumstances, will be less united and compact within itself than it has been heretofore? Or will it be imagined that its unity is to resolve itself into a mere invisible sentiment? And yet the idea of the Church[41] seems to involve unity, catholicity, and visibility, as its necessary elements wherever it has come to be felt as an object of faith. To God we commit the mighty problem. May he resolve it soon in his own glorious way.

MERCERSBURG. J. W. N.

---

41. [For the "idea of the Church," see Nevin, *The Church*, MTSS 5:138–58.]

Document 2

Human Freedom and a Plea for Philosophy

Editor's Introduction

The current volume's introductory essay for "The Year 1848" outlines the political crises in Europe and the U.S. of the era; the appearance of "Human Freedom" in *The Whig Review* in 1848 (later reprinted with "A Plea for Philosophy" in 1850) provides opportunity to further situate Nevin in his historical and political context.

A monthly periodical based in New York City from 1844 to 1852, *The American Review* (also known as *The American Review: A Whig Journal* and *The American Whig Review*) was published by Wiley and Putnam. The inaugural issue of *The American Review* (dated January 1845) was likely released as early as October 1844 in order to promote Whig nominee Henry Clay in the 1844 presidential election.[1] The Whigs were critical of Manifest Destiny, opposed territorial expansion into Texas and the Southwest, and were against the Mexican-American War. They drew support from a broad base, including entrepreneurs, professionals, planters, social reformers, and devout Protestants, particularly evangelicals, as well as the emerging urban middle class, garnering less support from poorer farmers and unskilled workers.

The emergence of the Whig Party, alongside the larger Democratic Party, dominated the "Second Party System" from the late 1830s to the early 1850s. This system began to take shape in the early years of the antebellum era, as factions in New England coalesced, paving the way for the arrival of the Whig Party in the 1820s. This group, which was largely made up of evangelical Christians, saw themselves as the progressive force in American politics, and their efforts helped to sustain the "benevolent empire" of social activism and voluntarism throughout the first half of the century. While sharing with Federalism a belief in the state's role in enforcing moral

---

1. Notably, there existed a rival publication, *The Democratic Review*, that backed James K. Polk. The magazine's co-founder and editor, John O'Sullivan, coined the phrase "manifest destiny" in an 1845 issue.

and social order, Whiggery brought about a realignment of supporters by introducing a new evangelicalism that extended beyond the confines of Yankee elitism.[2]

But was Nevin a Whig? James Bratt's work is highly beneficial in placing Nevin's political stance in context. According to Bratt, Nevin's organic conception of society and history, as well as his vehement opposition to American individualism, align him more closely with the Whig party than with the Democrats. His rejection of "party spirit" and his desire for the realization of the kingdom of God during his lifetime were also in keeping with Whiggery. However, his traditional liturgical inclinations and his connection to the Scotch-Irish and German immigrant communities suggest a Democratic perspective. Additionally, his support for the Mexican War, which he believed would provide more opportunities for communal autonomy and freedom by establishing new U.S. territory, revealed Democratic leanings. Nevin also stated that the era of "nativism" was rapidly coming to a close, demonstrating a pro-immigration, Democratic stance. Ultimately, however, Nevin was more concerned with whether a democratized America could successfully balance human freedom with submission to God's authority than with which party—Whig or Democrat—held sway.[3]

Theodore Appel, Nevin's biographer, recounted that for Nevin, "philosophy and theology had no interest or value, apart from their actual bearings on the welfare of man and the progress of society."[4] This is key for understanding Nevin's concerns about American philosophical trends and his attempts to counter them with viable alternatives. The political realignment of the antebellum era rested on several nuanced philosophical underpinnings, ideological shifts, and accompanying theological influences.[5] The emergence of republicanism as the new ideal for a free society was still seen as revolutionary, even radical. It involved a new way of thinking about governments—and especially the relationship between governments—in mixed-constitutional and democratic terms. This new structure was a catalyst for Americans to re-examine their role in society and their understanding of social relationships. As such, social activism and the concept of a "benevolent empire" were informed by a new confidence in moral causes and their potential to contribute to broader social agendas and the shaping of American society.[6] This shift emphasized the importance of moral responsibility in shaping American society, and owed much to the influence of Scottish Common Sense moral reasoning.

Traditional understandings of human identity and societal existence were therefore facing challenges from multiple angles during the antebellum era. The concept that an individual's identity was defined solely by their allegiance to authority or

---

2. Borneman, *Church*, 18.
3. Bratt, "Nevin and the Antebellum Culture Wars," 7–9; Borneman, *Church*, 47–48.
4. Appel, *Life*, ix.
5. On the following, see especially Noll, *America's God*, 209–10.
6. On the "Benevolent Empire," see Smith, *Revivalism and Social Reform*.

Document 2: Human Freedom and a Plea for Philosophy

adherence to a universal law, especially one of divine origin, was slowly eroding.[7] On the whole, the prevailing worldviews of the antebellum period tended heavily in the direction of the finite and the particular. John Locke and the Scottish Realists advanced this basic orientation, in which the individual entity takes precedence, and all relations are therefore regarded as the result of individual consent in the form of a "social contract" (which Nevin called a "monstrous fallacy").[8]

Nevin's modified German idealism and his emphasis on the whole and essential over individual "rights" and "freedoms" led him to temper and modify several fundamental principles of Enlightenment political theory. He found unacceptable many of the basic tenets of nominalism, which posits that terms and concepts exist only in name and without objective reference, and voluntarism, which holds that the will is fundamental to one's existence. This position left Nevin at odds with the majority of American intellectuals who largely assumed without hesitation the ability of republicanism to balance private character and public well-being, the fixed nature of virtue and liberty versus vice and tyranny, and the predictability of sociopolitical development governed by reason. Nevin, a great admirer of America and her role in the world, did not regard such principles or philosophies as inherently futile, but he lamented the lack of a more organic and all-encompassing theological vision in which to situate them. And he remained suspicious of what he viewed as the essentially sectarian origins of many of these principles, captured in Hume's famous praise of the Puritans: "By these alone the precious spark of liberty was kindled, and to these America owes the whole freedom of her constitution."[9]

Nevin's organic and idealistic view of the world played an important role in both his understanding of human identity and their place in history. In "Human Freedom" Nevin proposes a philosophical foundation for his beliefs on human ontology and freedom by emphasizing the "universal force" that underlies all existence and the ideal character that exists before individual objects. Nevin insists that life is both ideal and real, and that "the ideal can only exist in the form of the actual, and the actual can only have truth if it is filled with the presence of the ideal,"[10] a phrasing and formula that occurs frequently throughout the Nevin corpus.

Nevin argued that "Men are born for truth, as they are born also for freedom,"[11] which echoes the concept of "inalienable rights" from the American Revolution. However, he believed that the freedom worth seeking is not just any kind, but one that can only be found in the life of Christ. The essential expression of man's freedom

---

7. Borneman, *Church*, 59–60.
8. Nevin, "Philosophy of History," as noted by DiPuccio, *Interior Sense*, 170.
9. See Noll, *Civil War*, 17–19; Nevin, "The Sect System," MTSS 5:248–49. Nevin here uses a modified version of the Hume quote as it appears in Winebrenner, *History of All the Religious Denominations*, 57. Original quote in Hume, *The History of England*, 527.
10. "Human Freedom," 3.
11. Nevin, "Bible Anthropology," 363–64.

is demonstrated through personality, which is rooted both in the supernatural order and his natural, material state. Thus, the reconciliation of the created order depends on his intimate relationship with the earth. Despite his transcendent qualities, man's personality is "rooted in the earth, conditioned at every point by the material soil which it has sprung."[12] As such, in his created state, man's personality holds a unique relationship to both natural and supernatural existence, offering redemption to the former while seeking the latter.

One can see, then, why "Human Freedom" was later re-printed alongside "A Plea for Philosophy." The latter provides not only an important complement to Nevin's arguments in "Human Freedom," but in many ways serves as a prerequisite for such discussions. That is to say, for Nevin, philosophy matters because it demands an awareness of one's theological and epistemological assumptions for engaging in even the most basic theological tasks. Nevin is careful to point out that while it is true that philosophy poses risks for Christianity and life in general, it is important to recognize that the absence of philosophy is even more perilous. Religion cannot be so practical that it has no connection with intellect and contemplation. It always relies on a theory that shapes and conditions its impact on the world. If this theory is not based on sound philosophy, it will be erroneous and false. As a means of engaging with the world and its affairs, it will hinder the Gospel's rightful power to save.

---

12. See "Moral Order of Sex," below.

HUMAN FREEDOM

AND

A PLEA FOR PHILOSOPHY:

TWO ESSAYS

BY J. W. NEVIN, D. D.,

PRESIDENT OF MARSHALL COLLEGE.

[Originally published in the American Review.]

REPUBLISHED BY REQUEST.

MERCERSBURG, PA:
P. A. RICE, "Journal Office."

1850.

Human Freedom.[1]

[The Singular and the Universal]

All created life exists under two aspects, and includes in itself what may be denominated a two-fold form of being.[2] In one view, it is something individual and single, the particular revelation as such, by which, in any given case, it makes itself known in the actual world. In another view, it is a general, universal force, which lies back of all such revelation, and communicates to this its true significance and power. In this form, it is an *idea*; not an abstraction or notion simply, fabricated by the understanding, to represent its own sense of a certain common character, belonging to a multitude of individual objects; but the inmost substantial nature of these objects themselves, which goes before them, in the order of existence, at least, if not in time, and finds its perpetual manifestation through their endlessly diversified forms. All life is at once ideal and actual, and in this respect, at once single and universal. It belongs to the very nature of the idea (as a true subsistence and not a mere notion,) to be without parts and without limits. It includes in itself the possibility, indeed, of distinction and self-limitation; but this possibility made real, is nothing more nor less than the transition of the idea over into the sphere of actual life. In itself, it is boundless, universal, and

---

1. ["Human Freedom." *American Review: A Whig Journal Devoted to Politics and Literature*, n.s., 1, no. 4 (1848) 406–18. Reprinted in *Human Freedom, and A Plea for Philosophy: Two Essays*, 3–24. Mercersburg, PA: P. A. Rice, 1850.]

2. [The opening paragraph nicely summarizes key elements of the hermeneutic that pervades Nevin's theology and writing, elements which brought him into direct conflict with the theological vision of most American Reformed theologians of his day. The notion, "All life is at once ideal and actual . . . single and universal" figures prominently here, pitting Nevin at odds with the alleged nominalism of many of his Reformed and Presbyterian contemporaries, and also at odds with the particular brand of Transcendentalism hat had become influential in the United States. For Nevin, the dialectic is historical, taking into account individual and national history, and also world (or universal) history, through which the individual, the whole, the actual, and the ideal find their beginning and end in the Incarnation. See Borneman, *Church,* 64–88; Appel, *Life,* 591 ("Lectures on History"); Nevin, "Catholic Unity," MTSS 5:118–20; Nevin, "Natural and Supernatural" (document 12 below); DiPuccio, *Interior Sense,* 25–40.]

Document 2: Human Freedom.

always identical. It belongs to the very conception of the actual world, on the other hand, that it should exist by manifold distinction, and the resolution of the infinite and universal into the particular and finite. All life, we say then, is at one and the same time, as actual and ideal, individual also, and general; something strictly single, and yet something absolutely universal.

These two forms of existence are opposite, but not, of course, contradictory; their opposition involves on the contrary, the most intimate and necessary union. The ideal is not the actual, and the actual is not, as such, the ideal; separately considered, each is the full negation of what is affirmed in the other; and still they cannot be held for one moment asunder. The ideal can have no reality, except in the form of the actual; and the actual can have no truth, save as it is filled with the presence of the ideal. Each subsists only by inseparable union with its opposite; each is indispensable to the other, as the complement of an existence, that could otherwise have no force. The bond which unites them, accordingly, is not mechanical and outward merely. The life in which they meet, is not to be regarded as, in any sense, two lives. The two forms of existence which it includes, are at the same time the power of a single fact, in whose constitution they are perfectly joined together, in an inward way. The ideal and the actual, the general and the particular, are both present in all life, not by juxtaposition or succession, but in such a way as to include each other at every point. The very same life is both general and particular, at the same time—the ideal in the actual, and the actual in the ideal; and each is what it is always, only by having in itself the presence of the other, as that which it is not.

Take, for instance, the life of a particular plant or tree.[3] Immediately considered, it is something single, answerable to the outward phenomenal form under which it is exhibited to the senses. But it is, at the same time, more also than this. It becomes a particular plant or tree, in fact, only as it is felt to be the revelation of a life more comprehensive than its own, a life that appears in all plants and trees, and yet is not to be regarded as springing from them, or as measured by them, in any respect. The general vegetable life is not simply the sum of the actual vegetation that is going forward in the world. It is before this in order of being, and can never be fully represented by its growth; for in its nature it has no bounds, while this last is always necessarily finite, made up of a definite number of individual existences. Still it is nothing apart from these existences, which serve to unfold its presence and power; and which, in doing so, and only in doing so, come also to be what they are in truth. The life of each particular tree is thus at once the universal vegetable life, in which all trees stand, and the single manifestation to which this life has come in that particular case. Abstract from it the invisible, ideal, universal force or fact, which as a mere particular tree it is not,

---

3. [Nevin utilizes images of the natural world, and of nature in general, in several places throughout his writing. For examples, see Appel, *Life*, 591; Nevin, "New Creation in Christ," MTSS 4:39–43; Nevin, "Natural and Supernatural" (in this volume). For the biological metaphor at the root of Nevin's thinking, see Layman, general introduction to *Born of Water*, MTSS 6:23–24 and n129.]

but which belongs to it only in common with other trees, and you reduce its existence at once to a sheer nullity: an object absolutely *single* in the world, could never be anything more than a spectral prodigy for the senses. So also, if it be attempted to sunder the particular from the general. Vegetable life can have no reality, save as it shows itself through particular plants and trees. The claims of the particular here, are just as valid and full, as the claims of the general. We have no right to push either aside, in order to make room for the other. The ideal or general cannot subsist without the actual or particular; and it is equally impossible for this last to subsist without the first. They can subsist both, only in and by each other; and it is this mutual comprehension and inbeing of the two precisely, which gives life its proper realness and truth. The *real* is not the actual as such, nor the ideal as such, but the actual and ideal perfectly blended together, as the presence of the same fact.

The same order holds in the sphere of humanity.[4] Every man comprehends in himself a life, which is at once both single and general, the life of his own person, separately considered, and the life at the same time of the race to which he belongs. He is *a man;* the universal conception of humanity enters into him, as it enters also into all other men: while he is, besides, *this or that* man, as distinguished from all others by his particular position in the human world. Here again, too, as before, the relation between the general and the particular or single, is not one of outward conjunction simply; as though the man were, in the first place, complete in and of himself, and were then brought to stand in certain connections with other men, previously complete in the same way. His completeness as an individual involves of itself his comprehension in a life more general than his own. The first can have no place apart from the second. The two forms of existence are not the same in themselves, but they are indissolubly joined together, as constituent elements of one and the same living fact, in the person of every man.

[Man as Nature and Spirit]

All this belongs to our constitution, considered simply as a part of the general system of nature. But man is more than nature, though organically one with it as the basis of his being.[5] His life roots itself in this sphere, only to ascend by means of it into one

---

4. [The following sections about humanity and the individual "man" are further explored in significant ways in Nevin, "Wonderful Nature of Man," "Man's True Destiny," (both in this volume); "Christianity and Humanity"; "Bible Anthropology."]

5. [As will become clearer throughout this essay, humankind in Nevin's system plays a unique role in the constitution of history and nature and their teleological relation to Christ Incarnate. Like many other aspects of this essay, it's a line of thought that appears in many other writings of the Nevin and Mercersburg corpus. For example, in "Undying Life in Christ," Nevin posits that the relation of Christ to the world, "comes into still clearer view when we ascend from the sphere of mere physical existence into the sphere of *humanity and history*, where nature shows itself joined with the self-conscious mind, and the world stands sublimated to its highest sense in the free personality of man." Nevin, "Undying Life," in *Tercentenary Monument*, 23–24, emphasis original; also in Appel, *Life*, 612.]

Document 2: Human Freedom.

that is higher. It becomes complete at last, in the form of self-conscious, self-active spirit. The general law of its existence, as regards the point here under consideration, remains the same; but with this vast difference, that what was mere blind necessity before, ruled by a force beyond itself, is now required to become the subject of free intelligence and will, in such way as to be its own law. It is as though the constitution of the world were made to wake within itself to a clear apprehension of its own nature, and had power at the same time to act forth its meaning by a purely spontaneous motion. Reason and will are concerned in the movement of the planet through its appointed orbit, in the growth of the plant, and in the activity of the animal; but in all these cases, they are exerted from abroad, and not from within the objects themselves. The planet obeys a law, which acts upon it irrespectively of all consent on its own part. So in the case of the plant: it grows by a life which is comprehended in itself, but in the midst of all, it remains as dark as the stone that lies motionless by its side; its life is the power still of a foreign force, which it can neither apprehend nor control. The animal can feel, and is able also to move itself from place to place; yet in all this, the darkness of nature continues unsurmounted as before. The intelligence which rules the animal is not its own; and it cannot be said to have any inward possession whatever of the contents of its own life. This consummation of the world's meaning is reached at last, only in the mind of man, which becomes thus, for this very reason, the microcosm or mirror, that reflects back upon the whole inferior creation its true, intelligible image. Here life is no longer blind and unfree. The reason and will, by which it is actuated, are required to enter into it fully, and to become, by means of it, in such separate form, self-conscious and self-possessed. This is the idea of *personality,* as distinguished from the conception of a simply individual existence in the form of nature.[6] Man finds his proper being at last, only in such life of the spirit.

Personality, however, in this case, does not supersede the idea of individual natural existence. On the contrary, it requires this as its necessary ground and support. The natural is the perpetual basis still of the intellectual and moral. The general character of life, therefore, in the view of it which is before us at this time, is not overthrown by this exaltation, as has been already intimated, but is only advanced by it into higher and more significant force. It still continues to revolve as before, between the two opposite poles, which we have found to enter into it from the start, and exhibits still to our contemplation the same dualistic aspect, resulting from the action of these forces, whose inseparable conjunction at the same time forms its only true and proper unity. It is still at once actual and ideal, singular and universal; only now the union of these two forms of existence is brought to be more perfect and intimate than before, by the intense spiritual fusion to which all is subjected in the great fact of consciousness.

---

6. [On personality, see also Nevin, "Faith, Reverence and Freedom," 114; Nevin, "Moral Order of Sex," 551; Appel, *Life*, 407–10.]

Consciousness is itself emphatically the apprehension of the particular and single, in the presence of the universal.[7] The two forms of life flow together, in every act of thought or will. Personality is, by its very conception, the power of a strictly universal life, revealing itself through an individual existence as its necessary medium. The universal is not simply in the individual here blindly, as in the case of the lower world, but knows itself, also, and has possession of itself, in this form; so far, at least, as the man has come to be actually what he is required to be by his own constitution. The perfection of his nature is found just in this, that as an individual, inseparably linked in this respect to the world of nature, from whose bosom he springs, he shall yet recognize in himself the authority of reason, in its true universal character, and yield himself to it spontaneously as the proper form of his own being. Such clear recognition of the universal reason in himself, accompanied with such spontaneous assent to its authority, is that precisely, in the case of any human individual, which makes him to be at once rational and free. The person is necessarily individual; but in becoming personal, the individual life is itself made to transcend its own limits, and maintains its separate reality, only by merging itself completely in the universal life which it is called to represent.

Personality and moral freedom are, properly speaking, the same. By this last we are to understand simply, the normal form of our general human life itself. As such, it is nothing more nor less than the full combination of its opposite poles, in a free way. In the sphere of nature this union is necessary and inevitable; in the human spirit, it can be accomplished only by intelligent, spontaneous action, on the part of the spirit itself. The individual life in this form, with a full sense of its own individual nature, and with full power to cleave to this as a separate, independent interest, must yet, with clear consciousness and full choice, receive into itself the general life to which it of right belongs, so as to be filled with it and ruled by it at every point. Then we have a proper human existence.

Moral freedom then, the only liberty that is truly entitled to the name, includes in itself two elements or factors, which need to be rightly understood, first, in their separate character, and then in their relation to each other, in order that this idea itself may be rightly apprehended. It is the *single* will moving with self-conscious free activity in the orbit of the *general* will. The constituent powers by which it comes to exist, are the sense of self on the one hand, and the sense of a moral universe on the other, the sense of independence, and the sense of authority or law. It is the perfect union of the single and the universal, the subjective and the objective, joined together

---

7. [For a deeper exploration of the philosophical background of consciousness within Hegelian idealism, see especially chapters 3 and 4 of Hegel, *Phenomenology of Spirit.* In contrast to Kant who argued that the individual mind determines thought and guides access to knowledge, Hegel argues that there is also necessarily collective thought and knowledge. The tension between collective and individual knowing is what legitimates access to universal (and particular) concepts. For Hegel this dialectic constitutes the first two movements of "consciousness."]

DOCUMENT 2: HUMAN FREEDOM.

as mutually necessary, though opposite, polar forces in the clear consciousness of the spirit.[8]

[The Factors of Freedom]

Let us direct our attention now, for a moment, separately to each of these great constituents of freedom.

Freedom supposes, in the first place, entire *independence*[9] on the part of its subject.

It can have no place accordingly, as we have already seen, in the sphere of mere nature. God is free in upholding and carrying forward the world, in this form, according to its appointed laws; but the world itself is not free. Its activity is for itself altogether blind and necessary, accompanied with no self-apprehension, and including in itself no self-motion. It is actuated throughout by a foreign force, with no possible alternative but to obey, while yet its obedience carries in itself no light or love, no intelligence or will. Nature is held in slavish bondage to its own law, as a power impressed upon it perpetually from abroad, and in no sense the product of its separate life. The earth rolls round the sun, the sap mounts upward in the tree, the dog pursues its game, with like subordination to a force by which they are continually mastered, without the least power to master in return. Animal impulse and instinct are no better here, than the plastic power that fashions the growth of the plant.[10] There is individual existence in each case, included in the bosom of a general ideal life, and comprising action powerfully turned in upon itself; but there is no independence: the subject of the action hangs always, with helpless necessity, on the action itself, and is borne passively along upon the vast objective stream of the world's life, without concurrence or resistance of its own.

[Independence of the Individual]

It is only in the sphere of self-conscious spirit, then, that individual independence becomes possible. Hence it involves two things, the light of intelligence and the power of choice. Both of these, in their very nature, refer to an individual centre, or *self,* from which their activity is made to radiate, and towards which, again, it is found

---

8. [The way in which Nevin draws together the will, freedom, independence echoes "Bible Anthropology": "Men are born for truth, as they are born also for freedom. The first is the inalienable right of their understanding, the second is the inalienable right of their will" (363–64).]

9. ["Independence" is in "small caps" in the original.]

10. [Nevin learned the concept of "plastic power" from his first colleague at Mercersburg, the philosopher Frederick Rauch, who defined it as "the principle of individual life and its preservation" that produces "forms of individual life" in all of their diversity (Rauch, *Psychology*, 28–29). Also called "plastic nature," the concept was introduced by the Cambridge Platonist Ralph Cudworth (Edwards, ed., *Encyclopedia of Philosophy*, 2:272).]

continually to return. All knowledge begins and stands perpetually in the consciousness of self; and every act of the will may be denominated, at the same time, an act of self-apprehension.

It belongs to the conception of individual life universally, that it should be in itself a centre of the manifold activities by which it makes itself known. In the sphere of nature, this relation holds in the form only of a blind plastic law, or at least in the form of an equally blind instinct. In the sphere of consciousness, which is above nature, it is no longer blind, but clear. The subject is not simply an individual centre, but knows and seeks itself under this character. In such form first, it attains to what we call subjective independence.

By means of intelligence, the individual self emerges out of the night of nature into the clear vision of its own existence, and is thus prepared to embrace itself as a separate living centre. It is no longer an object merely as before, acted upon from abroad, but is constituted a *subject*, in the strict sense of this term, having possession of itself, and capable of self-action.

Mere intelligence, however, is not of itself independence.[11] If a planet were endowed with the power of perceiving its own existence, without the least ability to modify it in the way of self-control, it is plain that it would be just as little independent as it is in its present state. Consciousness in absolute subjection to nature, would be, indeed, a species of bondage, that might be said to be even worse than that of nature itself. And so if the intelligence were ruled and actuated, not by nature, but by some other intelligence in the like irresistible way, the result would be the same. No matter what the actuating force might be, if it were even the Divine will itself, which were thus introduced into the conscious life of the individual, so as to carry this along with overwhelming necessity in its own direction, the subject thus wrought upon from abroad, without the power of self-impulse, could not be regarded as having the least independence. The case calls for something more than mere intelligence. To this must be joined also the power of choice.[12]

The supposition, indeed, which has just been made, is in its own nature impossible. Reason and will necessarily involve each other; and the light of intelligence, therefore, can never be sundered in fact (but only hypothetically) from the motion of choice. Self-consciousness is itself always self-action.

Individual independence, we say, requires the power of choice; that the self-conscious subject shall not be moved simply from abroad, but have the capacity of moving itself, as though it were the original fountain of its own action. If the will be itself bound by a force which is foreign from its own nature, the man in whom it

---

11. [Nevin's underlying theological framework for this section of the essay is captured well by DiPuccio: "The whole idea of redemption, therefore, is to raise the fallen creation into just such a sacramental communion with the powers of heaven. But such a conjunction between God and creation can never be more than outward and mechanical unless it also joins with human will and intelligence." DiPuccio, *Interior Sense*, 26.]

12. [Nevin held to this psychology to the end of his life. See Nevin, "Bread of Life," MTSS 6:229–30.]

dwells cannot be free. It lies in the very conception of freedom, that the subject of it should have power to choose his own action, and that this power should involve the possibility of his making a different choice from that which he is led to make in fact. He acts from himself, and for himself, and not in obedience merely to an extraneous power, whether in the sphere of nature, or in the sphere of spirit. The action springs truly and fully out of his own conscious purpose and design, and is strictly the product of that separate living nature which he calls himself.

This is what Kant makes so much account of, in his philosophy, as the *autonomy* of the will.[13] The idea is one of vast importance, notwithstanding the great abuse which has been made of it in his school. The will, in its very nature, must be autonomic in order that it may be free; that is, it must be a law to itself, in such sense that its activity shall be purely and strictly its own in opposition to the thought of everything like compulsion exerted upon it from abroad. It is a world within itself, no less magnificent than that with which it is surrounded in the external universe; and it may not be invaded by any form of power, that is not comprehended from the beginning in its own constitution. All such power, proceeding from earth, or hell, or heaven, must be counted *heteronomic*, and contradictory to its nature. The will can endure no heteronomy. It must be autonomic, subjectively independent, the fountain of its own activity, wherever it is found in its true and proper exercise.[14]

This then is the first grand constituent of Moral Freedom. The idea implies universally the presence of an individual will, which, *as such*, is perfectly unbound from all heteronomic extraneous restraints, and carries in itself the principle of its own action, in the way of law and impulse to itself. There can be no liberty where there is no subjective independence.

[The Conception of Law]

But such autonomic will is not of itself at once, as some appear to think, the *whole* conception of freedom. This requires another constituent factor; no less essential than the first; the presence, namely, of an objective universal *Law*, by which the individual will is of right bound, and without obedience to which it can never be true to its own nature.

---

13. [Kant insisted "that a rational will must be regarded as autonomous, or free, in the sense of being the author of the law that binds it. The fundamental principle of morality—the Categorical Imperative—is none other than the law of an autonomous will. . . . Kant argues that the idea of an autonomous will emerges from a consideration of the idea of a will that is free 'in a negative sense.' The concept of a rational will is of a will that operates by responding to what it takes to be reasons. This is, firstly, the concept of a will that does not operate through the influence of factors outside of this responsiveness to apparent reasons. For a will to be free is thus for it to be physically and psychologically unforced in its operation." Johnson and Cureton, "Kant's Moral Philosophy."]

14. [For Kant, heteronomy is the condition of being under the sway of external influence and acting on desires not in accord with reason. See Andrews, *Agency and Autonomy*, 36.]

Part 1: Culture, Philosophy, Ethics, Anthropology

Self-consciousness is itself the power of a life that is general and universal, as well as individual. All life we have already seen to be the union of these two forms of existence in fact; though in the sphere of nature, of course, the fact prevails only in an outward and blind way. With the light of intelligence, however, including in itself the force of self-apprehension and self-action, it must itself enter into the life of the subject under the same character. That is, the union of the general and individual must hold in the form of consciousness itself; so that the subject of this, in coming to know himself properly as an individual being, shall have at the same time the apprehension of a life more comprehensive than his own, and, indeed, truly universal, in the bosom of which his own is carried as the necessary condition of its existence. It is the complete sense of this, theoretically and practically felt, that gives us the fact of personality; which is just the consciousness of an individual life, in the form of reason and will, as the universal truth of the world's life. Reason cannot be something merely particular or private. It is universal in its very nature. It is so theoretically, and it is so, also, of course, practically. In entering the sphere of thought and will, then, as distinguished from that of mere nature, man comes into conscious union with a life which is more than his own, and which exists independently altogether of his particular knowledge or choice. He does not create it in any sense, but is simply received into it as a sea of existence already at hand, and altogether objective to himself as a separate single subject; while he knows it to be in truth, at the same time, the only proper form of his individual life itself subjectively considered. If this were not the case, there could be no room, in his case, for the idea either of intelligence or freedom. A purely particular or single intelligence would be as blind as the stork, which knoweth, we are told, her appointed times in the heaven; and a purely particular or single will, in like manner, would be as little free as the wind, which is said to blow where it listeth, or as a wave of the sea driven of the same wind, and tossed hither and thither without object or rule. —Reason and will, to be truly subjective, must be apprehended always as truly objective, also, and universal. This necessity lies, as we have said, in the very idea of consciousness itself, and is the foundation of all personal life in the case of men.

But the idea now of such universal reason and will, is itself the conception of law, in its deepest and most comprehensive sense. This is nothing more nor less than this boundless objective authority or necessity, in which the individual life of the human subject is required to enter freely that it may be complete.

The *law*, in this character, is of course an idea, not an abstraction. It has in itself, accordingly, the two grand attributes of an idea, universality and necessity.

Its universality is not simply this, that it represents collectively all individual wills, or objects of will. On the contrary, it excludes every sort of distinction and comparison. No individual will, as such, can enter into the constitution of the law. It is absolute, and one within itself, merely revealing its presence through the single wills into which it enters, without deriving from them at all its being and force.

Document 2: Human Freedom.

So, again, its necessity is not simply this, that the world cannot be preserved in prosperity and order without it, or that the world itself may have been pleased to agree in establishing its authority as sacred. It is a necessity which is altogether unconditional, and which rests eternally and unchangeably in the nature of the law itself.

As thus universal and necessary, the being of the law is infinitely real. It is not simply the thought or conception of what is right, not a name merely or mental abstraction representing a certain order of life which men are required to observe; but it is the very forms of truth and right themselves, the absolutely independent power by which they exist in the world. As in the sphere of nature, the law is in no respect the product of the forces which are comprehended in nature itself, but forms rather the inmost life of its entire constitution, which could not consist at all if it were not held together by this bond; so here in the sphere of free intelligence also, it is by no other power that the order of life, as thus intelligent and free, can be upheld for a single hour. The world, in its moral no less than in its physical constitution, lives, moves and has its being, only in the presence of the law, as a real existence in no sense dependent upon it for its character. Not indeed as though it might be supposed to exist, with its own separate entity, in no connection with the actual world whatever. As the ideal life of nature, it cannot be sundered from the actual manifestation in which this consists; and as the absolute truth and right of the moral universe, it cannot subsist except through the consciousness of the thinking and willing subjects of which this universe is composed. Abstracted from all subjective intelligence, its objective reality is reduced to a nullity. It is only in the form of reason and will, which have no being apart from self-consciousness, that the law can have any true subsistence whatever. It supposes an intelligible and intelligent universe. But still it is no creature of the universe, no mere image abstracted from its actual constitution. In the order of being, though not of time, it is older than the universe. Without reason and will there could be no law, and yet all reason and will stand in it from the very start, and can enter into no living subject whatever except from its presence, as their ulterior objective source and ground.

Concretely real in this way, and not simply an abstraction, the law has its seat primarily, as Hooker expresses it, in the bosom of God.[15] Not so, however, as if God might be supposed, in the exercise of any private arbitrary will of his own, to have devised and ordained it as a proper scheme after which to fashion the order of the universe. The universality of the law excludes, as we have already seen, the idea of all merely private or particular will, even though it were conceived to be in this form the will of God himself. God's will, however, is not private or particular, but absolute; subjective indeed, in such sense as is required by the nature of personality, but objective and universal at the same time; these two forms of existence, subjective and objective, being with Him absolutely commensurate and identical. God is not the author of the law, as something standing out of himself and beyond himself; he does not *make* it, as

---

15. [Hooker, *Of the Laws of Ecclesiastical Polity* 1.16.8.]

a man might frame an instrument to serve some purpose which he has, under another form, in his own mind. Still less, of course, may the law be said, in any sense, to make *Him,* as though it were a power before Him in authority, determining the manner of his existence. It has its being only in God and from God; not however as something different from the Divine mind itself. It is the necessary form of God's infinitely wise and holy will, as exercised in the creation and support of the actual universe, considered both as nature and spirit.

Thus resident primarily in the Divine will, and identical with it throughout, the law at the same time, in its objective character, passes over into the actual order of the world, and reveals itself here also as a power to be acknowledged and obeyed, under the most real and concrete form. In the sphere of nature the universal and singular are brought together, not directly and immediately, but through the medium of the particular, constituting what we denominate the species or kind, as distinguished from the genus.[16] Thus the tree is not what it is, by receiving into itself at once the universal vegetable life; but only as this life has previously undergone a distinction within itself, by which it may be recognized as vegetation under this or that specific form; it can become a tree, only as it puts on at the same time the type of some particular tree, locust, for instance, or ash, or elm, so as to be known accordingly in this character and no other. And just so in the sphere of the moral world, where the law has to do with intelligence and will. As universal or ideal, it is not carried over at once into the consciousness of each individual subject in an original and independent way; but the case requires necessarily that it should, in the first place, resolve itself into certain particular orders or forms of authority, through which intermediately its presence may afterwards thus actualize itself in full for the single will. As no single man is the human race, but only a part of it, having the truth of his being in the organic relations by which he is comprehended, through the family and state, in the whole; so the law, which is an objective rule and measure for the whole, and only for the parts as comprehended in this, and not as sundered from it, can never come near to any man in the way of an absolutely singular and exclusive revelation. It can reach him really, only by passing *through* the organic system, in which alone it takes cognizance at all of his existence. Under such view, it has an actual concrete being in the world itself, and is wrought objectively into the very constitution of its rational and moral life, as imbodied [sic] in the form of human society and made to reveal itself continually in the process of human history.

Such, we say, is the conception in general of the law, which is the other grand factor or constituent of Moral Freedom; the first having exhibited itself to us before in the necessary independence or autonomy of the individual subject. It remains now to consider *how* these two great forces are joined together in its constitution.[17]

16. [See further commentary on these themes in Borneman, *Church*, 76–78.]

17. [For an excellent discussion of Nevin's view of human freedom in relation to divine law, see DiPuccio, *Interior Sense*, 188–92. DiPuccio writes, "Freedom involves a consubstantiality between will

Document 2: Human Freedom.

[The Organic Unity of Freedom and Law]

Separately considered, they seem to oppose and overthrow each other. If the will be absolutely autonomic and independent in its subjective character, how can it be absolutely bound at the same time by a force that comes from beyond itself, the purely objective authority of law? And if it be thus bound, placed under necessity, comprehended in a power which is broader than itself, and older than itself, how can it be said to be in any proper sense its own law, and the fountain of its own action?

It is clear that no merely mechanical union here can escape the power of this contradiction.[18] If we suppose the single will to be, in the first place, something complete by itself, and then think of the law as existing in the same separate way, each including in itself the claims which belong to it, as they have now been described, the two conceptions must necessarily contradict each other, and cannot be brought in such form to any true reconciliation. If the subject feel himself in mere juxtaposition with the law, having it over against his consciousness as a form of existence different from his own, it will not be possible for him to assert his own independence, without resenting and resisting the pretensions of the law at the same time, as a heteronomic, foreign force. Nor will it be possible for the law, in the same circumstances, to acknowledge or respect the independence of the human subject. It must necessarily assume the tone of command, arraying against him the majesty of its own everlasting nature, and with the weight of its terrible categoric imperative, *Thou shalt*,[19] crushing his liberty completely to the earth. In such a relation, there is no room for the idea of moral freedom. It is slavish in its very nature. The liberty which the subject may still pretend to assert for himself, becomes necessarily licentiousness and sin; while, on the other hand, any obedience he may seem to yield to the law, as being thus forced and external, can have no reality or worth in the view of the law itself.

Such is the relation which holds in fact between human consciousness and the law in a state of sin. The two forms of existence are still incapable of being absolutely

---

and law. The constitution or essential properties of the will must become one with the constitution of the law in order to be free" (189).]

18. [A brief note on Nevin's language of "mechanical" is in order. For Nevin, mechanical is associated with the outward, external, and strictly materialist, lacking the organic relationship to the inward constitution of nature, humankind, and Christ Incarnate. This is in opposition to much of the prevailing philosophical movements he encountered. As DiPuccio astutely points out, "Despite Nevin's appropriation of classic metaphysics, he rejected the mechanical and dualistic view of creation associated with Newtonian physics and Common Sense Realism. For Mercersburg the essential stuff of reality is neither passive matter, inert substances, nor static ideas (Aristotle and Plato), but dynamic 'laws.' In Nevin's hands, the analogy of being is not a static idea but a dynamic one in which the forces which uphold the cosmos spring fresh every moment from the will of God." DiPuccio, *Interior Sense*, 38.]

19. [A succinct version of Immanuel Kant's categorical imperative reads: "One must be able to will that a maxim of our action should become a universal law." Kant, *Groundwork*, 37 {Ak 4:424}. "Thou shalt" do *this* because *this* is what every rational being *ought* to *will*. Here Nevin emphasizes the "terrible" burden of the absolute *ought*.]

sundered; but they are bound together only in an outward, unfree way. The law cannot relax its right to rule the sinner's will; but it stands over him merely in the attitude of despotic commination.[20] The sinner, too, can never emancipate himself entirely from the sense of the law, for that were to lose his hold upon himself at the same time; but he has it over against him only as an objective might, in whose favor he is required to renounce the separate self, which he has come to regard as his true and proper life. Hence continual rebellion only, and continual guilt. The law, in such circumstances, has no power to bring light or freedom, strength or peace, into the soul. It is necessarily the ministration only of sin and death. Emphatically it works wrath.

In distinction from all such merely outward and mechanical conjunction of the two opposing forces, liberty and authority, from which can proceed at best only a powerless, unfree morality, the true idea of human freedom, we say now, requires their internal *organic* union as constituent elements of one and the same life. The opposition of the two forces, in this case, remains in its full strength; each is left in the possession of its separate independent character; neither is permitted to exclude or overwhelm the other; but the opposition is simply that which belongs to the contrary poles of the magnet, which fly asunder only that they may, at the same moment, be drawn together with the greater force, and whose union, as it is the result, is also the indispensable condition always of the separation out of which it grows. Such polar distinction enters, in fact, into the very idea of concrete existence. Where there is no distinction, there can be no concretion, but only meaningless and powerless abstraction, or, at best, the ideal possibility of an existence which has not yet become real. Distinction, however, involves opposition, or the setting of one thing over against another. Only where this has taken place, then, is there any room for the union that all proper reality implies. But such union shows the two sides thus sundered, to be at the same time necessary to each other. The opposition is polar only, and as such conservative and not destructional. All organized, concrete existence, physical or spiritual, will be found to carry in itself a polarity of this kind.

We may be assisted to a right apprehension of the point in hand, by referring again to the constitution of life, as we have already found it to hold in the sphere of mere nature. The ideal and the actual, a universal generic nature on the one hand, and a particular single existence on the other, enter jointly into the constitution of every plant that springs from the bosom of the earth. These two forces, at the same time, are in their own character truly different and distinct. Their distinction takes the form of actual, direct opposition. What the one is, the other *is not*. Each is in itself the negation in full of the other. And yet they are here brought perfectly together, in the constitution of the same life; not by mechanical juxtaposition, but in the way of mutual interpenetration and interfusion, so that each is made to grow into the other, and by such concrescence only, comes to be at last what it is found to be in fact. The two sides of the plant's life still continue to be distinct, and their opposition to each

---

20. ["Commination": "The act of threatening divine vengeance."]

Document 2: Human Freedom.

other is by no means abolished in such sense as to be taken wholly out of the way, it still exists, but it exists as something comprehended in a higher action, which is, at the same time, the perfect union and reconciliation of the forces from which it springs. The opposition is polar. The union is organic.

Bring all this into the sphere of consciousness, so that the union in question shall be, not blind and unavoidable, but the movement of clear, spontaneous intelligence, acting from itself and for itself, and we have the conception of Moral Freedom. The existence here is not a mere object, wrought upon by an action strange to itself, but a subject which has come to be possessed of its activity as the very form of its own being. It is as though the planet, moving in its appointed orbit, were made to awake within itself to the clear knowledge of its own nature, with full power at the same time to pursue any course through the heavens that to itself might seem best; while it should still continue true notwithstanding, as before, to the path prescribed for it, no less *bound* by objective law but bound always only by its own consent. Should such a rational planet, in the exercise of its liberty, strike off from its orbit, affecting to play the part of some wandering comet, it must in the same moment, become unfree; as much so, at least, as when carried forward in its true course by the force of mere blind natural law. Only the power of choice making it possible for it to become a comet, but yet spontaneously embracing the true planetary motion in fact, identified thus with the sense of law, could constitute it the subject of freedom. Neither as bound simply, nor as simply unbound, would the planet be free; but only as bound and unbound, at the same time, and in the same continuous action;[21] the two forms of existence joined together as the power of a single fact, in the sphere of consciousness; the law coming to its proper expression only in the independence of the subject, and the independence of the subject having no reality, save under the form of obedience to the law.

What may thus be imagined in the case of a planet, to illustrate the conception in hand, is the very constitution of man in his normal state. He is formed for freedom, and becomes complete only in this character, by the possibility he carries in himself of such a living, conscious free union, as has now been mentioned, of the great polar forces of the world's life. He has a will of his own, and he is at the same time under a law which is not himself; he is conscious of both, as making realities in his existence; and, to crown, all he is capable of so acknowledging both, that they shall actually grow into each other as the same consciousness. The union of the two powers, in such case, is not mechanical, but organic and real; as truly so as the flowing together of the ideal and actual, in the constitution of a plant or tree; only with the difference, that what is blindly necessary there, has become here the self-comprehending activity of the living nature itself. This is Freedom. In no other form can it exist for men at all. It is the action of the individual will, moving of its own accord and apart from all compulsion,

---

21. [In simple English: let us imagine a planet has the power to "choose" to become a comet. But if it so chose, it would cease to be what it "is," a planet. So it "chooses" to be remain what it is. It is bound (to being a planet), and yet it is unbound—it can choose (hypothetically) to be so.]

in the orbit of the law, with clear sense of its authority, and clear private election in its favor, at the same time. This implies, of course, that the will is of the same nature with the law. They are thus related, in fact, as we have already seen. In obeying the law, the will obeys in reality its own true constitution; as much so as fire does, for instance, in exhibiting the properties which show it to *be* fire, and not water. So, in breaking away from the law, it necessarily becomes false to itself, to the same extent. Thus all apparent contradiction is resolved in the idea of freedom as now described. Authority involves necessity, while liberty is the very opposite; and still both are here inseparably joined together, in such way, indeed, that neither can exist at all, in its true form, without the other. Freedom, in order that it may be free, *must* be bound. But in this case it is self-bound; not arbitrarily, however, to a rule of its own invention, which would be again to be unfree, but in obedience to the law, as the necessary form of its own existence. The will of the subject is ruled by a force that comes from beyond itself, and yet it is strictly autonomic at the same time; even as the rose blooms forth always its proper single life, though it is only as filled with the general law of vegetation that it has power to bloom at all. The law so enters the subject, as to become within him a continually self-originated obligation; while his private will is so comprehended in the law, as to find in it no foreign constraint whatever.

Such is the proper theory of human freedom, whether considered as religious or as simply political. It is formed by the union of liberty and authority, so joined together that neither is allowed to exclude or oppress the other; the two constituting thus the force of a single life. Where this inward organic conjunction of the elements now named is wanting, one of them either excluding the other altogether, or at best enduring its presence only in an outward way, the whole idea must be to the same extent necessarily overthrown. It matters not, in such case, which of the two factors may thus prevail at the cost of its opposite, the result will be the same. In the one direction, we shall have authority turned into despotism; in the other, liberty converted into licentiousness; both alike fatal to all true freedom. To be wholly bound, and to be wholly unbound, come here to the same thing in the end. Either state is to be deprecated as slavery.

[The Historic Dialectic of Authority and Liberty]

The world has a continual tendency to fall over, either to one or the other of these extremes. Thus we have, on one side, authority coupled with blind obedience, and on the other a spirit of insurrection against all legitimate rule, making up to a great extent the history of human life.

Our own age leans especially toward the extreme of exalting individual liberty at the expense of just authority.[22] Time has been, when the whole civilization of the world

22. [Nevin explicitly levels this critique against the "Sect System," which he describes as "full of zeal, apparently for human freedom in every shape, the rights of man, liberty of conscience, and the

Document 2: Human Freedom.

showed an opposite character. It was necessary indeed, in the nature of the case, that the process of our modern culture, the fruit of Christianity, and the only culture that may be regarded as worthy of the name, should commence in this way. Its foundations were to be laid deep, in the first place, in the sense of law and a corresponding spirit of obedience to its authority.[23] Long ages of discipline were required for this purpose, in the course of which it was hardly possible that wrong should not be done to the idea of freedom, by an undue depression of its opposite element, the liberty of the individual subject. The discipline became, in fact, as we all know, tyrannical and oppressive just in this way, by refusing to recognize the rights of those who were subjected to it, as the time of their minority came to an end, and made it proper that these rights should be brought into full and free exercise. Instead of making it their business to train their subjects for personal independence, the true design of all sound government, both Church and State pursued the policy only of repressing every aspiration in this direction, and sought to hold the world in perpetual vassalage to mere power on their own side; as though a parent, long accustomed to rule his children with absolute control, should, at last, insist on extending over their full adult life itself the same kind of rule, without any regard whatever to the wants and capabilities of their advanced state. The relation between authority and obedience became, in this manner, mechanical and altogether external. Free authority and obedience fell asunder, as though each belonged to a different sphere from the other. The authority claimed to be of divine force for itself, under a fixed outward form; while the merit of obedience was supposed to lie in its blind, uninquiring subjection to the will thus imposed upon it from abroad. In one word, the claims of the subjective were overwhelmed, and well nigh crushed by the towering pretensions of the objective. No wonder that this extreme should at length become insupportably onerous to the ripening consciousness of the Christian world. It opened the way gradually for a powerful reaction towards the opposite side. This gave birth finally, when the fullness of time had come, to the great fact of the Reformation; which may be regarded as a solemn *Declaration of Independence* on the part of the human mind, against the tyranny by which it had been wronged for centuries in the name of religion and law. A grand epoch certainly, in the history of the world's life, whose consequences must continue to fill the earth to the end of time. These belong of course, not simply to the Church in a separate view, but to every sphere, whether of thought or action, that is comprehended in our common human existence. Art, science,

---

privilege of every man to worship God in his own way. . . . Roger Williams is taken by his sect to be the father emphatically of our American Independence . . . . The truth is . . . [t]hose precisely which make the greatest boast of their liberty, are as a general thing, the least prepared either to exercise it themselves or to allow its exercise in others. The sect habit, as such, is constitutionally unfree." Nevin, "The Sect System," MTSS 5:248, 249–50.]

23. [Beginning with this paragraph, one notices Nevin's subtle shift into considerations of "Church and State," independence, and other elements of authority and law in a more concrete manner. For a thorough discussion of the political context and Nevin's engagement with it, see Borneman, *Church*, especially 15–58, and 149–60.]

government, and social life, all have been affected by the change. A new stadium is in progress, for the universal life of the world; having for its object now the full assertion of what may be styled the subjective pole of freedom, in opposition to the long historical process that went before, in favor of its opposite side. Protestantism is the fountain thus of all modern liberty, religious and political alike. Its tendency has been, from the beginning, to break the chains of authority as previously established, and to engage the human mind to a bold vindication of its own rights in opposition to all blind obedience of whatever kind. Nor is it to be imagined at all, that the new position which has been reached in this way, can ever be surrendered again, in favor of the order which prevailed before. The period of blind submission to the sense of the objective, whether in Church or State, when priest and king were held to be superior by divine right, to the divine constitution itself by which they were created, we may well trust, has forever passed away. But it does not follow at once from this, that the past was all wrong, or that the present is all right. A just consideration of history would lead us rather to suppose, that the new direction it has taken, may itself be liable to abuse, in a way answerable to the wrong which existed before on the opposite side; which would not imply certainly, that we must fall back again to the things we have happily left behind, but only that we should so far right our course, as to steer clear of the rocks that threaten us from either side, and so press forward to the true and proper destiny of our race. That the principle of individual liberty has been, in fact, thus carried to an extreme, at least in some cases, in the progress of the Protestant era, is acknowledged on all sides; and it needs no very profound or extensive observation, to see that our own age in particular is peculiarly exposed to danger just in this direction. It leans constitutionally towards an undue assertion of the prerogatives of the individual life, over against the idea of authority as something absolute and universal.

False liberty, in this form, does not consist, of course, in the open rejection of the law in itself considered. On the contrary, it usually affects to make great account of the law; but it is always only in a mechanical and outward way. The law is not viewed as a necessary constituent of freedom itself, but simply as an outward rule and measure of its supposed rights. The subject starts with his own independence as an interest full and complete in its separate character, and obeys the law accordingly, in his way, not by entering it as a life beyond himself, but by requiring it to come first into subjection to his own private will. He has no conception of freedom as the union of liberty and authority. It is for him, at last, the exercise only of separate personal independence on his own part. By the right of private judgment, he means to assert the right of thinking for himself, regardless of the thoughts of all other men; and so also in the case of private will.[24] He does not deny, indeed, that truth and right are universal in

---

24. [Nevin expresses similar sentiments in "Faith, Reverence, and Freedom," where he writes, "Why may not the man who disowns private judgement and private will be just as free in the reverent use of established law and tradition to say the least, as the man who scorns every such limitation" (114).]

Document 2: Human Freedom.

their nature, and as such not to be created or controlled by his particular mind. But the authority which belongs to them in this view, remains for him always more or less a mere abstraction. It does not come near to him under a concrete form, in the actual constitution of the world with which he is surrounded. He is without reverence accordingly for the powers by which it is properly represented. He sees nothing divine in history. The Church is to him the mere aggregation of a certain amount of private thinking on the subject of religion. The State is taken to be the creature only of its own members, standing by their permission, and liable of right to be taken down by them, or changed into a new form, at their own good pleasure.

All this involves, of course, an immense error; though it is one which it must ever be difficult to bring home clearly to the consciousness of the popular mind. Liberty without law is licentiousness, whether in the sphere of thought or will; and law, to be real, must be the sense of a general concrete authority, actually comprehended in the constitution of the living world to which we belong. Where this may be wanting, it is not possible that there can be any true religious or political freedom. The exaltation of private independence, the rights of the individual as they are called, at the cost of all proper objective authority, is just as fatal here as the exaltation of authority at the cost of individual rights. There is a vast amount of cant[25] and falsehood abroad on this subject, which it is important we should understand, and against which we have need to stand continually upon our guard.

With any right conception of the nature of freedom as now explained, it will not be possible for us, on the other hand, to fall in with the views of those who would persuade us that the only remedy for the evils of a licentious individualism, is to be found in casting ourselves once more blindly into the arms of mere outward authority. This were to fall backward to the period which preceded the Reformation, when we should seek rather to make our own period the means of advancing to one that may be superior to both. It is well to see and admit the difficulties of the present; but we are bound to remember also the difficulties of the past, that we may look for salvation only in the form of a brighter and more glorious future. It deserves to be continually borne in mind that mere authority is as little to be trusted for securing the right order of the world, as mere liberty. They are the opposite poles of freedom, and neither can be true to its constitution, except as this is made to include both in a perfectly inward and free way. The evils incident to private judgment are not to be corrected by referring us to an infallible public judgment, ecclesiastical or political, that may do our thinking for us in every case, and then make it over to us in a merely outward way, without any activity on our own part. And just as little of course are the irregularities of private will to be reformed, by handing us over to the rule of a foreign public will,

---

25. [A pejorative term Nevin uses regularly (see immediately following the second heading in "Plea" below). Webster, *American Dictionary*, 121 provides multiple nuances: "A whining, singing manner of speech," such as beggars might use, and thus "Whining pretension to goodness;" It can also mean "The peculiar words and phrases of professional men," and "Any barbarous jargon."]

as the measure of all right and wrong for our conscience.[26] It is not in this way, that Christianity especially proposes to make us free. The imagination of a mechanical system of notions and rules brought near to the mind from abroad, to be accepted by it in a blind way, on the ground of authority conceived to be divine, is wholly aside from the true character of the gospel. Christianity is indeed a law; but it is at the same time the "law of liberty," comprehending in itself the true normal mould of our general human life, into which it must be cast in every case, in order that it may be complete; but into which it can be cast, for this purpose, only by its own consent and choice. In truth, no government can be rational and good in the case of men, that does not aim at making them able to govern themselves. The only proper use of government is to educate its subjects for freedom, if they have not yet come to be capable of its exercise; and if this be not proposed, the government becomes to the same extent tyrannical. He is an unfaithful parent who seeks to hold his children in perpetual dependence upon his own judgment, and in perpetual vassalage to his own will, instead of training them as quickly as possible to think and act for themselves. So neither the State nor the Church can have any right to bind the understanding and will of their subjects in slavish obedience to mere authority. The case demands a different relation between the two interests with which it is concerned. Though the authority should be never so benevolent and wise, and the subject of it never so well satisfied to be ruled by it in this way, the result would still be slave and not freedom. No man can fulfil his true moral destiny, by a simply blind and passive obedience to law. His obedience, to be complete, must be intelligent and spontaneous. In other words, the law must enter into him and become incorporated with his life. The remedy, then, for subjective license, is not such an exhibition simply of outward authority as may supersede the necessity of private judgment altogether. Even an *infallible* authority in this form would not be desirable; for the Divine will itself, if it were made merely to overwhelm the human as a foreign force, must lead to bondage only, and not to freedom.

[Conclusion: the True Nature of Freedom]

The case requires, then, such an understanding of the true nature of freedom, as may serve to secure its constitution on both sides, Mere theory, indeed, will not be sufficient, here or elsewhere, to preserve life in its right form; but it is, at least, a most important auxiliary to this object. It is much to know clearly, and still more, steadily to keep in mind, that liberty and law, the activity of private will and the restraining force of authority, are alike indispensable to a right condition of human life; that they are required to enter into it always as polar forces, which organically complete each

---

26. [In other texts, Nevin situates consciences both individually and corporately. He speaks of the individual conscience, for example, in the context of polemical texts such as *Antichrist* MTSS 5:215–16; but also of the conscience of the church throughout *The Mystical Presence* (MTSS 1), and *Vindication of the Revised Liturgy*.]

Document 2: Human Freedom.

other; and that the exaltation of either interest at the cost of its opposite, must prove alike fatal to true moral order. It is much to know that the idea of freedom can never be reached by simply opposing one of these powers to the other on either side, as though to insist upon authority were necessarily to wrong liberty; or as though to press the claims of this last, required a rejection of the no less rightful pretensions of the first. That is at all times a very shallow philosophy, though it be unfortunately very common, which can see contradiction only in the polarity now mentioned, and is urged accordingly to affirm and deny with regard to it, in such a way as to exclude the possibility of any reconciliation between the tendencies thus opposed. No authority can be moral that does not seek liberty as its end; and no liberty can be free that is not filled with the sense of authority as the proper contents of its own life.

That it may be difficult to bring this theory of freedom into practice, is readily admitted; but this forms no proper argument against the truth and value of the theory itself. The difficulty lies in the nature of the subject to which it belongs. Still, however, there is no other way in which it is possible for the end to be secured that is here in view. Man must be at once independent and bound, self-governed, and yet obedient to authority, in order that he may at all fulfil his own destiny, in distinction from the system of mere nature with which he is surrounded. For this he is to be educated and formed, under the influences which are comprehended in human society for the purpose. He comes not to moral freedom at once, but is required to rise to it by regular development, out of the life of nature in which his existence starts, and in which it continues always to have its root. In our present circumstances, moreover, the process is greatly embarrassed and obstructed by a false law of sin, which is found too plainly seated in our constitution. It becomes accordingly a most complicated problem, to bring our common human life, in this view, into its proper form; a problem, whose solution in fact runs through the history of the world's entire social constitution, from the beginning of time to its end. The family, the State, and the Church, are all comprehended alike in the service of this great design. They surround the human subject with the force of law from the cradle to the grave, and from the rudeness of savage life onward through all stages of subsequent social refinement; but it is only that he may be educated for the full use finally of his own proper personal independence, in being set free from all bondage, whether objective or subjective, by the clear spontaneous union of his private will with the law to which it is necessarily bound.

It lies in the very conception of this vast educational process, including as it does not only all stages of the single life from infancy to old age, but all stages also of the general ethical life in the progress of nations, that the two great compound forces by which the problem of freedom is in the course of being solved, should sustain to each other, in their legitimate action, a constantly fluctuating relation; the pressure of authority being necessarily greater, and the sense of independence less, in reverse proportion to the actual development of the true idea of freedom in the subject. Here, of course, a wide field is thrown open for the exercise of political and ethical science, in determining the claims of duty and right, as related to each other in any given stadium of morality. On this, however, we are not called now to enter. It may be sufficient to conclude with the general rule, drawn from the whole subject, that no one can be true ethically to his own position, whether as a child or as a man, high or low, rich or poor, in power or out of power, who, in the use of his liberty, whatever it may be, is not ruled at the same time by a sentiment of *reverence* for the idea of an objective authority extended over him in some form, in the actual social organization to which he belongs. To be without reverence for authority, is to have always to the same extent the spirit of a slave. In no other element is it possible to think what is true, or to act what is right.

A Plea for Philosophy.[1]

[The Popular Cant about Philosophy]

Some will have it, that all philosophy is vain; and that the time bestowed upon it, in our colleges and elsewhere, is only wasted, or worse than wasted in the pursuit of a phantom that can never be reached, while it leads us away continually from the proper use of life. What men need in this world, we are told, is not speculation, but an active apprehension of the living realities with which they are immediately surrounded, and the proper practical use of these for the ends of their own existence. The world is a fact, broadly and palpably spread out before our senses; and our life is a fact, which we are required to turn to right account, by making the best of it for ourselves and others, in the circumstances in which we may happen to be placed. Why, then, should we occupy ourselves with things that lie wholly beyond the sphere of our actual existence, and that can only serve to disqualify us for understanding and using the world as it is? The sense of the world is sufficiently clear of itself for such as are disposed to take things just as they are, without troubling their heads about what they are pleased to call its inward spiritual constitution and design. We have had ample experiment besides of the vanity of philosophy, in the past history of its own achievements. The world has been philosophizing since the days of Pythagoras[2] at least, and from a still earlier date, and yet to what has it come in the end? Has its philosophy made it any wiser or better? Has it accomplished any solid gain whatever for the human race? Is the world improved in any respect by the long exploded systems of Greece, by the profound lucubrations of the schoolmen in the middle ages, or by the vast upheavings

---

1. ["A Plea for Philosophy," in *Human Freedom, and A Plea for Philosophy: Two Essays*, 25–45. Mercersburg, PA: P. A. Rice, 1850.]

2. [Pythagoras, the ancient Greek mathematician and philosopher known for his contributions to number theory and geometry, heavily influenced the political and religious philosophies of Plato, Aristotle and the west in general. While best known for "the Pythagorean theorem," he was also a pioneer in formulating the "transmigration of souls" concept which holds that every soul is immortal and, upon death, inhabits a new body. See Horky, *Plato and Pythagoreanism*; Joost-Gaugier, *Measuring Heaven*.]

of thought which have had place since the days of Immanuel Kant, in the modern metaphysics of Germany.³ Is it not, in fact, a history of contradictions and confusions, from beginning to end—one system continually surmounting another, only to be as certainly overwhelmed after the same fashion, in its turn? It will be time enough to challenge our respect for philosophy, when philosophy shall have come to some proper understanding, in the first place, of her own mind and meaning. When she shall have become once mistress of herself—a house no longer divided against itself, the very cavern of Æolus⁴ where all pent up minds are struggling perpetually in fierce conflict—it will be time enough to think of proclaiming her mistress of the world. Till then, let her be remanded to her proper dwelling place in the clouds, the land of far-off shadows and dreams. The world has too much serious business on hand, to be interrupted by her pretensions, and may reasonably say, in the language of Nehemiah to Sanballat and Geshem the Arabian of old: "I am doing a great work, so that I cannot come down; why should the work cease, whilst I leave it and come down to you?"⁵

All this is very comfortable doctrine, of course, for those who have no disposition and not much power, possibly, to think for themselves, while they have just as little wish or will to be bound by the thinking of others. Agrarianism, indeed, we may call it, of the most truly democratic order; for is it not something more to level thus the aristocracy of mind, than it is to bring down simply the aristocracy of birth or fortune? Is it not a species of self-exaltation, particularly soothing to the sense we commonly have of our own importance, to be able in this way to compare ourselves so favorably with what has generally been counted the highest order of the world's intellect, and the true nobility of its life? The man who can say of all philosophy, It is mere wind, must needs feel himself in this respect somewhat superior to the great minds which, in different ages, have counted it worthy of their attention and study. It is much, surely, for any one to have the thought clearly present in his own consciousness: "Pythagoras was a fool, Plato was a fool, Aristotle was a fool; all the old Greek philosophers were fools; the seraphic, irrefragable doctors of the school divinity, Thomas Aquinas, Bonaventura, Duns Scotus, the whole of them together, were fools; and the same character belongs most eminently to the modern German thinkers, Kant, Fichte, Schelling, Hegel, and all who think it worth while to waste any time upon their speculations;⁶

---

3. [Kant figures prominently in this essay. Highly regarded for his proposals in metaphysics, epistemology, and ethics; he insisted that human knowledge is limited by the structure of the mind and that concepts such as space and time are not derived from experience but are only necessary for understanding and interpreting experience. He famously proposed the "Categorical Imperative," a moral principle that one should always act in a way that can be willed as a universal law, a particularly important formulation for understanding Nevin's engagement with his thought and work.]

4. [Aeolus was the mythological keeper of the winds (*Odyssey* 10.20–25). Later artists depict his cavern as a place where all the winds are "struggling perpetually" with each other: e.g., https://www.metmuseum.org/art/collection/search/700488.]

5. [Neh 6:3.]

6. [Both students of Immanuel Kant, Johann Gottlieb Fichte and Friedrich Wilhelm Joseph Schelling are likewise key figures of German idealism (later overshadowed by Hegel), and hugely

Document 2: A Plea for Philosophy.

but *I am wise;* for I have sense enough to know that all philosophy is nonsense, and that the less the world is troubled with it the better. *My* life is more rational, and likely to be of far more account at last, than theirs." This, we say, is comfortable; and it is not much wonder, perhaps, that philosophy should be in bad credit with so many persons, when so fair a premium in this way is made to rest on unthinking ignorance and sloth.

And then, the case becomes still worse, of course, when the prejudice of religion comes in, as it is always ready to do, in favor of the same conclusion. It is bad enough, we are told, that philosophy should pretend to interfere with the actual world, in its common life, abstracting men's minds from its practical realities, and amusing them with its own theoretic dreams; but when the evil is made to reach over, in the same form, to the sphere of religion and faith, it is something still more difficult to be endured. And is there not in fact an original, necessary opposition between revelation and philosophy; Is not faith the simple contrary of speculation? Is it not written, "Let no man *spoil* you through philosophy;"[7] plainly implying that we should have nothing to do with it, in the business of Christianity! And is not the history of the church from the beginning full of instruction and warning, in the same direction? Have not all corruptions and heresies sprung from philosophy, undertaking to rule and set aside the simple doctrine of God's word? Witness the flood of Gnostic speculations in the second century; the subsequent errors of Origen and his school;[8] the scholastic subtleties of the Aristotelian theology, at a still later period; and above all, the rationalistic, pantheistic systems, to which the modern German philosophy has given birth. Philosophy and infidelity are found to have, in all ages, a close inward affinity for each other, The first may be considered the elder sister, if not in fact the proper natural mother of the second. That state of the church accordingly is to be accounted the most prosperous, in which religion is as little as possible the subject of speculation; and the man who meddles least with the contents of his faith, in the way of inward thought and reflection, is likely to show himself the best Christian, and make his way most successfully to heaven.

---

influential for Nevin. Fichte is perhaps most well known for his concept of the self, which he conceived as the starting point for all knowledge and experience. He argued that the self is the origin of all knowledge and that the self is free and autonomous. Schelling, for his part, established and advanced a system of transcendental idealism in which he argued that the mind and the world are interconnected and that the mind can access the basic, organic unity of the world through the intellect. See Beiser, *German Idealism*; Guyer and Horstmann, "Idealism."]

7. [Col 2:8.]

8. [Origen remains one of the most controversial figures in the history of Christianity. Nevin here may well be referring to Origen's rejections of the goodness of material creation, but would likewise be a critic of Origen's arguably hierarchical view of the Trinity. For more, see Mark Edwards, *Catholicity and Heresy*; Williams, "Origen: Between Orthodoxy and Heresy."]

PART 1: CULTURE, PHILOSOPHY, ETHICS, ANTHROPOLOGY

[The Necessity of Philosophy]

But now, in opposition to all such popular cant,—that can hardly be said for the most part to understand its own meaning,—it is at once an ample reply to say, that philosophy belongs to the very constitution of our life, and cannot be expelled from it therefore without the greatest violence and wrong. For what is it at last, more or less than the endeavor to know ourselves and the world, and the form in which, at any given time, this knowledge reflects itself in our consciousness? And can it be a question at all, whether it be proper and right for us to seek the knowledge of ourselves in this way? It lies in the idea of humanity itself, that it should comprehend within itself such a mode of existence, just as it necessarily includes also the life of art or the law of social or political organization. The question whether philosophy is to be tolerated and approved, is precisely like the question whether we should approve and tolerate government or art. These are all so many several spheres only of our human existence itself, which are necessary to make it true and complete, and which cannot be sundered from it, without overthrowing, at the same time, its essential constitution. It is not by any arbitrary option or will of ours, that they come to have the right of being comprehended in the organic structure of the world; their right is as old as the world itself, and must stand as long as man and nature shall be found to endure. If any number of men, for instance, in vast world-convention assembled, should pretend to sit in judgment on the right and title of the fine arts, music, sculpture, poetry and the rest, to retain their place in the world, and at last proceed in form to legislate them out of it, as useless, fantastic, and injurious to religion; to what would such legislation amount in the end, more than to expose the impotence and folly of the congress from which it might spring? The fine arts might say to such a convention: "What have we to do with *thee,* vain wretched apparition of an hour! Is the nature of man to be thus made or unmade, at thy puny pleasure? *Our* authority is broader, and deeper, and far more ancient than thine." And can it be any more reasonable, I would ask, to think of legislating philosophy out of the world or out of the church, in any similar way? Philosophy is no subject for human arbitrament and legislation, in such magisterial form. The question of its being tolerated and allowed, is not just like the question whether we shall have, or not, a tariff or a national bank. It asks no permission of ours, to exercise its appointed functions in the vast world-process of man's history; it has exercised them through all ages thus far, and it will continue to exercise them, no doubt, to the end of time, in virtue of its own indefeasible right to be comprehended in this process, as an original necessary part of its constitution.

Philosophy is the form, simply, in which all Science is required at last to become complete.[9] It is not, as sometimes supposed, one among the sciences only, in the way

9. [DiPuccio, *Interior*, 138, comments on Nevin's view of science's limitations. For Nevin, "One cannot use the scientific method to scale the invisible and transcendent. Religious knowledge does not come by way of dispassionate observation (though this is not wholly excluded), but by intuition, existential participation, and communion. Nevin's epistemology intersects postmodernism by

Document 2: A Plea for Philosophy.

in which this may be said of geography for instance, or chemistry, or mathematics; it is emphatically the science of science itself—the form in which science comes to master *its* own nature, in the way of conscious self-apprehension and self-possession. It belongs to the very conception of knowledge, that however distributed into manifold departments and spheres, it should nevertheless be at the last the power of a single universal life. All science is organic, and falls back finally upon the unity of self-consciousness as its centre and ground. This is, however, only to say that it comes to its true general end in the form of philosophy, which is for this very reason the mistress and mother of all sound knowledge in every other view. What can be more irrational, then, and absurd, than to cry out against philosophy as something unprofitable and vain? It were just as reasonable surely to cry out against science in any of its subordinate departments; as some, indeed, most consistent in their fanaticism, have at times pretended to do, in blind homage to a life of sense, or in the service, possibly, of a blind religion. All science has its chaotic disorders and revolutions, its sources of danger and its liabilities to corruption and abuse. But what then? Must we cease to think and inquire, in order that we may become truly wise? Shall we extinguish the torch of knowledge, that we may have power in the dark to fancy ourselves secure from harm? To do so were only to commit violent wrong upon our human nature itself. Man was made for science; he needs it, not as a means simply to something else, but as a constituent, we may say, in the substance of his own being. But his relation to science, in this view, is his relation at the same time to philosophy; for, as we have just seen science can have no reality, except as it includes in itself a reference at least to philosophy, as that in which alone it can become complete. Man then is formed for philosophy, as truly as he is formed for science; and if we did but consider it properly, we should see and feel that to undervalue and despise the first, is as little rational as it is to undervalue and despise the second. Philosophy is not a factitious interest, artificially and arbitrarily associated with our life, which we may retain or put away from us altogether at our own pleasure; it is the perfection of our intelligence itself, the necessary summit of self-consciousness, towards which all the lines of knowledge struggle from the start, and in which only they are made to reach at last their ultimate and full sense.

What has now been said, does not imply of course that all men are called to be philosophers, and to exercise the functions of philosophy on their own account. When we say of art, that it forms an original constituent sphere of our general human life, we do not mean certainly that every individual is required to be a painter, or musician, or poet, or all of these together, in order that he may fulfil his proper destiny in the world. *Non omnia possumus omnes*[10]; the life of the world is something far more comprehensive and profound than the life of any one man, or any ten thousand

---

recognizing that when it comes to religious and metaphysical knowledge, science knows no position of privilege from which to articulate truth."]

10. [Trans. "We can't all of us do everything."]

men, included in its course. Humanity has its measure in the whole, and not in the separate parts of which the whole is composed. The perfection of the individual does not consist in his being all that the general idea of human life requires, but in this, that he shall truly fill his own place in an organism, which is complete for the purposes that belong to it as a whole.[11] In this sense we say, that art is a necessary constituent of humanity, though few comparatively may be fitted as organs to exercise the functions for which it calls: these functions belong to the organic constitution of our life, as a whole, and for the use of the whole; and where they are not acknowledged or fulfilled, the life itself must be regarded as, to the same extent, mutilated and shorn of its true sense. So in the case before us. Science and philosophy are not necessary for all men, individually and separately taken; but they *are* necessary at all times to Man as an organic whole. The great fact of humanity, the process of the world's life, cannot go forward at all without their presence. It may be enough for the mass of men perhaps to be borne along by the spirit of the age to which they belong, without any clear insight into its constitution and course; but this is not enough for the age itself. Through organs proper for the purpose, it ought to come if possible to a clear understanding of its own spirit and will, so as to be self-conscious and not blind. As we have already said, however, this self-consciousness is philosophy; and towards it at least all human life must continually struggle, so far as it is vigorous and sound. Nay, a bad life must rest in some consciousness too, often, to be sure, very dark, of its own meaning and tendency; and so far this also will have its philosophy. Philosophy and life, in fact, whether men consider it or not, go ever hand in hand together.

It is perfectly ridiculous, therefore, to think or speak of the world as having power to accomplish its history without philosophy; as much so, as though we should dream that society might exist without government. It would be indeed something most strange and unaccountable, that the human mind should have shown such an inveterate propensity through all ages to speculate in this way, in spite of all discouragement and seemingly bad success, if there had been no reason for it other than its own vagrant curiosity or lawless self-will. The world has never been without its philosophy, as far back as we find it exhibiting any signs whatever of a moral or intellectual life. Christianity wrought no change in it, with regard to this point. Many in modern times have charged the early Church with unfaithfulness to her Master, in

---

11. [This language recurs frequently throughout Nevin's writings. One of the more unique passages that complements this line of thought is in Appel, *Life*, 118: "The social principle, which binds men together in large as well as small platoons, enters vitally into the constitution of human nature, without which individual men would be mere atoms, and man would no longer be man or the common unity of races, nations, tribes, and individuals. Without contact and communion with other spirits like himself, he would have no development worthy of his nature, and no history that constantly leads him from one grade of perfection to another. There is a common mind belonging to each age and to every country, to every province and class of society, which surrounds men as an atmosphere and in the end forms the character of the individual and the community." (This lecture, "Party Spirit," was originally delivered in 1839, and thus shows Nevin's thinking before he was exposed to German idealism in Rauch and Schaff. Appel excerpts most of the original.)]

Document 2: A Plea for Philosophy.

permitting the great truths of the Gospel to become a subject of school speculation; as though it might have been possible to have handed them down as mere traditional articles of faith, without their being made to enter thus, with new informing power, into the actual thinking of the world as well as into its actual life. And yet is not the thinking of the world, at all times, inseparably identified with its life; or rather, is it not the very soul through which this itself lives, the central stream that carries all forward in its own direction? If Christianity were to be something more than a religion of blind mechanical tradition; if it should at all make good its claim to be the absolute truth of the world, the eternal consummation of humanity itself; it *must* introduce itself into the actual process of the world's history as it stood, so as to fulfil and not destroy the original sense of it, in all its complicated parts. We might as well ask, that it should not meddle with the sphere of politics, as that it should abjure all interest in philosophy. The early Church soon found herself compelled to speculate. It was part of her mission in the world, to regenerate its intelligence and reason. And so in all periods since, we find philosophy closely interwoven with the activity of the church under other forms, and refusing to part with its authority for the human mind, so far as this can be said to have made any historical progress at all. The Reformers, in the sixteenth century, imagined at first, indeed, that their cause required its entire banishment from the territory of religion; but they were soon compelled themselves to have recourse again to its aid; and in the end, the old order of things in this direction was fully established throughout the Protestant world.

How vain, in view of all this, to quarrel with philosophy, as though it were an interest false and pernicious in its own nature. We might, with as much reason, quarrel with the waters of the Susquehannah[12], for making their way towards the sea. The world must think; would not be true to itself, if it ceased to think; and it is not possible that it should be thus actively intelligent, without moving at the same time in the channel of some philosophical system, that may represent more or less clearly the unity of its general life.

[Philosophy as a Historical Phenomenon]

It will follow, moreover, from this view of the necessary relation in which philosophy stands to the life of the world, that it is not so entirely without rule and method in its course, as is taken for granted by the wholesale objection we are now considering. If it form an original and essential part of man's constitution, it must have a history, comprehended in the general flow of human history as a whole. But history implies organic unity and progress. It is just the opposite of chaos. Such onward movement, exhibiting the present always as at once the birth of the past and the womb of the future, belongs to the very conception of humanity; as much so as it does also, that it should exist by

---

12. [A river flowing through central Pennsylvania, down to the Chesapeake Bay, and from there to the Atlantic.]

resolution into a vast system of nations, families and individuals. Distribution in time, and distribution in space, are alike necessary, to represent the one vast, magnificent fact, through which the idea of man is made real. To be human, then, is to be at the same time historical, in the sense here explained.[13] If we should say that the world is not bound together by the force of a common life, at any given time, but is made up of nations and men confusedly thrown into one mass in an outward and mechanical way; it would not be a greater wrong to our nature than it is made to suffer, when this life is not apprehended as a continuous process also, always different and yet always the same, extending perpetually from one generation over to another. In fact, the two conceptions cannot be held asunder. There is no alternative here between cosmos and chaos. To be organic at all, the world must be historical; and its history must show itself especially in the progressive development of humanity, as a whole, towards its appointed end.[14] This we might seem justified to assume, as a postulate of religion as well as reason; since in no other view can we conceive of the world as carrying in itself a divine sense and meaning, so as to be the mirror truly of an idea in the mind of God. God is not the author of confusion, either in nature or history. He upholds and rules the world by plan; and this plan takes hold of the end from the beginning, bearing all life steadily forward as a process in its own service. In this way, every sphere of our general human existence comes to its proper evolution only in the form of history; and so we should expect to find it pre-eminently in the case of philosophy, representing, as this does, the inmost consciousness of the race itself from age to age. The idea of an absolutely stationary philosophy, mechanically at hand as something ripe and done, for the use of the world through all time, is an absurd contradiction. How could it then represent the world's *life*, in its ever-flowing actual form? Change and revolution here are not at once contradiction and confusion. May they not be but the necessary action of history itself, as it forces its way onward continually from one stage of thought and life to another? For this process, it should be remembered, is not by uniform movement, in the same direction and under the same character. It goes by stadia or eras; not unlike those great world-cycles which geologists undertake to describe in the primitive formation of the earth, only compressed into much narrower dimensions. Each period has, of course, its own history, including the rise and decline again of its particular life, and the breaking up of its whole constitution finally, to make room for a new spiritual organization; and all this must necessarily be attended with some show of chaotic confusion, to the view, at least, of the superficial thinker; while it is still possible that the whole may be, notwithstanding, in obedience throughout to the same great law of development and progress.

Such an onward movement is found to characterize in fact the course of human thought, as it may be traced from its cradle in the ancient Oriental world, down

---

13. [For broader implications of this idea in Nevin's writings, see Borneman, *Church*, 59–88.]

14. [The Hegelian understanding of "historical development." For the current state of scholarship on the concept in Mercersburg studies, see Evans, *Companion*, 83–87.]

Document 2: A Plea for Philosophy.

to the present time.[15] Philosophy has its own history, capable of being studied and understood, like the history of any other sphere of human life. This may be so dark still indeed as to leave room, at many points, for uncertainty, and controversy, and doubt. All history is open more or less to the same difficulty; but still its general sense, and the force at least of its great leading epochs, are sufficiently clear. It is only the unphilosophical and uninquiring, who pronounce the record of the world's life in this form, a farrago of unmeaning, disconnected opinions and dreams. In proportion as any man can be engaged to direct his own attention to the subject, in the way of earnest thought, he will feel the deep unreasonableness of this presumption. The history of mind he will see to be something more than chaos, "without form and void." Alas for us indeed, if that were all the world here offered to our faith! Order in its outward material structure, only to make room for an interminable soul-chaos within!

It would go far at once to break the force of much of the prejudice that is entertained against philosophy, if only this idea of a historical development in the case of our world-life generally, as its necessary and proper form, were fairly familiar to our minds. We should then understand, that the very same life, in passing upwards through different stages, may be expected to show itself, under different phases or aspects without yet falling for this reason into any self-contradiction; and in this way we would be rescued from the narrow bigotry of measuring all past ages by our own, while at the same time we might be prepared to estimate intelligently the actual advantages of our position, in its advanced relation to the past. As the self-consciousness of the individual has different contents in childhood and riper age, and must necessarily migrate through a succession of forms in order that it may become complete; so we say of philosophy, which may be denominated the self-consciousness of the world as a whole, that it too can assert its proper reality only by living itself, from age to age, upwards into new and higher forms, till the process shall become complete in the full completion of humanity itself—the glorious, all-harmonious millennium of creation. It does not follow, then, that a system of philosophy has been nugatory and null in its own time, because it has come to be exploded, as we say, and superseded by some following system. We have no right to declare the wisdom of Plato and Aristotle vain, and just as little to deride the speculations of the medieval schoolmen as learned nonsense, merely because their authority has long since passed away. The Greek philosophy comprehended both truth and power for the use of the world, in its own time. It entered largely into the growth and education of the human spirit. And in this way it still continues to live also, in the organic progress of human thought. The acquisitions of the past in this form are not lost by the downfall of the systems in which they may have seemed originally to inhere; they are simply translated into the constitution of

---

15. ["Ancient Oriental World" generally refers to civilizations of the Near East and Asia that existed prior to the arrival of Europeans. It is a broad reference than can encompass China, Mesopotamia (Sumer, Akkad, Assyria, and Babylonia), Egypt, the Indus Valley, as well as the ancient empires of Persia, India, and the Levant.]

other systems, and so carried forward in the vast intellectual process to which these belong. In a deep sense we may say of all history, that it is thus a perpetual metempsychosis[16] of the world's life, by which it is always new and yet always the same.

[The Practical Use of Philosophy]

We may easily see, now, how little room there is for the fashionably vulgar imagination, that philosophy has little or nothing to do with the realities of actual life. There is indeed a latitude of meaning sometimes allowed to the term, especially in England and our own country, by which it is supposed to be saved from this reproach in part; though only in such a way as to fall more clearly under the power of it beyond the bounds of such exception. In the sense to which we refer, philosophy is taken to be a scientific insight simply into the nature and force of things empirically considered, as we find ourselves surrounded by them in the actual world. In this way we may have a philosophy of mind, by a sort of spiritual anatomical dissection, and then a philosophy of nature also as something altogether different; and however it may be with the first, it can easily be shown that this last is capable of being turned to many important practical uses. Witness only the wonders that are now wrought by steam, and the brilliant, though silent, action of the electro-magnetic telegraph. Philosophy in *such* shape means something, and has a value that can be made tangible to the world's common sense. It is the glory of our own age, too, in particular, that it is made to carry its salutary power into every nook and corner of our common material existence. We have a philosophy of farming, a philosophy of manufactures, and a philosophy of trade. We make our shoes and bake our bread philosophically. We talk, with equal ease, of the philosophy of the heavens and the philosophy of a plum pudding. We can go still farther, and admit also the practical use of philosophy, as occupied with the laws of our own reason and will, in the same Baconian style—provided always the process be not pushed too far. The science of mind, as handled by Locke, may help us possibly to think correctly; while the science of ethics, as unfolded in the same way by Paley, may serve to assist us occasionally in distinguishing between right and wrong. But here the concession is required to stop.[17] For philosophy, as the science of *ideas*, or as it is sometimes called, the science of the absolute,[18] which is after all the only proper sense of the term, our common system of thinking is apt to entertain no respect

---

16. ["Transmigration" (of a soul); here meant metaphorically of human thought.]

17. [Nevin has been describing the ruling American philosophy—which he seems to have regarded as no philosophy at all—called Baconianism (after Francis Bacon, the alleged innovator of the inductive scientific method) or Scottish Common Sense Realism. Holifield, *Theology in America*, 174–75, identifies three characteristics: "observation of particular facts" (whether nature, mental states, or biblical texts), avoidance of metaphysical speculation, and the taxonomic classification and ordering of the facts so observed. See Aubert's bibliography in *German Roots*, 236n25. For descriptions from within Mercersburg studies, see Evans, *Companion*, 37–40 and DeBie, *Speculative Theology*, 1–6.]

18. [À la Schelling.]

Document 2: A Plea for Philosophy.

whatever, in the general view now noticed. It is regarded as unprofitable metaphysics, of some service possibly for dialectic practice in the schools, but of no conceivable use besides in our ordinary mundane experience. For does it not in fact profess to go *beyond* the bounds of this experience; showing itself thus to be *transcendental*, as we say, and more fit to be referred to the visionary moon, than to this solid material earth we now inhabit? Is it not, by its own confession, the science of ideas and not the science of *facts*? It is in reference to such philosophy especially, that the question has been triumphantly asked: What has it done to improve the actual life of the world, from the days of Plato down to the present hour? Has it ever manufactured, not a steamboat, not so much as a *pin* only, in the service of the world's comfort? Has it descended at all into contact with the real wants of man? Has it added one luxury to his table, or coined a single dollar of new wealth for his pocket?

The whole force of this plausible representation, we say, is broken by the view we have now taken of the true nature of philosophy, and its necessary relation to the onward historical explication of the great mystery of humanity. The "chief end of man," after all, in this world, is not to create railroads, and telegraphs, and great Lowell establishments,[19] for his own comfort; to seize the reins of nature in a merely outward way, and force her chariot wheels to move subservient to his simply physical accommodation. All this is right, indeed, in its place, and we mean not to undervalue or condemn the march of improvement in such outward form. Man is appointed to be the tamer and subduer of nature, and it is reasonable and fit that this should be brought to serve him, with absolute and universal submission. It is the proper prerogative of Mind, its grand moral vocation, we may say, in the world, thus to assert and proclaim its supremacy over Matter; as it is the true glory of this last, again, to be ruled and filled by the self-conscious presence of the first. But this lordship, to be true and right, must be moral as well as physical, inward no less than outward; it must be the supremacy of man over nature *as man*, and not simply as the potent magician of science,[20] at whose bidding the spirits of the vasty deep stand ready, in shape of steam, tempest and lightning, to execute his pleasure. The only true mastery over the world at last, is that by which man is brought at the same time to master himself, in the clear apprehension and spontaneous election of goodness and truth in their absolute form. This is something more than agricultural chemistry, or the rattling machinery of cotton factories and rolling mills. It is by the power of the spiritual at last, that the full sense of the world, whether as spirit or nature, is to be evolved, and the full triumph of humanity, as sung in the eighth psalm, carried out to its grand consummation. The chief end of man is, not to know and rule the world simply as it stands beyond his particular person, but to know and rule it in the form of reason and will, as the inmost constitution of his own

---

19. [Francis Cabot Lowell was the inspiration for a factory town that integrated every aspect of the manufacture of cotton textiles at East Chelmsford, Massachusetts, using water-power. See Kenngott, *Record*, 6–27.]

20. [On the moral affinity of magic and science, see Lewis, *Abolition*, 82–85.]

life. As in the case of his person separately considered, the skillful use of his bodily organs for mere bodily ends is in itself no argument of either strength or freedom, but can become of account only as such active power may be itself comprehended in the higher activity of the soul, moving always in obedience to its own law; so here, also, it is nothing less than the same moral self-consciousness and self-government, that can impart either dignity or value to any dominion we may be brought to exercise over external nature, by virtue of our mere intelligence under any other form. But now this inward supremacy of mind over matter, constituting thus the self-consciousness of the world itself through the medium of the human spirit, is something which lifts us at once into the sphere of philosophy. It is emphatically at last the power of the ideal as compared with the power of the actual, the ascendency of the absolute (universal reason and universal will) over the force of all that is simply empirical and particular.

Philosophy, we say then, is supremely practical. It takes hold of life, not indeed upon its immediate surface, but in the very foundations of the great deep of which it consists. Away with the heresy, dishonorable to man and God alike, that this world is ruled supremely by material forces, or simply sensuous interests of any kind. In the face of Heaven, we proclaim it false. Of all forms of power that enter into its constitution, there is none to compare with that which belongs to mind, in the form of the Idea. This is more than tempest, lightning and steam; more than whirlwind, cataract and fire; more than the noise of many waters, or the tumult of the people surging and roaring with passion. Not by might, nor by power, but by my Spirit, saith the Lord,[21] shall the great purposes of this world be ultimately carried. There is nothing under heaven so omnipotent among men, as the presence of an Idea, in its true conception, representing, as it does always in fact, the inmost and deepest consciousness of the world itself. Amid all the thundering noise that marks the progress of history, it is only here at last we communicate with its soul, and are made to understand the true motive power which actuates its wheels. Men may talk as they please about their mechanics, and politics, and tactics—the world is governed, when all is done, by the power of Ideas; and the deepest thinkers, though far out of sight, it may be in the solitude of the closet, are still ever in the end, by divine right, the royal oligarchy, that preside over its affairs, and conduct them forward towards their proper end. No great revolution has ever yet occurred, that took not its birth first from the womb of an Idea. No department of our life can be advanced towards perfection, save through the presence of the same force. And shall we say, then, that philosophy, the science of the Idea, whose very province it is to bring the world to a consciousness of its own life in this form, is not practical? Can we understand ourselves, or possess our own nature fully, in any respect, without its aid? No general activity, whether in the form of thought or will, can deserve to be regarded as at all complete, that is not controlled by the light of philosophy, if not directly, at least in an indirect and circuitous way.

21. [Zech 4:6.]

DOCUMENT 2: A PLEA FOR PHILOSOPHY.

[The Contribution of Philosophy to the Christian Religion]

Such being the case, we may not admit, of course, that philosophy is necessarily unfriendly to religion. We have seen already, that it has entered largely into the history of Christianity from the beginning; though efforts have been made from time to time, with more zeal than clear knowledge, to sunder the church entirely from its connection.[22] All such efforts have proved to be of no account thus far, and will continue to be of no account always, just because philosophy is a necessary condition of our general human life; and to renounce the one in this absolute way, were to renounce the other also to the same extent. If Christianity be truly divine, and at the same time truly human, it must so adjust itself to the actual constitution of man in its previous form, or rather so take this up into its own constitution in the way of natural consummation, that nothing belonging to it of right shall be destroyed, but the whole on the contrary show itself, under a higher form, more perfect than before. No wrong to the Gospel can well be more egregious, than that by which its power is limited and restrained to a part only of the general organism of the world's life; while other spheres, clearly included in this from the beginning, are violently thrust out from the range of its action, as hopelessly profane, and incapable of sanctification. It is a libel on Christ, to say that his religion has nothing to do with politics, or the fine arts, or the sciences, or common social life. It must unite itself with all these, inwardly and profoundly, so as to transfigure them fully into its own image, before it shall have accomplished its mission in the world. For how else should it deserve to be acknowledged the universal truth of man's life?[23] And so it is something monstrous also in the same way, to affirm of Christianity, that it has nothing to do with philosophy. Is ignorance then, after all, the mother of devotion; or must the inmost walks of consciousness be barred against the approach of religion, in order to preserve this sound and pure? Christianity claims to be the proper rightful magistracy of man's entire nature, the power to which all belongs, and by which all requires to be occupied and ruled. It must enter then into the thinking of the world, as well as into its willing and working; and it cannot actualize itself in full, except as it is brought to reign thus, with proper symmetrical development, throughout its whole life.

To say that Christianity should have no fellowship with philosophy, comes simply to this in the end, that the contents of faith are not formed to become ever the contents

---

22. [Nevin's understanding of philosophy's relationship to Christianity is well summarized by DiPuccio, *Interior*, 133: "Though philosophy is not the actual power of this divine, it reflects the interior form of the world's life on which the divine power makes itself felt. It represents the self-consciousness of the world itself at any given time and the medium by which faith comes to reflection in an intelligible form. Only through philosophy, therefore can, the power of Christ take hold of the universal life of humanity in its actual forms, namely, art, science, and social life."]

23. [Nevin later more fully developed the claim that, speaking of the "the kingdom of God," "the grand test of its truth is its absolute adequacy to cover the field of human existence at all points, its *catholicity* in the sense of meaning the entire length and breadth of man's nature" ("Catholicism," MTSS 7:19, emphasis original).]

of knowledge; that religion is necessarily something blind in its own nature, incapable of being reflected in the consciousness of its subject under an intelligible form; that it is to be received and held, from first to last, in the way of mechanical outward tradition, on the ground, simply, of the foreign authority by which it comes authenticated to our confidence and trust. But is not religion the inmost life of our human being itself; and must not the precept, *Know thyself*,[24] extend to it always as the necessary issue, in which alone the knowledge for which it calls can become complete? Strange that any should hold it man's privilege and calling, by the indefeasible right of his intelligence itself, to penetrate the interior sense of the world around him in the way of knowledge, and yet count it little better than profane for him to think of penetrating the interior sense of his own nature, as unfolded to his consciousness in the Christian revelation. Is it not the prerogative of intellect, to be self-intelligent? And is it possible then for Christianity to be the absolute truth of humanity, the inmost substance of its very life, without including in itself, at the same time, a capacity at least for being made transparent to its own vision in this way? It lies in its very conception, that it should form thus, when complete, the *self-consciousness* of the world, in its deepest and most comprehensive sense.

This is not to make Christianity dependent on philosophy in any way, for its existence. No process of thinking, on the part of men, could ever originate or discover religion in this form; just as little as it might be supposed to originate or discover the constitution of the natural earth and heavens. Christ, and the new creation revealed through him, are not a *thought* simply, but a fact, such as philosophy has no power either to make or unmake. But this is only to say, that philosophy has no power to make or unmake the world's life in any view. The province of philosophy is not to create truth in any case, but only to make truth clear to itself in the reflected consciousness of its subject. It is truth itself in the form of self-knowledge; and in this view, there is no reason surely why Christianity should treat it as false and profane, but every reason on the contrary that it should be made welcome to the Christian sphere, as its rightful sanctuary and home.[25]

But we are pointed to actual history in proof of its pernicious power in the view now noticed. It has been from the beginning, we are told, the fruitful mother of heresies and corruptions in the church. And has it not ever shown a sort of native affinity with atheism and infidelity? Has it not, more or less, openly proclaimed itself the enemy of Christ, from the days of Ammonius Saccas and Origen[26] down to the days of Immanuel

---

24. [One of three aphorisms purportedly inscribed at the entrance to the Temple of Apollo at Delphi. It became a guiding maxim of Socrates's quest for truth.]

25. [This clarifies Nevin's central thesis: Christian theology cannot reject the philosophical tradition of the west, parallel to his argument that American Protestants cannot reject the spiritual and theological products of the *catholic* Christian tradition. Philosophy provides self-conscious reflection on the *Idea*, as the foundation for all other thought. So Nevin is defending his *idealism*, against what he perceives as the brutish empiricism of Common Sense Realism.]

26. [Ammonius Saccas (2nd–3rd century) was a Platonic philosopher and teacher of the Christian

Document 2: A Plea for Philosophy.

Kant, and from the epoch of the Critical Philosophy onward again, with rapid development, to the culmination of this modern movement in the pantheism of Hegel?

This only shows, we may reply, that philosophy is not of itself Christianity, and still further, that Christianity has not yet fully mastered the inward life of the world. But this is nothing more than we find abundantly made evident to us, in the manifestation of the world's life also under other forms. Art, science, government, all have exhibited, in the progress of Christian history thus far, a more or less unfriendly relation to the Christian consciousness, refusing to acknowledge and accept it as the only proper form of their own being. But what then? Shall we abjure all art, science and politics, for this reason, as necessarily unholy and profane? Or shall we say that their whole past history has been false and without value, as not springing directly from Christ? And why then should we entertain any such judgment in regard to philosophy, which at last is but the consciousness which enters into all these, and makes them to be what they are in fact? It comes simply to this, when all is done, that philosophy is not of itself Christianity, and that it must necessarily fall into an infidel position, if it assume to be in its own separate nature sufficient for the ultimate purposes of man's life, as comprehended in Christianity, and in Christianity alone. But although philosophy be not thus the actual power of the divine fact itself, it may be said to constitute, nevertheless, the interior fundamental form of the world's life, on which the power in question is required to make itself felt—the posture of humanity at any given time, in its relation to the great regenerative process by which it is thus to be transformed finally into the full image of God. In this view, philosophy is a great fact too—nothing more nor less, indeed, than the self consciousness always of the world itself, at such stage of its historical development as it may have reached at the time, and as such a fact, it *must* be respected by Christianity, in order that this may at all take hold on the vast world-process to which it belongs, in a real way. That is, Christianity, to conquer fully the world's life, must become philosophical, by endeavoring continually to work itself into the consciousness of the world as it stands, for the purpose of thus helping it forward into a form that may be found fully commensurate at last with its own divine contents. The ultimate problem, of course, is the full reconciliation of the two powers here brought into view, in such way that neither shall be allowed to do violence to the other, but both come finally to harmonious union, as form and substance in the actualization of all that is comprehended in the idea of humanity. But it lies in this conception itself, that they should continually seek each other in the resolution also of this problem, and be more or less interwoven through all the process by which it is to be accomplished. Christianity must enter the *mind* of the world as it is, to secure any permanent power in its life.—Philosophy, it deserves to be well remembered and earnestly laid to heart, is the only medium by which the new creation in Christ Jesus

---

theologian Origen. He was probably "originally a Christian who at some point renounced his faith to embrace Greek philosophy" (Lilla, "Ammonius Saccas," 1:104). Also see the earlier sources on Origen. Thus Nevin saw both as exemplars of how philosophy could lead a believer astray.]

can come into triumphant contact with the actual universal life of man, as it stands, in the form either of art, or science, or political organization. An unphilosophical Christianity may be sufficient to save a multitude of individual souls for heaven, but it can never *conquer the world*.

[The Modern Need for True Philosophy]

Admitting, too, that philosophy has its dangers for Christianity as well as for life generally, it must be kept in mind that the want of Philosophy is always something more full of peril still. Religion cannot be made so practical as to stand in no relation whatever to intelligence and thought. It must ever rest in a theory of some kind that will be found to rule and condition its influence upon the world. If this theory be not philosophically sound, it will be philosophically unsound and false; and as a medium of communication with the world's life, it will to the same extent be a barrier to the proper power of the Gospel, as appointed for its salvation. We have, indeed, a widely extended school, if we may so use the term, who affect to hold Christianity (greatly differing at the same time to be sure, about its true form) directly from Christ and the Bible, without the help of any theory whatever, as the medium of its apprehension. But it needs no very deep philosophy certainly—though the case itself shows that it calls for *some*—to perceive the utter vanity, nay, profound absurdity, of every such pretension. The greatest slaves of theory, commonly, are just those who profess to have none; only their theory includes in itself no life, but resolves itself at last into the power of blind, tyrannical, tradition.[27] If we need to be cautioned against philosophy, we need still more perhaps at this time, at least here in America, to be cautioned against the tendency that seeks to bring all philosophy among us into discredit, and which would exclude its authority, only the more effectually to bind the yoke of its own ceremonialism upon our necks.

However it may be with the rest of the world, it is clear indeed that what is wanted among ourselves, to bring our life generally into right form, is not less philosophy than we have at present, but, if it were possible, a great deal more. There is a sad disproportion, in our general American life, between outward activity and inward consciousness; which implies, however, so far as it prevails, a want of full self-possession and self-control, in the case of our outward activity itself; a want that is extensively felt already throughout the social system to which it belongs, and that may be expected to work itself out sooner or later, if not met with proper seasonable remedy, into the most disastrous, if not absolutely fatal, practical results. We need earnest, profound *Thought*,[28] born and cradled in the inmost philosophical consciousness of the age, by

---

27. [Once more a parallelism can be noted: in both philosophy and ecclesiology either one has a historical and *catholic* tradition or an unreflective, "tyrannical" one. On the irrationalism and tyranny of American sectarianism, see Nevin, "The Sect System," MTSS 5:258–61.]

28. ["Thought" is "small caps" in the original.]

Document 2: A Plea for Philosophy.

which to understand the problem we are called to solve as a nation, and so to turn our action to right account. Action of course, is all important for the proper use of life; it belongs to our nature, not simply to mirror in itself the sense of the surrounding world, but to mould this also into its own image and it is only under this form, that it can ever possibly show itself complete. Philosophy without action, is always something helpless, and liable to disease, as we see exemplified on a large scale in the history of speculation among the modern Germans. But then, action without philosophy will be found just as little worthy to be trusted also, in the end, for the great purposes of human life. No imagination can well be more false, than to suppose that our American practical talent is sufficient of itself to accomplish all that is comprehended properly in our vocation as a people. Power, to be efficient for moral ends, must be accompanied with light. The force of mind, sundered from the inward illustration that should of right go with it always, is made to resemble, more or less, the force of mere nature, and becomes of the same order with the strength of the whirlwind or mountain torrent. It may carry all before it for a time, but the action, at last, is neither rational nor free. We need not only the energy of will, which now distinguishes us above all the nations of the earth, but the clear insight of speculative reason, also, to clothe our will with its full right to be thus energetic and strong. Let our national spirit be brought to know and possess itself fully in a free way, so that the action of the nation, in all the spheres of its life, may be filled and ruled with the soul of a true self-consciousness, in the form of philosophy, and we shall then be prepared to fulfill indeed the high destiny that seems to be assigned to us on the part of Heaven. Such a union of action and speculation, joined with the vast resources of our outward life, and the mighty scope thrown open to us by the genius of our political institutions, might be expected to carry us, in due time, far beyond all the world has yet been permitted to reach, in the way of moral progress, under any other form. May we not say, indeed, that this is the very problem of problems, which our new-born America is called at this time to solve, for the universal benefit of men in all time to come?

At present, as already remarked, we are manifestly suffering through the want of speculation, and not from its excess. Action is allowed too often to overwhelm or crowd out thought. There reigns among us, indeed, a wide-spread prejudice against philosophy, in its true and proper character, which makes it difficult to secure any earnest attention to its claims in any quarter. In the meantime, besides, to make the case still worse, a false empirical scheme of thought, (since all action must have *some* spiritual bottom on which to rest in this way) claiming to be philosophy itself, though only its wretched caricature, in fact, has come to underlie our activity on all sides, and is now ready to resist all deeper thinking, as an invasion upon its own rights. The general character of this bastard philosophy[29] is, that it affects to measure all things, both on earth and in heaven, by the categories of the common abstract understanding, as it stands related simply to the world of time and sense. These categories, however,

---

29. [Scottish Common Sense Realism, described above.]

being in themselves the forms or types only of things in this outward world, and representing therefore the conditions merely of existence in space and time—something relative always and finite by the very nature of the case—become necessarily one-sided and false, the moment we attempt to carry their authority beyond these limits, and to apply them to the truths of the pure reason. This has been triumphantly shown by Kant, in his immortal work on the subject;[30] whose argument thus far, at least, can never be nullified by the skeptical use to which it was turned in his own hands, but only makes it necessary to surmount this skepticism by pressing forward to still higher ground. It should be understood, and borne in mind always, that the skepticism of Kant is not something from which we escape by falling back simply on the sensuous philosophy, once for all demolished by his gigantic criticism. As against *this*, his argument and the bad use he makes of it, are alike legitimate and sound. With the premises of Locke, it is not possible successfully to withstand the reasoning of David Hume; and the reasoning of David Hume, brought to understand itself, and pushed out to its proper universal form, conducts us over with like necessity to the critical idealism of Immanuel Kant.[31] If our knowledge can have no other ground on which to rest, than that which is offered to us in the forms of the sensible world, as apprehended through categories of thought, simply answerable to their outward and finite nature, it ought to be clear, surely, that it cannot reach, with any true force, and *as knowledge*, to objects that lie beyond this sphere. The system of Locke pretended to do so, indeed, building its faith in the absolute and infinite upon deductions from the simply relative and finite. This pretension, false from the beginning, Kant has fairly and forever overturned, leaving the world, so far as *that* philosophy could help it, without any sure hold upon a single truth beyond the range of its present experience. And yet it

30. [Kant, *Critique of Pure Reason* {*Kritik der reinen Vernunft*}. According to Kant, the "categories of understanding" include space, time, and causality. These are not "facts" as it were, objective phenomena directly known by sensation. They are "pure forms of sensibility," "intuitions containing a priori the condition for the possibility of objects as appearances" (145 {Ak B 122}). One cannot "know" them, for they are "a priori," prior to all sense experience. They are *forms* of sensibility, not the content of sensation. However, they make sense experience possible by "synthesizing" objects into an objective whole.]

31. [A philosophy textbook would explain the trajectory something like as follows: Locke thought that sensation generated ideas, which could then be verified by checking them against sensation. But this attempt at "verification" generates still more ideas. One never knows "pure" sensation, but only the ideas that sensation gives rise to. George Berkeley drew the logical conclusion that all we *know* are ideas: *esse est percipi* {"to be is to be perceived"}. Hume riposted that the only reality known is sense data ("impressions"); an idea is "meaningful" if one can describe the impression that gave rise to the idea. Hume's "empirical criterion of meaning" exacted a massive cost, philosophically speaking. Among other problems, one could not speak intelligibly of "cause-and-effect," since Hume showed that one has no "impression" of the cause-effect relationship. Rather, all one knows is that a given effect *habitually* (generally, but not of logical necessity) arises from a particular cause. Kant attempted to save cause-and-effect by arguing that it exists, not as a sensed phenomenon, but as a "category of understanding" (see previous note). Our mind works by *assuming* that "anything that happens" has a precedent cause. Causation is not experienced "in" the data, but is an a priori intuition brought *to* it, and thereby "synthesizes" it.]

is just this false and helpless system of thinking that still insists, too generally among ourselves, on its right to rule our whole life, and that is ready, alas! on all sides, to stigmatize as transcendental nonsense, if not something still worse, every attempt that is made to go beyond itself in the way of earnest and profound speculation.

The whole tendency of this philosophy is towards materialism and infidelity; as we may see abundantly exemplified by its past history in other parts of the world, particularly in France. It may be associated, it is true, with an opposite system; as commonly in this country, where it claims the spiritual and supernatural, indeed, as peculiarly its own province. But so far as such connection goes, it is outward only and traditional, not inward and real. The philosophy itself has no power to reach the spiritual and supernatural, and in pretending to do so, only drags it, in fact, downward into its own sphere, so that it is in the end truly neither one nor the other. It reasons from time to eternity with vast dexterity and ease; establishing, by strict Baconian comparison and induction, the existence of God, the immortality of the soul, and the truth of revelation; but it is all in such a way as turns eternity itself into time, and forces the whole invisible world to become a mere abstraction from the world of sense.[32] The empirical understanding affects to become transcendent, (as Kant calls it) and may please itself with the imagination of having actually grasped in this way the truth which lies beyond its own horizon; but it is the illusion of one who dreams himself to be awake, and, behold, he is asleep: the object grasped, when all is done, belongs to the sphere of sense, and not to the sphere of spirit. This philosophy makes no room at all for *ideas*, in the proper sense of the term; its ideas are all intellectual abstractions merely, that as such carry in themselves no necessary or universal force. How is it possible, that such a system should have depth or strength; that it should penetrate the interior sense of life, in any quarter; or that it should communicate true spiritual earnestness to the general character and conduct of men, in any direction? All the higher interests of our nature must necessarily be made to suffer, wherever it prevails.

The bad power of this system is widely exemplified among us, in our reigning indifference to philosophy itself, and our want of faith generally in the objects with which it is of right concerned. Speculation and action are very commonly regarded as opposite spheres, only outwardly related to each other; in which view, the first must ever be shorn of all earnest independent interest, on its own account. It is either held to be of no force for actual life at all—the unprofitable metaphysical pugilism, merely, of the schools, by which the world can never be made wiser or better—or else, to save it from such reproach, it is forced to quit the skies wholly, and become the mere shadowy echo of experience and "common sense," as it is called, in the service of directly material ends. It is pursued accordingly either as a pastime only, or as a restricted

---

32. [As noted earlier, Baconianism derives knowledge through inductions from empirical facts. As applied to theology then, the "facts" are the facts either of nature (e.g., William Paley's "watchmaker" argument for the existence of a cosmic "designer") or those of the Bible, through which one "proves" its veracity by its accounts of miracles and fulfilled prophecies.]

trade. Few have any faith in philosophy as the original and rightful mistress of life. Few have any firm, solid belief in the reality of ideas, as anything more than the generalizations of sense, or the wisely calculated results of common utilitarian experience. He is counted to generally to be the best philosopher, whose thinking is found to move most fully in the orbit of the common understanding, while it shows itself at the same time most skillful in discerning the relation between means and end, and is crowned at last with the largest percentage, in the way of practical benefit and profit. The bearing of all this on our national life, is sufficiently plain in every direction. Our literature and science, our economics and politics, nay, our very ethics and divinity, are all made to suffer in the same way. They are not properly scientific.

The defect is particularly obvious and worthy of notice, in our general system of education. Whatever advantage this may possess in other respects, it is characterized almost universally by a sad want of true philosophical spirit. The idea of a separate department or faculty of philosophy, as necessary to complete the conception of a university education, is almost gone from our minds. The prejudice of tradition is indeed too strong, to allow its total banishment from our colleges, in an open and formal way. Every institution feels itself bound to include in its course of studies something which it is pleased to dignify with the title of philosophy in the shape particularly of metaphysics and ethics, as a sort of crowning distinction in honor of the Senior year. But the crown, alas! is not what it ought to be, the keystone of the academic arch, that binds and supports the whole; it is at best an outside ornament simply, of most light and airy structure, set loosely on its summit, of which, in a short time, no trace whatever is to be found. We may safely say, that the way in which philosophy is taught and studied in our colleges generally, is suited only to bring it into discredit. It stands in no organic connection with the course as a whole; it is handled in the most mechanical and external way, as a thing of simple memory and report; and to complete the misery, it is acknowledged only in a form which subverts its whole sense, by substituting for it a poor parody that is wholly unworthy of its name. In its own nature the most earnest of interests, it is thus metamorphosed into the most frivolous and trivial. We need not wonder, that in such circumstances, it should appear shorn of all strength. We need not wonder, that the interest of liberal study generally, deprived in this way of its proper *soul,* should be made to suffer at every point. An earnest philosophy is indispensable to an earnest education, as through this again it is indispensable to all real earnestness in life.

Document 3

"The Moral Order of Sex"

Editor's Introduction

For four years, from January, 1849 to January, 1853, Nevin served as editor of *The Mercersburg Review*. These years, while encompassing a flurry of rich theological composition from Nevin that captured key elements of his thought, were hardly free from strife. At the close of 1851, Nevin resigned his position as professor at Mercersburg seminary, not only due to the financial struggles of the institution and the increased demands on his time, but also to Nevin's ongoing theological struggles and anxieties about American Protestantism in general. (He did, however, remain in his post as president of Marshall College until its removal to Lancaster in 1853.)

Correlated to his theological doubts and questioning, Nevin was suspected of a "Romanizing" tendency. Increasingly accused of setting up a strawman Protestantism to expose its negative aspects, Nevin was seen by a growing number of colleagues and interlocutors as overly sympathetic to Roman Catholic theology. In response Nevin published a steady stream of critiques of Roman Catholic theology, signaling that many of his Protestant convictions were surely more deeply rooted than his obvious despair over the state of American Protestantism and frustration with his own Reformed tradition.[1]

Even so, Nevin's wrestling with Roman Catholic theology is important for understanding the context of the second volume of *The Mercersburg Review*. It helps to shape the lens through which to interpret his reflections on the sacraments (indicated by the list of the volume's contents), and it is also a dynamic that pertains to "The Moral Order of Sex," for as Nichols observes, Nevin's views on matters of gender, sex, and marriage were always evolving, as he later (mid- to late-1850s) began to speak positively about celibacy, both as an honored vocation in early Christianity, and even as a viable contemporary option.[2]

1. Hart, *John Williamson Nevin*, 157.
2. Nichols, *Romanticism*, 204–5.

PART 1: CULTURE, PHILOSOPHY, ETHICS, ANTHROPOLOGY

The essay appears in the second volume of *The Mercersburg Review*, published in 1850. The volume is notable for its various ways of advancing Nevin's organic idealism and sacramental hermeneutic, whereby Nevin goes at great lengths to demonstrate how various spheres of the world's life as well as the life of the church are integrated into an organic whole most forcefully comprehended in the Incarnation. Other significant writings from *The Mercersburg Review* that year that likewise exhibit Nevin's overall theological program include, "Brownson Quarterly Review" (see below in Part 2 of this volume); "Faith, Reverence and Freedom" (a condensed version of *Human Freedom*, see above); "Wilberforce on the Incarnation" (republished in MTSS 3); "Noel on Baptism" (MTSS 6); "Bible Christianity;" and "Doctrine of the Reformed Church on the Lord's Supper" (MTSS 1).

One who has read any sampling of Nevin's writings will find familiar the opening pages of "The Moral Order of Sex," which display the broad idealist and hierarchical framework Nevin will use to eventually situate marriage and gender. To get there, Nevin's line of thought proceeds from religion's role with respect to the natural world, to society, and then to family. He believes that religion's transformative power is far reaching, giving meaning to art, science, and social interactions, and that church must grasp this role. And at the foundation of this scheme lies the fundamental institution of society—the family. Just as the Church embodies morality, the family serves as the origin of moral values, representing the essence of human nature itself. From that point, Nevin, emphasizes that society thrives on diversity and distinctions, and most fundamentally the division of humanity into two distinct genders—male and female. Among all the differences inherent in human nature, this gender division bears vital significance, preceding other differentiations and laying the foundation for all other relationships and connections to flourish.

At this point, and throughout the essay, one may begin to perceive some clear examples of Nevin's indebtedness to Platonism. Yet despite Nevin's emphasis on difference and division, this is not a Platonism that requires dualism in the formal sense. As DiPuccio points out, similar to Jonathan Edwards and other Puritan Platonists, Nevin believed that nature, particularly humanity, functions as a sacrament signifying the divine presence within creation. The interconnection between the spiritual and the tangible implies that nature serves as the external manifestation or embodiment of the spiritual and ideal.[3] However, Nevin's perspective diverges from Plato's in that he perceives the world of space and time not as a mere static reflection of the ideal, but as a dynamic embodiment of it. Nevin argues that while universal ideals hold logical precedence, these qualities are actually derived from a reservoir where the ideal has become intertwined with the real. This framework is essential for Nevin, as it allows him to emphasize the universal essence of humanity without diminishing the value of natural existence. It is crucial to keep this in view when interpreting those passages that sound especially "Platonic." As Nevin wrote, "Innumerable analogies,

3. DiPuccio, *Interior*, 40–41.

adumbrations, and correspondences, not obvious to commoner minds, seemed to be pressing habitually to his view, binding the universe into one sublime whole, the earth reflecting the heavens, and the waves of eternity echoing on the shores of time."[4]

Modern readers will find some of Nevin's views of gender and marriage to be antiquated. Based on his assumptions about the laws of nature, Nevin writes, the woman "participates more largely in the character of passive necessity and dependence," and, "The personality of man is more vigorous and concentrated, and if we may use the expression, more thoroughly and completely personal, than the personality of woman: showing him clearly thus to be the center and bearer properly of the human nature as a whole."[5] Nevin insists that this does not imply women's inferiority, advancing an argument based on his broader view of nature, mankind, and how God has ordered the universe. He argues that in Christ Jesus, the distinctions of gender and ethnicity, just like the divisions between Jews and Greeks, lose their significance. And yet for Nevin, this doesn't mean that these differences are completely eliminated, but rather that they find harmony and complementarity that goes beyond their opposing nature, resulting in some sort of reconciliation. This is of course largely in keeping with his hermeneutic described above. Readers will need to evaluate for themselves the framework, arguments, and conclusions.

In "The Moral Order of Sex," readers encounter a remarkable example of Nevin connecting his broad hermeneutical categories to matters that are perhaps even more relevant and pressing for our own time and place in the twenty-first century than they were for him in 1850. Some readers will conclude that Nevin's views on such matters are simply bound by his culture and tradition, while others will view them as theologically and scientifically flawed. Even so, the basic foundations of his idealist view of an organic, integrated reality can provide valuable raw materials for ongoing inquiry and conversation concerning society, family, gender, and marriage, especially in decidedly theological contexts.

---

4. DiPuccio, *Interior*, 41, citing Appel, "A Sketch of Marshall College," 540. (This is Nevin's description of the philosophy of Frederick Rauch, his predecessor at Mercersburg, but certainly applies to Nevin himself.)

5. *Moral Order*, 560.

The Moral Order of Sex.[1]

[Man[2] as the Center and End of Nature]

There are two great conceptions very generally altogether overlooked, which it is all important to hold in full view in our efforts to understand and interpret the mighty problem of human life. In the first place, this life, while it culminates and becomes complete only in the form of morality or spirit, has its root always in the sphere of nature, and can never disengage itself entirely from its power; in the second place, while it reveals itself perpetually through single individuals, it is nevertheless throughout an organic process, which necessarily includes the universal race, as a living whole, from its origin to its end.[3]

Nature, of course, can never be truly and strictly the mother of mind. The theory of an actual inward development of man's life, out of the life of the world below him, as presented for instance in the little work entitled the "Vestiges of Creation,"[4] is entitled to no sort of attention or respect. The plant can by no possibility creep upwards into

---

1. Originally an Address, delivered in Hagerstown, Md. Published afterwards in the *American Review*. Now reprinted by special request, in the present form. [*MR* 2 (November 1850) 549–73.]

2. [Some readers will find the use of "man" in the headings obsolete and inappropriate. Since the headings attempt to concisely reproduce Nevin's expressions and key ideas, it has been retained for the sake of consistency.]

3. [This formulation is ubiquitous in the Nevin corpus. Borneman, *Church*, 76, summarizes: "For Nevin, mankind's distinction from the rest of the natural order is marked by his morality, intelligence, and free agency; these are qualities that grant the possibility of freedom, personality, and sociality. As such, they are qualities which both demonstrate mankind's sanctified status from—yet still pending their organic relationship to—the natural world, allowing him to be the imago Dei that he was created to be. While intelligence, morality, and human agency find their concrete existence in the natural world, they find their genesis in the organic relationship between the natural and supernatural. According to Nevin, the universal ideals take logical precedence, but man actually derives these qualities from a repository where the ideal has embedded itself in the actual. This scheme is crucial for Nevin, who wishes to emphasize humanity's universal essence without debasing the value of natural existence."]

4. [Chambers, *Vestiges of the Natural History*.]

Document 3: The Moral Order of Sex.

the region of sensation, and just as little may we conceive of a transition on the part of the mere animal, over into the world of self-conscious intelligence and will. The sundering gulph is just as deep and impassable in one case as it is in the other. But we must not so understand this, as to lose sight at the same time of the mysterious life union which holds notwithstanding between nature and mind. The world in its lower view, is not simply the outward theatre or stage on which man is to act his part, as a candidate for heaven. In the midst of all its different forms of existence, it is pervaded throughout with the power of a single life, which comes ultimately to its full sense and force only in the human person. This should be plain to the most common observation. Nature is constructed, or we should say rather exists, on the plan of a vast pyramid; which starts in the mass of inorganic matter, and rises steadily through successive stages of organization, first vegetable then animal, till at length it gains in man the summit and crown, towards which it has been evidently reaching and tending from the start. So, in the first chapter of Genesis, we have the process of creation described in this very order, and all conducted to its majestic conclusion finally, only towards the close of the sixth day, in that oracle of infinite majesty and love: "Let us make man in our image, after our likeness; and let them have dominion over the fish of the sea, and over the fowls of the air, and over the cattle, and over all the earth and over every moving thing that moveth upon the earth."[5] Man is the centre of nature, without which it could not be in any of its parts the living constitution which it is in fact; for the parts in this case subsist not, by themselves or for themselves simply, but in virtue only of their organic comprehension in the whole. Nature of course then rests in man as her own universal sense and end, and can never be disjoined from his life. The union is not outward simply, but inward and vital. Man carries in himself the full mystery of the material world and remains from first to last the organ of its power. He is indeed, in another view, far more than nature. Reason and freedom, as they meet together in the idea of personality, belong to a wholly different order of existence; in virtue of which, he towers high above the whole surrounding world, as the immediate representative and vicegerent of God in its midst; made in the image, and after the likeness of his glorious Maker, as we are told, and for this reason clothed with supremacy over the entire inferior creation. But still, in all this dignity, his native affinity with this creation is not in the least impaired or broken. Nature clings to him still, as the noblest fruit of her own womb, in whose mysterious presence is fulfilled the last prophetic sense of her whole previous life, while at the same time this is made to pass away in something quite beyond itself. His personality, with all his world-transcending heaven-climbing powers, remains rooted to the earth, conditioned at every point by the material soil from which it has sprung, and reflecting in clear image

5. [The citation is Genesis 1:28. In a passage that could be read as complementary, Nevin elaborates on these verses of scripture in "Wonderful Nature of Man." See next document, p. 124; also in Appel, *Life*, 516: "In the midst of all these wonders of Nature, however, it is easy to see that the central place belongs to *Man* himself.... All its mysteries and glories culminate at last in his person, and find here only their full significance, their proper conclusion and end."]

the outward life which has become etherealized in its constitution. The process of nature is thus rising upwards perpetually into the process of morality, by which in the end the problem of the world is to become complete in the history of man. The first is the necessary basis and support of the second, as truly as the stock is made to carry the flower in which it passes away. Man is the efflorescence of nature, the full bursting forth of her inmost sense and endeavor, into the form of intelligence and will; and his whole thinking and working consequently can be sound and solid, only as they are in fact borne and carried by a growth that springs immediately from her womb.[6]

There is no opposition then, as is sometimes dreamed, between the natural and the moral. They are indeed widely different, but not in such a way as to contradict each other. On the contrary, they can never be rightly sundered or disjoined. Nature, in order to be true to itself, must ascend into the sphere of morality; and morality, on the other hand, can have no truth or substance, except as it is found to embody in itself the life of nature, thus emancipated into a higher form. Daughters of heaven as they all are, there is still not a single virtue, which is not in this respect at the same time truly and fully earth-born; as much so, we may say, as its own sweet image, the natural flower, be it modest daisy or stately dahlia, that quietly blooms at its side. A morality that affects to be purely of the skies, can never be other than sickly and sentimental. The more of nature our virtues enshrine, the more vigorous will they be found to be and worthy of respect.[7]

[The Individual and the Unity of Humanity]

This is one universal law, in the constitution of our human life. Another presents itself, as already stated, in the conception of an organic process, in virtue of which the

---

6. [Nevin's use of biological metaphor is hardly unique to this essay, and he utilizes it in a variety of ways. With respect to faith, for example: "It is like the progressive development of leaf, flower, and fruit, in all plant life, where foliage and efflorescence are but stages, through which the life of the fruit works from the beginning to bring itself to pass. So faith in the mere understanding first, by virtue of the divine force of the truth which is in it as the word of God, finds itself gradually lifted more and more into positive communion with the interior lightsphere of the word, as this proceeds from the Lord of life and glory himself; brightens thus into Christian hope, and through this comes to full fruitage finally, and in that which has been all along the inward scope and power of the movement, 'charity out of a pure heart and of a good conscience and of faith unfeigned' (1 Tim. i.5)." Nevin, "Bread of Life," MTSS 6:237.]

7. [The philosophical framework behind much of Nevin's biological metaphors is very likely—and significantly—indebted to Rauch, who, as Layman notes: "thought {Aristotle's concept of} 'potentiality' was equivalent to 'genus' (e.g., 'tree'), itself invisible but becoming manifested in the 'species and individual' (e.g., 'white oak tree,' '*this* tree'). To close the circle, Rauch then claimed that genus/potentiality was approximately equivalent to the Hegelian 'idea.' This formulation enabled Nevin to synthesize his underlying biological metaphor of a plant that grows and manifests its 'germ' with the idealism that was becoming increasingly attractive to him." Layman, general editor's introduction to *One, Holy, Catholic, and Apostolic, Tome 2*, MTSS 7:3.]

Document 3: The Moral Order of Sex.

problem of every individual life is from the start involved in the problem that includes humanity as a whole.

Morality, by its very nature, is something social.[8] It does not simply require the relations which society creates, as an outward field for its action, but stands also only in the sense of these relations as a part of its own being. The idea of man, which is of course originally one and single, in order that it may become actual, must resolve itself into an innumerable multitude of individual lives, whose perfection subsequently can be found again in no other form than that of their general union is a free way. Provision is made for such a union in the natural constitution of humanity, bound together as it is by a common origin, and up held by perpetual evolution from itself in the way of history. But mere nature here is not sufficient to secure all that is required. Humanity comes to its full sense only in the sphere of intelligence and freedom; and its proper wholeness therefore is something to be reached, only by the activity of the will, recognizing and embracing, with full consent, the relations in which it is required to move. This again supposes a process, growing forth continually from the law of natural evolution and growth just noticed, by which the individual life, in finding itself under its higher form of self-consciousness, may be still engaged to seek its true place in the integration of life as a whole, flowing into this by the spontaneous force of love, and resting in it as the proper and necessary perfection of his own being. The unity of the race can be fully accomplished thus, only through the free action of the living elements into which it is resolved for this purpose. The process of the union is moral, and in no sense physical, except as conditioned by a natural constitution, which adumbrates and supports the spiritual structure that springs from its presence. It is possible in such case, of course, that the freedom of the individual subject may be abused, and the law of love denied which he is bound by his nature to honor and obey. He may so cling to his own separate and single life, through selfishness and sin, as to wrong perpetually the claims of the general life in which this should become complete. But in all this he wrongs at the same time the inmost sense and meaning also of his own individual being. Whether he choose to make account of it or not, he is formed for morality, that is for free inward union with his race, through the social relations in which he stands; and his life can come to no right development in itself, but must suffer rather perpetual violence in its nature, if it be not allowed to unfold itself in this its only normal and legitimate form. Morality, including as it does the conception of personality, or the self-conscious and self-acting force of reason and will, is something general and universal by its very nature. It implies throughout the idea of fellowship and union, the organic marriage of reciprocally necessary and mutually supplemental parts, working into each other and conspiring towards a common whole. In the power

---

8. [This social element is crucial for understanding what we might call the "horizontal" element of what often seems like a predominantly "vertical" dynamic of nature and mankind ascending and descending. This social element shows up in several other places throughout Nevin's writings, including "Party Spirit," in Appel, *Life*, 118; Nevin, "Catholicism," MTSS 7:17–18; Nevin, *Human Freedom*, 23; see also, Binkley, *Mercersburg Theology*, 85–86.]

of this universal, omnipotent and irreversible law, the life of every man stands from the beginning, in virtue of its spiritual and moral constitution. He can never be true to himself at a single point, he can never exercise a single moral function, a single act of intelligence or will, in a free way, without going beyond his own person, and mingling, with conscious coalescence, in the sea of life with which he is surrounded.

[The Forms of Human Society]

By one of the greatest discoveries in modern science, placing the name of Schleiermacher[9] in the sphere of ethics on the same high level with that of Kepler[10] in the sphere of physics, the general moral function, as it may be styled, in man, is found to resolve itself, by a process of analysis which we have no time here to follow, into four cardinal forms of action, two lying on the side of the understanding and two on the side of the will. Each of these can hold properly only under a social character, by which the individual in order that he may be at all complete in himself, is forced to enter into fellowship with his race. Thus arise four great spheres of moral union, in the proper constitution of the world's life. The first is exhibited to us predominantly in the idea of *Art*; the second, in the idea of *Science*; the third, in the idea of *Sociality* (*Geselligkeit*) corresponding very much with the conception of *Play*, in its widest and most dignified sense; the fourth and last in the idea of *Business*. These four orders of life are not to be regarded, indeed, as standing wholly out of each other in the way of external distinction; the case requires, on the contrary, that they should grow into one another with inward reciprocal embrace, and it is only their complete concretion in this way at last, as the power of a single life, that can bring the moral process to its rightful conclusion. Still they are for the most part, as the world now stands, more or less out of each other in fact; and each has a nature also of its own, which it must always be important to understand and cultivate under such separate view. They are the four grand departments of humanity, each an organism of universal power within itself, in whose organic conjunction alone we have revealed to us the full idea of morality, as the proper life of man.[11]

---

9. [Friedrich Schleiermacher (1768–1834), German theologian best known for his emphasis on personal religious experience, argued that religion should be understood as a feeling of absolute dependence on God. He advanced a biblical hermeneutic that insists that a text's meaning can and should be shaped by the context in which it is read and interpreted. DiPuccio, *Interior*, 80, summarizes Nevin's appropriation well: "Like Schleiermacher and other romantic exegetes, Nevin believed that the presuppositions which guide the biblical interpreter must emerge out of the essential character of Christianity itself. The meaning of Scripture can only be grasped when we hear it speak from its own element which is the life and power of Christ. The proper context of Scripture, therefore, is none other than the new creation in Jesus Christ considered in its universal scope. This is the presupposition of all sound interpretation."]

10. [Johannes Kepler (1571–1630), German mathematician and astronomer, and a seminal figure of the modern scientific revolution, most well-known for his laws of planetary motion.]

11. [For explanations of these four "forms" or "orders," see Crossley, "Schleiermacher's Christian

Document 3: The Moral Order of Sex.

[Catholicity as the Unity of Human Society]

Not as co-ordinate in any sense with these, but as above them all, and as constituting indeed the only form in which they can become complete, stands the idea of Religion, as fully actualized in the glorious union of the One Holy Catholic *Church*. In one aspect, we may style such a moral whole, the *State*. But in a perfect state of society, this idea itself must become merged in the broader and deeper idea of the Church, in which alone we reach the final and adequate expression for our universal human life. Religion of course then stands in no opposition to any of the great divisions of this life, as they have just been named; for this would imply an original contrariety between it and the actual constitution of the world, which the nature of the case must be held to exclude. On the contrary, it must have power finally to lift them all into its own sphere. Art, science, social and civil life, must all be capable of being sanctified by its transforming presence. It belongs to the very conception of Christianity and the Church thus, that they should take full possession of the world at last, not extensively alone in its outward population, but intensively also in the entire range of its inward life; and it is only in proportion as we find their actual form commensurate with the idea of such catholicity, that this can be said to have reached in any given stadium of their history, its true significance and design.

[The Family and Sexual Difference]

Underneath this whole magnificent superstructure, on the other side, appears the primitive fundamental form of society, in the constitution of the *Family*. As the four-fold organism of morality terminates in the idea of the Church, so it takes its start here from an organization, that may be regarded as the root of its whole process, rising into view immediately from the mysterious life of nature itself. The domestic constitution stands in no way parallel simply, with the four forms of society that make up the union of humanity as a whole; it includes them all rather in its single nature, in the way of beginning and germ. It is the rich well-spring, out of which flows the river of Eden, that is parted from thence into four heads, and carried forward with fruitful irrigation over the fair garden of life, till all its streams become one again in the deep bosom of the sea.[12]

All society rests on distinction and difference. So the primary form of fellowship now mentioned, lying as it does at the ground of our universal life, is at once provided for and secured, by a radical disruption of the entire race into two great sections or halves, in the form of *sex*. Of all distinctions that exist in our nature, this must be held to be the most significant and profound, as entering before all others into its universal constitution, and forming the basis on the ground of which only all other relations

---

Ethics," 96–100; Schleiermacher, *Lectures on Philosophical Ethics*, xxviii–xxix.]

12. [The four rivers of Eden are the Euphrates, the Tigris, the Gihon and the Pishon. They are first listed in Gen 2:10–14.]

belonging to it become possible and real. It comes into view accordingly in the first mention of man's creation; where we are told that he was made in the image and likeness of God, and at the same time under the two-fold character of male and female, as the necessary form of his perfection. His nature became complete, only when woman was taken from his side, and he was permitted to hail her bone of his bone, and flesh of his flesh, in the new consciousness to which he first woke by her presence.

Thus radical and original in the constitution of our nature, the sexual difference must necessarily pervade, not simply a part of its being, but the whole. The life of man is indeed always a complex fact, made up of widely different forms and spheres of existence; but it is always nevertheless, in the midst of all these, a single undivided unity within itself, bound together and ruled throughout by the presence of a common principle or law. The life of the body is ever in strict union with the life of the soul, and this, on the other hand, stands wedded again to that continually, as its own proper self under an outward material form. No less intimate and necessary, in the next place, is the connection that holds between the individual natural constitution, thus inward and outward, and the proper personality of the subject to whom it belongs. It lies in the very conception of personality, it is true, being as it is the life of the spirit, in the form of intelligence and will,[13] that it should not be ruled blindly by the force of mere nature, as comprehended in the individual organization. It is a principle and fountain of action for itself, and is required to act back upon the natural life with such independent force, as may serve to mould and fashion this continually more and more into its own image. But still, this original and independent action, however free it may be in its own nature, can never escape from the particular organization in which it has its basis, and which it is called to fill with its presence. In other words, the inmost life of man, his personal spirit, though absolutely universal in its own character, is made to individualize itself by union with the inferior part of his nature,[14] while at the same time it seeks to lift this into its own sphere. Reason and will accordingly are not the same thing exactly in all men. Personality is conditioned and complexioned, all the world over, by the individual physical nature, somatic and psychic, out of which, and by means of which, it comes to its historical development.[15] It is not possible then of course, that it should not participate in the force of a distinction so broad and deep as that which is involved in the idea of sex. It results necessarily from the organic unity of every single life as a whole, that the order which thus severs the human world into the two grand sections of male and female, should extend to the most spiritual part of our nature as well as to that which is simply corporeal. There is a sex of the mind or

13. [See above, "Human Freedom," 56–68.]

14. [According to Aristotle, every form (μορφή: *morphe*) is individualized by "matter" (ὕλη: *hyle*). Matter then is what differentiates say, one cow from another, or similarly, every human being from every other human being. Any definable being is a unity of form (e.g., "cow-ness") and matter (thought of as undefined "stuff").]

15. [Nevin's indebtedness to Rauch should once again be noted. For some background to Nevin's thinking on the themes of this section and the essay more generally, see Rauch, *Psychology*.]

Document 3: The Moral Order of Sex.

soul, just as there is a sex of the body, an inward difference of structure in the one case, including the whole economy of the spirit, fancy and feeling, thought and volition, as broadly marked and strikingly significant, to say the least, as any outward difference of structure which may show itself in the other.

It is altogether preposterous, to think of resolving this difference into the influence of education or mere social position; as though nothing more were needed to convert men into women, or women into men, so far as character and spirit are concerned, than simply to make them change places for a time in the order of society, confining the male sex to the employments of the nursery and the kitchen, and throwing open to the female sex the active walks of business, politics and trade. The difference as we may all easily see, is original and constitutional, and in this view co-extensive in full with the entire range of our common life. It shows itself even in the character of the infant, as soon as it begins to discover any signs of character whatever. The tastes and tendencies of the boyish nature are peculiar to it as such, from the first hour of its activity in the nursery, clearly distinguishing it from the nature of the girl. The distinction reigns through all the sports of childhood, and accompanies the entire subsequent development of the spirit onward and upward to mature age. It prevails in full force over the whole broad range of middle life, imparting to it its highest interest and value in a moral view. Finally it ceases not with the decay of bodily vigor and beauty induced by old age itself, but reaches forward still, with a radiant light that grows only more mellow as it is less tinged with the coloring of sense, far down into the vale of years; covering thus in truth the universal tract of our existence, from the mystery of the womb to the still more impenetrable and solemn mystery of the grave.

Nor can the distinction possibly terminate here. It has been made a question indeed, whether the difference of sex extends to the other world; and it is characteristic of the Hegelian way of thinking in particular, that it allows but little room for any such supposition, having the tendency always to merge the individual in the general, and to make men mere passing exemplifications of humanity. But this view overthrows in the end the doctrine of a future state altogether; since without the distinctions of individual nature, as something continued over from the present life, there can be no sense of personal identity, no true resurrection, or other world consciousness, in any form, in the very conception of our being as we have here described it, that its individual distinctions should reach throughout the whole man in a permanent and enduring way.[16] Personality cannot be evolved at all, except in such union with a particular natural organization, as to have wrought into it from first to last the same particularity, as a necessary part of its own constitution. It is one of the great merits of Schleiermacher again, to have perceived and asserted, with proper force, the claims

---

16. [Here we have the problem of applying Aristotelian hylomorphism (matter-form) to the Christian understanding of the eternal life. If the human form is simply the generic essence of being human, then what is eternal about the individual human identity? Nevin gives one solution, aided by his interpretation of Schleiermacher.]

of the individual over against the authority of the universal and absolute, as a permanent element in the constitution of man.[17] The question before us then, according to this view, is already answered. The multiplication of the race will not extend, it is true, over into the other world, and with this must come to an end also the present significance of the sexual relation as concerned in that object; our whole present physical state indeed being but the transient process, by which our being is destined to emerge hereafter into a higher order of existence. In that higher state, we are told, they shall neither marry nor be given in marriage, but resemble in this respect the angels in heaven.[18] The family constitution, in its strict sense, though it be the basis of all morality in its process of revelation, belongs only to the present order of things, and will not be continued in the complete kingdom of God. But we may not suppose that the vast and mighty distinction in our nature, out of which this radical constitution now springs, will come to an end in the same way. Entering as it does into the life of the entire person, it cannot be overthrown by the simple elevation of our mortal individuality into the undying sphere of the spirit. On the contrary it may be expected rather to appear now under its most purely ethical, and for that reason its highest also and richest form. In Christ Jesus there is neither male nor female, as there is also neither Jew nor Greek;[19] not however by the full obliteration of all such differences, but only through their free harmonious comprehension in a form of consciousness that is deeper than their opposition, and able thus to reconcile them in an organic way. It is on the back ground of such universal unity precisely, that the differences stand out after all in the clearest delineation which their nature admits. There will be races and nationalities and temperaments, strongly marked, in heaven, no doubt, as we find them here in course of sanctification upon the earth. And so there will be, not in the flesh but in the spirit, the difference of sex there too. Humanity made forever complete in the new creation will comprise in itself still, as the deep ground-tone of its universal organic harmony, the two great forms of existence in which it was comprehended at the beginning, when God created man, we are told, male and female after his own image.[20] In this view, it involves no extravagance to extend the idea of sex even to the angels themselves, although they neither marry nor are given in marriage.[21]

---

17. [Schleiermacher "assert[s] . . . the fact and value of *diversity* or *individuality* even in the moral sphere." He "champions not only a (moral) distinctiveness of different human societies vis-à-vis the human species as a whole . . . but also a (moral) distinctiveness of the individual vis-à-vis his society . . . ." Forster, "Friedrich Daniel Ernst Schleiermacher," emphasis original.]

18. [Matt 22:30.]

19. [Gal 3:28.]

20. [See Nevin, "New Creation," MTSS 4:32–45; Nevin, "Man's True Destiny," below in this volume. In another passage, Nevin explains that the new creation must "take up into itself the entire compass and power of the old creation; not destroying its constituent elements and laws, but fulfilling their inmost sense rather and raising them to their highest power." Nevin, "Noel on Baptism," MTSS 6:100.]

21. [Matt 22:30.]

Document 3: The Moral Order of Sex.

[The Constitution and Relationship of the Two Sexes]

We are now prepared to notice more particularly, though of course still only in the most general way, the constitutional character of the two sexes in a comparative view. The case requires of course, as already intimated, a glance at the simply physical side of our nature, in the first place, and then at its moral or spiritual side, in which only the first comes finally to its full human significance and force. So intimately interwoven however, are these two spheres of existence, that no full view can be had of one apart from the other, and it is only in their union at last that we are enabled to complete properly the comparison we have in hand.

The *physical* difference of the sexes, is not limited by any means, in the first place, to any particular organs and functions of our simply corporeal structure, but extends to the body as a whole. This is in no sense a mechanical composition merely of various parts outwardly filled together, but a living whole pervaded throughout with the presence of a common principle and constitution. It is not possible accordingly, that a peculiarity so broad and deep as that of sex should appear as something adventitious and accidental only, in some particular parts of the general organization, without affecting the rest. It must impress itself, more or less clearly, upon the whole. This we find accordingly to be the case in fact. Both anatomically and physiologically considered, the whole body is made to participate in the sexual character. Man and woman are so completely different in their whole organization, that as it has been remarked no single part of the one could be properly substituted for the corresponding part of the other. Bones and muscles, the turn of the limbs, general height and bulk, the conformation of the head and breast, the show of the skin, the expression of the face, the tones of the voice, the bearing and carriage of the person, all are comprehended in the same universal distinction. So also in the case of the several great systems of which life is composed; the action of liver, lungs and brain, is subjected to corresponding modification. In man the arterial and cerebral systems prevail; in woman, the venous and glanglionic; creating a preponderance of irritability in the first case, and in the second a similar preponderance of sensibility, conditioning thus throughout their different capabilities and tendencies, and indicating with sure necessity the different spheres in which they are appointed to move.—In the next place with the purely corporeal or somatic difference now stated, corresponds also the inward or psychical region of what must still be denominated our physical nature. This includes the whole natural consciousness, the product directly of our animal organization as such, which the true spirit within us is required to raise into its own native sphere of freedom, that it may become the vesture, subsequently, of its own life. Such consciousness from the start is not the same thing in man that it is found to be in woman. Sensation and perception, feeling and affection, appetite and tendency, inclination and desire, are all modified by the power of sex. The whole inward and outward nature, harmoniously constructed in each case within itself, is comprehended in the same distinction, and carried always in the same direction. Man is characterized by superior strength and activity, while woman is more delicately tender and passive. Thought predominates in man, in woman taste and feeling. All goes to indicate that man is formed to exercise authority and protection, and to wrestle both physically and spiritually with the surrounding world; while woman is led by her whole nature rather, to cultivate a spirit of submission and dependence, and finds her proper sphere in the retirement of the house and family. We are in this way, however, conducted over to a still higher apprehension of the difference under consideration. It is only as nature passes upwards, as its constitution here requires it to do, into the sphere of the spirit, that the full sense and force of the distinction, thus sublimated by the ethical process, is brought finally into full view.

In this character, the difference is no longer natural simply, but in the fullest sense *moral*. Personality unites in itself the presence of a spiritual universal life, which is strictly and truly the fountain of its own activity in the form of intelligence and will, and a material organization as the necessary medium and basis of its revelation. In this relation, the spirit, while it must remain always the centre of the whole person with power to assert its own proper primacy, is notwithstanding capable of being acted upon and influenced in various measures by the power of nature, as brought to bear upon it through the organism of the body. In proportion, at the same time, to the independence it may be urged and enabled to assert in its own sphere, will be the strength and force of the personality thus brought into view. Now it results from the whole peculiarity of her organization, as already described, and so of course lies also in the proper purpose and destiny of her sex, that woman should possess less of this independence than man. Her life springs more immediately and directly from nature, even under its true ethical form. There is a specific difference, in this view, between the personality of the sexes, taking up into itself and completing the sense of all differences in a lower sphere. It resolves itself ultimately, we may say, into this, that the universal side of our common humanity prevails in man, and its individual side in woman. Self-consciousness in man runs readily into the general form of thought, disposing him for comprehensive observation, speculation and science; in woman it takes more the character of feeling, which is always something single, closely coupled with fancy and art; her thoughts are her own inward states and impressions mainly, and the product immediately of the outward occasions from which they grow. So again self-activity in man takes naturally the broad character of will, carrying him forth into the open world, involving him in business and conflict on the arena of public life; while in woman it is exercised more in the form of impulse and desire, falls more fully within the flow of nature as embodied in her own particular organization, and for this very reason, at the same time, participates more largely in the character of passive necessity and dependence, as the law by which nature is ruled. The personality of man is more vigorous and concentrated, and if we may use the expression, more thoroughly and completely *personal*, than the personality of woman: showing him clearly thus to be the centre and bearer properly of the human nature as a whole. This implies no inferiority on the side of woman; she is just as complete and whole in her own sphere as man can possibly be in his; and this sphere is just as necessary also as the other to the true perfection of human life. It lies however in the nature of the case, that this life should be, not a dualism, but an inward unity; and that the distinction therefore in which it starts, reaching as it does into the personal consciousness itself, should be so ordered nevertheless as to return in upon itself again to a common personal ground. The relation of the sexes then requires, that their two-fold constitution, dividing as it does the proper wholeness of humanity, should be supported at last as a single personality from a common basis on the one side or the other. The general nature accordingly is made to centre in man; and woman taken in symbolic vision from his side, while she forms the necessary complement of his being, comes to her full spiritual development and gains her true native freedom and independence, only by seeking in him the central support which she lacks in herself, and by bringing her whole consciousness thus into profound union with his life, as the inmost and deepest ground of her own.

[The Contrasting Mission of the Two Sexes]

With such natural and personal differences, the sexes are designated from the start to different spheres of life, and have widely different missions to fulfil in the social system. Neither the duties of the man on the one hand, nor his virtues and perfections on the other, are the same in general that belong to woman; and so also the vices which most dishonor the one, are not always of exactly parallel turpitude for the other. Man's vocation is to go forth into the world, to wrestle with nature as its rightful lord and master, to make his understanding and will felt on the general course of life. The forest-felling axe, the soil-subduing plough, the mason's hammer and the joiner's saw, the wand of judgment, the scepter of authority and the sword of war, belong properly to his hand, and to his alone. Business, politics, outward enterprize, learning and science, are all computed in his legitimate domain. Woman on the other hand, finds her true orbit, as we have already said, in the quiet retreats of private and domestic life. Her highest glory and greatest power are comprehended in the sacred names of wife and mother. She is not indeed shut out from society, in a wider view. On the contrary, she is filled to exert the largest influence in the social sphere strictly taken, as distinguished from that of business and science. But it is always under her domestic character only, and in virtue of her peculiar constitution, as representing the individual side of the world's life, rather than that which is general and universal. The moment she affects to overstep this limit, by the personal assumption of public and general functions, in which she can have no part properly except through the medium of the other sex, she makes herself weak, and forfeits her title to respect. The popular platform, the rostrum, the pulpit, are interdicted to her nature, no less than the battle field and crowded exchange. All public primacy is unsuitable to her sex; nor is it easy to see certainly, how the "monstrous regimen of women" as denounced by the Old Scottish Elijah, in his memorable "*Blast*," should not be as fair an object of indignation and scorn when seated on the throne, as it is felt to be in all inferior stations.[22] Christianity here is always deep, and at the same time true to nature. "Let your women keep silence in the churches: for it is not permitted unto them to speak; but they are commanded to be under obedience, as also saith the law. And if they will learn anything, let them ask their husbands at home: for it is a shame for women to speak in the church."[23] So again: "Let the women learn in silence with all subjection. I suffer not a woman to teach, nor to usurp authority over the man but to be in silence. For Adam was first formed, then Eve. And Adam was not deceived, but the woman being deceived, was in the transgression."[24]

The order of society, springing as it does from the sexual relation first of all, imperiously requires that the opposition in which it holds should be sacredly regarded and preserved, throughout the whole economy of life. All that serves to neutralize it, or to thrust it out of sight, should be reprobated as an unfriendly to the best interests of the human race. Civilization and culture, morality and religion, while they call for the free intercourse of the sexes, as polar sides of one and the same social constitution, call no less clearly at the same time for their constant distinction and separation in all that pertains to inward character and outward life. They need a different education. The accomplishments which adorn the one, are not those which most become the other. It is not without reason that they are required to distinguish themselves in their outward dress. "Doth not even nature itself teach you," says the apostle, "that if a man have long hair, it is a shame unto him? but if a woman have long hair, it is a glory to her; for her hair is given her for a covering."[25] All confusion of the sexes, all removal of the lines and land-marks that show the true and proper boundary between them, is a crime against society of the most serious order. For either sex to forsake its own

---

22. "Who would not judge that body to be a monster," says Knox, "where there was no head eminent above the rest, but that the eyes were in the hands, the tongue and the mouth beneath in the belly and the ears in the feet? [. . .] No less [. . .] is the body of that commonwealth, where a woman beareth empire; for either doth it lack a lawful head, as in very deed it doth, or else an idol is exalted instead of the true head. An idol I call that which hath the form and appearance, but lacketh the virtue and strength, which the name and proportion doth resemble and promise. [. . .] I confess a realm may in despite of God—he of his wise judgment so giving them over unto a reprobate mind—exalt up a woman to that monstriferous honor to be esteemed as head. But impossible it is to man or angel, to give unto her the properties and perfect offices of a lawful head; for the same God that denied power to the hands to speak, to the belly to hear, and to the feet to see, hath denied to the woman power to command man, and hath taken away wisdom to consider, and providence to foresee, the things that be profitable to the commonwealth."—First Blast. [Nevin's edition is unknown. See Knox, *First Blast* in *Works of John Knox* 4:391. Either Nevin or his source modernized the spellings; he also reordered the phrases of the sentence beginning "I confess a realm . . . ."]

23. [1 Cor 14:34–35.]

24. [1 Tim 2:11–14.]

25. [1 Cor 11:14–15.]

sphere, and to intrude into that which belongs of right only to the other, though it should be even in the most trivial things merely, is ever something revolting to all reason and taste. To be unsexly, in costume, habit, spirit or occupation, is to be at the same time unnatural also and immoral.

[Unity in the Difference of the Two Sexes]

This opposition and distinction however, as we have already seen, are intended only to make room for the more perfect union of the two interests thus flung asunder. It is because they are different in this way, and in proportion also as the difference is understood and respected, that the sexes are capable of entering into the intimate union, which lies at the ground of our whole human life. Physically, psychologically, and morally, man shows himself to be at all points what woman is not. The one is the opposite of the other. But for this very reason, the relation is one of reciprocal want and supply. Neither section of the race is complete in its own nature, while the defect which exists on each side is met with its proper complement precisely in the comparative advantage of the other. Humanity is the unity of the two sexes; which as such accordingly can never rest in one apart from the other, but must seek continually the full conjunction of both, as original, necessary component sides of its proper constitution. In the nature of the case it can never be satisfied with such conjunction, except under the most inward and spiritual form, as the power ultimately of a single individual life. The sexes are made complete only in and through each other; and this necessarily by such a union only, as extends to their whole constitution, physical and spiritual, embracing thus the entire inward life full as much as that which is exhibited outwardly in the sphere of flesh and blood. Each is needed to fill out and complete the personality or moral nature of the other, no less than its material organization. The qualities of man's spirit require to be softened and refined by communion with the mild nature of woman; as she on the other hand needs the strength and firmness of his more universal life, on which to lean as the stable prop of her own. The personality of man is enriched and beautified, through woman, on the side of nature; the personality of woman is consolidated and perfected, through man, on the side of the idea.

In this view, of course, the union which the case demands, can not overthrow but must serve rather to establish in full force, the order we have already found to hold between the two sexes in their personal constitution. It is emphatically the fact of this order, involving as it does a certain primacy on the one side and a corresponding subordination on the other, that makes it possible for the union to take the vital, fundamental form, that is here required. Two strictly co-ordinate personalities could not be expected to flow thus into the power of a single life. It is because woman has her true and proper centre at last in man, and not in herself, that it is possible for the sexes to become, not simply one flesh, but one mind also and one soul. Her consciousness thus poised upon the personality of man, is brought to such harmony and freedom and active force within itself, as it could never be advanced to in any other way. All this implies no sort of dishonor or degradation. It is simply the necessary form of our general human life itself, whose perfection demands this distinction of sexes, as something which, to be real at all, must hold in such proportional relation and no other. It is precisely the strength and glory of woman, to be thus dependently joined to the personality of man, as the vine is carried upwards by clinging to a trunk more vigorous and rough than its own, which it serves at the same time gracefully to ennoble and adorn. Marriage is indeed in this view, more significant and necessary, we may say, for woman, than it can be held to be for man. It is the appointed and regular process of her full emancipation from the power of sense and nature over into the sphere of a firm and enduring spiritual independence. She needs it to make her own personality, whether as intelligence or will, sufficiently central and deep to sustain itself as it should against the force of the surrounding world. It is by the mighty energy of love, in this form, that she comes at last fully to herself, and is enabled to bring into clear revelation the true wealth of her nature. In a deep sense thus we may apply to the case, that mystic word of the apostle "She shall be saved (διὰ τεκνογονίας) by childbearing." Connected as it is immediately with the thought of her moral weakness, as exemplified in the fall, (1. Tim. ii. 14, 15) it seems to refer not obscurely to the like mystic word of the curse pronounced against her, Gen. iii. 16, in consequence of that catastrophe.[26] The relation which is made the fountain of her deepest sorrows, under the iron reign of sin, becomes itself the well spring of her salvation, through the law of "faith and charity and holiness" revealed in Jesus Christ. So profoundly true again is that other declaration: "The head of every man is Christ, and the head of the woman is the man;" or as we have it in another place: "The husband is the head of the wife, even as Christ is the head of the Church" (1. Cor. xi. 3; Eph. v. 28). So intimately close is the union, for which the sexual distinction opens the way and in which alone it comes finally to its true meaning.

On this union, the primitive and most fundamental form of human fellowship, depends not simply the perpetuation of the race, but the entire problem besides of its social and moral history. It is by means of it, in the first place, that the generic or universal life of man is brought to assert its proper authority, over against the life of the individual singly and separately considered. The individual is forced to feel that he is no complete whole in himself; that his nature can be true to its own constitution, only by passing beyond his single person and seeking its necessary complement in another; that, in one word, to be a true and full man at all, he must enter into communion with his race, and make himself tributary, in a free way, to the high ends for which it has been placed in the world. This subordination of the single life to the general, is of such vast consequence to the entire plan and structure of the moral world, that it must be secured by an invincible guaranty in the constitution of the world itself. It is

---

26. ["To the woman he said, 'I will surely multiply your pain in childbearing; in pain you shall bring forth children. Your desire shall be contrary to your husband, but he shall rule over you.'"]

Document 3: The Moral Order of Sex.

curious and instructive to see accordingly, how the law of society, lying as it does at the foundation of all ethics, is here made to take root, as it were, "in the lowest parts of the earth;"[27] illustrating on a grand scale, the proposition affirmed in the beginning of this article, that all morality has its basis in nature, and is to be regarded as genuine only as it shows itself to be in very truth the efflorescence of this lower life, bursting upwards into the ethereal region of the spirit.

The bond by which the sexes are thus drawn together is lodged, in the first instance, deep in the physical constitution of those who are under its power. In this form it is the sexual appetite or instinct, a purely natural tendency, which has for its object the preservation of the race, as the instinct of hunger is designed to secure the preservation of the single individual. It is the power of the general nature over its own constituent factors or parts, by which these are urged to seek, each in the other the full sense of their proper being, and thus to constitute, in the way of reciprocal appropriation, a living union that may fairly represent both.

But nature here as elsewhere is required to lose itself always in the power of a higher life, in which its action shall no longer be blind and unfree, but the product of the spirit itself in its own. As the sexual relation extends to the whole person, the union for which it calls can never be complete except as it is made to embrace this in its full totality, under a strictly central and universal form. It must be a union of mind and will, a process of mutual apprehension and reciprocal personal appropriation, in the farthest depths of the soul. In no other form can it be truly normal, and answerable to the high purposes it is designed to serve. The sexual tendency *ethicised* in this way, and sublimated into the sphere of personality, becomes love. This is always in its very nature something moral and spiritual, springing from the will, and having regard to the inmost person. Still in the case before us, it is in the fullest sense also sexual. It rests throughout on the distinction of sex, and regards the spirit only as beheld and apprehended under such modification. Hence the legitimate power of beauty, as constituting on the side of either sex to the eye of the other, the outward image and expression of the inward life in its sexual form. All true beauty, of course, in this view, falls back upon the spirit, while at the same time its proper revelation to be sought in the outward person. A sexual interest that includes no regard to beauty, must necessarily be immoral, as falling short of the high spiritual region in which only love finds its suitable home. The merely animal nature, in such case, is suffered to prevail over the human. It belongs to love, not to overthrow absolutely indeed the power of mere sense, but still so to cover it at every point with its own superior presence, that it shall not be permitted to come into separate view.[28]

Love, as now described, includes in itself always a regard to the sexual character as such; and so far there is truth and force in the observation of Sterne, that no man

---

27. [Ps 139:15. "My bones were not hidden from thee when I was made in secret, curiously wrought in the lower parts of the earth."]

28. [For an extended treatment of beauty, see Nevin's lectures on aesthetics, in Appel, *Life*, 667–85.]

ever loves any one woman as he should, who has not at the same time a love for her whole sex.²⁹ This however is only one side of the subject. Love, to be complete, must be also strictly and distinctly individual, determined towards its object as a single person to the exclusion of all others.

The single plant is only a specimen of its kind, the particular animal a copy of the tribe to which it belongs. But it is not thus in the human sphere. The individual man is vastly more than a passing exemplification simply of the generic life that flows through his person. He comprehends in himself an independent specific nature, that can be properly represented by no other. His individuality is always at the same time personal, and as such something universal and constant; as on the other hand his personality is always individual, taking its special complexion from the living material nature out of which it springs.³⁰ Every such individual personality is a world within itself, existing under given relations to other worlds of corresponding nature around it. No two of these are exactly alike, and all by these differences fall short of the measure that belongs to humanity as a whole. This is constituted only by the society and union of the individual personalities into which its falls, joined together morally, not with indiscriminate conjunction, but according to specific reciprocal correspondence, in the way of inward want and supply. The general law of moral association then being such, it must extend of course in full power to the primary and fundamental union which we have now under consideration. It lies in the very conception of love, as already explained, that it should concentrate itself upon the spirit, as revealed under a sexual form; but to do this fully, it must be carried by inward elective affinity towards its object as a particular person. It is not simply the general attraction of sex, that can satisfy its demands; it requires besides that this attraction shall lodge itself in the presence of a specific personal life, which is felt to be as such the necessary complement of its own nature. Under no other form can the union here in question, be regarded as moral. It is not every woman that is adapted, physically or spiritually, to be a helpmeet for every man; but as the sexes are formed for each other in a general way, so each individual of either sex may be said to be formed for some corresponding individual of the other, and it is of the highest consequence of course, for themselves and for the race also, that they should be able to find and know each other in the confused wilderness of the world's life.

[Marriage]

We may go so far as to say, perhaps, that in a perfectly normal state of the world, this pairing and matching of individual natures would be so complete as to exclude, in

---

29. [A "man who has not a sort of an affection for the whole sex, is incapable of ever loving a single one as he ought." Laurence Sterne, *A Sentimental Journey*, 248.]

30. [At this point Nevin's psychology moves beyond Aristotle's hylomorphism. Each person not only has a unique body (matter) but a unique personality.]

Document 3: The Moral Order of Sex.

every case, all possibility of different choice. Each would be for each, by absolute singularity of mutual suitableness and want, in such a way as to shut out the whole world besides. Of course our actual life, disordered as it is by sin, cannot be expected or required to conform strictly to this rule of ideal perfection. But still it should include at least an approximation towards it; and it must be regarded as defective, in proportion precisely as it is found to fall short of such high measure. In a state of barbarism, but small account comparatively is made of individual personality, in the commerce of the sexes; which however is simply itself an expression of the barbarous life to which it belongs, showing it to border close on the merely animal existence below it, in which as there is no personality so there is no room also for the idea of love in any form. The savage takes his wife, very much as a specimen simply of her sex, just as he selects his dog, in the same view, to accompany him in the chase. It is remarkable too, that in such low stage of moral development, the individual nature itself stands out to view for the most part, only under dim and indistinct lines. It is the sense of personality in the end, that advances the single life to its legitimate rights and claims, investing it with clearly marked distinction under its own form, and challenging towards it in this way the attention and respect it is entitled to receive. We are furnished here accordingly with an unerring standard of civilization and social culture, which in the case before us especially is always of plain and easy application.

The sexual union, representing thus the general relation of the sexes to each other on the one hand, and involving the elective personal affinity of individual natures on the other, mediated throughout by the sacred power of love, comes to its proper expression in the idea of *marriage*; whose nature at the same time is defined and explained, by the whole analysis through which we have now passed. This is simply the true and normal power of that commerce and communion, in which the distinction of sex comes at last to its full sense, as the necessary completion of humanity, and the primitive basis of all history and society. The attributes that belong of right to this union, are the true and proper attributes also of marriage; which is not therefore something joined to our nature, as it were, from abroad, and in the way of outward order or device, whether human or divine; but should be considered rather as part of our nature itself, a simple fact in its organic constitution, without whose presence it must cease to exist altogether.

Marriage, of course then, is the process of reciprocal appropriation, by which the sexes according to their original destination, become one, and so complete themselves each, in the power of a single personal life. In the nature of the case, this double appropriation is required to extend to the entire being of the parties concerned in the transaction: for the sexual difference is such, as we have already seen, that each side of the relation requires the opposite, not in part only but in full, to make itself complete. This implies, at the same time, a corresponding act of self-abandonment, on each side, in favor of the other, as the necessary condition of full mutual appropriation in return. Each yields itself up to be the property of the other, in the very act of embracing this again as its own property. So as regards the merely outward and natural life. The parties are made "one flesh." This of right, however, only in virtue of the inward spiritual embrace, by which the personality of each is brought to rest in that of the other, by the deep mysterious power which belongs to love. The case, in its own nature admits of no compromise or reserve. Marriage calls solemnly for the gift of the whole being, on the altar of love, and can never be satisfied with any sacrifice that is less full and entire. In proportion as the relation comes short of such inward, central, community of soul and life, it must be regarded as an imperfect approximation only to its own true idea.

There is a difference indeed in the form of this mutual self-surrender on the part of the two sexes, corresponding with the order of their general relation as already noticed. As the united person constituted by marriage is required to centre ultimately in man, it follows that the union calls for the largest measure of such free sacrifice on the side of woman. For this also she is happily disposed by her whole constitution. Love is emphatically the element of her life. She needs the opportunity of going fully out of herself in this way, in order that she may do full justice to her own nature. There is nothing in life accordingly more deep, and beautiful, and full of moral power, than the devotion of woman's love. It goes beyond all that is possible, under the same form, on the side of the other sex. The perfection of marriage so far as she is concerned, turns on the measure in which she is prepared to make herself over, in body, mind, and outward estate, without limit or reserve, to him whom she has chosen to be her head. The husband is not required to quit himself, exactly to the same extent and in the same way. He may not resign the sense of his more central and universal character, by which precisely he is qualified to become the personal bearer of the united life involved in the marriage bond. All this however gives him no right to exercise his independence in a selfish way. It lays him under obligation only, to make himself over, in this character, to the possession of his wife, answering thus with full unbounded fidelity and truth, the full unbounded measure of her confidence and trust. "So ought men to love their wives as their own bodies: he that loveth his wife loveth himself."[31]

The idea of marriage, as now presented, clearly excludes, not only all promiscuous concubinage, but all polygamy also and divorce. In its very nature it is the full and enduring union of one man with one woman, according to the law of sexual difference and correspondence. Many outward reasons may be urged against the irregularities now mentioned; but the grand argument in the case at last is just this, that they contradict the true conception of the sexual union itself. This can never take place normally, excepting the way of mutual self-surrender and *whole* appropriation of each other, on the part of those who are its subjects, that is in the way of marriage. Polygamy necessarily violates this law, and the same is true also of divorce, which is tolerated by Christianity accordingly only where the marriage bond has been already nullified, in fact, by the crime of adultery.

---

31. [Eph 5:28.]

Document 3: The Moral Order of Sex.

[Concluding Reflections and "the Emancipation of Woman"]

We cannot bring the whole subject to a conclusion better perhaps, than by making use of it to expose, in a direct way, as has been done in some measure indirectly already, the entire theory of what is sometimes styled *the emancipation of woman*, as held with various modification, by our modern Fourierites[32] and Socialists of every description. Of all forms of agrarianism,[33] this is to be counted, as it is in some respects the most plausible, so also the most mischievous and false. No maxim universally taken, can be more impudently untrue, than that which asserts the general liberty and equality of the human race, in the sense of this disorganizing school. The freedom and independence of all, not only outwardly but inwardly also, is conditioned always by the position assigned to them of God in the social organism to which they belong. All are free only as comprehended in given social relations, and in the measure of their correspondence as parts with the idea of the whole. The proper unity of life, as an organic system, involves of necessity the conception, not simply of manifold distinction, but of relative dependence also and subordination. Of this we have a broad, perpetual exemplification, in the constitution of the sexes. The school which we have now in view, affects to vindicate what it calls the rights of woman against the authority of the stronger sex, as though this had taken advantage of its accidental physical superiority in this view, to assert a primacy and lordship here, which is in full violation of the original and proper equality of the race. The savage, it is said, turns his wife into a slave, the instrument of his own pleasure and convenience; and it is only a higher order of the same barbarism, by which in the reigning structure of our present civilization, the whole sex is shorn of its political and public rights and forced to devote itself to the service of man in the nursery and kitchen. We need in this respect, we are told, a reconstruction of society in such a way, as that among other abuses this Mohammedan prejudice also may be fully abolished, admitting woman thus to a free participation in all public counsels and transactions, so far as she may show ability for the purpose, and placing her on full level with the opposite sex both at home and abroad. So runs the theory. It has the universal custom of the world against it, and also what would seem to be the most explicit testimony of the bible. But of this we speak not at present. We meet it here with the moral geology, if we may so term it, of our human nature itself, drawn forth with overwhelming evidence, from the everlasting mountains of its original constitution. The theory in question is just as unphilosophical, as it is unbiblical and contrary to all history. It violates morality and nature alike.

It is by no accident, or violent wrong merely, that woman is made to occupy a secondary rank in the economy of human society. Her outward weakness makes it

---

32. [François Marie Charles Fourier (1772–1837) was a French philosopher, economist, and early socialist thinker. He believed that a system of "phalanxes" or communes could solve social problems and produce a more just society.]

33. [Any movement for the equal distribution of land.]

necessary, to some extent; but this itself is only the index of a still deeper necessity for it in her spiritual constitution. All the purposes of her being, all the conditions of her welfare and peace, all the laws of her interior organization require this subordination to the other sex, and urge her towards it as the only possible way in which her personality can be made complete. This relation of dependence needs to be well fortified indeed against abuse, as it may run easily otherwise into vast tyranny and wrong; but still it remains forever indispensable in itself to woman's proper life, and under its normal character constitutes emphatically her spiritual salvation. It is not in her physical nature merely that she is formed to lean on man as her necessary prop and stay. He is the ultimate centre also of her personality, through which alone she can stand in right organic communication with the general world, and so attain to true and solid freedom in her own position. No agrarian radicalism can ever change the moral order of humanity here; for we may say of it, precisely, as the Psalmist does of the constitution of the planets: "Forever, O Lord, thy word is settled in heaven!"[34] The emancipation of these heavenly bodies from their appointed orbits, were just as rational an object of reforming zeal, as to set woman free from her natural subordination to the headship of man. All such freedom is monstrous in its very nature; and the wrong which it involves can never fail to avenge itself, with terrible moral retribution on all concerned in it, wherever it may be allowed. Most disastrous will be its action on woman herself, if she can be tempted thus to forsake her own character and sphere. She must unsex herself more or less in the very step; and by doing so, she is necessarily shorn, to the same extent, of all her native dignity and strength. The more thoroughly masculine she may prove herself to be in this way, the more fully and certainly will it be at the cost of all true respect whether public or private. The process of such unnatural self-dereliction exerts unavoidably, at the same time, a demoralizing influence on her own spirit. She becomes in reality coarse, and the fine gold of her nature is turned into what must be counted at best but common brass. Society too is made to suffer necessarily by the perversion. It requires a certain amount of moral fanaticism, in the first place, to endure at all any such aberration of the sex from its proper sphere, and the thing itself can never fail subsequently to aggravate the evil out of which it thus springs. The influence of woman exercised in this form, is not at all to refine the face of life, but to render it vulgar and harsh. Such an "emancipation," made general in any community, would involve the overthrow ultimately of all taste and refinement, the downfall of all morality and civilization.

It deserves to be well considered, at the same time, that this doctrine of the full co-ordination of the sexes in the social system, strikes necessarily at last at the sanctity of the marriage relation itself. It is the subordination of the female nature to that of man precisely, which makes room for that peculiar union of the two, in which the true idea of marriage consists. The possibility of such an inward personal oneness as it requires in the case of husband and wife, turns not simply on their difference of sex,

34. [Ps 119:89.]

Document 3: The Moral Order of Sex.

but on the order also in which this relation is found actually to hold. The common personality which is thus created, must have a real centre on which to rest; and the correspondence between the sexes is such, that this is fully and necessarily determined to the one side only, and not to the other. The help which each needs here in the other, is not at all, in this respect, of parallel character. The whole nature of woman urges her towards man, as the necessary centre of her own being; her personality is so constituted, that it can be perfected only by falling over upon the deeper and broader consciousness of man, as its ultimate support. The personality of man on the contrary, is constitutionally formed to take this central position, and is made complete by woman, not as the basis of his being, but as the necessary integration simply of its proper compass and volume. So related the two are suited to flow together in the power of one and the same life, and may be expected to do so when the proper conditions are present, by the mysterious union of marriage; which, in such view, is no outward temporary contract of merely civil nature, no simply moral partnership, however high and solemn, for purposes beyond itself; but a mystical sacramental bond rather that reaches into the inmost sanctuary of life, and is thus of indissoluble force by its very nature. All this however is made to assume a different aspect, as soon as we lose sight of the order which holds in the original interior economy of the sexes, and under the pretence of restoring woman to her inborn rights, admit such a view of her nature, as sets it in full parallel with the opposite nature of man. There is no room then for the idea of marriage, as the organic comprehension of two lives in the power of a single personal root. It is impossible to withstand the fatal error, by which it is resolved into the conception of a simply outward compact, between independent parties, for mutual convenience and profit. Then of course its inviolable sanctity is gone, and no good reason can be assigned why it should not become as free finally as social partnerships of any other kind. So it is that all Socialism, having no sense of the true nature of the sexual union, as the basis of all morality and society under a settled and necessary form, shows a tendency always in fact, whether it be owned or not, to run into that worst form of agrarian disorder, by which the marriage tie itself is proclaimed a mere social abuse. In its pretended regard for the freedom and dignity of woman, it robs her of the entire glory of her sex and takes away the last bulwark of her independence and strength.[35]   J. W. N.

---

35. The reader interested in a critical analysis of Nevin's perspective in this essay can consult De-Bie, *John Williamson Nevin*, 256–57.

Document 4

"The Wonderful Nature of Man"

Editor's Introduction

On August 31st, 1853, Nevin stood before the student body and faculty of Franklin and Marshall College to present a baccalaureate address to the first graduating class in Lancaster. The theme was "Man's True Destiny."[1] For Nevin, humanity is not simply an offshoot, accident, or even a product of the natural world. As the climax of God's creation, humanity is more than nature but still organically one with it as the basis of nature's being and longing for the divine.[2] As Nevin put it, he is "the perfection of nature, the crown of its glory, the very centre of its light," finding his elemental constitution in the whole and transcendent rather than the particular and the finite. As such, he is to serve as a means for creation's reconciliation with God. "The organization of the world," Nevin said, "as a system of nature, comes to completion in his person."[3]

The occasion and content of the address anticipates similar themes found in "Wonderful Nature of Man." He entered into a period of retirement, leaving his posts at Franklin and Marshall College and Mercersburg Seminary.[4] He would never again write or publish at the same furious pace that he had in the 1840s and early 1850s. As D. G. Hart notes, from 1853 to 1876 (when he stepped down from Franklin and Marshall for the last time), Nevin averaged three published articles per year, compared to the nine per year during the seven years following publication of *Mystical Presence* (1846). The decline in output was manifested both in the lesser number, as well as a drastic reduction in length, of essays.[5]

---

1. Nevin, "Man's True Destiny," 492–520. Republished by M. Keiffer, 1853. Document 11 below.
2. See Nevin, "Human Freedom," 5. Document 2 above.
3. Nevin, *Man's True Destiny* (Keiffer), 4.
4. Hart, *John Williamson Nevin*, 169–96, provides a remarkably helpful summary of this period. The following biographical material is highly indebted to his account.
5. Hart, *John Williamson Nevin*, 188.

DOCUMENT 4: "THE WONDERFUL NATURE OF MAN"

The year 1853 also marked the beginning of several relocations of the Nevin family. In 1854, Nevin moved his family from Mercersburg, Pennsylvania to Carlisle, approximately twenty miles from the Nevin homestead, and home of Dickinson College, where Nevin's father had studied. A year later, the family moved again eighty miles east to Windsor Place, in the northeastern corner of Lancaster County.[6] Here, Nevin was closer in proximity to Franklin and Marshall College, and enjoyed participating in occasional college and faculty events, but remained detached from the college's administration. Perhaps too far removed from the life of the city, the Nevins moved once again in 1858, closer to the outskirts of Lancaster City, residing on a fifteen-acre farm. This was adjacent to the residence of President James Buchanan, with whom Nevin developed a long-term friendship. In the 1860s, he once again took up official capacities at Franklin and Marshall.

Given the many significant changes in Nevin's life and his overall reduction in writing projects during this period, "Wonderful Nature of Man" stands out as unique, a publication arguably more substantive than others at the time, one which captures key tenets of his overall theological framework. Even so, themes of the essay are evident in a variety of writings across the Nevin corpus.[7] For Nevin, the transition from the world's natural state to its divine life is found within the moral, intellectual, and bodily existence of human beings. This dynamic emerges in the opening chapters of Genesis, where humanity stands as the pinnacle of God's creative endeavors. Humanity, created in the image of God, possesses a distinctive, reconciling role as having intimate connection to the natural world, God's creative and moral character, and the common, bodily humanity of Jesus Christ. "Undying Life in Christ" also expressed this:

> In the spirit of man, past and future are brought together in the power of the present—the transitoriness of time surmounted in the apprehension of the Infinite. He was made, we are told, in the image and likeness of God, to be the head of the natural world and to exercise lordship over it in every lower view—to be in it and of it through his bodily organization, and yet to be above it at the same time through his intelligence and reason, disclosing within himself a new and higher order of life altogether.[8]

Humanity for Nevin is a singularly important creation that gradually unfolds its true essence over the course of history, progressing towards its ultimate fulfillment in Christ, transforming creation along the way. Humanity thus represents the ultimate fulfillment and perfection of nature via union with the divine. All aspects of human existence, which exist on a lower organic level, are reconciled with God, and the fragmented elements of the world's life are integrated into the divine and made whole. In

---

6. Windsor Place was the home of his father-in-law, Robert Jenkins. It is outside of Churchtown, Pennsylvania.

7. In addition to "Man's True Destiny," the following are worth noting: *Human Freedom and A Plea for Philosophy*; "Christianity and Humanity;" "The New Creation in Christ," MTSS 4:29–45.

8. "Undying Life," in Appel, *Life*, 613.

this way, humanity is the culmination or "end of nature." Though in its present natural condition fallen and incomplete, humanity is created to experience union with the divine through Christ Incarnate. The natural world, which is transformed into a moral and intelligent realm via humanity, achieves its ultimate purpose. This connection is most fully realized in the second person of the Trinity, Jesus Christ, who comprehends all of creation and humanity in his person.[9]

It should be evident, then, that "Wonderful Nature of Man" is hardly an outlier in the Nevin corpus in terms of its themes and argument. It serves as an important link for drawing together common themes of his overall project, not least those which seemed to carry so much weight for multiple decades, forming the basis for so many other strands of Nevin's theological reflection.

---

9. Nevin, "New Creation in Christ," MTSS 4:39–40; Nevin, "Christianity and Humanity," 469.

The Wonderful Nature of Man.[1]

Science, as it has to do with the world of Nature, unfolds to our view, in every direction, objects and scenes of surpassing interest. Each different province of knowledge is found to embrace a whole universe of wonders, in some sense, within its own separate bounds. Who shall pretend to set limits to the grand significance, in this way, of Astronomy, of Geology, of Chemistry, of Natural History in all its divisions and branches?[2] Nay, who may pretend to exhaust the full sense of any single object or thing, included in these vast fields of scientific research? The relatively small here has its mysteries of wisdom, its miracles of power, no less than the relatively great. Vistas of overwhelming glory, stretching far away in boundless, interminable perspective, open upon us through the microscope and telescope alike. Every drop of water shows itself to be, in the end, an ocean without bottom or shore. The flowers of the field, the leaves of the forest, the worm that crawls upon the ground, the insect that sports its ephemeral life in the air, all, all are telling continually—in full unison with the everlasting mountains, with the rolling waves of the sea, with the starry firmament on high-the endless magnificence of God's creation; the music of earth rising up everywhere, like the sound of many waters, responsive to the music of the spheres, and echoing still forever, in universal triumphant chorus, *The hand that made us is divine*.[3] In whatever direction our eyes are turned, under the guiding light of science, above, beneath, around, we are met with occasions for adoring admiration, and may well lead to exclaim with the Psalmist: "O Lord, how manifold are Thy works! In wisdom hast Thou made them all; the earth is full of Thy riches."[4]

1. [MR 11 (July 1859) 317–37.]

2. [Throughout Nevin's writings there are reflections on the relationship of science to nature, mankind, and the Incarnation, but rarely does he refer specifically to these "harder" sciences. The opening paragraph is otherwise typical of Nevin's idealistic dialectic.]

3. [The last line of the hymn, "The spacious firmament on high," by Joseph Addison (1672–1719). See *Poetical Works of Joseph Addison*, 137–38. It was eventually set to the tune "Creation," adapted from Haydn's chorus, "The Heavens are Telling," from *The Creation*. This may have been the tune Nevin had in mind.]

4. [Psalm 104:24.]

Part 1: Culture, Philosophy, Ethics, Anthropology

[Man as the Glory and Goal of Nature]

In the midst of all these wonders of Nature, however, it is easy to see that the central place belongs to *Man* himself.[5] This indeed is plainly signified to us by the Mosaic account of the Creation, in the first chapter of Genesis; where the different parts of the world are represented as coming into existence in a certain order and course; each lower stage opening the way always for a higher, and one part of the process leading over continually to another; until all is made to end at last, on the sixth day, in the formation of Adam—as though the whole work previously had been concerned with the preparation simply of a fit platform or theatre, on which he, the last sense and crowning glory of all, was to be finally ushered into being. On which account, moreover, a new special solemnity is thrown around his advent, a sort of heavenly circumstance and pomp, showing forth sublimely the greatness of the occasion. All else being complete, and the preliminary arrangements of creation brought forward in order to this point, there follows as it were a pause in the process; and then the voice of God is heard once more: "Let us make man in our image, after our likeness; and let them have dominion over the fish of the sea, and over the fowl of the air, and over the cattle, and over all the earth, and over every creeping thing that creepeth upon the earth."[6] Man thus is declared to be something higher and greater than the whole world of nature besides. He is the head of the natural creation. All its mysteries and glories culminate at last in his person, and find here only their full significance, their proper conclusion and end.[7]

The actual structure of the world, as it unfolds itself continually more and more to the observation of science, is found to be in striking agreement with this ancient representation of the Bible. It is plainly a single system throughout, subject everywhere to the presence of a common law, pervaded universally by the power of a common idea or thought, and reaching always, with inward restless nisus, toward a common end. The inorganic is in order to the organic. The crystal is a prophecy of the coming plant. Rising continually from lower to higher and more perfect forms of existence, the whole vegetable world serves to foreshadow, in like manner, the sphere of animal

---

5. [Here, Nevin articulates the central role of "Man" in relationship to the progression of the opening chapters of Genesis. Other times, he makes a similar argument from more decidedly philosophical or naturalistic grounds. See for example Nevin, "Man's True Destiny," 612: "The organization of the world, as a system of nature, comes to its completion in his person.... Man is himself... the end of nature, the point where its whole process reaches its ultimate destination."]

6. [Gen 1:26.]

7. [As Borneman, *Church*, 5, comments: "Mankind, as the image of God, serves uniquely as the creature that possesses both an organic relation to the lower, natural, created order and possesses qualities that manifest God's character. As such, mankind serves as the end and perfection of nature insofar as he becomes truly human in his union to the divine. By virtue of this process, the lower organic sphere of social and political existence is reconciled unto God sacramentally, and the fragmented elements of society are incorporated into the divine, objective whole. The visible locus of this whole is the church, who, by way of the ministry of word and sacrament, reigns in the disparate remnants of the fallen, splintered creation."]

life above it. This again is an upward movement throughout, an ever ascending series of types and forms, reaching always toward an ideal, which on to the last it has no power to actualize, but can faintly prefigure only as something far more exalted and far more glorious than itself. The organic order comes to its rest ultimately in Man. He is the true ideal of the world's universal life, the last aim and scope, we may say, of the whole natural creation. He is the fulfilment of all its prophecies, the key to its mysteries, the exposition of its deepest and most hidden sense.

As being then, in such view, the last, full sense and meaning of the world, Man necessarily represents to us its main interest and glory, and must be more worthy of our regard than all it offers besides to our contemplation. It can be no extravagance to say, that his existence and presence in the system of nature set before us the greatest and strangest part of its wonderful constitution—a fact, which surpasses in significance, and transcends in interest, all its other phenomena and facts combined. Man is an object immeasurably more lofty and grand, in the universe of God's works, than the towering hills, the swelling seas, or the stars even, that look down upon him from their infinite distances in the calm, blue vault of heaven. He ranks higher in the scale of creation. He embraces in his being more stupendous realities, profounder mysteries, wider and far more enduring interests. Well might the Hebrew Singer cry out, overwhelmed as it were with the contemplation of his own nature: "I will praise Thee, O Lord; for I am fearfully and wonderfully made: marvellous are Thy works; and that my soul knoweth right well."[8] Yes, of a truth, fearfully and wonderfully made. The declaration applies in full force to the entire being of Man. He is to be gazed upon with a sort of trembling admiration, first of all, in his simply physical nature; still more so, afterwards, in his intellectual nature; but most of all, finally, in his moral nature—where only, at the last, the full boundless significance of his life, and along with this, the whole terrible sublimity of it also, may be said to burst completely into view.

[The Wonders of Man's Physical Nature]

I. Look at him first in his simply *physical nature*. The human body offers itself to our consideration at once, as the greatest and most finished work of God in the outward world. When we compare it with other natural objects, there is none which can be said to be equal to it, or like to it, either in conception or in actual execution and effect.

So under a merely anatomical view. The more closely and carefully we study its conformation and structure, as they are laid open to our observation by the dissecting knife—its framework of bones, its muscles and tendons, its nerves, its curious apparatus of the senses, its organs of action and motion, its marvellous dispositions and arrangements of stomach, lungs, heart, brain, the perfection, in one word, of all its parts, and their most admirable fitness for their several purposes and ends—the more

---

8. [Ps 139:14.]

deeply and thoroughly shall we be made to feel, that taken altogether, even in this dead mechanical light, there is indeed nothing so absolutely wonderful and complete, in the whole range of nature besides.[9]

But the case becomes of course still stronger a great deal, when we pass from anatomy to physiology, and fix our attention not simply on the mechanism of the body in a state of rest, but on this same mechanism animated and set in motion everywhere by the powers and forces of life itself, working by it, and through it, for the accomplishment of their proper ends.[10] Such a sphere of wonders is here thrown open to our contemplation, as may be easily seen at once to leave far behind, in significance and interest, all that can be brought into comparison with it under any like physical form. Vast as the powers of nature may show themselves in other quarters, grand as the scale of their action may be, and however much of strange, amazing mystery may seem to enter into their processes, they bring after all no such results to pass anywhere, as can be said to match in any measure what is going forward continually in the living constitution of the human body.

What, for example, is the chemistry of nature, its dark mysterious processes going forward always in the deep places of the earth, its laboratory of wonders in the air and in the sky—where the winds are born—where the clouds come and go—where rain, snow, hail, lightning, and tempest issue continually from the same awful womb; what is all this, we say, in comparison with what is taking place every day in every such living body, by the process of digestion and assimilation; through which, all sorts of foreign material are received, in the shape of food, into the stomach, wrought silently into blood, and converted out of this finally into the very substance of all the different parts of the system—meeting thus its perpetual waste with perpetual renovation and supply.

What is the ocean, with its world-embracing circulation—its waters lifted into the air, borne in every direction by the clouds, made to descend in showers upon the earth, gathered into streams, and poured at last through mighty rivers back again into their original bed; what is "this great and wide sea, wherein are things creeping innumerable, both small and great beasts," where the ships go, and where leviathan is made to play;[11] what is the whole of it at last, in all its greatness, over against that wonder of

---

9. [Prior to and during Nevin's lifetime, significant advances were made in the fields of anatomy and physiology. From the late eighteenth century to the early nineteenth century, the work of Giovanni Batista Morgagni, Scott Matthew Baillie, and Xavier Bichat advanced and popularized "pathological anatomy," a "clinical pathology that applied the knowledge of opening up corpses and quantifying illnesses to treatments." Along with the popularity of anatomy and dissection came an increasing interest in the preservation of dissected specimens. See Lindemann, *Medicine and Society*, 112.]

10. [During Nevin's lifetime, the differentiation of organs and their working relationship to one another rapidly developed as a key physiological insight. The famed French physiologist Henri Milne-Edwards wrote that the "body of all living beings, whether animal or plant, resembles a factory . . . where the organs, comparable to workers, work incessantly to produce the phenomena that constitute the life of the individual." On this concept and more from the era, see Brain, *Pulse of Modernism*, 48.]

11. [Ps 104:25–26.]

wonders, the human heart, with its tidal flow of blood kept up day and night, and year after year, through the arteries and the veins!

What is the action of the winds, which come no one can tell whence, and go no one can tell whither, now fanning the earth in gentle zephyrs, and now sweeping over the face of it in hurricanes and storms, penetrating all things, purifying all things, stirring all things into motion and life; what is the action of the winds, we ask again, in this outward view, compared with the proper breath of life in man, received through his nostrils, and made to fulfil its unresting twofold ministry by the marvellous economy of his lungs?

Or the still more subtle forces of electricity and magnetism, as they are found to be constantly and powerfully at work everywhere, through the universal realm of nature, or as they are made to perform miracles, at the present day, in obedience to the will of science and art; what are they, under either view, in comparison with the brain of man, and its dependent system of nerves, extending with infinite ramification to all parts of the body, and causing the whole to be filled at every point, and through every instant of time, with the unity of a common life?[12]

It is true indeed, that these physiological wonders themselves come before us, to a certain extent, on the outside of man's nature. They belong to the animal world in general. Here too the phenomena of sentient life, upheld and carried forward by organs and functions strangely adapted to its use, challenge in every direction our profound admiration. Bodily senses are here, vital activities, powers of digestion, secretion, and self-reparation, blood coursing through arteries and veins, the curious play of lungs, and the working more curious still of nerves and brain. Many animals seem even to surpass man, in particular aspects and features of their organization. He is excelled by some in strength; by others, in speed; by others again, in special forms of natural art and ingenuity. Some have a more quick and acute sense of hearing; others a far more keen and wide reaching vision. In all directions around him, they show themselves qualified and fitted for modes of existence, which are for him impossible altogether. But all this detracts nothing in the end from the proper superiority of his being, even in that merely physical view with which only we are now concerned. For it is easy enough to see, that any points of advantage which may seem to belong to other animal organizations hold only in single subordinate particulars; going thus to show the comparatively partial and narrow order of their life; while in any whole view, considered either singly or collectively, they fall short, immeasurably, we may say, of the full proportioned harmony and perfection of the human body. Their completeness in all cases is something relative only, the dim foreshadowing of something higher and greater than itself, a defective one-sided approximation at best to the idea of the absolute under some entirely different form. Thus do these organizations, in fact, give

---

12. [The pace and degree of advances in understanding of electricity and electro-magnetism during Nevin's lifetime are astounding. See Morus, *Michael Faraday* and Marvin, *When Old Technologies Were New*.]

glory to the body of man from all sides, doing homage to it as being far more honorable than themselves, and proclaiming it to be, what it is in truth, the complement and crown of the whole physical creation.

In this view, it is not in virtue of his spiritual nature simply, that man is to be considered the end and consummation of the present world. As a physical system, it comes to its conclusion, first of all, in the organization of his body, through which alone it can make room for his presence under any higher form. Toward this grand final result, accordingly, all its processes may be said to reach and struggle from the beginning; while the universal order of things, as they now stand, finds here also its proper meaning and full central rest, through all time. Even the vast geologic periods, which are supposed to have gone before the creation of the world in its present form, are not shut out from the force of this rule. Through all its precious, grand, and mighty cycles, the history of the earth, as it remains still written in the rocks, was one long course of preparation for what it was brought to be finally, in being made a fit abode for man; and the signification of its manifold forms of life, its successive worlds of animated nature—rude, imperfect, and often monstrous as they were—lay mainly in this, that they served to anticipate and prefigure in their way, through the ages, the living order of the world as it is now, and so looked through this continually to the advent of man himself, by which, in the fulness of time all was to be conducted at last to its proper end.

This is sufficient to show, what small account is to be made of mere outward powers or magnitudes in nature, set over against the living person of man. He stands before us, intrinsically greater, in his bodily organization itself, than all the geologic creations, which served so many ages beforehand to prepare the way for his coming. They were in order to him throughout; and in such view could be only of secondary and subordinate rank, as compared with him, in the scale of creation. We need not wonder then, if the whole world, in its constitution, be found owning and confessing his superior dignity in the same way. The forms and processes of nature converge from all sides toward man as their grand centre, and gather themselves up finally in his person. He is the world concentrated, consolidated, reduced to its last most comprehensive unity. All its elements and forces come together, we may say, in the wonderful constitution of his body; which becomes in this way a microcosm, the world in its inmost essence, reflecting and showing forth continually the sense of what it is in its widest macrocosmic view. Man unites in himself thus the powers of the whole creation around him. All cosmical influences stream into him and through him. Fire, earth, air, and water, mingle in his composition. The majesty of his nature, in such view, towers above the everlasting hills. Winds, cloud, storms, volcanoes, and earthquakes, do homage to his presence, proclaiming it to be something greater than themselves. The broad ocean of life, spread out in the animal world beneath him, rolls toward him, in like manner, its universal tribute of respect. Reptiles, fishes, birds, and four-footed beasts, join in seeking his presence and heralding his praise. He is said,

Document 4: The Wonderful Nature of Man.

indeed, actually to travel through all these orders of existence in his embryonic state, beginning with the lowest conformation, and passing up through the highest finally into his own proper human shape; a process, that involves in every case, a resumption or new taking up, as it were, of the life of the world in its lower forms—curiously repeating in this way the original work of creation, and verifying in the most striking manner the idea of its organic oneness and wholeness, as we have it so graphically represented in the old Mosaic record.

Among all the works of God in the world, then, there is none which may be considered comparable, in dignity and perfection, to the human body. How could it be otherwise, if nature was to become in this form the shrine of intelligence, the organ of thought, the dwelling place of free, self-conscious mind? Must it not, for any such purpose as this, be raised into its highest state, and wrought into its most perfect mould, so as to be made as nearly as possible analogous and conformable to the quality of that superior life, with which it was to be so mysteriously conjoined? Must not the temple of the soul, in the midst of the natural world, be so framed and ordered, as to be, even in its own merely physical constitution, more honorable and glorious than the whole world of nature besides? The primacy of man in the world, the proper sovereignty of his nature, is not a prerogative belonging to him through his soul only; it comes into view most immediately, and first of all, in his body also. That of itself proclaims him at once monarch and lord of creation. His erect form, his countenance lifted heavenward, the harmony and symmetry of his parts, his firm walk, his commanding port, his spiritual aspect, the lightning of his eye, the moral thunder of his voice—all announce his imperial distinction, and authenticate his title to universal reverence and respect.

One other thought here we have no right to pass by, as going to show, beyond all that we have yet said, the incomparable excellence and worth of the human body. God has put infinite honor upon it, through the mystery of the Incarnation. "*Tu ad liberandum suscepturus hominem*," the Church sings in her grand, old Ambrosian Hymn, "*non horruisti Virginis uterum*."[13] The Word became flesh, and was made in the likeness of men![14] Simply to state this awful fact is enough, in the present connection.

[The Wonders of Man's Intellectual Nature]

II. Wonderful and glorious as man may be, however, in his physical constitution, his mere bodily organization either considered in itself, or viewed in its relations to the

---

13. [The "Ambrosian Hymn" is a Latin liturgical text, more commonly known as the *Te Deum*. Trans., "When thou tookest upon thee to deliver man: thou didst not abhor the Virgin's womb" (*Book of Common Prayer*).]

14. [John 1:14.]

world of nature on the one side and the world of mind or spirit on the other—he is found to be a great deal more glorious and wonderful still in his *intellectual nature*.[15]

Nature is in order to Mind. All her productions and processes look toward this continually, in the way of general direction, as their common end. It is as though thought or intelligence lay bound and imprisoned in her mighty empire of laws and forms, and were forever struggling to rise by means of them into the clear, full possession of its own life. We have seen already how this universal order comes to its conclusion physically in the human body, showing it to be thus the summit and crown of the natural creation. But that first conclusion is itself only in order to another and far higher end, the revelation of the human soul in the world as a new order of existence altogether. Nature culminates in the physical constitution of man, just because she can rise no higher in her own sphere, and there at last, if ever, must come into communion with free self-active mind. This it is which constitutes in fact the perfection and dignity of the human body, that it stands so nearly related to the world of mind in its whole conformation, and is so eminently fitted to become the organ and medium of its presence in the world of nature. Here, accordingly, the necessary complement of the body, and the last full meaning of the world, are reached at the same time in the knowing and reasoning soul of man; in rising to which, however, nature must be regarded as transcending herself, efflorescing as it were into a higher life, and so finding her end in another system of existence altogether. Grand and magnificent, beyond the power of language to express, is the epiphany of Mind in this way, pouring its effulgence over the dark face of nature. It is equivalent in truth to the rising of a new sun in the universe, far more glorious than that which rules the day in its common form. When God commanded the light to shine out of darkness in the beginning, dispersing the deep night of chaos, and opening the way for its transformation into a world of order and beauty, it was after all an imperfect symbol only of what took place in a higher form, when "the Lord God formed Man of the dust of the ground, and breathed into his nostrils the breath of life,"[16] causing him to become thus, through his own inspiration, a rational and intelligent soul. It was as if the whole work of creation, in its previous form, had been suddenly flooded with fresh heavenly light, and kindled into new sense. For such in truth is the mysterious relation, which mind, as it lives and reigns in man, sustains through all time to the outward material world. In a profound sense, it may be said actually to make the world, imparting to it its whole form and meaning as it now stands.[17] Not as if the system of nature had no existence, on the one

---

15. [The following paragraphs exhibits one of Nevin's primary influences, Friedrich Wilhelm Schelling, who constructed a transcendental idealism that insisted the mind and the world are interconnected and that the mind can access the basic, organic unity of the world through the intellect. See Beiser, *German Idealism*, and Guyer and Horstmann, "Idealism."]

16. [Gen 2:7.]

17. [The *idea* imparts to the physical world whatever meaning it has. Thus Nevin's idealism was anticipated by the formulation of George Berkeley, *esse est percipi*, "to be is to be perceived." The "being" or "essence" of all phenomena is discerned in being intellectually recognized and understood.]

Document 4: The Wonderful Nature of Man.

side of man's intelligence and thought. It has a being of its own, we believe, apart from all such apprehension. But what that is, we can never either know or guess. It offers to our contemplation nothing better than thick, impenetrable darkness.[18] In such view, it is for us as though it did not exist at all. To become real for us, in any way, the world must not only be; it must come into us also in the way of knowledge; and the forms of this knowledge, in the nature of the case, can be imparted to it only by our own minds. It is for us, therefore, only what it is made to be through our intelligence itself, and nothing more. Not only so; but we must say the world itself is made for this mode of existence—what it comes to be by entering into the types and moulds of actual knowledge[19]—as its only true and full perfection; so that, short of this, it must ever be a rude and unformed mass, carrying in it no right sense, and representing no proper reality whatever. Thus it is that the whole world is literally brought out of darkness into marvellous light, and reduced at the same time to full order and form, by the power of intelligence made to bear upon it through the mind of man. In the waking of consciousness, all nature may be said to wake together with him into new life. It takes shape everywhere in conformity with his perception and thought. It shines, and blooms, and sings, in obedience to the magical authority of his spirit. It lives, and has its being—such phenomenal being as we know it by—only in the orb of his mind.[20]

We have seen before, that the physical creation centres in the human body; and that this may well be dignified with the title of *microcosm*, for this reason, as gathering up into itself finally all the forms and forces of nature in its larger view, and so representing in small compass its universal sense. But what is all this, in comparison with the centralization that is here exhibited to us, in the constitution of the human soul? By this emphatically it is, that man becomes in the fullest sense a living microcosm, taking up into himself the very being of the great and mighty world around him, and so reflecting and showing forth the full sense of it, as it is not possible for it to be known in any other way. The vast, the manifold, the multitudinous in nature, is not simply reduced here to relatively small bounds, as in the other case; it is brought down to absolute unity, and so made to pass away entirely in another order of existence altogether. In such view, the microcosm is more than the macrocosm—the world intelligible than the world diffused and spread abroad in space; since it is wholly by the first alone, that the latter can ever be at all, what it seems to be in any such outward form. Here, therefore, mere physical bulk and force, set over against the being of man, shrink into still greater insignificance than before. Are not mountains and

---

18. [Kant held that the objects of sensations are phenomena: we experience them, but do not know what they "really" are, since they are mediated through the "categories of understanding." Inversely, behind the experienced phenomena are noumena. We know that noumena must exist (otherwise we would experience nothing) but have no mental access to their content. This is a highly simplistic summary; see Stang, "Kant's Transcendental Idealism."]

19. [Kant's "categories of understanding."]

20. [For more on the philosophical background with which Nevin may be engaging in this section, see Pinkard, *Hegel's Naturalism*.]

seas, bellowing thunders, roaring cataracts and storms, comprehended truly in his spirit, and made to pass through it, in order that they may be for him either outward or real? Why then should he stand aghast before *them,* and not feel rather in them, and by them, the yet more awful grandeur and overwhelming vastness of his own nature. Mind is infinitely greater than all that is not mind, enlarge the conception of this as we may. It towers above the whole material creation. It outshines the stars. It is a force more active and powerful by far, than that which bears along comets and planets in their course. The sun itself, in all its majestic splendor, is an object less high and glorious, than the soul even of an infant, carrying in it the latent power of thought, the undeveloped possibility of reason.

We have spoken of the physical action of the brain, as something greatly more wonderful than that of the most subtle forces in nature under any different form. But what is this in its turn, when we come to compare it with the activity of thinking itself, which, however it may depend upon the working of the brain, is yet not that simply, but another order of force and energy altogether? Thought is more free than air, more penetrating than fire, more irresistible and instantaneous in motion than lightning. It travels at a rate, which causes the velocity of light to appear sluggish and slow. It traverses the earth, and sweeps the heavens, at a single bound. In the twinkling of an eye, it passes to the planet Saturn, to the sun, to the star Sirius, to the utmost bounds of the universe.

We have spoken of the circulation of the blood, as something more fearfully grand than the waters above the firmament, and the waters under the firmament, revolving continually through the heart-resembling ministry of oceans and seas. But what is all this to the mystery of consciousness—that broad, unfathomable sea in the human spirit, which serves to set in motion all its activities and powers, out of whose depths all knowledges proceed, and into whose bosom again they continually return!

Every faculty of the mind is a subject for admiration, from mere sensation up to the use of reason in its purest and most perfect form. The images of conception, the reproductions of fancy, the new combinations and grand creative processes of the imagination, the operations of judgment, the intuitional apprehensions involved in the power of ideas—time would fail us, to speak of them in any way of particular detail; but what realms of interest, what worlds of thrilling wonder, do they not all throw open to our view!

Let any one consider only for a moment what is continually going forward within us, in the familiar process which is known to us by the name of memory. Nothing so simple, it might seem, at first view; and yet, the moment we stop to think of it, nothing more profoundly mysterious and strange. Images and thoughts are continually entering the consciousness of the mind, and then disappearing from it again, as though they were entirely lost. But they are in fact only buried, and hidden away, in the secret depths of the mind itself, so as to be capable of being resuscitated, and called back again, whenever their presence may be required; and in this way they are in truth all

Document 4: The Wonderful Nature of Man.

the time coming and going, appearing and disappearing, in our ordinary thinking. What we hold in our intelligence thus is only in small part ever contained in our actual consciousness, at any given time. By far the most of it is in us always under a latent, slumbering form. And yet all enters into our spiritual being, is truly part of ourselves, and goes to make up continually the proper contents of our personality. But what a marvel this is; that so much of our knowledge should be in the mind, and yet out of mind, at the same time; that our sense of self should hold joined with it in this way such a vast multitude of conceptions, thoughts, and ideas, such a whole world of past experiences and affections, which nevertheless are in general as much unperceived as though they did not exist at all, and only come into view occasionally and transiently, ever rising and ever sinking, ever entering and ever departing—an endless succession of vanishing forms, in what remains throughout after all the indivisible, unbroken unity of one and the same consciousness. To stand on the shore of such an ocean to look forth on its broad, boundless expanse—to send the imagination down among the secrets that lie buried, far out of sight, in its dark and silent depths—may indeed well produce in any thoughtful mind an overwhelming sentiment both of astonishment and awe. There is neither height nor depth, nor show of vastness and sublimity under any other form, in the simply physical world that may bear to be placed in comparison with it for a single moment.

The case swells upon us into its full significance, only when we come to ask, Can that which has once been in the mind, so as to be part and parcel of its consciousness, ever so pass out of it again as to sink into everlasting oblivion? Some thoughts, we know, return upon us readily and easily in our ordinary experience, lying as it were near at hand to us all the time; others are recalled with more difficulty, as having got farther out of reach; while others again, the largest class of all, seem to have sunk like lead in the mighty waters, to be remembered by us no more forever. But who will pretend to distinguish here, between what is still within the reach of memory, and what has become for it thus as though it had never been? Who will undertake to say at what point of time, or under what terms and conditions otherwise, that which has once been the property of the spirit, in the way of thought, shall be so sundered and alienated from it as to pass irrecoverably and entirely out of its possession? The grand wonder is, how the past should return at all, and become thus the matter of present consciousness and knowledge—a thing past and yet present at the same time; that it should do so after a short interval, or do so after a long one, would seem to be in the case a distinction of no material account. If the power of memory may bridge in this way the chasm of an hour, why not with equal ease the oblivion of a year, or the dark void of a thousand years? We know in fact, that what has thus slumbered in us through long periods of time does often wake up within our consciousness at last, in the most surprising manner. In old age especially, nothing is more common than such a resurrection of long buried images and thoughts. In many cases, the circumstances and experiences of childhood and early youth, after being forgotten for scores of years, are so restored to memory again as to seem only of recent date. Persons recovered from drowning have said, that in the middle state to which they were brought between life and death, a whole world of such buried recollections seemed to pass before them in panoramic vision. We have been told of others, who, in circumstances of extreme danger, falling from a precipice for instance, or exposed to the jaws of death in some like violent way, have had their whole past lives, as it appeared, brought back upon them with a sort of instantaneous rush. Who, in view of such cases, may presume to limit the possibilities of memory? And who that thinks of it may not well be filled with amazement, rising even to terror itself, in considering what is involved for himself, in the awful abyss, which is found thus yawning before him continually in the depths of his own soul?

[The Wonders of Man's Moral Nature[21]]

III. But it is in his *moral nature* most of all, that Man comes before us finally in the full terrible sublimity of his being—"fearfully and wonderfully made,"[22] beyond all the wonders of creation under any different form.

There is a close, necessary connection, of course, between the moral and the intellectual. Reason and Will, thought and action, flow together, and as it were interpenetrate each other continually, in the constitution of the mind.[23] There can be no act of intelligence without volition; and there can be no exercise of volition without intelligence. Still thinking and willing are not the same thing; and there is full room, therefore, for distinguishing between the intellectual nature of man as based upon his reason, and the moral nature of man, as based upon his will. It is easy enough to see, moreover, that the relation is of such a kind as to place the moral nature, in point of dignity and worth, above the intellectual. If it be asked, where the economy of the mind is to be regarded as coming to its main end, its grand ultimate purpose and meaning, the answer must be, in that part of it which is represented to us by the idea of the will. Thought is rightly in order to action; knowledge in order to freedom. The practical reason is greater than the speculative reason. Truth in the understanding must become truth in the will also, if it is ever to be either spirit or life.

We have seen already, that the human mind is in fact the revelation in the world of a new order of existence altogether; a result, which serves to satisfy and fulfil the universal sense of the physical creature, struggling up to it through all its realms of existence, and that might seem to be thus, in one view, the last product of this process

21. [The section repeats the arguments of "Human Freedom," document 2 above.]

22. [Ps 139:14.]

23. [Concerning reason, will, and mind, for Nevin: "Mind is not just the completion of nature, but a new order of existence. In humanity, 'the world process, the divine idea which underlies creation puts on a new form.' . . . The human mind (consisting of reason and will) is the most perfect mirror of the Universal Mind of God." DiPuccio, *Interior*, 47, quoting Nevin, "Philosophy of History. I. The General Idea of History," *College Days,* January 1873.]

Document 4: The Wonderful Nature of Man.

itself; while it is yet plain, that in reaching it nature is actually carried beyond itself, and met, as it were, in its own sphere by the power of a higher life, descending into it from above. Considered as the mere passive counterpart of nature under a spiritual view—the mirror simply of its multitudinous forms, the echo only of its manifold voices and sounds—such a manifestation is indeed wonderful in the highest degree. But the full force of the wonder comes into view, only when we look beyond this, and see the mind to be at the same time a fountain of power, a principle of free spontaneous action, in its own nature, not only open to impressions receptively from the world around, but capable also of working back upon the world again, and as it were over against it, in the most original and independent way. This is the idea of the *Will*.

There is no power or force like it, under any other form, in the system of creation. Physically considered, the world is a constitution carried forward in the way of inward, settled and fixed law, causes producing effects continually, and effects following causes, with a certainty which admits of no variation or exception. The whole process, in such view, is necessary, blind, and unfree. So in the sphere of mere lifeless matter; so in the sphere of vegetation; and so in the sphere also of animal life. The actions of animals are determined absolutely by influences exerted upon them from without, through their natural appetites and instincts. Neither is the case different with the animal nature of man, in itself considered. This likewise stands connected with the physical world by organic relations, which involve the same kind of subjection to its laws that is found to prevail in lower spheres. Appetite, desire, inclination, passion, in man, are in this view, so far as their original form is concerned, responses simply to other forces in the system of nature, and as such include in themselves neither light nor freedom. The difference here, however, is the conjunction in which these forms of merely natural life are set with a power above nature in man, which may indeed lend itself to their service in a base passive way, but whose rightful prerogative it is rather to rule them always in subserviency to its own ends. This power, the practical reason—the will in its proper form—is no agency that serves merely to carry into effect, what has been made necessary by the working of causes going before. If that were the case, it would at once lose its distinctive character, and be nothing more at last than the continuation of nature itself, under a new sublimated and refined form. But the very conception of will implies and involves the contrary of this. It is, by its very constitution, a self-determining power. It is no blind, necessary force, like the laws of nature, but a free, spontaneous activity, which knows itself, and moves itself optionally its own way; giving rise thus to a whole universe of relations, interests, actions and systems of action, which but for such origination could have no existence whatever, and which, however it may be joined with the constitution of nature, and made to rest upon it in some sense as a basis, is nevertheless in fact a new world altogether of far higher and far more glorious character.

Let it be considered only, for a moment, what this *hyperphysical* economy—the moral world as distinguished from the world of nature—is found to comprehend and contain. It comprises in itself all the powers, functions, and operations of mind; the thinking of men; their purposes and aims; their affections, emotions, and passions; their acts of whatever kind, whether inward only or extending out into the surrounding world; the full unfolding and putting forth, in one word, of all that is involved in their spiritual being. In it are embraced, at the same time, the idea of society, the order of the family, the constitution of the State, the organization finally of the Church; all social, political, and religious relations; all virtues and opposing vices; all human privileges, duties, and rights. It is the sphere emphatically thus, of whatever is comprehended in the conception of education and history; being made up mainly in fact, not so much of present experiences simply at any given time, as of a whole world rather of past experiences, consolidated together, and handed forward continually from one generation to another. What a mass of material, accumulated in this way through ages, goes to form the proper ethical life of civilized nations—the historical substance, we may call it, of their nationality—strangely treasured up in their language, their institutions and laws, their manners and customs, their traditions and hereditary memories of the ancient past. Among animals there is no education, and no history. The ideas are purely and exclusively human. They belong only to the world of intelligence and freedom.

We have spoken of the self-moving nature of the will, its independence of all outward constraint, its power to originate action in its own way. This freedom, however, forms only one side of its marvellous constitution. Under another view, it is just as much bound by the force of necessary law, as the constitution of matter itself. The only difference in the two cases is, that in nature the law carries itself into effect as it were by its own force, while in the moral world it cannot go into effect at all, unless by the free choice and consent of the will itself which it thus necessitates and binds. The necessity, to prevail at all, must pass into the form of freedom. But this does not detract in the least from the idea of its authority and force. The distinction serves only, in truth, to clothe it with greater dignity and glory. In this view, the law of nature, in all its generality and constancy, is but the type, in a lower sphere, of the universal and unchangeable character of the law, as it exists for freedom in a higher sphere. The first mystically adumbrates, for all thoughtful minds, the wonderful presence of the second. Some such thought seems to have been in the mind of the ancient Psalmist, when he was led to exclaim: "Forever, O Lord, Thy word is settled in heaven! Thy faithfulness is unto all generations; Thou hast established the earth, and it abideth."[24] How many have been made to feel at times, in the same way, the sense of God's glorious moral government mirrored upon them from the contemplation of the natural world.

"There are two things," the celebrated philosopher Kant was accustomed to say, "which I can never sufficiently wonder at and admire—the starry heavens above me, and the moral law within me."[25] The thought is at once beautiful and profound; for

24. [Ps 119:89–90.]
25. [Kant, *Critique of Practical Reason*, 133 {Ak 5:161}.]

Document 4: The Wonderful Nature of Man.

there can be no more fitting image, in truth, of the grandeur and sublimity of this inward law, than that which is offered to our gaze in the silent, tranquil, ever during[26] majesty of the stars.

Along with the presence of the law again, in this department of our being, comes into view what is in some respects the most wonderful part of our whole nature, the power with which we are so familiar under the name of conscience. As a necessary and binding rule for freedom, it lies in the very conception of the moral law, that it should be able to assert its presence, and make its authority felt, in the mind itself, and not be brought near to it merely in the character of an outward and foreign force. And thus it is in truth, that the will is found to be actually autonomic, affirming and laying down in one direction the very rule, which it feels itself called upon to obey in another. Not as if it could be supposed actually to originate the law in this way, according to its own pleasure. That would be a monstrous imagination, subverting the whole idea of morality. The will does not make the law; but still it is through it alone, that the law comes to any positive legislation in the soul. In no other way, can the full force of the categorical imperative, *Thou shalt*,[27] be brought fairly home to its consciousness. What a strange spectacle, then, we have exhibited to us here. Two forces in the same mind, transacting with one another in such solemn personal way. Here the will commands; while there again the very same will is required to obey. Nor is that all. The power that legislates in the case, goes on also to sit in judgment on its own conduct, and then to execute sentence upon itself according to the result of such trial.[28] Obedience brings at once self-approbation, and is followed with peace. Disobedience leads just as certainly to self-condemnation and self-inflicted pain. Such is the terrific mystery of conscience—the knowing of God brought into man's knowing of himself, and made to be thus an inseparable part of his proper spiritual being and life.

We conclude the whole subject with the obvious reflection, that the richest and most interesting field of science for man, is that which is offered to him in the constitution of his own person, and especially in the constitution of his person under its ethical or moral view. The world may be worthy of our thoughts and studies, in its other aspects; but it can be properly so, at all times, only as it is studied, under such aspects, with full regard to what must ever be considered its last central interest in the form now stated. No wonders of the simply outward creation, no mysteries of mere nature, can ever signify as much for us, as the world we carry about with us continually in our own being.

    Lancaster, Pa.   J. W. N.

---

26. ["Ever during": i.e., "ever continuing or lasting." Webster, *American Dictionary*, 1846.]

27. [Kant's categorical imperative: one must act in accordance with the moral law, which is determined by the *duty* of every rational being. Also see next note.]

28. [Here Nevin restates the Kantian principle that willing the moral law is an act of self-legislation, and through that act the rational being becomes "subject to the law." Kant, *Groundwork*, 44 {Ak 4:431}.]

Document 5

"Our Relations To Germany"

Editor's Introduction

The backdrop for Nevin's "Our Relations to Germany" is in one sense his entire theological project and career, given the many hermeneutical lenses and structures he employs from German influences. But the immediate context was the ongoing liturgical controversy within the German Reformed Church,[1] Isaak Dorner's critique of Nevin's theology, and more generally the impasse between German idealism and American philosophical trends, especially as expressed in the criticisms by Charles Hodge of Nevin's work.

As we saw in *Human Freedom and a Plea for Philosophy* above, America was a society and culture enamored with the philosophy of Common Sense Realism.[2] Among the advocates of this philosophy was Charles Hodge, a theological giant of nineteenth century America and one of the most prominent critics of Nevin's German theological influences. In his famed *Systematic Theology*, Hodge weaved throughout his arguments an attempt to dismantle what he perceived as a pantheistic realism advanced by German idealism and his more immediate theological adversaries at Mercersburg. Over the course of their decades of theological engagement, Hodge repeatedly accused Nevin of fully adopting Schleiermacher's theological system[3] and replicating

---

1. While the need for new resources for ministry in the German Reformed Church was generally recognized, two distinct trajectories developed. Nevin, his co-professor Schaff, and their disciples supported a liturgy that was both "catholic and Reformed" (Evans, *Companion*, 122). J. H. A. Bomberger, who had been on the original committee, came to view the proposals of the committee as "ritualistic." The standard study of the movement and the ensuing controversy is Maxwell, *Worship and Reformed Theology*. A good contemporary overview is in Evans, *Companion*, 120–27. A study of the texts that emerge in the liturgical controversy is planned for a future volume of MTSS.

2. For a comprehensive discussion of these divergent theological tendencies and Nevin's debates with Hodge, see Bonomo, *Incarnation and Sacrament*.

3. Hodge regularly critiques Schleiermacher in his *Systematic Theology*, see esp. 1:6–9, 1:173–79; 2:440–54.

Document 5: "Our Relations To Germany"

the broader structures of that idealist, and arguably semi-pantheist, nineteenth century German theology for American audiences.[4]

In response, Nevin posed the following rhetorical question: "But am I not a teacher in the German church, and as such bound, in common honesty, to cultivate a proper connection with the theological life of Germany, as well as with that of Scotland and New England?"[5] The Reformation had originated in Germany, and therefore it was the scientific resources of German theology that would determine whether "the *idea* of the Reformation" "has a right to exist."[6] But he denied following Schleiermacher (or any other German theologian) "slavishly, for my master and guide.... [T]he most I lay claim to is the exercise of some proper independence in thinking after others."[7]

Nevin followed Isaak Dorner in the claim that Christian theology must be Christocentric. He was therefore astonished when Dorner came out against his theology, as Nevin had summarized it in *Vindication of the Revised Liturgy*.[8] Nevin had somehow learned that his American adversaries were presenting the "great German Christologist"[9] as an opponent, and wrote the present essay to outline what he regarded as the inconsistency, and indeed absurdity, of their attacks. Dorner's more detailed critique, "Der liturgische Kampf in der deutsch-reformirten Kirche Nord-Amerika's"[10] would come out the following year, and Nevin responded with "Answer to Professor Dorner."

> We have been able to see and own thankfully the service which has been rendered to the cause of Christianity, through the intonation of this great [Christological] principle, by Schleiermacher, and other master minds, who have followed him with far more orthodoxy than he ever had himself, without feeling ourselves bound in the least to accept in full all that any such master mind may have been led to deduce from the principle as belonging to the right

---

4. Hodge's critiques were leveled at multiple elements of the Nevin's theological system and the influence of German thought more generally. See, in chronological order, Hodge, "Review of *The Principle of Protestantism*," MTSS 3:213-22; "Short Notices: *Antichrist*;" "Doctrine of the Reformed Church on the Lord's Supper"; "What is Christianity?" In the secondary literature, see DiPuccio, *Interior*, 173-77 and Littlejohn, *Mercersburg Theology*, 56-87.

5. Nevin, *Antichrist*, MTSS 5:176n35.

6. Nevin, "Wilberforce on the Incarnation," MTSS 4:50, emphasis original.

7. Nevin, *Antichrist*, MTSS 5:165.

8. *Vindication* was originally published in Philadelphia: Jas. B. Rodgers, 1867. The current modern edition is Yrigoyen and Bricker, *Catholic and Reformed*, 313-403. Nevin's surprise is stated in "Answer to Professor Dorner," 551-52.

9. Nevin, "Answer to Professor Dorner," 551.

10. Trans. "The Liturgical Conflict in the Reformed Church of North America." See Dorner, "Der liturgische Kampf;" English translations, *The Liturgical Conflict* (Philadelphia: Loag, 1868); and *The Reformed Church Monthly* 1 (1868) 327-81. Nevin also responded with an essay "The Church Movement" in the church's *Weekly Messenger* (see citation in DeBie, *Speculative*, 108).

construction of Christian doctrine. Our theology, in this view, has not been built upon Schleiermacher, or Ullmann, or Dorner, ...[11]

Nevin then repeated words he lifted from the penultimate paragraph of the present essay: the Christological principle that he had gratefully learned from German theology had to be "supplement[ed]" with the confession of the "old Creeds," "We believe in the Holy Catholic Church," even if this meant that "our theology is more Anglican than German."[12] *Vindication of the Revised Liturgy* argued at length how Christocentrism was guided by the confessional framework of the Apostles Creed, and required an understanding of the Church that was "the organ through which Christ works in world (His body), the medium of his presence . . . , the sphere of his grace."[13] The German theologians could not provide adequate guidance on this "Church Question," for reasons stated at the end of this essay.

A generous, simple interpretation of Nevin's relationship to German thought would say that he borrowed ideas when it seemed appropriate and offered constructive critiques where necessary. Moreover, such borrowing and critiquing was always with a view toward integrating what he deemed valuable and praiseworthy in the mediating theologians ideas into his own brand of Reformed confessionalism and his reverence for the teachings of the early Church Fathers, particularly as expressed in the creeds of the early Church.[14]

---

11. Nevin, "Answer to Professor Dorner," 542. My thanks to Bonomo, *Incarnation*, 69–70, for bringing the passage to my attention.

12. Below, 145. Also, Nevin, "Answer to Professor Dorner," 542–43.

13. Nevin, *Vindication*, 60–80; repr. Yrigoyen and Bricker, *Catholic and Reformed*, 370–90. Quotation 79/389. Scholars see *Vindication* as one of the more mature summations of Nevin's theological project (Hart, *John Williamson Nevin*, 216).

14. See Littlejohn, *Mercersburg Theology*, 179, and Bonomo, *Incarnation*, 69.

Our Relations to Germany.[1]

It has been occasionally charged against our theology heretofore, that it consisted very much in a blind following of German modes of thought. Because it made large account of German learning, and of the results of German speculation in the different departments of theological science, it was considered proper to make the fact a reason for viewing its peculiarities with suspicion and distrust. This could be done in different ways to suit occasions. Sometimes it had the purpose simply of disparaging our views, as being without any sort of original force. Again, it was to hold them up to contempt, as unintelligible and obscure; German thinking, at best, being a sort of dreamy idealism, and *our* version of it of course an incompetent rendering into English, that was sure to turn it into something worse. What came in such form was of questionable shape. It might be set down at once as transcendental nonsense; in so far forth precisely as it failed to fall in with the stereotyped notions of those whose perspicacity, thanks to their want of all German training, had never become clouded by any similar mysticism. Then again, however, the charge of *Germanizing* was pitched upon a new key. Could any good thing, in the way of Christianity and theology, come out of Germany?[2] Was it not the land of neology, rationalism, and pantheism? Had not its philosophy, from Kant to Hegel, been in the service throughout of skepticism and unbelief; and was it not notorious that its old religious orthodoxy had been swept away completely by the influence of its philosophical speculations?[3] To be in any communication with German thinking, in such circumstances, was counted enough in certain quarters to justify the apprehension of a somewhat latitudinarian or unsound faith. The idea seemed to be, that a man was the more to be relied upon as a competent scholar in philosophical, theological, and moral science, the less he knew of the great writers on these subjects in modern Germany. Rauch's *Psychology*,[4] for

1. [*MR* 14 (October 1867) 627–32.]

2. [Nevin here is perhaps alluding to Nathanael's question to Phillip regarding Jesus in John 1:46.]

3. [For an overview of the key philosophical and theological moves made by Kant, Hegel, and associated thinkers, and the long-term implications in the modern west, see Rosen, *Shadow of God*.]

4. [Rauch's *Psychology* was a basic text of Mercersburg thought, since it introduced idealism and Hegelian philosophy to the German Reformed Church. Rauch, a German émigré who came to

example, might have been better without the knowledge of Hegel; it detracted from the value of his Lectures on Ethics,[5] that he had studied Fichte and was thoroughly familiar with the teaching of Daub; and that Mercersburg theology, as it was called, should find any thing at all to admire or approve in the magnificent Schleiermacher, was held sufficient to bring upon it the reproach of all his errors. Here, moreover, was ground for looking askant on its professed regard for the first class of evangelical German theologians generally belonging to the present time. For who among them had not been influenced, more or less, by the thinking of Schleiermacher? It was no help to our cause then, that it could plead in its favor at certain points the authority of such men as Neander, or Ullmann, or Julius Müller, or Dorner, or Rothe, or Ebrard, or Martensen, or Liebner, or Tholuck, or Lange.[6] These might be all good enough for Germany; but they could not pass muster here, of course, among the evangelical sects of America; and any school or tendency among us, therefore, that might pretend to be in good understanding with them theologically, could but deserve for this very reason, to be looked upon with some measure of misgiving and doubt.

We have been blamed heretofore, we say, in these different ways, for being too much ruled by the authority of the Germans in matters of theology and religion; and many are no doubt still ready, as much as ever, to renew the blame on what they may feel to be suitable occasion. It is somewhat surprising, however, to find this charge against us turned of late into precisely the opposite form. On the strength of an opinion got at second hand from Dr. Dorner, in regard to our new Liturgy,[7] occasion is taken to make it out that our views are *not* endorsed by the standard-bearers of modern evangelical theology in Germany, and that this now must be taken as a powerful presumption against them without any farther consideration. If it was our heresy before to be too much German, it is our no less serious heterodoxy now to be too little German. The case of difference with us on the part of Dorner, is indeed ludicrously small. It reduces itself to a single point, set over against three other main points, in which he agrees with us in full, against those who wish to overwhelm us with his condemnation. Dorner is in favor of a true people's Liturgy; Dorner approves of our seeking to incorporate the spirit of the primitive Liturgies with the theological life of the sixteenth century; Dorner declares the sacramental doctrine of our Liturgies to be the true doctrine of the Reformed Church as it was taught by Calvin in the age of the Reformation. All great points, on which the Puritanic anti-liturgical party among

---

America in 1831, soon thereafter joined the tiny faculty of the seminary and college of the Church. He taught until his death in 1841, nine months after having been joined by Nevin. For a brief biography and explanation of his relevance to Mercersburg, see Evans, *Companion*, 14–17; for his philosophy, see DeBie, *Speculative Theology*, 46–49.]

5. [Rauch left unfinished a work entitled "Christian Ethics."]

6. [For a thorough exploration of these men and the school of thought in general, see Aubert, *German Roots*.]

7. [See Nevin's explanation of Dorner's distance from the discussion in "Answer to Professor Dorner," 541.]

us, and on the outside of us, has been at issue with us, more or less angrily, all along. But then, the same Dr. Dorner takes exception, it is said, to our view of Ordination and the Christian Ministry, pronounces it Anglican (not German), and sees involved in it the conception of a third sacrament not in proper harmony with Protestantism;[8] and this at once is seized upon as sufficient to turn his otherwise favorable judgment into a wholesale testimony against us, with which, it is complacently assumed, we ought to feel ourselves altogether confounded and put to shame. With the Christological theology of Dorner, Ullmann,[9] and other such German divines, the Puritanic anti-liturgical party among us, and on the outside of us, have in the nature of the case no sympathy whatever. It is that order of thinking precisely which they are ever ready to exclaim against as unevangelical, whenever it comes in their way. But in the case before us, all that is forgotten. To serve an occasion now, these German authorities (though they are themselves mostly not Reformed at all, but either Lutheran or Unionistic),[10] are made to be an infallible standard for the German Reformed Church here in America, which we, as belonging to that Church, are bound to respect, on pain of being held heretical for any deviation from it whatever. The authorities in question, it is well known, are not in full harmony among themselves, and agree with no sect or confession in this country; but no matter for that; if they can be made to tell against our so-called Mercersburg theology in any way, it is at any rate so much clear gain. Does not this theology claim to be German, as professing to represent the German Reformed Church? But here we have the Germans themselves objecting to at least something in it, as not according to their mind. Is not that enough to condemn it?

It is hard enough certainly, that we should have charged upon us as a fault in this case, what it has been considered our fault at other times to be wanting in; the power, namely, of not following blindly in the wake of German theological speculation. But let it pass. We are used to such unfair polemics. All we have in mind now, is the improvement of the occasion here offered, for setting forth in general terms briefly what our relations to Germany have been actually all along, and still continue to be, in the whole sphere of religion and theology.

We honor German learning and thought, and stand largely indebted to them for such views as we have come to have of man and the world, of Christianity and the Bible. We are not of that class who pique themselves on being good philosophers,

---

8. [The primary statement of this allegedly "Anglican" view is Nevin, "Christian Ministry," MTSS 7:38–56. See Nichols, *Romanticism*, 275–80; Evans, *Companion*, 110–20; Littlejohn, "Sectarianism," 410–12.]

9. [In spite of Nevin's negative reaction at the end of this essay, Karl Ullmann (1796–1865) was important for Nevin's theological development: he used a "free compressed translation" of Ullmann's "The Distinctive Character of Christianity" to introduce the argument of *Mystical Presence*, MTSS 1:15–39 (quote p. 15).]

10. [Frederick William III, king of Prussia 1797–1840, organized the Prussian Union Church, bringing together Lutherans and Reformed with a common liturgy (Nichols, *Romanticism*, 73). The theological and liturgical agenda of the Union Church had a significant influence on Schaff and thus on Mercersburg theology (Nichols, *Romanticism*, 73–77).]

because they have never read a line of Kant and have not the remotest conception of what was dreamed of by Fichte and Schelling;[11] or who consider themselves good and safe theologians, because their dogmatic slumbers have never been for a moment disturbed by Schleiermacher or the dangerous school of Tübingen.[12] We confess our obligations both to the philosophers and the theologians of Germany. They have done much to deepen our religious convictions, and to widen the range of our religious thought. We are perfectly sure that the central stream of all spiritual science in the modern life of the world, is in that country; and that it is worse than idle, therefore, to dream of any live, progressive thinking, philosophical or theological, in England, America, or any other country, which shall not be impregnated largely with the results of German study and speculation.

With all this high opinion, however, of the German mind and learning, we belong to no German school, and have never pretended to follow strictly any German system or scheme of thought. Neither have we been blind at all, or insensible, to the dangers of a too free and trustful communication with these foreign forms of thinking. There has been no disposition with us, either to commit ourselves passively to any such guidance, or to set up an independent system by its help. We have all along disclaimed everything of this sort. Theory and speculation have been with us subordinate always to the idea of positive Christianity, as an object of faith exhibited to us in the Bible and the history of the actual Church. The Christological principle has been for us immeasurably more than the requirements of any school of philosophy; its practical consequences have weighed more with us than the logical necessities of any metaphysical system. We have been able to see and own thankfully the service which has been rendered to the cause of Christianity, through the intonation of this great principle, by Schleiermacher, and other master minds, who have here followed him with far more orthodoxy than he ever had himself, without feeling ourselves bound in the least to accept in full all that any such master mind may have been led to deduce from the principle as belonging to the right construction of Christian doctrine. Our theology in this view has not been built upon Schleiermacher or Ullmann, or Dorner, however much of obligation it cheerfully owns to each of them, as well as to others,

---

11. [As noted previously in this volume, Johann Gottlieb Fichte and Friedrich Wilhelm Joseph Schelling, students of Kant and key figures of German idealism (later overshadowed by Hegel), were hugely influential for Nevin. Fichte is perhaps most well known for his concept of the self, which he conceived as the starting point for all knowledge and experience. He argued that the self is the origin of all knowledge and that the self is free and autonomous. Schelling, for his part, established and advanced a system of transcendental idealism in which he argued that the mind and the world are interconnected and that the mind can access the basic, organic unity of the world through the intellect. Beiser, *German Idealism*.]

12. [School of German New Testament theologians founded by F. C. Baur that applied Hegel's notion of historical development to early Christian movements (specifically by setting up Petrinist and Paulinist movements in dialectical tension). The influence of the Tubingen school was greatest during the 1840s, but was gradually abandoned. F.C. Baur, *History of Christian Dogma*; Dietrich and Himes, *Legacy of the Tubingen School*.]

DOCUMENT 5: OUR RELATIONS TO GERMANY.

whose more or less variant systems of thought go together to the conception of what is called the evangelical theology of Germany in its most modern form.

Whatever of force and worth the Christological studies of these great men carry with them for our thinking, all is felt to rest ultimately only in their bearing on the actual life of Christ, and the relation they hold to the development of the mystery of godliness in the actual history of the Church. Here we reach what we feel to be surer and more solid ground than any such studies of themselves furnish; and just because these studies seem too often to stop short of what is involved for faith in the full historical apprehension of the Christian mystery, as a continuous presence in the world, they are found to be at certain points more or less unsatisfactory in the end to our religious feeling. Here it is that, with all our respect for German divinity, we consciously come to a break with it in our thoughts, and feel the necessity of supplementing it with the more practical way of looking at Christianity which we find embodied in the ancient Creeds. In this respect, we freely admit, our theology is more Anglican than German.[13] We stand upon the old Creeds. We believe in the Holy Catholic Church.

In this way the Church Question, in particular, has come to have for us an interest and significance which it has not, and cannot have, even for the best thinkers in Germany.[14] With us, the whole Christological interest is felt to run into it as its necessary issue and end. The Church challenges our faith as an essential part of the Christian salvation; a mystery, to the acknowledgment of which we are shut up by the inward movement of the Creed. But in Germany, they cannot look at the matter in the same way. Their circumstances forbid it. Their churches are dependent on the State, are ruled by civil authority, have no proper ecclesiastical authority or power of their own. How, standing in the bosom of such Erastian[15] systems, can German theologians be considered good authority for any thing that has to do with the proper solution of the Church Question? We profess no agreement with them here, and ask

---

13. [For an excellent discussion of Nevin's relationship to the Oxford Movement and Anglicanism, see Littlejohn, *Mercersburg Theology*, 88–123.]

14. [Bratt, "Nevin and the Antebellum Culture Wars," 11, is correct to suggest that Nevin "saw the church question as paramount, absorbing all other problems of the age. All naturally conceived and secularly wrought solutions, he insisted, shared humanity's fateful limitations. Life required a supernatural redemption, which had begun only in the incarnation of Jesus Christ. Here was the objective fact of a new life, a divine and supernatural force present in history, offering power for real change. But that power was available only in the Church, Christ's living body in the world, and there preeminently through the sacrament." In his "Lancaster Commencement Address," Nevin comments: "Above all in interest for us, here must be settled the great ecclesiastical issues, with which the whole Christian world is wrestling at the present time, and which are felt by thousands everywhere to involve nothing less than the question of life or death for the universal cause of Christianity itself.... Here on this Western Continent is to be the arena where the Church Question, which all truly earnest men feel and know to be the greatest question of the age, is to be fought out, if I may use the expression, to its last consequences and results." Appel, *Life*, 643. See also Hart, *John Williamson Nevin*, 230–32.]

15. [A theory that gives the state authority over the church, even in theological and disciplinary matters. Named after Thomas Erastus (1524–83), a Swiss theologian. "The Anglican Crisis" (document 9 below) is Nevin's critique of Erastianism manifested in the Church of England.]

from them no endorsement of our views. We know that we stand upon higher ground. Who among us can think of accepting Rothe's idea of the Church, by which it is made to merge itself at last formally in the Christian State?[16] Who that has had the least insight into the miserable church relations of the late Dr. Ullmann, Prelate so called of the Church in Baden,[17] would be willing to take him as a sound expositor of what the article of the Church means in the Apostles' Creed? And just so with the judgment of the excellent Dr. Dorner, quoted against our Liturgy on the subject of Ordination.[18] It is only what was to be expected. It carries with it for us no weight whatever. God forbid that we should be bound here by Prussian examples or Prussian opinions in any form.

---

16. [Richard Rothe (1799–1867), professor of theology at Heidelberg. Nevin describes Rothe's view that the church will ultimately be absorbed in the state in "Early Christianity," 40–43; repr. Yrigoyen and Bricker, *Catholic and Reformed*, 296–99. For Rothe's positive influence on Nevin's doctrine of revelation late in life, see editor's introduction to Nevin, "The Bread of Life," MTSS 6:214–15.]

17. [Ullmann became the prelate (similar to bishop) of the united church of Baden (a state in southwest Germany), 1853–61. He came into conflict with the other directors of the ecclesiastical council, over (ironically enough) the introduction of a new liturgy (Beyschlag, "Ullmann, Karl," 3:2416).]

18. [Nevin answered Dorner in series of articles in the *Reformed Church Messenger*. These were collected in Nevin, "Answer to Professor Dorner." Publication is expected in a later volume of this series. DeBie gives a thorough analysis of the debate (beginning with the present essay) in *John Williamson Nevin*, 328–35.]

Document 6

"The Church Year"

Editor's Introduction

Nevin's insistence that philosophy, theology, anthropology, and Christian practice be rooted concretely in history and in the course of the world's life is ubiquitous throughout the Nevin corpus, but rarely as clearly—and at times poetically—as it is in "The Church Year." Here, Nevin most explicitly links the cycles and seasons of the natural world, humanity's general religious desire, liturgical practice, and mankind's rhythmic movement toward and fulfillment in the Incarnation, Jesus Christ. In sum, in Nevin's own words, "Religion in the form of nature, and religion in the form of history, come here (in Christianity) to a perfect understanding and agreement. The constitution of the world is sanctified, by being taken up into the constitution of grace. The year of religion is now truly and properly a Church Year."[1]

The essay, penned in 1856, was prompted by several key trends in both in American Protestantism and in the German Reformed church more particularly.[2] By the mid-nineteenth century, emerging awareness of and access to historical liturgies and related texts prompted renewed interest in liturgical forms. In 1840, John Knox's liturgy become more widely available in Scotland, upon which a resource for families was produced and distributed (1841). This was followed by Ebrard's publication of *Reformiertes Kirchenbuch* (1846), a collection of prayers and liturgies from Continental sources that had particular appeal to German-speaking Protestants, and the Scottish Presbyterian's publication of Calvin's *Form of Prayers* in 1849. Many students of Nevin and the era in general would have been especially familiar with Charles Baird's collection of Reformed liturgies and other liturgical resources, published in 1855,[3] followed by an anthology in 1857, *A Book of Public Prayer*.

---

1. Nevin, "The Church Year," 474–75.
2. For the historical context, I am highly indebted to the excellent account in Hart, *John Williamson Nevin*, 197–223.
3. Baird, *Presbyterian Liturgies*, reprinted by Wipf & Stock, 2006.

As such, between 1850 and 1880, the German Reformed Church embarked in a variety of ways on an inventory, evaluation, and possible revision of its liturgy, a task which included substantial engagement with the Mercersburg theology and theologians. For many, this engagement was undertaken to determine if the catechetical system that Nevin had previously advocated, as opposed to the revival program of Anxious Bench, could be applied in other regions (the implementation of Nevin's liturgy was primarily restricted to the Eastern Synod of the German Reformed Church). Accordingly, Nevin and Philip Schaff spent time on—and at different points chairing—committees appointed by the German Reformed synod to produce liturgical resources. Nevin was ambivalent about much of the work, due to personal spiritual and theological anxieties, as well as a general skepticism about the American free church impulse. Although his interest and investment in the work waned for much of the 1850s, in 1856 Nevin published an article surveying Christian hymnody and the present essay, and played a key role in the publication of the Provisional Liturgy in 1857. *Vindication of the Revised Liturgy*[4] was published a decade later, after opposition from John H. A. Bomberger and members of the western synod.[5]

Nevin's particular interest in the church year was rooted in his belief that being rooted in God's work of creation, it provided the most logical and natural framework for understanding and liturgically participating in the eternal mystery of Christ's birth, death, resurrection, and ascension, and for celebrating these events in ways that Nevin believed were divinely initiated and instructed. It was essential to connect humanity with the life and work of Christ, through the Eucharistic liturgy and broader sacramental life of the church, to the ongoing historical continuity of the Church's. The "Church Year" for Nevin was not only a way of ordering the "time" in which these events and practices took place, but also a means of wholeness and catholicity, unifying the church across time and space, as Christians around the world and throughout history shared in the same rhythms and rituals.

Accordingly, Nevin viewed seasonal changes as corresponding with the progress of salvation history. In keeping with this broader theological project, he believed that God established the natural cycles of the seasons to symbolize movements in redemptive history, where the supernatural takes up the natural world into itself in eternal, organic union in Christ. "The course of the year in time, with its revolving material changes, serves to shadow forth in a real way the idea of a higher spiritual orbit, through which man is to be regarded as moving towards his proper destination in another world. Time is made to be the mirror thus of eternity."[6] For example, the newness of spring symbolized the victory over death in Christ's resurrection at Easter, while the triumphant progress of the sun toward its summer solstice and its effects on the earth appropriately represented Christ's ascension and the outpouring of the Holy

---

4. Nevin, *Vindication*.
5. Maxwell, *Worship and Reformed Theology*, 254–311.
6. Nevin, "Church Year," 463.

Document 6: "The Church Year"

Spirit at Pentecost. In these ways, the liturgical year showcased the sacramental nature of the whole creation, finding its fulfillment in the Incarnation.[7]

Richard Wentz provides this fine summary:

> The church year makes true ritual possible because religion in the form of nature and religion in the form of history are integrated. The constitution of the world (nature and history) is raised to a constitution of grace, the realm of Incarnation. Humankind is now provided with the occasion of true worship, a liminal action that contemplates the life of the world. Liturgy celebrates what has taken place; liturgy is the coming together of those whose lives are constituted by the constitution of grace. Liturgy is bound up with the church year. Liturgy and the church year are expressive of the heart of Christianity.[8]

---

7. See Farley, "Liturgical Theology," 218.
8. Wentz, *John Williamson Nevin*, 133, see further 131–34.

The Church Year[1]

The idea of a sacred or ecclesiastical year is not something peculiar to any particular people or time. It grows forth naturally from the religious constitution of man, and reveals itself spontaneously in his religious history, among all nations and through all ages. Paganism, Judaism, Christianity, show themselves here of one mind and feeling. All alike seek to link themselves in this way with the course of nature, by bringing it into standing connection with the high sphere of religion under their own several forms.[2] The only difference is in the order and quality of the spiritual conceptions, with which they are severally occupied and employed. These, as they may be of a higher or lower grade, condition necessarily the way, in which the idea in question may be reduced to practice. But the idea itself is of universal authority and force; and if, in any case, it be hindered from coming into view, it must always be with some measure of violent restraint put upon the religious life of the communities in which such exception may prevail. The unnatural and artificial here have place, not in seeking to join the solemnities of religion in this way with the circling course of the year, but in affecting rather to dispense with all such conjunction as something superfluous and vain.

[The Correspondence between Nature and Spirit in Man]

The general ground of this is easily explained. It lies in the close necessary connection, which holds universally between the spiritual life of man and the constitution of nature. Two worlds, two different orders or spheres of existence, are joined together in man's person. He is composed of body and spirit. In virtue of his spirit, he is above the whole system of a mere nature, and beyond it, possesses in himself a life which is no product or continuation simply of its powers, but the result of a new and higher

1. [*MR* 8 (July 1856) 456–78.]
2. [For further reading on Nevin's theology of the Christian year and the liturgy more broadly, see Maxwell, *Worship and Reformed Theology*. For more on the history of the ecclesiastical year and liturgical calendars, see Talley, *Origins of the Liturgical Year*; Bradshaw, *Origins of Feasts*; Senn, *Christian Liturgy*.]

principle; and looks to his ultimate destination in an order of things, to which plainly it is intended to minister only as a scheme of transient preliminary preparation. On the other hand, however, he is just as truly and really, for the present, comprehended by means of his body in this same system of nature, as the very home of his being. Its entire organization comes to its last sense, completes itself in his person.[3] The material creation culminates in man, as the point towards which all its powers struggle from the beginning, and whose presence alone serves finally to impress upon its manifold parts the unity, roundness, and symmetry of a common whole. He is thus the highest and most perfect birth of nature, the full efflorescence of its inmost life. Its powers reach him, and affect him, on every side. In this way his whole existence, spiritual as well as physical, is rooted in the natural world around him, and conditioned by it continually, from the cradle to the grave. For the two parts of his being, spirit and matter, mind and body, are not united in a merely outward and mechanical way.[4] They flow together in the constitution of a single life. Hence the material organization underlies the spiritual throughout, supports it, enters into it, determines more or less its entire form and complexion. Mind, in the case of man, is never a power wholly abstract and free from matter; it is always, in a most important sense, derived from and dependent upon the body. The true relation between the two, requires, indeed, that this last should be ruled by the first, as the higher power; that the material organization should be in the end so taken up by the spiritual, as to pass, in some sense, over to this out of its own sphere; that the body should be glorified into full harmony with the superior nature of the soul. But still, with all this, the soul can never free itself absolutely from the power of the body. Such is the law of humanity.[5] However it may be with other intelligences, man is made up of both matter and spirit. His whole being is conditioned by the natural basis, in which it starts, and from which it continues ever afterwards to

---

3. [Michael Farley summarizes the scheme well: For Nevin, "The natural cycles of the seasons were established by God to be a symbol of the course of redemptive history in which the supernatural takes up the natural world into itself in a permanent, organic union in the person of Christ. These typological correlations come to liturgical expression in the celebration of the life, death, and resurrection of Christ in the seasons and festivals of the liturgical year. . . . Thus, the liturgical year exhibits the sacramental reality of the whole creation and expresses the cosmic significance of the incarnation." Farley, "Liturgical Theology," 216–17.]

4. [The tension of inner-outer, organic-mechanical is throughout Nevin's writings. For one example, in the preface to *The Mystical Presence*, Nevin writes, "The whole conception that the externalization of the Christian life is something accidental only to the constitution of this life itself—a sort of mechanical machinery, to help it forward in an outward way—is exceedingly derogatory to the Church, and injurious in its bearings on religion. An outward Church is the necessary form of the new creation in Christ Jesus, in its very nature; and must continue to be so, not only through all time, but through all eternity likewise." MTSS 1:12.]

5. [On the relationship of body and soul see e.g., his typical formulation in "The Wonderful Nature of Man": "Must not the temple of the soul, in the midst of the natural world, be so framed and ordered, as to be, even in its own merely physical constitution, more honorable and glorious than the whole world of nature besides? The primacy of man in the world, the proper sovereignty of his nature, is not a prerogative belonging to him through his soul only; it comes into view most immediately, and first of all, in his body also" (above, 129).]

grow; just as the plant which blooms towards heaven, draws the quality of its leaves and flowers at the same time from the soil that secretly gives nourishment to its roots.[6] Primarily and immediately, this natural basis, for every man, is his own body. But as we have just seen, the human body is no separate and isolated existence in the world of nature. The world of nature is a system, a single grand whole, bound together in all its parts, and looking from all sides towards a common centre; and this centre is precisely man himself, in his material organization. To be dependent on the body then, is to be dependent also through this on the general system or constitution in which it is thus centrally comprehended. Mind modified and conditioned by its union with the body, is in fact necessarily also mind modified and conditioned, in its universal existence, by the whole world of nature to which the body belongs. Man stands in sympathy and correspondence with the material universe on all sides. It acts upon him continually through all his senses. It gives form to his affections and color to his thoughts. In his highest flights of intelligence, he owns still its authority and presence. It surrounds and pervades his spirit at every point, and forms the very element in which he lives, moves, and has his being.

Such is the general law of correspondence between the inward and outward sides of our existence in the present world, between the higher life of the soul in man and his lower life in the body. We feel the force of it every hour, in the influence which is exercised over us by the forms of nature as they surround us in space. Skies, mountains, seas, plains, forests, rivers, enter into us, and become part of our spiritual being.[7] All natural scenery, in one word, is educational. Our interior life is conditioned by it in every stage of its development. Our thinking and feeling, from first to last, owe to it a large part of their peculiar character and form. And what is thus true of nature as a system existing in space, is no less true of nature as a system existing in the continual flow of time. The changes, movements, revolutions, and periods, through which the world is continually passing, connect themselves with the economy of our inward being, no less really than the material objects which are perpetually subject to their law. Days, months, years, and cycles of years, carry with them a plastic educational force for the human spirit, full as profound and far reaching, to say the least, as any that is exercised over it by seas, plains, mountains, and skies. Indeed of these two forms of nature, existence in space and existence in time, it would seem that the last here must be allowed even to surpass the first in power. It lies nearer to the soul, and holds more

---

6. [Nevin frequently insists on the natural world's vital and proper role in God's process of redemption. Nevin also uses the images analogously to describe the process of the individual's spiritual growth and ultimately their redemption. As Layman notes, one's "surrender {to the gospel} led to a 'process of regenerating and sanctifying grace,' which was like the 'development of a plant,' and 'carries in itself the germ of its own most perfect state from the beginning, and grows by unfolding itself from within.'" Layman, general introduction to *Born of Water*, MTSS 6:17, quoting "Religion a Life" (1834).]

7. [Ultimately, as nature becomes part of humanity, the natural world, becoming a moral, intelligent world through mankind, reaches its fulfillment as it is linked with the divine through the second person of the Trinity. See Borneman, *Church*, 84, and Nevin, "Christianity and Humanity," 469.]

direct affinity with its spiritual constitution. It is by the sense of movement in the way of time especially, that the more outward sense of matter in space is etherialized and made to enter into the service of intelligence and mind.

[Time as a Measure of Human Existence]

Our whole existence, spiritual as well as physical, is continually influenced in the most powerful manner by the course of nature, as thus measured by periods and seasons. We feel it in the succession of day and night. This is for us no merely outward index of time. It marks a law of regular revolution in our life, which corresponds in full with what goes forward in the world around us. The force of this law shows itself in our souls as well as in our bodies, in the activities of our mind no less than in the pulsations of our heart. Day is the time for action, night for sleep. There are strong sympathies in us also with particular hours. We make inwardly the circuit of morning, noon, and evening. Midnight constitutes a crisis for our universal being. Diseases come and go, have their remissions and intermissions, at certain points of the orbit. Good health and sound understanding alike depend on proper conformity with the order, which God has been pleased thus to establish for us in the general constitution of the natural world. So too the revolutions of the moon have their effect upon our life, as well as upon the growth of plants or the ebb and flow of tides. And still more the grand period which is accomplished by the revolution of the earth round the sun. The year, with its four seasons, makes its full circle continually in man himself, as really as in the world around him. Spring, Summer, Autumn, and Winter, repeat themselves perpetually in the onward movement of his existence. Clouds and sunshine, all atmospherical changes, all the varying phases of nature, are mirrored in his consciousness and responded to by his inmost sensibilities, in the order of the rolling months. His existence is not just a continuous line in one and the same direction. It proceeds by cycles that are always returning upon themselves. It is made up of years, which repeat themselves with perpetual recurrence in the progress of his experience, ever the same and yet ever new, from infancy to youth, from youth to manhood, and from manhood to old age. The Year, it has been well remarked, is the most perfect and complete measure of time belonging to the earth. It is not merely a full revolution for itself in which the end comes back to the beginning, but it forms also a distinct whole in the organic process of all terrestrial life. In many cases this begins and ends with the annual circle; and where that is not the case, the circle marks at least a full round period in the process, which may very fairly be taken as an apt representation and image of the whole. Each single year forms for every man a significant epitome, first of the several ages of his life, and then of his life itself in full. Nothing is more natural, as nothing is more common, than the sense of this analogy. And thus it is, that all the world over men are led to look upon the year as the type and symbol of their universal existence upon the earth, and under such view seek to make it the vehicle and bearer of what is most inward and spiritual for their experience, as well as of that which is merely outward and physical.

[The Conception of the Religious Year]

Here then we reach the proper conception of the religious or sacred year. Two ideas are brought it together in it, which are materially different and yet closely related, religion and nature. Starting in nature, the life of man is required to complete itself in religion, as an order of existence above nature, and involving relations which go altogether beyond the present world. In the religious year, all this is expressed by an easy and natural symbolism. The higher sphere is made to link itself with the lower, in such a way as to show at once, both the necessary connection of the two, and the proper subordination of the last to the purposes and ends of the first. Religion lets itself down, as it were, into the sphere of nature, in order to raise this into its own sphere.

The lower constitution in this case is made to carry in itself the sense of the higher, in the way of figure or type. Nature passes into an allegory of religion. We should err greatly, however, if we should imagine that there was nothing more here than a mere outward resemblance, arbitrarily established by the wit and fancy of man. We have already seen, that there is an inward, real correspondence between the spiritual and physical sides of man's being; and that this last is organically comprehended, by means of his body, in the constitution of nature as a whole.[8] From this it follows as a necessary consequence, that the entire physical order of the world must look towards the spiritual in all its parts, and find there always its last, most true and perfect sense. Could we understand in full the economy of creation, we should see the first of these spheres to be in its very nature a perpetual parable of the second. So it was evidently to the mind of Christ; and so we too feel it to be, when listening to its most simple and yet most profound lessons, as interpreted under this view from his lips. It is by no mere figure of speech, no simply rhetorical metaphor or comparison, that the forms of nature in space, or its powers in time, are taken to be significant of facts and truths in the higher world of the spirit. There may be much of mere fancy and conceit, much ignorance and blindness, in particular attempts to make out and express the full force of the correspondence at different points. But the correspondence itself is for all this none the less certain and real. The natural carries in itself an affinity with the spiritual; tends towards it as its own proper complement and end; forms everywhere an adumbration of its invisible presence and power. So in the case before us, where the year is made to assume a sacred or religious form, by having the ideas or facts of religion lodged in its natural revolution, we are not to conceive of the relation as being simply outward and artificial; but are bound to see in it rather a real inward connection between the things which are thus brought together. In no other way can we do

---

8. [For later development of this "correspondence between the spiritual and physical sides of man's being," see the 1878 sermon, "Bread of Life," MTSS 6:218–44.]

full justice to the subject, or be able to understand and explain the position it occupies in the actual history of the world.

The existence of such inward necessary cause or reason, in the case, is at once established by the fact, already mentioned, that the notion of a sacred year is found to prevail among all people and through all times. It enters spontaneously, as it would seem, into the thoughts of men, and can be repressed and set aside only by a certain violence inflicted upon the spirit of religion itself. What is thus natural and universal can never be accidental merely or arbitrary. It must have its ground always in the real nature of things. A sentiment or practice in which all forms of religion come together with common agreement, cannot be absolutely false or without meaning. It cannot be an empty prejudice merely, or a hurtful superstition. Error and falsehood, perversion and extravagance, may correct themselves with its use. But no such corruption can turn the principle itself, which may be thus wronged and abused into a wholesale lie. They form rather part of the evidence, which goes to establish its truth. Back of all such wrongs and abuses, this still stands firm and secure, as being by the universal consent of mankind something grounded in the religious constitution of the world itself, and so beyond all rational contradiction or doubt.

The force of this in reference to the religious year becomes more striking, when it is considered that the universal consent in question reaches far beyond the mere general notion of making the year in this way a religious remembrancer, the bearer of religious thoughts and ideas. Were this all, we should find unbounded freedom in the manner of carrying out the conception. There would be no fixed order or rule in the location of particulars, in the determination of details. All would be at the mercy of fancy or caprice. Such, however, is not the way, in which we find this universal conception carried out in the actual practice of the world. The conception determines also, to a very material extent, the order and mode of its own reduction to use. It is not satisfied with having the year hung around with religious garlands and festoons, the ornamental imagery of a higher life, in a merely loose and external manner. It involves always the supposition of some necessary order and method, growing out of the correspondence of the natural and spiritual worlds themselves, according to which only the arrangement can be rightly carried into effect. It is assumed throughout, that the course of the year in time, with its revolving material changes, serves to shadow forth in a real way the idea of a higher spiritual orbit, through which man is to be regarded as moving towards his proper destination in another world. Time is made to be the mirror thus of eternity. The visible is held to reflect the invisible. The lower sphere is felt to include in itself parabolically the sense of the higher. The natural, accordingly, is not taken to represent the spiritual at random, in any and every way, but only according to a law fixed in its own constitution. This we see exemplified in the actual judgment and practice of the world. The natural year, all the world over, is made to underlie the religious or sacred year, and to lead the way in determining its order and form. The relation between them is such, that the first refers as it were of its own accord to the second, and offers itself throughout as its proper utterance and expression. The ideas of the religious year are apprehended as having an actual representation in the facts of the natural year, as meeting in them their own picture or echo. Hence we have, in the midst of all that may seem to be confused and fantastic in the filling up of different forms of this spiritualized year, a certain uniformity of scheme at the same time that serves to impress on the whole a common character. The more closely the matter is examined, the more clear it seems to become that these various forms are themselves in some way inwardly related; the only difference being that some are far more perfect than others, in the measure of their approximation to the truth, which all in their way propose to reach and express. This fact, still more than the mere universal notion itself of a sacred year, goes conclusively to show how truly and really the whole conception is grounded in the natural constitution of the world.

[The Conception of Time in the Order of Grace]

Religion in the case of man, however, requires more than the simple development of his own spiritual faculties and powers in what may be denominated the order of nature. It supposes, as necessary to its own completion, an order also of grace, a supernatural revelation descending into the bosom of the world in the form of actual history and fact. The absolute fulness of this revelation is reached at last in Christ, "in whom are hid all the treasures of wisdom and knowledge."[9] In the form of promise, prophecy and type, it runs away back to the beginning of the world, preparing the way through the whole period of the Old Testament for his glorious advent. Necessarily this system of grace, under such historical view, must be vastly more for the religious life of man, than the system of nature; and it might seem, in one view, that the idea of religion thus based on what is above nature, and virtually opposing it as a power antagonistic to faith, would require no such union with it, and no such help from it, as is implied in the conception of a sacred or ecclesiastical year; that its true interests rather would be much better consulted in every way, by separating it wholly from all such connection with the merely natural order of time, and joining it in thought and association only with the supernatural facts which are presented to us in the Bible, in their own higher order and form. But here three thoughts offer themselves to our view.

First, these supernatural facts are themselves historical; and having thus entered into the sphere of nature and time, they need to be held in permanent connection with this for our thinking, in order that they may be apprehended as facts, and not as notions merely or imaginations.[10] Like all other historical events, they must have for us a local habitation in our sense of chronology, to be realities at all for our belief. This of itself at once leads to the conception of anniversaries, monumental solemnities,

9. [Col 2:3.]
10. [Nevin held that Christianity was a supernatural fact manifested in history. First clear statements are in 1847: *The Church*, MTSS 5:148, 153–54.]

seasons of commemoration; to the conception, in one word, of an ecclesiastical or sacred year. It is in this way great national facts perpetuate their force in the mind of a nation. Other forms of tradition, oral or written, are not enough for the purpose. They must be lodged monumentally in the ever recurring circuit of the year, that grand image of all time, that proper epitome of man's life, both in dividual and universal; so as to be in this way reproduced and called up anew in the national consciousness, age after age. This gives us the idea of a political year; which is constituted, not just by a system of anniversary observances in memory of all separate events possessing national historical interest, but rather by singling out such events as are felt to be of cardinal and fundamental account in the history, and making them to represent the whole. Without some arrangement of this sort, serving to keep alive the memory of the past in the consciousness of the present, no true national spirit can be long maintained. But now the very same law which requires the great facts of political history to be kept thus alive, for the purposes of patriotism, requires just as much the great facts of sacred history to be kept alive in the same manner, for the purposes of religion; and so we are brought here again to the idea of an ecclesiastical year, precisely as in the other case we come to the idea of a political year. As historical events, the facts of revelation need to be domiciliated for our minds, in this way, in our natural sense of time. Without this, they must ever be in danger of becoming for us mere shadows and abstractions.

Secondly, whilst it is true that the order of grace, resting on revelation, is something far above the order of nature, resting upon the constitution of the present world, and that this last, regarded as a separate system, involves a certain opposition to the first; it does not follow from this, by any means, that the two systems are in absolute contradiction to one another, and capable of no agreement whatever. On the contrary, it is certain, from the very nature of the case, that as different parts of the same creation they must be inwardly related, and closely bound together, in the harmony of a common divine purpose and plan. The case demands not the destruction or exclusion of nature, not a Manichean fanatical hostility[11] to its presence in any and every form; but its proper subordination merely to the authority of grace, as the sphere in which it is formed to find properly its own true significance and end. In such right order, nature appears no longer as the foe, but only as the handmaid of grace, and this relation too is found to be in no sense compulsory, but most perfectly free. The lower sphere shows itself to have been in truth created and formed for the higher. Nature becomes the prophecy of grace, its universal type and symbol. The two systems flow thus easily and of their own accord together. There is no reason, therefore, why the facts of revelation, regarded as the ground of religion, should be taken to exclude or thrust out of sight the facts of nature in the same view.

11. [Manicheanism was a dualistic salvation cult that competed with early Christianity. There were two fundamentally opposed realities: light and darkness, spirit and matter. Salvation was the process in which spirit turned away from matter, in order to return to the light.]

In the third place, the more we look into the subject the more we shall see that these two classes of facts do in very deed, as it were, run parallel the one with the other, so as most readily to admit the harmony of which we have just spoken. So much might be presumed, as an *a priori* anticipation, on the supposition that both systems proceed from God. There is no room properly for the thought of such correspondence, in the case of any simply national or political year. Who would dream, for example, of setting the Birth Day of Washington, or the Declaration of American Independence, in any sort of connection with the astronomical character of their anniversary seasons, unless it were in the way only of acknowledged fancy or conceit? Ordinary national history is too narrow and partial an interest to be separately symbolized, in such fashion, by the constitution of nature. It can be so symbolized at best, only as it is comprehended in the general movement which represents the history of the world as a whole. The political year, accordingly, is not expected to fall in with the full constitution of the natural year; it is enough, if it be brought simply to rest upon this as an outward and artificial arrangement. But with the religious year the case is altogether different. This has to do with the most universal of all hu man interests. Religion is for no nation as such, but for the whole world. The facts which underlie it historically in the form of revelation, are necessarily of the same universal and abiding force; and we have a right to expect, accordingly, that the constitution of nature, related as it must be to the destiny of man under the like broad view, should be found to include a certain inward correspondence with the order and course of these supernatural facts, as well as with the spiritual economy itself which they underlie.[12] And what might thus be anticipated, we find to be in truth strikingly verified in the actual relations of the two systems. The main historical facts here have been so ordered, in the wise providence of Him who rules all things for his own glory, as to fall in chronologically with the very facts in nature which properly symbolize their sense and power; thus rendering it perfectly easy to bring both systems into the construction of one and the same Church year. It is easy to see how this goes, on the one hand to attest the truth of revelation, by showing its correspondence with the typology of nature; while it serves, at the same time, no less clearly, to interpret and corroborate on the other hand the true sense of this lower sphere, as being throughout, the terrestrial parable of spiritual and heavenly things.

[Summary of the General Conception]

The sum and organic comprehension of the entire symbolism of nature comes to view in the *Year*, as being the completion of a full circle in the process of all earthly life. By being taken up into the sphere of grace, not only is the year itself glorified, but along with it at the same time, the whole constitution and course of nature may be said to

12. [Continuing the idea that nature is an analogy of supernature.]

Document 6: The Church Year

be glorified also, and sublimated into a new and higher sense. For the higher sphere, on the other hand, the relation involves the idea of a real victory or conquest, enlarging its rightful power. The sense of this expresses itself in the ordinary conception of *festival* days. They carry with them the feeling of joyful solemnity, elevation above the common level of our earthly life, rest from the hard work-day character of our natural worldly existence in the bosom of a higher order of being, which is made to descend upon us by the power of religion. The ecclesiastical year becomes thus a system of symbolical festivals; in which is celebrated continually the true and proper relationship of the two economies of nature and grace.

Such is the conception of the religious year in its perfect form. As such, it must be of course, at the same time, the Christian year. But it does not necessarily appear at once in this completeness. Rather it has a history, a genesis, through which it reveals itself under various forms, rising from what may be considered its rude beginnings only to that which constitutes at last its absolute consummation. Wide differences characterize these forms; but through all such differences, they are still found to represent and express fundamentally the same idea of law. So much indeed is implied by the supposition of any real history in the case. The idea of a religious year, as we have before seen, is universal, a fact seated in the religious constitution of the world. Under all manifestations, accordingly, it is the same force always working in the same direction. Its different forms are but so many different stages, in the progress of which, it is carried forward to its true ideal perfection.

Regarded in this light, the sacred year falls, for our observation, into three grand historical types—*Pagan, Jewish, Christian.* To these the subject requires us now to turn our attention.

[The Pagan Sacred Year]

In the *Pagan* religious year, we have the symbolical apprehension of nature in its most elementary and rude form. The visible material creation is felt to carry in itself the traces of its divine origin, and becomes to the consciousness in this way the sign and type of powers existing mysteriously behind itself, on which it is always dependent and whose presence it serves to reveal. But there is still no clearness in the perception; and so no power of steady discrimination between the sign and the thing signified. Hence the two are made to flow together, at the expense of the higher thought. Nature is confounded with the divine powers it represents, and superstitiously invested with their proper dignity and right. The divine, in this view, becomes earthly, as the earthly also is taken to be divine.

It fares with the religious nature of man here, as in all other cases where it labors to fulfil its constitutional destiny, without the help of an objective revelation. The effort to do so proves an abortive nisus merely in the right direction, which terminates at last in an empty shadow, throwing the spirit helplessly back upon the sphere of nature which it had thus vainly struggled to surmount. In all such cases, however, the abortion is not without its meaning. It shows what the religious constitution of man universally needs and seeks; and becomes in this way a testimony and argument for the truth, which it has no power to reach; just as the blind force which turns and leads the roots of a plant towards the water, or its upward growth towards the light, shows its necessary relation to these elements, even before this may be established in fact. Such unsuccessful endeavors on the part of the religious spirit, in the sphere of Paganism, can never be more of course than sad caricatures of the truth itself, as brought into full view by the glorious light of Christianity. But caricatures are still in their way correspondences; and the old Greek Fathers, therefore, were perfectly right, in looking upon Paganism itself as a real preparation in such view for the Gospel. We need not be disturbed at all, then, by any parallelisms it may seem to offer with Christianity. We need not shrink from owning them in their utmost force. We should be glad rather to meet them, wherever they may come in our way. They are just what we are bound to expect if Christianity be indeed the absolute truth of religion, that in which all its partial and defective manifestations come to their final end. What comparative anatomy and physiology are to the structure of the human body, or comparative psychology to the true idea of the human soul, that precisely comparative religion, as we may call it, or the scheme of religious systems in general, is to Christianity. If this stood in no agreement or correspondence with religion in other forms, we might well question its pretensions. They show themselves unquestionable, just because analogies of this sort do press upon it from every side, and find in it the universal and harmonious fulfilment of their own sense.

The Pagan sacred year, through all its variations among different nations, proceeds always on the theory of a merely natural or physical religion. The relation of the sun to the earth is felt darkly to signify, and then in some way to actually involve the higher spiritual destinies of the world, as well as its simply outward changes. The active and passive forces of nature, represented in this relation, are confounded with the notion of divine powers. All becomes mythology, a play of the religious fancy, constructed on the basis of purely physical facts and changes. This may be clearly seen especially in the Roman Heathenism, which is to be regarded as the last result only or falling together of all older Pagan religions. It is throughout pure naturalism, based upon the movements of the astronomical or solar year. Its twelve superior deities personify the system of the twelve months, the course of the year through the signs of the zodiac, the great leading changes wrought by the sun, during this period, in the life of the earth. We have no room here to follow out the correspondence in its details; nor is it necessary. It is enough for our purpose to state the general fact.

The equinoxes and solstices form the four cardinal points of the process, and rule throughout the order of its symbolism. The oldest Pagan years were made to commence in the Fall, equinoctially. The later Roman year, on the other hand, was solstitial, opening in the Winter. In both cases, however, the order and sense of the symbolism is substantially the same. It starts with the time, in which the powers of nature are shut up, as it were, in its interior economy; the life of the earth in a state of deep slumber; the strength of the sun in a great measure unfelt. Through the winter months, we have a struggle between the forces of darkness and light, resulting continually more and more in the triumph of the last. The heavens gain power. With the progress of Spring, this power descends into the air and earth, causing the whole sphere to wake into new life. In Summer the victory becomes complete. The sun culminates in the June solstice, and exercises universal dominion in the form both of light and heat. He shines as Mercury; burns and thunders as Jupiter. The earth is made to teem with living spirit. Afterwards the heavens seem to bury themselves in its bosom. All becomes fruit, harvest vintage. Then follows a new equilibrium, and sort of second Spring, more spiritual than the first, in the grave form of Autumn. The process completes itself as the full maturity of terrestrial life; which thus returns back again from its outward action into its own original stillness (the gloomy reign of Proserpine,) only to make room for a new circuit afterwards under the same form.

In all this, there was for the Pagan mind a reference to the general conception of religion; that is, to the idea of *redemption*, as a process of deliverance from the powers of darkness and evil, which are felt universally to press upon the life of man in this world. To be real, this process must begin in the soul, must be spiritual. For the natural religious consciousness, however, it has its mirror in the life of nature as set forth by the process of the solar year. This, unfortunately, has no power to bring into view the positive supernatural realities, through whose power alone it is possible for the symbolized idea to become fact. That requires the historical intervention of a higher life, in the form of revelation. Having no such help, Paganism could never make its escape, as we have seen, from the sphere of nature. Matter and spirit fell confusedly together. All ended in a purely physical mythology, of the most fantastic and barren kind.

But shall we say, for this reason, that there is no connection really between the course of nature and the process of redemption in its true and proper form? By no means. The Pagan feeling on this subject was right, although dark and confused. The enigma did not lose its sense, nor cease to be a real prophetical burden for the human soul, merely because it came to no true interpretation. There exists, we have good reason to believe, a real analogy or parallelism, between the natural year and the system of redemption, in virtue of which, the last is typified by the first throughout, in a way far beyond all simply fanciful conceit. This can be fully apprehended, of course, only where the system of redemption itself comes fully into view; that is to say, only in the full light of Christianity, the end and completion of religion in every other view.

PART 1: CULTURE, PHILOSOPHY, ETHICS, ANTHROPOLOGY

[The Jewish Sacred Year]

The *Jewish* religious year was of a vastly higher order than the Pagan.[13] It was established by divine law, and rested immediately on historical facts, miracles of grace actually wrought in the world, and serving to reveal in the bosom of nature the intervention of a supernatural life. What nature struggled in vain to reach and express without revelation, was here to a certain extent supplied by its presence. With such higher character, Judaism necessarily stood opposed, at the same time, to the way in which the religion of nature was carried out by Paganism, involving, as this did, an apostacy which changed the truth of God into a lie, and drew after it all the abominations of idolatry. Its mission was, to prepare the way, on the one hand, for the coming of Christ, and on the other, to turn the human mind away from nature, that it might be fixed upon itself and made to know its own need of redemption. Both these purposes called for laws and positive institutions. Nature was not to be set aside; it was still, with all its yearly changes, a manifestation of divine powers; but it must not be confounded with the notion of these powers themselves. The symbol must pass into a better sense, by being made an allegory of history, an image in the world of sense representing God's actual dealings of grace with men.

The peculiarity of the Jewish year is, that it has not only yearly but *weekly* sacred days. It starts from the *Sabbath*, as the centre which rules and conditions its whole construction. It has yearly festivals also; but they are made to hinge on the weekly institution, as the primary power. This of itself had a tendency to break the force of the simply physical year, as it ruled the religious thinking of the Pagan world; and contributed very materially, beyond all question, to raise the idea of worship out of the element of nature into a different and far higher region, that of history, God's supernatural conduct and providence employed for the redemption and salvation of his chosen people.

But with all this care taken to guard against perversion and abuse, regard was still had to the natural year, as being of itself in true harmony and correspondence with the life of religion in man. This appears at once from the fact, that the great annual festivals were made to fall in with those parts of the year precisely, which corresponded parabolically with their proper signification and sense. They were not founded directly on these; all of them rested on grand historical facts, which they served to commemorate from age to age; but these facts themselves had been so ordered, as to concur with the times in question. The epochs of history fell in wonderfully with the epochs of nature. The Passover, commemorating the deliverance of Israel from the bondage of Egypt, answered in this way to the time when the whole Pagan world celebrated the renewal of nature through the return of spring. So in like manner, Pentecost and the Feast of Tabernacles, resting on the memory of other dispensations of God's favor towards the same people, had their significant analogies also in the positions assigned to

---

13. [For a more recent scholarly account, see Stern, *Calendar and Community*.]

them in the natural year, which it is by no means difficult to discover and understand. Have we any right to look upon this as a merely, accidental, and therefore unmeaning concurrence? We think it must be plain to all, that we have not. It must be viewed as belonging to the plan of the world; and goes to confirm what we have already said, that according to this plan a real original and necessary parallelism holds between the two systems of nature and grace, in virtue of which the first is to be regarded as everywhere adumbrating the sense of the second.

[The Christian Sacred Year]

True, the sacred year of the Jews was made to commence in the Spring; differing in this respect from that of Paganism, which dated from Autumn or the first part of Winter. But then the system took no account comparatively of the period between Autumn and Spring. This suited the character of the Old Testament dispensation, under which the process of grace preparatory to redemption lay, back of the fact itself, in a sort of hidden mystery, like the powers of nature during the reign of Winter. With the coming of Christ, this mystery clears into magnificent light. The process of redemption is found moving its course, first in his person, in order that it may break forth in the full victory of Easter as a fact accomplished for the world at large. Here the mystery of Winter finds at last its proper spiritual meaning. The year of religion falls back again in its order, and is brought thus once more to commence where the year of nature also of right begins. Only the correspondence is now such as to light up the movement with celestial splendor from beginning to end. Nature appears transfused throughout with spirit and life. Grace reigns triumphant over all the months and seasons.

This is the *Christian Year*. The universal character of Christianity, as compared both with Judaism and Paganism, is fulfilment or completion. Judaism stood far above all simply natural religion. It was a system of revelation. It rested on supernatural history. Still it was only a relative and partial exhibition of the truth in such form, the shadow of blessings to come. For this reason, it could never do full justice to Paganism. It was the direct, broad contradiction of the wholesale lie into which this had fallen, by substituting mere nature for the proper idea of God; but such contradiction had no power of itself to harmonize with their true end the principles and tendencies, out of whose corruption the falsehood sprang. There was, accordingly, an antagonism here, that called for reconciliation in a still deeper and more comprehensive sphere of life. In the fulness of time this appeared in Christ, the Word made Flesh. "He is our Peace," says the Apostle,[14] the end of all previous discords; the last full sense of man's relations to himself, the world and God. In Him, Judaism was fulfilled and Paganism explained. Christianity is the absolute truth, in which both the types of the one and the dark endeavors of the other, are satisfied and brought to rest. This general character appears

---

14. [Eph 2:14.]

in its universal constitution; and so among other things embraces also the structure of its sacred year. Religion in the form of nature, and religion in the form of history, come here to a perfect understanding and agreement. The constitution of the world is sanctified, by being taken up into the constitution of grace. The year of religion is now truly and properly a *Church Year*.

If the correspondence between the historical facts of Judaism and the course of nature be striking, as we have just seen, the correspondence between the great facts of Christianity and the same course of nature is more wonderful and instructive still; showing most manifestly the presence of a common thought in both, by which the one is to be considered a true type and figure of the other. Who in his senses can imagine, that no such significance attaches to the time of our Saviour's death and resurrection; or that the Festival of Easter has been determined thus, by a fortuitous correspondence only, to the period of the vernal equinox? Who that thinks can fail to see in the Festivals of Ascension and Pentecost, a similar relation to the triumphant progress of the sun towards the summer solstice, and the changes which are brought to pass by it on the earth? And so much being allowed, who can have a right to consider it an empty play of fancy only, when the months going before Easter, from the beginning of Winter, are taken to symbolize the process of redemption, as carried forward previously to that point in the mystery of Christ's own person; or when the months following Pentecost, on to the close of Autumn, are made to symbolize in like manner the progress of the same work, as carried forward subsequently in the life of the Church? In both cases, what a field for pious contemplation! Analogies, of the most interesting sort, thicken upon our view, just in proportion as we give the subject our earnest attention.

Our limits will not allow us to enter here, into any more particular consideration of the organism or structure of the Christian Year. The object of this article has been merely to bring into view the general nature of the conception, and the grounds on which it properly challenges our religious respect.

Those who fancy, that the use of any such scheme of worship is without reason or meaning, or who, it may be, permit themselves even to stigmatize it as an unprofitable and hurtful superstition, betray at once their own want both of earnestness and knowledge.[15] There is in truth a deep foundation for it in the constitution of nature, and it falls in with the universal spirit of religion. Christianity differs from other religions here, only by passing beyond them in the fulness and perfection of its image. The feeling which justifies and prompts the conception of a religious year, found nothing to counteract it in the coming of Christ, but much to favor it, much to assist and carried it forward in the right direction. The great facts of Christianity served powerfully of themselves to call it into exercise. The lively apprehension of them which prevailed in the mind of the early Church, made it impossible to avoid so natural an

---

15. [See the editor's introduction describing the work Nevin was doing on the Liturgical Committee of the German Reformed Church at the same time he wrote this essay.]

observance. The Christian year, accordingly, is as old as the Christian Church itself. What an amount of interest do we not find clustering around the solemnity of Easter, from the earliest times! The idea of such a year, and its general outline, leaving room of course for much filling up afterwards in its details, entered into the universal thinking of the Church, and conditioned the entire system of its worship, from the beginning. It did so, moreover, spontaneously, and by the necessity, as it were, of an inward law. It came not primarily by art and reflection, but grew forth rather as a natural product from the Christian consciousness itself. And so, we may add, its true sense and force can never be fully measured by any merely logical standard. It speaks, not just to the understanding of man, but far more to his feeling and heart. Its voice is for the deep places of the soul, where life reigns as a full power back of all partial forms of expression. Hence the authority it has carried with it for the Christian world, through all ages. Only since the Reformation, has the attempt been made, not by Protestantism in general, but by a fragmentary section of Protestantism, to set aside the whole conception and practice as a "relic of superstition," serving to encumber more than to assist the proper spirituality of Christian worship. But of what force can any such isolated judgment be, over against the united mind of the Church in all past centuries, backed as this is, at the same time, by the religious constitution of the world, and by its religious history also, in the most universal view? The exception is too violent, too monstrous, we may say, to stand.

Any attempt to set aside the proper Church Year, involves necessarily an attempt also to substitute for it some other scheme of religious solemnities contrived to serve the same end; for there is a natural instinct or impulse here, which will not allow itself to be long absolutely disregarded. But no such scheme can ever carry with it anything like the same worth for the ends of religion. Every other scheme must be in comparison mechanical merely and superficial. All experience goes to show, that no system of Christian instruction, no method of Christian worship, can ever be so effective for Church purposes, as that which is based on the proper use of the ecclesiastical year. As it is always an unnatural, so it is always a poor and hurtful exchange, where this is given up in favor of any other arrangement; and it is certain that no such new arrangement can be able to compete successfully, in the long run, with the infinitely more respectable authority of the older system.

The principle of the Church Year is of vastly more consequence than is commonly imagined. It goes deep into the very heart of Christianity. So it must do, necessarily, if we have now taken any right view at all of its nature. There is a most intimate connection between the use of such a scheme of worship and the practical apprehension of the great facts of Christianity in their own proper form. Puritanism,[16] in this case, pretends to be more spiritual than the old Church faith, as it does also in so many other cases, by setting its worship above all outward forms and conditions. But such

---

16. [For what Nevin meant by "Puritanism," see the essay "Evangelical Radicalism," document 10 below.]

spiritualism is something very different from real spirituality. It is only in keeping with the general character of the Puritanic heresy—the heresy which disowns the Apostles' Creed, and turns the idea of the Church, as there taught, into an obsolete "figment."[17] The difficulty with this whole habit of mind, is its want of power to receive and hold the historical truths of the Gospel, not as ideas, merely, but as realities and facts. It is sadly infected throughout with the old leaven of Gnosticism, which is ever in disguise again nothing else but the secret virus of Rationalism.[18] It is but the natural result of such character, that it should be unfriendly to the Church festivals, and to the whole idea of the Church Year; and so, on the other hand, it may be assumed, that this ancient system cannot anywhere go into general disuse or neglect, without serious loss to the true interests of religion just in the direction of such Gnostic or Rationalistic thinking. The system forms a necessary part of the churchly scheme of Christianity. Where it has fallen to the ground, there can be no right sense of the Church, no proper faith in the holy sacraments, no sound liturgical feeling, no active sympathy with the grand facts which are set forth in the Creed, no firm hold on the abiding power of these facts, as an order of grace moving onward in sublime correspondence with the order of nature to the end of time.

---

17. [Nevin argues for this claim in "Puritanism and the Creed," MTSS 8:103–21.]

18. [Nevin interpreted American sectarianism as an exemplification of Gnosticism in *Antichrist*, MTSS 5:177–232.]

PART 2

The Church Question and Supernaturalism

Edited by Patrick Carey

General Introduction, Part 2

John Williamson Nevin was, in my view, the foremost American Protestant theologian of the church and the sacraments in the antebellum period. He based his theology on his examinations of the Scripture, the confessional statements of the Protestant Reformation, the Apostles' Creed, the history of the early church and the Church Fathers, and the works of some nineteenth-century German historians and theologians. Yet, his theology was not well received by his contemporaries and had little influence on American Protestant theology in the nineteenth century. The mark of a good theology, however, is not always how well it is received in a particular era, but how it relates to the sources, the history of Christianity, and the experiences of the Christian people.

During the 1850s, Nevin's emphasis on the Christological and Incarnational foundation of the church, its organic, communitarian, and developmental nature became the basis for his critical essays on persons and movements in Part 2.[1] He opposed the popular Protestant and Catholic supernatural rationalism that had arisen in England and the United States since the eighteenth century, even as he defined his position on the church and the supernatural. By 1850, Nevin was speaking and writing for an American audience that had developed very different conceptions of what constituted theology and the church, what shaped Christian life and holiness, and what counted for Christian experience. The remaining essay in this part, "Man's True Destiny" (1853), describes the goal of Nevin's emphases: the supernatural end of all human life, an end that is ever-present in history.

Nevin worked out his theology in an American religious context that was overwhelmingly Protestant, and by the 1850s that Protestantism was split into various denominations and varying theological orientations.[2] The theological and doctrinal

---

1. Nevin, "Brownson's Quarterly Review," 33–80; "Brownson's Review Again," 307–24; "The Anglican Crisis," 359–98; "Evangelical Radicalism," 508–12; "Natural and Supernatural," 176–210.

2. For an excellent introduction to the theological diversity in the antebellum period, see Holifield, *Theology in America*, 159–513. Holifield divides his study into two major divisions of theology: those Protestant theologies that were influenced by Baconian science and the British and Scottish Enlightenment (especially Scottish Common Sense Realism), 159–394; and those theologies that were outside the Calvinist or Reformed traditions (Lutherans and Catholics) and those Protestant theologies that were influenced by British Romanticism (especially Samuel Taylor Coleridge's *Aids to Reflection*) and by German post-Kantian and idealist philosophies, 397–504.

differences that characterized the antebellum period were substantial. The Universalists attacked the Calvinist doctrine of predestination and the Unitarians assaulted the orthodox doctrine of the Trinity and Christology. Harvard came under the influence of Bostonian Unitarians, and Princeton retained much of the Calvinist orthodoxy, while Andover and Yale sought to revise elements of the Puritan-Calvinist inheritance.

Nevin, educated under Charles Hodge at Princeton, considered the Puritan-influenced theologies of the church to be inadequate and in fact submissive to the democratic élan of the American political system. Even the more orthodox Calvinist Hodge had what Nevin considered a "very low" conception of the church. In 1857, Nevin published two review articles on Hodge's commentary on the Epistle to the Ephesians in which he criticized Hodge's view of the church as "grossly dualistic" by denominating the outward visible church as an external community and the true church as the invisible one, which included only those individuals elected by God from the beginning. For Nevin, Hodge's visible church accounted for little as a means of grace and as an article of faith. Hodge's Puritan view of faith, too, was "really independent of the doctrine of the church altogether."[3] Nevin periodically made similar charges against others he designated as modern Puritans.

By the 1830s, three other developments—Transcendentalism, Evangelicalism, and the Oxford Movement—within American Protestantism reinforced the diversity and changed the dominant Protestant orientation. In New England, Ralph Waldo Emerson (1803–82), attacked the inductive and rationalistic approaches to religion within Unitarianism itself, which gave rise to American transcendentalism. The Boston Transcendentalists began to emphasize Christianity as a life force rather than a doctrine, and intuition rather than the inductive method as means for grasping the universal reality hidden within the concrete expressions of the Christian tradition.[4] Some Unitarians went even further. Theodore Parker (1810–60) claimed that Christianity could exist even if "Jesus of Nazareth had never lived."[5] Although Nevin shared something of the romantic and idealist philosophy of the Transcendentalists, he never accepted the radical rationalist consequences of their thought. His own understanding of the church was far removed from the subjective idealism that characterized their approaches to religion.

In the 1830s, too, Charles Grandison Finney (1792–1875), educated by a Presbyterian pastor in upstate New York, rose to prominence in the United States as an effective revivalist preacher and theologian. Like eighteenth-century American Protestant evangelicals, Finney focused upon the necessity of conversion, but he stressed, as never before, the importance of the right use of revivalist means to bring sinners to an

---

3. Nevin, "Hodge on the Ephesians," in *One, Holy, Catholic, and Apostolic, Tome Two*, MTSS 7:62–125, quotes on 62, 77, 78, 121.

4. Besides Coleridge's *Aids*, the influences here were the French Eclecticism of Victor Cousin and the philosophy of Immanuel Kant and German idealist philosophies.

5. In his essay *A Discourse on the Transient and the Permanent*; see Collins, *Theodore Parker*, 90.

experience of grace and conversion. His revivalist tactics, as articulated in his *Lectures on Revivals of Religion* (1835), shocked some Orthodox Presbyterians, particularly those at Princeton, but those lectures responded well to the American democratic *élan* and contributed to the dominance of Evangelicalism in the antebellum period. Finney's emphasis upon free will and the protracted revival meetings separated him significantly from Calvinists who highlighted divine agency and moral incapacity in the conversion process. Finney stressed human effort to such an extent that some from the Puritan tradition considered him a Pelagian or semi-Pelagian. He did represent, however, something of the Arminian side of the Reformed tradition. His style of Protestantism attracted large crowds to his revivals and resonated with those smaller colonial denominations (e.g. Methodists and Baptists) whose church membership grew to such an extent that they became the largest Protestant denominations by 1860. Long before the 1850s, Congregationalists and Presbyterians "could no longer claim predominance in membership."[6]

Nathan Hatch has examined these Evangelical-revivalist-populist traditions in the United States in his *The Democratization of American Christianity* (1989). He argued that the Evangelicals, Mormons and others had no problem breaking with the dead past: outdated traditions, creeds, theologies or an educated clergy. American democratic citizens lived in a new order of the ages (*novus ordo seclorum*), and by the use of their own reason they could discover Christ and the means of salvation in the Bible. They created a populist theology that appealed to common sense, the right to think for oneself, and the individual's personal experiences of conversion. By the 1850s, this mass religious movement dominated the American Protestant landscape and was the primary target of Nevin's theological criticisms. He did not oppose free will, democracy, or the subjective dimensions of evangelical theology, but he did oppose theologies of the church that were founded on them.

In the 1830s, moreover, the Oxford Movement (also referred to as Puseyism or Tractarianism) in England drew some attention in the United States and had some effects especially on the Protestant Episcopal Church. That movement in the Anglican Church was almost the polar opposite of the American Evangelical movement in the United States. In England, it was led by a few prominent Oxford Anglican divines: Edward Bouverie Pusey (1800–82), John Henry Newman (1801–90); John Keble (1792–1866); and Richard Hurrell Froude (1803–36). They called for a historical reexamination of the early church traditions and a restoration of traditions that had been lost after the Protestant Reformation but were a part of the seventeenth-century Anglican tradition that had been forgotten or neglected in recent times in the Church of England. In 1833 and for a few years thereafter they protested that the Anglican Church had become too submissive to the British Parliament's interferences in purely ecclesiastical matters. In 1833, for example, John Keble opposed the British

---

6. Holifield, *Theology in America*, 10.

government's decision to reduce the number of Anglican dioceses in Ireland.[7] British opponents of the Oxford movement charged that the leaders of the movement were attempting to reform the Anglican Church on Catholic, not Anglican, theological principles. By 1845, a few leaders of the movement, including most significantly John Henry Newman, converted to Catholicism. The conversion of Newman and a few others severely curtailed the movement.[8]

In the United States, the Oxford movement also had a divided response. That was especially evident in the Protestant Episcopal Church, which was already by the 1830s divided into High Church and Evangelical Episcopalians. Bishop Benjamin T. Onderdonk (1791–1861) of New York, Bishop George W. Doane (1799–1859) of New Jersey, Samuel Seabury (1801–72), editor of *The Churchman*, and Bishop Levi Silliman Ives (1797–1867) of North Carolina were aligned with the High Church party and were sympathetic to some Oxford movement reforms. Some of the High Church party, including Bishop Ives and more than thirty Episcopal priests, eventually converted to Catholicism.[9]

The Protestant Evangelical Episcopal party, however, opposed the movement, seeing in it the danger of Romanism. In the Episcopal Evangelical party, Bishop William Meade (1789–1868) of Virginia and Bishop Charles Pettit McIlvaine (1799–1873) of Ohio became the most forceful opponents of Oxford. The Virginia Protestant Episcopal Convention, under Bishop Meade, condemned Oxford Divinity as heresy.[10] McIlvaine thought that the Oxford movement was "a systematic adoption of that very root and heart of Romanism, whence has issued the life of all its ramified corruptions and deformities."[11] Bishop John Henry Hopkins (1792–1866) of Vermont compared the Protestant Episcopal Church with the primitive church in 1835, arguing that the primitive church (i.e. the church before the Nicene Council) was nearest to the Apostolic pattern still evident in the Protestant Episcopal Church in its acceptance of the

---

7. Newman considered Keble's "National Apostacy" sermon on July 14, 1833 the beginning of the Oxford Movement. See Newman, *Apologia Pro Vita Sua*, 50.

8. On the Oxford Movement, see Faught, *Oxford Movement* and Ker, *John Henry Newman*.

9. Holifield, *Theology in America*, 238. Ives converted to Catholicism in 1852, and in 1854 he published an apologia for his passing to Rome: Ives, *The Trials of a Mind*. Clarence A. Walworth, a pro-Oxford participant and a former student in the Episcopal General Theological Seminary in New York published in 1895, after his 1845 conversion to Catholicism, an account of *The Oxford Movement in America* that had influenced General Theological Seminary. George D. Wolff, a graduate of Marshall and an admirer of Nevin, wrote an account of "The Mercersburg Movement" in 1878, after his 1871 conversion to Catholicism, outlining grounds on which Protestantism and Catholicism might unite. On the movement of Episcopalians and other Protestants to Catholicism between 1840 and 1858, see also Gorman, *Catholic Apologetical Literature*, 123–47, and Lincoln A. Mullen, "The Contours of Conversion," 1–27.

10. On this, see Kenrick, *The Catholic Doctrine of Justification*, 7.

11. McIlvaine, *Oxford Divinity*, 6. Vanbrugh Livingston, an Episcopal layman, published his *Remarks on Oxford Theology* (1841), 81, to warn the public "against the errors of his [McIlvaine's] theological system." Two years later he converted to Catholicism.

divine institution of the episcopacy, among other apostolic teachings.[12] "Innovation has been the plague of the Church of Rome" and has always been the parent of heresy and schism.[13] Many of the episcopal attacks on Oxford were also attacks on Catholicism, and some American Catholics responded.

Since McIlvaine's work badly misrepresented Catholic doctrines on faith, justification, baptism, and the sacraments in general, the Catholic Bishop of Philadelphia, Francis Patrick Kenrick (1796–1863), responded with *The Catholic Doctrine of Justification* (1841). Kenrick agreed with the Oxford divines and Newman in particular that justification was the communication of a divine gift whereby the soul was justified and made holy. Christ was the cause of justification, but a living faith formed by charity, was the necessary condition of its fruitfulness and not the cause of the forgiveness of sin and the creation of a new heart. Faith for Catholics, moreover, was not a naked assent. On the gratuitousness of justification, Kenrick asserted, there was "more misunderstanding than difference."[14]

By the 1850s and until the Civil War, immigrations primarily from Ireland and Germany brought thousands of Catholics into a predominantly Protestant country, increasing the religious and theological diversity. Between 1800 and 1860, the Catholic population increased from about 50,000 (1% of the total American population) to about 3,000,000 (about 11% of the population), making Catholicism one of the largest denominations in the country by 1860, although still a minority within the American religious community.[15] Catholics, too, spread geographically across the country, establishing the first diocese in Baltimore in 1790, and creating thirty-three new dioceses from the east coast to the west coast by 1853.

This numerical and geographical expansion stirred up the inherited Puritan hostilities to Catholicism and produced what Ray Billington has called *The Protestant Crusade*. That crusade was widespread. Protestant elites as well as ordinary pastors and lay and clerical journalists published popular attacks on Catholic moral life, doctrines, and Catholic understandings of religious liberty and the relationship between

---

12. Hopkins, *The Primitive Church*, viii–ix, 1–12, 237–66, 312–15.

13. Hopkins, *History of the Confessional*, 271. Hopkins belonged to that part of the high church party that emphasized the unity of the Episcopal Church with the primitive church and who separated himself from those in the high church party that were sympathetic to the Oxford movement, emphasized the indefectibility of the church, and were open to much in the Catholic tradition. Since the 1830s, Hopkins had not only opposed the Oxford movement, but also attacked various doctrines and practices within the Catholic Church. On Hopkins, see Mullin, *Episcopal Vision*, 101, 157–59. For a Catholic assessment of Hopkins' *Confessional* and many other Episcopal works on that Catholic practice, see [Brownson], "Sermons on the Obedience of Faith," 448–65.

14. Kenrick, *Catholic Doctrine of Justification*, 30, 63, 93–94. Bishop John Hughes of New York also focused on the doctrine of justification, especially in the Anglican Church, in his 1843 introduction to Livingston's *An Inquiry into the Merits*, v–xx. Hughes highlighted the social as well as doctrinal consequences of the Catholic doctrine of justification. Livingston was an Episcopal layman who by 1843 had converted to Catholicism.

15. Almost a million Catholic immigrants came during the 1850s alone. These statistical estimates come from Gerald Shaughnessy, *Has the Immigrant Kept the Faith?*, 145.

church and state. The American public was bombarded with conspiracy theories about the growth of Catholicism in the United States and its threats to the nation's moral character and political liberties.[16] Theologians agreed, with Charles Hodge of Princeton asserting "Romanism is immeasurably more dangerous than infidelity"[17] and Horace Bushnell, when examining the westward movement, thought "Our first danger is barbarism—Romanism next."[18] In antebellum America it would have been difficult for Protestants to escape the pervasive influence of anti-Catholicism.

While American Catholics were occupied with establishing the institutions that supported their spiritual life, they did not neglect their theological traditions. The dominant theological tradition in the period was apologetical, defending and vindicating Catholic doctrines and practices that were being attacked in the Protestant press and in public religious debates that periodically occurred. The most systematic and best informed American Catholic theologian of the period was the Roman-educated Bishop Francis Patrick Kenrick. His systematic theologies were written for seminarians in Latin, while his apologetical works in English were generally more irenic than polemical. For example in his *Catholic Doctrine on Justification* (1841), he tried not to overemphasize the differences that separated Protestants and Catholics on the issue and recognize agreements. He was hard on those who intentionally or unintentionally misrepresented Catholic doctrinal statements and practices.[19] Some of the Catholic defensive responses could be particularly obnoxious to Protestants because of their failure to find anything good in the Protestant Reformation or in the Christian life and teachings of the various Protestant traditions.[20] The religious polemics in antebellum America created an atmosphere that led to conspiracy theories and to the misrepresentation or falsification of each other's respective traditions. Real differences existed, but many times those differences were exaggerated or misrepresented, reflecting the tribal religious mentalities of the day.

Nevin worked out his theology in this antebellum American Protestant-Catholic religious atmosphere. He distinguished his Reformed theology from much of the Princeton theology he had learned in his early years. As he studied sixteenth-century Protestant sources, he developed a theology of the church and sacraments that did not fit into the parameters of the American Protestant theologies of the elite schools nor into the popular theologies of Evangelical revivalism. His theology—which matured at Mercersburg in the 1840s and 1850s within the German Reformed Church, the Seminary, and Marshall College—was a minority theological tradition in American

16. E.g., Lyman Beecher's *A Plea for the West*; Maria Monk's *Awful Disclosures*; Samuel F. B. Morse's *Foreign Conspiracy* and his *Immigrant Dangers*.

17. [Hodge], "Critical Notices," 626. Also Hodge, *Systematic Theology* 3:545.

18. Bushnell, *Barbarism*, 5.

19. On misrepresentations, see, e.g., Kenrick, *Catholic Doctrine of Justification*, 132–33.

20. Bishop John Hughes of New York, for example, revealed much of his anti-Protestantism in *Decline of Protestantism*, as did Brownson in many of his articles in *Brownson's Quarterly Review* especially in his early years as a Catholic convert (1844–55).

Protestantism.[21] The documents published in Part 2 of this volume focus primarily on Nevin's theology as he articulates it in response to the theologies of the Catholic Orestes Brownson (1803–76), the Oxford movement, Evangelical (primarily Baptist) theology, and the thought of Horace Bushnell (1802–76).

Nevin and Brownson

Nevin published two articles on Brownson.[22] The first was Nevin's examination and critique of articles Brownson had written in his *Quarterly* from 1844 to 1849. The second was a response to Brownson's analysis and critique of Nevin's first article and a reiteration of what he had argued in the first article. It is not clear why Nevin singled out Brownson's works, but by 1850 Brownson was considered by many as the most forceful and articulate defender of Catholicism in the United States. In his youth Brownson had been associated with the Congregational Church and had experienced a Methodist revival in Vermont. In his late teens, he joined the Presbyterian Church for a brief period and then became a Universalist minister. In his late twenties, he identified himself for a short period of time as a religious skeptic and departed from all organized religion, siding with social reformers like Fanny Wright (1795–1852). In the early 1830s, he became a Unitarian minister and in Boston joined the Transcendentalist Club. In the late 1830s and early 1840s, he came under the influence of Victor Cousin's (1792–1869) eclecticism and then Pierre Leroux's (1797–1871) doctrine of life by communion. Leroux's philosophy eventually moved him toward a Catholic understanding of the church and the sacraments. In 1844, then, he converted to Catholicism and began publishing his *Quarterly Review* (1844–64; 1873–75). Because of Brownson's frequent religious and ideological changes, many in Boston considered him unstable and unpredictable. James Russell Lowell made this sentiment famous in his *A Fable for Critics* (1848):

> [H]e shifts quite about, then proceeds to expound
> that 'tis merely the earth, not himself, that turns round,
> and wishes it clearly impressed on your mind,
> that the weather-cock rules and not follows the wind; . . . .[23]

After his conversion and for the next decade, Brownson departed from the theology that had moved him toward Catholicism and defended a post-Cartesian rationalist Catholic apologetic that he later claimed was a "method of authority."[24]

---

21. Major influences include Romanticism, the German historian of Christianity, Johann August Wilhelm Neander, the theologian Friedrich Schleiermacher, the philosopher Immanuel Kant, and forms of German philosophical idealism.

22. Nevin, "Brownson's Quarterly Review," 33–80; "Brownson's Review Again," 307–24.

23. Lowell, *A Fable for Critics*, 33–34.

24. On Brownson's intellectual journey, see Carey, *Orestes A. Brownson*, and especially 389–401 for an extensive bibliography on Brownson. On the "method of authority," see [Brownson], "Reunion

Nevin was well aware of Brownson's reputation as a chameleon and of his attempts "to gulp a Gregorian bull," as Lowell put it.[25] Nevin, however, considered this characterization of Brownson as a great disservice to the man and to his Catholicism. Brownson was a hard-hitting polemist and Nevin had a certain respect for his forthrightness. Brownson's tone and language was bold and confident, but also overbearing and harsh and condescending.[26] Nevin considered the dismissal of Brownson to be a major mistake. Like Brownson, Nevin had opposed the "pseudo-protestant" crusade against Catholicism as a form of bigotry that accepted "every sort of polemical assault upon Rome, without proof or examination."[27] That whole campaign against Catholicism was also inconsistent with religious liberty. He also shared Brownson's criticisms of the sect mentality in the United States, the recurring divisions in the Protestant religious denominations, and his emphases on the church catholic, the sacraments, the early creeds, and the apostolic succession of the church throughout history.

Nevin, however, had his difficulties with Brownson's presentations of each of these agreements and with what he, like most of English-speaking Protestants, referred to as "Romanism." Protestants, both ordinary and educated, saw Romanism as the total corruption of Christianity and its complete separation from the Bible and primitive Christianity. Nevin distinguished between Romanism and Catholicism. For him, catholic was one of the foundational marks of the church and it referred not only to numerical universality but to an organic wholeness. The church was commissioned to carry that organic life of Christ to all throughout history and gradually to deepen that life in individuals and in the social order. The extensive and intensive universality of Catholicism was realized in history, but was also eschatological and could never be

---

of All Christians," 4–5. The post-Cartesian Catholic rationalist apologetic, analogous to an early nineteenth-century American Protestant apologetic influenced by Scottish Common Sense Realism, was an attempt to demonstrate the reasonableness of faith in response to the rise of the physical sciences and Enlightenment philosophies. Catholic apologists of this era tried to demonstrate respectively the possibility, necessity, and factual existence of supernatural revelation and the church. In this regard, the New Testament miracles were viewed as incontestable supernatural facts that provided evidentiary proof of Catholic Christianity. Many early nineteenth-century Catholic bishops and priests were educated in this tradition and apparently Brownson was influenced in this direction by John Bernard Fitzpatrick (1812–66), the auxiliary bishop (1843–46) and later bishop of Boston (1846–66).

25. Lowell's reference is to a papal bull, that is, an official papal decree or letter that has a seal (bulla) attached to it to authenticate the document.

26. Nevin, "Brownson's Quarterly Review," 37.

27. Nevin, "Brownson's Quarterly Review," 36. Nevin repeatedly criticized the "Protestant Crusade." In the early 1840s, Joseph F. Berg, pastor of the Reformed Church in Philadelphia and editor of the *Protestant Banner*, a particularly bitter anti-Catholic paper, assaulted Nevin for his tendency to Romanism. Berg accused Nevin of teaching that the Catholic Church was part of the church of Christ. Nevin responded with a series of articles arguing that a church might be impure, have errors and corruptions and little piety in it, and still be a Christian church. See Nevin, "Pseudo Protestantism," August 13, 20, 27, 1845; September 3, 10, 1845. Appel, *Life*, 398–401, gives a brief summary of these articles. Nevin also criticized Nicholas Murray's (alias Kirwan) polemical assault on the Catholic Church and Bishop John Hughes as part "of the whole popular style of Protestantism." Nevin, "Kirwan's Letters," 229–63, quote on 231.

completely realized in any historical period or identified with any single institution.[28] Catholicism, existed within Romanism, even though inadequately. In May 1849, Nevin gave a fuller definition of what he meant by Catholicism:

> Catholicism stands in the sense of the outward and objective in Christianity, as a supernatural constitution at hand in the world under a historical form; the idea of the Church, as the bearer of heavenly powers; submission to authority; resignation of individual judgment and will to the apprehension of the divine rule, embodied and made concrete in the Church as a whole; sympathy with the symbolical, mystical, sacramental interest in religion.[29]

Romanism in fact referred to the corruptions and errors that Rome had accumulated over time. Romanism has made claims to its Catholicity and universality, but, Nevin asserted:

> Whole territories and spheres of human life here, have never yet been brought to any true inward reconciliation and union with the life of the Church. Romanism has pretended indeed to bring them into subjection; but so far as the pretension has yet been made good, it has been ever in a more or less outward and violent way only; whereas the problem from its very nature requires that the relation should be one of free loving harmony and not one of force.[30]

Nevin's quarrel with Brownson and more generally with modern Roman Catholicism was clearly stated in the thesis of his first article on *Brownson's Quarterly Review*: "Unitarianism and Romanism are contrary poles of Christianity, freedom and authority, the liberty of the individual subject and the binding force of the universal object, carried out each, by violent disjunction from the other, into nerveless pantomime and sham."[31]

Nevin believed that truth could be found in extreme positions and that opposing or contrary positions needed to be reconciled or brought together. His extensive examination of Brownson's works, however, did not aim to reconcile opposing religious systems of thought. In the 1840s he had criticized the wrong-headedness in modern American Puritanism and Evangelicalism. Now he was similarly criticizing extremes in Brownson's defense of Catholicism. Thus, he was arguing that his own position was *not* tending towards Romanism, as his opponents claimed.

---

28. On this, see Nevin, "Catholicism," in MTSS 7:11–32.

29. Nevin, "Kirwan's Letters," 262. The German Catholic theologian Johann Adam Moehler, known to Nevin, expressed a similar view of Catholicism in Möhler, *Symbolism*, 253–71, especially 254 where Moehler calls the church "the Christian religion in its objective form—its living exposition."

30. Nevin, "Catholicism," MTSS 7:21. See also Nevin, "The Lutheran Confession," 471, where Nevin is speaking of reconciling "the Protestant principle, as a whole, not with Romanism as it now stands, but still with the deep truth of Catholicism, from which, by abuse, the Roman error springs."

31. Nevin, "Brownson's Quarterly Review," 33.

Nevin's primary charges against Brownson can be briefly summarized. First, Brownson separates the objective dimension of Christianity from its subjective dimension. He emphasizes the outward and authoritative dimensions of the church to such an extent that he fails to bring it into harmony with the freedom and capacity of the human mind and will to appropriate the outward in any internal way. His view of Christianity is extrinsic, formal, and without consideration for the activity of the intelligence and will of the individual believer. Romanism puts an end to all private thinking in religion.

According to Nevin, the same disconnect is evident in Brownson's distortion of the relationship between the supernatural and the natural. The supernatural is everything with him, but it is abstract, extrinsic, purely outward, and formal. It is outside of the individual and outside of history; it is an abstract supernaturalism, characteristic of Romanism. Likewise, faith is separated from or disjoined from reason. The motives of faith are based on external evidences or on the authority of the church. This discounts the internal motives that engage the mind and heart of the believer to freely accept and respond to the supernatural object. The motives of credibility, for Nevin, are internal as well as external; the believer is drawn to the supernatural because it appeals to what is lacking in the natural and engages the mind and heart. Brownson instead makes the individual believer a passive recipient of a foreign action and thereby wrongs human nature. "The mind must fulfill its mission, not by following blindly a mere outward force of any sort, but by the activity of its own intelligence and will, both as general and individual."[32]

Brownson's view of the church emphasized its supernatural authority. The church or general life of Christianity, Nevin charged, was identified with the teaching magisterium (the *ecclesia docens*). For Brownson, the church was perfect from the beginning, coming like Minerva from the brain of Jupiter.[33] It was unaffected by human errors, sins within the church, or historical and cultural changes, and he denied explicitly any notion of historical development.

Like many American Catholic leaders, Brownson followed Jacques Bossuet (1627–1704), the bishop of Meaux, who held that truth was unalterable; only error and heresy changed: "Variations in faith a certain proof of falsehood."[34] The church for Brownson was a supernatural fact, *semper eadem*. Nevin, too, accepted the fact that the church was always the same, but what was always the same was the supernatural life that was organically and historically present throughout the ages, not simply an outward institution divorced from nature and history. Brownson's view of the church was ahistorical, and in fact "Romanism is, by its very constitution, unhistorical."[35] Nevin's criticisms of Brownson were analogous to arguments he had been making

---

32. Nevin, "Brownson's Quarterly Review," 56.
33. Nevin, "Brownson's Quarterly Review," 47.
34. See Bossuet, *History of the Variations*, 1.
35. Nevin, "Brownson's Quarterly Review," 46.

in the 1840s against those Protestants who had interpreted Christianity through the lenses of Baconian science and Scottish Common Sense Realism. The major difference between the Catholic Brownson and the major American Protestant apologetic was the fact that Brownson made the church authoritative while the Protestants made the Bible the supernatural object, and Protestants made the individual rather than the authoritative church the interpreter of the supernatural.[36]

In his interesting conclusion to this article on Brownson, Nevin acknowledged that he was dealing with two extremes: the modern Puritan forms of Protestantism and Catholicism, both suffering from the same illness, rationalism. The two extremes needed to be reconciled, but, he admitted, in the present circumstances he did not know how to bring the two extremes together into a dialectical unity: "The best preparation for solving the problem of the age, is to be well satisfied that the problem really exists, and so to feel earnestly that it calls for a solution."[37] Nevin had been describing this need for reconciliation for some time. In November of 1849, for example, when he forecasts his article on Brownson, he told the readers of his *Review* that he had within his own bosom the two systems that needed to be brought into some kind of harmony:

> The hardest Puritan we have to do with always, is the one we carry by birth and education, in our own bosom. But the misery of it is, for our quiet, that the Catholic is there too and will not be at rest. . . . We are deeply persuaded, too, in the case before us, that Catholicism and Puritanism both enter of right into the constitution of Christianity, and that neither can legitimately exclude the other. The problem of their true and proper union, is indeed one of no common difficulty; the great problem, as it would seem, for the new era of Christianity which is now so generally supposed to be at hand.[38]

Brownson responded to Nevin's critique with a defense of his own positions and a criticism of Nevin's interpretations of the Christian tradition.[39] Unfortunately, at least from my perspective, Brownson was too polemical to meet Nevin's concern for reconciliation. Brownson's apologetic at the time of his review was what he would later call a "method of authority" primarily focused on providing evidence for the church's authority. In the introduction and conclusion to his essay, Brownson acknowledged his respect for Nevin as a man, a scholar, and a writer. He also reminded his readers

---

36. For a description of this abstract (or, rationalistic) supernaturalism, in critique of "Puritanism," see Nevin et al., *Born of Water*, MTSS 6:76n23. Holifield explains its application in the apologetics of Evangelical theology, *Theology in America*, 186–90.

37. Nevin, "Brownson's Quarterly Review," 80.

38. Nevin, "Puritanism and the Creed," 602; repr. MTSS 8:117.

39. [Brownson], "*The Mercersburg Review*," 191–228. Some of the major studies of Nevin's life and works present Brownson primarily from Nevin's critique and rarely examine Brownson's own works. See, for example, Nichols, *Romanticism*, 180–82; Wentz, *John Williamson Nevin*, 54–55, 57–58; Hart, *John Williamson Nevin*, 158–60.

that his criticisms were directed to Nevin's theological system, not to his person. Nonetheless Brownson's language was at times arrogant.

Brownson protested first against Nevin's charge that when Brownson went from Unitarianism to Catholicism he went from one extreme to another and was never able to reconcile freedom and authority. If Nevin would have read Brownson's early writings prior to his conversion he would have understood that Brownson never accepted the extreme rationalism and individualism of Unitarianism and that the key to his conversion to Catholicism was in fact his attempts to reconcile liberty and authority. However, Nevin never consulted or referred to these early sources.[40] Nevin in fact misrepresented Brownson (and more generally Catholicism) as separating liberty and authority.

Brownson called Nevin's system eclectic, meaning by that that Nevin sought, as he repeatedly noted, to reconcile opposites, especially "the liberty of the individual subject with the binding force of the universal object." The Catholic system, in Nevin's view, made these two opposites antagonistic and mutually destructive. In Brownson's interpretation of Nevin's charges, Brownson had placed Christianity as a supernatural object of faith outside of the subject, the supernatural wholly above the natural, and made faith the mediate rather than immediate apprehension of the truth. Nevin, in Brownson's opinion, went to the opposite extreme by placing the supernatural object of faith in the subject, failing to make the supernatural transcend the natural, and presenting faith as the immediate apprehension of the truth of Christianity.[41]

Some of Nevin's charges against Brownson's apologetic, it seems to me, are spot on. Brownson's system, Nevin correctly noted, was unhistorical, opposed to the idea of development. Brownson saw nothing good in the Protestant Reformation or in the post-Reformation Protestant developments. There was, moreover, some justification in Nevin's criticism that by separating nature and supernature, Brownson's apologetic made Christianity purely extrinsic, and authoritarian. These last charges, however, are exaggerations of Brownson's tendencies. Brownson protested, rightly I believe, that he never made the kind of abstract philosophical separations that Nevin found in his writings. The Catholic understanding that grace presupposes nature compensated for these distinctions. It sustains an intrinsic relationship between object and subject, super-nature and nature, faith and reason; it distinguishes these opposites without separating them. Faith, too, in Catholic theology was a gift of God (*donum fidei*, 1 Cor 12:9) and came to the individual subject as a revelation that did not depend on flesh and blood (Matt 16:17). Faith was not simply the result of the church's testimony, even though testimony was integral to faith, since faith comes from hearing (Rom 10:17).

Brownson made his own exaggerated charges against Nevin's theology. By uniting or trying to harmonize subject and object, nature and supernature, without making

---

40. See Carey, ed., *The Early Works*, vols. 6 and 7.
41. [Brownson], "*The Mercersburg Review*," 198–99.

proper distinctions, Nevin's principles led logically to pantheism and subjectivism.[42] Nevin rightly founded his theology on the doctrine of the Incarnation, but he interpreted it in the light of German pantheistic philosophies. Thus "Christianity is a new and higher life in the world, and that this new life is literally 'God entering into human nature.'"[43] The new creation, furthermore, "is indistinguishably the Incarnate God; and that we are Christians, are introduced into the Christian order, only by being literally, organically, physically, adunated [elevated] into his living substance."[44] Although Nevin upheld the objectivity of the object and asserted that faith did not create reality, the language he used with respect to what was real indicated to Brownson that the reality of the object depended on the immediate appropriation or apprehension of the subject. Faith had become for Nevin the immediate apprehension of Christ. In this, according to Brownson, Nevin destroyed the objectivity of the object and opened himself to the charge of subjectivism.[45] For Brownson, Nevin failed to give sufficient attention to the mediation of the object.

There were real differences in language and philosophies between Nevin and Brownson. Furthermore, they both extended the principles of the other to what each considered their logical consequences. Thus the differences were exaggerated. Nevin spoke in Romantic and organic categories (e.g. life, growth, development); Brownson in nineteenth-century post-Enlightenment Catholic rationalist categories (e.g., evidence, credibility, substance, universality, permanence). Nevin was influenced by post-Kantian German idealism, Brownson by an early nineteenth-century Catholic evidentiary tradition analogous to the Scottish and British evidentiary tradition.

Nevin's second article in response to Brownson's charges[46] legitimately defended himself against the accusations of pantheism and subjectivism and reiterated charges he had made against Brownson and Romanism. Nevin focused on what he called Brownson's dualism, but the substance of the charges remained the same. Brownson then responded a second time to Nevin's charges of dualism, but his arguments were similar to his first article on Nevin.[47]

If nothing changed in the debates between Nevin and Brownson, what consequence did the exchange have? It is difficult to find a direct causal relationship between

---

42. For various places where Brownson implies or makes this charge, see [Brownson], "*The Mercersburg Review*," 195–99, 205, 209–10, 216, 225–26. Hodge, "The Doctrine of the Reformed Church," 275, made analogous charges against Nevin's supposed pantheism.

43. [Brownson], "*The Mercersburg Review*," 195.

44. [Brownson], "*The Mercersburg Review*," 196.

45. [Brownson], "*The Mercersburg Review*," 206, where Brownson quotes Nevin's language: "'The word lives,' he says, 'and is word, only by faith.'" "'The existence of truth is objective, and in such view, of course, universal and independent of all private thought and will; but as thus objective, it must be at the same time subjective, must enter into particular thought and will, in order to be *real*'" (Brownson's emphasis). The two quotes are respectively from Nevin, "The Apostles' Creed," 209 (repr. MTSS 8:60) and "Brownson's Quarterly Review," 56–57.

46. Nevin, "Brownson's Review Again," 307–24.

47. [Brownson], "*The Mercersburg Review*," 353–78.

subsequent events in their lives and the debate. Nonetheless, immediately after the debate and for the next four or five years, Nevin ceased to make the charges against Catholicism (e.g. formalism, authoritarianism, blind faith, magical and mechanical interpretations of sacraments, and dualism—typical Protestant protests) that he had made in his exchange with Brownson. In 1852, moreover, Nevin wrote Brownson telling him that he no longer wanted to get into any public controversy, which he had "no heart for," with Brownson or any other champion of Romanism. "I find much of the truth and right on your side, and so much of the falsehood and wrong on ours." His difficulty with Protestantism, however, "is no positive conversion to Catholicism."[48] Within five years of the debate, moreover, Brownson gave up his former rationalistic apologetic and returned to a modified doctrine of what he once called "life by communion." It seems to me that his polemic with Nevin was one of the causes of this development in his life.[49]

Anglican Crisis

"The Anglican Crisis" in September 1851 was one of Nevin's major essays after his debate with Brownson.[50] James Hastings Nichols interprets the text as a turning point in Nevin's more favorable view of Catholicism during the next three years.[51] I don't see it so much a turning point but a continuation of the favorable views of Catholicism he had been articulating for a few years.[52] Nevin sought, even in his critique of Brownson's perspectives, a reconciliation of what some have called the Catholic substance and the Protestant principle. Protestantism was in fact the product of the old Catholic Church itself "and the very channel in which was carried forward the central stream of its history, the true significance of its life."[53] Protestantism was not, as some Anglicans and some in the American Puritan tradition claimed, the restoration of primitive Christianity. Protestantism was in continuity with Christian life that flowed through the historical Catholic community, despite its errors and abuses.

Nevin interpreted the "Anglican Crisis" as a fundamental problem for all Protestants. The debate over the Oxford Movement had been going on in the United States since the mid-1830s, but Nevin did not give it an explicit systematic response until 1851 after the so-called Gorham case in England. In 1847, the Anglican priest George

---

48. Nevin to Brownson, August 18, 1852, in Brownson Papers, University of Notre Dame Archives.

49. On this change, see Carey, *Orestes A. Brownson*, 193–281.

50. Nevin, "The Anglican Crisis," 359–98.

51. Nichols, *Romanticism*, 194–95. After Nevin's death, Schaff also said this essay—along with "Cyprian"—made a "wrong & reactionary turn" (unpublished letter to Theodore Appel, February 13, 1889, Schaff Papers, ERHS). See the analysis in Layman, editor's general introduction to *Born of Water*, MTSS 6:24–25.

52. See, for example, Nevin, "Kirwan's Letters," 237, 257–58; Nevin, "Short Notices," 153–56, a review of Wiseman's three-volume *Essays on Various Subjects*.

53. Nevin, "Kirwan's Letters," 258.

Cornelius Gorham (1787–1857) was nominated as vicar of the Anglican church in Brampford Speke in the diocese of Exeter. The bishop of Exeter, Henry Phillpotts examined him for the position and refused to appoint him because of his rejection of the doctrine of baptismal regeneration and his holding that by baptism infants do not become members of the Body of Christ, the church. Gorham then appealed to the ecclesiastical Court of Arches to overturn the bishop's decision. The Court sided with the bishop. Thereafter Gorham appealed to the Judicial Committee of the Privy Council, a lay civil court, which decided on 9 March 1850 that Gorham's position on baptism was consistent with the Anglican tradition and ordered the bishop to appoint Gorham as vicar. The civil court's decision angered Anglicans in the Oxford Movement, and many of them joined the Catholic Church, including Henry Edward Manning, a future Cardinal Archbishop in England.

Nevin protested against what he and others, British Catholics as well as some Tractarians, considered an abuse of civil authority and a lack of Anglican support for the independence of the church in matters that were exclusively doctrinal.[54] Nevin had high praise for the Catholic hierarchies in Ireland and England who solemnly committed themselves on the church's behalf "to the old catholic principle (very apostolic too, as it strikes us, both in sense and sound,) that powers and rights ecclesiastical, come not from kings or civil parliaments, but from the divine constitution of the church itself upheld and maintained by the perpetual presence of its own head."[55] Nevin wanted to call American Protestant attention to the Anglican crisis because he believed it had much to teach the Americans. Religious liberty of course protected the freedom of the American churches, but the Anglican crisis was about more than the independence of the church from political entanglements. It involved an understanding of baptismal regeneration, but even more so a notion of the church as the objective presence of the incarnate life of Christ, the sacraments in general as the means of salvation and holiness, and the apostolic succession of the ministry in the church.

Many of the Oxford dons who were participants in the Tractarian movement were students of the history of the church and especially of the early church. Unlike Anglicans and Puritan Protestants, who saw their own churches as a restoration of

---

54. The Catholic archbishop of Westminster, Nicholas Patrick Wiseman (1802–65), and John Henry Newman (1801–90) spread out the Catholic welcome mat for those Anglicans upset by the lack of Anglican support for church prerogatives. Even prior to the Privy Council's decision on the Gorham case, Wiseman protested against the state's involvement in matters that belonged to the church, saying that Anglicans made no clear reference to the true character of imperial and episcopal powers, especially when they clashed (as in the days of St. Chrysostom and St. Ambrose). See Wiseman, "Position of the High Church Theory," and, more generally, "The Catholic and Anglican Churches," in Wiseman, *Essays on Various Subjects*, 2:464–65, 203–62. Nevin was aware of Wiseman's essays and arguments. See his "Short Notices," 153–56. Newman also protested the Anglican Church's failure to uphold ecclesiastical doctrine and its submission to a governmental decision. He also noted that the Oxford Movement had no influence on the national church. See Newman, *Certain Difficulties*, 1:5, 8–12.

55. Nevin, "The Anglican Crisis," 382.

primitive Christianity, the Oxford dons understood the church as the continuation of the Incarnation over time and as continuous organic development of the Christian life, doctrine, and institutions. Nevin shared much of this framework: he saw the "Church as a living supernatural fact, . . . having its ground and force in the mystery of the Incarnation, according to the order of the ancient creed, and communicating to the marks and signs by which it is made visible every particle of virtue that is in them for any such end." The church question preceded the issue of baptismal regeneration and sacramental grace, the sacraments in general, and the Episcopacy or the ministry in general. "We must believe in a divine church, in order to believe in divine sacraments, or in a divine ministry under any form."[56] Both Nevin and Oxford dons were calling all Protestants to reconsider their inherent connection and continuity with the church of the ages and to transcend the sect mentality and their own exclusive claims to authentic Christianity.

The issue of baptismal regeneration, which occasioned the current Anglican crisis, presupposed a conception of the church as the bearer of the means of grace and the object of belief as was evident in the early creeds. Baptismal regeneration involved an understanding of sacramental grace as an "objective mystical and supernatural virtue."[57] Evangelicals thought baptism a mere outward sign of commitment, done because it was commanded in Scripture. Nevin denied this was the view of the magisterial Protestants or the ancient church, and saw Oxford as recovering this older understanding of the sacraments. However, Nevin thought the Oxford Movement dons in particular made too much of the divine institution and apostolic succession of the episcopacy. It was "a secondary and subordinate particular only, and by no means the central or main thing." What Nevin objected to most in the Anglican system of church government, whether low church or high church, was its support for episcopacy on the basis of an outward precept "rather than in the very bosom of the system itself."[58] In other words, how does episcopacy flow from the very life of the church itself?

The Oxford Movement raised the church question of the age and called for more attention to the substance of the catholic tradition. However, Nevin thought it did not go far enough to address the Protestant problem. It was incapable of reforming Protestantism in ways that could reconcile the benefits of the Protestant Reformation with those of the previous Catholic tradition. Thus, the end of "Anglican Crisis" echoed the conclusion of the first article on "Brownson's Quarterly Review." In the latter Nevin said there were truths in both extremes (the Roman emphasis on authority and the Evangelical stress on liberty) that needed to be reconciled "in a form of life which shall be the union of both."[59] In "Anglican Crisis," the Oxford Movement could never be expected to solve "the great church problem of the present time." The only

56. Nevin, "The Anglican Crisis," 377, 379.
57. Nevin, "The Anglican Crisis," 371.
58. Nevin, "The Anglican Crisis," 361, 375.
59. Nevin, "Brownson's Quarterly Review," 80.

solution to that question was to be found in "the idea of historical development" that acknowledged the earlier Catholic tradition and Protestantism as "a real advance on this [Catholic tradition] in modern times" while admitting the faults in both systems. He also argued that the present state of the church was "transitional only and interimistic." Following the German theologian Heinrich Wilhelm Thiersch (1817–85), the crisis could influence "true historical progress," Nevin argued, by transcending the faults and false views of both the Catholic Petrine and the Protestant Pauline traditions and by moving toward a new Johannine tradition that united the benefits of both into a new synthesis. That would preserve the "rich wealth of the old Catholic faith" and the improvements of the older Protestant tradition. In his theory of development, Nevin wanted to make Protestantism itself "the main though by no means exclusive stream, by which the general tide of the original Christian life is rolling itself forward."[60] Oxford and Anglicanism could not achieve this goal.

In the early 1850s, his articles began to sound to many Protestants as if he was moving toward Rome. In 1851 and 1852, he began a series of articles on "Early Christianity" and "Cyprian." Nevin argued that the Puritan and Evangelical forms were not, as claimed, the restoration of the primitive church and that the early church was more in line with Catholicism.[61] Brownson and a few others encouraged Catholics to read those articles and to pray for Nevin's conversion, believing that he was indeed headed to Rome. After abandoning his earlier Catholic apologetic, which he called the "method of authority,"[62] Brownson became progressively more positive about Nevin and the Mercersburg theology in the mid-1850s and throughout the rest of his life. In 1854, for example, he wrote that Nevin "is a man of great ability and earnestness, and as a scholar, as a logician, and as an original and vigorous writer, inferior to no Protestant divine in the country. His papers in the *Mercersburg Review* on *Early Christianity* and *St. Cyprian* are masterpieces of their kind, and indicate a mind of the first order."[63]

James A. McMaster, editor of New York's *Freeman's Journal*, published excerpts of Nevin's articles on "The Anglican Crisis,"[64] "Berg's Last Words,"[65] and "Cyprian,"[66] and

60. Nevin, "The Anglican Crisis," 395, 396, 398.

61. "Early Christianity was in its constitutional elements, not Protestantism, but Catholicism" (Nevin, "Cyprian," 561).

62. [Brownson], "Reunion of all Christians," 4–5. I believe that Nevin's criticisms of Brownson's earlier Catholic theology (1844–50) was one of the contributing factors in Brownson's change to a new synthetic approach to theology in the mid-1850s. On this, Carey, *Orestes A. Brownson*, 234–81.

63. [Brownson], "The Mercersburg Hypothesis," 254. For Brownson's other positive assessments of Nevin's writings, see also "Church Organism," 112–13; "Christianity or Gentilism?," 17; "Union with the Church," 1–16.

64. "The Anglican Crisis," *New York Freeman's Journal*, August 9, 1851, 3, 6.

65. "Dr. Nevin and Dr. Berg," *New York Freeman's Journal*, June 19, 1852, 5.

66. "Dr. Nevin on the Theology of St. Cyprian," *New York Freeman's Journal*, August 14, 1852, 6, quoting from Nevin, "Cyprian," 357–64; and "The Mercersburg Review: July No. Dr. Nevin on Cyprian," *New York Freeman's Journal*, August 21, 1852, 1, 4, quoting from Nevin, "Cyprian," 365,

told his Catholic readers that those articles "convince us that the day is not distant when another triumph will be added to the faith in the conversion of this profound and learned scholar." He also asked "the prayers of all our pious readers, that God would be blessed to give to this distinguished and honest scholar the grace of conversion, and the gift of faith."[67] Francis Patrick Kenrick, the archbishop of Baltimore (1851–63), also paid particularly close attention to Nevin's writings, and in the fourth edition of his *Primacy of the Apostolic See Vindicated* (1855), he quoted extensively from some of Nevin's most recent works. In its preface, moreover, he acknowledged: "The many striking avowals made by Dr. J. W. Nevin, late President of Marshall College, Mercersburg, Pennsylvania, are freely quoted in support of the authority of the Catholic Church and of the Holy See, although it may perplex the reader to understand how he should still remain out of our communion."[68]

In 1852, in the midst of writing his third article on Cyprian, Nevin wrote privately to Brownson, thanking him and other Catholics who were praying for his conversion to Catholicism and telling him that his third article on Cyprianic Christianity was about to be published and that it presented Cyprian's doctrine on the church, a doctrine that went back to the Apostles.[69] Nevin, however, could not reconcile that doctrine with the cause of the Protestant Reformation, and especially with the American Evangelical conception of the church. He found much truth on the Catholic side and much falsehood on his side. Although he had many difficulties and doubts with respect to the current Protestant understandings of the church, he was not prepared to bring those doubts to an end. Nevin's difficulties with American Protestant conceptions of the church did not, however, make him doubt the benefits of Protestantism, rightly understood. Like John Henry Newman, Nevin could say "Ten thousand difficulties did not make one doubt."[70] Nevin was attracted to the Catholic understanding of the church, but he still had a hard time reconciling Catholicism in its modern form with the "powers and privileges" claimed by the early church. He also told Brownson

---

366–67, 370–71, 376–77.

67. See "The Mercersburg Review," *New York Freeman's Journal*, August 21, 1852, 1, 4. McMaster and Archbishop John Hughes of New York were among those American Catholics who took an interest in Nevin's writings and anticipated his conversion. See, for example, Nevin to McMaster, June 8, 1852, in McMaster Papers, University of Notre Dame Archives; Nevin to McMaster, July 14, 1852, in Brownson Papers, University of Notre Dame Archives; and Nevin to McMaster, February 26, 1853, in McMaster Papers, University of Notre Dame Archives.

68. Kenrick, *The Primacy of the Holy See Vindicated*. Kenrick quoted several times Nevin's articles on "Early Christianity," 56, 87, 103, 145, 148, 240, 406, 407; on "Cyprian," 36, 65, 101, 118, 150, 150, 219; and on "The Anglican Crisis," 226. Kenrick began writing his *Primacy* in a series of letters to Bishop John Henry Hopkins, Episcopal bishop of Vermont, which was published as *The Primacy of the Apostolic See, and the Authority of General Councils*. In 1845, then, he published the first edition of *The Primacy of the Holy See Vindicated*. Thereafter he revised and enlarged the text several times; it continued to be republished several times in the nineteenth and twentieth centuries, and was translated into German in the 1850s.

69. The reference is to Nevin, "Cyprian," 417–52.

70. Newman, *Apologia Pro Vita Sua*, 238.

that his studies of early Christianity were historical, not dogmatic, statements. He could not understand, too, how Brownson could continue to deny Newman's doctrine of development, especially in light of the difficulties and hesitancy that current Catholics were having in bringing forth the article on the Immaculate Conception of the Blessed Virgin Mary. If the article was always a part of the explicit faith, as many Catholics believed, why any hesitancy in bringing it to a definition?[71] Nonetheless, it was clear to American Catholics and to many of his fellow Protestants that his early 1850s essays clearly indicated his leaning toward Catholicism. Brownson responded with two letters, trying to make Nevin comfortable in moving toward Catholicism.[72] In 1852, though, Nevin was not ready to go to Rome, and did not in fact do so.

Evangelical Radicalism

In the midst of his historical examinations of primitive Christianity, Nevin also wrote a short article on "Evangelical Radicalism."[73] The article was the most devastating criticism of what Nevin called the "Baptistic spirit." That spirit, which identified the divine element in religion with the outward precepts of the Bible, "has ever shown itself prone to make common cause in the end with all sorts of rationalistic radicalism in its open assault on the mysteries of Christianity." By focusing on the Bible as a mere outward or legal institute, the Baptist system had become another form of legalism that led to a mechanical view of Christianity, treating the letter of the Bible before the life that flowed into it. The Baptist system was unchurchly and unsacramental.[74]

The Baptist denomination was one of the largest Protestant denominations in the United States by the 1850s, and Nevin saw it as "very perfection and *ne plus ultra* [most extreme example] of evangelical religion." That system needed to be brought before the "bar of the ancient system" of Christianity where it was judged to be out of touch with the primitive churchly and sacramental view of Christian life. Nevin argued in "Evangelical Radicalism" that "we must break" with this modern Puritan system or else break with the whole of Christianity of the first ages.[75] Nevin's thesis reflected his recent historical studies of early Christianity as well as his more general hostilities to what he had repeatedly called modern Puritan Evangelicalism.

By making the Bible the law of the church and private judgment, even if enlightened by the Holy Spirit, its authentic interpreter, Baptists had separated the Bible

71. Nevin to Brownson, August 18, 1852, in "Brownson Papers," University of Notre Dame Archives. In 1854, after consulting theologians and bishops around the world, Pope Pius XI defined the doctrine of the Immaculate Conception of Mary, meaning that she was freed from original sin from the time of her conception.

72. Brownson to Nevin, August 23, 1852; August 28, 1852, in Brownson Papers, University of Notre Dame Archives.

73. Nevin, "Evangelical Radicalism," 508–12.

74. Nevin, "The Anglican Crisis," 375, 376, 395.

75. Nevin, "Evangelical Radicalism," 510.

from the life of the historical church and the creeds, exaggerated the Protestant sense of liberty, and fostered a spirit of independence and individualism that was contrary to the Bible's own sense of the church's unity as the body of Christ. In the end, Nevin charged Baptists with a form of supernatural rationalism, a criticism that he had also made against Brownson and modern Catholicism.

Man's True Destiny

During the early 1850s as Nevin continued these battles, he began to separate himself from his activities in the German Reformed Church. In 1851 and 1852, he resigned as professor of the Mercersburg Seminary, editor of the *Mercersburg Review*, and president of Marshall College. These resignations worried some of his friends in the German Reformed Church, and some believed that he was headed to Rome, as a few of them had predicted even in the 1840s. In 1854, on a trip to Germany, Philip Schaff told a German audience that "not only his opponents but also some of the friends of Dr. Nevin have entertained the fear that he might submit to the claims of Rome, and there find rest for his troubled spirit." Schaff went on to say that Puritanism drove Nevin to this state because of its failure to regenerate itself in line with the churchly and sacramental realities of the Christian tradition. Nevin, nevertheless, had a clear understanding of the weaknesses of Rome, and thus he would not be drawn to Rome.[76] Schaff was correct. Nevin had difficulties with much of American Protestantism and had hoped for a regeneration of it along lines he had indicated in his articles in the *Mercersburg Review*, but he had all along believed that Protestantism was a developmental advance over Catholicism. He did not believe that a reconciliation between Protestantism and Catholicism was possible in the current circumstances and was willing to wait for that to happen in the future. His basic loyalties were to the German Reformed Church.

Nevin's resignations did not prevent him from taking care of the German Reformed institutions that he served. He continued, for example, to shepherd the union of Marshall College with Franklin College in Lancaster. He was also invited to give the Baccalaureate Address to the first graduating class of the new Franklin and Marshall College in August 1853. That address, "Man's True Destiny," reflected Nevin's hopes that the graduating seniors would have been taught to examine their lives and the society in light of their eternal destiny. The talk articulated theological themes that Nevin had been teaching for the past two decades: individual freedom and autonomy, human nature's yearning for fulfillment beyond itself, an openness or capacity for religion that needed to be brought forth, the necessity and value of faith, and a focus on the "actual

---

76. Appel, *Life*, 416. Appel was here translating Schaff's talks that were published as *Amerika* (1854), which included a chapter on Nevin. The English edition of *America* (1855) did not contain the chapter Appel had quoted from the German edition.

presence of the supernatural as a real force in the world."[77] The Commencement address was a substantive nineteenth-century theological treatise and was intended not only for the seniors but also for those citizens in Lancaster and Mercersburg who were members of the local communities and of the German Reformed Church.

Bushnell, Nature and the Supernatural

Since 1852 Nevin had been living in retirement from his previous official functions within the German Reformed Church, but he continued publishing articles in the *Mercersburg Review*, serving periodically in the church, and on occasions lecturing and teaching at the Franklin and Marshall College in Lancaster. In 1859, on the brink of the Civil War, Nevin reviewed Bushnell's *Nature and the Supernatural, as Together Constituting the One System of God* (1858).[78]

Nevin's review reiterated themes he had been developing throughout the 1850s. He and Bushnell shared some of the same misgivings about American Protestant theology at the end of the 1850s. Both were disturbed by what they saw as a rising confidence in the physical sciences and in the human capacity for perfectibility, which both men criticized as manifestations of naturalism or supernatural rationalism. Both agreed that the Transcendentalist emphasis on God in nature, Theodore Parker's view of Christ as a good but dispensable teacher, and the American Protestant propensity to organized voluntary societies for the reform and perfection of society were all signs of an increasing loss of faith in the supernatural.

Nevin had more in common with the theology of Horace Bushnell than he did with most other American Protestants. He was sympathetic with Bushnell's understanding of the church's role in Christian life and the relationship between nature and the supernatural. Nonetheless, there were vast differences between Nevin's and Bushnell's conceptualizations of nature, sin, the supernatural, and the church, as was already evident in Nevin's earlier reviews of Bushnell's *Discourses on Christian Nurture* (1847) and *God in Christ* (1849).[79] Nevin's response to Bushnell's *Nature* can be better understood within the context of Nevin's earlier reactions to Bushnell's first published book, *Discourses on Christian Nurture*.[80] Bushnell's book has been considered the forerunner of the modern twentieth-century Protestant religious education and the Sunday School movement. Bushnell saw in Samuel Taylor Coleridge's understanding

---

77. Nevin, "Man's True Destiny," 512.

78. Nevin, "Natural and Supernatural," 176–210.

79. For a republication of Nevin's reviews on *Discourses*, see Nevin, "Educational Religion," MTSS 6:38–63. See also Nevin, "*God in Christ*," 311–12.

80. For good introductions to Bushnell's *Discourses*, see Edwards, *Of Singular Genius*, 86–94, and Layman, "Nevin and Bushnell," MTSS 6:34–37. For a good introduction to the 1860 edition of Bushnell's *Christian Nurture*, see Mulder, "Introduction," vii–xxx. Mulder, however, pays no attention to Nevin's review of that work.

of language and nature a way of escaping the divisions in New England theology.[81] Nevin considered Bushnell's *Discourses* a theological move in the right direction as his 1847 review articles on "Educational Religion" in the *Weekly Messenger of the German Reformed Church* indicated.[82] Those articles also outlined his major agreements and corresponding disagreements.

Nevin agreed with Bushnell's basic thesis: "A child is to grow up a Christian," or as the 1860 edition articulated it: "That the child is to grow up a Christian, and never know himself as being otherwise."[83] Like Nevin, Bushnell opposed the mechanics and machinery of revivalism, although they both valued an emphasis on conversion. Conversion, however, was not just a radical and sudden change brought about by an exercise of free will, reflecting the extreme individualism in American society, but an organic communal, ecclesial, and developmental formation and education of the child in the Christian tradition.[84] Christian nurture started, as the older Puritans held, with infant baptism.[85] Bushnell asserted against the Baptists that infant baptism was a presumptive entrance into the Christian life. Children, as all human beings of whatever age, lived in the context of families and within the church, which helped to form children into Christian adults who could be led to a conversion experience that would make them full members of the church, rather than presumptive members.[86] Nevin shared this acknowledgement of infant baptism and a child's gradual education and formation within the church (a view held in common with the older, pre-revivalist, tradition of Puritanism).

Nevin, however, was not entirely satisfied with Bushnell's approach to Christian nurture. Bushnell's views were based, Nevin believed, too much on the natural constitution of human nature, the family, and the church, and not enough on the church and the constitution of grace.[87] Bushnell did not take into account, moreover, the radical consequences of original sin and the disabilities that were the result, making human beings incapable of rising above their own condition.[88] Bushnell's understanding of baptism, moreover, was deficient because he did not consider it a divine sacrament

---

81. On the influence of Coleridge, see Cherry, *Nature*, 161–69.

82. Nevin, "Educational Religion," MTSS 6:38–63.

83. Bushnell, *Discourses on Christian Nurture*, 6–7, and Bushnell, *Christian Nurture*, 10.

84. Nevin, "Educational Religion," MTSS 6:45–47.

85. Nevin, "Educational Religion," MTSS 6:42.

86. "Presumptive membership" was a technical term, especially used by theologians who adhered to federalism: any baptized person was "*presumed* to be Christian and potentially the subject of God's electing and converting grace, but no one could claim certain knowledge of this election: thus the truly regenerate were 'invisible'" (Nevin et al., *Born of Water*, MTSS 6:159, emphasis original; see the longer discussion, 156–60).

87. Nevin, "Educational Religion," MTSS 6:50. See also Layman, "Nevin's Holistic Supernaturalism," 195–97.

88. Nevin, "Educational Religion," MTSS 6:50.

that actually communicated grace.[89] While he valued the role of the Christian family and the Church in the process of Christian nurture, he failed to see the church itself as "a new supernatural constitution," a means of grace, and an object of faith as in the creeds of the early church.[90]

In his review of "*God in Christ,*" Nevin asserted:

> We believe him [Bushnell] to be wrong. But we are very sure, at the same time, that he is struggling in his spirit towards great truth, and that the things he is warring with in the actual theology of New England, are no spectres [sic] simply of his own imagination, but very substantial realities at bottom, that greatly need in some way to be dragged into the light and properly exposed.

Bushnell was dealing with the primary issues of the age: "The constitution of Christ's person, and, as determined by this, the true idea also of the Christian Church." Yet Nevin had problems with Bushnell's Christology, the doctrine of the Atonement, sin, his opposition to dogmatic statements, the church, and the creed. "Bushnell is not prepared to do justice to the historical objective character of Christianity, as it meets us in the Universal Church."[91]

Nevin had similar reactions to Bushnell's *Nature and the Supernatural*. By the late 1850s, Nevin considered Bushnell one of the most creative theologians in the United States. Nevin appreciated especially Bushnell's attempt to relate the natural and the supernatural in the "One system of God." Bushnell was trying to restore belief in the supernatural dimension of Christianity without denying the legitimate role of nature. For Nevin, however, Bushnell's revisions dismissed or left out too much of the theological substance of the Reformed side of the Protestant Reformation. Nevin singled out four major problems with Bushnell's theology: his understandings of nature, sin, the supernatural, and the church. Bushnell, following Coleridge, had an excessively restricted notion of nature, defining it as "a chain of causes and effects, or the scheme of orderly succession, determined from within the scheme itself."[92] For Nevin nature included human nature with its intelligence and free will, which had the capacity to act upon the natural chain of causes and effects. Nature, moreover, was itself "a divine revelation. A supernatural presence underlies it, and works through it, at every point."[93] Human nature, however, was affected by the fact of sin, the "disorder which underlies the universal nature of man as it now stands" and could not be removed by humanitarian remedies.[94] Bushnell's theory of sin made the Fall and sinning the result

---

89. Nevin, "Educational Religion," MTSS 6:58–60, 63. On this, see also Payne, "Nevin on Baptism," 127–31.

90. Nevin, "Educational Religion," MTSS 6:56, 60–62.

91. Nevin, "*God in Christ,*" 311–12.

92. Bushnell, *Nature and the Supernatural*, 37.

93. Nevin, "Natural and the Supernatural," 203.

94. Nevin, "Natural and the Supernatural," 191.

of a primitive condition that made sinning inevitable even though nature itself was not its positive cause. Such a notion of original and actual sin, Nevin asserted, was a naturalistic explanation of what was a fundamental mystery. Bushnell and Nevin, however, agreed that their understandings of sin called for a supernatural remedy.

Bushnell then defined the supernatural as that which is "not in the chain of natural cause and effect, or which acts on the chain of cause and effect, in nature, from without this chain."[95] Nevin said that made the supernatural extrinsic to the natural, and even though Bushnell put the person of Christ at the center of his conceptualization of the supernatural, he failed to understand the full significance of the Incarnation. The Incarnation brought "the presence of a new supernatural life in the world" and was the "organic root . . . of all true revelation from the beginning of the world." Bushnell's extrinsic supernaturalism failed to allow "any real union with the sense of the natural in the way of faith."[96]

Bushnell also failed to acknowledge the full significance of the Incarnation in the doctrine of the church. The church was the organic continuation of Christ's life in history, bringing the supernatural and the natural into real union. For Bushnell, as for many American Protestants, the church was a positive institution, a voluntary human community, where the gospel was preached and heard, but it was not, as it was for Nevin, a supernaturally established body that communicated the means of grace and was an object of faith, as it was in the ancient Christian creeds and in the church Fathers.

Conclusion

By the Civil War, Nevin had mapped out the contours of his own Mercersburg theology. Many of his articles throughout the 1850s repeated his emphases on the historical, developmental, organic, objective, and supernatural dimensions of Christian life that had been preserved in the church catholic, even though the full objective and subjective dimensions of that life were not always preserved in harmony throughout history. Nevin's interpretation of the Reformed tradition had minimal support within or influence on the antebellum American Protestant denominations that were significantly aligned with American democracy. Since the 1960s, however, Nevin's theology has received much more sympathetic scholarly attention than it had received in the 1850s.

---

95. Bushnell, *Nature and the Supernatural*, 37.
96. Nevin, "Natural and Supernatural," 188, 203, 204.

DOCUMENT 7

"Brownson's Quarterly Review"

Editor's Introduction

During the 1840s Nevin had been developing his organic, incarnational, and developmental theology of the church and his understanding of the relationship between nature and the supernatural. For Nevin the church and sacraments were the objective bearers of Christian consciousness and of the presence of Christ in history. He critiqued the Protestant sect-mentality predominant in the United States for viewing the church as a collectivity of individual wills rather than a communion in the body of Christ. During the 1840s, Nevin developed this theology through critiques of revivalism (*Anxious Bench*, 1843–44), evangelical sectarianism (*Antichrist*, 1848 and "The Sect System," 1849)[1] and the reigning American Puritan view of the sacraments. According to *Mystical Presence* (1846), the Eucharist was not a mere sign relying on the subjective faith of the believer for its efficacy. Rather it provided a real mystical union with the humanity and person of Christ.[2]

In the next decade, Nevin engaged with several interlocutors to clarify his understanding of the relationship between Christ and the church, between the objective and subjective dimensions of Christianity, and between nature and the supernatural. The first was the Catholic Orestes A. Brownson (1803–76).[3] Nevin sympathized with the Catholic emphasis on the church and the sacraments and forcefully opposed the "Protestant Crusade" against Catholicism that had asserted itself in the United States

---

1. These three texts are in Nevin, *One, Holy, Catholic, and Apostolic*, Tome 1, MTSS 5:27–103, 165–232, 238–71.
2. "The participation is not simply in his Spirit but in his flesh also and blood. It is not figurative merely and moral, but real, *substantial* and *essential*." Nevin, *Mystical Presence*, MTSS 1:48, emphasis original. Nevin's analysis of the modern Puritan view is presented in *Mystical Presence*, MTSS 1:92–137. He thought the modern view of the sacrament tended to divorce the incarnate life of Christ from the atonement. Nevin, "The Doctrine of the Reformed Church on the Lord's Supper," MTSS 1:240–41.
3. Nevin, "Brownson's Quarterly Review," "Brownson's Review Again."

since the 1830s.[4] Nonetheless, he demonstrated in his two essays on Brownson's theology that his own Reformed theology did not lead to Rome, as some like Charles Hodge of Princeton had charged.[5]

Brownson had had some limited contact with the Mercersburg theology prior to 1850. In 1845, shortly after leaving his position as a Unitarian minister and converting to Catholicism, he published in *Brownson's Quarterly Review* a short notice of Philip Schaff's *Principle of Protestantism*. In the review, Brownson promised to make a lengthier report on Schaff's *Principle* because it was "a work of some ability." He never did so, however. The review acknowledged that Schaff, following Neander, argued that revelation was given "in the form, not of *doctrine* but of *life*." It was an argument Brownson himself had made in an article he wrote on life by communion in 1842 in opposition to Theodore Parker. Although Brownson saw the value of what Schaff had done, his review was negative, condescending, and polemical, as were many of his reviews of Protestant works during the 1840s.[6]

Brownson acknowledged Schaff's *Principle* again in 1846 when Brownson was attacking John Henry Newman's theory of the development of doctrine. Both Newman and Schaff had adopted "very nearly the same fundamental principles, but one concludes in favor of Protestantism, the other of Catholicity."[7] Brownson had opposed the theory of development throughout the 1840s, and Nevin criticized Brownson's position in 1850 as one of the issues that separated Nevin from the Catholic tradition.

In 1847, Schaff wrote to Brownson, asking him to review Nevin's *Mystical Presence* (1846) and his own *What is Church History?* (1846) because, Schaff noted, the Mercersburg theology had received very little notice in New England. Because of Brownson's support of the church and his criticisms of Protestants whose only rule of faith was the Bible and private judgment, Schaff believed that Brownson was open to a dialogue with Mercersburg, would give a substantive analysis of the two texts, and would like both texts because of their criticisms of popular Protestant evangelicalism and the "hard things" Nevin had to say about Puritanism.[8] Brownson, however, did not review these texts and there is no reason given for the failure.

Nevin had been reading Brownson's *Quarterly* after the latter's conversion to Catholicism, and in 1850 he published two extensive critical reviews of Brownson's

---

4. Billington, *The Protestant Crusade*.

5. Hodge, "Doctrine of the Reformed Church," 270 and 273, said that Nevin's views on the sacraments and the church were not Reformed teachings. His understanding of the Eucharist should be placed between the Romanist and Lutheran doctrines, and his doctrine of the church as the mystical body reflected the fundamental error of the Romanists. Nevin had made clear in his *The Mystical Presence*, MTSS 1:162, that he accepted neither the Catholic doctrine of transubstantiation nor the Lutheran doctrine of consubstantiation.

6. Schaff, "The Principle of Protestantism," MTSS 3:546–47. See also, [Brownson], "Parker's Discourse," 385–512.

7. [Brownson], "Newman's Development of Christian Doctrine," 351.

8. Schaff to Brownson, February 8, 1847, in Brownson Papers, University of Notre Dame Archives.

works. Brownson responded in his *Quarterly* with an equally extensive review of many of Nevin's *Mercersburg Review* articles. Nevin then replied to Brownson's critique, and for all practical purposes, that ended the public debate, even though Brownson published a second article reiterating his former critique.[9]

Brownson's articles (1845–49), which Nevin critiqued, reflected a post-Cartesian Catholic apologetic that Brownson had accepted after becoming a Catholic.[10] Years later, he gave up that post-Cartesian apologetic, which he called a "method of authority"; in 1862, he outlined what that method meant. The method emphasized the motives of credibility that were based on the authority that God had delegated to the Catholic Church. It was a strictly logical method, but it "has practically very little, if any, efficacy, in convincing non-Catholics of the truth of our religion. It silences, but it does not convince." It is an inadequate apologetic because it does not present truth in its unity and universality and is extrinsic in that it must live and operate "in the convictions of all Christians." Truth is above us and is ours "only as it lives in our convictions, and informs our lives." Brownson, like many other converts to Catholicism, was not led to the Catholic Church by this method, even though many converts used the method after their conversions.[11] Brownson's 1862 assessment was similar to Nevin's 1850 critique of Brownson's works.

Nevin argues in his examination of Brownson that "Romanism," one of the extreme contrary poles of Christianity, exaggerates the role of authority, the binding force of the universal object, without reference to freedom or the liberty of the individual subject, which Unitarianism, the other extreme of Christianity, overemphasizes. Authority in Brownson's perspective was so disjointed from liberty that it tended to distort the Christian tradition, though it manifested (in the extreme) a valid dimension of Christianity. Nevin's thesis is a caricature of the longer Catholic tradition, but Nevin finds solid evidence for it in Brownson's post-conversion articles (1845–49).

Nevin made six charges against Brownson's theology that were central to his overall thesis. First, Brownson's one-sided emphasis put an end to "all private thinking in religion" by reducing everything to an external, supernatural revelation and authoritative church. Such a view did a fundamental wrong to the human

---

9. The four articles are, in order: Nevin, "Brownson's Quarterly Review," 33–80; [Brownson], "Reply to Mercersburg," 191–228; Nevin, "Brownson's Review Again," 307–24; and [Brownson], "The Mercersburg Theology," 353–78.

10. The post-Cartesian Catholic apologetic, analogous to an early nineteenth-century American Protestant apologetic influenced by Scottish Common Sense Realism, was an attempt to demonstrate the reasonableness of faith or the compatibility of faith and reason in response to the rise of the physical sciences and Enlightenment philosophies. Both versions of this apologetic tried to demonstrate respectively the possibility, necessity, and factual existence of supernatural revelation and the church. In this regard, the New Testament miracles are viewed as incontestable supernatural facts that provide evidentiary proof of Catholic Christianity. This was similar to eighteenth-century Catholic Scholasticism, under which many Catholic priests and bishops in the United States were educated.

11. [Brownson], "Reunion of all Christians," 4–5.

constitution because it allowed no room for the law of freedom and the personal subjective appropriation of faith. The human mind "must fulfill its mission, not by following blindly a mere outward force of any sort [Bible or Church], but by the activity of its own intelligence and will, both as general and individual."[12] Brownson makes the individual a passive recipient of a foreign action. Second, he denied or failed to recognize the unity of subject and object by overemphasizing the role of the objective and the general to the exclusion of the subjective and the activity of the intelligence and will of the believer. Third, he reduced the church to the teaching magisterium (*ecclesia docens*) and thereby almost identified the general life of Christianity with the church's ministry. What Brownson does with the church, many American Protestant apologists do with the Bible, making the church (not the Bible) the rule of faith. Fourth, he disconnected the supernatural from the natural, making the supernatural abstract and extrinsic to the natural and placing the supernatural outside the course of history. Fifth, he confuses and distorts the relationship between faith and reason because his motives for faith are extrinsic and have no relationship to what really appeals to or moves the believer's mind and will. Although Brownson's emphasis on the *donum fidei* (the gift of faith) modifies somewhat this criticism of extrinsicism, Nevin admits it does not erase the criticism because for Brownson the motives for faith have little to do with the object of faith. Faith arises from something entirely extrinsic to the mind and to the object of faith. Faith is thus limited to an intellectual assent to a doctrinal proposition defined by the church. Sixth, throughout Nevin argues that Brownson is unhistorical. He sees no good in the Protestant Reformation (and especially in the post-Reformation movements), has no understanding of the development of the church, and presents the church as unaffected by historical and cultural changes. For him, the church is the same in every age, unchanged like Minerva from the brain of Jupiter.[13] "Romanism," Nevin asserts, "is by its very constitution, unhistorical."[14] Brownson has little understanding of the human, sinful, and historical side of the church and is unwilling to acknowledge the wrongs of the past, thereby making the church an abstraction. In this he is very much like those American Protestants who separate the Reformation from the pre-Reformation church and believe they are reproducing the primitive Christian community.

Nevin's charges against Brownson arise from his own organic, incarnational, developmental, and dialectical view of Christianity that he also used against those American Protestants who were more influenced by the Scottish Common Sense tradition than they were by the Romantic and Hegelian philosophies of the early nineteenth century. Both pseudo-Protestantism and Romanism were absorbed in rationalism and extrinsicism. Nevin wanted to avoid both extremes because the truth

---

12. Nevin, "Brownson's Quarterly Review," 56.

13. Nevin, too, admits that there is in the church something that is unchanging, but he identifies the divine life in the church as that which is *semper eadem* (always the same).

14. Nevin, "Brownson's Quarterly Review," 46.

was not in either alternative. The union of both pseudo-Protestantism and Romanism was needed, but, he admitted, he had no answer for how to unite the two in the current atmosphere in the United States.

Brownson's Quarterly Review.

We are not among those who consider O. A. Brownson, Esq., a mere weathercock in religion, whose numerous changes of faith are sufficient of themselves to convict his last position of falsehood and folly.[2] We can see easily enough in all his variations, a principle of steady motion in the same general direction. He started on one extreme, only to be carried over by regular gradation finally to another. Unitarianism and Romanism are the contrary poles of Christianity, freedom and authority, the liberty of the individual subject and the binding force of the universal object, carried out each, by violent disjunction from the other, into nerveless pantomime and sham. Thus seemingly far apart, however, they are in reality always closely related; just as all extremes, by the force of their own falsehood, have an innate tendency to react, pendulum-wise, into the very opposites from which they seem to fly. Hence, the familiar observation, that Romanism in many cases leads to rationalism and infidelity. In bursting the bonds of mere blind authority, a Ronge[3] has no power to stop in true Protestantism, but swings clear over into the dark void of full unbelief. So it is not unnatural, on the other side, that Rationalism should lead the way occasionally to popery and superstition. This transition we see exemplified in the case of Mr. Brownson.

---

1. [*MR* 2 (January 1850) 33–80.]

2. [See the general introduction to part 2 for a description of these chameleon-like changes, made famous by Lowell's 1848 satire *A Fable for Critics*. For major biographies and studies of Brownson's thought, see Carey, *Orestes A. Brownson*, 389–401.]

3. [Johannes Ronge (1813–1887), German Catholic priest and pastor of a parish at Schneidemühl in East Prussia, separated himself and his parish from the Catholic communion and in October 1844 declared the parish an independent Catholic congregation. He also organized other Catholic communities to join him in a schismatic German Catholic Church. Ronge rejected the Catholic hierarchical system, clerical celibacy, idolatry, indulgences, auricular confession and several Catholic religious practices and abuses. He was eventually excommunicated. He formulated a new rationalist creed for the new German Catholic Church that denied the divinity of Christ. In 1845, Harper and Brothers published Ronge's *John Ronge, the Holy Coat of Treves* to make Ronge and his new schismatic movement better known in the United States. Philip Schaff eventually considered Ronge's new movement to be "idea-less, destructive and rationalistic." See *What is Church History?* (1846), MTSS 3:239–40. By 1850, Nevin, too, saw Ronge as a specimen of rationalism and ultimately of infidelity—one of the tendencies of those who departed from the Catholic community.]

He himself, indeed, speaks of his conversion at times, as if it had come upon him by a sort of miracle, without any such preparation in his previous life. But it is easy enough to see that such was not the case. Forced to feel the hollowness of the ground on which he first stood, his mind had been for years before seeking some better settlement, by a succession of experiments, which, though not, of course, to his own consciousness, yet in truth and in fact, looked all along towards the full spiritual somerset [*sic*], in which they came at length to an end. That they reached this end finally, instead of stopping in some intermediate position, was owing in his case, not to the levity and inconstancy of his mind, but to its earnestness rather and logical severity. We should be very sorry to consider him here the counterpart simply of the infamous Ronge. As a general thing, we may say, it requires far more earnestness to pass from rationalism to popery, than it does to make a like transition from popery to rationalism; and it must ever argue a most vitiated state of religious feeling, where the second case is regarded with more toleration and respect than the first; where the conversion of a Ronge, for instance, is glorified as the triumph of reason and truth, while the conversion of a Brownson is resolved into sheer dishonesty and caprice. Had the last seen proper to bring his wanderings to an end in Orthodox Congregationalism, in Presbyterianism, in old Lutheranism, or in Protestant Episcopacy, his mutability in either case, *thus far*, would have seemed consistent and rational enough, at least within the bosom of his chosen communion. And yet it was simply because he was more consistent and rational than multitudes in these several positions, that he could not thus pause in his movement, but found it necessary to leave them all behind, and to seek shelter for his wearied spirit in the bosom of Rome. We mean not by this, that others may not occupy in good faith such intermediate ground, without having been brought to surmount in their own minds the inward difficulty which made this impossible for Mr. Brownson. They may do so, just because they have never come to be sensible at all of the antagonistic powers out of which the difficulty springs. Let the true nature of this antagonism come to be felt, and their position will be found at the same time to involve a contradiction, out of which, with their reigning principle of religion, they can make no rational escape. So it was in the mind of Mr. Brownson. The very principle which led him to renounce Unitarianism, made it impossible for him to stop short of Romanism. With less light in his understanding, or less firmness in his will, he might have forced it to come to a halt somewhere between. But this would have been for him error only and not truth. The case demanded, for its right solution, a new religious principle and theory altogether. Without this, he felt himself shut up to the alternative already mentioned. He could not be a Congregationalist, Presbyterian, Lutheran, or Episcopalian. He must be either a Rationalist or a Romanist. Had it been possible, he might have liked to be at once both; but as the case could not allow this, he made up his mind finally to bow as he best could to the authority of the Pope. In all this, as we have said, we find no occasion for disparagement or contempt. Our condemnation, rather, is mingled with respect. We reverence earnestness and moral courage, wherever they may come in our way; and we know not that they are more entitled to such homage in the form of perpetual stability and sameness, than they are in the form of necessary revolution and change. Calvin and Melanchthon[4] are both great, the one in the uniformity, the other in the fluctuations, of his faith. It is neither by moving, nor by standing still, that men prove the worth of their religion. A faith which has never found occasion to stir an inch from its first moorings, *may be* of far less value than that which has been carried by wind and wave to a wholly different shore. Nay, even a bad faith, in this view, may be entitled to greater regard, than a faith which is in form more sound; on the well-known principle, that a living dog is better than a dead lion.

[Brownson's Defense of Catholicism]

We are not among those again, who look upon Mr. Brownson's championship of Romanism as either weak or of small account. It is vain to affect, as some do, a supercilious contempt for it, in this view. His mind is naturally of a very acute and strong character; and long, earnest and vigorous exercise has served to clothe it with a measure of dialectical agility and power, such as we rarely meet with on the field at least of our American theology. His reading evidently is extensive and varied; though he is not free from the infirmity, we think, of passing it off frequently, in an indirect way, for something more than its actual worth. He allows himself, for instance, to refer at times, to the German philosophers and theologians, as if he were perfectly at home in their speculations; whereas we have never met with any evidence of his having any more thorough acquaintance with them after all, than that second-hand information which is to be had through the medium of a foreign literature, particularly that of modern France. On the contrary it is sufficiently clear, that he has *not* by any means mastered the best and most profound results of the later German thought; he makes no proper account of the history through which it has passed; affects, indeed, to make light of all history, as applied to the progress of philosophy; and shows himself at fault especially, where the discipline of this thought precisely should come to his help, or, at all events, be intelligently refused, if found wanting, and not merely waved with magisterial hand to the one side. After every necessary drawback, however, in this way, there can be no question of Mr. Brownson's actual knowledge, as going in the walks of philosophy and history, quite beyond the measure of our reigning American education. He is well fitted thus for taking the lead in this country, as a defender of the Roman faith; not because of his having been trained to the science of it in the usual way; for he

---

4. [Philipp Melanchthon (1497–1560), a follower of Martin Luther and a professor of theology at the University of Wittenberg from 1518 to his death, was a major author of the *Augsburg Confession* (1530). He was more conciliatory to Catholic theologians than were some other Lutheran theologians of the Reformation era and periodically called for Christian unity. See Robert Stupperich, *Melanchthon*.]

Document 7: Brownson's Quarterly Review.

acknowledges himself that no such study went before his conversion; but in virtue of his general Protestant training, his familiarity with American life, and the dexterity with which, as a practised athlete, he is able to throw his whole strength now into the direction of this new creed. There is a freshness and force in this way in his polemics, which they could not so well possess, perhaps, under any different form. However superior the drilled generalship of a Möhler[5] may be for the theological atmosphere of Germany, or that of a Wiseman[6] for the ecclesiastical relations of England, it may be doubted[7] whether either of them is as well prepared as Mr. Brownson for carrying the war home to the special habit of thought that prevails with Protestantism on this side of the Atlantic. He is a born Puritan, steeped by education in the element of New England life; the first, probably, who with anything like the same amount of intellectual culture, has made the transition to Romanism from this most uncatholic coast. He is intimately familiar thus with Puritan modes of thought and forms of life, and is able to take direct account of them continually in the management of his own cause. He deals with Protestantism mainly, as he finds it living and working, at the present time, in these United States, though not without an eye always to its condition and character also in other countries. His Review altogether for one who is prepared to take any real interest in theology and the Church, must be felt to carry with it more than common weight and force; with all its scholastic subtleties and offensive dogmatism, is possessed of much vivacity and point; and is far more readable, it must be confessed, than a large proportion of our current controversy on the opposite side.

It is just one of the miseries of our fashionable pseudo-protestantism, that it legitimates and accepts so readily every sort of polemical assault upon Rome, without proof or examination; as though it were the easiest thing in the world, to fight this battle to purpose; in consequence of which, we are flooded here with more insipid trash, in the name of religious argument, than is to be met with probably in any other

---

5. [Johann Adam Möhler (1796-1838), German Catholic theologian at the Universities of Tübingen (1823-1835) and Münich (1835-1838), was particularly influential in ecclesiology and comparative symbolics. Philip Schaff called Möhler "the most important Roman Catholic theologian of the present age." *The Principle of Protestantism*, MTSS 3:86n. Möhler was influenced by the organic categories of German Romanticism and idealism. Two of Möhler's studies, *Die Einheit in der Kirche* (*The Unity of the Church*) and *Symbolik*, became widely influential in Catholic circles. Brownson reviewed Robertson's 1843 translation of *Symbolism* ("Symbolism," 408-410), defended Möhler in "Professor Park," 485-87, and periodically cited Möhler's texts, especially those that referred to the church as "the visible continuation of the Incarnation." See, for example, [Brownson], "Evangelical Alliance," 95. On Möhler, see, in particular, Fitzer, *Moehler and Baur*; Wagner, *Die eine Kirche und die viele Kirchen* (The One Church and the Many Churches).]

6. [Nicholas Patrick Stephen Wiseman (1802-65), first Cardinal archbishop of Westminster (1850-65) after the restoration of the Catholic episcopacy in England, had received his doctorate in theology at Rome and while there became a professor of Oriental languages and curator of Arabic manuscripts for the Vatican Library. He published several theological and apologetical works, including *Twelve Lectures* and *Lectures on the Principal Doctrines*, which were republished many times throughout the nineteenth century. On Wiseman, see Ward, *Life and Times*, Jackman, *Nicholas Cardinal Wiseman*, and Schiefen, *Nicholas Wiseman*.]

7. [Due to a missing cross-stroke, this word appears as "doubled" in the printed text.]

quarter. It is with a most wretched grace, that such easy literature, whether figuring in the newspaper, catch-penny book,[8] rostrum, or pulpit, allows itself to overlook and despise the vigorous pen of such a man as Brownson, as though it were a flourish of mere empty words and nothing more. There is nothing gained in the end, but much lost, rather, by such imbecile self-conceit. Over against its blind though proud pretensions, it is no wonder that true learning on the other side should be excited at times to indignant scorn. Mr. Brownson has full right to retort on this spirit, as he often does with withering sarcasm, its own commonplace charges against Romanism. It will not reason; it sets all logic at defiance; it shrinks from the light; it goes blindly and dumbly by its own tradition; it substitutes cant for argument and thought; it turns the Bible into a nose of wax, to suit its own taste; it plays pope as fully as though it were itself the bearer of the triple crown, and held all the thunders of the vatican [sic] in its hand. As compared with a very large amount of our popular literature against Popery in this form, we are constrained to admit, however humiliating the confession may be, that the Review before us bears away the palm completely, as regards both dignity and strength.

It is not unnatural, that Mr. Brownson himself, with such sense as he must have necessarily of his own superiority to the false Protestantism now noticed, (which he of course is very ready to accept also, as the only proper representative of Protestantism in its true form) should feel his championship of the Roman faith to be of more than ordinary account. He takes pains, it is true, to speak very modestly and humbly of his own deserts; as though he felt himself to be a learner only in this school, and had no right to open his lips in any other capacity. But it is still plain enough, through all this show, that he secretly considers himself notwithstanding, to be something of a giant in the Protestant controversy, and has good hopes of making himself appear so also to others. His tone is bold, confident, overbearing and harsh. He moves throughout with the air of a man, who takes himself to be thoroughly master both of his own cause, and of that of all his opponents besides.[9] He deals his blows like a conscious Hercules,

---

8. [A cheap booklet lacking any intrinsic value, printed only for the purpose of getting the readers' money.]

9. Mr. B. is fond of appealing to his own past history and experience, in a way that shows he has not lost the sense of his personal importance towards the world, however much of a child he may feel himself in the arms of the Church. He takes it for granted always, that he has made the whole circle of Protestant knowledge, and has no need to go beyond himself to understand any question here thrown in his way. "Think you that we," he exclaims, "who, according to your own story, have tried every form of Protestantism, and disputed every inch of Protestant ground, would ever have left the ranks of Protestantism in which we were born, and under whose banner we had fought so long and suffered so much, if there had been any other alternative for us."— [Brownson], "Protestantism Ends in Transcendentalism,"] July, 1846, p. 386. Prof Park, Emerson, Neander, Newman, Schaff, Bushnell, &c., in their most profound attempts to get at the intrinsic reason of things, simply go over ground which was familiar long since to his feet, but which a logic still deeper than theirs compelled him afterwards again to abandon.— [Brownson, "Professor Park,"] Oct. 1845, p. 511, ["*The Principle of Protestantism*," Oct. 1845,] p. 546. [Brownson, "Newman's Theory,"] Jan. 1847, p. 84. [See also {Brownson,} "Newman's Development," (July 1846) 357, on Neander.]—[Brownson, "R. W. Emerson,"] April, 1847, p.

Document 7: Brownson's Quarterly Review.

sent forth on divine errand to reform the world. And what is of still more account in the case, his mission in this view seems to receive, not doubtfully, the approbation and sanction of the Church of which he has now become so zealous and dutiful a son. His conversion is counted an important gain, with that of Hurter[10] and Newman,[11] we may well suppose, throughout the Roman world. At all events, it is felt to form a sort of epoch for Romanism in America. Already he has succeeded in gaining fully, as it would appear, the confidence of his ecclesiastical superiors in this country; and neophyte and layman though he be, is counted worthy to take a foremost place among the expounders and defenders of the Roman faith. At the close of the late Council in Baltimore, through the suggestion of Bishop Kenrick, of Philadelphia, a brief note was addressed to Mr. Brownson, signed by both the archbishops and twenty-three bishops, for the purpose of seconding and encouraging his literary labors in defence of his newly adopted creed, of which he is acknowledged to have proved himself an able and intrepid advocate.[12] This, it must be confessed, is no ordinary recommendation. Com-

---

276.— [Brownson, "Bushnellism,"] Oct. 1849, p. 497. [Edwards Amasa Park (1808-1900), Congregational minister and theologian, taught theology at Andover (1836-80) and represented a conservative mediating position in theology between the Calvinism of the New Divinity theologians and the Romantic theology of Horace Bushnell and the emerging liberal Protestant theology. He was a staunch critic of Roman Catholicism. On Park, see Cecil, *Theological Development of . . . Park*. Ralph Waldo Emerson (1803-82), Transcendentalist essayist and poet, had been a Unitarian minister in Boston, but left the ministry to continue writing and lecturing. He represented the European Romantic influence in the United States and in *Nature* he argued for the superiority of spirit over the rigidity of the law. In his "Divinity School Address" of 1838 he emphasized the fundamental importance of intuition and dared the students "to love God without mediator or veil." On Emerson, see Allen, *Waldo Emerson* and Richardson, *Emerson*. Johann August Wilhelm Neander (1789-1850), influential German church historian who taught at the University of Berlin, had significant influence on the Mercersburg theology of Nevin and Schaff. Neander's organic and developmental view of the church's life in history was represented in his *Allgemeine Geschichte der christlichen Religion und Kirche* (1825-52). For a Mercersburg view of Neander, see Schaff, *Confessions and Letters of St. Augustine*. Horace Bushnell (1802-76), a Congregationalist pastor and theologian significantly influenced by the Romantic strain of thought, published *Christian Nurture* and *Nature and the Supernatural* that reflected his organic view of reality and drew Nevin's attention and critique. On Bushnell, see Edwards, *Of Singular Grace* and Haddorff, *Dependence and Freedom*.]

10. [There were three Von Hurters from Switzerland who converted to Catholicism in 1844: Friedrich Emmanuel Von Hurter (1787-1865), a Swiss clergyman and historian, and his two sons, Heinrich (1825-95), who became a Catholic priest, and Hugo (1832-1914), who became a Jesuit and a distinguished theologian and historian. More than likely Nevin was referring to Friedrich Emmanuel because by 1850 the two sons would not have been as widely known as the father who had published a significant four-volume biography of Pope Innocent III prior to his acceptance into the Catholic communion. See *Geschichte Papst Innocenz des Dritten und seiner Zeitgenossen*, 4 vols.]

11. [John Henry Newman (1801-90), an Anglican priest and theologian, was received into the Catholic Church in 1845 and the same year published his widely-read *Essay on the Development of Christian Doctrine*, which was, among other things, a defense of his change of religious allegiance. Nevin and Schaff were sympathetic to Newman's argument on the organic development of doctrine, but Brownson, particularly in the early years after his conversion, became highly critical of the idea of development, as is evident in many of his articles on Newman from 1845 to 1850. On Newman, see Ker, *John Henry Newman*.]

12. [Bishop Francis Patrick Kenrick (1796-1863), archbishop of Baltimore and presiding bishop

ing from such a quarter, and under such a form, it carries with it peculiar significance and force. No wonder that Mr. Brownson should be pleased with it, and thank the prelates "again and again for their act of unexpected and spontaneous kindness." It is, in truth, a solemn *imprimatur*[13] affixed to his Review, by the universal Roman Catholic Church in America; which, of course, in such view, well deserves the attention also of those who stand on the outside of this Church and seek only its destruction. "No higher testimonial could be asked," says the happy editor,

> and no higher, out of Rome, could be given; and to say we are grateful, is to say nothing. We thank the eminent prelate [Kenrick] who drew up the letter, and each and all of the illustrious Archbishops and Bishops who generously signed it, and gave us their approbation and a pledge of their support. It was more than we deserved, more than we can deserve, more than any editor can deserve; but we will do our best not to make them regret their generous act. We should be oppressed with their approbation, did we not know that whatever merits this journal may have, as a Catholic journal, they are due not to us, but principally to the distinguished Bishop of this diocese,[14] and his learned and venerable clergy, who have always been ready to instruct our ignorance, and to advise and direct us in the course proper for such a journal to pursue, and in the proper views to be taken of the several important theological questions we have discussed. To them pertain the merits of the Review; to us alone its faults and imperfections, which we hope will diminish with time and experience.—July, 1849, p. 412.[15]

This extract goes to illustrate both sides of the relation, which it brings ostentatiously into view. The favor of the reigning priesthood is conditioned and reciprocated, by the unlimited obedience that is found basking in its sunshine. Mr. Brownson makes a point of being, in this respect, a Roman of the Romans, with whom no halfway measures can go down. His theory, from the start, is a sort of violent protestation against Protestantism, the absolute negative of all that this affirms, by which he holds himself bound to part with his own independence altogether in matters of religion, and place his faith submissively in the hands of the Church, as an outward authority ordained of God for such purpose. The alternative with him is, law from within or

---

of the 1849 Seventh Provincial Council of Baltimore, wrote periodically for *BQR* and was perhaps the best theologian among the antebellum American Catholic bishops. In May 1849, the bishops of the council endorsed *BQR*, acknowledging Brownson's "literary labors in defense of the faith" as "an able and intrepid advocate." For the episcopal commendation, see "We cannot resist." On Kenrick, see Nolan, *The Most Reverend Francis Patrick Kenrick*.]

13. [Trans. "it is permitted"; that is, an official ecclesiastical permission to publish a religious book.]

14. [John Bernard Fitzpatrick (1812–66, bishop of Boston, 1846–66) became a theological advisor to Brownson after his reception into the Catholic Church. Fitzpatrick's post-Reformation scholastic theology had a conservative impact on Brownson's theology while he was living in Boston, 1844 to 1855.]

15. ["We cannot resist."]

law from without; one *or* the other, and one always so as to exclude the other; and having satisfied himself that the first, in such abstract view, runs out inevitably into rationalism and nihility, he considers himself shut up to the necessity of accepting the opposite rule, as the only form in which it is possible to have part at all in a really supernatural religion. To this necessity, thus apprehended as a law of logic merely, Mr. Brownson, wearied and worn out with his own long attempt to find bottom in the miserable bog of a churchless independency, holds himself now bound, it would seem, as a rational man, to bring all his powers into subjection, cost what it may in any other view. Such an outward authority of the Church being granted to hold in any form as the necessary medium of faith, it follows plainly enough that the best claim to it lies with the Church of Rome. He is the best Christian, then, who most resolutely brings both his reason and will into captivity to the authority of this Church, as it is found embodied from age to age in the voice of its hierarchy. Having reached this conclusion, Mr. Brownson seems resolved to follow it to the death. He feels rightly enough, that if it be good for anything at all, it must be good for everything; as a well built arch is only made more firm and strong, by piling new weight upon its shoulders; and he is determined, accordingly, to let the world see that he has confidence in his own logic, and power also to bend his New England nature to its iron requisitions. As he tells us himself somewhere, his soul recoils from the mortal sin of being inconsequent, or holding premises which he is not prepared to follow out to their natural and necessary end. Has it become thus a maxim of reason with him, to obey with unquestioning faith the Roman Church? He will be *rational* then in such style, to the full end of the chapter. He will allow no sort of compromise with any rule besides. He will play the very *Yankee* himself in this new game; he will be a Puritan Romanist; making a king still of his own mind, and wilfully forcing his very will itself, to fall in with the new theory of faith he is thus brought to embrace. He will abjure philosophy in religion, and take all in the way simply of authority. It shall be his reason here to silence reasoning, and his will to have no freedom whatever. Thus firmly set in his own mind to follow out his new principle at all hazards, Mr. Brownson has had no trouble apparently in complying with even its most extreme demands. He is at once a very ultramontanist, a downright Italian, in the plenitude of his obedience and faith, who can swallow even a camel, if need be, in the way of edifying example to less vigorous believers. Not content to affirm the infallibility of the Roman Church, he is willing to lodge this divine attribute, without farther ado, in the person of the ruling Pope.[16] He

---

16. "The Papacy is the Church, the Pope the Vicar of our Lord Jesus Christ on earth, and if you war against the Pope, it is either because you would war against God, or because you believe God can lie. If you believe God has commissioned the Pope, and that God will keep his promise, you must believe his authority is that of God, and can be no more dangerous than would be the authority of our Lord, were he present to exercise it in person."— [Brownson, "Religious Novels," {review of Henry Major's *Reasons for Acknowledging*}] Jan. 1847, p. [129-]130.—"We copy below the Encyclical Letter of our Holy Father, Pope Pius IX. We have no room for comments, and should not offer any if we had. In it God speaks to us by his Vicegerent on earth, and it is ours to listen, believe, and obey."— [Brownson,

pays his devotions to the Virgin Mary, as though he had been born and bred to it in the natural way. He makes himself quite at home in the region of Roman Saints, legends, relics and miracles, as if he had been used to it all his life. At all times, and in all things, he carries himself most dutifully towards the priesthood, who form to his eyes the medium of all truth and authority in the Church, and from whose lips in such view the common layman is required to accept both without doubt or contradiction. His tone towards these spiritual superiors, as contrasted especially with the confidence and self-reliance he is accustomed to exhibit in other directions, is to affectation humble, we might almost say at times sycophantic and servile. "It would be presumptuous in us," he says in relation to Bishop Kenrick's work on the Primacy of the Apostolic See,

> to speak of the doctrines set forth in this book, either to commend or to censure. The layman, because an editor or reviewer, is not relieved from his obligation to submit to his spiritual superiors, or to learn his faith from those the Holy Ghost has set in the Church to teach and to rule the flock. Yet on matters of private opinion, each man, whether layman or not, may entertain and express, reverently, his own opinions.—April, 1845, p. 263.[17]

So throughout He is not simply a learner, but a passive receiver of theological knowledge, professedly, at the feet of the bishops and priests. He is careful to let us know, that in the conduct of his Review, he is to be considered, theologically, the echo simply of the proper masters of his faith, the bishop of Boston and his learned clergy.

> The Catholic Church, faith and worship, as they are, always have been, and always will be till the end of time, is what we have embraced, what we love, what we seek to defend, not relying on our own private judgment, but receiving the truth in humility from those Almighty God has commissioned to teach us, and whom he has commanded us to obey.—Jan. 1846. p. 136.[18]

This is Romanism in full force; such as may be held to be fairly entitled to its reward, in the smiling approbation with which so many bishops and archbishops have seen fit to honor it before the world.

Mr. Brownson having thus violently given himself away to a theory of the Church which puts an end to all private thinking in religion, makes a merit apparently of the most violent consistency, in following it out to its most difficult consequences on all sides. The Christian salvation is for him a process that goes like clock-work. To his New England mind, the operation of the *machine* is all settled, as clearly as two and two make four, by the fixed nature of its pullies and wheels.[19] The maxim, *Out of the*

Review of "Recent Publications,"] April, 1847, p. 249. "Certainly, when the Pope decides, we submit, for we recognize his right to decide, and we believe his decisions are infallible."— [Brownson, "Methodist Quarterly Review,"] Jan. 1846, p. 100.

17. ["*The Primacy of the Apostolic See.*" See also Kenrick, *The Primacy of the Apostolic See* (1845).]
18. [Brownson, "The New Volume."]
19. [In Nevin's mind then, Brownson's intellectual activity is *mechanical*, Nevin's antonym of *organic*.]

Document 7: Brownson's Quarterly Review.

Church no salvation, he applies at once to the Roman communion exclusively, and takes pains to shut out as much as possible every sort of hope in favor even of the best men beyond. Out of this Roman Church indeed, as his theory requires, he holds that there can be no act of true faith. Protestantism then, in its best shape, is a sham, that leans always towards open infidelity; and its virtues are to be counted hollow and deceitful, even where they may seem to carry the most pious and heavenly show. The Reformation was wholly without reason or necessarily, and had its rise in worldly motives far more than in any true zeal for the glory of God. Luther and Calvin were bad men, and tools besides of men worse than themselves. The Church, as it stood before, was steadily moving in the right direction; while this revolution, so far as it prevailed, served only to hinder and embarrass the march of true christian improvement, causing the sun mark to go back on the dial plate of the world's civilization, God only knows how far. Protestantism rolls forward from the very start, by its own weight, to infidelity and nihilism. Its *life* is to be sought always on the side nearest this result, and not in its more respectable forms; for these are always more or less ossified and dead. Its only fair representation at this time accordingly, is found in transcendentalism, pantheistic atheism, and communism. Not only is the history of the Roman Church before the Reformation full of testimony to her divine character, as the patron and prop of all good in the world, whether in the form of religion, science, politics or social life; but her history *since* also, as compared with that of Protestantism, is powerfully suited to inculcate the same lesson. The advantage often claimed in favor of Protestant nations, is more specious than solid.[20] Puritanism especially, here

---

20. "We deny, positively deny, that in moral and intellectual science, properly so called, Protestants have made the least progress, or that their philosophers have assertained a single fact or a single principle not known and recognized by the Schoolmen.—You talk of 'the Dark Ages'—dark forsooth, as Coleridge, one of your own number, tells you, because you have not light enough to read them. We know something of your Protestant philosophers, and there are absolutely only four Protestant names, that it is not discreditable to one's own knowledge to call a philosopher, and it is doubtful if any one of these was really a Protestant. We mean Leibnitz, Kant, Hegel and Hobbes.—In theology you are as badly off as you are in philosophy. You have no more respectable theological work than Calvin's *Institutes*, which none of you now accept—unless with a qualification.—Saving some branches of physical science, in which the progress effected is far less than is imagined, Protestants have really contributed nothing of any real importance to the progress of the human mind. We know the Protestant boasts, and we know what Protestants have done. Not one of the great inventions or discoveries, which have so changed the face of the modern world, with the exception, perhaps, of the mule and jenny, and a few other inventions in labor saving machinery, all of which we look upon as a curse, are due to them. Everything degenerates, except material industry, in their hands; and yet, they have the singular impudence to accuse the Catholic Church of injuring the mind."—[Brownson, "Professor Park,"] Oct. 1845, p. 492–494. [Samuel Taylor Coleridge (1772–1834). English Romantic poet and idealist whose *Aids to Reflection* (1825) had a significant impact on American theology. On Coleridge, see Ashton, *Life*. Gottfried Wilheim Leibnitz (1646–1716), German philosopher and mathematician, promoted the idea that the universe was governed by a law of continuity. His optimism, expressed in the view that this world was the best of all possible worlds, influenced his advocacy of international peace and Christian unity. Thomas Hobbes (1588–1679), political philosopher, advocated a form of political absolutism and psychological determinism that had an important impact on modern political science. *Leviathan*, his major work, argued that although political sovereignty comes from the people, it is

in America, is little more than a bag of wind.[21] Professor Park only raves, when he tell us that "Rome has trained a smaller number of original thinkers, for the last three hundred years, than have arisen from even half the number of Protestant churches." If the assertion mean, not soap bubble blowers, but men of solid learning, and clear as well as profound thought, Mr. Brownson denies it, and pledges himself, "after making all proper allowance for the excess of Catholic population over the Protestant, to produce ten Catholics to every one Protestant the Professor will bring forward."—1845, p. 495.[22] "The Catholic cantons of Switzerland are more truly enlightened than the Protestant." Spain, Portugal, and Ireland, bear comparison favorably with Holland, Denmark, and Scotland.[23] The laboring classes are much more degraded in England, than they are in Austria, in Italy, or in Spain. The Austrian clergy are not inferior to the Prussian, nor the Bavarian to the Saxon; and "to represent the present body of the French clergy, whether of the first or of the second order, as inferior to the English, betrays an ignorance or a recklessness that we were not prepared for even in our Andover Professor."—1845, p. 495-497.[24] So everywhere. Mr. Brownson forces himself to see only evil in Protestantism, and in Romanism only goodness, beauty and grace. However black this last may seem to other eyes, it is still comely to his as the tents of Kedar or the curtains of Solomon.[25] Out to Ireland and Mexico even, he is ready to say of it: "Thou art all fair, my love, there is no spot in thee" [Song 4:7].

---

transferred to the monarch who holds it absolutely, though it is not of divine right.]

21. "The literature of our country, such as it is, and it is nothing at best to boast of, we owe to authors not of the Puritan or Calvinistic school. The profoundest works of the Puritan school in this country are Edwards *On the Will*, and *On the Affections*, Hopkins' *System of Divinity*, and Dwight's *Theology*. The school does little else than republish from England and Scotland, translate from the German, or compile from foreign scholars. And yet our Puritan Professor, (Park) with the tail of a Dutch goose in his cap for plume, steps boldly forward, and accuses Catholicity of being hostile to the mind, and seriously charges the Catholic Church with being deficient in great philosophers and eminent preachers."— [Brownson, "Professor Park,"] Oct. 1845, p. 494. [Samuel Hopkins (1721–1803), Congregationalist minister and theologian, followed in the theological footsteps of Jonathan Edwards and established after Edwards what became known as the New Divinity Theology; see Hopkins, see Conforti, *Samuel Hopkins* (1981). Timothy Dwight (1752–1817), Congregationalist theologian and educator, was the grandson of Jonathan Edwards and although he followed Edwards's Calvinist theology in some respects, he tended to emphasize human activity in the conversion process. In this, he joined those theologians who supported the Great Awakening in the antebellum period. On Dwight, see Berk, *Calvinism Versus Democracy*.]

22. [Brownson, "Professor Park."]

23. "Not to Catholicity, but to the policy of England and the Church by law established, must we look for Ireland's degradation. We would willingly let the question itself turn on the instance of Ireland. We want no better evidence to prove the superiority of Catholicity over Protestantism."— [Brownson, "Professor Park,"] 1845, p. 496.

24. [Brownson, "Professor Park."]

25. [Here Nevin is referring to Song 1:5, "I am black and beautiful, Daughters of Jerusalem—Like the tents of Kedar, like the curtains of Solomon." Where others see only blackness in Romanism, Nevin argues, Brownson sees only beauty.]

Now to our mind, all this wholesale sweeping style is adapted to beget distrust, rather than to inspire confidence. It seems to involve a desperate determination to carry out a given theory, at all costs. Mr. Brownson's new orthodoxy sits on him with an air of stiff unnatural mannerism and constraint. It is too much a thing of logic and outward rule. It is so bent on being straight, that the very effort causes it to lean over from its own perpendicular. Its want of full inward security is betrayed, by the perpetual tendency it shows to assert itself in an extreme way.

[Brownson on the Reformation and History]

The man draws enormously on our faith, who requires us to take the vast fact of the Reformation, with all its consequences down to the present time, as either a mere zero, or as something far worse than zero, in the history of the world and the Church. It comes before us, not as a side current simply in the stream of life, but as a force belonging plainly to its central channel. It had its ground and necessity in what went before. Whole ages looked towards it previously as their proper end. It is not more clear that the civilization of the modern world grew up in Europe, than it is that its growth and progress produced the Reformation. The fact carries in itself a universal significance, a force that reaches into politics, literature, and philosophy, as well as religion, and is capable thus of scientific exposition, as a necessary crisis in the course of Christianity. That it was in truth of such universal sense and force, is made evident by the vast agitations and changes that grew out of it in the sixteenth century, and the consequences, broad, mighty, and deep, that have continued to proceed from it down to the present time. Whatever our estimate may be of the worth of these, in themselves considered, it seems not possible for any sober mind to call in question their historical significance and moment. Protestantism, plainly, has not been an interlude simply, during the past three hundred years, in the drama of the world's life. It belongs to the *history* of the period, in the fullest sense of the term. So far as the world can be said to have had a universal historical life at all, since the time of Luther, it must be acknowledged to have had its stream mainly in the line of Protestantism. Whether for weal or for woe, Protestant nations have taken the lead in the onward movement of humanity; and Protestant principles and interests have controlled, to a great extent, all its more prominent developments and positions. Unless, then, we choose to give up all faith in history, as a revelation of God's mind and will,[26] we must bow before this great fact of three hundred years with earnest reverence, and admit that it has a meaning in it for the kingdom of God, in some way worthy of its vast proportions. Suppose the worst even in its case, that Protestantism, namely, is destined to prove a failure altogether, still it would be in the highest degree unphilosophical and irrational to deny its significance at least in this view, as the medium of transition for the Church to a better

---

26. [Nevin's assumption—that history was the revelation of God's mind—was taken from F. H. W. Schelling, via Schaff: see Nevin, *One, Holy, Catholic, and Apostolic, Tome One*, MTSS 5:148n15.]

and brighter state, that could not have been reached without such a period of inward contradiction going before. The honor of God, the credit of religion, require that a movement which has so covered the field of history for so long a time, should in *some* form be acknowledged to carry with it a truly historical force, and to enter into the universal mission and plan of Christianity for the salvation of the world. If the space filled by Protestantism may be violently set aside as a blank in history, it would be hard to name any other period of equal duration which we might not as easily set aside in the same way. We ought to have no patience with men, who turn the first three centuries of Christianity into a sheer waste of sand, to suit their own miserable prejudices; and just as little too with those, who see only a long night of unmeaning desolation in the centuries that follow the downfall of the old Roman civilization; regardless, in the first case, of the world triumph by which Christianity was steadily conducted to the throne of the Cæsars, and in the second case, making no account of the no less magnificent new world triumph, which was accomplished in its mastery of the wild elements from which Europe draws its present life. Our faith in God, above all our reliance on Christ's special promise *not* to forsake his Church to the end of the world, will not allow us to acquiesce in the thought of any such vast hiatus or inorganic chaos in the history of Christianity. But why, we ask, should we have any more patience with this style of thinking, when we find it applied to the period since the Reformation, than we have for it as applied to the period before? Is it less arbitrary and pedantic, less frivolous and profane, to treat the great fact of Protestantism, clearly belonging for three hundred years past to the central history of the world, as a nullity, a dream, the oversight of a sleeping Christ,[27] than it is to look upon a like term of centuries a thousand years since, in the same dishonorable light? The fact is too wide, too deep, too overwhelmingly significant, to be set aside in that way. Make Protestantism to be as bad as you please, still springing as it has done from the inmost depths of modern civilization, and filling as it does the middle channel of modern history, we are bound by all faith in God and in Christ, to hold it of necessary sense and value in some way, for the final triumph of Christianity under its true and right form. History here, as well as elsewhere, must be allowed to be *rational*, worthy of the Mind by which it is actuated, and not the sport simply of wild winds and waves. Christ, Head over all things to the Church, has not been asleep, nor out of the way, in the rise and progress thus far, of a movement so vast in its consequences. It is something monstrous, on the part of Mr. Brownson, then, that he affects to make such small account of Protestantism, and will not allow it to be of any historical significance whatever, for the last end of Christianity. Such an assumption is a great deal too violent; and for one who has come to have any sense at all of the divine character of history, overthrows itself, while it destroys at the same time the credit of the source from which it proceeds. Romanists must learn to find some sense, and not mere Devil's play, in the Reformation, if they

---

27. [An allusion to the familiar story of Jesus's calming of the Sea of Galilee: Mark 4:35–41. Nevin regularly uses this metaphor to say that the apparent chaos of history does *not* catch Jesus asleep.]

expect to be heard respectfully in the scientific world in opposition to its claims. If Mr. Brownson should set himself to denounce and ridicule the Allegheny mountains or the Mississippi river, as useless or absurd accidents in nature, we do not see why it would be more reproachful to his philosophy and religion, than it is for him to put scorn in like style on the vast creations of history, that come before us during the past three hundred years in the form of Protestantism; for sure we are, that a continent, shorn of its highest mountains and mightiest streams, would not miss its own universal sense more, than the tract of the world's general life must do, if the events of the last three hundred years were swept from the face of it as a mere impertinence or blank nothing.

Mr. Brownson however, is consistent with himself, and true also to the genius of his Church, in this violence offered to history. He abjures the true idea of history, and will not allow it to be of force for the period before the Reformation, any more than for the period following. History, in its very conception, implies progress; not fixed sameness, but unity in the form of movement and change; the counterpart in time of what the manifold is in space, for an organic whole, as distinguished from mere number without unity. The sense of this is what we mean by historical feeling, and faith in history as the immanent force of a divine, and so of course supremely rational thought.[28] But all such sense Mr. Brownson appears entirely to lack, or else resolutely to resist. History for him is no continuous living creation, that actualizes always more and more its own interior sense, and never falls away from a steady urgency towards its own last end; but a system rather of outward combinations and changes, over which God presides in a mechanical way, much at best as a chess player, whose business it is to keep the game in his own hands, through every new phase of the checkered board on which it is carried forward. The celebrated English convert, Mr. Newman, made an attempt to enlist the idea of *development*, which it is becoming so hard, in the face of modern science, for any truly scientific mind to withstand, in the service of the Roman Catholic Church. Against this pretension, however, it will be remembered, Mr. Brownson, a mere novice himself still in Romanism, but under the safe guidance of course of the powers above him, came out with the most determined contradiction and opposition.[29] He saw and felt, correctly enough, that Romanism could not stand successfully on that ground; and he is to be acknowledged here, accordingly, a true and faithful expounder of its proper spirit and sense. Romanism is, by its very constitution, unhistorical. It lays claim indeed to history and tradition as wholly on its side, over against the abstract thinking that pretends to fetch all faith plump from the Bible; but the claim is overthrown by the fact, that it withdraws from history the idea of inward moving life, without which it has no title to its own name, and turns

---

28. [Nevin stated this several months earlier in "Historical Development." (Forthcoming in the next volume of MTSS.)]

29. [On Brownson's opposition to Newman, see "Newman's Development," 342–68; "Newman's Theory," 39–86, and "Doctrinal Developments," 525–39.]

it thus into an existence, which is just as abstract on its own side, as the abstraction it pretends to fly from on the other. Romanism takes the truth of Christianity for an outward fact, entrusted for safe-keeping to its own hands, out of which it is to be dispensed of course in an outward way for the use of men in all ages. In this form, it must be taken to be perpetually the same, not simply as a living law in the life of the world itself, but as a formal deposit, also, and tradition in such outward style. Its history in such view, is that of a mountain, always the same through all changes of sun and storm that may play upon it from age to age. Only so, can the conception of its line-and-plummet infallibility be fairly carried through. Immense difficulties, it is true, lie in the way of this view, when we try to make it square with facts. Romanism, as it now stands, seems to be anything but a facsimile of primitive Christianity, and the evidences of change may be said to meet us from almost every page of Church history. No two centuries appear to be alike. Still the theory requires it to be otherwise, and to this all facts must be made to bend, by violent hypothesis at least, if in no other way. Mr. Brownson has his fixed *idea* here, like every other good Romanist, and shows himself a perfect Hegelian in requiring it to underlie and rule the construction of history from first to last. The Church has been monotonously one and the same, if we are to take his word for it, from the beginning. Only error and heresy change; truth stands like a rock, against the face of which their rolling waves beat, age after age, without impression or effect.[30] All Christian doctrines came forth from God full and complete in the beginning, and have been handed down by the Church, as an outward deposit, to the present time. The law of history is allowed to hold in other spheres of life. There is growth in nature. Humanity too, in its natural form, subsists by evolution and progress. Religion moreover meets us as a moving fact in the Old Testament. But all such growth contradicts, we are told, the proper conception of Christianity. Only sects here have any development; and then it is always away from the truth and against it.[31] Mr. Newman's theory is applicable to the sects, but not at all to the Church.

> He forgets that she sprung into existence full grown, and armed at all points, as Minerva from the brain of Jupiter; and that she is withdrawn from the ordinary law of human systems and institutions by her supernatural origin, nature, character, and protection. If he had left out the Church, and entitled

---

30. [Like many nineteenth-century American Catholic apologists, Brownson followed Jacque Bossuet's *History of the Variations*, 1, in asserting that variations and changes in faith were a certain proof of falsehood.]

31. "Catholicity is immovable and inflexible, one and the same always and everywhere; for the truth never varies. He who knows it in one age or country, knows it in all. But with the sects it is far otherwise. They must needs obey the natural laws of development, strengthened and intensified by demoniacal influence. Their spirit and tendency, indeed, are always and everywhere the same, but their forms change under the very eye of the spectator, and are rarely the same for any two successive moments. Strike where Protestantism is, and it is not there. It is in perpetual motion, and exemplifies, so far as itself is concerned, the old heathen doctrine, that all things are in a perpetual flux. You can never count on its remaining stationary long enough for you to bring your piece to a rest and take deliberate aim. You must shoot it on the wing."—[Brownson, "The Great Question,"] Oct. 1847, p. 417.

> his book, *An Essay on the development of Christian Doctrine, when withdrawn from the Authority and supervision of the Church*, he would have written, with slight modifications, a great, and valuable book. It would then have been a sort of natural history of sectarism, and been substantially true. But applying his theory to the Church, and thus subjecting her to the law which presides over all human systems and institutions, he has, unintentionally, struck at her divine and supernatural character. The Church has no natural history, for she is not in the order of nature, but of grace.—[Brownson, "Newman's Development,"] July, 1846, p. 366.

This is sufficiently clear. Christianity has no history, and enters not into the law of time, as this holds of all human existence besides. It owes nothing to history, but in truth stands wholly on the outside of it, as an unvarying supernatural fact, preserved by mechanical tradition from the start exactly as it is now held and taught in the Roman Church. With such a theory, it is easy to set aside Protestantism as a nullity; just as false Protestantism on the other hand, finds it easy to set aside all that crosses its humor in the ancient Church; in the same way precisely, in both cases, that the facts of geology are shorn of all their force, for those who have no sense of what belongs to the organic constitution of nature, and think it enough simply to resolve all phenomena into the abstract fiat of Jehovah.

Here, however, Mr. Brownson stands on common ground, for the most part, with those who have entered the lists with him in this controversy; and it must be admitted that the advantage, in such view, falls altogether to his side. He will have it that it is only sectarism, or dissent from Rome, that moves in the way of history. But our Protestant sects generally deny this. Rome has moved, they tell us, by apostacy and corruption; *they* represent the primitive faith, as we find it in the Bible. History, in the true sense, they reject and disown. Christianity must be accepted as "a full grown Minerva;" only not from the living Church, but from the written word; or as the Episcopalians take it, from the word and ancient tradition combined. It becomes necessary, accordingly, to assert and defend Episcopalianism, Presbyterianism, Methodism, or whatever else it may be, as the identical form of primitive Christianity, rightly of force for all ages, and to treat all intervening variations in Church history, as corruptions and aberrations from the truth. It is easy to see, however, that no form of modern Protestantism can successfully affirm its identity with primitive Christianity; if such identity be taken to stand in the same forms of Church thought and Church life.[32] And if this be laid down as the necessary condition of ecclesiastical legitimacy, we see not truly how any effectual stand can be made, by any of these bodies, against the pretensions of Rome. Both sides claim divine right, in the same unhistorical way, in defiance of all historical difficulties, on the ground simply of abstract supernatural revelation. It needs of a truth a supernatural commission, to legitimate such a claim

---

32. [Two years later, Nevin would make the full argument for this claim in "Early Christianity," 538–62; repr. Yrigoyen and Bricker, *Catholic and Reformed*, 232–56).]

under such circumstances. This Romanism pretends at least to show in favor of itself; while the opposite interest requires us to take in lieu of it, simply what is by confession its own merely human judgment and word. If Christianity be thus unhistorical, it is easier on the whole to accept it under the Roman form, than it is to be satisfied with it under any other. The theory still remains unreasonable and violent in its own nature; but it wins at least a relative apology, by being made to appear the necessary alternative of a scheme still more at war with reason than itself.

The false position thus taken by such unhistorical Protestantism, serves to entangle it in other wrong views, which it is not hard to turn to the advantage of the opposite side. In this way, candor constrains us to acknowledge, Mr. Brownson too often triumphs in argument over his opponents, not so much because he is himself absolutely right, as because they unhappily place themselves in the wrong.

[Brownson's Arguments Against Protestantism]

In this warfare he wields a most active pen; not confining himself by any means, as some of his opposers might wish, to the business of parrying and warding off thrusts from the contrary side; but seeking rather to carry the main brunt of battle into the very heart of the enemy's country; fiercely assailing Protestantism in its own strongholds, and defying it to mortal combat where it is accustomed to look upon itself as most secure and strong. His attacks in this way have been renewed and repeated in various forms, particularly during the first two years after his conversion, according to the different aspects under which the war was to be met; for Protestantism, though a common interest in one view, as opposed to Romanism, is still a divided interest within itself, that is not to be approached from all sides exactly in the same way. Mr. Brownson seemed to lay himself out systematically, from the start, for the demolition of its several divisions and sections in detail. We have him at one time, accordingly, directing his artillery against the pretensions of the High Church Episcopalians; then in an article on the British Reformers, against Bishop Hopkins, routing the theory of Low Church Episcopalians; then, against the Unitarian Examiner, exposing the vanity of the No-church theory, which admits the Church in name, but denies it in fact—a theory not confined by any means to Unitarians. Again we find him doing battle with Methodism, then with Presbyterianism, then with Congregationalism, then with Transcendentalism and Socialism, which form in his view the natural and proper end of the whole Protestant movement. In the midst however of all this variety of warfare, conducted in all these different directions with so much versatility and spirit, the fundamental argument of Mr. Brownson against Protestantism remains always the same, and is capable of being reduced to comparatively narrow dimensions. He may be said thus to have exhausted the whole force of it in his first onset, or series of assaults, so that his later polemical articles involve necessarily, in this respect, a considerable amount of self-repetition, which for the intelligent reader can hardly fail to detract somewhat at times from their interest.

[Brownson's Catholic Apologetic]

The course of reasoning, which thus underlies Mr. Brownson's whole faith in Romanism,[33] and to which we are continually referred as the ultimate argument in his manifold debates with Protestantism, may be reduced briefly to the following statement:

I. Christianity is a revelation made to men by God through his Son, Jesus Christ, in other words, "the truth which Jesus Christ taught or revealed."[34] As such, it belongs, at least in part, to the *supernatural* order, transcends nature, comes from beyond the limits of human knowledge. It is something superadded to nature. "Grace, though having the same origin, is above the order of creation, is not included in it, nor promised by it. It is, so to speak, an excess of the Divine Fulness not exhausted in creation, but reserved to be superadded to it according to the Divine will and pleasure."[35] In this form, it is indispensably necessary for our salvation, but can be apprehended only by faith, whose vocation and prerogative it is, as distinguished from science, thus to make us sure of what transcends sense and reason. The object of faith here must be the very truth itself of this supernatural revelation, and not something else in its stead. The problem of our salvation requires, that the supernatural, as revealed by Christ and transcending our knowledge, should be appropriated to our minds notwithstanding in the way of faith or sure belief, so as to act upon us with the reality which belongs to it in its own sphere.—II. "Faith, as distinguished from knowledge and science, rests on authority extrinsic both to the believer and to the matter believed."[36] Knowledge is intuitive, finds its motives of assent in the subject or person knowing. Science is discursive, finds its motives of assent in the object or thing known. "But in belief I must go out of myself, and also out of the object, for my motives of assent."[37] It rests on *testimony*. All turns then of course on the authority, or credibility of the witness, extrinsically considered. The supernatural cannot be attested or made sure in this way by any merely natural witness but only by supernatural authority, that is, by God

---

33. "We had already convinced ourselves of the insufficiency of Naturalism, Rationalism, and Transcendentalism; we had also convinced ourselves of the necessity of Divine revelation and of the fact that the Christian revelation was such a revelation. From this, by a process of reasoning which may be seen in the first article of this number, we arrived infallibly at the Catholic Church. The process is simple and easy. It requires no metaphysical subtlety, no long train of metaphysical reasoning. All it needs is good common sense, a reverent spirit, and a disposition to believe on sufficient evidence."—[Brownson, "Catholic Magazine,"] April, 1845, p. 262.

34. [Brownson, "The Church Against," 146.]

35. [Brownson, "The Church Against," 146–47.]

36. [Brownson, "The Church Against," 151. Closing quotation mark added.]

37. [Brownson, "The Church Against," 151.]

himself. Nothing less than Divine testimony can be a sufficient ground for faith in what transcends nature. This however, we may rationally trust in such case, if we have it;

> because enough is clearly seen of God from the creation of the world, and understood by the things that are made, to establish on a scientific basis the fact that he can neither deceive nor be deceived; for we can *demonstrate scientifically*, from principles furnished by the light of natural reason, that God is infinitely wise and good, and no being infinitely wise and good can deceive or be deceived.[38]

But now to place our faith in contact truly with the authority of God, in the case of a Divine revelation, the fact of the revelation must be authenticated to us by a competent witness, and also the true sense of it made certain in intelligible propositions; for if it be a question whether the revelation is really from God, or if it be taken in a wrong or doubtful sense, there can be no apprehension of God's testimony as it is in the case, and so no apprehension through this of the supernatural to which it bears witness, "Faith in the supernatural requires, then, in addition to the witness that vouches for the fact that God has made the revelation, an interpreter competent to declare the true meaning of the revelation."[39] And as faith is required in all times and places, these necessary conditions of its exercise must be no less universal, at hand for all nations and through all ages, and of unmistakable authority for the poor and illiterate as well as for the high and learned. The witness and interpreter, moreover, must be *infallible*. Faith is a theological virtue, which consists in believing, without doubting, what God has revealed, on the veracity of God alone.

> He who has for his faith only the testimony of a fallible witness, who may both deceive and be deceived, has always a reasonable ground for doubt, and therefore no solid ground for faith. Therefore, since, with a fallible witness, or fallible interpreter, we can never be sure that we are not mistaken, it follows, if we are to have faith at all, we must have a witness and interpreter that cannot err, therefore infallible.[40]

—III. As God requires faith in his word, in order to salvation, and this can have no place without the conditions now mentioned, we are bound to believe that these conditions *sine qua non* are by him provided for this end. Where then is the infallible witness and interpreter of God's word, thus indispensable to the exercise of faith in what it reveals, to be sought and found. It is not *reason*, whether as intuitive or discursive. It is not the *Bible*; because this itself needs to be authenticated and interpreted by some infallible authority beyond itself. It is not *private illumination*; for that at

---

38. [Brownson, "The Church Against," 152. Biblical allusion to Rom 1:20. The argument that an infinitely good being could not deceive us comes from Descartes, *Philosophical Works* 1:171.]

39. [Brownson, "The Church Against," 154.]

40. [Brownson, "The Church Against," 155.]

best would give only a private faith, while what we are required to have is a public faith, such as can be sustained by public evidence, by arguments which are open to all and common to all. "No witness, then, remains to be introduced but the Apostolic ministry, or *Ecclesia docens*."[41] Either this, or we have no witness.—IV. This conclusion is abundantly supported and made good also, in the way of historical fact. "The ministry is the organ through which Jesus Christ *supernaturally* bears witness to his own revelation."[42] It is infallible, not in virtue of what it is naturally, but by his supernatural presence. Such supernatural qualification or competency might seem to be a fact itself requiring again supernatural witness; but it is not so; the credibility of the witness may be "supernaturally established to natural reason by means of miracles."[43] A miracle connects the natural and supernatural, "so that natural reason can pass from the one to the other."[44] Natural reason can determine whether a fact be or be not a miracle; and if it be so, can conclude from it legitimately to the supernatural cause, and to the Divine commission or authority of him by whom it is wrought. The miracle is God's own assurance to natural reason, that he speaks in and by the person who performs it; in which case we have the veracity of God for the truth of what the miracle-worker declares, and therefore infallible certainty; "for God can neither deceive nor be deceived."[45] So then the process of proof for the fact before us, namely the infallible authority of the *Ecclesia docens*, is simple and easy.[46] The miracles of Christ, historically certified or made sure for natural reason, are sufficient to accredit his Divine commission,[47] and authorize the conclusion that whatever he said or promised was infallible truth; for whether you say Jesus was himself truly God as well as truly man, or that he was only divinely commissioned, you have in either case the veracity of God as the ground of faith in what he said or promised. Suppose then the fact that Jesus Christ appointed a body of teachers, and promised to be always with them to make them infallible, and suppose also this fact made infallibly certain to natural reason, by proper historical evidence; have we not, in such case, infallible certainty that Jesus Christ does speak in and through this body, and that it is absolutely secure thus from error in all it believes and teaches? Here we have recourse to the New Testament, which as a simple historical document may be infallibly clear for private reason alone, in *some* of its contents, though not in the whole. In Matth. xxviii. 18, 19, 20, Mark xvi.

41. [Brownson, "The Church Against," 173. *Ecclesia docens*: trans. "the teaching church."]
42. [Brownson, "The Church Against," 174.]
43. [Brownson, "The Church Against," 174–75.]
44. [Brownson, "The Church Against," 175. Closing quotation mark added.]
45. [Brownson, "The Church Against," 175. Quotation marks added.]
46. [Original quotation mark here deleted because misleading and inaccurate. Brownson's exact quotation is: "The supernatural, it follows, is provable. . . . The process of proof is simple and easy." Brownson, "The Church Against," 175].
47. [The quotation marks here have been deleted because misleading. The actual text reads: "The miracles of our blessed Lord were all that was necessary to establish his divine authority to those who saw them." Brownson, "The Church Against," 175.]

15, Eph. iv. 11, we have the well known apostolical commission; which is declared to reach to the end of the world, and to have regard to all nations. In such view, it requires and implies a corporation or body, always identical with itself. This is the *Ecclesia docens*, which with such constitution must be considered corporately infallible, and whose voice all men consequently are bound to obey as the voice of God.—V. Where now is this corporate ministry to be found, at the present time. It cannot be in the Greek communion; still less in the Protestant. It is then the Roman Catholic ministry; because it can be found nowhere else, and because also its regular succession can be clearly identified here from the beginning.

> Then we sum up by repeating, that Jesus Christ has instituted and commissioned an infallible and indefectible body of teachers, and this body is the congregation of the Roman Catholic pastors in communion with their chief. The Catholic Church then is the witness to the fact of revelation. What its pastors declare to be the word of God, is the word of God; what they enjoin as the faith, is the faith without which it is impossible to please God, and without which we are condemned and the wrath of God abideth on us. What they teach is the truth, the whole truth, and nothing but the truth; for God himself has commissioned them, and will not suffer them to fall into error in what concerns the things they have been commissioned to teach.[48]

Out of this Church, of course, no act of faith can take place; for faith is a theological virtue, which can be elicited only in obedience to God's authority, propounding truth in a supernatural and also public way; which we have only in the body of pastors, and teachers belonging to the Roman Catholic Church. See the article particularly entitled, *The Church against No-Church*.—April, 1845; also *The British Reformation* in the same volume; *Faith not Possible without the Church*.—Jan., 1846; *The Two Brothers, or why are you a Protestant*.—July, 1847; &c., &c.

[A Protestant Apologetic: Bible and Private Judgment]

The main force of this reasoning lies in this, that the view maintained is made to appear the only and necessary alternative to another view, starting from the same premises, which is found to be irrational and untenable. In both cases, Christianity is taken to be a revelation of supernatural truth, which men are to receive by faith, as something wholly out of themselves, that is brought near to them for their use in a purely outward way. As it has its source and seat beyond their proper nature altogether, so it cannot be allowed to find in this any rule or measure whatever for its apprehension. It must be taken as a matter of mere authority. The relation between the receptivity of faith on the one side, and the propounded truth on the other, the subject natural and the object supernatural, is held to be in no sense inward and living,

---

48. [Brownson, "The Church Against," 191.]

but mechanical only and juxtapositional, the one remaining always on the outside of the other. How now is the necessary connection between the two to be mediated, so as to secure for faith a real possession of the heteronomic supernatural? We take it only on God's testimony; God is true, and we may rationally trust his word, if we have it, in so great a case. Very good; agreed so far on all sides. Now comes however another question. How are we to be sure that God has spoken in the first place, and then in the next place that we have his very mind or sense in what he has spoken? It is not enough here to send us to the Bible; the question still returns, How do we know that the Bible is his word, and how are we to ascertain the mind of the Spirit in what it teaches? Inspiration is itself something supernatural, of which faith needs to be infallibly assured, in order that it may be infallibly sure of what it reveals. Here however a certain system of thought, which claims to be Protestantism, although it is not Protestantism in its true and genuine sense but a corruption of it rather on the side towards Rationalism, is ready at once to respond: "We need no infallible witness to assure us of the revelation, other than the inspired Bible itself; the proofs of its divinity lie open to reason, and every man may there get the mind of God out of it for himself." But with the theory of revelation before noticed, by which it is taken to be wholly outward and transcendent, and which resolves faith into an assent to grounds which are extrinsic both to the object and the subject, and to be found only in an authority that lies between, it is plain that this short method of settling the matter must land us at last in something very like infidelity itself. It is in truth to subordinate the supernatural to the natural, and to make the private reason of every man the seat and certification of God's oracles, sounded forth from world which has this same reason wholly on its outside. To say "Man needs no revelation, but only the full development of his nature;" and to say: "He may by his nature assure himself infallibly that he has a revelation on the outside of him, and also make out what it means in the same outward view;" are declarations that come to very much the same result in the end. In either case we have substantial rationalism, or a faith that has to do immediately and really, not with the supernatural at all in its own kind, but only with the natural shoved in as a supposed intermediate witness in its name and stead. Faith becomes a conclusion of logic, and not the substantiation of things invisible, immediately and directly, as they are in their own nature. The case labors under a twofold difficulty. First, the merely individual judgment is made to be the measure of truth, without regard to the claims of mind in its general character; which is in contradiction to the idea of humanity itself, as it comes before us on all other sides. Private judgment, like private will, has no force of reason ever *as private*, but becomes rational only by ceasing to be private and showing itself to be truly general. Then again, if it *could* be regarded as sufficient and complete, it must still be held of no power to bridge over effectually, in a real way, the impassable gulph by which it is here taken to be sundered from the object, of which faith needs to be infallibly certified and assured. The theory of the *Bible and Private Judgment*[49] then,

49. [A theory illustrated and critiqued in "Evangelical Radicalism," document 10 below.]

under this abstract form, cannot possibly bear examination. It is not only false, but pernicious to the very life of faith. It runs at last into mere naturalism and rationalism. Over against it, the argument for the idea of the Church, the claims of Christianity in its universal or catholic and historical character, and the necessity of a truly Divine certification or witness of supernatural truth for faith, is overwhelmingly conclusive. Without all this, Christianity has no power to save its proper divine credit. The alternative is, faith in this form or infidelity.[50] Romanism thus far is fully in the right; and if it can cause it to appear that its own theory, as exhibited by Mr. Brownson, is the only way of escape from what is thus opposed, we must feel ourselves bound certainly, as we fear God and value his salvation, to throw ourselves into its arms.

At present, however, we do not see this theory to be such a necessary way of escape from the ruinous system it so justly condemns on the opposite side. On the contrary, it seems to us intrinsically defective in its own constitution, as being nothing less in truth than the reverse side of that bad system itself; which as such is found, on close inspection, to labor under substantially the same difficulty and contradiction. Here, as there, the difficulty is again of a double sort. The general is made to exclude the individual, as there the reverse; in contradiction to the idea of humanity, as we find it in the natural world. And then, as before, no real bridge is made to span the gulph that divides the visible from the invisible. Both views are alike in this, that they make faith to rest on a conclusion of mere natural reason, and will not allow the supernatural, as such, to come by means of it into any real union with the natural. We will try to make our meaning clear, as regards Romanism, by the following general observations, in the way of criticism on Mr. Brownson's argument in its defence.

[Nevin's Critique of Brownson's Apologetic]

[Brownson's Neglect of Freedom]

I. The theory involves a general wrong against our human constitution, naturally considered, inasmuch as it will not allow its ordinary law of freedom to have force in the sphere of religion, which is that precisely in which it is required to make itself complete.[51] The general law of our nature is that mind must fulfil its mission, not by following blindly a mere outward force of any sort, but by the activity of its own intelligence and will, both as general and individual. It must move in the light that springs from itself, and by the power it generates continually from within. This moral constitution includes complex relations, laws, organic interdependence, action and reaction,

---

50. We propose to take up this subject again, sometime hereafter, in the way of a review of two interesting and profound tracts by the justly celebrated Dr. Owen, on the *Reason of Faith* and [*Synesis Pneumatikē,*] the *Causes, Ways and Means of understanding the mind of God as revealed in his word.* [John Owen (1616–83), British Puritan theologian, wrote numerous theological treatises that supported the independent Puritan movement in England.]

51. [See *Human Freedom*, document 2 above.]

as in the world of nature, on a vast and magnificent scale. Still to the idea of it as a whole the conception of freedom appertains, in the form now stated, as a necessary universal distinction. The theory of Mr. Brownson however, if we rightly understand it, requires us to assume that in the highest form of religion, that which is reached in Christianity, the human mind ceases to be directly active in the accomplishment of what is brought to pass in its favor, and is a passive recipient simply of foreign action brought to bear on it in an outward way. It does not help the matter, that it is taken to be active with regard to Christianity in a different sphere; the difficulty is that no activity is allowed to it in the realization of Christianity itself, as the highest fact of the world. Christianity claims to be the perfection of man's life; this, in its ordinary constitution, unfolds itself by its own self-movement, in the way of thought and will; but just here all this is superseded by another law altogether; the supernatural comes in as the outward complement of the natural, in such sort as to make the force of this last null and void in all that pertains to its higher sphere.

[Brownson's Separation of Subject and Object]

II. This wrong against human nature becomes most immediately plain, in the violence which the individual mind is made to suffer, by the theory, in favor of what is taken to be general. The existence of truth is objective, and in such view of course universal and independent of all private thought or will; but as thus objective it must be at the same time subjective, must enter into particular thought and will, in order to be real. As object merely, without subject, it becomes a pure abstraction. Mere single mind can never be, in and by itself, the measure of either truth or right; it must be ruled, and so bound, by the objective or the authority of the general. On the other hand, however, the general as such, mere law or object, is no such measure either, in and by itself; to be so, it must take concrete form in the life of the world, which resolves itself at last into the thinking and willing of single minds. But now, in the case before us, Romanism sets aside the authority of this order, which is found to be of such universal force for the constitution of our nature in every other view. Christianity is taken to be of force for the world under a simply abstract form; an outwardly supernatural revelation, transcending the whole order of our common life, and not needing nor allowing the activity of man himself, as an intelligent and free subject, to be the medium in any way of its presence and power. Authority is made to be all, and freedom nothing. The authority too is cut off and sundered from the proper life of the subject, and in this way comes to no real union with his intelligence and will. It comes from abroad, stands over him in an outward way, and requires him to submit to it as a foreign force. Authority thus is not mediated at all by man's actual life; is in no sense living and concrete, but altogether mechanical, rigid, and fixed. It is from the start a given quantity, just so much, and nothing either more or less. It excludes private thought and will, according to Mr. Brownson. "The two authorities," that of private thought and that of the Church, "may indeed co-exist," we are told, "but not in regard to the same matters; for one is the negation of the other."[52] The right of private judgment is taken to be of force only where the authority of the Church ceases; as though each had its own territory separate from that of the other, without the possibility, ever of any truly common jurisdiction. "To assume the authority of both private judgment and the Church on the same matters, is, [as we have said,] absurd. One authority necessarily excludes the other. If it is private judgment, then not the Church; if the Church, then not private judgment."[53] The office of reason ends, where authority begins.

> We accept private judgment, as well as the Bishop (Hopkins),[54] and give full scope to the individual reason, but only within its legitimate province. We reconcile reason and authority by ascertaining the province of reason, and confining it within its legitimate province. Questions of reason are to be decided by reason, but questions of faith are to be decided by authority; for all faith rests on authority, and would not be faith if it did not. See article on the British Reformation.—Jan. 1845 [p. 45].

Authority may override private reason, and make it null. Its teachings and commands, in the case of the Church, "constitute the rule of truth and falsehood, right and wrong, good and evil. It is no matter what you prove she teaches and commands; for if it be clear that she teaches and commands it, we will maintain that it is true, right, and good, against all gainsayers, even to the dungeon, exile, or the stake, if need be."[55] Articles of faith are first principles, or axioms in religion, over which "reason has no natural rights, never had any, never can have any; because they lie out of her province, and belong to the supernatural, where her authority does not extend."[56] So again:—"The articles of faith are not taken from the dominions of reason, but they are certain grants made gratuitously to her, extending, instead of abridging, her authority, and therefore serve instead of injuring her."—Oct. 1845, p. 448-451.[57] This, and a great deal more to the same purpose, shows clearly enough the relation in which Mr. Brownson makes faith stand to reason; and so the view he takes of authority, or the claims of the general, as related to the rights of the individual mind. He sees rightly enough that a purely unbound freedom, liberty without law, is the very conception of slavery itself; but does not stop to take into view the other side of the truth, this namely, that a purely bound authority, law without liberty, is slavery also. "Liberty to

---

52. [Brownson, "The British Reformation," 41.]
53. [Brownson, "The British Reformation," 41.]
54. [John Henry Hopkins (1792–1868), bishop of the Protestant Episcopal Church of Vermont, opposed the Oxford Movement and wrote an historical account of the British Reformation, *Sixteen Lectures* (1844), that Brownson reviewed and criticized in the article that Nevin cites here.]
55. [Brownson, "Professor Park," 448.]
56. [Brownson, "Professor Park," 451.]
57. [Brownson, "Professor Park."]

hold and teach," he tells us, "what the Sovereign Pontiff says we may, is all the liberty we ask;" for this is liberty to obey God's law, the only liberty he allows to any man.

> Law is the basis of liberty, and where there is no sovereign authority there is no law. Liberty is not in being free of all law, but in being held only to the law. We believe the Church, and the Pope as visible head of the Church, is the organ through which Almighty God promulgates the law. Consequently, in our own estimation at least, in submitting to the Pope, we find, instead of losing our liberty. —Jan. 1816, p. 101.[58]

Good. No law, no liberty. But still, the planet is not free in being true simply to the law that carries it round the sun; and the animal is not free, that follows the law of its own instincts. Law here is not enough. It must be met by the spontaneity of a free subject, which with the power to go aside from its orbit, makes the law notwithstanding the very form of its own action, producing its authority purely and truly from within. Certainly, the theory before us is ready to say, the law must be obeyed freely, by the option and choice of the obeying subject; but this requires no autonomy of the subject, in the constitution of the law, no voice in its legislation; all the case demands or allows, is that on grounds extrinsic wholly to its constitution the subject be rationally persuaded that obedience is wise and right. Is this however, more at last, we ask, than mere prudence, or a skillful calculation of profit and loss? Is the man free who obeys the law, *Thou shalt not kill*, to avoid the gallows? Is it liberty to say white is black or black white, though it should be said never so pleasantly and glibly, because we are required to do so by an authority which we feel it unsafe to resist?[59] Am I free when I renounce my own intelligence and will, and accept in their place another measure of truth altogether *in no union whatever with my personal reason*, whether from the hand of an earthly prince to buy political distinction, or from the hand of a pope to buy a place in heaven? Freedom is more, a great deal, than any such outward consent to the authority of law. It is life in the law, union with it, the very form in which it comes to its revelation in the moral world. Place the law as an objective force on the outside wholly of the intelligence and will of those who are to be its subjects, and at once you convert it into an abstract nothing. This is the natural extreme of Romanism. Against it, the Reformation formed a legitimate and absolutely necessary reaction and protest. It is quite in the order of history, that this protest should itself lead again to extreme results on the opposite side, making the subjective everything and the supernatural objective next to nothing. But the cure for this is not just the old error; and however

---

58. [Brownson, "Methodist Quarterly Review."]

59. [Nevin seems to be referencing Ignatius Loyola's "Rules for Thinking with the Church" (1534-35): Rule 13, "What seems to me white, I will believe black if the hierarchical church so defines." The rule is generally misunderstood. It emphasizes church doctrinal definitions. On this, see Loyola, "Rules for Thinking," no. 365, pp. 129-30. He might further have in mind the Platonic problem raised in the story of "Gyges' Ring": if one is just only because one is compelled by fear of punishment or desire for reward, is one truly just (*Republic* II, 359b-360d)?]

much of force there may be in Mr. Brownson's polemics, as directed against Parkerism, Socialism, and Pseudo-protestantism universally, (a force which *we* have no wish certainly to deny or oppose) it does not follow by any means that Protestantism, as simply opening the way for such abuse, is to be considered unsound and false from the start; just as little as the abuses of Popery show the Catholic truths to be false, from which they can be shown to have taken their rise. It is still as true now, as it was at the beginning of the sixteenth century, that the *actualization* of truth in the world, is something which can be accomplished only through the medium of intelligence and will on the part of the world itself; that liberty, in its genuine sense, is not simply the outward echo of authority, but the very element of its life, and the co-efficient of its power, in that which it brings to pass; that man is no passive machine merely in the business of his own salvation; that the free activity of the individual subject in the world of mind, never can be paralyzed or overwhelmed by the sense of law, as a nature foreign and transcendent wholly to its own nature, without such bondage as involves in the end the overthrow of reason altogether.

The force of this position does not depend on the kind of authority, that is to be obeyed. Whether it be divine or human is all the same thing, if it is taken to be something wholly on the outside of the subject, in no way congenerous[60] with his natural constitution, a law beyond his own reason altogether and foreign from his life. It is not in such view, that God exercises authority. His will is never arbitrary, and so never abstract. Where it touches men, it forms in truth the inmost and deepest reason always of their own being; and in such view, though it may not be fully comprehensible, and though it could never have been dreamed of without supernatural revelation, still it must be allowed, even to the mystery of the Blessed Trinity itself, to carry in itself such an organic agreement with the world's life as otherwise known, and such a felt suitableness to the demands of reason, as may serve to evidence its rationality at least afar off, and create thus a presumption in its favor from the start. It will not do to say, that reason is absolutely passive in the reception of what is propounded by Divine authority; in such way, for instance, that it would be as easy to allow five persons in the Godhead as it is to allow three, or that a Hindoo avatar[61] might be believed as fully as the Christian Incarnation, on the strength simply of God's outward word. It may be said indeed, and with truth also, that to be sure of God's word in the case is to be sure of the intrinsic rationality of what it is thus supposed to proclaim; but this just shows, that we *cannot* be sure of his word without some regard to the intrinsic reasonableness of what it propounds, and that this itself accordingly is ever to be taken as part of the evidence for the other fact. In other words, the authority of the revelation is not abstract and foreign wholly from the nature of the life, for which it is made. Our difficulty here with Mr. Brownson, then, is not just that he arms the Pope with divine

---

60. ["Of the same kind or nature." Webster, *American Dictionary*, 178.]

61. [In Hinduism, the millions of gods are incarnations or embodiments of the universal power, Brahman.]

authority, whereas he might seem to be only a common man; but that such authority, in the hands of the Pope or anywhere else, should be taken to supersede and nullify so completely the true idea of human freedom. The theory rests on a wrong conception of what authority is in the world of mind, and so on a wrong conception of the true nature of the Church, as the divinely constituted organ and bearer of Christ's will among men, (as we too take it to be) to the end of time.

[Church More than Teaching Magisterium]

III. For as already intimated in some measure, the necessary result of such a separation of liberty and law, the rights of the subjective and the claims of the objective, is vast wrong in the end to the second of these interests as well as to the first. The true idea of authority in the moral world, requires that it should come to its revelation, under a concrete form, through the medium of the general life and in the way of history. With the theory of Mr. Brownson, however, all this fails. The Church is taken to be the infallible witness of God's mind in the Christian revelation; but not in virtue of her living wholeness as the Body of him that filleth all in all, her life serving in such universal form, as the natural medium for unfolding the full sense of its own contents; all this is precluded by the conception of an abstract ministry, or *ecclesia docens*, on which the gift of infallibility is conferred in a purely outward supernatural way. This gift is not mediated at all, in any way, by the life of the Church as a whole. The *ecclesia docens* is no organic product and outbirth of the new creation generally, which it is appointed to serve. Its prophetical, priestly and kingly functions,[62] are not the activity of Christ's mystical body working itself forth collectively in such form, by appropriate organs created for the purpose. The ministry rather is independent of the Church; it has a life of its own; it is a separate organization, through which the higher powers of Christianity are carried forward, by a wholly distinct channel, for the use of the world from age to age. These higher powers too belong to it in a mechanical, magical way, and not according to the ordinary law of truth and power among men. It is objected to Mr. Newman, that he makes the general mind of the Church the medium of christian knowledge. "This view, if followed out," we are told,

> would suppress entirely the proper teaching authority of the Church, competent at any moment to declare infallibly what is the precise truth revealed; or at least would raise the *ecclesia credens* [believing church], above the *ecclesia docens*, and reduce the office of the Church teaching to that of defining, from time to time, the dogmatic truth which the Church believing has gradually and slowly worked out from her implicit feelings. The secret supernatural

---

62. [In Reformed dogmatics, these are the three "offices" of Christ. See Calvin, *Institutes*, ed. McNeill, 2.15.1–6 (1:494) and n. 2. Nevin criticized the doctrine as making Christ's work external to his person (Nevin, "Bread of Life," MTSS 6:225 and n. 11). Thus here it is doubly externalistic, since the "activity" of the *ecclesia docens* is a "separate organization" from the Church.]

assistance would then attach to the Church believing, and superintend the elaboration, rather than to the Church teaching; and if to the Church teaching at all, only so far as to enable it faithfully to collect and truly define what the Church believing elaborates.—July, 1846, p. 354.[63]

There is no room with this view, of course, for the conception of anything like a progressive actualization of the life of the Church, in the form of authority. As the infallibility which belongs to her is independent of her natural constitution, abstract and not concrete, so it lies also wholly on the outside of her proper human presence in the world. To be out of history, is to be out of humanity. All this is encumbered with difficulty. We find no clear account of it in the New Testament. What is said there of the Church and its ministry, leads of itself to no such conception. The two forms of existence are exhibited rather as one; the second proceeding organically from the first; the entire constitution holding moreover under the character of life, real human life, in unity with itself throughout. It is not easy again, to withstand the universal analogy of the actual world in favor of the same view. Humanity, in all other cases, accomplishes its destiny by organic co-operation, carried forward in the form of history. Truth is brought to pass for it, through the medium of its own activity, the whole working towards its appointed end by the joint ministry of the parts, in such a way however, as to be something more always than these separately taken. So it is in the sphere of science; so in the sphere of art; so in the sphere of politics and social life. In each case, we have association, organization, historical movement; intercommunity of powers and functions; in one direction activity to guide and rule, in another direction activity to obey and follow; but this distinction conditioned by the life of the corporation itself in its whole character, and so always more or less free and flowing, not fixed by arbitrary ordination from abroad. The same law is allowed to have place in the sphere of religion too, beyond the precincts of Christianity. Even Judaism, we are told, was not exempt from its operation. But in the sphere of the Church, as it stands since Christ, we are required to take all differently. As a supernatural constitution, it must not conform to the order of nature. It must be neither organic, nor historical, nor human, in its higher life; but one long monotony rather of mere outward law and authority, superseding the natural order of the world, and contradicting it, age after age, to the end of time. The Roman system carries in itself thus a constant tendency to resolve the force of Christianity into magic, and to fall into the snare of the mere *opus operatum* in its bad sense.[64] It must be confessed, at all events, that the theory, right or wrong, labors here under a difficulty, which it is by no means easy for a truly thoughtful mind to surmount.

---

63. [Brownson, "Newman's Development."]
64. [Literally, "the work wrought." The phrase is used by theologians like Thomas Aquinas to mean that by the merits of Christ, the sacraments have the power to confer grace. In the "bad sense," the phrase has been thought to mean that grace is conferred irrespective of the receiver.]

Document 7: Brownson's Quarterly Review.

[Relationship of Nature and the Supernatural]

IV. This brings us to notice more particularly, in the next place, the general relation in which the supernatural is taken by this system to stand to the natural, and its corresponding view of divine revelation. The two worlds are held to be wholly disjoined and separate the one from the other, so that any connection which is formed between them is regarded as outward only and not in the way of common life. The truth with which faith has to do belongs to the "supernatural order," which transcends altogether, we are told, the order of nature; holds out of it, above it and beyond it; and cannot come to any organic union with it, under its own form. The two worlds are sundered by an impassable gulph, as regards inward constitution and being; only by the word of God, as an outward report, it is possible for faith, in the sphere of nature, to be infallibly assured of what lies beyond in a higher sphere.[65] This abstract conception of the supernatural, as something that refuses utterly to flow into one life in any way with the natural, may be said to underlie the whole theory of Romanism, as we find it set forth by Mr. Brownson; and it is of so much the more force to lend it plausibility, as it is for substance very generally accepted as correct, only with a less broad application, by those who are most forward to oppose the pretensions of this system as vain and false. Much of our Protestant orthodoxy, it must be confessed, rests on precisely the same abstract supernaturalism,[66] in the view it takes of the Bible as the medium of divine revelation; without seeing that from such premises we are shut up at last, without help or escape, to the Romanist conclusion; since if the matter of revelation be wholly without self-evidencing power for faith, and such that it can be received on the ground of outward divine authority or testimony only, it follows plainly that we need also an infallible outward witness in the Church, to assure us in like mechanical style

---

65. We have a strong assertion of such *transcendence* in the article, "Natural and Supernatural."—Jun. [Jan.] 1847, p. 110, 111, in reply to the allegation of an opponent that man's capacity of knowing God, as far as it goes, can be only through kindred powers. "Why could not Newton's dog know Newton? Because he had not the kindred powers [110]." Mr. Brownson accepts the case as in point, and turns it to his own use. The dog did know his master within the range of a dog's nature; but not in the order in which Newton transcended this; "no one can know naturally above the order of his nature," [110] and so no one can know naturally the supernatural. But will the objector deny, asks Mr. B., "that Almighty God, if he had chosen, could, by a special act of his power, have so elevated the dog's powers as to have enabled him to know his master in the full sense in which one man may know another [111]?" And so the mind of man may be supernaturalized, by the gift of faith, into a capacity for apprehending the supernatural; while all this implies no fitness in his nature previously for any such apprehension. But is not this power, we ask, to set the higher sphere wholly on the outside of the lower, and to make the translation from the second to the first a simple miracle? The dog, to ascend into the order of man's life, must be essentially changed, created over again altogether; and if the supernatural entering man's life be a like process, it must be virtually his demolition and the construction of a new being, by Divine fiat, in his place.

66. [For Nevin's meaning of "abstract supernaturalism," see Nevin et al., *Born of Water*, MTSS 6:76n23. Evangelical Protestantism appealed to reason as an external "proof" of Biblical revelation; in place of that Brownson appealed to "Romanist" authority. But the need for some "externalistic" authority was parallel. Here Nevin clearly thinks that Brownson's position is more consistent.]

where this authority is really and truly at hand. The reasonableness of faith turns not at all, according to this school, on any correspondence in which it stands directly with its own contents, but purely and exclusively on its relation to the extrinsic authority on which they are accepted as true. The principle, that we must judge the speaker by the word, however sound within the sphere of nature, is taken to involve infidelity, or at least a strong leaning to it, when adopted in the sphere of religion; "for it cannot be adopted in the sphere of religion without first denying, that in religion there is anything to be believed which transcends natural reason; therefore it cannot be adopted without denying supernatural revelation; and to deny supernatural revelation is what is meant by infidelity."— Oct. 1845, p. 510.[67]

It might seem enough to convict this theory of error, so far as the Bible is concerned, that this bears on the face of it throughout clear proof of a real union of the supernatural with the natural, in the persons of the sacred writers. The truth it reveals is conditioned in the form of its manifestation always, by the mind and education of the men who give it utterance, and through them by the living human relations in the midst of which they stood. No two prophets think alike or speak alike. Their inspiration then is no abstraction, no divine mechanism, but something that truly descends, with all its divinity, into the order of nature. And what shall we say of Him, in whom all prophecy and inspiration became at last complete? Was it his office simply to stand between the two worlds that met in his person, and report *mysteries* over from one to the other, for the use of faith, in a purely outward way? What is meant then by the declaration: The *Word* became *Flesh*, and dwelt among us, and we beheld his glory, the glory as of the only-begotten of the Father, full of grace and truth [John 1:14]. Surely if the gospel means anything, we have here at least the supernatural order linked in real organic union with the natural, and showing thus the capacity of this last, as well as its need, to receive into itself such higher life as its own proper complement and end. It will not do, in the face of such a fact as the *Incarnation*, to say that the realities with which faith has to do in distinction from reason are wholly without light or evidence for this last in their own nature, and as such to be taken on the mere authority of God ascertained in some such sense that a man might be supposed to be infallibly sure first that he has this authority to go upon, and so be prepared to accept any and every proposition as true, on the strength of it, with equal readiness and ease. What is revelation, if it be not the actual entrance of the supernatural in some way over into the sphere of the natural? That which remains wholly beyond the orb of man's life, naturally considered, and in no living contact with it at any point, cannot be said surely to be revealed at all for his apprehension and use. All revelation, as distinguished from magic, implies the self-exhibition of God, in a real way, through the medium of the world in its natural form. To a certain extent, we have such a revelation in the material universe. The outward creation is the symbol, mirror, shrine and sacrament, of God's presence and glory, as a supernatural fact, in the most actual way. The word

---

67. [Brownson, "Professor Park."]

of prophecy and inspiration is the gradual coming forth of eternal truth into time, in a like real way, through the medium of human thought and speech; a process, which completes itself finally in the full domiciliation, we may say, of the Infinite Word itself in the life of the world by Jesus Christ.[68] It is an utterly unevangelical conception of this fact, to think of Christ only as an outward teacher or reporter of secrets, belonging to another order of existence wholly from that in which he appeared among men. Such a conception involves in fact the old Gnostic imagination, by which the supernatural side of his existence was never allowed to come to any really inward and organic union with its natural or simply human side; in consequence of which this last became always a phantom, and the first at the same time an extra-mundane abstraction. In Christ, most literally and truly, the supernatural order came to a living and perpetual marriage with the order of nature; which it could not have done, if the constitution of the one had not been of like sort with that of the other, (man made in the image truly of God) so as to admit and require such union as the last and only perfect expression of the world's life. It lies then in the nature of the case, that Christ can be no abstraction, no solitary portent, in the midst of the world. If his incarnation involved a real entrance into its life at all, (and not simply an avatar, whether for an hour or for ten thousand years,) it must stand in living inward relation, and this fundamental too and central, with its entire organization and history under every other view. The lines of truth must fall in upon it as their necessary centre, from all sides, out to the farthest periphery of nature. It must be found to carry in it the inmost and deepest sense of the universal sphere to which it belongs. It is a fact therefore which must come harbingered and heralded by voices from the deep, and long shadows thrown before, signs, prophecies, and types, from every quarter; all made clear at last indeed only by the event itself; whilst with equal necessity, the powers of history may be expected to throw themselves subsequently, always more and more, into its train, the world before and the world behind joining thus in one and the same loud acclamation : "Hosannah to the Son of David! Blessed is he that cometh in the name of the Lord [Matt 21:9]!" But now, if this be the relation of the supernatural in Christ himself to the sphere of nature, it is not easy certainly to acquiesce in any theory of the Church, by which this is taken to be the medium of divine revelation in a wholly different style. An abstract Church, is as much at war with the true mystery of Christianity, as an abstract Christ. The Church, according to Mr. Brownson, is the infallible witness of God's word, not in the way of any really human mediation in the case, but in a wholly outward and unearthly way, by a special fiat of grace investing it with such infallibility, as a fixed mechanical fact, in no union whatever with the laws of our life under its ordinary form.[69] This we find it by no means easy to admit. The view works back unfavorably

---

68. [Near, the end of his life, Nevin develops these themes in "The Testimony of Jesus" and "The Spirit of Prophecy."]

69. Mr. Brownson sees the Church always as an order extrinsical to the life of nature, or to humanity in its own proper form. Human institutions, he admits, allow a mixture of good and bad; but the

on the whole idea of revelation; and especially wrongs, in the end, the character of Jesus Christ. We are very far from believing, that the divinity of a revelation turns on its having no common life with humanity; on the contrary it seems to us to become complete, in proportion precisely as the supernatural, by means of it, is brought to enter most fully and truly into the conditions of the natural.

[On Faith and Reason]

V. The theory carries with it finally, as it seems to us, a wrong conception of the true nature and power of faith, involving in the end the very consequence it seeks professedly to shun, namely the subordination of faith to reason or its resolution into mere logic. It goes on the assumption that the supernatural, with which faith has to do, is so sundered from the natural, as to admit no direct approach or apprehension from that side; that truth in such form is inevident for the mind wholly in its own nature, and without force of reason intrinsically to engage its assent; that the mind is moved to such assent in its case accordingly, not by any motives either in itself or in the object set before it, but by something extrinsic to both, the weight of an intermediate authority which is felt to be fully valid as a ground of certainty, without regard to the nature of what is thus taken on trust one way or another. "In belief," says Mr. Brownson, "I must go out of myself, and also out of the object, for my motives of assent."[70] Subjective and objective come to no union or contact whatever. The gulph between them is sprung only by means of outward *testimony*. The case requires indeed Divine testimony; but still it is this always as something *between* the subject and object, in a purely separate and external way. As such, the testimony itself needs of course to be authenticated, before it can be rested upon as sure and certain; and this authentication must be again infallible. Such a witness of God's veracity we have in the Church, whose voice accordingly is to be taken as the true sense always of his word. The Divine authority of the Church, it is supposed, may be established for natural reason in its own sphere; although this of itself is not enough to produce faith. For that we need what is termed the *donum fidei* [gift of faith], a supernatural benefit conferred by the ministry of the Church itself through the holy sacrament of Baptism.

Church, he will have it, is no *human* institution. "If Christian, she is divine—for Christ is God; and then she is not a human institution, unless God and man are identical;" and so she must be taken as only and wholly true, right, and good.— [Brownson, "H. M. Field's,"] July, 1849, p. 310. But Christianity in the individual believer is divine too; does it then make *him* to be also free from all error and sin? Even an apostle, it seems, might do wrong. And is the Church in fact so good, as to be literally *sinless* as well as infallible? Her divine side of course is both one and the other; but she has also her human side, her divinity shines through humanity; she is not only the heavenly leaven of Christ's life in the world, but the true and proper life of the world itself also *in the progress of being leavened*. The progress here is not at once the end.

70. [Brownson, "The Church Against," 151.]

Document 7: Brownson's Quarterly Review.

We object to the way in which faith is here opposed to reason. Its opposition is properly to sense, and to nature as known through sense; to reason, only so far as this is taken for the understanding in its relation to such knowledge. Faith is the capacity of perceiving the invisible and supernatural, the substantiation of things hoped for, the certification of things not seen (Heb. xi. 1); which, as such, does not hold on the outside of reason, any more than this can be said of sense, but opens to view rather a higher form of what may be called its own proper life, in which it is required to become complete, and without which it must always remain comparatively helpless, blind, and dark. It requires of a truth, in our present circumstances, a supernatural influence to call faith into exercise; no force of logic, and no simply natural motives, can bring it to pass; there must be for the purpose a new life by the Spirit of Christ. But still all this forms at last but the proper education, or drawing out, of the true sense of man's life as it stood before. Faith does not serve simply to furnish new *data* for thought in an outward way, but includes in itself also, potentially at least, the force of reason and knowledge in regard to its own objects. It stands in rational correspondence with its contents, and involves such an apprehension of them as makes the mind to be in some measure actually in their sphere. Faith touches its object as truly as sense. This requires indeed the medium of God's veracity; we can perceive the supernatural, only as we feel and know that God exists; faith thus sees all things in God. But the veracity of God here is no abstraction; it reaches us in and by the things it verifies and affirms. So in the world of nature. Mr. Brownson will not allow the revelation of God in nature to be for faith at all; we have it, he says, by mere reason; "regarded solely as the author, upholder, and governor of nature, he is natural, and hence the knowledge of him as such is always termed *natural theology*." In this character, "he is naturally cognoscible, according to what St. Paul tells us, Rom. i. 20."— [Brownson, "The Church Against"] April, 1845, p. 146[-47]. But surely mere logic can never conclude from the world of sense to the world of spirit, from the finite to the infinite. To perceive God in nature requires far more than any syllogism. We see him there, only when he authenticates himself to us by his works, as the immediate felt symbol of his presence; and then our perception is faith. So St. Paul, Heb. xi. 3: "*Through faith* we understand that the worlds mere framed by the word of God, so that things which are seen were not made of things which do appear." Through the world of sense, faith looks continually, not the logical understanding, to the vast and glorious Reality that lies beyond,[71] and of which it is only the outward type or shadow. Nature in this view is a divine word (as in the 19th psalm) always showing forth the supernatural;[72] having its seal or witness

---

71. [Nevin's exact meaning here is uncertain. Is "logical understanding" being contrasted to "faith" or "Reality"? The "world of sense" is the "type" of "Reality." "Mere logic" does not disclose God; it is faith that sees God in the sensual world. That much is clear, and supports the rephrasing "faith, not the logical understanding, looks continually . . . to the . . . Reality." However, one could also rewrite it: "through the world of sense, faith looks continually, not {to} the logical understanding, {but} to the . . . Reality."]

72. [Ps 19:1, "The heavens declare the glory of God; and the firmament showeth his handiwork."]

too in the veracity of God, that is, in his being, as a fact underlying the phenomenal creation; while however, at the same time, this fact makes itself immediately certain, not from beyond, but in and by the very document, which it thus seals and certifies for faith. And why should it be different in the case of revelation, under its higher view? God speaks in the Bible; and he must himself authenticate his own voice. This implies however no merely outward certification, apart from the word itself. He reveals himself for faith, in and by the word, as the very medium of his own presence. This becomes most clear in the person of Jesus Christ, the Word Incarnate, by whom all previous revelation is made at last complete. How is *He* authenticated for faith? By Divine testimony. In what form? Miracles, according to Mr. Brownson. "From the miracle the reason concludes legitimately to the supernatural cause, and to the Divine commission or authority of him by whom it is wrought."[73] Jesus Christ performed miracles, and stands accredited by them as a Divine teacher. But could a miracle legitimate the pretensions of the Mormon prophet, Joseph Smith?[74] Certainly not. The miracle itself needs to be authenticated, by the living person and word of him whose commission it is appointed to seal. This is plain from Deut. xiii. 1–3; which is of itself sufficient to show that reason is concerned, in faith, not simply with the seal of God's word outwardly considered, but with the intrinsic reasonableness also of the word itself. A miracle in favor of a lie proves nothing. Is the word itself then enough, without the miracle? By no means. Only they are not to be sundered one from the other. They are wedded together as body and soul. The body authenticates the presence of the soul; but it is only as the soul, at the same time, authenticates the life of the body. Christ's miracles then are indeed a divine attestation of his character and mission; but their true force for this end holds at last in their relation to his person. *That* underlies all truth in the world besides; and how then could it be proved or made sure by any other form of truth, taken as something separate from itself? Christ thus authenticates himself, and all else that is true. Not abstractly again however, but concretely, in and by the living relations of his presence in the world. The supernatural in his life, including his miracles, forms but the natural and proper expression of what his life was in its own power. The force of all falls back finally on his person itself; and it is with this accordingly that faith has to do primarily, in accepting his Divine mission. The voice of God for it, attesting the revelation comes not from abroad, but in and through the revelation itself. Thou art the Christ, it says with Peter, and to whom else shall we go; thou hast the words of eternal life. "He that believeth on the Son of God," says St. John," hath the witness in himself; he that believeth not God—in and by this revelation—hath made him a liar" (1 John v. 10). Not to own and obey Christ, is the greatest possible wrong to truth which any man can commit. It is such a blow at God's veracity

---

73. [Brownson, "The Church Against," 175.]

74. [Joseph Smith, Jr. (1805–44), founder of The Church of Jesus Christ of Latter Day Saints (Mormons), published in 1830 *The Book of Mormon*. He was murdered by a mob in Carthage, Illinois, near where his followers had located themselves. On Smith, see Bushman, *Joseph Smith* (1984).]

as can be aimed at it in no other way; for the Truth of truth itself is Christ, the alpha and omega of life, the same yesterday, to-day, and forever. Faith here is not indifferent to the word and work of Christ; but still it sees these in the light of his person, and does not so much conclude to this as from it, in the view it takes of their significance. It is not by establishing his miraculous conception, or the fact of his resurrection, in an abstract separate view, that we prove him to be the Son of God; but we must feel him in the first place to be the Son of God, with Peter, before we can truly believe, on any evidence, either the first of these facts or the last. *He* is the last proof of both. So in the Creed. Christ authenticates himself for faith, not by mere outward warrant and seal of any sort, but by direct communication, in some way, with the rational nature of men, as being himself indeed the life of reason and the only true light of the world. Faith here, as in all other cases, is led by motives of assent in its object, and not simply by motives drawn from some other quarter; or in other words, the authority of God moving it is not on the outside of the object, but comes to view in and by the object bearing its proper seals, these last having no conclusive force save in union and connection with the first.[75]

Mr. Brownson himself is forced to allow something like this in the end, though as it seems to us not without contradiction to his own general theory. Reason may conclude in its own sphere, he says, from the natural to the supernatural by the miracle; but not so as to generate faith; this comes in another way as a free donation from God. It is not given to us in the fact that we are human beings, but supernaturally, so as to lift us from the order of nature to the order of grace. Supernaturalized in this way,

> the creditive [believing] subject is placed on the plane of the supernatural credible object, and they are thus *correlatively* creditive and credible; and if no obstacle intervene, the act of faith is not only elicitable, but elicited, *without other motive than is contained in the subject and object,* as is the case with every act of faith, whether human or divine.[76]

Faith then is not blind and regardless of its object. "The *donum fidei* is not a general *vis creditiva* [power of belief], but simply *vis creditiva* in relation to its special correlative, the supernatural credible object." What it believes is the authority of God, but this authority in identification always with the object it commends to faith; just as light, in the natural world, bears witness to the objects of sense, shows them as they are for

75. [For Nevin, faith was the "organ by which we perceive and apprehend the spiritual and eternal; . . . the very eye . . . that enables us to 'look at things unseen,' and causes their presence to surround us as a part of our own life." "The Apostles' Creed," MTSS 8:59; see also the 1838 sermon, *"The Seal of the Spirit,"* 6. I see and touch a tree, and the tree verifies itself to my perception. Through the organ of faith, a believer "knows" Christ, who thus discloses himself to the believer. Therefore, his objection was that, according to Brownson, faith needed an external "motive of assent," the authority of the church, rather experiencing the self-authenticating power of Christ. In a parallel manner, most Protestants used reason as a motive for believing in Scripture, as he states below. (David Layman acknowledges DiPuccio, "Nevin & Coleridge," 61, for reminding him of these sources.)]

76. [Brownson, "Liberalism and Catholicity," 299, Nevin's emphases.]

the eye, by making them at the same time the medium of its own revelation. Such is the view given of the subject in the article, "Liberalism and Catholicity" July, 1846 [299, 311]; which however, as we have just said, seems not to agree fully with what is said, when we are told, April, 1845,[77] "that faith or belief, as distinguished from knowledge and science, rests on authority extrinsic both to the believer and the matter believed." If this be meant simply to exclude the notion that reason is the mother of faith, the so-called *Vulgar Rationalism*, it is all very well. But in the hands of Mr. Brownson, it is made to mean much more. It sets faith out of the sphere of reason altogether, and reduces it to the character of a mere blind assent to outward authority; contrary to what we find him saying again of the *donum fidei*, as an actual bringing of the subject into inward correlation with the object believed. Where the authority for faith is thus taken to be extrinsic to the supernatural object, as with the system generally, we are thrown at last on the very rationalism, which it is sought in this way to avoid. So our common abstract supernaturalism, on the Protestant side, is in the habit of concluding *logically*, from miracles and other evidence in the sphere of nature, to the supernatural authority of the Bible, and then pretends to make this, in such outward view, a complete succedaneum[78] subsequently for all reason besides—as though reason and revelation were only contiguous spheres, the one ending where the other begins; not considering, that the whole authority of the Bible itself thus can be no better at last than the strength of the logic, on which as an arch it is made in this way fundamentally to rest. To make the Church however a succedaneum for reason, in like outward style, comes precisely to the same thing. Allow the *donum fidei*, as an elevation of the mind to the plane of the supernatural, and the case is changed; but then also it is no longer easy to see, why faith should be bound so mechanically to the voice of the Church, as an authority extrinsical to the truth itself. The Church we hold too to be the medium of the Christian revelation, the organ by which Christ makes himself known in the world, and which is to be reverenced on this account, through all ages, as his body, the fulness of him that filleth all in all [Eph 1:23]. But it is all this, not in a mechanical quasi-magical way, as a witness set forward to propound the truth in outward style only, a supernatural automaton with the Pope at Rome for its mouth piece. The Church is the body of Christ, only as it serves to reveal Christ, under a truly living and historical form, in the history of the world; in which view all the power it has to propound Christ as an object of faith, is found in the fact of its being itself an object of faith[79] through Christ and from him, the form in which his life completes itself among men. Faith starts then in Christ. *Because* we believe in him, we believe also the Holy Catholic Church; and not in the reverse order. The Church is still necessary as an indefectible witness to the truth; but her indefectibility is a moral fact, not a physical necessity, made good through this activity

---

77. [Brownson, "The Church Against," 151.]

78. ["Succedaneum" is something that is used as a substitute, as a medical drug or agent that may be taken in place of another.]

79. [On the church as an object of faith, see Nevin, *The Church*, MTSS 5:148–56.]

of the general Christian life itself, the life of Christ in his people, working out its own problem in a truly human way. Why should not the supernatural in this form be quite as accessible for the *donum fidei*, as when exhibited or propounded in a purely outward and abstract style? Nature, we know, is not grace. This pertains to a higher order. But why may not the higher order reveal itself through the very life and constitution of the lower, supernaturalizing it for its own ends, as well as in an abrupt outside way; in such sort as to be for faith still all the authority that is needed, to place it in the infallible possession of Christ's word?

[On Infallibility of Church and Pope]

It may be made a question, whether the Roman system itself, rightly understood, actually claims in its own favor any such purely outward and mechanical infallibility, as we find attributed to it by Mr. Brownson and others of like wholesale zeal. At least, there is much in its order and history to conflict with the supposition, and to show that it is not the true original sense of what the Church is required to be for our faith in this view. A somewhat curious exemplification is furnished here by a late work entitled, *Mornings among the Jesuits at Rome*; in which, among other discussions, there occurs a friendly disputation with two learned professors of the Roman University on this very topic, the infallibility of the Church. The ground is taken on the Protestant side, that the Church of Rome does not formally claim to be infallible, that there is no decree of any general council, no bull of any pope, no canon or article of an authoritative nature, asserting any such attribute in her favor. This was at first treated with derision by the Jesuit professors; but on being seriously challenged to prefer proof to the contrary, they showed themselves completely puzzled and perplexed, and in the end were compelled fairly to give up the point. With all their learning, no such decree, bull, or canon, could be quoted.[80] It is one thing to affirm that the Church is

---

80. [Michael Seymour,] *Mornings among the Jesuits at Rome. Being Notes of conversations held with certain Jesuits on the Subject of Religion in the City of Rome. By the Rev. M. Hobart Seymour, M. A.*— [New York: Harper and Brothers, 1849] p. 138-144. The work has some things that read strangely. So far as we know, however, it is allowed to pass as authentic. Since the date of these conversations, we have a pretty explicit claim to infallibility, in the form required, on the part of the present Pope [Pius IX], if his Encyclical Epistle [*Qui Pluribus*], Nov. 9, 1846, is to be taken as of any canonical force. "Hinc plane apparet," he says, "in quanto errore illi etiam versentur, qui ratione abutentes, ac Dei eloquia tamquam humanum opus existimantes, proprio arbitrio illa explicare, interpretari temere audent, cum Deus ipse jam constituerit auctoritatem, quæ verum legitimumque cælestis suæ revelationis sensum doceret, constabiliret, omnesque controversias in rebus fidei et morum infallibili judicio dirimeret, ne fideles circumferantur omni vento doctrinæ in nequitia hominum ad circumventionem erroris. Quæ quidem viva et infallibilIts auctoritas in ea tantum viget Ecclesia, quæ a Christo Domino supra Petrum ædificata, suos legitimos semper habet Pontifices sine intermissione ab ipso Petro ducentes originem, in ejus Cathedra collocatos, et ejusdem etiam doctrinæ, dignitatis, honoris ac potestatis hæredes et vindices. Et quoniam ubi Petrus ibi Ecclesia, ac Petrus per Romanum Pontificem loquitur, et semper, in suis successoribus vivit, et judicium exercet, ac præstat quærentibus fidei veritatem, iccirco divina eloquia eo plane sensu sunt accipienda, quem tenuit ac tenet hæc Romana Beatissimi

indefectible, as the pillar and ground of the truth, and another thing quite to predicate infallibility of all her judgments and decisions in an abstract magical way. The Church is constitutionally holy, called to holiness and formed for holiness; yet never in such form as to be absolutely free, here on earth, from corruption and sin. So too she is constitutionally true, and the truth can never fail from her communion, as it can have no place also beyond it; yet all this in the midst of present error, confusion and contradiction. The truth is in her life, considered as a whole, and is to be sought in such form by the individual believer, with child-like though still free and independent docility and obedience. Even the Church of Rome is compelled to allow this to some extent, in her own way. If the case required only an outward oracle on the one side, and implicit passive obedience on the other, how has it happened that the authority after all is not offered, in every case, in the most direct and universally accessible form, for all to read or hear at any moment without the possibility of mistake? This, we all know, is not the case. The infallibility attaches, not to the ministers of the Church separately, but to the ministry as a whole; and so it is only in certain circumstances, and under certain conditions, that the Pope himself, the head of the corporation, is to be taken as its true voice. Seven requisites must be at hand, we are told, to show a decision of the pope infallible; 1st. communication with the bishops of the universal Church, asking the assistance of their prayers; 2nd. the possession of all available information on the point in hand; 3d. a formal assertion of authority; 4th. universal promulgation; 5th. universal reception by the Church as infallible authority; 6th. limitation to proper sphere, having for its matter a question of faith or morals; 7th. freedom, on the part of the pope, from all outward compulsion or constraint.[81] This is something wide away

---

Petri Cathedra, quæ omnium Ecclesiarum mater et magistra fidem a Christo Domino traditam integram in violatamque semper servavit."—This is sufficiently bold and strong, it must be confessed. [Trans. "This consideration {that "Human reason is convinced that it is God who has given everything the faith proposes to men for belief and behavior"} too clarifies the great error of those others as well who boldly venture to explain and interpret the words of God by their own judgment, misusing their reason and holding the opinion that these words are like a human work. God Himself has set up a living authority to establish and teach the true and legitimate meaning of His heavenly revelation. This authority judges infallibly all disputes which concern matters of faith and morals, lest the faithful be swirled around by every wind of doctrine which springs from the evilness of men in encompassing error. And this living infallible authority is active only in that Church which was built by Christ the Lord upon Peter, the head of the entire Church, leader and shepherd, whose faith He promised would never fail. This Church has had an unbroken line of succession from Peter himself; these legitimate pontiffs are the heirs and defenders of the same teaching, rank, office and power. And the Church is where Peter is {St. Ambrose on Ps 40}, and Peter speaks in the Roman Pontiff {Council of Chalcedon, Act. 2}, living at all times in his successors and making judgment {Synod of Ephes. Act. 3}, providing the truth of the faith to those who seek it {St. Peter Chrysologus, epistle to Eutyches}. The divine words therefore mean what this Roman See of the most blessed Peter holds and has held." See, Carlen, *The Papal Encyclicals 1740–1878*, 279.]

81. [Seymour, *Mornings Among the Jesuits*, 156–61, list these seven conditions of papal infallibility, which he obtained from a Jesuit canon lawyer in Rome. These conditions were at least one line of development up to the definition of papal infallibility in 1870 at the First Vatican Council. Kenrick's *Primacy of the Apostolic See*, 222–24, does indicate some, but not all, of the conditions Nevin listed for infallible papal statements. Nonetheless, Kenrick focused his study on the primacy and not

from a mere mechanical infallibility. There is no safety in the mind of the pope, any farther than it is found to hold in living communion with the mind of the universal Church; and of this no assurance can be had by the common christian, without active, waking, and earnest attention on his own part. Plainly the infallibility here claimed is not inspiration. Mr. Brownson himself makes it to be different. If however it were wholly above the ordinary law of knowledge, by which truth is apprehended through the activity of mind in its general living character, it must be fully equivalent to inspiration or else mere magic. The very fact then that this is disclaimed, goes to show that the infallibility in question is conditioned after all by the working of the universal mind of the Church, that it is a result of the concrete life of the Church, and that it belongs thus to the process of history and must bear also a truly historical form. If it were not so, why should the pope ever hesitate or pause, when any new decision is to be made, instead of fetching forth at once from the promptuary[82] of his infallible stewardship the precise answer required. Just now, it seems, he is travailing in pain with the article of the immaculate conception of the Virgin Mary, and has called on the bishops of the universal Church to assist him by their prayers, in the business of bringing it, if possible, to a satisfactory official decision.[83] But if there be no *history* for christian doctrine, no development, no growth or progress; if on the contrary all is to be regarded as a full grown Minerva from the beginning; why, we may well ask, the suspense of centuries on this great article heretofore, in the midst of interminable strife and war; and why this difficulty in bringing the infallibility of the pope to bear upon it forthwith, for its final settlement at the present time. It shows two things; first,

---

infallibility. On the *origins*, not conditions, of infallibility, see Tierney, *Origins* (1972).]

82. ["A storehouse; ... a repository." Webster, *American Dictionary*, 646.]

83. See his late Encyclical [*Ubi Primum*], dated Gaeta, Feb. 2, 1949 [See Carlen, *The Papal Encyclicals*, 291–93]; where he represents the subject as weighing heavily on his mind, announces that he has appointed a special commission of eminent theologians and cardinals to investigate its claims, and calls upon the bishops to have prayers solemnly offered in all the churches for his illumination and guidance in so great a concern, as well as to report to him the mind and feeling of the faithful in regard to it throughout the Catholic world. This surely is something more than simply affirming an old truth, clearly possessed from the beginning in the face of a new error. "If there be anything in which Catholic theologians are agreed," says Mr. Brownson, "it is in these two points; that the revelation in the beginning was perfect, and that nothing can be proposed by the Church to be believed, *fide divina*, not revealed from the beginning."— [Brownson, "Newman's Theory,"] 1847, p. 66. "If there be anything uniformly taught by our theologians, it is that the faith of the Fathers was perfect, that the revelation committed to the Church was complete and entire, and that the Church has, from the first, faithfully, infallibly, taught or proposed it. If this be true, as it would at least be temerity to question, there can be, there can have been, no latent or merely virtual doctrine, waiting for heresy and controversy to call it forth, and to render it formal and actual. There is implicit belief,—for individuals may be ignorant, some on one point, and some on another; but there is, save in a very restricted sense indeed, no implicit teaching."— [Brownson, "Newman's Theory,"] p. 77. Has the Immaculate Conception of the Virgin been part of this formal teaching from the time of the Apostles? If so, why all this hesitation and care on the part of the Pope, about erecting it into an article or faith in the year 1849? [The Dogma of the Immaculate Conception was defined by Pope Pius IX in 1854 after consultation with the world's Catholic bishops.]

that Christianity, for Rome itself, is *not* full grown from the start, and one always in the form of its faith; secondly, that the pope, to have authority even for Rome, must be more than a divine automaton, must be incorporated actively with the life of the Church, must be the organ of truth for it through the mediation of this life itself, reaching him at last in a perfectly human and historical way. With any such view as this, however, the theory of infallibility against which we have been arguing, and which seems to us to be held by Mr. Brownson, at once falls to the ground.

[Brownson's Wrong View of History]

We have a striking, and as it appears to us very significant, illustration of Mr. Brownson's wrong view of history, in an article on "The Church in the Dark Ages," published July, 1849 [330–57]. While he shows off with just severity the stupidity of the slang, which is often employed against this period, by men who show themselves profoundly ignorant of the whole glorious mission accomplished by the Church after the downfall of the Roman empire,[84] he has no mind at the same time to fall in with the undue glorification of mediæval history into which some have been carried latterly, by a sort of reaction against that other extreme. Digby's *Mores Catholici, or Ages of Faith*, he considers not sufficiently guarded on this side.[85] With all that was good in the Church, as such, those ages were full of abominations under a different view. She had by no means a clear field and her own way, for a thousand years, as her enemies now say, but stood in constant battle with hostile forces that sought to bring her down to the dust. It is well enough, Mr. Brownson thinks, for Protestants, of the Romantic and Puseyite Schools, to seek a rehabilitation of this old, long misunderstood and abused, mediæval life; their own Church is a mere corpse, and they may be pardoned for seeking to deck her off in the robes of the dead past, instead of those that belong to

---

84. "Never indeed did she give more unequivocal proofs of her supernatural origin and support, than in those ages of ignorance, violence and blood; never did she struggle with more manifest supernatural constancy and force, or with more glorious trophies to her celestial prowess." [Brownson, "Church in the Dark Ages," 335.] Those ages open with the destruction of the Western Roman Empire, and the permanent settlement of the Northern Barbarians on its ruins. Society was reduced almost to chaos, a new civilization was to be created out of the most wild and rude material. The church, after having subdued the world as it stood before had her own work to do over again. "Far more disheartening were her prospects than when she concealed herself, in the catacombs, or bled under Nero, Decius, Maximian, and Diocletian; and far more laborious was the task now before her, than that which she had accomplished in passing from that upper room in Jerusalem to the throne of the Cæsars." [Brownson, "Church in the Dark Ages," 337.] Alas, how much of the argument for the divine power of christianity as found in the form of church history, is obscured or altogether lost for those who yield themselves to the prejudice, (blind as Erebus [the personification of darkness and one of the primordial deities in Greek mythology], though wiser in its own conceit than seven men who can render a reason [Prov 26:16]) that the darkness of the Middle Ages sprang from the Catholic Church. [For a modern argument that the "Dark Ages" were not "dark," see Stark, *The Triumph of Christianity*, 237–52.]

85. [Kenhelm Henry Digby (1800–80), an English Romantic author, converted to Catholicism in 1825 and sought to glorify the Middle Ages as in his *Mores Catholici*.]

the present; but with Catholics (Roman) it is different. "They seek their Lord not in the dead past, but in the living present, in the Church that is, and is to be until the consummation of the world, unvaried and invariable."[86] The distinctive human side of the Middle Ages, the new element which then came into society, Mr. Brownson seems anxious rather to disown, as something outward and foreign altogether to the proper Christian life. As far as the Church was active in the phenomena of the time, we accept them and glory in them, he tells us, but as it regards all lying beyond, we feel comparatively indifferent. "Under the point of view of humanity, it matters little to us, as Catholics, how dark, how superstitious, how turbulent, violent, or barbarous" these ages were.[87] Strange to say, we find the advocate of Romanism here joining hands, to some extent, with Pseudo-protestantism, in the view that the proper sense of the world was interrupted and stopped by the overthrow of the old Roman civilization; that there is no meaning in the chaos that follows, farther than it gave room to labor for the recovery of what had been lost; and that the great task and problem for a whole millenium of years following, was simply to fill up its own blank by the reconstruction of the Christian life once more in its first form. How does this happen? Pseudo-protestantism sees in the Middle Ages only the growing power of Rome, and gives them up accordingly as a "grand apostacy" from first to last, (the Devil's millennium [sic], Christ asleep and the gates of hell triumphant,) for the purpose of making short and easy its own argument against the Pope. Mr. Brownson, on the other side, with much better perspicacity, begins to see in these same Middle Ages, Dark Ages, or as they are sometimes called Ages of Faith, the embryonic life of Protestantism itself, ripening in the womb of Catholicism, by a pregnancy of centuries instead of months, under the forms of the Roman faith and worship, for the mighty birth that followed by due course of time in the Reformation of the sixteenth century. Such undoubtedly is the true view of this great fact. Protestants, who insist on sundering the Reformation from the Church life of the previous period, do as much as they well can to ruin their own cause. Unless it be the product of all earlier church history, it can deserve no faith. Let it appear on the other hand, that the causes which led to it, under God, were in full force for centuries before; that they were seated in the life of the modern world as a part of its intrinsic nature and constitution; that their operation is to be traced back even to the world-historical epoch, which laid the foundations of modern society amid the crumbling ruins of that which went before; and it becomes at once to the same extent difficult to resist the conviction, that it belongs to the true sense of Christianity, and that it came to pass by the finger of God. Such in truth is the actual state of the case. The new form of humanity brought in by the Northern Barbarians did not merely furnish material for re-civilizing Europe in its old form, but offered elements which were not previously at hand for the creation also of another order of civilization; by which in the end Christianity was to become more complete, than

86. [Brownson, "Church in the Dark Ages," 345.]
87. [Brownson, "Church in the Dark Ages," 346.]

it could ever have become under the first order. Out of this new order of the Christian life, made possible only through the Germanic nature as distinguished from the old Roman, sprang with inward necessity at last the *Protest* of the Reformation. Mr. Brownson, as we have said, sees this; more quick of vision here than many Protestants; and sets himself to forestall, as he best can, the weight it carries against his own cause. "We frankly confess," he says, "we are Græco-Roman, and to us all tribes and nations are barbarian, just in proportion as they recede from the Græco-Roman standard."[88] This is the climax of culture, humanly considered. "Nowhere else does history show us man receiving, under all the aspects of his nature, so high, so thorough, so symmetrical, and so masculine a cultivation, as under this wonderful civilization."[89] Add Christianity to it, "and you have a civilization beyond which there is nothing to seek."[90] Tried by this standard, the Middle Ages cannot stand the test. The Church labored to re-civilize them, as well as she could, according to the old norm, with which she has a native affinity; but this could be done only so far as the nations were brought to exchange the Barbaric nature for the Roman.

> Wherever the barbaric element has remained predominant in the national life, as in Russia, Scandinavia, Prussia, Saxony, Northern Germany, or where, through exterior or interior causes, it has regained the preponderance, as in England and the once Christianized Oriental nations, the nation has relapsed into heathenism, or fallen off into heresy or schism. In several of the nations which have fallen off from the Church, the old barbaric institutions, traditions, customs, and hereditary hatred of Graco-Roman civilization, always survived in the heart of the people, and nourished a schism between its national life and its Christian faith.[91]

In all this there is much truth. The Romanic nations remain Papal; while the Germanic nations, in virtue of a new element peculiar to themselves, could never make over their will in the same way to mere outward rule, and so in the end have become Protestant. It is perfectly clear that *nationality* has exercised a determining influence on this great issue, from the beginning. Protestantism is the child of the modern civilization, the Teutonic life, and not of the Græco-Roman.[92]

---

88. [Brownson, "Church in the Dark Ages," 346.]
89. [Brownson, "Church in the Dark Ages," 347.]
90. [Brownson, "Church in the Dark Ages," 347.]
91. [Brownson, "Church in the Dark Ages," 349.]
92. American life might seem to be, in this view, the very efflorescence of the Protestant spirit, and as such the worst possible for the admission of Catholic influences. Mr. Brownson, however, judges differently. "Our civilization," he tells us, "is founded on a right basis, is Roman and Christian in its ground work; and there never has been a State constituted throughout more in harmony with Catholic principles than the American." [Brownson, "Civil and Religious Toleration," 307.] True, our American fathers had unhappily turned their backs upon the Church; but they had been nursed, notwithstanding, in the bosom of her civilization. "That civilization they brought with them to this New World, purged of the barbaric leaven which was still in some measure retained in the Mother

Document 7: Brownson's Quarterly Review.

But what now is the true significance of this fact? The old Græco-Roman civilization, says Mr. Brownson, must be held normal for all ages; your Teutonic life consequently is at fault, just in the measure of its variation from this rule; and so Protestantism is found to be simply part and parcel of the same general abnormity, the final upshot, we may say, of the war carried on with the authority of the church by the refractory spirit of these Northern Barbarians from the beginning. A convenient theory truly. But how violent, at the same time, and arbitrary. Only see what it involves. The normal order of the world naturally considered, its best possible form and true ultimate sense, just as it was ready to go fully into the arms of Christianity, suddenly dashed to the ground and turned into universal wreck by the inundation of an entirely new life, uncivilized, unlettered, absolutely wild and rude: Europe planted with elementary nations, requiring the growth of centuries io bring them to any mature and settled political form: The work of a thousand years laid upon the church, only to regain in some measure the loss created by this sad catastrophe: A new civilization in time, which refuses however to fall fully into the true Christian order; carries in it more or less a semi-barbarous, heathenish character; and issues finally in an open rebellion against the Church, which at the same time bears away with it palpably the central powers and activities of the world's natural life, with a momentum which centuries have no power to check or restrain. It needs surely no small gift of faith seriously and steadily to give credit to all this. Was the wreck of Græco-Roman culture an *accident*? Did the Northern Barbarians come on the stage of Europe, without God's will and plan? Was there no end to be answered for Christianity and the world, by the taking down of the former civilization, the bringing in of new material, the open field created for the building up of another life, and the work of so many centuries employed in the accomplishment of this great object? These questions, it seems to us, carry in them their own answers. The true use to be made of the whole case, then is just the reverse of Mr. Brownson's view. God moves in history. It must therefore have meaning. It must especially minister to Christ and his Church; for is not *he* head over the while of it, for this very end? If a sparrow fall not without his eye, how could the *Völkerwanderung* [the migration of peoples] take place by chance? The fact that he should so remove the old, and make room for the new, and call in

---

country, and against which the Popes and the whole spiritual society had protested for ten centuries. Whoever will examine the respective civil institutions of England and this country, will hardly fail to perceive, that what of England we have rejected is what she owes to her barbarous ancestors, and what we have added, which she has not, has been borrowed from Roman and Catholic civilization. Indeed, just in proportion, under a civil and political point of view, as we have receded from England, we have approached Rome and Catholicity."—*Civil and Religious Toleration.*—July 1849, p. 307. Here is a discovery worth looking at certainly. The precious spark of liberty, to which we owe our Constitution, is after all not from Geneva but from Rome! The Pilgrim Fathers stand in the same line, politically, with the Popes! Puritanism belongs of right to Popery. The body is here already prepared; "it is moulded from fine, rich, red earth, in a form of majestic proportions, and of surpassing beauty, wanting nothing but the Divine Breath to be breathed into its nostrils in order to become a living soul." [Brownson, "Civil and Religious Toleration," 308.]

the historical process of a thousand years to come to his object, is itself enough to show, not only that the new civilization thus sought was to be different from that which was rejected in its favor, but also that it was to be of a superior order, of more vigorous constitution, better suited to the wants of humanity and more answerable to the interior demands of Christianity. This superiority of the modern civilization, then, turns on the new element which has been brought into it by the Germanic or Barbarian life, in distinction from the old Roman. It amounts to nothing that Mr. Brownson stigmatizes this as heathen; for the old Roman life was originally heathen too; and it is purely gratuitous to assume that Christianity might not appropriate and assimilate to itself the peculiarities of a Barbarian nationality as fully and completely as those of the Graeco-Roman. Its province is not to stand on the outside of nature in the way of foreign help, but to enter into it, to clarify it, and to fill it with divinity after its own form and type. The new civilization thus brought to pass carried in itself, from the beginning, the principle of *freedom*, which gave birth finally, as Christ had all along designed, to the fact of Protestantism. Its distinctive power, of course, fell in with this fact. The Romanic nations were left behind; not without some great ulterior purpose, we presume; while the Germanic nations, obedient to the law of their life, are carrying the sense of history in the Protestant direction. It does not follow at once, we know, that Protestantism is all that the world needs for its salvation, because it now carries all temporal interests in its stream. Outward activity and strength are not of themselves the guaranty of grace. The Protestant movement *may* prove morally unequal to its own problem. Still this cannot change the significance of the fact as now stated. It belongs to the reigning power of the world's civilization. It has its seat in the spirit of the nations that go with it, and their spirit now rules the course of humanity, as something plainly in advance of the spirit that meets us in nations still bound to the authority of Rome. In this view, if we believe in Christ, we are bound to acknowledge in it, if nothing more, yet surely the necessary medium of transition at least for the Church of God into a higher and better state. Not to do so, turns the past into a riddle and shrouds the future in despair. Protestantism, as the world now stands at all events, has the floor of history, carries the word of the age; and the last sense of Christianity, the grand scope of Christ's Mediatorial reign, is to be reached *through* it, by its help and intervention in some way, and not by its being hurled aside as an impertinent accident, or mere nullity, in the course of this all conquering dispensation.

It is high time for us, however, to bring this long article to a conclusion. It will be perceived that our object has been to convict the general Roman principle of falsehood, by showing it to run into untenable consequences and to be at war with the true conception of our life. This is not with us, of course, an argument for the mere negation or denial of the same principle, as the true meaning and force of Protestantism. We have before tried to expose the rock on that side; and our object now in setting forth the dangers of the whirlpool, is not certainly to recommend the first, as on the whole less false and terrible than the second. Rationalism, the resolution of faith into the mere mind and will of man (with the Bible or without it) under all its forms and shapes, we religiously abhor and hate. With the reigning slang on that side, we have no sympathy whatever. Here then the question comes, how are these extremes to be at once both avoided? And no question can well be more great and solemn. We pretend not now, however, to answer it. Enough so far, if we have been able to show that it needs and demands an answer; that the truth is not, in this case, in either of the alternatives, separately taken, which for the common understanding seem to cover the whole ground; that Christianity, in one word, must find its true sense between them, in a form of life which shall be the union of both. It is much to be sure of what is false and wrong here, even if at a loss still to master the full meaning of what is right. The best preparation for solving the problem of the age, is to be well satisfied that the problem really exists, and so to feel earnestly that it calls for a solution.

J. W. N.

Document 8

"Brownson's Review Again"

Editor's Introduction

After Nevin's January 1850 article on Orestes Brownson's Catholic theology, Brownson responded with an analysis and critique of Nevin's *Mercersburg Review* writings. Nevin, in May 1850, replied to Brownson. The published exchange between these two ends with Nevin's reply, even though Brownson reiterated much of his first response in another article on Nevin in July 1850.[1]

Brownson's response to Nevin's January 1850 article reflected Brownson's apologetical approach to theology but also his respect for Nevin and his abilities. In fact, Brownson told his readers that the *Mercersburg Review* was conducted "with spirit, learning, and ability" and Nevin's arguments presented Protestantism "in as plausible form as it admits, and give[s] it the most respectable vindication that it receives in our language." Nevin, too, Brownson noted, agreed that Brownson's arguments against popular Protestantism—which took "private judgment, with or without the Bible, for its rule of faith"—were invincible.[2] But, Brownson held that popular Protestantism was the major form of Protestantism in the United States and that Nevin's views reflected an aberration or a minority perspective.

Brownson rejected Nevin's charge that Catholicism, or Romanism, as Nevin preferred to call it, represented an extreme pole in Christianity. Nevin argued that in converting, Brownson went from the extreme of private judgment (represented by Unitarianism) to that of external authority. Brownson responded, correctly I believe, that he had tried to unite and reconcile the two poles in the period immediate before his conversion in articles on his doctrine of life by communion in 1842 and 1843.[3]

---

1. The three articles are, in order: [Brownson], "Reply to Mercersburg," 191–228; Nevin, "Brownson's Review Again," 307–24; and [Brownson], "The Mercersburg Theology," 353–78.

2. [Brownson], "Reply to Mercersburg," 191.

3. [Brownson], "Reply to Mercersburg," 192. Brownson referred to his article on "Parker's Discourse" in 1842 and articles on the "Mission of Jesus" in *The Christian World* in 1843. For a recent edition of these articles, see Carey, *The Early Work*, 6:280–387; 7:43–109.

Document 8: "Brownson's Review Again"

It was, moreover, a "gross misapprehension" to assert that when he converted, he had moved from an extreme rationalism to Catholicity, or from an extreme individualism to authority.[4]

Nevin made three subsidiary charges: first, that Brownson placed Christianity, as a supernatural object, out of the subject; second, that he placed the supernatural object wholly above the sphere of the natural; third, that he made faith the mediate, instead of the immediate apprehension of the truth of the matter believed. Brownson constructed his own objections to Nevin's theological system by inverting the charges: Nevin placed the supernatural object of faith *in* the subject; the supernatural does not wholly transcend the natural; and faith is the immediate apprehension of the truth of the matter believed.[5] All three of these charges boiled down to the overriding accusation of pantheism. Brownson did not say that Nevin was personally a pantheist, but pantheism was the result of Nevin's system.[6]

Brownson sees pantheism in Nevin's emphasis on the intimate union between the church and the substance of Christ's life, in the union of subject and object, in his understanding of the Incarnation as the continuous development of Christ's life in history, in the unity or identity of the natural and supernatural, and in his progressive and optimistic view of history as the unfolding of the divine life in time. In all these charges, Brownson seeks to maintain the distinctions that he believes Nevin's system fails to make clear. Nonetheless, Brownson's polemical charges are caricatures of Nevin's positions, as Nevin indicates in his response to Brownson.

One of the problems in this exchange between Nevin and Brownson, common to many polemical religious debates, was their tendency to focus on what they considered the ultimate logical consequences of the other's positions without considering the larger context and conditions their opponents put on their own positions. In this second article on Brownson, Nevin reiterates many of the arguments he made against Brownson in his January 1850 article, but under the new categories of pantheism and dualism. Nevin asserts that there is truth in both extremes of pantheism and dualism, but the truth is found not in the extremes but in the unity and mediation of both systems. He denies completely the charge of pantheism because he repeatedly emphasizes both the unity, not the identity, and the distinctions, not the separations, between the natural and the supernatural, Christ and the church, faith and reason, freedom and law. His own theology mediates between both extremes. He thinks Brownson is dualistic because he exaggerates the distinctions between subject and object, Christ and the Church, the natural and the supernatural.

Nevin defends his own position by countering Brownson's accusations that ultimately Nevin's theology ends up in pantheism and subjectivism. He reaffirms that

---

4. [Brownson], "Reply to Mercersburg," 193.
5. [Brownson], "Reply to Mercersburg," 198–99.
6. Charles Hodge, like some other Protestants, charged that Nevin's theology led to a "pantheistic mysticism." See Hodge, "Doctrine of the Reformed Church," 275.

God is indeed in nature and in history, but this did not mean, as Brownson charged, God's self-evolution or development in history. "History is not necessary to complete God himself; as nature is not necessary either for any such end." For Nevin "History is not an emanation of the Divine life."[7] God is in and above history and nature.

Nevin's emphasis on human freedom and morality, moreover, did not lead to subjectivism, as Brownson asserted. Subject and object were not separated or divided from each other, as they were in Brownson's system. Human freedom did not mean that human beings make the law by their own independent wills. Nevertheless, law (like nature) is not only outward, as Brownson insisted, but inward and subjective. Law comes to actualization in the world by being apprehended and willed by its subjects. Nevin wanted to make sure that his point on freedom and the subjective appropriation of law did not make the individual will the creator of law, which would lead to licentiousness. "It is the union of law and will, necessity and liberty, not outwardly but inwardly, which brings the life of man emphatically to its proper form."[8] Nevin argued in "Human Freedom," "the individual will is of right bound" by the presence of an objective, universal law in such a way that the individual will is simultaneously autonomous and bound.[9]

Truth, as well as law, was not, as Brownson seemed to hold, purely objective and external to the subject. For Nevin, "Truth exists, as truth, only by being known."[10] This was not an admission of subjectivism because for Nevin "Men make neither truth nor law;"[11] both, however, need to become concrete in human intelligence and will—not just in the individual or private mind, but in the collective will and intelligence. God's will and law came to human beings, as Horace Bushnell[12] held, through family, right public opinion, art and science, the civil state, the course of history, and most of all, through the church as it moved in history from the time of the Apostles down to the present.

Brownson's dualism, finally, is manifested in his division of the supernatural and the natural and in his accusation that Nevin had so united them as to lead logically to pantheism. Brownson claimed that Nevin had confused the supernatural with the supersensible, and Nevin denied the accusation. He did not deny the full objectivity of the supernatural as "an order of life above nature," but insisted upon a "corresponding subjectivity" in human beings.[13] For Nevin, the supranatural in fact draws the subject who "depends on a certain inward sympathy and correspondence with the

---

7. "Brownson's Review Again," 314.
8. "Brownson's Review Again," 316.
9. Nevin, *Human Freedom*, 10, 17.
10. "Brownson's Review Again," 317.
11. "Brownson's Review Again," 319.
12. See final essay in this volume.
13. "Brownson's Review Again," 322.

truth revealed."[14] The supranatural, by drawing the subject, creates a receptivity in the subject, even though only some persons in fact have that receptivity.

As we saw in the general introduction to Part 2, in "Early Christianity" and "Cyprian," Nevin was attracted to the Catholic understanding of the church, but he still had a hard time reconciling Catholicism in its modern form with the "powers and privileges" claimed by the early church. He could not understand, too, how Brownson could continue to deny John Henry Newman's doctrine of development, especially in light of the difficulties and hesitancy that current Catholics were having in bringing forth the article on the Immaculate Conception of the Blessed Virgin Mary. If the article was always a part of the explicit faith, why any hesitancy in bringing it to a definition?[15]

After his letter to Brownson, Nevin continued to support American Catholics during the Protestant Crusade against them, but his contacts with Brownson ceased, as far as I know, with his letter of 1852.

14. "Brownson's Review Again," 323.

15. Nevin to Brownson, August 18, 1852, in Brownson Papers, University of Notre Dame Archives. See also Nevin, "Cyprian," 417–52. In 1854, after consulting theologians and bishops around the world, Pope Pius XI defined the doctrine of the Immaculate Conception of Mary, meaning that she was freed from original sin from the time of her conception.

Brownson's Review Again.

The last number of *Brownson's Quarterly Review* contains an article of some length, in the way of reply to our January paper on its championship of Romanism.[2] We have no reason to complain of the tone and spirit with which it is written. It gives us full credit for sincerity and honesty of purpose, and takes pains to treat us with manly consideration and respect. It shows itself duly sensible also of the merits of our argument for Protestantism; as far as this could be considered at all possible for a standpoint so thoroughly Roman, as we have already found that to be which is occupied by the respondent. As a whole, of course, our reasoning is set down as fallacious and false; and an effort is made to burden it with consequences which are fatal to the whole idea of Christianity; but care is taken, at the same time, not to charge these consequences upon us directly as part and parcel of our own faith. We are supposed to be entangled in them unconsciously and by implication, rather than with clear logical insight. This is all polemically right and fair. The true consequences of a system have legitimate force against it, whether its advocates have ability to perceive them or not; and it is always proper to drag them into view for this purpose, so far as a superior logic may render it possible. We object not to the severity of some of Dr. Brownson's representations, in this view. If the results he tries to fasten upon us were indeed necessarily involved in our arguments it would deserve much of the censure it is made to receive at his hands. We should ourselves join him heartily in its condemnation. We own no such results as our own. If they belong to our system, they have no place at least in our mind or heart. It is our logic which must be taken to be at fault in this case, and not what we cherish and value as our faith. We are not yet brought, however, to acknowledge any such dualism here between these two orders of thought. Not only do we repudiate the irreligious consequences in question, as no part of our faith; we do not allow them either to be fairly deducible from our philosophy or theology. On the other hand, the positions taken by Mr. Brownson, at certain points, seem to us clearly to confirm what we have already urged in the way of objection against the Roman

1. [*MR* 2 (May 1850) 307–24.]
2. [{Brownson,} "Reply to Mercersburg," 191–228.]

system. It is not necessary to say that he shows himself at once acute and profound, and that the weapons of his warfare are handled with dexterity and power. The argument belongs to a field, where few are so much at home, and has to do with topics which few are so well fitted to manage with effect. But with all this, his dialectics, on the great subject here at stake, are by no means equal to the task he has undertaken, in pretending to vindicate Romanism at the bar of reason. To our mind at least, the plea remains as before defective and unsatisfactory.

[Brownson's Charge of Pantheism]

The grand aim of Mr. Brownson, in this article, is to run us into *pantheism*; such a view of the universe as confounds it with the idea of God, and so resolves itself at last into pure autotheism or nihilism; "to which" he says, "we have shown over and over again, all Protestantism, whatever its form, has an invincible tendency."[3] To this end flows, he tells us, the view we take of the relation between subject and object in the constitution of the world, as well as what we say of the relation of the general to the particular. To affirm that the object without subject is unreal, or a pure abstraction, amounts with him to an affirmation that all reality is subjective, in the sense of Fichte,[4] and that the objective as such has no existence whatever. This, we are told, is to make God himself dependent on the thinking and willing of men. He is reduced at best to the character of infinite void, mere abstract possibility, seeking to become *plenum*, full, or real in the life of the world. But such abstract possibility is a nullity, can do nothing, bring nothing to pass; "then there is no world, and if there is no world, and God is a nullity, nothing is or exists,"[5] and so we are landed in pure nullism or nihilism, as just now said. To the like result is carried out by the Critic our view of the relation between the natural and the supernatural. To affirm an organic or inwardly living correspondence between these different spheres of existence, is to confound and overthrow, he thinks, the distinction by which they stand apart. God must be out of the world, and beyond it altogether, in order to be truly self existent and independent. So in the sphere of nature; and so also in the sphere of mind or will. The Critic will hear accordingly of no *autonomy* in this latter world. "Nothing can be worse than this," he tells us," for it supposes the law is created, and in part at least by man himself."[6] To make man active at all in the constitution of the law, is taken to be tantamount to a claim of self-creation in his favor; which must be regarded of course as a full lapse again into the vortex of

---

3. [{Brownson,} "Reply to Mercersburg," 207.]

4. [Johann Gottlieb Fichte (1762–1814), was a German philosopher between Kant and Hegel. We begin to understand knowledge by "disregard[ing] external objects and our mental states and focus exclusively on the I that apprehends both external objects and mental states." *Oxford Companion to Philosophy*, 299. Thus a simplistic reading might have been that reality is wholly subjective, in the "knowing I."]

5. [{Brownson,} "Reply to Mercersburg," 207.]

6. [{Brownson,} "Reply to Mercersburg," 213.]

pantheism or nullism as before. Our view of the relation between faith and divine truth, is made to plunge headlong over the same awful precipice. To require a real inward union of the two, in such sense that the first shall appear the very form under which the second has its subsistence for men, is to reduce this last to the character of a simple abstract possibility. "It is the object that gives the form or species," the Critic tells us, "and to contend that it is the subject, is simply making man, if creation is supposed, the creator, and God the creature,—that is, man makes God, and not God man!"[7] Such a theory leaves no room, of course, for the idea of revelation, in any true and proper sense. And so, finally, our Christology, the view we take of Christ's person and the mystery of the incarnation, is charged with the same general fault, as tending to break down the distinction that should of right hold perpetually between the order of nature and the order of grace. Christ, we are told, is the author of the new creation, but no part of it in his own person; just as he is the old creation, only *mediante actu creativo* [by means of the creative act], by the act of creating it, and in no more intimate way. To make him the real fountain of Christianity itself, is gravely represented as a full identification of his life with that of his people, and runs, we are told, into palpable pantheism.

Mr. Brownson, as we have before said, does not mean to lay all this to our charge, as something contemplated and proposed on our part with heresy prepense.[8] He means only, that our premises lead necessarily to such end. We think it well, however, to put in here a formal disavowal of the pantheistic conceptions, one and all, which are supposed thus to lurk in our system. The idea "that God is real being only in that he is creator, and actually creates *ad extra*," is none of ours.[9] We have not the slightest sympathy with the theory of Spinoza.[10] We believe the world to be God's free act, and as such in no sense necessary to the fulness of his own being. We have never dreamed of any such autonomy on the side of the created will, as might make it the source or reason of the law. This we hold to be of absolute and universal necessity, though ten thousand worlds should conspire to set its power aside. We recognize fully the distinction between the natural and the supernatural, and the necessity of revelation for the purposes of religion. Faith never makes the truth it is brought to embrace; it simply makes it to be truly present, and so authenticates its existence, for the sphere of created intelligence into which it is thus actually introduced. We carefully distinguish Christ from his Church, while yet we hold them to be in a deep sense one, even as

---

7. [{Brownson,} "Reply to Mercersburg," 211.]

8. [Heresy prepense, that is, deliberate or intentional heresy.]

9. [{Brownson,} "Reply to Mercersburg," 208. The quotation reads "Following modern philosophy, which teaches that God is real only in that he is creator, the Reviewer . . . ." Nevin adds to the quotation: "and actually creates ad extra" but the addition does not change the meaning of the quotation.]

10. [Baruch Spinoza (1632–77), Dutch philosopher, is sometimes accused of being a pantheist because of his view that the world is a part of God or that God was the sum of the natural and physical laws of the universe and not an individual entity or creator. Nonetheless, he did try to maintain a distinction between God and the world in one of his most important works, *Tractatus Theologico-Politicus*.]

the head and members are indissolubly joined together in the living constitution of one and the same body. Most certainly, "we are not made one with him in the sense of identity with him, nor are we *deificated*."[11] The position of Christ, as we have taken occasion often to say, is absolute and central; while that of his people is relative only and peripheral. He is the only begotten Son of God; we are sons only through him, by adoption and living insertion into his life, the process of what the Scriptures call eating his flesh and drinking his blood, as the true condition of all righteousness and immortality [John 6:53–58].

[Dualism in Religion]

But now, as we take it, the truth, in opposition to these several pantheistic consequences charged upon us by Mr. Brownson, does not stand on the other side in their simple negation and contradiction. There is another class of conceptions in this form, and which the common understanding is always prone to lay hold of as the necessary and only alternative in the case, that go just as directly and surely in the end to exclude God from the world, and to unsettle all the foundations of religion. These are comprehended collectively in the idea of *dualism*, or abstract deism, which may be taken as the immediate reverse of what is properly pantheism in the bad and false sense. It may be said that dualism involves a great truth, the actual distinction of God and the world; and this we are freely willing to admit; but it is just as certain, on the other side, and just as necessary too to be affirmed always, that pantheism also involves a great truth; such a truth indeed as may be said to meet us on almost every page of the Bible, as well as from the inmost and profoundest depths of our own religious nature. That is a poor and cheap orthodoxy, in any case, which stands barely in the rejection of error in some one direction, while it makes no account of the danger, always at hand, of falling under the power of its natural counterpart in a direction just the opposite. We are bound to do justice, in the case before us, to the truth which underlies pantheism, as well as to that which underlies dualism; and we are not more bound to fear and avoid heresy in the first shape, than we are bound to avoid and fear it also in the second shape. It has been our wish at least, and our honest endeavor, to keep clear of both extremes, as well as to acknowledge and honor the great truths out of which both grow. Mr. Brownson, we are sorry to say, in common with a large amount of what we conceive to be bad Protestantism, (the almost universal thinking, we might say perhaps, of New England) turns the two phases of thought into the form of a simple syllogistic dilemma, where one horn is the only resting place from the other, and avoids and rejects thus the pantheistic extreme only in such a way as to lay himself open, in our estimation, to the charge of dualism. We distinguish of course, as he also has done in our case, between his theory and himself, and speak of what the first is

---

11. [{Brownson,} "Reply to Mercersburg," 226, Brownson's emphasis.]

by necessary consequence, as it strikes our own mind, rather than by open and direct avowal; although at some points, the general consequence itself might seem to be not indistinctly allowed, in the particular propositions by which we find it indirectly affirmed. The facility with which he throws us continually into the wrong, serves only to illustrate, as we take it, the fault and wrong of his own position. It shows this to be itself a dialectical extreme, whose very character it is always to condemn in a wholesale way, as its own opposite, all that is different from itself, or that carries towards it in any way the aspect of negation. No such extreme can ever live by simply killing its opposite; but only by coming to a true inward reconciliation with it in the power of a higher idea, whose province it is, in such case, not to destroy absolutely on either side, but rather as regards both to complete and fulfill.

Abstract deism, as distinguished from the true *theism* of Christianity, it is hardly necessary to say, is not in and of itself an exclusion absolutely of God from the world. It prides itself rather in being an acknowledgment of God, under the character of the great first cause and end of all things. In this view, however, he is taken to be always out of the world, beyond it, over and above it, and in no sense truly immanent in its constitution and life. His relation to the world is that of a mechanician to a machine. It is the product of his mind and hand; it works according to his will; it goes forward under the superintendence of his eye; while he remains himself, whether near at hand or afar off, wholly on the outside of it, abstract and independent altogether as another order of being. Such dualism may refuse the idea of revelation entirely; but it can with equal ease also allow it, after its own fashion. In the first case, it is mere naturalism or rationalism, in the most direct form; teaching that man has no need to go beyond the world as it now stands, for the solution of the problem involved in his existence; and that he must be necessarily inaccessible indeed to the literally supernatural, for the reason simply that it *transcends* his own nature, and so cannot enter it in the way of real knowledge, or appropriation. In the second case, we have abstract supranaturalism; which owns and seeks the supernatural, in the Bible or in the Church, as the necessary and at the same time possible complement of the natural, but will not allow still the chasm to be in any way filled that sunders the one from the other. The relation remains at last, what it was at first, extrinsical and mutually exclusive; while all conjunction in the case is found to be mechanical only, and thus more or less magical and unfree. A general convenient illustration of both these errors, is furnished by the question concerning inspiration. Rationalism reduces it at once to a nullity, by resolving all into the natural activity of the human mind. Abstract supranaturalism asserts on the contrary a higher activity, the moving power of the Holy Ghost; but in doing so, at the same time, sets the Divine wholly on the outside of the human; in consequence of which, this last sinks into the character of a mere passive organ or instrument, in the service of the first. The error in this form is of course more respectable than the error in the other form; but in both cases the proper truth of the doctrine is missed, and its rightful authority more or less overthrown. Inspiration transcends nature; but it is on the other hand a real entrance of the supernatural into this lower sphere. The Bible in this respect is just as thoroughly human, as it is found to be also heavenly and divine. The evidence of this meets us from every page and line. Not merely are the words human words; but the thoughts also are human thoughts, as intimately joined with these words as thoughts are in any other case with their own language, which we know to be the very intimacy itself of soul and body. No two of the sacred writers think alike or speak alike. On the contrary the individual nature of every one of them is exalted, and so made to be more specifically peculiar and characteristic, through his gift of inspiration, than it would be if presented to us under any other circumstances. *How* all this is accomplished, is not here the question. We have to do only with the fact. This includes two sides; one natural and the other supernatural; which however do not stand each on the outside of the other, in such a way that the action of one becomes all and the action of the other nothing; but are so brought together as to be both truly and really concerned, as joint factors, in the result which is brought to pass. Holy men of old *spake*, as they were *moved* by the Holy Ghost [2 Pet 1:21]. The speech is *human* speech, in all respects, under Divine motion. Any theory of inspiration which leaves this out of view, or which implies the contrary in any way, is of course radically defective and false.[12]

[Beyond Pantheism and Dualism]

And so, we say, in the relation which God sustains to the world generally, as its Creator and Preserver, we are required to see neither pantheism nor dualism; neither a necessary self-explication simply of his own being, on the one hand, nor yet such an outwardness and disjunction, on the other hand, as implies in fact two different worlds, two separate and independent spheres of being. Even Nature itself has a constitution and life of its own; it is no mere apparition or shadow, its powers are real powers; its laws are true laws; it is not in this respect a mere system of *occasionalism*,[13] the inefficient show only of what is taking place, while all in truth proceeds by immediate act of God. And still under this form, it can never, for one moment, or at a single point, be sundered from God; it subsists in Him continually, as the very ground of its whole constitution; its powers and laws are of no force, save as they flow forth unceasingly from the activity of his will. This activity is just as full, as omnipotent, as universally present, in the preservation of the world from hour to hour, as it was in its original

---

12. [Nevin's view of biblical inspiration at the end of his life is summarized in Layman, general introduction to *Born of Water*, MTSS 6:30 and n161.]

13. [Occasionalism was a theory of causality, namely that God is the direct efficient cause of everything and that creatures or created things are not the efficient causes, but only the occasions of divine activity. The French Oratorian priest and philosopher, Nicolas Malebranche (1638–1715), was a major supporter of the theory in the modern period. In the sacraments, for example, he held that God was the efficient and direct cause of grace in the sacraments, the signs (e.g. water in baptism) were merely occasions of the Divine communication of grace.]

creation. Not a sparrow falls without his hand [Matt 10:29]. In Him, really and truly, we live, and move, and have our being [Acts 17:28]. Of him, through him, and to him, (ἐξ αὐτοῦ, καὶ δι' αὐτοῦ, καὶ εἰς αὐτόν τὰ πάντα, Rom. xi. 36) from him as their beginning, in and by him as their constant cause and medium, and to him again as their absolute and universal end, are all things. *Such* pantheism the Bible teaches, and we are bound to admit. It is the very character of a true childlike religious faith itself, thus to *see* God in the stars, to *hear* him in the winds, to *mark* his stately goings in all the processes of nature. And so when we rise from the world of mere Nature up to the world of Mind, as this meets us in the constitution of man, it is still always the same mystery we are called to admire and adore. God is different from the thinking, and willing, and working of men; and yet all thought and will are conditioned and made possible, only through the universe of life which has its seat in himself. He is the foundation of the moral world. It holds throughout in the presence of his intelligence and the activity of his will. Truth and freedom exist from him, and by him, as their necessary ground. The law which upholds all ethical relations, and by which the organical structure of society subsists, is the utterance continually of his very life. History, unfolding from age to age the progress of humanity, is not something separate from God; full as little certainly, to say the least, as any such thought may be tolerated of the course of dumb blind nature. It moves throughout, though in a free way, in obedience to an all comprehending law or plan, as truly as this may be said of the planets; and this law resolves itself finally into the intelligence and will of Him, who is at once the beginning, the middle, and the end of all things. The intelligence and will of God are immanent in the process itself; so that it may be said truly to be a revelation of what he is in the world; just as we may say the same thing of the natural heavens, which *declare* his glory and *show forth* his presence in the most direct and real way [Ps 19:1]. This is not Buddhism.[14] History is not necessary to complete God himself; as nature is not necessary either for any such end. It is no process of self-evolution, by which he is to be regarded as coming to be actually what he is otherwise only potentially, the transition of the logical Nothing into the logical Something; God as pure being into God as the living universe. History is not an emanation of the Divine life, in any such sense as to be the necessary form of this life itself. God is complete without it, and lives with absolute fulness beyond it in the way of personal self-consciousness and freedom. He is the free cause even of his own being; and how much more then of all his works. But still in such free view, we have a right to speak of history as the actual presence notwithstanding of his life, as the very form in which he reveals himself so as to show forth in an actual way the sense of what this life contains. By being free, it does not

---

14. [Several pages later, Nevin equates the ultimate reality of Buddhism with an "infinite Nothing," the "nirvana" which is goal of Buddhist practice. Nirvana is not utter nothingness; in the simplest, probably the oldest, sense it is the "extinguishment" of suffering. As in all great religions, there is a considerable development in the traditions regarding what it is and how it is achieved. In some strands of the Mahayana (the "Great Vehicle") it comes to mean an all-inclusive yet transcendent "realized ultimate reality." (The editor thanks Harold O. Koenig for the wording of this clarification.)]

Document 8: Brownson's Review Again.

cease still to be God's act, and in this view a process of real self-explication, by which he comes forth from the depths of eternity into the syllabled speech of time, and so makes himself known for the adoration of angels and men. We see no pantheism in this; but only the pure living theism of the Bible, in opposition to the dead mechanical abstractions of that dualistic deism, which converts the world into a grand watch, and sees in the Maker of it the clever artist only who has contrived and set in motion its wheels and springs.[15]

"Following modern philosophy," Mr. Brownson says,

> which teaches that God is real only in that he is creator, the Reviewer can assert that God lives, is living God, only by asserting that he lives in the life of the world, that is, as he explains it, "in the thinking and willing of single minds." His system seems to us to be based on the supposition, that God comes to reality only in the life of the universe, and that the universe, whether natural or supernatural, is simply the evolution or development, that is, realization, of the abstract potentialities or possibilities of the Divine nature. ——Hence the significance and sacredness of history. It is God's realization of his own potentiality, in space and time, or his coming to reality.— [{Brownson,} "Reply to Mercersburg,"] P. 208.

This, it will be seen, is a wholly false view of what we have wished to say. It makes no distinction between a necessary emanation and a free act, and reduces to the conception of a physical process what we hold always to be the work of intelligence and will in their highest form. Even the necessity by which God himself exists, what is sometimes called his *aseity*,[16] we hold to be a free necessity, and not a blind fate excluding thought and will; for this would shut us up to the everlasting impersonal *substance* of Spinoza. The being of God is his own eternal act, resting in nothing and conditioned by nothing beyond the free activity from which it springs. All his works of course are no less free. But for this very reason, on the other hand, they have no subsistence save by the immanent force of his all-producing will at every point. The world has its end no less than its beginning, its *terminus ad quem* full as much as its *terminus a quo*,[17] in God only. It is not in this respect like a plan which an artist projects, and then carries into execution. Plan and execution fall here completely together. To suppose an outward reason or aim of any sort, in the Divine Mind, is in truth to subject his action to a foreign force, and so to overthrow the absolute aseity of his nature. The universe must be taken, from first to last; as wholly and only from himself. The law itself in this view is his work. True, it is eternal, and has its seat in the very nature of God; but it has its seat there, not out of any necessity by which his will may be supposed to be ruled from behind itself, but by the infinite activity of this will itself.

15. [The English minister and rationalist philosopher William Paley (1743–1805) used the watchmaker analogy in his *Natural Theology* (1802) as a teleological argument for the existence of God.]

16. [Self-originating, self-subsistent existence.]

17. [The end to which, i.e., goal; and the end from which, i.e., beginning.]

PART 2 : THE CHURCH QUESTION AND SUPERNATURALISM

[On Human Freedom and Law[18]]

It may now appear in what sense, and in what sense only, we have ever dreamed of allowing man a will or voice in the constitution of the law by which he is required to be governed. "To assert man's authority, or right to be governed only by his own will," according to Mr. Brownson, "is to deny that he is under law, or bound at all to seek God as the Sovereign Good. Does the Reviewer maintain that we are not morally bound to seek God as our ultimate end? Does he deny all morality, and assert that man is free to live as he lists?"[19] Nothing of this sort, we reply; nothing of this sort whatever. All we mean to say is, that mind is not matter; that morality is not nature; that the law of freedom, to be different from the law of blind necessity, must come to its actualization in the world, not in the way of merely outward force under any view, but through the self-moving spontaneity of its own subjects, the thinking and willing of the created minds in which it works and reigns. The planets obey a law which they have no power to accept or not accept; it is in them, but not from them or of them in any way; and for this very reason their action is blind and unfree. So throughout *Nature*, as such. Its very character is to be without autonomy in its own order of existence. The Moral, on the contrary, as distinguished from the Natural, is self-conscious, self-active, in a certain sense we may say even self-productive, and in such form truly free. It is not made, except as it at the same time makes itself. It is not moved, save as it originates its own motion. It stands, like all created existence, in the power of law; but the law here is not from abroad simply, as in the case of mere nature, not objective and outward only, but inward also and subjective; it is brought to pass, comes to its actualization in the world, only in the form of being apprehended and willed by its subjects. On the outside of such self-conscious life it can have no being in the world whatever. Turn it in any way into mere blind force, simple outward compulsion, and all proper morality is at an end. The necessary medium of its revelation, the very element in which it exists and makes itself felt, is the self-moving activity of the life it is formed to bind; which at the same time has full power to be untrue to itself by refusing the authority of its proper law, and which can be rightly bound by this in the end only as it receives the law freely into its own constitution, and so enacts it into force for its own use. Mind thus, by its very constitution, is required to be autonomic, self-legislative, a true fountain and source of law for itself; while the law notwithstanding has its ultimate ground only in God, and can be of no force whatever as the product merely of any lower intelligence. Objective and subjective here must fall absolutely together. The will without the law is false; denies its own proper nature; falls over to the sphere of bondage and sin. But the law, on the other hand, without the will, has no power either to accomplish its proper work. Only as the law, previously necessary by Divine constitution, is *willed*, freely embraced, affirmed and constituted, by the created intelligence it is ordained to rule,

18. [See document 2 above, *Human Freedom*.]
19. [{Brownson,} "Reply to Mercersburg," 218.]

so as to be at the same time the product of this, its own act virtually and deed, can there be any true escape from the idea of slavery, any true entrance into the sphere of freedom, any morality or religion in the full and right sense of these terms. It is this union of law and will, necessity and liberty, not outwardly but inwardly, which brings the life of man emphatically to its proper form. This is what we mean by the autonomy of the human subject, the right of man to be governed by his own will and not simply by a heteronomic force acting upon him from beyond his will, the voice that belongs to him properly in the constitution of the law which he is called to obey.

Our objection to the Roman doctrine, as we understand it to be exhibited by Mr. Brownson, is that the law objectively taken is so far sundered from the activity of the obeying subject, as to be in fact set over against this in the character of another nature altogether, and under a wholly outward form. Objective and subjective are made to fall apart dualistically into two distinct worlds. We do not wish to confound them, to mix them together, or to make one absorb and destroy the other; we recognize their difference; but still we object just as strenuously also to this abstract separation. Allow that we may not be able to show in what way precisely the two interests of authority and freedom flow together, this is no reason still why we should give up the claims of either in favor of the other. We may not subordinate authority to the independence of man, so as to make him his own lord and master, with liberty to follow simply his private pleasure; but just as little have we any right to affirm such separate mastery in favor of the law, to the exclusion of man's mind and voice. Authority on the outside of the will, in no union with it, standing over against it simply as a foreign force, though it should be the authority of God himself, can bring with it no strength, no freedom, no life. The case demands an inward mediation; such an entrance of the law into the sphere of the subject's own life, that it shall seem to be part of his very nature, and to grow forth spontaneously from the activity of his will. It is the "law of the spirit of life in Christ Jesus,"[20] the law as the power of self-moving spirit in the soul itself, that makes it free from the law of sin and death. This implies oneness of nature between the power that binds, and the activity which allows itself thus to be bound; and it is only on the ground of such correspondence that the relation requiring them to be so joined can be said to hold from the beginning.

[Relation of Object and Subject]

Mr. Brownson charges us with great confusion, as well as fundamental error, for making object and subject dependent on each other in the realization of truth, and for resolving the first separately taken into the general, as distinguished from the particular; which is he tells us, to make the object the product of the subject, and in the end to overthrow the existence of particular concrete objects altogether. We still say however,

---

20. [Rom 8:2.]

that there can be no truth or law in the world of mind under a purely objective form; for the reason that intelligence and will are needed to make room for any such existence, and to bring it actually to pass. Truth exists, *as truth*, only by being known. Blot out all knowledge, all consciousness, all thought, and you blot out all truth at the same time. Intelligence is the light in which it reveals its presence, the very form in which it becomes real.[21] Will it be said, that is to make God himself dependent on the thinking and willing of men, and so to resolve his being into mere void, or abstract possibility, seeking to become plenum, full and real in the life of the world? We reply, by no means. God is at once Object and Subject, in the most universal sense. His existence is the absolute union of both. As object merely, without self-knowledge and self-activity he would not be the God of the Bible, but the very abstraction of Buddhism itself, the infinite Nothing from which it is pretended here so anxiously to fly on the other side. To conceive of God as necessarily existent under a purely objective form, without regard to his own intelligence and will; as though these had to do with the first in a secondary way only, finding the object at hand previously for their use; is a thought in its own nature fatal to all sound theology, full as much as the imagination which allows him no independent personality whatever. Dualism in this shape, is only pantheism back upon us again with a new face. The necessity by which God exists, as we have before said, is a free necessity; it has ground, not from beyond his own will, but in the activity of his will itself. He is eternally self-produced. His being is not merely an object, but an *act*, his own act, going forth always from an exercise of thought and will. In this consists his Personality; which at the same time is *absolute*; carries in itself no reference to any object or thing beyond itself, but affirms itself with illimitable self-sufficiency from within as the Infinite I AM, which is at the same time and must be the everlasting ground of all life and being besides. And so there in the constitution of the universe under God, object and subject can never fall absolutely asunder, but are required to go always together as joint factors in the determination of all proper *reality* in the world. Nature itself exists only for mind; and in this view, moreover, the proper truth and sense of it are found not at all in the single particular things belonging to it as these may be perceived by the senses merely, but in the ideas rather they reveal and represent, which come from beyond, which are always general or universal in their nature, and which can have no being or presence in the world whatever, save under the form of thought and by the activity of self-apprehending and self-moving intelligence. Truth thus, in the moral world under God, considered as objective merely is always something general. So is law. In such form exclusively, however, they can have no force in the concrete constitution of man's life. For this purpose, they must become subjective, or in other words enter into the sphere of particular thought and will. This is not to subordinate them in any sense to the power of such thought and will; as though truth and law might be considered the product simply of men themselves.

---

21. [Similarly Plato: the Good illuminates objects of reason and makes them intelligible, just as the sun illuminates objects of sense and makes them visible (*Republic*, VI, 508b-c).]

Document 8: Brownson's Review Again.

Men make neither truth nor law. These have an absolute necessity beyond their will, and underlie the very order out of which their whole existence springs. But still truth and law actualize themselves in the world, become concrete and thus real for men, only as they are incorporated with their life, and pass over in this way from a purely objective character to a character which is at the same time subjective and individual.

[Organic and Objective Wholeness of Truth]

In this realization of reason and law, however, their character as general is not lost. It is not every man's thinking and willing privately taken that can thus make room for them in the world; but only such private thinking and willing as are comprehended in the life of the world as a whole. In this way mind collectively taken is more always than mere single thought and will; not simply as it is the aggregate of individual opinions numerically joined together, but as it brings us nearer also to what may be considered the proper wholeness of truth under its objective form. Reason and law work thus objectively in the constitution of the moral world, as a most real power lodged in the very structure of our collective life; something which is in such view wholly different from all merely private intelligence, as well as independent of it while it is only by means of this at the same time that it can ever bring itself to pass or make itself felt. This objective revelation forms the medium accordingly, the necessary and only medium we may say, through which mind in its individual capacity is brought to communicate with truth in a truly living way. The communication is not separate and direct, but by the intervention rather of a more general rationality, in the bosom of which the single mind is of necessity born and matured and perpetually carried. Purely private reason is an absurdity; and so just as much is private will. The absurdity is not relieved, however, by setting authority over against either, in the form of truth or in the form of law, in a purely abstract and outward view. The abstraction here is full as bad as the negation. The case calls for a concrete mediation of the single and the general. This we have in the actual structure of the human world; where reason and law are found touching men continually, not in an abrupt and isolated way, (what Dr. Bushnell styles the ictic method)[22] but mediationally always, through the organism of

---

22. [Horace Bushnell was a near contemporary of Nevin and a Congregationalist preacher and theologian. In the 1847, Nevin and Bushnell discussed the nature of conversion or regeneration as it applied to infant baptism. They were both critics of a revivalist conversionism separated from the nurture of a Christian child in the community. Bushnell described the typical revivalist conversion as a "divine stroke or *ictus*," a divine act coming from above, breaking into the normal pattern of religious life (Bushnell, *Views of Christian Nurture*, 103, emphasis original, see also 93, 107). While Nevin agreed with this much, he interpreted Bushnell's theory as *naturalistic*, where the child became a Christian through the natural nurture of the child in a Christian family, whereas Nevin understood regeneration as happening *supernaturally*, through the sacramental life of the church. For the entire debate from Nevin's side, see Nevin, "Nevin and Bushnell: Christian Nurture," MTSS 6:34–77. Bushnell responded in *Views*, 100–109. For a three-sided debate among Bushnell, Nevin, and Charles Hodge on Christian nurture, see Layman, "Holistic Supernaturalism," 194–200.]

the human life itself collectively taken, and by means of relations that bind the single subject indissolubly at all points to the great living, rational and moral mass, of which he is a part and without which he can be nothing. God does not bring his will nigh to men in a direct way, but through some living constitution more broad and general than themselves, which they are bound, as well as naturally prompted, to regard and reverence for this very end. His authority utters itself through the family; through right public opinion; through art and science; through the civil state; through the course of history; and above all, though in full conformity with the same general law, in the Church catholic as this has stood from the time of the Apostles down to the present day, and is destined to stand also to the end of the world, the pillar and ground of the truth, against which the gates of hell can never prevail.

[Private Judgment and Romanism]

In this way, we recognize fully the vanity of mere private judgment, in the great business of religion, and the need of authority to assist us in settling rightly the high and solemn questions with which it is concerned. This authority too, we see plainly enough, must be something more than the letter of the Bible, as each man separately taken may have power to read it for his own use; since this necessarily resolves itself at last, under such view, into that very private judgment and will, from which the problem is to find some sufficient escape. It is in truth the essence of rationalism itself, to make the single mind, in such style, the source and measure of Christianity, and it is only a circumstance in the case, that the Bible may happen to be taken as the ostensible platform of such independent thinking, while another sort of rationalism sets this also aside, and falls back fairly and openly on its own resources in the most naked form. We acknowledge the need of something more here than the Bible, thus made the sport and plaything of private judgment. Christianity is a living fact in the world, which as such carries along with it, to the end of time, its own evidence and its own authority. In this form it constitutes the Church. We own and confess the authority of this body, the one holy catholic Church of the Creed, as both legitimate and necessary for the proper constitution of the Christian faith in all ages and lands. When those who would make the Bible *per se* the source of Christianity, refer us at the same time to the influence of the Holy Ghost as going along with it and securing its right use, we see clearly enough that all such illumination must be regarded as fanciful and vain, if it fall not in with the general law of our nature just noticed, by which the presence of truth for the individual mind is conditioned and mediated by its relations to mind in a more comprehensive view. We have no right to conceive of the Spirit, as working in any such abstract way. It is against philosophy, against experience, and against the clear representations of the New Testament itself. As the Spirit of Christ especially, the medium of the new creation which began to be revealed on the day of Pentecost, he is at the same time the Spirit of his Church, the one and the self-same power that is active in all the saints, as they form collectively his mystical body, and are thus the fulness of him that filleth all in all.[23] The authority of the Spirit then is to be expected and sought, like all other manifestations of God's will in the world, not under an abstract character, but under the form of concrete life; that is, in the bosom of the Church, by which and through which only it comes to such revelation. But now when the Romanists, to meet this acknowledged want, refer us to their Church outwardly considered, or to the Pope as its visible head, for an authority which is declared to be infallible at all points, and always at hand, for the solution of all religious questions, we seem to ourselves at least to encounter, under a slight change of aspect only, the very same difficulty we have wished to escape from on the opposite side. The Church or the Pope here is made to stand mechanically in the place of the Bible, as the organ of the Holy Ghost; whose authority is then supposed to reach over to the single believer, through such outward medium, in a purely abstract quasi-magical way, without any regard whatever to the standing order of our life, which demands in every such case, as we have seen, a concrete living revelation, by the force and power of which objectively the individual mind may be brought io assert a corresponding activity in a truly free way. We object not to the idea of authority in the case; but we wish an authority that may show itself truly moral, answerable to the constitution of humanity, compatible with the idea of freedom. No authority, it seems to us, can be of this character that is absolutely abstract, that comes upon the subject as an abrupt and isolated *mandamus*,[24] from a higher sphere. To be really from God, it must legitimate itself by entering the sphere of the life it seeks to rule; it must take concrete form in the world; it must win for itself a living human activity in the social system, which in the case before us becomes the Church, whereby it may have access to individual thought and will in conformity with the general law of our nature. Let it appear that the decisions of the Pope, though taken to be moved by the Holy Ghost, are the product in some way of the general life of Christianity, rationally working out the result through such central organ, according to the law of man's nature as otherwise known; and we can at least listen patiently to the plea that is put in for his infallibility. But this is not the view that Romanism is willing to allow. The infallibility must be set quite above the standing order of our life. The authority is lifted clear out of the process of humanity, and in this way ceases to be concrete and historical altogether. It has no objective mediation in the actual constitution of the world. It is wholly abstract, transcendent, superhuman; and so in the end it is not moral; leaves no room for freedom; but runs into despotism, spiritual legerdemain, and magic.

23. [Eph 1:23.]
24. [A judicial order or command to carry out some duty.]

Part 2: The Church Question and Supernaturalism

[The Supernatural and Faith]

We have never meant to deny the supernatural; nor yet to make it the same thing simply with the supersensible, the world of pure thought as distinguished from the world of sense. Our objection to Mr. Brownson is, not that he sets the supernatural out of nature over it and above it, but that this *transcendence*, in his hands is carried to the point of such an absolute disruption of the one world from the other as amounts at last to downright dualism, and leaves no room for the accomplishment of any real conjunction between them in the life of man; which, however, at the same time is the necessary conception of all religion, and the very form especially in which the idea of Christianity becomes complete. We see not how such a real conjunction should imply anything like a full sufficiency on the side of nature, left to itself for the actualization of the supernatural as its own product; but it does seem to us certainly to require a constitutional fitness and capability on the part of the first, for apprehending with some inward connatural grasp, the presence of this last when brought within its reach. We question not the full objectivity of the supernatural, as an order of life above nature; only we ask that a corresponding subjectivity be allowed also on the part of man, whereby he may be able to receive the object which is thus higher than himself into true union with his life, so as to be lifted by the power of it, not magically but rationally, into its own superior sphere. Such directly receptive capacity we take to be inherently at hand in the gift or faculty of faith. Faith carries in it a real inward living and rational correspondence with the truth it is called to embrace; and in this view it belongs to the proper original nature of man, though a divine influence is needed certainly to bring it into exercise. Such drawing out of the subjective capacity of our nature, however, by no means implies that the truth itself is drawn out in this way; just as little as the awakening of sight in a previously blind eye would imply, that the surrounding world was brought to pass by its becoming thus an object of vision.[25] What else does our Saviour mean when he says: No man can come to me, except the Father *draw* him; He that is of God, heareth God's words; If any man will do my will, he shall know of the doctrine whether it be of God.[26] For the reception of Christ, all depends on a certain inward sympathy and correspondence with the truth revealed in his person, a real receptivity for the supernatural on the side of the human soul itself, such as all men ought to have, but only some men have in fact.

To affirm such a rational correspondence between faith and its object, is not to affirm by any means the full intelligibleness of this last for the human mind. The world of sense is not at once understood, by being apprehended as an object of sense. Still this apprehension carries in it the relation of a real inward connection with the intrinsic

---

25. [Faith must be able to "see" the (supernatural) truth. However, faith does not "cause" that truth to *be*, any more than eyes that were previously blind "cause" the external world to come into being because they can now see. Nevin extends this analogy in the next paragraph.]

26. [Biblical references are, in order: John 8:47, John 6:44; John 7:17.]

nature of what is thus perceived as real and true. So here. The object supernatural, according to the measure of each particular revelation, is substantiated and made to be real, not objectively of course but in the sphere of the human mind, by the power of faith, touching it, falling in with it, embracing it, and so admitting it into union with man's life, though it be still by no means fully comprehended. Faith is not itself the truth it embraces; just as little as the Holy Ghost is the same truth, in making way for it to the believer's soul; but it is nevertheless truly the very form under which truth exists *in the soul*, as the Holy Ghost also is the real medium by which such result is brought to pass. Supernatural truth is for man no truth at all except as it is "mixed with faith" in them that hear it. The language of St. Paul, Heb. xi. 1, taken in connection with the whole chapter, clearly implies, we think, that faith is such a power of grasping invisible and eternal things, as serves to authenticate them, and to make their reality actually felt, as truly as the things of sense are felt in their own way. By it, for instance, we know that the worlds were framed from nothing by the word of God [Heb 11:3]. We get that by no ratiocination, and by no outward testimony; but in the form rather of a direct response on the part of our religious nature, to the word that addresses faith directly out from the constitution of the world itself.

But this, Mr. Brownson tells us, is to exclude testimony, as the necessary medium of faith. "Even Divine testimony is not to be credited, it seems, according to our German Reformed Doctor, till we have examined what it testifies to, and satisfied ourselves by our own light that it is true, and worthy to be believed" ["Reply to Mercersburg,"] p. 204. But this is not a fair representation of our meaning. What we have objected to is the idea of a purely outward evidence in this form, coming between the believer and the truth to be believed, and engaging his assent to this on grounds wholly extrinsical to the truth itself. Certainly we allow the testimony or word of God to be the true foundation of faith. The question is simply, how this testimony is to be obtained. *Can* it be conclusively ascertained in a purely abstract way, as something sure and full on the *outside* of the revelation to which it requires our assent; according to the view taken of faith, if we understand Mr. Brownson rightly, in the Roman system? We think not. The whole revelation, be it less or more, commencing with the miracle or primary seal and reaching out to all that is spoken, must be regarded as entering into the evidence by which the presence of the Divine Speaker is authenticated and his testimony accredited.[27] This is not to make the word more certain than the Speaker, but only to set the Speaker before us under a form worthy of himself, and sufficient to command faith. When we have, in such circumstances, the Presence of God joined with its proper concrete relations, these serve of course to complete the evidence of the adorable fact; but it is still the Presence itself, as the centre of all,

---

27. [Beginning in 1870, Nevin more fully develops the theme that revelation in Scripture is a self-authenticating reality, in accordance with the Reformed dogma of *testimonium spiritus sancti internum* {trans. "internal witness of the Holy Spirit"}. Nevin, *My Own Life*, 112–14; "Christ and His Spirit," 363–64, 379–84; editorial introduction to "Bread of Life," MTSS 6:214–15.]

which at the same time legitimates and proves the reality of the whole revelation. So the world of Nature proclaims the being and glory of God; but only as the idea of God himself, discerned by faith, comes into view through Nature, and in the midst of it, to authenticate it as his own spoken handiwork and word. The miracle seals properly a Divine commission; but not abstractly; not magically; otherwise no direction could have been given (Deut. xii. 1–5) to destroy a wonder-worker using such argument in favor of idolatry and falsehood. The miracle, to prove truth, must have a certain moral constitution; must be surrounded with right relations; must proceed from a worthy quarter and look to a worthy end.

So Christ stands commended to faith certainly by evidence *ab extra*[28] as the Son of the living God; only however as he is himself the *Light*, which sheds on all such evidence its full significance and power. The knowledge which Peter had of Christ (Matt. xvi. 17) came not of course by mere sense; it was from God, and not in any way from flesh and blood; but still it was not a secret whispered in his ear in this form from beyond Christ's person. The truth was *there* before him, with self-authenticating force in Christ himself; and it was his peculiar privilege to see and feel *in Him* the living glorious *Shekinah*[29] which he was in fact.

But here our limits require us to stop.

J. W. N.

---

28. [Trans. "from outside."]

29. ["God's presence in the world." Not a biblical term, but used in post-biblical Jewish literature. Harrelson, "Shekinah," 222.]

Document 9

"The Anglican Crisis"

Editor's Introduction

Nevin weighed in on the Oxford Movement in his "Anglican Crisis" article of 1851.[1] Nevin like others also referred to that movement as "Puseyism," after Edward Bouverie Pusey (1800–82) who was one of its leaders, or as "Tractarianism," which referred to the theological *Tracts for the Times* published by the Oxford don leaders (John Henry Newman, 1801–90; John Keble, 1792–1866; and Richard Hurrell Froude, 1803–36). The movement had its origins, as Newman acknowledged, after John Keble's "National Apostasy" sermon in the Oxford University pulpit on July 14, 1833.[2] According to C. Brad Faught, the "formal phase of the Oxford Movement ended in 1845 with Newman's conversion" even though "the ideas of the Tractarians lived on."[3] Keble's sermon was a vehement protest against Parliament's 1833 Church Temporalities Bill, which suppressed ten Anglican bishoprics in Ireland. For Keble, as well as the other Oxford participants, the church was independent from the government, and the state had no right to interfere in internal ecclesiastical matters. This sense of the independence of the church was one of the major themes that ran through the entire movement. The protest created a crisis in the Anglican Church and tensions with the government. The issue for the Oxford dons was one of principle (the freedom of the church). There were, however, justifiable practical reasons for reducing the number of Anglican dioceses in Ireland, where the sparse Anglican population did not justify the great number of Anglican dioceses in a country that was overwhelmingly Catholic.

The Oxford Movement called for a re-examination of the primitive church and a reformation within the international Anglican communion based on that

---

1. Nevin, "The Anglican Crisis," 359–98. For previous analyses of this essay, see Nichols, *Romanticism*, 195–99; Black, "A 'Vast Practical Embarrassment,'" 264–73; and Layman, general introduction to *Born of Water*, 25.
2. Newman, *Apologia Pro Vita Sua*, 50.
3. Faught, *The Oxford Movement*, 151.

re-examination. It was a minority campaign within the Church of England, but it had adherents in other parts of the world where there was a renewed interest in the so-called "church question." Nevin paid close attention to the publications produced by the Oxford dons and asserted that "The Anglican Crisis" had major implications for all of Protestantism, and he called especially for American Protestants to take seriously what the movement had to contribute to its own revitalization.

In addition to their support for the independence and freedom of the church, the leaders of the Oxford Movement supported other issues that they believed were consistent with the longer tradition of the Christian church, issues that were being neglected in the contemporary Church of England. They called for a more thorough examination of the Church Fathers and the doctrines and piety of the early church. They emphasized the organic continuity, development, unity, and universality of the church throughout the ages; the recovery of baptismal regeneration; the centrality of the Eucharist in the church's life and piety; and Apostolic succession in the episcopacy.[4]

For Nevin, the Anglican crisis within Protestantism should awaken Protestants to what the Anglican divines were trying to do by focusing their attention on the present church's continuity with the church of the past. That pre-Reformation church was the womb of the present and future church. But, Nevin argued, the Anglican emphasis on antiquity and retrieval was not the answer for the present or the future.

Nevin's thesis was consistent with his view of development, namely that Protestantism was in continuity with the substance of the earlier Catholic tradition but was a development and "real advance" of that tradition. The Oxford Movement fit into that Protestant development but did not carry forward or perfect or improve either the Catholic or Protestant traditions.

Although Nevin articulates his thesis at the end of his article, he had the argument in mind as he evaluated the contributions and weaknesses of the Oxford Movement. Raising the church question was the most important contribution of Oxford in Nevin's estimation. This was especially important for what Nevin called the no-church crowd or the "unchurchly and unsacramental school" within Protestantism and those Protestants who had broken faith with the past and considered Oxford "nonsense and folly." Oxford was a "revival of the catholic tendency in the English church." Oxford called into question many taken-for-granted Protestant assumptions about the church. The unchurchly school of Protestants ignored the church's "proper supernatural character as we find this asserted in the Apostles' Creed." That creedal faith in the church "as a living supernatural fact" was grounded in the mystery of the Incarnation, made visible in history. Some Protestants have turned that "concrete mystery into a pure abstraction" by asserting that the church universal is purely invisible or a collectivity of individual wills.[5]

---

4. Faught, *The Oxford Movement*, 71.
5. Nevin, "The Anglican Crisis," 362, 363, 368, 377, 378.

Document 9: "The Anglican Crisis"

Oxford was restoring a sense of the church that was consistent with the longer tradition of Christianity, but Oxford put a false emphasis on polity and especially on an Apostolic succession limited to the episcopacy. The genuine notion of the church went well beyond polity (whether episcopacy or Presbyterianism or any other outward structure). Episcopacy was only a secondary and subordinate part of the church, and the Oxford men and Anglicans in general made it a priority. In his review of Brownson's work, too, Nevin asserted that the authority of ministers within the church was the result of the "progressive actualization of the life of the Church" and was not, as he believed Brownson held, "independent of the Church."[6]

The Oxford men, though, rightly emphasized and tried to restore the church's understanding of baptismal regeneration in opposition to Baptists and low-church Episcopalians. Nevin supported this stress on baptismal regeneration for two reasons:[7] First, it was in conformity with the early and medieval and the major Reformed churches' views of baptism as a sacrament. Sacraments were considered divine acts that accomplished what they signified, and their efficacy and value came "not from the mind of the worshipper, but from the power of the transaction or the thing done." From the beginning of Christianity, this view of baptism was considered "a necessary part of the Christian faith." Baptism flowed from a correct understanding of the powers and grace given to the church itself. Second, in response to the Gorham case, as indicated in the General Introduction, Nevin approved the Tractarian's assertion that civil supremacy in matters of religion was "an abuse." In this the Oxford participants were reaffirming the ancient notion of the independence and freedom of the church in matters that related to the divine constitution of the church.[8]

Nevin focused most of his attention in "The Anglican Crisis" on the doctrine of the church and the sacraments, particularly on baptism. The Eucharist, however, was also a central issue for the Tractarians, but Nevin gave it little explicit attention in this essay. Instead, he examined the sacraments in general as efficacious signs and not mere outward forms that led to a kind of mere formalism in religion. He stressed this general point throughout the essay against what he consider the Puritan, Baptist, and "unchurchly and unsacramental" churches in England and the United States. For him, though, the sacraments were essentially tied to ecclesiology: "We must believe in a divine church, in order to believe in divine sacraments, or in a divine ministry under any form."[9]

---

6. Nevin, "Brownson's Quarterly Review," 61.

7. For Nevin's own developing perspective on baptismal grace and regeneration, see Nevin et al., *Born of Water*, MTSS 6, esp. 1–4, 19–22; "Baptismal Grace," 64–68; Nevin, "Noel on Baptism," 83–115; Nevin, "The Old Doctrine," 192–213. See also Payne, "Nevin on Baptism."

8. Nevin, "The Anglican Crisis," 370, 382.

9. Nevin, "The Anglican Crisis," 379.

Part 2 : The Church Question and Supernaturalism

Nevin's "Anglican Crisis" was another step in the early 1850s in demonstrating a more favorable view of Catholicism[10] and a more rigorous criticism of what he called, along with Brownson, the no-church tradition. In fact, he indicated at the end of this essay that Romanism was to be preferred to all other options available in current Protestantism, but that preference did not in fact have to be made because of the possibilities of a more perfect development in the future. The perfection of the church was for him an eschatological project that transcended all current manifestations of the church catholic.

---

10. In 1851, Nevin was also examining documents from the early church and was preparing essays he entitled "Early Christianity." In 1852, too, he wrote a series of essays on "Cyprian." American Catholics interpreted these essays as signs that Nevin was moving toward Rome. But Nevin expressed even in these essays, as in others, enough difficulties with modern Catholicism to keep him from going to Rome. On the American Catholic responses, see Nevin to Brownson, August 18, 1852; Brownson to Nevin, August 23, 1852, August 28, 1852, in Brownson Papers, University of Notre Dame Archives; see also Nevin to J[ames] A[lphonse] McMaster, February 26, 1853, in McMaster Papers, University of Notre Dame Archives.

The Anglican Crisis.[1]

The man who takes no lively interest in the present ecclesiastical troubles of England, under the notion possibly that they belong only to a standpoint of prejudice and superstition which he and the American world generally have happily left forever behind, has good reason to suspect some fatal flaw in the constitution of his own piety. Never since the age of the Reformation, has the progress of the Church presented practical questions of more solemn moment, or issues of more thrilling significance for the future. The course of events there now may be regarded as eminently *historical*, in the true and proper sense of this term; which is not reached by any means with the notion merely of passing years and their budget of facts, but implies the idea of actual movement in the world's inward life, the development of tendencies and principles into new results of general and lasting force for the nation and the race. Such palpably is the nature of the great church agitation, which has been for some time shaking England to its centre, and the end of which no one is able yet to calculate or foresee.[2] It is no superficial or merely transient commotion. It is no play of simply pragmatical contrivance and policy, in the hands of men intent on altogether other ends; however

---

1. [*MR* 3 (July 1851) 359-98.]

2. [The Anglican Crisis to which Nevin refers is sometimes called "Puseyism," "Tractarianism," and more frequently "The Oxford Movement." Nevin uses these terms interchangeably. Puseyism refers to the reform movement within the Church of England that Edward Bouverie Pusey (1800-82), Regis professor of Hebrew and a Canon of Christ Church at the University of Oxford, organized and was a chief representative. Tractarianism was a contemporary title for the same movement. Tractarianism, though, refers in particular to the theological Tracts for the Times, which Oxford representatives wrote to advocate a return to more organic and historical understanding of the church. The Oxford movement called for a re-examination of the primitive and medieval church and its theology and piety and had its origins after Parliament's Church Temporalities Bill (1833), which suppressed ten bishoprics in Ireland. In reaction, John Keble (1792-1866), a second leader of the movement, delivered a sermon, "The National Apostasy" (July 14, 1833) at Oxford, protesting the government's involvement in decisions that belonged properly to the Church of England. The movement had its most fruitful period between 1833 and 1845 when John Henry Newman (1801-90), another prominent leader at Oxford, converted to Catholicism. Other Tractarians (e.g., William George Ward, Henry Edward Manning, Frederick William Faber) eventually were received into the Catholic Church. See Ward, *The Oxford Movement*; Faught, *The Oxford Movement*; Brown and Nockles, *Oxford Movement*.]

ready the art of courts and political parties may show itself, as in all similar cases, to turn the movement into its own service. Under all such false purposes and aims, the ruling power of the agitation is undoubtedly a true interest of humanity, the working of religion, the most fundamental of all forces in history, in a form which it is quite possible that kings and parliaments may find as much beyond their control at last as the whirlwind itself.

[Significance of the Oxford Movement]

Serious men feel this in England; and they are coming to feel it, more and more, also in other countries. Nor is this feeling confined by any means to those who are members of the Episcopal Church. It extends to all Protestant communions, just in proportion to their intelligence and their knowledge of what is going forward in the world. This itself may be taken as a criterion of the real general historical significance of the problem, which is here in the course of practical solution. It is only what is thus universally significant in its own nature, that has power to engage in this way general attention and concern; and then it is not so much through any personal reflection that this takes place, as in obedience rather to a sort of instinctive consciousness, by which men feel themselves sympathetically borne along with the authority of such a movement, whether it suit their judgment and taste otherwise to make much account of it or not. It is curious to observe, how this law works in the case now under consideration. With all their professed indifference or hostility to the Establishment, Dissenters of every hue find themselves forced to mix themselves up to a certain extent with its controversies and quarrels, though hardly able to tell in in any cases *where* exactly it becomes them to take their position. The Presbyterianism of Scotland too is not able to sit still; and even the Puritanism of this country, while it affects to despise the whole doctrine of the Sacraments and of the Church as it is here in controversy, sees itself constrained notwithstanding to acknowledge indirectly the deep solemnity of the struggle, as one in which some interest of its own is felt to be ultimately at stake.[3] All this goes to show, we say, the profound meaning and far reaching importance of what is taking place. It is indeed a great crisis in the history of Protestantism, not for England only but for all countries; and *not* to see and feel the solemnity of it in this view, as we have said before, is to betray by the very fact a sad want of earnestness in

---

3. [Some Presbyterians in Scotland, led by Thomas Chalmers (1780–1847), withdrew from the established Church of Scotland in 1843 to form the Free Church of Scotland. They protested the state's encroachment on the spiritual independence of the church when the state approved lay patronage—that is, the legal right of wealthy landowners to select ministers for the church. In the late 1830s and early 1840s, the so-called church question arose in the United States not only within the Episcopal Church but also in the works of some Congregationalist ministers and theologians like Horace Bushnell, and even in the works of some Unitarians like Orestes Brownson, James Freeman Clarke, and William Henry Channing. Except for Brownson, these other Americans were not focused on an organic and sacramental, but a contractual or voluntary, view of the church.]

Document 9: The Anglican Crisis.

religion altogether. Only the ignorant or frivolous can be indifferent to the progress of so great a question.

The critical character of the movement is shown, not only by the general feeling of anxious awe now mentioned with which it is fixing upon itself more and more the gaze of the world, but by the central relation also in which it stands plainly to the bearings of previous history. It is no sudden excitement, that comes no one can tell whence and looks no one can tell whither. In all parts of the world, Protestantism has been for some time past in a course of inward preparation, either theoretically or practically, for just such a powerful reaction in favor of the old idea of the Church, with its corresponding principles and doctrines. There must have been in this way a mighty predisposition in the English mind towards Catholicism, or at least a mighty dissatisfaction inwardly with Puritanism, to account at all for the rapid growth of the Tractarian system, since its first appearance fifteen years ago in Oxford. It is easy enough moreover to point out powerful tendencies, which have been working either negatively or positively in other lands also, in the same general direction. The time has not yet fully come indeed, to estimate these in their whole strength. But it is plain enough, for all thinking men, that the problem of the Church Question, as it enters into the controversy between Catholics and Protestants, has been for some time past challenging reconsideration and demanding new settlement; and that this call is powerfully enforced from all sides, by what we may style the whole experience of the age, in a political and secular as well as ecclesiastical view. The English movement falls in with this wide spread and manifestly providential tendency, as it is clearly also the fruit of it and one of its most startling and awakening results. This of course shows again its vast historical significance and force. It lies at the very heart undoubtedly of the general life of the age; and it is all in order accordingly, that the earnest and thoughtful, who stand in the nearest sympathy always with this life, should regard what is passing with more than usual interest and concern.

Taking the controversy in the broad view now noticed, there is no reason whatever for restraining this interest to the bounds of the Episcopal Church. The question in agitation is something far deeper at last, than the proper view to be taken of the Protestantism of this particular body, or of its rights and claims over against the Church of Rome. It looks directly to the whole constitution of Protestantism, and grapples at once with the deepest and most universal issue that holds between it and Romanism. Episcopacy here becomes a mere circumstance; it may be in itself an element of some considerable account for the final settlement of the subject in hand, but it is still a secondary and subordinate particular only, and by no means the central or main thing, the very root and marrow, as some affect to think, of the whole question that is to be solved. To make it so, either on one side or the other, is sheer pedantry of the poorest and most pitiful kind. The question which lies at the heart of this movement, and communicates to it all its depth and power, is of no such shallow range. It goes far below this, to the very foundations of the whole cause of the Reformation. It is not necessary that one should be an Episcopalian, to feel himself brought into direct contact with its vastly solemn scope. He may feel this also, and ought to feel it, as a Presbyterian, as a Methodist, and even as a Congregational Puritan. For under every such character, he is still bound to take a lively interest in all that concerns the general constitution of that common Protestantism, out of which these unfortunate distinctions spring. And this interest is due to the case before us, independently altogether of the view that may be taken of the main question in debate. Let it even be supposed, that the whole drift and aim of the Catholic tendency is false, and that the true perfection of Protestantism is to be sought only in its being stripped of the last shred of churchly feeling, (after the taste of the Baptists) then will there be only the more reason of course to watch anxiously the progress of the present movement, and to look forward earnestly to the day when this desirable consummation shall be reached. The sacramental and the unsacramental alike have a deep interest at stake, in the present transitional crisis of the Anglican Church; and just in proportion to their earnestness, may they be expected accordingly to turn towards it their most solemn regards.

[Oppositions to the Anglican Church Question]

Of the last class we know indeed that there are many, who make it a point to treat the whole subject with an air of easy superiority and disdain; as though there were no room in truth for any rational controversy in the case, and so of course no ground for apprehension with regard to its ultimate issues, and no occasion therefore for any special interest in its progress. It is wonderful really how easily and how soon this unchurchly and unsacramental school in general are able to make a full end of this deepest problem of the age, and to gain a height of serene conviction in relation to it, that sets them quite beyond the reach of all the doubts and difficulties that seem to surround it for minds of another cast and make. To *them* the whole church question, as it now disturbs the peace of England, is nonsense and folly; they see to the bottom of it at once, and only wonder that men of education and sense in the English Church should find the least trouble in bringing it to its proper solution. Romanism is a tissue of abominations and absurdities from beginning to end; Puseyism is made up of silly puerilities, that cannot bear the light of common sense for a single moment; and it only shows the misery of Episcopacy and the English Establishment, that it should have given birth to so sickly a spawn at this late day, or that it should now find it so hard to expel the thing from its bosom. The proper cure for all such mummery is to give up the church mania altogether, to discard the whole idea of sacramental grace, to fall back on the Bible and private judgment as the true and only safe rule of Protestantism, and to make Christianity thus a matter of reason and common sense. This too is clearly the order and course of the age; all is tending, by political and ecclesiastical revolution as well as by the onward march of science, towards this glorious result of independence and freedom; and it may well be expected therefore, that all these

Document 9: The Anglican Crisis.

church crotchets will soon follow the other rubbish of the Middle Ages into the darkness of perpetual oblivion and night.

But it is just one of the great uses of instruction to be drawn from this movement, that it is eminently suited to convict all such flippant thinking of falsehood, and to expose it for the seriously thoughtful in its true nakedness and poverty. The entire history of Christianity indeed, for one who is able to study it, is replete with instruction in the same form; it is impossible to have any tolerable familiarity with it, and not be filled with a sort of moral nausea towards all such crude and empty declamation, as being a libel on its whole divine significance from the start. But it is well to have the lesson brought home, as it is here, to the very door of our own life and day. And no one will pretend, that it is not so here under a form that carries with it extraordinary weight. So much is this the case, that even the class of whom we now speak, with all their self-complacent flippancy, find themselves forced, as we have already seen, to do some homage instinctively to the inherent solemnity of the crisis which is passing. With all their tone of contempt for it, they have no power to avert from it absolutely their eyes, or to speak of it with calm indifference; which they should be able to do certainly, if it were in its own nature really so puerile and weak as they pretend. And who may not see, that the instinctive feeling here is more to be trusted, than the empty judgment to which it gives the lie. If ever a movement deserved to be honored, for its religious earnestness and for the weight of intellectual and moral capital embarked in it, such title to respect may fairly be challenged by this late revival of the catholic tendency in the English Church. The movement is of far too high and ominous a character, has enlisted in its service far too great an amount of powerful intellect and learning and study, and has gone forward with far too much prayer, and fasting and inward spiritual conflict, and has taken hold far too deeply of the foundations of the best religious life of the nation, and has led and is leading still to far too many and too painful sacrifices, like the dividing of soul and spirit or of the joints and marrow [Heb 4:12]—to be resolved with any sort of rationality whatever into views and motives, so poor as those which are called in to account for it by the self-sufficient class of whom we now speak. To charge such a movement with puerility, to set it down as destitute of all reason and in full contradiction to the clear sense of religion, as a mere rhapsody of folly without occasion or meaning in the proper history of the Church, is but to make ourselves puerile and silly in the highest degree. Plainly it is the part of true wisdom, rather to pause before such an imposing fact with a certain measure of reverence, whether our sympathies fall in with it or not, to study it carefully in all its proportions, and thus to turn it to some purpose of instruction and profit that may be helpful in the end to others as well as to ourselves. There is no excuse for treating such a fact with mere ribaldry and scorn. We are bound in all right reason, as well as in all good conscience, to take it for granted that it is not without meaning, whether we have power to understand the sense of it or not. It is high time, we think, in view of what has taken place already in the history of this Anglican movement, and of what is now taking place—not to speak of events that are as yet only casting their shadows before them—that our popular declaimers on the subject, whether of the rostrum or the press, should pull in their zeal a little, and learn to proceed somewhat more moderately in their philippics and squibs. They are, in the usual style, quite too wholesale and sweeping. All excess at last cuts the sinews of its own strength; an argument which proves too much destroys itself; and so there is some reason to apprehend, that this anti-catholic and anti-sacramental ammunition may in the end lose its effect altogether, by being simply pushed too far and so made vile and cheap. The method is indeed short and easy, and answers an admirable purpose especially for our May anniversaries, where many of the orators, as we all know, would be sadly at a loss to get along at all, without the opportunity of such wholesale never-come-amiss vituperation of Romanism and Puseyism, with all that belongs to the sacramental system.[4] But for all this, it is high time, we say again, that men who lay claim to so large a portion of all the knowledge and piety that are going, should begin to be a little more reserved at least in the practice of such polemics, as being more and more likely to make an impression on thinking people the very opposite of that which they themselves seek and wish.

We do not mean of course, that the personal credit of the party embarked in the Tractarian cause, whether still in the Church of England or gone over to Rome, is to be taken as an argument for the truth of the cause itself; or that this is to be made right and good, by any consideration simply of the learning and piety, the labors and sacrifices, which it has had power thus far to engage in its service. There are learning and piety also on the other side; and the question is not to be settled at once by any proof of this sort in either direction. All we mean is, that a cause which is thus circumstanced is no fit object of wholesale contempt. It has a right to be looked upon with respect, and to challenge sober and serious examination. More than this, it must include in its constitution some real meaning and reason, well entitled to consideration, which it is perfectly certain that those have never yet come to see or understand, who affect to dispose of its pretensions in any such summary and sweeping style.

The catholic and sacramental tendency in religion is something too great, to be set aside lawfully by a flippant dash of the tongue or pen, or by a mere magisterial wave of the hand. All superficial criticism here is egregiously out of place. Never was there a case, in which it could be less reasonable and becoming to sit at the feet of fools for instruction; and it is truly humiliating to see, how readily this is done by a large part of the nominally Protestant world, to whom every strolling mountebank is welcome that comes among them as a lecturer on Romanism; as though the deepest and most sacred themes of religion, and questions that have carried with them the earnestness of death itself for the most earnest and profound minds age after age,

---

4. [Annual May anniversary celebrations usually occurred sometime around May 21, the date commemorating the opening of the First General Assembly of the Presbyterian Church of the United States of America in 1789.]

Document 9: The Anglican Crisis.

might be satisfactorily settled in five minutes' time with a flourish of idle declamation, by men whose want of serious thought is as it were visibly stamped on their whole face. Such championship of Protestantism is of course disgraceful, and tends directly to kill its own cause; on which account we are not much surprised to learn, that a somewhat notorious renegade brawler of this sort, who is now scouring the country, has come to be regarded by some with suspicion as being possibly himself still only a cunning Jesuit in disguise.[5] But the championship may be of a much more respectable order than this, and yet fall fairly notwithstanding under the same general charge of frivolous superficiality. It may proceed, not from fools and blackguards but from men of respectable education and apparently very serious piety, and yet be of such form and spirit throughout as to show manifestly, that it is dealing with a subject which it has never taken any, serious pains to understand, and the merits of which therefore it has no power either to fathom or explain. So it must ever be, where it is assumed from the outset that the subject carries in it no real difficulty, that two or three obvious common sense maxims are sufficient to settle it immediately and entirely one way, and that it is only a sort of palpable hallucination to think seriously for a moment of settling it in any other way.

In the case before us, all such sweeping criticism, we repeat, is in danger more and more of fairly capsizing by its own spread of sail. Of this some seem to be growing at least partially aware, and we notice accordingly in the late Tabernacle oratory, as reported in the newspapers, an occasional lowering the usual high tone in regard to the intrinsic folly and wickedness of the whole Catholic system.[6] A few of the best speakers have condescended to acknowledge, that this system is not so utterly destitute of all sense and piety as is often imagined, that the main power of it after all lies in the appeal it makes to some of the higher principles of our nature, and that it may be found in this way to carry in it a perilous charm, a true siren's voice, even for religiously earnest and learned men, nay, for this class perhaps, in certain states of thought, beyond all sorts of people besides. "The sacramental system," in the language of one of these speakers,

5. [This "notorious renegade brawler" may well be Louis Giustiniani, an anti-Catholic Evangelical Lutheran Church minister. Nevin wrote of the "notorious Giustiniani" in "Early Christianity," 475. Billington, *Protestant Crusade*, 308, noted that he traveled about the country converting Germans to Protestantism. He was from a prominent Italian family, was raised a Catholic, but left the church and became a missionary in Australia before coming to the United States. I am indebted to David Layman for identifying Giustiniani and his work. While in the United States, he published two anti-Catholic tracts in the midst of the "Protestant Crusade": *Papal Rome* and *Intrigues of Jesuitism*. Nevin's reference to him as a "cunning Jesuit in disguise" may be a reference to Calvin Colton's *Protestant Jesuitism*, 34–35, where Colton asserts that Protestants cannot claim that "there is no Jesuitism" in their crusade against Popery because they have "taken the weapons of their adversaries to fight them with." Jesuitism, according to Colton, is evident in "a religious society governed by principles of human policy for worldly ends," 46.]

6. [The Broadway Tabernacle Congregational Church was established in lower Manhattan in 1832 and became a center for major addresses on important nineteenth-century issues: e.g., the Evangelical Revival, the women's movement, anti-slavery, as well as Catholicism.]

is susceptible of such an expression, that its repulsiveness may be concealed, and it may be rendered attractive and full of spiritual meaning; and this was the reason why it attracted many of the learned and refined. It was impossible to read the Oxford tracts, or to converse with some of those who had gone from among us, and not feel that Popery is a system that may be rendered attractive to certain minds. But, nevertheless, it is a false system; and it is in this *plausible* aspect that it needs to be met, as a false theory.[7]

But even this sort of concession, we feel bound to say, gentlemanly as it is in comparison with the tone too often adopted by others, falls altogether short of the respect that is justly due to the subject, and that *must* be felt as well as professed towards it, before it can be approached in any case with truly successful controversy and debate.

The air of *condescension* here is quite too palpable, implying as it does the sense of most complete personal superiority to the entire issue in hand, to allow the supposition that there has been any real mastery after all of its proper difficulties and merits. No man can be justified in the use of this tone in such a case, we say it respectfully but still with the most firm decision, who has not been led in the first place through much profound thought and earnest prayer to the platform on which he is brought finally to stand; and then the fruit of his experience will have been such, beyond all doubt, that it will be morally impossible for him not to allow a great deal more still in favor of the system, which he ventures thus intelligently and not blindly to condemn. It is not enough, to say that the sacramental system is very childish, and contrary to the Bible, and at war with the whole idea of evangelical religion; but that we may easily see still how it can have charms for persons of a sentimental and poetical turn of mind; and so are bound to acknowledge the learning and religious sincerity of many who are now yielding themselves to its power, while we pity and deplore their blindness as contrasted with our own light. The apology itself, in any such form, is intolerably superficial and slim. It may go down, as a nice morsel of philosophical wisdom, with some dreamy audience of the Broadway Tabernacle, but it can never bring any true and solid satisfaction to wakefully inquiring souls that hunger after truth. All such see at once, that it needs something more than sentimentalism to explain a movement so vast and deep. The very fact that the system in question has carried in it such power, through all past times, to lead captive the minds of the cultivated and learned, as well as of the rude multitude, and that it is doing this now in so earnest a way, should be taken as itself solemn proof that it is not without some sort of cause and reason, in the religious wants of men and the revelation of grace with which they are met in Christianity. Why should the system be so hard to destroy, and whence should it have come

---

7. [I could not identify the quotation. Something of the spirit of the talks given on Catholicism at the Broadway Tabernacle, however, is evident in Nicholas Murray's (1802–61) *Decline of Popery and its Causes* (January 1851), a polemical attack on Catholicism given at the Broadway Tabernacle. Murray's text was an unacknowledged response to New York's Archbishop John Hughes's equally polemical November 1850 lecture at St. Patrick's Cathedral on *The Decline of Protestantism and Its Cause*.]

to so powerful a revival in the very bosom of Protestantism itself, and by what means shall we account for its energy and zeal, if it be in itself after all so void of reason, and so diametrically opposed to every right conception of religion, as is taken for granted even by the more liberal representation of which we now speak. No such system could ever so prevail, if it were altogether without reason. No such system could so turn the heads of the best scholars in the English Church, if it were made up of mere puerilities and dreams. No such system could produce so much uncommonly earnest fruit, in the way of fasting and prayer and sacrifice, if it were a simple trick of Satan got up to put down Christ. Every assumption of this sort is violent, outrages reason, and flies in the face of clear facts; and no opposition which is made to the system on any such ground, however respectable it may be in other respects, will be found of any true weight in the end. We have a right to say to such opposition always:

> You have never yet so studied this system, as to be justified in using towards it the tone of superiority with which you affect to speak: It may be open to censure in the form here noticed, and it is in truth of the utmost account, in such case, that its faults and defects should be brought fully and clearly into view: But *you* evidently are not yet prepared for any such work: Your supposed superiority to the party on whom you pretend to sit in judgment, is imaginary only and in no sense real: You must think more a great deal, pray more, wrestle more, before you can deserve to be regarded as in any state answerable at all in these respects to the moral weight of the movement on the other side: That all is so clear and easy to your view, only shows how dark in fact your view still is: The first and most necessary condition for fighting Puseyism and Popery to purpose, let it be well understood and borne in mind, the most indispensable *sine qua non* of all right to be heard in the controversy at all, is power to perceive and acknowledge the vast body of awfully solemn and most deeply interesting and vital truth, which enters into these systems, and clothes them with their strange and mysterious authority for so many earnest minds.

[Oxford Challenges to Protestantism]

What makes this Anglican crisis particularly solemn for serious thinkers, is the force it has to bring out sensibly the difficulties and contradictions that belong to the present state of the Church on different sides. In this respect, it may be taken as of a truly diacritical[8] nature; for it goes to probe and expose the doubtful character at least of much, which was before rested in with a sort of passive acquiescence as good and sufficient, simply because it was put to no practical inquest and trial. It sometimes happens that what has seemed to work well enough for ages in this way, is at last suddenly found wanting, to the view of all who do not choose wilfully to shut their

---

8. ["Diacritical": "that which separates or distinguishes; distinctive." Webster, *American Dictionary*, 244.]

own eyes, by some new experiment it may be of a very few years; a particular turn or juncture in history, that serves of itself all at once to bring out, with glaring revelation, huge flaws and defects of which the world generally seemed to have no sense whatever before. Such a juncture, to our view, in the progress of modern church history, is the movement now under consideration. It is in this light especially, that we look upon it as eminently entitled to attention, and as more than usually pregnant with instruction.

Who that thinks seriously, for instance, can fail to be struck with the fearfully ominous posture, into which the whole open and professed no-church interest is thrown by the progress of this controversy. By such interest we do not mean of course those who repudiate the name and notion of a church out and out, but that large class of Protestants rather which has come to look upon the Church as only a notion or a name, disclaiming all faith in its proper supernatural character as we find this asserted in the Apostles' Creed.[9] The opposition which holds between this sort of religion, whether on the outside of the Episcopal church or in the bosom of it, and the old catholic faith, has been all along felt; but there has been room generally for a certain amount of vague uncertainty and disguise in the case, which has kept the full sense of the issue always more or less out of sight. The no-church interest contrived too commonly not to come to any clear understanding with its own theory, finding it more convenient to take the general orthodoxy of it for granted, and to assail negatively the views of the other side at given points as unevangelical and absurd. But one grand effect now of the crisis which is going forward in England, is to put a full end to all such dubious and deceitful twilight, and to drag this question so into the blaze of day, that all men may see and know where they stand with regard to it, and judge of themselves and of one another accordingly. The main significance of the crisis lies just here, that it goes so thoroughly to the heart and core of the church question, and shuts men up to the necessity of answering it in it direct way, if they answer it at all, with full view of what their answer means.

The force of the question in the end is nothing less than this: Whether the original catholic doctrine concerning the Church, as it stood in universal authority through all ages before the Reformation, is to be received and held still as a necessary part of the christian faith, or deliberately rejected and refused as an error dangerous to men's souls and at war with the Bible? No one will pretend to say surely, that this is not a great question, and worthy of being met with a feeling of sacred awe. It is so, whatever view we take of the proper answer; for let it be considered never so plain and certain, that the rejection of the old doctrine is required by common sense, and that to uphold it is the perfection of folly and superstition, it is still something exceedingly solemn to come in this way to full rupture with a creed, which has been of such wide dominion and of such ancient date, and that must be acknowledged by all too to have been crowned in times past with extraordinary power and fruit. To break faith and

---

9. [See Nevin, "The Apostles' Creed," MTSS 8:55–88, for the argument that the Creed firstly embodies faith in the church as supernatural reality and then theologically outlines that faith.]

Document 9: The Anglican Crisis.

communion in this way, not only with such men as Anselm, Bernard, and others of like spirit in the Middle Ages, but with the fathers also of the fifth and fourth centuries, the Gregories, Basils, Augustines and Chrysostoms, who shine as stars of the first magnitude in that older period of the Church, and still more with the entire noble army of martyrs and confessors in primitive times, clear back as it would seem to the very age at least next following that of the Apostles;[10] to break faith and communion, we say, with all this vast and glorious "cloud of witnesses," [Heb 12:1] not on a merely circumstantial point but on a question reaching to the inmost life of christianity itself, is beyond contradiction a thought of such momentous gravity as might well be expected to fill even the most confident with some measure of concern.

[Baptism as Sacrament]

Here comes into view the proper significance of the controversy with regard to Baptismal Grace.[11] The idea that the holy sacraments are divine acts, that they carry in them a mystical force for their own ends, that they are the media of operations working towards salvation which have their efficacy and value, not from the mind of the worshipper, but from the power of the transaction or thing done itself, reaches back plainly to the earliest times of the Church, and has been counted a necessary part of the christian faith by the great body of those who have professed it through all ages. Baptism has been held thus to be for the remission of sins, and to carry with it in some way an actual making over to the subject, on the part of God or Christ, of the grace it signifies and represents. In this view, we find it identified very directly from the first with the idea of regeneration itself. So through the whole period before the Reformation. The mystical sense of the sacrament, and its real relation to the new birth, are everywhere acknowledged, and appear intertwined with the universal system both of doctrine and worship. The use of infant baptism in particular turns altogether on the assumption of such an objective force in the ordinance, and must be surely undermined indeed, sooner or later, wherever this assumption is renounced.

---

10. [Anselm (c. 1033–1109), archbishop of Canterbury (from 1093), was one of the major theologians of the Middle Ages. Contemporary theologians continue to read his many writings, including *Monologion, Proslogion, De Incarnatione Verbi,* and *Cur Deus Homo*. Bernard (1090–1153), Abbot of Clairvaux, was at the center of many theological and ecclesiastical issues in his day. He too wrote many tracts on the spiritual life that guided not only his Cistercian monks but also other theologians and church leaders. Nevin singles out the three Cappadocian church fathers, all of whom supported the Nicene Creed, and wrote significant works on the Trinitarian doctrine. All three Cappadocians were bishops as well as theologians: Gregory of Nyssa (c. 330–c. 395); Gregory of Nazianzus (329–89); Basil of Caesarea (c. 330–79), the brother of Gregory of Nyssa. Augustine (354–430), bishop of Hippo, was perhaps the greatest theologian of the western church prior to Anselm and Thomas Aquinas. John Chrysostom (c. 347–407) was bishop of Constantinople; his preaching earned for him the title Chrysostom ("golden mouthed").]

11. [See the debate between Nevin and an anonymous reader of the *Weekly Messenger* in "'Baptismal Grace': A Conversation," MTSS 6:64–68, and the editor's commentary in the same volume, MTSS 6:2–3.]

PART 2 : THE CHURCH QUESTION AND SUPERNATURALISM

Protestantism in the sixteenth century had no thought of breaking here with the faith of previous ages; and the Baptists of that time were regarded accordingly with little less horror than the Socinians themselves. Luther insisted on baptismal regeneration in the strongest terms. Calvin is more guarded, but very firm also in maintaining the mystical supernatural power of the sacrament, as parallel in full with the virtue he supposed to go along with the holy eucharist. The baptism of infants was continued in the Protestant Church on this ground alone, and has been spoken of from the first as in their case emphatically the sacrament of regeneration.[12] So we have it broadly and plainly represented in the English Liturgy. With Puritanism however, the tendency has been all along to make but little of sacramental grace, and to turn the laver of regeneration in particular into a mere bold figure; and we find it now taking its stand openly and decidedly against the ancient church spirit, in its late Anglican revival, just on the platform of this question, as one of central and main account for the whole controversy to which it belongs. The question in truth is thus central in its nature. It involves at bottom the whole force of the alternative, *Church or No-church,* in the form already presented, as a solemn choice in fact between owning or disowning the creed of all Christendom in former times. And the alternative is brought home in so practical a way, that it is no longer easy to evade the full sense and point of the issue, which is comprehended in it under this broad view. This it is that makes the "Gorham case"[13] of such high moment and far-reaching significance at the present time, far beyond what many see or imagine, not only for the Church of England but for the cause of Protestantism in general.

For let it be well observed, that the controversy now at last regards not simply the use of the word *regeneration,* nor some one sense in which it may be taken on either side, nor the doctrine merely of the English Service Book in any sense, but the whole idea of *baptismal grace,* and along with this the whole conception of sacramental grace in any form, as an objective mystical and supernatural virtue going along with the

---

12. [There are two puzzles here: Nevin ignores the role of covenantal theology ("federalism") grounding infant baptism in Reformed theology, and he sidesteps what should have been obvious from his earlier debate over child nurture: "Baptismal regeneration evoked a visceral reaction among all thinkers within" that tradition (Layman, general introduction to *Born of Water*, MTTS 6:19; also 4–10 on covenant theology, 20 on regeneration and Whitefield).]

13. [George Cornelius Gorham (1787–1857) was a priest of the Church of England in the diocese of Exeter. He did not believe in baptismal regeneration, saying that the baptism of infants did not make them members of Christ and his church. When Gorham's bishop, Henry Phillpotts (1778–1864; bishop of Exeter, 1830–69) discovered his views he declared Gorham unfit for an appointment to a parish in the Church of England. Gorham appealed to an ecclesiastical court, which confirmed the bishop's decision. Gorham then appealed to a civil court, which overturned the bishops' decision in 1850. "The Gorham case" became a *cause célèbre* especially for those in the Oxford movement who opposed the interference of the state in theological issues and internal ecclesiastical affairs. And, since the Church of England, under the leadership of John Bird Sumner, the archbishop of Canterbury (1848–62), did not protest the civil court's ruling, after Bishop Phillpotts urged him to do so, several members of the Oxford movement, including Henry Edward Manning, left the Church of England and joined the Roman Catholic Church. Nevin sided with Bishop Phillpotts's protest.]

Document 9: The Anglican Crisis.

holy sacraments, in distinction from all states and acts accompanying the use of them in the minds of men.[14] We have no right to make this a question for Episcopalians only or for the English Establishment; as though it were a contest properly only between a high party and a low one in that semi-catholic communion, touching the construction of a few unfortunate clauses in their Liturgy; while other denominations may be considered as out of its range altogether. We ought to see and feel, that it is a question, not for Episcopalians as such only, but for all Protestants.

It comes just to this now more and more plainly, whether the old notion of baptismal grace, as it reigned through all ages before the Reformation, is to be still retained in any sense, or fairly expelled from the bosom of Protestantism as a foreign heterogeneous element which had no business to be there in the beginning, and that never can be brought to amalgamate with it in an inward and true way. The Puritan party in the English Establishment, and still more readily of course the Puritan and Baptistic tendencies on the outside of it, are in the way of taking openly and with full consciousness more and more the broad ground, that the doctrine of the Prayer-Book on this subject is a pure superstition, as bad as the old dream of transubstantiation itself, and that the farther the Protestant world can get away from it the better. It was all a pernicious mistake, we are told, that the old church made so much of the supposed mystical force of the institution; there is no particular mystery in it; baptism is a sign simply of spiritual benefits to be received in truth in quite another way; and to attach to it any higher significance, to make it in any view a vehicle of grace, is to endanger seriously the interests of *evangelical* religion. It is to fall into the vortex of the sacramental system, against which the entire evangelical host of God's elect—whether known otherwise as Congregationalist, Baptist, Methodist, Presbyterian, Quaker, or what not besides—is bound to exercise watch and wage war forever, as part and parcel of the policy of Antichrist; to deceive the nations and destroy the Church.

Such is the issue here joined, between the churchly and unchurchly tendencies which are now brought to wrestle, as it were in final deadly conflict, for the mastery of Protestantism, in this great English movement. Need we say, that so apprehended the struggle is one of intense interest and solemn as the grave? We see not how it can well stop, till the question is practically settled, not whether regeneration in some particular sense of his term is always accomplished by baptism, but whether baptism is to remain a sacrament at all for Protestantism, in the old universal church sense. Sacrament or no-sacrament, is in truth the question to be decided; and decided it will be, with consequences of unutterable moment, accordingly as the Protestant world is brought to rest now prevailingly in one or the other side of this ominous controversy. We wonder how any person of serious and intelligent mind can fail to regard the controversy, in such view, with profound solemnity and concern. For let it be taken as indeed destined to settle finally the question now presented, the question namely whether Protestantism is a "sacramental system" at all, or carries in it any

---

14. [The collection of Mercersburg's texts on these topics is Nevin et al., *Born of Water*, MTSS 6.]

acknowledgment whatever of sacramental grace, as this idea ruins through the whole previous faith of the Church back to the days of Ignatius, Polycarp, and the Apostles, and who may not see that it is in fact a crisis for the whole Protestant cause (and not for Episcopacy only) equal to any perhaps through which it has been called to pass since its origin in the sixteenth century.[15] In the naked and broad form in which it has come up for practical decision in the English Church, we are not surprised at all that so many of the best men in that communion have been led to look upon it as the very Thermopylae[16] of the whole church controversy, a question of life and death in truth for English Protestantism. It is only surprising that Evangelical Dissenters so generally, as well as Low Church Episcopalians, should have so little power apparently to look at the crisis in the same way. That the Baptists should desire to see the last trace of the old sacramental system obliterated from Protestant Christianity, is all in order; but how can Lutherans and the Reformed, Methodists, Presbyterians, or even Congregationalists of the old stamp, fall in with their perfectly unchurchly humor, and not be struck with some feeling of anxiety and dread at the thought of making Protestantism by its own voice and vote constitutionally baptistic and unsacramental, in any such open revolutionary style? Can they look the present issue solemnly and steadily in the face, and say:

> Away with this whole doctrine of the mystical objective force of baptism; we hold it for no part of pure Protestantism; we deliberately renounce here all fellowship with the Holy Catholic Church of other ages, and with the clear sense of the ancient creeds, and count it a gain for evangelical religion to get clear also of all such absolute mystification as we find on this subject even in Luther, Calvin, and the English Prayer Book.

Is *this*, we say, what such warfare against the sacramental system means? Is it at last in league with the Baptists and Quakers out and out, for the overthrow of the sacraments altogether?

So much for the no-church, no-sacrament party of the day, whether in the English Establishment or on the outside of it, whether in Great Britain we may add or in this country. It is exposed here to a sifting probation, which is well adapted to bring out the true nature of its principles, and to make them for considerate men an object of wholesome apprehension and dread. But the crisis carries with it a sifting efficacy also in other directions.

---

15. [Ignatius (c. 35–c.107) was bishop of Antioch who wrote a series of letter that reveal much about early Christianity in Syria. He was martyred in Rome. Polycarp (c. 69–c. 155), bishop of Smyrna and a martyr, was reputed to have been a disciple of Saint John the Evangelist. He also wrote letters that have been preserved as witnesses to early Christianity.]

16. [Thermopylae is a narrow mountain pass in Greece where the Spartans in 480 BCE battled the Persians and finally died to the last man rather than yield to the Persians. As used here, Thermopylae refers to the life and death situation within Protestantism with respect to the sacramental system.]

Document 9: The Anglican Crisis.

[On the Pretensions of Episcopacy]

It bears with trying severity on the pretensions of Episcopacy. This system, as it prevails in England and this country, admits either too little or too much for the stability of its own claims.

Take the Low Church ground in its communion, and it sinks at once plainly to the order of the sects around it, which have by open profession discarded the proper church theory altogether; it is one simply among the various denominations of the christian world, arguing from scripture and reason as it best can for its own peculiarities, but not venturing to make them in any way of the very essence of faith. In this view, Episcopacy becomes at best a simply outward institute, a matter purely of authority and so in truth a matter of mere ceremonial and form;[17] of the same order precisely with the law and letter of other distinctions, on the strength of which the Baptists, the Scotch Seceders, and such like bodies, are accustomed to make a parade in true Jewish style of their great regard for God's will. The Baptist pleases himself with the notion of his strict conformity to the "*law* of baptism," without note or comment, in the rejection of its use for infants, involving the repudiation of the whole idea of sacramental grace; while the Episcopalian pleases himself, in exactly the same way, with the notion of following the primitive and apostolical law of church government and worship, by acknowledging three orders in the ministry and the necessity of a public liturgy. This feeling indeed may go so far, that he shall appear to be anything but a low churchman in the assertion of it; for as the distinction runs most commonly perhaps between high and low here, it regards rather the stress which is laid on this mechanical notion of Episcopacy, than the truth of the notion itself. The low churchman, in this view, rests his cause more on the ground of expediency and rational preference; whereas the so called high churchman affects to build upon the outward precept as the very rock, beyond which no church whatever can be supposed to exist. In this sense, the rigid Baptist is also a high churchman, who counts all baptism a nullity that is not suited to his own scheme; and so too is the stiff Seceder, who refuses to hold communion with such as stick not exclusively to the use of David's psalms. In truth however Episcopacy of this sort is low enough, and the difference between it and that which more generally bears that name, is more circumstantial than real. Nay, it is in some respects more unchurchly even than the other order of thinking, just because it goes more decidedly to resolve the idea of the church into the notion of an external law, and so into mere Jewish mechanism and form. The true high church theory requires something far beyond this, and is virtually surrendered in fact where it is made to rest on any such false and insufficient foundation.

17. [This becomes the foundation of Nevin's critique, a few months later, of the Episcopalian version of restitutionism, that *it* has "restored" the true Christian practice of the Nicene period: "Early Christianity," 482–83 (*Reformed and Catholic*, 198–99). In the present essay, over the next three paragraphs, Nevin unpacks the claim that Episcopalianism has the form, but not the spirit, the "inner life," of patristic episcopacy.]

Part 2: The Church Question and Supernaturalism

The progress of the present Anglican agitation, extending as it must of necessity do more and more also to this country, is serving powerfully to illustrate and confirm what is now said. The false and suicidal position of that large class of Episcopalians, whose church principles are confessedly only Evangelical Puritanism under the drapery of Episcopal forms, is becoming fast apparent to all men. Their peculiarity of faith and worship is vastly too small, their Protestant maxim much too large and wide, to justify the ground they take over against the other divisions of God's sacramental host, confessedly as evangelical as themselves. Nor is it any excuse, that all this is a matter of church order for their body, and not directly of their own choice and will. We all know the original meaning of this order; it turns on the old doctrine of no salvation out of the church, and assumes that the measure of the church is its own communion. What must we think then of those who reject every such thought, and yet show themselves as exclusive as though it were still the full object of their faith? It would be far more honest and manly, we think, if the school here noticed, both in England and in this country, would it once forsake Anglicanism as it now stands, and either pass over into the bosom of other denominations, or if more to their taste form a new Episcopal sect in open and free fellowship (like a part of the Baptists) with other sections of orthodox Protestantism. How can they reconcile it with a good conscience, to postpone such an interest as this, with all that is staked upon in their own view for the cause just now of evangelical Protestantism, to the consideration of keeping up what they themselves regard as no better than a shadow and a lie—the Episcopal system claiming the prerogatives of a church, to which they allow it no title in fact! If this bold Puritanic view be correct, the Episcopal system, with its manifold reminiscences and echoes of the old church life, must be regarded as a perfect wilderness of contradictions, from which the party in question, one might suppose, would count it both a privilege and a duty to clear themselves as quickly as possible, for the sake of a purer and better faith. If Protestantism mean what *they* take it to mean over against Rome, they put the whole cause into peril by pretending to stand up as they do for *Episcopalian* Protestantism, as being of any real account for the general interest. Their principles should carry them farther. Admit the force of their logic[18] *quoad hoc* [with respect to this], and no one can see why it should not be of force very far beyond. It is childishly wilful, to stop where they insist on stopping, and then pretend to play off the exclusiveness of Rome itself towards all who exceed such arbitrary bounds. If we are to have a *Thus far but no farther* in any case, let us be saved from it at least, in all conscience, under every such purely capricious form! Romanism is more reasonable a great deal than Episcopalianism of this stamp, which first sinks its own authority to the same level with that of all surrounding sects, and then breaks fellowship with every sect besides to uphold it, as the imaginary palladium of the Protestant Reformation.

But what shall we say now of that other form of low Episcopacy, which calls itself *high* only because it is more exclusive in theory as well as practice, and lays greater

---

18. [The text reads "logid."]

Document 9: The Anglican Crisis.

stress on the legal obligation of its system, while the whole is taken still in the light of a merely mechanical appointment or law? We see not truly, how Episcopalianism in such shape deserves to be considered a whit less pedantic, to say the least, than the exclusiveness of the Baptists or Seceders under a like outwardly legal form. In both cases alike, the Divine element in religion is regarded as holding on the outside of it, in the way of precept, rather than in the very bosom of the system itself; the letter is made to go before the life, to underlie it as first in order and importance, instead of being joined with it in concrete union, and so deriving from it continually all its force. Thus the Baptist pretends to be scrupulously exact in obeying the law of baptism, according to his own view of the particularities belonging to the rite in the time of the New Testament; the value of it in his eyes, its true use and necessity, is to be sought only in the notion of its being commanded and enjoined by God; and so he makes a religious merit of following the injunction, as he supposes, to the letter, unchurching practically all others—on the principle that the essence of religion is implicit submission to God's authority as made known by the Bible, and that it is rationalistic to vary from this a jot or tittle in any way. In truth however, the rationalism lies wholly on his own side; for the factors of his religion in such form are, not the word as life and spirit, and faith yielding to its plastic force, but the dead letter of the Bible merely and his natural intelligence making out of it what sense it best can. So with the greatest scrupulosity for the form and shell of the sacraments, the true heart and inward substance of them are discarded as a miserable superstition; the circumstantials of baptism are made to be everything and its proper essential mystery nothing; the entire conception of the Church, as anything more than a natural human society, falls to the ground; and the glorification of God's authority in the Bible, (just because it is thus turned into a dead rule for the natural intellect of man to work by) becomes in the end a horribly grinning satire upon itself, by resolving faith into common sense and subordinating the whole interest of religion to private judgment and private will. It is not by accident, in this view, that the Baptistic spirit, loud as it is at the outset in its profession of being more bound than others by the "law and testimony" of revelation, has ever shown itself prone to make common cause in the end with all sorts of rationalistic radicalism in its open assault on the mysteries of Christianity; as it is not by accident either, on the other hand, that this radical humor, when it affects as it often does to be on the side of Christ, falls in with the Baptistic tendency, in thought and tone, more immediately and readily than with any other short of open infidelity—having, with all its veneration for the Bible, the same dislike precisely of the Church, and the same horror of everything like sacramental grace. Such, we say, is the fallacy here of resting the idea of religion on the supposed word of God, taken in the light of a merely outward or legal institute. And now we ask, what better is it than this to make Episcopacy, with its outward succession from the time of the Apostles, in and of itself the article of a standing or falling church—on the principle simply, that Christ and his Apostles are supposed to have prescribed this form, and that we have no right therefore to vary from what must be regarded thus as a strictly Divine rule? It is possible to take very high ground with this view, to be very aristocratic and very exclusive; but the view itself is low, and proceeds on the want of faith in the proper supernatural character of the Church rather than on the presence of such faith; on which account, the further it is pushed it only becomes the more plainly empty and pedantic. Being of this character, it is found to thrive best, like all pedantries, in periods of mechanical humdrum and sham; while it is sure to be exposed in its true vanity, when the religious life is called to pass through a great general crisis, as at the present time. The more the church question is agitated in an earnest and serious way, and the more men's minds are fixed on its real meaning, the more evident must it become always that no such mechanical view of it as this can ever solve its difficulties or satisfy its requisitions. And such precisely is the way in which the profound Catholic movement now going forward in England, is making itself felt on the pretensions of Episcopacy in this simply outward style all the world over. It is showing them to be hollow and vain, no better in truth than an idle sham. It is causing the earnest minded, both in that communion and out of it, to see and feel, that either the church rights and prerogatives of which it makes a parade are nothing and form no special property whatever in its case, or that they must have far deeper and more solid ground on which to rest than the order of bishops or the use of a liturgy, regarded as a simply outward appointment. No *juro divino* constitution, in any such style as this, can uphold in a real way for faith the mystery of the one, holy, catholic and apostolical Church. The premises are either too narrow for the conclusion, or else a great deal too wide.[19]

[The Church and Faith]

Faith in the Church, in the old ecclesiastical sense, is not a stiff persuasion merely that certain arrangements are of divine appointment, and a disposition to stickle for them accordingly as the lines and stakes that go to fix the conception; it is the apprehension rather of the Church as a living supernatural fact, back of all such arrangements, having its ground and force in the mystery of the Incarnation, according to the order of the ancient creed, and communicating to the marks and signs by which it is made visible every particle of virtue that is in them for any such end. This idea goes vastly beyond the notion of Episcopacy, Presbyterianism, or any other supposed divine right ecclesiastical polity of this sort; it looks directly to the original promise, *Lo I am with you always to the end of the world*; and lays hold first and foremost of the mystical being of the Church, as no mechanism of dead statutes, but the actual presence of an

---

19. [To summarize the two groups of Episcopalianism and Nevin's critique: "low church" Episcopalianism is simply "Evangelical Puritanism under the drapery of Episcopal forms." It "wears" episcopacy out of legalistic obligation, but does not believe in the ecclesiology that could justify and maintain it. "High church" Episcopalianism believes it is maintaining episcopacy out of principle, but that principle is "merely mechanical appointment or law." He contrasts this perspective to what he regards as genuine "faith in the church" in the next section.]

Document 9: The Anglican Crisis.

ever living revelation of grace, (no less divine than the Bible itself) a higher order of history, a strictly heavenly constitution on earth, (Christ's *body*, the fulness of Him that "filleth all in all" [Eph 1:23]) in virtue of which only, but in virtue of which at the same time surely, all organs and functions belonging to it have also a superhuman and heavenly force. This does not imply that such organs and functions may be indifferently in any form, or in no form whatever, (a theory of *invisibleness* that turns the concrete mystery into a pure abstraction) but it does mean certainly that the organs and functions make not of themselves the being of the body; they are parts only in any case, which owe their whole vitality and vigor to the general system in which they are comprehended, and away from this are of no worth whatever. If episcopacy and a liturgy be found to grow forth conclusively from the nature of the Church, in such catholic view, it is all well and good; let them then come in legitimately for their proper share of respect. But it ought to be plain "unto all men diligently reading holy scripture and ancient authors,"[20] we think, that the grand weight and burden of the question concerning the nature of the church rest not at all on these distinctions, and that to put them therefore ostensibly in any such form must ever smack of pedantry, and betray a poor and false sense of what this question means. All turns here on the *idea* of the Church, and this not only may, but must be settled to some extent in our minds, before we can go on to discuss to real purpose the divine obligation of Episcopacy, Presbyterianism, or any other polity claiming to be of such necessary force. Is the idea of a really supernatural constitution under this name, as it once universally prevailed, a sober truth still for Christian faith, or has it become a dangerous though beautiful *fiction*? That is the question; the first and most fundamental question here, before which the whole controversy about bishops and elders, liturgical forms and free prayer, becomes of only secondary account. For it is the answer we give to this question first of all in our minds, that must determine the sense of what we contend for at other points, or show it to be worth contending for one way or another. What is a *jure divino* polity, whether Episcopal or Presbyterian, or a *jure divino* system of rites and ceremonies, for a church that shrinks from proclaiming *itself* divine, and that has no faith practically in the supernatural character of its own constitution, as anything more than that of the American Tract Society or any other outward league of evangelical sects! In this view it is, that the question of sacramental grace is more profoundly interesting, than the question of episcopacy. It goes much nearer to the heart of the main question, the grand ultimate subject of controversy and debate; for the sacraments are the standing sign and seal of whatever power is comprised in the Church; and as we think of this, so invariably also will we think of them; the one conception giving shape and form always directly to the other. But even here the right church sense is something more general and deep, than the right sacramental feeling. The notion of grace-bearing sacraments, sundered from the sense of the Church

---

20. [From the Preface to "Form and Manner of Making . . . Bishops, Priests, and Deacons." See *Book of Common Prayer* (1945), 529.]

as still carrying in it the force of its first supernatural constitution, would be indeed magical, and must prove quite as pedantical in the end as a supreme regard for bishops in the same dead way. We must believe in a divine church, in order to believe in divine sacraments, or in a divine ministry under any form.[21]

The feeling of this enters deeply into the Anglican movement; forms we may say the very soul of it; and is extended by means of it also far beyond the movement itself, with new and unusual force. This we take to be a great benefit, whatever may be thought of Puseyism, or of the tendency it shows just now to pass over to full Romanism. Be its issues as they may, the question here agitated is in itself of the most vast and solemn import, and we have reason to be thankful that it is thus carried from the mere outworks to the inmost citadel of the cause in debate. This Anglican controversy, and most of all we may say the form it is now taking as an open reconsideration of the controversy with Rome, is in itself and for Protestantism something far deeper than the strife for Episcopacy in the usual style of past times; no such strife, as holding simply between Episcopacy and Dissent, deserves to be considered of any real account in comparison; and we may well be glad, that both Episcopalians and Dissenters are now in the way of being forced to see and confess this more and more. The controversy here has to do, not with the accidents and circumstances of Protestantism only, but with the very foundations of its life; and we rejoice to believe accordingly, that it is fast turning into impertinence, for thoughtful men everywhere, the agitation of the church question in every lower view.

[Church and State in the Oxford Movement]

It cannot be denied again, that the course of this controversy, as thus reaching to the very heart and soul of the church question, is powerfully sifting and trying the ecclesiastical pretensions of the English Establishment as a whole. These proceed on the old catholic doctrine of the Church, and claim to be in harmony with it throughout. But the near and close competition in which it is now placed with Romanism, is causing it to appear in a very different light. Think as we may of the aggressive movements of this last, in themselves considered, it must be confessed that so far as mere general *principle* is concerned the Catholic cause carries with it a better show at least of reason and right than that to which it is so daringly opposed. First in view is the high and solemn question of ecclesiastical supremacy, the true and rightful headship of the Church and its legitimate relation to the State. Who can doubt, but that the ground here taken by Cardinal Wiseman, and the Romanists in general, is of a higher character than that occupied by Lord John Russel and the English Establishment?[22] On one side, the civil

---

21. [Nevin returns to this line of argument in "Thoughts on the Church," MTSS 7:143–46.]

22. [Cardinal Nicholas Wiseman, the first Catholic archbishop of Westminster after the Reformation, consistently asserted that the church was above the state in its origins and in its internal ecclesiastical operations and teachings. Lord John Russell (1792–1878) was Prime Minister of the United

Document 9: The Anglican Crisis.

power is made to be the fountain of ecclesiastical authority; on the other, this authority is taken to be of an order wholly distinct from that of the State, independent of it, and for its own ends above it—derived originally from Christ, and having its seat perpetually in the spiritual kingdom of which he is the glorious though now invisible head. Can there be any question, which of these two views is most honorable to religion, most congenial to faith, most in harmony with the New Testament, most true to the authority of past history? It has been a great reproach to English Protestantism from the beginning, that it put the King into the place of the Pope, and referred all church offices and functions to him as their ultimate source. For refusing to acknowledge this royal supremacy in the affairs of the church, the Roman Catholics have been subjected in past times to persecutions and penalties, which those who are forever harping on the theme of Protestant liberality, as contrasted with the bigotry and intolerance of Rome, would do well to acquaint themselves with even in a superficial way. In the Establishment itself also, many have felt all along the disgrace and burden of the relation, and have often with feeble voice protested against it or tried to explain it away. But never before probably was there such a glaring exposure of the misery of it, as that which is taking place just at the present time. The whole Tractarian movement has been *against* the notion of such civil supremacy in ecclesiastical matters, in proportion precisely as it involved a revival of church principles generally, and a return to old catholic sentiments and ideas. The Gorham controversy might seem to have been providentially ordered, to bring out in broad caricature and irony the true sense of the farce, when it was sure in this way to receive the most earnest attention. Here, a theological question, not of secondary but of primary consequence—going just now as we have before seen to the very root of Protestantism—is settled in the last instance by purely civil authority; and the English hierarchy, with his Grace of Canterbury at its head, in the presence of the whole world dutifully succumbs to the insolent and profane dictation! How unlike the spirit of the Third Innocent truly, of Hildebrand, of Anselm, of Athanasius! No wonder the Bishop of Exeter, with such earnestness as he has in his soul, should feel such a crisis to be tremendously solemn.[23] And now,

---

Kingdom (1846-52; 1865-66). As a member of the Liberal (Whig) party in England, he pushed for the passage of the 1832 Reform Bill, which reduced the number of Irish bishoprics and which many in the Oxford movement opposed as the state's interference in the church's internal operations. Nevin sees Russell as a supporter of civil supremacy over the church.]

23. [During the Gorham controversy, Archbishop John Bird Sumner of Canterbury refused to oppose the 1850 civil court's approval of Cornelius Gorham's right to hold a clerical position in the Church of England even though Gorham's views on baptismal regeneration conflicted with church teachings. Innocent III (1160-1216, Pope from 1198) exerted papal authority even over secular matters and repeatedly asserted the independence of the church from secular control. Hildebrand, that is, Gregory VII (c. 1021-85, Pope from 1073), was a strong opponent of lay investiture (or lay patronage), calling for the freedom of the church in the appointment of bishops and clergy to their offices. Saint Anselm (c. 1033-1109), Archbishop of Canterbury (1093-1109) consistently opposed the kings of England (William II and Henry I) when they tried to interfere in church affairs. Athanasius (c. 296-373), bishop of Alexandria, battled with emperors Constantine and Constantius over the Arian heresy, which he consistently opposed. Nevin chose all of these as examples of the church's

to set the case in its worst possible light, England beholds in her bosom the sudden revelation of a full Catholic hierarchy, asserting the independence of the church in its own sphere, and taking thus with natural ease the very ground which the Tractarian tendency has been reaching after as necessary and right, but reaching after so far in vain.[24] The contrast could hardly be exhibited under a more noticeable or clearly intelligible form; and it is full of disadvantage to the cause of Anglican Episcopacy.

For let it be kept in mind, what we speak of is not the Papal system as such over against the State system of Queen Victoria and the British Parliament, but the general *principle* merely that enters into this contest. That is capable of being considered and settled without regard to actual forms of administration; and must be so settled indeed, in order to be acknowledged at all in any true way. It is a very important question certainly, whether the headship of the visible church shall be taken to reside in a General Assembly, or an Episcopal Convocation, or a Pope; but of still greater importance than this, because back of it and under it in the order of truth, is the question, whether the church shall be allowed to have any such headship of its own at all, or be regarded as a mere branch and dependency of the civil government, like the judiciary, the army or the marine. This is the question, on which issue is now joined by the Catholic and State Church parties in England; and we have no right to close our eyes to the true significance of the principle involved in it, merely because it may seem to go in favor of Popery here, as they call it, and not in favor of Protestantism. The exodus of the Free Church of Scotland has been widely glorified, as a grand exhibition of martyrdom for the very principle now in view, the independence of the church in church matters, the "rights of King Jesus," as the Scotch phrase it, in opposition to all worldly political power whatever. The fountain of ecclesiastical law and order, the true and proper primacy in matters of religion, was loudly proclaimed in this case to be, not the British throne or parliament, but the supreme judicatory of the church itself; and in defence of this principle, the best men of Scotland, with Chalmers at their head, showed themselves ready to brave, if need were, the greatest penalties and pains. Puseyism too has gained credit deservedly, for only seeing clearly, and saying plainly, that the civil supremacy in matters of religion is an abuse, at war with every right conception of the church, and for proposing, though thus far only in a weak and ineffectual way, a return to the old doctrine of ecclesiastical independence; and for all right minded men certainly, the Bishop of Exeter just now, by even the partial stand he is trying to make for this doctrine in the midst of the universal defection from it that surrounds him, is a spectacle of more moral dignity than the Archbishop of Canterbury with the whole bench of bishops besides at his back, truckling in base subserviency to the nod

---

independence from the state.]

24. [Pope Pius IX reestablished the Catholic hierarchy in England in 1850 and named Nicholas Wiseman as the first archbishop of Westminster. Prior to that date, Rome was represented in England by Vicars Apostolic, that is titular bishops usually sent to mission countries. The reestablishment of the hierarchy was an official recognition that Catholic bishops rightfully held the episcopacy in England.]

Document 9: The Anglican Crisis.

of the civil power. And why then should we refuse to see or own the same moral significance, in the controversy between the Queen and the Romanists? In their own way these last claim the right (indefeasible in its own nature and now solemnly guaranteed also by the British laws) to render unto God the things that belong to God, and to carry out the full idea of a church, without dictation from Cesar or dependence in any sort on Cesar's will. But against this, Lord John Russel and the great majority of the English nation loudly and violently protest—calling it Papal aggression, a violation of the proper liberties of the country, an attack on the Queen's supremacy; as though it were not by act of Parliament years since settled, that allegiance to the Pope in things spiritual is perfectly compatible with the acknowledgment of this supremacy in things political, full as much as allegiance to the General Assembly of Scotland. The principle of the controversy thus is clear and plain. And so far as this is concerned, we say, the right is with the Catholics, and the wrong glaringly and grossly on the other side. We sincerely admire for our part the firmness and constancy of the Irish hierarchy in the case of the Government colleges,[25] and the calm intrepidity displayed in the organization of the new hierarchy for England; and only wonder that so many otherwise sensible people should have no power apparently, through the mist of their prejudice against Popery, to look upon the matter in the same light. Let Popery be never so foul and false, in itself considered, it is still something great, in this age of mechanism and sham, to find a large body of men thus solemnly committing themselves on its behalf to the old catholic principle, (very apostolical too, as it strikes us, both in sense and sound) that powers and rights ecclesiastical, come not from kings or civil parliaments, but from the divine constitution of the church itself upheld and maintained by the perpetual presence of its own head. There can be no question in this issue, which side answers most impressively to the true ideal of the old church life, as it comes up to our minds when we think of such men as Cyprian, Athanasius, Chrysostom, Ambrose, or Augustine.[26] There is a moral majesty in the present position of the Pope's hierarchy both in Ireland and England, which, poor and mean as it may outwardly appear, has the effect just now undoubtedly of casting a very sensible shade on the Queen's hierarchy, in spite of all its pomp and wealth. Why should Wiseman not stand as high here at least as Chalmers? Who among the Anglican bishops or archbishops can be said to present anything like the same imposing and sublime figure?

---

25. [In 1850, at the Irish Catholic Synod of Thurles, the nation's bishops began a transformation of the Catholic Church in Ireland and one of the questions raised at the Synod was: who will control the education of Catholics, the church or the proselytizing state? The majority of bishops prohibited clergy from accepting offices in the state-sponsored colleges and encouraged the Catholic laity to avoid them because of the grave dangers to faith and morals. On the Synod, see Macaulay, "Strong Views," 87–92.]

26. [Cyprian (d. 258), bishop of Carthage and a martyr in the face of opposition from the Roman Empire. Nevin was drawn to Cyprian and wrote four articles on him for the 1852 *Mercersburg Review*: 259–77, 335–87, 417–52, 513–63. These essays should be published shortly in this series. Ambrose (c. 339–97), bishop of Milan, battled against paganism and Arianism and periodically invoked the independence of the church from civil powers.]

PART 2: THE CHURCH QUESTION AND SUPERNATURALISM

[On Religious Liberty]

But the issue here is not simply as between two hierarchies, the one culminating in the Pope and the other in the Queen, in the form now stated; it goes beyond this to the universal question of religions liberty, the right of men to worship God according to the dictates of their own conscience, the principle of church toleration in the broadest sense; and in this view it concerns directly all sects and parties on the outside of the Government church, no less than the membership of this favored communion itself. Is it not the pride of the age, to be considered liberal, enlightened, tolerant in matters of religion? Is not this in particular the boast of Protestantism? Above all is it not the boast of English Protestantism, whether in Great Britain or in these United States? Has not England moreover only a few years since, after ages of most unrighteous persecution, solemnly *emancipated* her Catholic population, and admitted them to a gracious comprehension in this grand privilege of the nineteenth century?[27] But how now does the case before us comport with all this; in which the first movement of the Catholics to carry out in earnest their own ecclesiastical polity, is met with noise and clamor from one end of the nation to the other, and mob and parliament and church-by-law-established are summoned angrily to unite for the purpose of putting it down! Thus ends the farce of toleration and freedom. One can hardly help being reminded by it of Pharaoh's liberality to the Israelites, when he graciously allowed them to go abroad for the worship of Jehovah, but at once set terms and bounds again to his own grant which made it no better than a hollow pretence. The liberty comes just to this: "You may live and serve God as good Catholics, provided only you consent in doing so to hold your ecclesiastical rights and privileges as a fief in fine from the English crown, and do homage for them accordingly, as is done by the regular government church, to her Majesty the Queen, as true *Pontifex Maximus* of the British realm." Pagan Rome in the first ages, and the Persian Monarchy in the fourth and fifth centuries, might easily have been reconciled to the church on the same Erastian terms.[28] But no true Catholic of course could so part with the substance of his faith, to be thus graciously *tolerated* in keeping the name of it afterwards and its mere empty shell. Say what men please of it then, the contest now going forward in England, between the Papal and Royal interests, is in truth a contest for religious freedom and the rights of conscience; and the fact is not to be disguised, that in this view, according to the established Protestant doctrine of the nineteenth century—the age of light, the flower of all ages—the wrong is palpably and egregiously on the Protestant side. This is so plain indeed, that the main body of

---

27. [In 1829, British Parliament, under the forceful campaigning of the Irishman Daniel O'Connell, agreed to emancipate British and Irish Catholics from the penal laws of the immediate past and allowed Catholics for the first time to be elected to Parliament. This Catholic Emancipation bill was not well received by some Protestants both in England and the United States. Nevin, however, supported the bill.]

28. [Erastianism takes its name from Thomas Erastus (1524–83), a Swiss physician and Zwinglian theologian who advocated the doctrine of state sovereignty in ecclesiastical affairs.]

the English nation itself, it seems to us, must soon be ashamed of its false position, and quarrel with its own passion for so upsetting the fair and even tenor of its way. It is only strange that the universal interest of Dissent should not at once have been prepared, to make common cause openly in such a case with the *persecuted* party—so far at least as the principle of religious toleration is concerned. A most curious commentary it is certainly on the reigning song of this class in particular about "freedom to worship God," the inalienable rights of conscience, &c., to find not only the Independents, Baptists and Methodists, of England, but the Presbyterians also of Scotland, holding up their hands for the royal supremacy in matters of religion against the Catholics, while yet professing to disown it for themselves. And what is if possible still more remarkable, even the Puritanism of this country, with all its antipathies for Episcopacy and law religion, is led by its still greater hatred of Popery to lean visibly in the same direction—as though in the presence of this Medusa's head the memory of Plymouth Rock itself should turn to stone![29] The doctrine of freedom to worship God according to his private judgment and conscience, and without dictation from the State, is good it seems for every fanatic who chooses to act the part of pope or pontifex maximus separately in his own behalf; but it is *not* good for such as acknowledge any such primacy in the Roman Catholic form. The question comes to this in the end; and is it necessary to say, that under such form it wears just now a very bad face, not only for the Protestant Episcopal church in England, but for the cause of Protestantism in general.

It amounts to nothing to say, that the Catholics are themselves constitutionally intolerant and exclusive, and therefore deserve no toleration from Protestants. *That* is not the true modern doctrine of toleration to allow the rights of conscience and "freedom to worship God" only to such as could be trusted to do the same thing, if they had full power in their hands. Tyrants reign and kill on precisely the same maxim. Protestantism is bound here to take the measure of its conduct from itself, and not from abroad, from its own theory of Christianity and not from any that may be held by others.

[Religious Liberty and Catholicism]

But Romanism is to be excepted from the law of universal toleration, we are told, on another account. It involves allegiance to a foreign power, and in such view is politically unsafe and so unworthy of trust. The settlement of a religious constitution under such form in the land, not holding as such from the British throne but from the Bishop of Rome, is taken to be an aggression, an invasion of the Queen's right, which looks finally to treason and revolution, and fully justifies accordingly the most stringent action on the part of the Government to put it down. We have sometimes heard the same cry of the *Republic in Danger*, on this side of the Atlantic also, to get

---

29. [In Greek mythology Medusa was a goddess and a protective symbol with the ability to turn men into stone. Medusa's head symbolized the power and ability to destroy one's enemies.]

up a crusade against the Catholics, though the trick is happily waxing now rather stale and grannyish for much effect.[30] The whole plea we hold to be perfectly idle and false. It is not upheld by either reason or history. No part of the English nation has shown itself—even through water and through fire, the persecution of the nation itself, almost forcing it the other way—more true to the government, more loyal and patriotic and worthy of trust in all respects, than just the body of whom we now speak. Nor has there ever yet been given in this country the shadow of an occasion (other than the noise made by alarmists themselves) for apprehending the least danger to our civil institutions; and for ourselves, we say it plainly, we believe the acknowledgment of the Pope's spiritual primacy is just as little at war with a true American spirit, and carries in it just as little peril for our American liberties, as the acknowledgment of any like primacy in in either of the Presbyterian General Assemblies, or in the American Episcopate, or in the private judgment simply of any true blooded Puritan Independent, who holds himself at liberty, if need be, to brave on the plea of conscience all human authority besides.

But into this question it is not necessary to enter at length in this place. What we wish to urge is, the wrong that is done practically to the Protestant cause itself, let the case be as it may with regard to the political character of Romanism, in supposing that this cause may not be left to take care of itself, even where it has every outward advantage on its side, but is to be cared for only by a system of wardship and police, in which the free action of mind is to be as much as possible forestalled and forced into a given form. The genius of Protestantism, we are told, is not *lucifugous*[31] like that of Rome; it seeks the light, has large trust in common sense and an open Bible, and asks only a clear field and fair play to get the better of Romanism in a short time even in France or Italy itself. Romanism indeed is so absurd as well as wicked, such a dark mass of fallacies and fooleries and vile abominations, that it might seem to have no chance of standing a moment in any such unequal contest, unless under cover of some such Egyptian darkness as brooded formerly over the Middle Ages. But now in the case before us the conditions of this trial are all against it, and in favor of the antagonistic cause. The Protestantism of England is not in its infancy, but of full age and growth, with its roots reaching out in every direction into the soil of the national life. It has learning, and wealth, and vast moral respectability, on its side. The government is in its hands, with boundless patronage and power. What can such a cause fear, thus inwardly and outwardly strong, from an interest so poor and weak and vile as the

---

30. [The *Southern Religious Telegraph* of Richmond, Virginia published on July 1, 1831 an article titled "The Republic in Danger," attacking Catholicism as unfit to live in a Republic and as hostile to American freedoms. Bishop John England (1786–1842) of Charleston responded with a long series of letters entitled "The Republic in Danger," defending Catholic support for American freedoms, especially religious liberty. See *The Works of Right Rev. John England*, 4:13–68. Nevin was aware of England's various publications and viewed favorably his support for the Catholic Church in the United States. See Nevin, "Early Christianity," 480.]

31. [Having a dislike of light.]

Document 9: The Anglican Crisis.

thing called Popery? One might suppose the English nation would only laugh at any show of serious competition, on British ground and in the middle of the nineteenth century, proceeding from such a quarter. And yet, strange to say, the simple erection of a Roman hierarchy, which can never be of more force than the mind and will of the people allow, has been sufficient to throw the nation into a sort of wild panic. There is a solemn self-contradiction in this, and what might seem to be an involuntary confession of weakness, which to the mind of an earnest Protestant, on either side of the Atlantic, can hardly fail to carry with it a somewhat portentous look. And it only makes the matter worse, when piety here turns into patriotism, and affects to be concerned—not just for any peril into which religion may be brought by so contemptible and barefaced an enemy—but for a future and distant peril of the State. This supposed political danger all depends of course, at the same time, on the *growth* of Romanism far beyond its present bounds; and such growth in England can come only by the activity of the British mind itself, exercised on the problem of the two opposing systems under the full meridian blaze of modern knowledge, with an open Bible and all sorts of outward force besides to stem the movement; in which case it would seem as if it must have some *right* to prevail, if a people have any right ever to think for themselves or to follow their own mind. But the conservative humor of which we now speak, with all its faith in Protestantism, its huge contempt for Romanism, and its high opinion of Anglo-Saxon intelligence and common sense, is by no means willing after all to trust things in this way to their natural course. England must not have the opportunity even of making a fool of itself by turning Catholic, though this should take place with never so much intelligence and freedom. If a man is likely to become a maniac, and in that state to commit suicide, his friends think no harm of chaining him for his own good; and just so here, in view of this possible fit of Romanism and the farther *possibility* by it of political self-destruction, it is held to be wise and right to clap a strait jacket on the patient forthwith, for the benevolent purpose of keeping him in safety from his coming self. The imagination of John Bull is terribly frightened with the chimera that he is in danger of losing his senses, that his mind is not safe in his own care and keeping; and he comes to the sage conclusion, that the best thing he can do to avoid so deplorable a catastrophe is to part with his mind altogether, to put it into the hands of his own Prime Minister, the British Parliament, the Anglican Bishops, or anywhere in short that may seem fit, only so as to be fairly rid of it himself and in no peril thus of becoming crazy.

What a Circe[32] after all this Popery must be, if the full grown Protestantism of England in the middle of the nineteenth century, with all sorts of patronage and prejudice to back it, may not be allowed to meet the hag or look her fairly in the face, even on its own soil, for fear of being bewitched by her sorceries into the similitude of a swine.

32. [In Greek mythology, Circe was the goddess of sorcery, skilled in the magic of transmutation, illusion, and necromancy.]

And how kind of the popular spirit now happily in the saddle, which is so well assured of its own sanity and can see this danger afar off, to break through its visual cant of free inquiry and free speech, its favorite cry of liberty and light, and to invoke the strong arm of power for the suppression beforehand of any and all workings of British mind that may look this way.

We have the same spirit in this country, officiously concerned to persuade the American people that Romanism is at war with the idea of a Republic, and that to guard against the danger of itself turning Catholic in time to come, and so by its own free choice committing political suicide, the part of wisdom is now, in obedience to the counsels of this far seeing and profoundly patriotic school, to forestall and cut off the exercise of all freedom in any such form, or in other words, by pulling out the light in season, to save the weak eyes first and then the weak life of the nation.

Seriously, we say, the cause of Protestantism is wronged, the cause of Romanism powerfully complimented, by every concession which implies in this way that there is any danger of an enlightened people, at this time of day, with its eyes open and its hands unbound, being led deliberately to exchange the boasted beauty and perfection of the first for the supposed ugliness of the second, at the cost of losing besides its most cherished privileges and institutions. Such extreme sensitiveness to danger, such spasms of morbid jealousy and fear, where the foe at the same time is represented as so poor and silly, so loathesome and vile, so miserably decrepit and weak, is to our mind we confess one of the most uncomfortable symptoms in the case of Protestantism at the present time. Why should a very ordinary Address of Archbishop Hughes, on its *Decline*,[33] set so many angry pulpits and presses in motion, all over the land, to prove that it is in the full zenith of its prosperity? Why should our evangelical papers, of every denominational hue, feel it necessary to let no week pass without at least two or three squirts of foul water cast towards Rome, when on their own showing it were quite as wise to do battle in the same style with the Grand Lama of Thibet? Why should this English demonstration, which if Protestantism is to be believed in its own favor, deserves to be counted little better than some outbreak of Bedlam, have power nevertheless apparently to move the heart of the Queen of England, and the heart of her people, "as the trees of the wood are moved with the wind?"[34] It would tell vastly more certainly for a cause that takes itself to be so good and strong, over against one that is reproached as rotten to the core and ready to fall to pieces by its own rickety weight, if it could only afford to enjoy this happy feeling of such vast superiority in a calm and quiet way, and with some corresponding self-reliance and self-possession. Why should the bellowing of a Roman *bull*[35] disturb, even for a moment, the serenity of the British lion?

---

33. [A reference to New York's Archbishop John Hughes's (1797–1864) *The Decline of Protestantism*.]

34. [Isa 7:2.]

35. [A papal bull is an official decree, letter, or document that a pope issues and stamps with a lead seal (*bulla*).]

Document 9: The Anglican Crisis.

The truth is however, that there is real room in the whole case for uneasiness, not just because Romanism may be seen to have power, but because Anglicanism is felt to be weak. The constitutional deficiency of this system, its want of ability to assert and carry out in full the proper functions of a church, is in the way of being exposed as never before by the progress the present crisis; and so searching has this become in its operation, that there is now good reason to expect that it will lead in due time to the breaking up of the Establishment altogether. It is becoming more and more difficult for the two tendencies it carries in its bosom, to move in any sort of union together; and we are not surprised to find that which still makes earnest with catholic truth leaning powerfully towards secession, whether it be to form a new body or to fall into the arms of Rome. The secessions which have already taken place in this last form, are exceedingly significant. No movement of the sort equally grave has occurred since the Reformation. The importance of it lies not just in the number of the converts, though this is serious enough; but in their character rather, and the circumstances of the change. Newman was the greatest theologian in the English church, and next to him probably Archdeacon Manning.[36] The converts generally have been men of learning and piety, filling prominent stations and connected with the best families. Of their great moral earnestness, the step they have taken is itself the strongest proof. It has been well remarked that every one of them must have gone through a process of fiery probation, of which the world generally can have no conception, to break in such style with his whole previous existence, and pass over through all sorts of sacrifice to his new position. Every single conversion in such circumstances is a true *martyrdom*, in the full sense of the word. No single case of such martyrdom can ever pass without weight; and in such a time of crisis especially as the present, a hundred cases of the sort coming together must be allowed to carry with them a truly startling and awakening power. It is only the perfection of insipidity to pretend indifference to the fact, in the old world or in the new. The fact itself however, as is well known, is but part of a much wider and still more serious fact. It is no more than the beginning probably of a great church-slide, which is destined soon to shake the whole world with its thundering sound. Nearly two thousand ministers at least are reported as holding ground with regard to the Queen's supremacy, and the late governmental settlement of the question of baptismal regeneration, which will hardly allow them to stay much longer with a good conscience in the Government church. It is difficult to see how Bishop Philpotts can avoid going along with the movement. Such an exodus, whether it may lead at once to Rome or not, must be followed with still more failing of heart and confusion of mind in the Establishment, and with such palpable self-contradiction before the

---

36. [Nevin was sympathetic with John Henry Newman's (1801–90) *Essay on the Development of Doctrine* even after he left the Church of England and became a Roman Catholic. More generally, Nevin respected him as a scholar of the early church. Henry Edward Manning (1808–92) left the Church of England in 1850 after the Gorham controversy was decided by a civil court. Manning eventually became the Cardinal Archbishop of Westminster (from 1865) and was a primary supporter of papal infallibility at the First Vatican Council (1870).]

whole world, that it will have no power finally to uphold itself even in form against the forces that are at work on all sides for its overthrow.

In this way it is that the crisis before us, as we take it, is bringing the pretensions of this Established Church to such a course of fiery trial as it has never been called to pass through before; and the result of the trial is sure to be, that Anglicanism will be found wanting, having no power to make good its own high sounding promises and claims. It is some instinctive apprehension of this, we doubt not, that excites it so much just now against the so-called Papal aggression. With all its superiority of patronage and wealth, and Protestant prejudice to boot, Anglicanism very plainly is afraid to meet Romanism on fair terms, before the tribunal even of the Anglican mind itself. It ritually confesses judgment, and condemns itself by its own verdict. It must either give up the church doctrine altogether, and so fall down openly to the level of the lowest Puritanism, or else be led by it to proclaim itself the sham only of what Romanism has the show at least of being in fact; and either horn of such a dilemma is "sharper than any two edged sword, piercing even to the dividing asunder of soul and spirit."[37] Hard enough it is of a truth, in such circumstances, to be calm and quietly self-possessed. But the exposure is only aggravated by the want of power to meet it in this way. The style in which both parties in the Establishment, High-church and Low-church, allow themselves too generally to rail at Romanism and the late conversions, is anything but dignified or rational, and must in the end rebound with righteous retribution on the credit of their own cause.

[Episcopalianism in the United States]

It is easy enough to see moreover, that Episcopalianism in general, even as it exists among us here in America, is sorely tried also by this Roman movement in much the same way. It has had already a few secessions of its own, and cannot help feeling at the same time that the secessions in England, and the assumptions that go along with them on the side of Rome, strike directly at the very root of its own life.[38] Hence we have no small display of the same sort of blustering petulant humor that is at work in England; which however tells all the more badly here, in the case particularly of the high toned church party, that it contrasts so strangely with the bland liberality towards "our Roman sister" which was in vogue in this quarter only a few years since,

---

37. [Heb 4:12.]

38. [A few members of the American Episcopal Church converted to Catholicism in the early nineteenth century. Among them were Elizabeth Ann Seton (1774–1821), founder of the Sisters of Charity of St. Joseph and later declared a saint of the Catholic Church; James A. McMaster (1820–86) who became editor of the *New York Freeman's Journal* (1848–86); Jedediah Vincent Huntington (1813–62, an Episcopalian priest, influenced by the Oxford movement, who converted in 1849 and became a respected author; and Levi Silliman Ives (1797–1867), the Episcopalian bishop of North Carolina who converted in 1852 and became thereafter a director of Catholic charities in the Catholic diocese of New York.]

Document 9: The Anglican Crisis.

and finds besides not even an inch of ground on which to build its pretensions in the political constitution of the country. In such circumstances it argues anything but a strong sense of truth and right, anything but real faith in a *jure divino* title, to fall upon nicknames and all sorts of unfounded scandal, the missiles always not of reason but of irrational passion, for the purpose of fighting off the opposite cause. It is ridiculous for Anglicanism to claim an exclusive right to this country, over against Romanism, unless it be on the ground that this last has lost all church character, and that Anglicanism accordingly is the only true Catholic succession—ground which in fact this communion does not venture to take. What a farce then to talk as if Romanism *here* in America (whatever it may be in England where Queen Victoria is the fountain of all church unity and life) could have no right to exist, and must be held only an apostacy and *schism* if it dare to exist, on the outside of the Episcopal communion! "Perverts," apostates and schismatics, all are taken to be, who fall away from this communion, whether it be to the side of Geneva or of Rome. It sets itself up thus for the one holy catholic church of these United States, out of which on either side there is no salvation. But why then should this same Anglicanism not go to France, or Spain, or even Rome itself, and there play off the same pompous pretense? By what right political or historical does it claim precedence here in such high-handed style, that would not be of equal force in Italy or Austria? Why should the true and only valid ecclesiastical jurisdiction of Maryland for instance, originally settled as it was by Catholics, be taken to lodge now in the hands of the excellent Bishop Whittingham only, and not in the See of Baltimore made vacant recently by the death of the no less excellent Archbishop Eccleston?[39] The question may be answered different ways; but let the answer go as it may, it will be found to bear hardly on the cause of exclusive Episcopalianism, involving in one view a great deal too little as in another a great deal too much for its hierarchichal claims. In this way, if we are not greatly mistaken, the present course of events is serving to unfold the weakness of such Episcopacy far more than its strength. The stream of the church question, so easy to wade through seemingly at first, is fast getting too deep for the legs of this system to touch bottom, and it must either swim beyond itself or sink. Plainly it has no power to give a satisfactory response to the problem of a truly Catholic Protestantism, the last and deepest interrogation of the present time.

It affords us no satisfaction to come to this melancholy conclusion. We would feel it a great relief rather, to be able to find in Anglican Episcopacy a truly rational and solid answer to the problem of which we speak, an Ararat[40] of rest for the ark of Protestantism, so long drifted by any and every wind over what has been thus far a waste of waters only without island or shore. For most firmly are we convinced, that

---

39. [William Rollinson Whittingham (1805–79) was the fourth Episcopal bishop of Maryland (1840–79). Samuel Eccleston (1801–51) was the fifth Catholic archbishop of Baltimore (1834–51).]

40. [Mount Ararat, located in Turkey near the borders of Iran and Armenia, was traditionally considered the place where Noah's ark landed.]

no *other* sect or fragment of the general movement carries in itself, as such, the power and pledge of any such rest, or is ever likely to prove hereafter more than a weak approximation at best, on the most narrow and partial scale, to the true ideal and proper perfection of its own cause. The whole reflection is suited to make one sad. But it is still a gain always, to have fallacies exposed and delusions brought to an end; and in this view, as we have said before, there is reason to rejoice at what seems to be taking place in the ecclesiastical world, in the way of historical judgment and dissolution, by the winnowing process that has now begun. It is a great matter to have subordinate issues thrown back on their deepest and last ground, in such sort that men may be compelled to deal with this in a really wakeful and earnest way. So it is coming to be now more and more with the question concerning the true sense of Protestantism, and its right to exist, over against the pretensions of the Church of Rome. There are difficulties in Protestantism, which are not to be settled by the common issues between its sects, let the decision here go as it may. These need to be acknowledged and seriously looked in the face, in order if possible that they may be surmounted or set aside. To make no account of them, is only to make them worse. It is well therefore that the course of history is forcing the world to their solemn consideration, and causing it to see that the right settlement of them calls for something deeper and better than any of the schemes that are now paraded as sufficient for this end.

[Implications of the Anglican Crisis for Protestantism]

The day of mere outward tradition here, and blind passive trust in authority, is fast passing away. The mind of the Protestant world is in the course of being roused more and more, to a full revision of the first principles and primordial elements of its own life. What is the real meaning of its *protest* against Rome? Was it in truth, though not so meant at first, a complete rupture with the idea of the Church as it stood before, a full casting off of the old sense of this mystery as it was held for faith in the first ages; in which view Puritanism becomes right, and the best course for ending difficulty would be undoubtedly to give both Episcopacy and Presbyterianism to the winds, and fall over at once in mass to the cool latitude of Baptistic Independency; or is it essential to Protestantism still to carry in it the sense of divine powers, and to assert them in the form of true sacraments and keys that are taken actually to open and shut the kingdom of heaven? And in this last case, can Anglicanism as it now stands be trusted to bear the whole weight of what is thus required, as being under Protestant form, by reason merely of its ecclesiastical machinery, what no Protestantism besides has any power to be under a different shape? And if no such trust be found to stand, is there no help save in a return to Rome; or may the whole cause of Protestantism be supposed to carry in it the promise of a better future, in which it shall be brought to leave all these difficulties behind, by passing forward to a new and higher position that shall be both Catholic and Protestant at the same time? These are the deep questions that are

Document 9: The Anglican Crisis.

coming home silently to the inmost heart of the age, by the church agitations of the present time; and so far have thought and doubt been stirred already with regard to them, that we hold it altogether idle and vain to think of a quiet and contented return hereafter to any past habit as in itself conclusive and sufficient. The past is not thus sufficient for the cause of Protestantism, in any part of the world. To say of it that it is so in any of its forms, is only a very bold or else a very ignorant lie; and no such lie now can long satisfy the mind of the age.

The Anglican crisis in this way involves far more than at once appears on its face. It is undermining confidence in much that has heretofore had a show of truth and strength, writing *Tekel* upon it, and turning it for the consciousness of men into mockery and sham.[41] How far this reaches already, or where it shall reach hereafter, no one can tell. One thing is certain; the way is opening for a new revival of infidelity in England, in close connection with the latest and worst form of German rationalism,[42] which is likely to go beyond all that has appeared there under this name before, and which can hardly fail to be felt powerfully also on this side of the Atlantic. It is remarkable too, that this alarming development seems to run in some measure parallel with the revival of the church tendency, as though it formed its natural alternative and reverse. It has entered the Universities, both Cambridge and Oxford. Puseyism in some cases has fallen over, with easy somerset, to sentimental Straussism.[43] The movement includes a brother of *Froude*, and a brother also of *John Henry Newman*.[44] To some, this connection may seem to be an argument against the church tendency; but in truth it is an argument in its favor; for darkness in the moral world follows light always as its shadow, and through the corruption of man's nature what is good is ever[45] ready to call forth what is bad, nay even to recoil seemingly itself at times into such conclusion, as a sort of Mephistophelian satire on its own beginning.[46] Nor is it at all difficult

41. [Tekel was the mysterious term written on the wall of King Belshazzar of Babylon's palace during a feast he celebrated with his friends. He was disturbed because he did not know what it meant. He, therefore, called upon the Hebrew prophet Daniel to interpret it (Dan 5:25). Daniel tells the king he was been weighed in the scales and found wanting, forecasting the collapse of his kingdom.]

42. [Actually, the challenge to the church came from another direction: Darwin's *Origin of Species* was published at the end of this decade.]

43. [Sentimental Straussian is probably Nevin's swipe at a kind of sentimentalism that is the reverse of David Friedrich Strauss's (1808–74) rationalism. Strauss's *The Life of Jesus* (1834) questioned, among other things, the historicity of miracle accounts in the Scriptures and reflected in general a rationalist approach to Christianity. His radical theology was a polar opposite of the Oxford movement.]

44. [James Anthony Froude (1818–94) was Richard Hurrell Froude's brother. Hurrell was a major leader of the Oxford Movement. James Anthony began in the Oxford movement but quickly departed from it, raising doubts, too, about major doctrines of the Church of England. He became a historian after leaving the Church of England. Francis William Newman (1805–97), John Henry's brother, also left the Oxford movement and became a historian of England. Both brothers represented for Nevin the historical dialectic of the early nineteenth century in England.]

45. [The text reads "every."]

46. [Mephistopheles was a demon in German folklore. The spirit of Mephistopheles refers to what is diabolical, sardonic, jeering, and irreverent.]

to see, in the case before us, how the very same need in the course of religious thought, which urges some to lay new stress on the mystery of faith, may throw others into the stream of unbelief, or carry the same persons indeed first in one direction and then in the other. Let the foundations of a reigning creed or habit in religion begin to give way, and there must be of necessity a movement on the part of such as think at all, towards either a more consistent supernaturalism or else a more clearly conscious rejection of the supernatural altogether. This, we doubt not, is just the relation that exists between the revival of infidelity, and what some take to be the revival of superstition, at the present time in England. Both tendencies in truth grow forth from the same ground; both argue the insufficiency of the established tradition, the breaking up of its authority, and the felt necessity of finding for the mind a surer and better resting-place. Both go in this way to show the truth of what we say, in regard to the far reaching character of the religious movement which is now at work. It cannot pass as a mere transient and partial excitement, to be followed by a full relapse afterwards into the old order of life and thought. The hollowness of this has been too far disclosed, all real faith in it is too far gone, to allow any such re-settlement under more than a facticious and hollow form. Politics and the interest of trade may prevail to bring back for a time such a reign of order in Warsaw;[47] but it will be a reign at the same time of violence, of indifferentism and conscious sham, opening the way certainly to new and greater revolutions in time to come. The idea of the Church must become practically far more than it has been for English Protestantism, or it will inevitably become far less. And this alternative is comprehended itself in a more general issue, which will be found of force finally for the Protestantism of the whole world.

To some it may seem possibly, that putting the matter in this form is equivalent to a full surrendry of the church question in favor of Rome. If it were so, we ought not to shrink certainly from the confession of clear and open truth, just for the sake of avoiding that consequence. Whether we choose to see it or not, the crisis now noticed is solemnly at work, and is sure to lead in the end to its appointed judgment and result. Protestantism must render a plain intelligible answer to the challenge:—"Church or No-church—Sacramental or Non-sacramental—Fidelity to the mystery of the ancient creed, or broad and full rupture with it as the opening revelation only of the Man of Sin?" We will not bear the thought of this answer falling the wrong way, to the side namely of a purely Gnostic naturalism, substituting its own spiritual common sense for the proper mysteries of faith; for that would amount at once to a sentence of condemnation on the whole cause of Protestantism, as complete as any its worst enemies could wish. The problem is then, How shall the demands of the old Catholic faith be satisfied in true union with Protestant freedom? And for this, we say, no sufficient

---

47. [The apparent origin of this phrase is Committee of Polish Emigrants, *Address to the British Nation* (1836), 9. After protesting the failure of the European powers to support the Polish struggle, the Committee "heard with indignation and disgust, . . . one of the ministers of France proclaiming in the chamber of deputies, 'Order reigns at Warsaw!!!'" The only "order" the Committee saw was death of Poland's soldiers, "desolated towns," and the slavery of her people.]

Document 9: The Anglican Crisis.

solution is found in the existing state of Protestantism, as any one may see who is honest enough to look at the matter earnestly with his own eyes. Not in the system as a whole; for it is intrinsically at war in such form with the whole conception. Not in any one part or section of it separately taken, whether in Europe or America. Can any thinking man seriously persuade himself, that Presbyterianism, under any of its multiplying constitutions, or Methodism, or American Lutheranism, or such chaos as now represents the notion of the church in Germany, carries in it the last sense of Christianity, and is in the way of solving hereafter the full burden of its awful riddle for the world's universal use? Can this be hoped of Anglicanism, or such Episcopacy as we have from this source in our own country? The times are working out a negative reply, in tones that are too loud to be overlooked and too clear to be misunderstood. Anglicanism can never cause itself to be accepted, with general faith, as in and of itself an adequate solution for the great church problem of the present time. These we say are *facts,* which we have no right to blink, let them lead where they may. The ostrich changes no truth, by simply plunging her own silly head into the sand. A cloud of arrows shot into the air may darken for a moment, but have no power to put out, the keen light of the sun.

There are however not simply two general alternatives here, but we may say four.[48] The first is a deliberate giving up of the sacramental system altogether, the only proper end of which —short of parting with the Trinity and the Incarnation—is Baptistic Independency, the extreme verge of unchurchly orthodoxy. The second is full despair of Protestantism, and reconciliation in form with Rome, as we have it exemplified with thrilling solemnity in the present English secessions. A third way of escape may be sought, in the belief or hope of a new miraculous dispensation on the part of God himself, through some special agency armed from his presence with fresh apostolical commission and corresponding powers, such as may supersede at once both Romanism and Protestantism as systems that have become historically powerless and dead. Swedenborgianism plants itself on this ground; and it is the ground taken also by Irvingianism—a far more respectable and significant birth of the modern church life than many, having no insight into its natural history, are disposed to allow; not to speak of the wretched caricature we have of the same tendency in Mormonism, which also in its own way claims to be a revival in full of the otherwise lost gifts and powers of the apostolic age.[49] A fourth and last resort is offered, the only one it seems

48. [This schema should be compared to the contrasting schemata in Nevin, "Early Christianity," 49 (*Reformed and Catholic*, 305) and Nevin, "Cyprian," 561–62.]

49. [Swedenborgianism refers to the system of philosophical and religious doctrine of Emanuel Swedenborg (1688–1772), the Swedish philosopher and theologian who emphasized the spiritual structure of the universe, the possibility of direct contact with spirits, and the divinity of Christ. Some in the United States, like Ralph Waldo Emerson, appreciated his works, and other followers established new religious communities to promote his religious views. Nevin was influenced by Swedenborg late in life: see the discussion in Nevin et al., *Born of Water*, MTSS 6:214–16, and the references in "The Bread of Life" in that volume. Irvingianism was a movement in the early 1830s, initiated by Edward Irving (1792–1834), a clergyman of the Church of Scotland. The movement helped to create what

to us which is left for the thoughtful, in the idea of historical development; by which, without prejudice to Catholicism first in its own order and sphere, or to Protestantism next as a real advance on this in modern times, though with the full acknowledgment of the faults and views of both systems, it is assumed that the whole present state of the church is transitional only and interimistic; and that it is destined accordingly through the very crisis which is now coming on—not just by a new miracle setting aside the whole past as a dead failure, but in the way of true historical progress, which makes the past always the real womb both of the present and the future—to surmount in due season the painful contradictions, (dialectic *thorns*) of the Protestant controversy as this now stands, and so to carry it triumphantly forward to its own last sense (the type neither of St. Peter nor of St. Paul but of both rather as brought together by St. John) in some form that shall be found at the same time to etherealize and save, in the same way, the last sense also and rich wealth of the old Catholic faith.

One of the most interesting and richly suggestive books that have appeared in our times, is Thiersch's Lectures on Catholicism and Protestantism (*Vorlesungen über Katholicismus und Protestantismus von Heinrich W. J. Thiersch*, son of the distinguished grammarian of this name, and professor of theology in the University of Marburg).[50] Through this whole article we have had it more or less in our eye, though it takes no reference directly to the course of things in England; and it is not impossible that we may make it hereafter the basis of another article on the same general subject, in the way of carrying out still farther the momentous discussion to whose threshold we have now come.[51] It detracts not at all from the interest of the work in question, that its highly accomplished and most amiable author, since the first edition of it was published in 1845, has been led to adopt the third general answer, just stated, to the great question of the age, by espousing the cause of the Irvingites, which strangely enough has won for itself in Germany quite a number of converts. This fact rather only goes to show the more affectingly the trying nature of the subject, and the deep

---

some called the new Catholic Apostolic Church, a Protestant denomination that spread to Germany and the United States. Irving was a charismatic preacher who emphasized the human ability to receive revelations, see visions, and speak in tongues. He was a pre-millennialist and predicted the coming of the end of the world. He also became an early proponent of the Rapture, and has been called a forerunner of the modern Pentecostal movement. Mormonism was initiated by Joseph Smith, Jr. (1805–44). He founded The Church of Jesus Christ of Latter Day Saints (Mormons) and on the basis of new revelations from the angel Moroni he published in 1830 *The Book of Mormon*. The new revelation was at the heart of the movement.]

50. Author also of the best work we have ever seen on the Canon of the New Testament, a. 1845, in opposition to the destructive criticism of the Tübingen school. [Nevin is referring to the German theologian Heinrich Wilhelm Josias Thiersch's (1817–85) *Versuch zur Herstellung des historischen Standpuncts für die Kritik der neutestamentlichen Schriften.* {Trans. Essay to establish the historical foundation for criticism of the New Testament.} In that text, Thiersch contrasts the theology he discovered in the early church not only with that of the Greek and Roman Churches, but especially with modern Protestantism.]

51. [An aspiration Nevin to some degree fulfilled in "Early Christianity: Third Article," *MR* 4 (January 1852) 1–54. Nevin began this series in the next number of *MR* (September, 1851).]

Document 9: The Anglican Crisis.

earnestness of the man. The frivolous and superficial not seldom find all easy, where the truly serious in proportion it may be to the very amount of their knowledge itself are brought into the greatest straits. No one can question the learning of Thiersch; it is of the very highest order. And just as little room is there to question his piety and profound practical sincerity. He wrestles with the problem of his book evidently, not merely as a theoretic scholar, and much less as the organ merely of a theological party, but as one who feels that issues of life and death are suspended for himself and for the world on its proper solution. No one can follow him, without feeling that the subject is full of embarrassment, as well as big with importance, and that it is regarded throughout by the lecturer himself, whatever it may be for others, with intense interest and concern. When we hear such a man seeking refuge from the difficulties of the church question, by falling in with the belief that nothing less than a new apostolate, sent forth with fresh commission directly from Christ himself, can restore Christianity to its proper form, and that such new apostolate has in fact appeared of late among the Irvingites—we may be well assured that there is here truly a *nodus vindice dignus* [a knot worthy to be untied], that the difficulties in consideration are neither few nor of light account, and that to meet them properly is a task which calls for more than common earnestness in any part of the world. It is hardly necessary for us to add, that we have no sort of faith in the solution of the knot in this way. No scheme can command our regard, which nullifies virtually the doctrine of the indestructible life of the church, as well as the Divine promise on which that doctrine rests, by assuming a full failure and frustration of all the sense the church had in the beginning. We have no patience on this ground with that bald Puritanism, which fairly buries the church for a thousand years and more, in order to bring it to a more striking resurrection in the sixteenth century. As little can we be satisfied, on the same ground, with the visions of Emanuel Swedenborg; they proceed throughout on the assumption that the church as it started with the Apostles has run itself out, both as Catholicism and Protestantism, and that the world is to be helped now only by a new revelation appointed to take its place. Irvingism involves more or less distinctly, as it seems to us, the same dismal thought; and if this be so, it needs no other condemnation. If it come to a necessary choice between such a view and Romanism, the advantage lies decidedly we think on the side of this last. It is easier to believe that the original powers of the church still flow in this communion, though hidden for the most part from our common Protestant sight, than it is to suppose that they have perished entirely, and now need a "*Lazarus come forth*," or a second edition of the word "*On this rock*," to come once more into full play for the salvation of a dying world. But, as we have seen, we are not thrown at once on any such desperate election. We may cast ourselves upon the theory of historical development, so as to make Protestantism itself, with all its painfully acknowledged miseries, the main though by no means exclusive stream, by which the general tide of the original Christian life is rolling itself forward, not without fearful breaks and cataracts and many tortuous circuits, to the open sea at last of that grand

and glorious ideal of true Catholic Unity, which has been in the mind of all saints from the beginning.

It is but fair to add in the case of Thiersch, for whom we entertain a more than common affection and respect, that he is by no means unhistorical in his own mind, but altogether the reverse; and that so far as the objection here noticed has any weight, it is to be regarded as holding by implication only against the system, in whose plausible meshes he has allowed himself to be recently caught. His theory agrees in many respects with the scheme of historical development; only he counts it necessary to include in this the idea of such a failure of the first life of the church, as makes it necessary now that it should be called forth again from the grave as it were of its own past history by a second supernatural gift of the same sort.   J. W. N.

Document 10

"Evangelical Radicalism"

Editor's Introduction

Nevin's "Evangelical Radicalism" (September 1852) continued his criticism of the sect mentality and its understanding of the church and the Bible.[1] The text was in fact a review of William Crowell's *Church Member's Manual* (1852), a guidebook that outlined Baptist principles, doctrines, practices, and church polity. Crowell was a Baptist minister who served churches in Vermont, Massachusetts, Illinois, Missouri, and New Jersey. His *Manual* was reprinted several times after its first publication in 1847 and continued to be published in 2022. At the same time he was reviewing Crowell's *Manual*, Nevin was also working on his third article on "Cyprian," which focused on Cyprian's doctrine of the Church.[2]

Crowell's *Manual* was subjected to some of the sharpest attacks that Nevin made against what he called the modern American Puritan and Baptist concept of the church and the Bible, a view he considered out of touch with much of the pre-Reformation and Reformation church. He declared the Baptist "rationalistic unsacramental system . . . a dangerous delusion."[3] Nevin's criticisms of "Evangelical Radicalism" were consistent with many of the charges he made in his articles on "Early Christianity" and "Cyprian."

In 1850, Nevin had criticized Brownson's authoritarian understanding of the church and his emphasis on the identity of the primitive church with the current Catholic Church. By 1852, though, Nevin's emphases shifted, and he was willing to admit that he preferred[4] those churches that underlined the organic continuity (not identity) of the present Christian church with the early church, rather than those

---

1. Nevin, "Evangelical Radicalism," 508–512.
2. Nevin, "Cyprian," 417–52. In the last article (October 1852), Nevin argued that early Christianity was "in its constitutional elements not Protestantism, but Catholicism." "Cyprian," 551.
3. Nevin, "Evangelical Radicalism," 510.
4. Nevin to Brownson, August 18, 1852, in Brownson Papers, University of Notre Dame Archives.

Evangelical churches who radically disassociated the contemporary church from the church's organic development. By 1850, moreover, it was clear to Nevin and many others that private interpretations of the Bible had been responsible for many of the divisions in Christianity, and the slavery controversy in the United States had only increased that tendency to undermine the church's unity.[5]

Nevin's thesis had two parts. First, he argued that the whole Baptist system "is completely at war . . . with what was held to be Christianity in the first ages."[6] The Baptist view of the church as based solely on the Bible and the natural right to interpret it by one's reason. That view was "preeminently rationalistic"[7] even when Baptists acknowledged the need for the illumination of the Holy Spirit. For Baptists, as for many other Evangelicals in the United States, the church was a kind of democracy or a contractual arrangement whereby the reason and will of individual persons constituted the church. In this sense, the church had become an "association of believers" or a collectivity of wills.[8] Such an approach appeared to be an application of Jean-Jacques Rousseau's *Social Contract* to the church.[9]

Nevin made a sharp contrast between what he considered the Christianity of the first ages and the modern Puritan and Baptist conception of the mid-nineteenth century. The two systems had very different conceptions of Christian salvation. The first was based on the Creed, while the second considered the Creed heresy or falsehood. The first believed the church was supernatural and the medium of salvation; the second thought of the church as a social contract. The first declared the ministry to be commissioned by God; the second understood the ministry as a human creation. The first saw sacraments as seals and bearers of heavenly grace; the second attributed no such "mystic force" to them. "We must break with this modern Puritanic system or else break with the whole Christianity of the first ages."[10]

The second part of Nevin's thesis dealt with the Bible as the sole guide to all things Christian. The Puritan-Baptist view of the Bible alone, interpreted by everyone's isolated reason, common sense, private judgment, and religious illumination

---

5. Prior to the Civil War, major religious communities separated into northern and southern denominations over slavery. The Presbyterians split in 1838, the Methodists in 1844, the Baptists in 1845. On these divisions within the churches, see Goen, *Broken Churches*.

6. Nevin, "Evangelical Radicalism," 509.

7. Nevin, "Evangelical Radicalism," 508.

8. Nevin's metaphor for this social atomism was "living sand-heap." *Mystical Presence*, MTSS 1:146; "New Creation," MTSS 4:39; "Nevin and Bushnell," MTSS 6:46.

9. Jean-Jacques Rousseau (1712–78), a Genevan political philosopher, wrote *The Social Contract* (*Du contrat social*, 1762) to argue that government obtains the right to govern by the consent of the governed. His emphasis on the general will of the people had an enormous impact on modern political philosophy and on many Americans who applied his principles to religious as well as political organizations in the United States. For a general introduction to social contract thinking and its influence on the United States, see Hulliung, *The Social Contract in America*.

10. Nevin, "Evangelical Radicalism," 510.

Document 10: "Evangelical Radicalism"

was "rationalism almost without disguise."[11] This had become for Nevin the basis of his charge of radicalism. Such an approach to the Bible was truncated and violated the understanding of the Bible in the early ages of the church. The Bible in the early church was read and interpreted in and through a creedal understanding of the church as one, holy, catholic, and apostolic. This reading presumed the concrete, objective, communal, and incarnational view of the church as the organ of salvation, and understanding the Bible through the church brought a wider and fuller sense of its meaning than was possible through private judgment.

In "Evangelical Radicalism," Nevin focused on the objective over and against the subjective, a reversal of the emphasis he placed in his article on Brownson. For him, the subjectivism and individualism of the Puritan-Baptist system neglected and overturned the creedal and ecclesial approach of the first ages.

---

11. Nevin, "Evangelical Radicalism," 511.

Evangelical Radicalism.[1]

The Church Member's Manual of Ecclesiastical Principles, Doctrine and Discipline: Presenting a systematic view of the structure, polity, doctrines, and practices of Christian Churches, as taught in the Scriptures. By William Crowell, &c. Boston: Gould and Lincoln. 1852.[2]

A truly interesting and suggestive book—though not exactly in the way of its own intention. The author is a Baptist, who proposes to set forth a scheme of the Church to suit the rationalistic standpoint of his own sect; "his only desire being to follow truth, wherever it may lead." To answer the question, "What and where is the church??" he scorns the thought of taking counsel of the Church itself. "I might as well go to Delphi or Dodona," he tells us, "or the shrine of Jupiter Ammon, to inquire who is the god, and where is his temple."[3] Pagan and Christian theocracies, it seems, are alike without truth and entitled to no trust. The whole appeal must be "*to the Bible*;" which means, of course, to the Bible as read by William Crowell and his Baptist brethren, in distinction from the reading of Presbyterians, Lutherans, &c., &c., as well as from the sense attached to it by the ancient Fathers and the Catholic Church of all past ages. "Hitherto Baptists have paid but little attention to the subject of church polity;" too busy with the interests of "*spiritual Christianity in its primitive form*,"[4] to give much attention to any such outward concern. We will not pretend here to go minutely into the theory now concocted out of the Bible, for their special accommodation and use, by this *Church Member's Manual*. Suffice it to say, that it is preeminently rationalistic. The idea of a general church, save in the sense of a mere abstraction, is discarded; the

---

1. [*MR* 4 (September 1852) 508–12.]

2. [William Crowell (1806–71), a Baptist minister, served churches in Vermont, Massachusetts, Illinois, Missouri, and New Jersey. In Missouri, he edited the *Western Watchman*, a Baptist weekly paper. His most important publication was *The Church Member's Manual*, which was revised and reprinted several times after 1847 and was still published in 2022. The 1852 edition not being available, the editor will use the 1857 edition, since the pagination Nevin provides corresponds to this later edition.]

3. [Crowell, *Church Member's Manual*, v.]

4. [Crowell, *Church Member's Manual*, vi.]

Document 10: Evangelical Radicalism.

only true order in the case, is that of *many distinct churches*, each perfectly original and independent in its own sphere. A church thus is simply an association of believers, who join together in this way for their common advantage in the Christian life, under the pledge of baptism.

> Men have a natural right to associate by mutual agreement for the accomplishment of any innocent or useful purpose. In this way civil government was first formed, and God owned the institution as one of his own appointment. The disciples of Christ have the right to unite themselves together in churches, for the promotion of their piety and the spread of the Gospel, unless he has forbidden them in his revealed word. This he has not done. It is, therefore from the nature of the case, proper that men should unite in a mutual, voluntary covenant for religious purposes. The objects in view are more important than those attained in the civil compact, in which men unite in a mutual covenant for a common benefit; and the act is as reasonable and as necessary in itself. —P. 55, 56. Every particular church, so formed by *social contract*, holds its powers directly and exclusively from Christ, who alone is head over all things to the *churches*, without the intervention of Pope, Bishop, or General Assembly. "Each one," as the celebrated Dr. Wayland[5] dogmatizes the matter, "is a perfect and complete system. The decisions of one are not binding on another. Each one is at liberty to interpret the laws of Christ for itself, and to govern itself according to that interpretation. Each church is therefore as essentially independent of every other, as though each one were the only church in Christendom."—P. 80.

So runs this *Bible* scheme of the Baptists. We have no room here to go into any close consideration of its merits. But it speaks for itself. Only think of Rousseau's theory of *social contract*, deliberately applied to the grand and glorious mystery of the *Holy Catholic Church*.[6]

The scheme is completely at war, it will be readily seen, with what was held to be Christianity in the first ages. Of this its patrons may not feel it necessary to make any account. Enough that they can pretend to have the Bible at all events on their side. Weighed against such authority, of what worth or force is Christian antiquity—even though it *should* reach back to the very age next following that of the Apostles? Still however the fact is one, which ought to be distinctly seen and acknowledged. Let it pass for what it may, it deserves to be fully understood and held up to view. This Baptist theory of Christianity is not what was held to be the "mystery of godliness,"[7] in the early church. Neither is the difference circumstantial only and accidental. It

---

5. [Francis Wayland (1796–1865), Baptist minister, was president and professor at Brown University (1827–55), where he lectured and published texts on *Moral Science* (1835), *Political Economy* (1837), and *University Sermons* (1849). He grounded most of his moral issues in the natural law and Scottish Common Sense philosophy.]

6. [See document introduction for comments on Rousseau. "Holy Catholic Church" is in "small caps" in the original.]

7. [1 Tim 3:16.]

goes to the heart of religion. It has to do with its universal system. We have in the two cases actually two gospels, two altogether different versions of the Christian salvation. In one case, all rests on the Creed;[8] in the other this fundamental symbol is charged with heresy and falsehood. In one case, the church is made to be supernatural, and is honored as the real medium of salvation to her children; in the other she is treated as a "figment" in every such view, and falls into the conception of a social contract. The ministry in one case holds its commission and its powers from God; in the other case it is the creature of man. In the one case, the sacraments are seals and bearers of heavenly grace; in the other, they possess no such mystic force whatever. The creed of the ancient church, this modern system openly turns into a lie. What all antiquity believed, it takes a pride in refusing to believe; and affects to be *spiritual*, by treating with contempt the real mystery of the Spirit's presence, in the only form in which it was to all Christian antiquity an object of faith. How can two such contrary systems be considered for one moment the same? They exclude each other. If one is to stand, the other must fall. Brought before the tribunal of this modem system, the ancient Christianity is found to be altogether wrong and false. We have only however to reverse the procedure, by bringing the modem system to the bar of the ancient, and at once the falsehood and wrong fall just as conclusively over to the other side. The two schemes are completely at issue. The contest between them is one of life and death. When the modern system challenges our faith, it asks us in fact to renounce all connection with the faith and religious life of the Church of the first ages. And so on the other hand if we feel it necessary to hold fast to the communion of this primitive piety—if we cannot bear the thought of giving up all spiritual fellowship with the martyrs, confessors, fathers and saints, of the early ages, and are not willing to set them all down for fanatics and fools—if we tremble to stigmatize the Christianity that conquered the Roman world as the invention of Satan, root and branch—we must not, and dare not, shrink from the responsibility of declaring the rationalistic unsacramental system now before us a dangerous delusion, which all who value the salvation of their souls are bound religiously to avoid. It would have been so regarded, beyond all controversy, by the universal church in the beginning. There would have been as little patience with it precisely, as there was with Gnosticism.[9] It would have been branded openly as a virtual denial of the entire mystery of the Gospel. Of this, we say, there can be no doubt, and in regard to it there should be no equivocation or disguise.

Shall we be told then, that it is harsh to think and speak as we do of the religious system now under consideration, because it embraces a large amount of respectable Christian profession at the present time, and is nothing more in fact than the last phase of what is called orthodox Puritanism, which many hold to be the very perfection and

---

8. [For Mercersburg's interpretation of the Creed (especially the Apostles' Creed), see Nevin et al., *The Early Creeds*, MTSS 8.]

9. [Nevin correlated the Christian sectarianism of his day with Gnosticism in *Antichrist*, MTSS 5:189–216.]

Document 10: Evangelical Radicalism.

ne plus ultra[10] of evangelical religion? We reply by asking, How is it to be helped? We are shut up to a sore dilemma here, from which there is no possible escape. We must break with this modern Puritanic system, or else break with the whole Christianity of the first ages.[11] No sophistry can cause them to appear the same. The Creed of the one, is the Lie of the other. What was the mystery of godliness in the old church, this new faith unblushingly declares to be the mystery of iniquity. In such circumstances we have no choice, except to say with which of the two interests we hold it best to make common cause. To justify the one, is necessarily to condemn the other. To show respect towards this new faith, because it is outwardly respectable, must we cover with reproach and disgrace the old faith from the days of Polycarp and Ignatius to those of Ambrose and Augustine?[12] Do we owe no respect also, and no charity, to the first Christian ages? What right indeed can those have to demand our tenderness and forbearance, in so grave a case, who make no account whatever of the reputation or credit of whole centuries of past Christian history, but modestly require us to set them all down as heretical and false over against themselves? What is the peculiar merit of this Baptistic Puritanism, a thing comparatively of yesterday, that it should be allowed thus to insult all Christian antiquity, and have full exemption at the same time from every unfavorable judgment upon its own pretensions and claims? "What!" we may well say to it in the language of St. Paul, "Came the word of God out from you; or came it unto you only?"[13] Who art thou, upstart system! that thou shouldst set thyself in such proud style above the universal church of antiquity—the immediate successors of the Apostles, the noble army of martyrs, the goodly fellowship of the fathers, the vast cloud of witnesses that look down upon us from these ages of faith—charging it with wholesale superstition and folly, and requiring us to renounce its creed, the whole scheme and habit of its religious life, and to accept from *thy* hands, in place of it, another form of belief, another scheme of doctrine altogether, as infallibly true and right? Who gave thee this authority? Whence came such infallibility?

With immense self-complacency, the system lays its hand on the Bible, and says: This is my warrant. Aye, but who is to interpret this written revelation? *Reason*, replies the system. "The Bible is the church's supreme law, reason is her court. The Bible is the compass; reason, lighted by the Spirit of God, is the binnacle lamp."[14] There we have it. Reason, every man's reason for himself, the world's private judgment and common sense with such religious illumination as it may come to in its own sphere, is the court,

---

10. [Literally, "no more beyond," or best example.]

11. [Nevin wants to make clear that he is not speaking of early Puritanism, which had a covenantal view of the church. Nevin considered modern Puritanism a departure from the older forms of Puritanism that had an organic rather than a collectivist or voluntary view of the church.]

12. [Nevin repeatedly refers to these fathers of the early church to indicate the disparity between the contemporary "pseudo-Protestant" experience of Christianity and that of the early church.]

13. [1 Cor 14:36.]

14. [Crowell, *Church Member's Manual*, vi.]

the tribunal, by which the law in this case is to take the form of truth and life.[15] Is that not rationalism almost without disguise? What more could the worst radicalism ask or want? But for the present, let that pass. Baptistic Puritanism appeals to the Bible. We now boldly deny, that it has the Bible on its side. This goes on the contrary full as much against its claims and pretensions throughout, as Christian antiquity itself. When it seems to have any part of the Bible in its favor, it is only by reading into it in the first place its own sense, by begging before hand the whole question in debate, by taking for granted what is to be proved, and by making its own rationalistic hypothesis in this way the standpoint from which is taken afterwards every observation of the Divine text. Even then the result is at best but a lame and forced construction. The New Testament is as far removed, as it well can be, from the Baptistic and Independent habit of mind. It proceeds throughout on the assumption, that Christianity is a mystery, a constitution above nature, objectively at hand under a real historical form in the world, to which men must submit by faith in such view in order to be saved. This of itself involves the whole doctrine of the Church, with its Divine jurisdiction and heavenly powers, its ministry starting from Christ, its grace bearing sacraments, its unity and catholicity, the universal course of the new creation, we may say, as it is made to pass before us in the Creed.[16] Only let the standpoint of this old faith be taken, in reading the Scriptures, the same that was occupied by the church in the beginning, and it will soon be found all that is needed, to expose the huge illusions of the Baptistic exegesis, and to set the Bible before us in a wholly different light and sense.

And why should *not* this old standpoint be taken, when we thus approach the Bible? Why should we renounce the posture of faith in which the ancient church stood, and take, at the bidding of Puritanism, what must be considered as compared with it a posture of infidelity or no-faith, that we may be supposed to study God's word to purpose and effect? The absurdity of such a requirement is greater than can be easily expressed. Its most enormous presumption may well fill us with wonder and surprise.   J. W. N.

---

15. [Nevin was here addressing a mode of evangelical biblicism that based the authority of the Bible on the allegedly rational evidences of its supernatural truth. The primary evidences were fulfilled prophecies and the miracles recorded in the Bible. These evidences "proved" the Bible was true, and thus it could be used as a textbook of supernatural revelation. See Holifield, *Theology in America*, 186–90.]

16. [For Nevin's mature statement of the nature of the church, see "Hodge on the Ephesians," MTSS 7:98–101.]

Document 11

"Man's True Destiny"

Editor's Introduction

"Man's True Destiny," a commencement address Nevin gave to the first graduating class of the newly-formed Franklin and Marshall College on August 31, 1853, reflected theological themes that Nevin had been articulating since the 1840s.[1] The address occurred at a time in his life when he was gradually withdrawing from direct involvement in the institutional activities of the German Reformed Church in Mercersburg. In 1851, he resigned as professor of theology from the Mercersburg Seminary where he had been teaching since 1840. In 1852, he gave up his position as president of German Reformed Marshall College in Mercersburg, where he had been president since 1841. He stayed on, however, for another year, serving the institution until it merged with the Franklin College in Lancaster, Pennsylvania, forming the united Franklin and Marshall College. In 1853, moreover, he withdrew from the editorship of the *Mercersburg Review* where he had been the most prominent contributor since 1849. Nevin gave up his previous active participation in these German Reformed institutions because of failing health and a crisis of conscience over his attraction to the Catholic Church. Theodore Appel, Nevin's friend and first biographer, noted that Nevin told him he retired from the college because he was "not satisfied with the present state of Protestantism and much less so with that of Romanism," and he did not want to embarrass the new college because of his recent theological writings.[2] During these years Nevin had become more and more outspoken on his understanding of the resemblance of the Catholic Church with primitive church, and some leading American Catholics in particular believed that his conversion to Catholicism was imminent.[3]

1. Nevin, "Man's True Destiny," 492–521.

2. Appel, *Life*, 439. Appel also noted (432) that prior to the merger, Franklin College (named after Benjamin Franklin) was owned by three communities: one-third by the Reformed Church, one-third by the Lutheran Church, and one-third by representatives of the Lancaster community.

3. On American Catholic interests in and expectation of Nevin's conversion, see Nevin to Brownson, August 18, 1852; Brownson to Nevin, August 23, 1852, August 28, 1852 in Brownson Papers,

Nevin was well aware of the importance of his denominational college and became a major supporter of its merger with Franklin College at Lancaster as his speech at the formal opening of the new college demonstrated in June 1853. In the presence of James Buchanan (1791–1868)—Pennsylvania politician, former United States diplomat, and future President— and a large crowd of supporters of the Franklin and Marshall College, Nevin called for financial and moral support for the new institution and called attention to the value of the college especially for the German Reformed community and for the good of the entire state of Pennsylvania. The kind of religious informed education the school could provide and the influence of the German mind upon that education would distinguish such a college from those well-endowed New England colleges where the modern Puritan and empirical mind dominated the educational systems. The newly-formed Franklin and Marshall College would enhance the value of diversity in American education and avoid a tendency to "monotonous sameness" in the American educational system. In other words, the New England system was not the universal standard of education.[4]

Antebellum college presidents, many of whom were ministers, perceived the importance of educating the people "politically, morally, and religiously," as Nevin asserted.[5] Francis Wayland (1796–1865), Baptist minister and president of Brown University (1827–55) in Providence, Rhode Island, shared many of Nevin's views on education, but his own concerns were much more focused on the need for reforms in higher education in order to democratize its benefits. In 1842, he argued that higher education in the United States had previously aimed primarily to serve the professions of law, medicine, and ministry. He called for expanding the benefits of education to meet the needs of the wider society, and, therefore, to educate the merchant, the mechanic, the manufacturer, and the farmer. A "knowledge of moral and intellectual philosophy, of the fundamental principles of law, of our own constitution, of history, of vegetable and animal physiology, and many other sciences" are just as important and necessary to the newer professions in society as to the traditional classes.[6] Society, though, was going to have to enlarge the provisions for the education of the newer classes. Wayland was preoccupied with the practical side of higher education. Nevin, while aware of the practical needs, focused his attention on what he considered the most important aim of education.

Nevin's baccalaureate address of 1853 demonstrated his view of what constituted a genuine liberal arts education. Such an education was not just to develop practical skills, provide useful knowledge, or prepare for meaningful employment, but to inculcate a wisdom that prepared students for life and for their supernatural destiny.

University of Notre Dame Archives, and Nevin to James Alphonsus McMaster, February 26, 1853, in McMaster Papers, University of Notre Dame Archives.

4. On Nevin's talk, see *Formal Opening*, 9–35; for quotation, 19.
5. *Formal Opening*, 18.
6. Wayland, *Thoughts on the Present Collegiate System*, 154–55.

Document 11: "Man's True Destiny"

He spoke as a father, a Christian, a theologian, and a former college president. The lengthy discourse was heavy on theology and, as D. G. Hart noted, Nevin's "fairly ethereal reflections" would have been difficult for many teenagers to follow attentively.[7] It contained long series of familiar biblical quotations and references to many prominent scholars and politicians (e.g., Kant, Hume, Humboldt, Davy, Kossuth, Mazzini, Rollin) that only a few graduating seniors may have followed with interest and understanding. It would have required from the graduates, for example, a knowledge of Kantian philosophy to comprehend the following sentence: "It is not hypothetically or problematically only, but with full categorical imperative, that the chief end of man is referred here to another world, and that he is required to subordinate to this all other ends as of merely secondary account."[8] The primary thesis, however, was clear to all.

That address was not entirely unusual in antebellum American colleges. Charles Philip Krauth (1797–1867), Lutheran minister and president of Pennsylvania College in Gettysburg Pennsylvania, for example, delivered a commencement address in September 1850 similar to Nevin's, focusing on the ultimate religious end of human existence.[9] In many antebellum colleges religion, science, and education were perceived as harmonious and not in conflict with each other. Scottish Common Sense Realism and Baconian science, with their emphases on the inductive method in science and religion, pervaded the halls, antebellum college classrooms, and seminaries where that harmony was clearly acknowledged. The days of John William Draper's *History of the Conflict between Religion and Science* (1874) and Andrew Dickson White's *History of the Warfare of Science with Theology in Christendom* (1897) were in the distant post-Civil War future. Although Nevin had criticized the overemphasis on the empirical methods in religion and philosophy in the United States, he too saw harmony between religion and science and education. For him, though, reason was more than induction. He was influenced more by German idealism and Romanticism than by Scottish Common Sense and Baconian science; he found the foundation of the harmony not in empiricism, but in a more profound and integral view of the relationship between nature and the supernatural.

Nevin argues throughout the text that true human destiny "lies beyond the present world in an order of things which is supernatural" and that it was necessary to have a knowledge of this end and to reduce that knowledge to practice in order "not

---

7. Hart, *John Williamson Nevin*, 181.
8. Nevin, "Man's True Destiny," 497.
9. Krauth, *Human Life: A Baccalaureate Address*. For a small sample of other antebellum commencement addresses with religious content, see Lord, *Paul a Model*; Verplanck, *The Influence of Moral Causes*; Sherman, *The Bible a Classic*; Mark Hopkins, *The Manifoldness of Man*. The religious and moral dimensions of baccalaureate addresses did not end after the Civil War and in fact continued well into the twentieth century as is evident in the addresses of Arthur Twining Hadley, president of Yale University (1899–1921). See Hadley, *Baccalaureate Addresses*. However, increasingly after the Civil War, those speeches, unlike Nevin's, reflected a diminished confessional and creedal character that explicitly appealed to faith and the student's supernatural destiny.

to live in vain."[10] He told the graduating class that human beings according to the biblical account of creation were at the apex of the natural order of things and in fact were the perfection of nature. As such, all had a religious nature and a capacity for religion that needed to be called into exercise. All of nature, and especially human nature yearned for fulfillment beyond itself, conscious that there was something more than nature itself could provide. Revelation came as a response to that inner impulse, but sin always hindered or blocked that receptivity. Sin, though, made human beings aware of the need for a savior. This explicit Christian message to the graduating seniors was a reminder of what had been the ultimate aim of their education at Marshall.

For Nevin, the summit and "crowning excellence of all education" was the acquisition and perfection of wisdom and knowledge.[11] But wisdom, in distinction from mere knowledge or science, was a practical virtue that affected the will as well as the intelligence and was manifested most clearly in the understanding and practical decisions that led to one's supernatural destiny. Ultimately the acquisition and perfection of that kind of wisdom required revelation and faith that put believers "in a real communication with things unseen and eternal."[12] Nevin wanted to make it clear in this address, as he did in so many of his previous articles, that he was not speaking of an other-worldly notion of the supernatural or of a kind of gnostic spirituality that existed only in the minds of individuals. The supernatural destiny that he was speaking of existed in this world as well as in a kingdom beyond this world, and the "actual presence of the supernatural" was "a real force in the world." He asserted, too, that this view of the supernatural end of all life was so contrary to a prevailing spirit in nineteenth-century America, which he characterized as "rationalistic, humanitarian, politico-economical."[13] That prevailing view he also found in large segments of American Protestantism.

To illustrate that point of the false spirit of the age, he criticized those many American Protestants who welcomed Louis Kossuth (1802–94), the Hungarian revolutionary, when he came to the United States in 1851 and 1852 to drum up support for his fight for freedom in Hungary. Nevin was particularly opposed to the way many Protestants had identified Kossuth's political and socialistic aims and programs with Christianity itself. Liberty, philanthropy, and human rights were indeed righteous goals, but they were natural ends and were being treated as if they were the end and goal of Christianity. Natural and social goals were of worth, he told his graduating seniors, only if they were subordinate to the supernatural and eternal. "Socialism is not Christianity."[14]

---

10. Nevin, "Man's True Destiny," 493.
11. Nevin, "Man's True Destiny," 503, 505.
12. Nevin, "Man's True Destiny," 508.
13. Nevin, "Man's True Destiny," 512.
14. Nevin, "Man's True Destiny," 519.

Document 11: "Man's True Destiny"

Nevin, however, was in the minority in his reaction to Kossuth. Many American politicians like Daniel Webster and a host of American Protestant religious leaders as well as many local citizens had warmly welcomed Kossuth and gave him financial and moral support for his cause.[15] Kossuth, the governor-president of Hungary during the European revolutions of 1848–1849, led the unsuccessful revolt against Austria, seeking to win Hungarian political and social independence. After his defeat, he toured the United States from December 1851 until he left in July 1852, giving numerous speeches and stirring up much support throughout the country.[16] Many of his Forty-Eight-freedom fighters who participated in the Hungarian revolution fled the revolt after it had been defeated and came to live in the United States after 1848.

College students and their parents would have been aware of the Kossuth speaking tours because they were given widespread publicity in local as well as national newspapers. Nevin's purpose of drawing attention to Kossuth and especially to the favorable reaction to him and his cause was to demonstrate the dangers of identifying social and political movements with Christianity. He warned students to be critical of some of the socialist and radical tendencies in American society—tendencies he characterized as "the *Antichrist* of the present age." If students thought first of the Kingdom of God and sought its righteousness, they would have the critical mindset to avoid the allure of "rationalistic speculation, sectarian fanaticism, radicalism, socialism, and wild revolutionary republicanism,"[17] and to have the wisdom to prioritize eternal over penultimate goals.

---

15. See, e.g., Daniel Webster, *Sketch of the Life of Louis Kossuth*.
16. For his speeches and tours, see Kossuth and Várady, *The Life of Governor Louis Kossuth*.
17. Nevin, "Man's True Destiny," 519.

Man's True Destiny.[1]

A Baccalaureate Address to the First Graduating Class of Franklin and Marshall College, August 31, 1853. By the Rev. J. W. Nevin, D. D., late President of Marshall College.

Young Gentlemen:

By invitation of the Board of Trustees of Franklin and Marshall College, and at your own special and earnest request as a Class, I stand before you on this occasion to pronounce a few parting words in the name of the Board, in the name of the Faculty, and in my own name, in the way of *Baccalaureate Address*.[2] The position is to myself one of more than usual interest and solemnity. The duty which it calls me to discharge, belongs of right to the relation I have borne to you for years as the President of Marshall College. It is not as a stranger, nor as the temporary representative simply of the government of this new institution for the service in hand, that I now speak to you, as a class, for the last time. I appear before you rather in the character of a father, whose responsible privilege it has been to preside over the course of your college education from its commencement to its close, and whose concern for your future welfare is conditioned thus by innumerable cares, and sympathies, and reciprocal affections, the proper growth of such endearing connection, which reach away back into days and years that are past. This relation itself, however, so far as the idea of outward office is concerned, has also passed away. All that remains of it is its moral life and power, which ought to be perpetual. In the present transaction, accordingly, the official in every view may be regarded as overwhelmed and lost in the personal; while all the circumstances of the occasion conspire to crowd the personal, at the same time, with memories and associations of the most solemnly affecting kind. Any College

1. [*MR* 5 (October 1853) 492–521.]

2. [Since 1841 Nevin had been president of Marshall College in Mercersburg, where he also taught theology in the German Reformed seminary. As president of Marshall, he negotiated with leaders of Franklin College in Lancaster (a Lutheran school) to unite the two colleges in Lancaster. The two colleges came together in 1852 and Nevin resigned his position as president of Marshall. His 1853 commencement address to the seniors of the combined Franklin and Marshall College reflected a theological position that he had been developing since the early 1840s and came at a time in his life when he was gradually withdrawing from his public involvement in the German Reformed Church. But his talk was consistent with his organic and incarnational understanding of Christianity.]

Document 11: Man's True Destiny.

Commencement is solemn, mirroring as it does, for every thoughtful mind, the great law of change, by which, in the drama of full life, one generation is continually passing away to make room for another. But on this occasion, we have something more than such an anniversary in its ordinary form. I see before me the first Graduating Class of one institution, which is, in a certain sense, at the same time, the last of a whole series of such Classes belonging to the history of another. These seem to rise in long review before my mind, and to join their presence with yours in the tender solemnities of this parting hour. You will not take it amiss then, if I consider myself speaking to them along with you, in the present address. It is in virtue of a past relation only, at all events, a relation which has now come to an end, that I am here to speak at all. Let this relation then be owned to-day in its broadest extent. Let me feel that the farewell words I now utter, are dedicated as a tribute of affection to all the Alumni, to all who have ever been students of Marshall College.

[Nature and the Supernatural Goal of Human Life]

The true destination of man, the proper end of his being and life, lies beyond the present world in an order of things which is supernatural; and it is absolutely necessary that he should know this, and have supreme practical regard to the fact, in order that he may not live in vain.

This is the theme on which I propose to speak; the one great thought I wish to bring before you, and to leave with you, in the full earnestness of its own proper consequences and relations. May the Spirit of all truth and grace so hallow the naturally sacred associations of this present occasion, that they may serve to fix deeply and lastingly in your minds the living force of the thought itself, so that it shall be found hereafter the pole-star of your existence, lighting it till life shall end onwards and upwards always to the glorious immortality of the saints in heaven.

The necessity of owning a supernatural destiny in the case of man, lies to a certain extent in his natural constitution itself, in the relation he is seen and felt to bear to the world around him in his present mortal state. This relation in one view is of the most close and intimate kind. The organization of the world, as a system of nature, comes to its completion in his person. This is signified to us very plainly in the Mosaic account of the creation; where the whole magnificent process, rising gradually from one stage of order and life to another, is represented as reaching its climax finally on the sixth day, when God said: "Let us make man in our image, after our likeness, and let them have dominion over the fish of the sea, and over the fowls of the air, and over the cattle, and over all the earth, and over every creeping thing that creepeth upon the earth."[3] Man thus is strictly the perfection of nature, the crown of its glory, the very centre of its life. In him the world comes to its last, deepest, fullest significance

---

3. [Gen 1:26.]

and sense.⁴ So to some extent even in his mere bodily organization. But far more still in his soul, in his intelligence, in the self-acting power of his will—that higher life of reason, of which only the most dim and remote foreshadowings are to be met with in the lower spheres of creation, but whose appearance here at once proclaims itself to be the central light, that reflects back on every other part of the system its true meaning and form. In such relation simply to the present world, our human intelligence and will, notwithstanding the spirituality which belongs to them in their own character, are to be regarded as appertaining still to the constitution of nature. They are the sublimation of this indeed to its highest potency, its most ethereal quality and sense, and present it thus under a form where to be true to itself it *ought* to pass away in the presence of a higher and more enduring economy; but the sublimation itself, the taking up of the world of nature into the world of mind, is now in and of itself the subjection of it in this way, to the claims and purposes of every such economy above nature. The process may stop with the mere *intellectualization*, so to speak, of the present order of things, the world as it now stands; and then it matters not how far the activity of thought may seem to go, exploring the depths or scaling the heights of God's creation; it matters not with what flights of science or art it may appear even to pass over the boundaries of time and space, and to hold communion in its own way with what it is pleased to denominate the absolute and the eternal, all will remain in the end a revelation of the life of nature merely, and nothing more. The mind of Humboldt, regarded as a mirror simply of the outward world he describes, is of one order with *Cosmos,* whose image it serves so magnificently to reflect.⁵ Mirror, image, and object, belong alike to the sphere of nature, and have to do only with its organization as such. So deep and far-reaching is the relation, by which man belongs to the present world, stands in it, moves in it, finds in it his natural and congenial home. He is the consummation of nature. It unfolds the entire volume of its wealth; it comes to its full efflorescence, only in his person.

But with all this, or rather we may say for this very reason, the life which belongs to him in the order of nature, is for him always something incomplete, a form of existence which manifestly does not find its full and proper end in itself, but needs and seeks this continually in some higher and different constitution of things. In this respect, man differs from the mere animal and the plant. Though the fulness of nature be in him, far more than it is in them, he cannot, like them, rest in it as the whole comprehension of his being. They do so, just because they are less than nature in its full sense. Their existence is rounded in by it on all sides, and made complete after its own kind, in the bosom of the general life by whose stream they are borne. But man

4. [See document 4, "The Wonderful Nature of Man" above.]

5. [Friedrich Wilhelm Heinrich Alexander von Humboldt (1769–1859), German scientist, explorer, and Romantic philosopher, was author of the five-volume *Cosmos* (1845–62), which argued for the harmony, wholeness, and coherence of the universe. Human beings existed in that cosmos and needed to be aware of the universal laws that govern the apparent chaos of the terrestrial world. Human beings should live in harmony with the universe, but they could upset it.]

is himself, as we have just seen, the end of nature, the point where its whole process reaches its ultimate destination. How then should he find in it his own destination or end? The universal constitution of the present world, viewed in its relation to man, carries in it thus a plain intimation that he is formed for a higher sphere of existence, that the life of nature is designed to be in him the beginning only and preparation of a life above nature, and that he can fulfill his destiny only by entering into felt communication with the powers of this *super-natural* life, and by proposing it to himself always as his last object and aim. The world, as a system of nature, completes itself in man, becomes in him a moral world, a world of intelligence and active will, in order simply that it may, through him, become linked, under such form, with another economy far more glorious than itself. Without such object and end, it must be regarded as an insupportable vanity. In itself, it is made up of perpetual revolution and change. The fashion of it is forever passing away. Its best realities are always like a dream or a shadow. It is everywhere an effort after that which is not, a type that labors to express its own sense, an unfulfilled prophecy which struggles towards its accomplishment in something beyond itself. To suppose such an order of things brought to its full conclusion in man's consciousness, made clear to itself here, as it were, in the full perfection of its vanity, without any farther promise or prospect, would be to turn this human consciousness, the high prerogative of reason, into the greatest vanity and most deplorable misery of all. That cannot be the meaning or end of God's natural creation. It looks upward towards man from all sides, not that it may stop there as an eternal irony upon itself, but that by him and through him it may be enabled, as it were, to transcend itself, and to make room thus for a new, higher creation, in which all its transitory show shall be brought finally to an end. Nature reaches its chief purpose and ultimate destination in man, and, in doing so, refuses to be acknowledged as in any way *his* end, but shuts him up rather to the necessity of seeking this in some other order of existence altogether.

And is it necessary to add, that what is in this way continually proclaimed by the general constitution of the world, finds its full echo in the moral nature of man himself? Whatever relation his intelligence and will may bear to the present world as such, they carry in their very constitution at the same time, no less distinctly, a necessary reference also to something beyond this world, to a higher economy, which is felt to extend over it in the form of truth and law, and in which alone is to be sought and found its highest and last end. The human mind, while it forms the natural summit and necessary crown of the whole inferior creation, includes in itself also what surpasses entirely the measure of this creation, capacities, affinities, tendencies, inborn necessities and wants which it has no power to satisfy, and that call continually for that which it does not contain. It is only in virtue of such higher nature indeed, that man is set rightfully over the world, and appointed to rule it for the glory of God; the intelligence that qualifies him for this being in truth a superior order of existence, which places him above the world as well as in it, by reason of what it is in such more than simply natural view. It is only as made in the image of God, that mind in this case is commissioned to exercise dominion over nature and matter; which at once implies, that to be faithful to itself, and true to its high trust, it must hold itself steadily in union with God, and seek in Him always its last destination and end. Thus it is, accordingly, that the soul of man finds it forever impossible to be either wholly or finally satisfied with the present world, and so long as it seeks to be so is tormented continually with a sense of falsehood and vanity. Whatever it may be for inferior orders of life, the present world is not, in any true sense, an end for man, and the attempt to make it so must always be felt as the power of a perpetually living lie, which carries along with it its own damning punishment wherever and however it may prevail. There is no material difference here between one form and another of such a worldly life. It may be rude or refined, grossly sensual or eminently spiritual; all comes to the same thing at last, an overwhelming confirmation of that old experience: "Vanity of vanities—all is vanity and vexation of spirit!"[6] The desires of the mind, as Paul terms them,[7] have no advantage in this respect over the desires of the flesh. Nay, the greatest vanity of all, perhaps, is science, walking among the stars in its own way, and yet never, in fact, transcending the universe of nature, the order of the world as it now stands, by a single act of faith.

[Religion and Conscience]

But it is in the sphere of religion and conscience, especially, that the necessary relation of man's life to an order of things which is above and beyond nature, so far as his own consciousness is concerned, comes most of all into view. Religion has no meaning except as it carries with it a reference always to some order of this sort, and without such reference there could be no place for it in the human spirit. Whether the religion be true or false is of no account as regards this point. What we are concerned with is simply the general idea of religion, the possibility of it in any form. This, of course, is something which lies back of all positive systems, to which the name may be applied. No outward teaching or tradition, no divine revelation, even, could cause religion to exist in any form among men if there were not in them previously a religious nature, a capacity for religion, needing to be called into exercise in this way. Now it is of this general capacity we say, lying, as it does, at the ground of all religions and making them possible, that it carries in it a necessary reference always to an economy which is beyond and above nature, and thus becomes an unanswerable argument, throughout the world, for the truth and importance of the thought we have in hand, namely, that the true end of man's life, his proper destiny, is to be sought in the world to come and not in that which is now present. For the sense of religion, in some form, is as universal as our human nature itself, and forms an inseparable part of its constitution; and it includes in itself everywhere, also, the assurance of its own legitimate authority,

6. [Eccl 1:2, 14: Nevin combines the two verses.]
7. [Eph 2:3.]

Document 11: Man's True Destiny.

and its right to be regarded as a supreme power in the organization of our life. The want it expresses is felt to be the deepest, the end it seeks the most absolute, in the mysterious economy of our being. It is not hypothetically or problematically only, but with full categorical imperative,[8] that the chief end of man is referred here to another world, and that he is required to subordinate to this all other ends as of merely secondary account. Such is the natural testimony of the soul, with regard to its own destination. No force of error or corruption can ever reduce it to silence. It speaks in the individual conscience of every man. It is heard in the religious faith and worship of nations, handed forward as a sacred tradition from one generation to another, deep answering unto deep,[9] as it were, in the vast and mighty abyss of the human spirit, and the voice of ages, like the sound of many waters, uttering itself forever in one and the same awfully solemn tone.

Infidels sometimes make it an argument against the whole idea of a revelation, and so of a strictly supernatural destiny for man, that the organization of nature is complete within itself, and that it offers no room directly for the apprehension or acknowledgment of any higher system. The supernatural as related to the natural must, of necessity, be miraculous; and the miraculous, according to the celebrated sophism of Hume,[10] must ever meet an overwhelming contradiction from the universal experience of our present life, which is conditioned throughout by the constitution of the world as it now stands. In these circumstances, all positive systems of religion, falling back, as they do necessarily, on some supposed revelation, are to be regarded as visionary and false; and still further proof of which may be found in their contradictory character, as well as in the palpable absurdity and immorality by which most of them belie at once their own high claims. These manifold superstitions in the name of religion, monstrous abortions as they are of the human spirit, all pretending to rest on supernatural facts, show only how liable men are to deceive themselves in this direction, and how little weight is to be attached to any such pretension in any quarter. Thus runs, in brief, the sceptical argument. But its show of wisdom is entitled to small respect. It comes, at most, simply to this, that the order of nature is not itself the order of the supernatural, that the second absolutely transcends the first, and that

---

8. [The categorical imperative is at the heart of Immanuel Kant's (1724–1804) moral philosophy: "Act only in accordance with that maxim through which you at the same time can will that it become a universal law." See *Groundwork* (2018), 34 {Ak 4:421}. Here Nevin abstracts from its specifically ethical meaning: if a person is to have any end at all, there must be a "super-natural" end to which all natural ends refer and in which they are grounded. This end is necessary ("imperative") and universal ("categorical").]

9. [Ps 42:7.]

10. [David Hume (1711–76), Scottish empiricist philosopher, argued in Section 10 of his *An Enquiry Concerning Human Understanding* that miracles were a violation of the law of nature and contrary to our contemporary human experiences. For him, it is never reasonable to believe that a miracle has occurred because it is contrary to evidence and our experience. For Nevin, it is true that empirical evidence and reason cannot prove the supernatural, but the world is not confined to the empirical and to reason.]

there is no room, therefore, to conceive of the first as itself producing or demonstrating the second. Most certainly nature includes no provision in its own constitution, as nature merely, for the production or verification of that which is positively above nature. Such want of capacity, however, to go beyond or transcend itself, to be at one and the same time what it is and what it is not, is something very different from the supposition of its being actually at war with all that may be supposed to exist beyond its own sphere. Between the natural and the supernatural in this view, as we have now seen, no such antagonism in fact has place, but just the reverse. The world as it now stands, the cosmos whether of Humboldt or of Kant, has no power, it is true, to affirm supernatural realities in their own proper form; they lie *over* its horizon; but it goes far to show negatively and indirectly their necessity, and to turn the eye of expectation and desire towards the region in which they are found. Time points always towards eternity. Nature cries aloud for that which is higher, greater, and more enduring than itself. The world that now is, with man in the centre of it, is a riddle whose burden can find no relief except in the thought of a world to come. The whole moral and religious side of man's life especially proclaims, with uncontrollable witness, his supernatural destiny, and leads him to acknowledge his relation to the invisible and eternal through all ages and times. It is not true, that the ideas of miracle and revelation do violence to his nature; on the contrary, he feels them to be in full harmony with its inmost wants, and, as it would appear, is unable to live without them indeed in any part of the world. False religions, in this way, are no argument against the truth of religion itself. They only show how deeply seated the idea of religion is in the very constitution of humanity; how irresistibly this looks and tends towards what is beyond the world of nature for its proper completion; and how natural and reasonable it is, therefore, to believe, that provision should be made for the satisfaction of so deep a want in some real way. This universal demand among men for religion in some form, both proves the reality of the supernatural relations on which the whole idea rests, and creates a presumption at the same time, not against, but powerfully in favor of any system which may present itself with the proper credentials of a true revelation.

[Revelation and the Supernatural End]

Such a revelation, it is plain, the whole case requires. The voice of nature, and the testimony of the soul, refer man for the end of his being to another world; but they have no power to set before him the actual realities of this world in their own proper form; their utterances, as we have already seen, are negative rather than positive in their character; and, for this reason, even the truth which they proclaim may be said to be wanting in full security and force. To the solemn question: "Where shall wisdom be found; and where is the place of understanding?" the answer they return is: "Man knoweth not the price thereof; neither is it to be found in the land of the living. The depth saith, It is not in me; and the sea saith, It is not with me. It cannot be gotten for gold, neither shall silver be weighed for the price thereof. It cannot be valued with the gold of Ophir, with the precious onyx, or the sapphire." In other words, the true destiny of man, the proper end of his life, is something which, according to the testimony of the world itself, is not to be found in all that it contains, nor to be represented for a moment by its richest forms of wealth. It belongs to another order of existence altogether. "Destruction and death say, We have heard the fame thereof with our ears." Natural religion points darkly to God, as comprehending in Himself in some way what the case is felt to require, and brings all to the momentous conclusion: "Behold the fear of the Lord, that is wisdom, and to depart from evil, that is understanding." But to give full effect to this conclusion, the voice of revelation must be added to the voice of nature. The supernatural must make itself known, not as a notion or thought merely, but as an actual reality, comprehending in it the very end itself for which man is thus required to live. This has been done, as we know, by the Gospel; which is to be regarded as a single revelation, shining more and more "as a light in a dark place" through the times of the Old Testament, till it burst forth finally with full effulgence in Him who is the "sun of righteousness," who, by the mystery of his incarnation, became himself among men the full manifestation of the truth under a living personal form; who, by his death and resurrection, "brought life and immortality to light," and who now reigns "Head over all things to the Church," a Prince and Saviour at the right hand of God, to give repentance and remission of sins, redemption and eternal salvation, to all who draw near to God in his name. "God, who, at sundry times and in divers manners, spake in time past unto the fathers by the prophets, hath in these last days spoken unto us by his Son."[11]

To say now that this glorious Gospel of the Blessed God places the chief end of man, the only true and proper destination of his life, in an order of things which is above and beyond the present world, is simply to declare what no one in his senses pretends to dispute. The only difficulty is, that the sense and meaning of it in this view are so common, so universally at hand, so much a matter of course, that the thought, by its very familiarity, fails to gain with most persons any distinct attention. Not only is it assumed throughout, that the constitution of nature is destined to pass away, and that the soul of man is formed for eternity; but the ground is everywhere taken, also, that the world, as it now stands, is under a curse, that the relation men hold to it naturally in their present state is the result of an original universal apostacy or fall, by which they have lost their proper relation to God and their right to eternal life, that it is in these circumstances under the power of Satan, and subject to a law of sin and death, and that there is no room, therefore, to conceive of any harmony or agreement between its interests and purposes, in such view, and the true last object of man's creation. All this comes before us abundantly in the general teaching of the Bible; but most of all, with overwhelming emphasis, in the actual life of our Lord

---

11. [The Scriptural texts in this paragraph are, in order, Job 28:12; Job 28:13–16; Job 28:22; Job 28:28; 2 Pet 1:19; Mal 4:2; 2 Tim 1:10; Eph 1:22; Heb 1:1.]

Jesus Christ. In him we see the truth itself, confronted in living form with the fallen world in the midst of which he moved without sin; and in no other way, certainly, could the full sense of what this world is in its relation to our human life generally be so effectually brought home to our minds. He came to seek and to save that which was lost, by conquering death and him that had the power of death, and by revealing or bringing to pass in and through his own person the kingdom of heaven, in which room is made for the complete fulfilment of man's destiny in a higher order of life that shall never come to an end. In calling us to such glory and honor and immortality, the Gospel, in the very nature of the case, requires us to enter into his spirit, to walk in his steps, to propose to ourselves the same supernatural end, and to aim at reaching it by renouncing and forsaking the present world. "Seek ye first," it is said, "the kingdom of God and his righteousness."[12]—"He that seeketh his life, shall lose it."[13] —"The kingdom of heaven is like unto treasure hid in a field, the which when a man hath found he hideth, and for joy thereof goeth and selleth all that he hath, and buyeth that field."— "Be not afraid of them that kill the body, and after that have no more that they can do; but I will forewarn you whom ye shall fear: Fear him, which after he hath killed, hath power to cast into hell; yea, I say unto you, Fear him."—"One thing is needful; and Mary hath chosen that good part, which shall not be taken away from her."—"Sell that ye have, and give alms: provide yourselves bags which wax not old, a treasure in the heavens that faileth not, where no thief approacheth, neither moth corrupteth. For where your treasure is, there will heart be also."—"For what is a man profited, if he shall gain the whole world, and lose his own soul? or what shall a man give in exchange for his soul?"—"Verily, verily, I say unto you, He that heareth my word, and believeth on him that sent me hath everlasting life, and shall not come into condemnation; but is passed from death unto life."—"I am the resurrection and the life: he that believeth in me, though he were dead, yet shall he live; and whosoever liveth and believeth in me shall never die."—"These things have I spoken unto you, that in me ye might have peace. In the world ye shall have tribulation; but be of good cheer; I have overcome the world." These are specimens merely of the way, in which Christ continually enforces the thought, that men are formed for an eternal destiny, and that this is to be reached only through himself as "the way, the truth, and the life,"[14] by giving up this world and living supremely for another. And so throughout the New Testament, the idea of Christianity is made to consist, especially, just in this, that we are saved from the vanity and misery of a simply natural life, and placed in real, felt communication with a life that is supernatural, of which Christ is the source

---

12. [Matt 6:33.]

13. [As worded here, the quotation is not in the Bible. Nevin may be quoting Luke 17:33: "Whosoever shall seek to save his life, will lose it." Or, he may have in mind parallel passages in Luke 9:24, Mark 8:35, or Matt 16:25.]

14. [Beginning with "The kingdom of heaven is like unto treasure . . . ," Scriptural texts are, in order: Matt 13:44; Luke 12:4–5; Luke 10:42; Luke 12:33; Matt 16:26; John 25:24; John 11:25–26; John 16:33; John 14:6.]

and the Holy Ghost the medium, and which carries in it thus the sure guaranty of an everlasting victory over all the powers of sin and death and hell.

The true destiny of man, the grand object and purpose of his existence, being thus not in the present world at all, but in an order of things which is out of it, above it and beyond it, and so in relation to it strictly supernatural, it becomes at once, of itself, plain, that no one can live to purpose, who does not know and acknowledge this end in its own proper character, so as to make it, in reality, the governing power of his life. It is not enough that we have been created for such end; nor yet that we may see and feel the necessity of it, as something beyond this world. The case calls for purpose and will, in view of an object which is known to be real. This comes before us here in the form of a supernatural revelation, brought to its full accomplishment in Christ; and the power by which we are set in actual communication with it, is what we denominate faith, "the substance of things hoped for, the evidence of things not seen."[15] Only where the soul comes to understand its true destination in this way, and is led to regard and follow it with active resolution as a supreme end, can there be room to speak of it as fulfilling, in any measure, the object of its existence. Human life universally must be regarded as a failure, no matter what it may seem to accomplish in any other view, if it be not ordered in harmony thus with its own proper purpose and design, as something which is to be reached in another world and not in the present.

[Wisdom, the End of all Education]

This, then, is the summit of all education, the perfection of knowledge and wisdom, that a man should comprehend and practically pursue the true end of his being, by seeking first the kingdom of God and his righteousness. It is so, not simply from the worth of the object, in itself considered, as weighed against all other interests, but still more immediately, also, because it serves to bring into the soul, at once, order, harmony, light, freedom, and strength, by setting it in right relation to the law of its own life. All things are beautiful and strong in their place, only as they obey the law of their nature, stand in their appointed sphere, and fulfill their original destination; and so man, as made at first in the image of God and formed for immortality, can never be true to himself in any stage of his existence, in any sphere or department of his life, except as he is brought to live supremely for this supernatural end and no other. This is for him emphatically the *truth*, the fundamental reality of things as they are and ought to be, in the apprehension of which as a living fact consists the idea of all *wisdom* rightly so called. For wisdom, as distinguished from mere knowledge or science, has to do with actual life, with truth in its practical relations to the will, as well as in its merely theoretic relations to the understanding; and it necessarily reaches its highest form, accordingly, where it comes to the perception and acknowledgment of what

---

15. [Heb 11:1.]

is in reality the chief end of our life. Hence it is said, that the fear of the Lord, which is only another name for religion, or the practical sense of our relations to God and another world, is the beginning of wisdom; for the simple reason, that here begins, in fact, for man, all apprehension of that which is for him the actual truth of his own nature, and so the true sense and meaning also of the universe to which he belongs. The living sense of this comprehension in an economy which is higher than nature, and the issues of which belong to eternity, carrying along with it the practical submission of the soul to its authority, is literally both the commencement and the perpetual foundation and ground of all right thinking, no less than all right acting, on the part of men, in any and every direction. This is to be in the truth, and so to possess it under its own highest and only complete form, instead of having only the notion or shadow of it in the understanding. Such right posture with regard to the actual order and end of our own being is of more account than any condition besides, for understanding whatever pertains to the welfare and dignity of our life, whether in this world or in that which is to come. "If any man *will* to do my will," our Saviour says,—if it be his mind and purpose to be thus in the truth—"he shall *know* of the doctrine, whether it be of God." And of the same import is that most significant word: "The light of the body is the eye: if therefore thine eye be single, the whole body shall be full of light; but if thine eye be evil, thy whole body shall be full of darkness. If therefore the light that is in thee be darkness, how great is that darkness." All depends on the inward bent and habit of the soul with regard to its own proper destination, whether it be itself in conformity thus with the law of truth, or under the power of a lie. In this last case, the condemnation is, we are told, "that light is come into the world, and men loved darkness rather than light, because their deeds were evil." Their unbelief is simply the result of their wish and determination to make the present world their end and portion. To men of this sort Christ says: "*Because* I tell you the truth, ye believe me not.—He that is of God, heareth God's words; ye *therefore* hear them not, because ye are not of God." The minds of such, according to St. Paul, are blinded by the god of this world, "lest the light of the glorious Gospel of Christ, who is the image of God, should shine unto them;" for which reason the reigning course of this world is said also, in another place, to be "according to the prince of the power of the air, the spirit that now worketh in the children of disobedience." St. John abounds in the same thought. Truth with him is always life. "We know that we are of God," he writes, "and the whole world lieth in wickedness. And we know that the Son of God is come, and hath given us an understanding, that we may know him that is true; and we are in him that is true, even in his Son Jesus Christ. This is the true God and eternal life."[16] To be on the outside of this supernatural system of grace, in which is comprehended the highest relations and interests, and so the highest realities, of the proper life of man, is to be by that very fact involved in all falsehood and error. The error is not a false proposition simply,

---

16. [The Scriptural texts in this paragraph are, in order, John 7:17: "If any man will do his {God's, not my} will"; Matt 6:22; John 3:9; John 8:45–46; 2 Cor 4:4; Eph 2:1; 1 John 5:19–20.]

for the understanding; nor yet a partial mistake only of purpose and practice at some particular point; it embraces the entire man, mind, soul, and body, we may say, and turns his whole existence into a falsehood. He becomes by means of it, and remains continually, a *living personal lie*. What room can there be in a case so dreadful as this, to speak rationally of knowledge, learning, wisdom, under any different form? How can any amount of science and culture avail to redeem from vanity, a life which is thus false throughout to its constitution, and which is itself no better than a hollow dream, and for which in this state the whole world must prove to be at last but shadow and sham? With what depth of meaning the Bible applies to every one, who is under the power of such a false life, the emphatic title *Fool*! All other forms of folly are in truth small, compared with this.

Here indeed is wisdom, the crowning excellency of all education, and of all knowledge and art besides, that a man should be in the truth, and know that which is for him in reality the deepest meaning of the universe, by having it for the very form of his own life. How easy it is to see, that the smallest measure of understanding in this form is of infinitely more worth, than the largest stores of learning or skill in any different view. What shall it profit a man, we may say, though he should know the whole world besides, and have no true knowledge of himself? What truth can there be in any other science or art for him, to whom the "light of life" is wanting in his own soul? We have no right to undervalue education and learning in any direction; and I have no disposition to do so certainly on the present occasion; but we must not shrink still from seeing and owning here what is after all, but the simple truth, namely, that no conceivable amount of such culture can deserve to be placed for one moment in comparison with the inward habit of piety which consists in fearing God and keeping his commandments. Without this, the greatest philosopher is less wise in fact than the unlettered rustic to whom it may belong. The science of the saints is something far more high and glorious than any mere learning of the schools. It has to do with vastly superior objects, moves in loftier and wider regions of thought, and brings into the soul an immeasurably clearer illumination. "The entrance of thy words giveth light, says the Psalmist, "it giveth understanding unto the simple." The revelation of the *Logos*, the Divine Word, by the mystery of the incarnation, "in whom are hid all the treasures of wisdom and knowledge," the most pure and perfect manifestation of truth in the world, was not to teach men the hidden secrets of nature, the laws of matter, the principles of government, or any other knowledge of this sort belonging merely to the present life, but to set them in right relation to God and their eternity; something which for this very reason must be accounted of more consequence than any other kind of knowledge which it is possible for them to possess. "In him was life"—not theory, merely, or outward doctrine—"and the life was the *light* of men," served to bring them into the truth itself under its highest form. "I am the light of the world," our Saviour says accordingly; "he that followeth me, shall not walk in darkness, but shall have the light of life." Such illumination is, of course, practical. There is no separation here between the understanding and the will. Knowledge is at the same time charity; without which, all gifts and accomplishments are pronounced by the apostle Paul to be of no worth whatever. With this comes also true freedom and strength. "If ye continue in my word," Christ says, "ye shall know the truth, and the truth shall make you free."[17] To know, in this case, is to *be* at the same time in what is known; and it is easy enough to see, how such living union with the truth, such settlement and consolidation of the mind, on the true last ground of its own being, where it is set in harmony also with the will of God and the actual order of things, must prove at the same time, its happy emancipation, so far as this right order prevails, from all false authority and power; and how utterly impossible it is, I may add, that liberty should exist at all, or be anything more than an empty chimera, under any other imaginable character and form. And to be thus in the truth, is to be strong also in the only proper and full sense of the word. We often hear it said, that knowledge is power; and this is true to a certain extent, no doubt, of all merely secular knowledge, as related to the ends of the present life. It is more in this respect than money, which is power also in a very high degree. In our own day especially, science rules the earth, and is fast subduing it to the service of secular purposes and ends. But it is after all only where knowledge takes its highest form, in the character of that practical, heavenly wisdom, which consists in understanding and acknowledging the true end of life as something to be found only in God and the eternal world, that it comes to be, at the same time, what is truly comprehended in the idea of power for man. Short of this, all science and art are at best but triumphs of mind over matter, in the sphere of nature itself. What is really needed, however, is that the soul should be brought to surmount the life of nature altogether, to acquire the mastery of itself, and to overcome the world, in the prosecution of its own proper destiny beyond the grave. For every purpose of this sort, all such secular science and art are perfectly powerless. But here precisely comes into view, the true nature and dignity of the power that is comprehended in a practical obedience to the truth as it is in Jesus Christ. Paul is beyond comparison greater than Alexander or Julius Cæsar,[18] "He that is slow to anger is better than the mighty; and he that ruleth his spirit than he that taketh a city."[19] To walk in the Spirit, so as not to fulfil the lusts of the flesh, is more a great deal than to tunnel mountains and bridge vallies [sic], curb the lightning and imprison steam, for the transitory uses of trade. "This is the victory that overcometh the world," says St. John, "even our faith. Who is he that overcometh the world, but he that believeth that Jesus is the Son of God?"[20]

17. [Scriptural texts in this paragraph up to this point are: John 8:12; Ps 119:130; Col 2:3; John 1:4; John 8:12, 32.]

18. [Alexander the Great (356–232 BCE), king of the ancient Greek kingdom of Macedonia, was a military genius who created a vast empire from Macedonia to Egypt and from Greece to part of India. Julius Caesar (100–44 BCE), also a military general, helped to create the vast Roman Empire that would last for centuries.]

19. [Prov 16:32.]

20. [1 John 5:4–5.]

No wonder, that this heavenly wisdom, carrying in it thus the highest perfection of man's life, should be so commended to our regard as it is in the Holy Scriptures, and that such glowing terms should be employed to set forth its praise. The price of it is indeed above rubies. The topaz of Ethiopia cannot equal it, neither may it be valued with pure gold.[21]

> Happy is the man that findeth wisdom, and the man that getteth understanding: For the merchandise of it is better than the merchandise of silver, and the gain thereof than fine gold. She is more precious than rubies; and all the things thou canst desire are not to be compared unto her. Length of days is in her right hand; and in her left hand riches and honor. Her ways are ways of pleasantness, and all her paths are peace. She is a tree of life to them that lay hold upon her; and happy is every one that retaineth her.[22]

[Revelation and Faith]

The whole subject reveals to us the nature, necessity, and value of *Faith*. The chief end of man, the last meaning of his life, is not comprehended in the present order of things, the passing diorama in the midst of which he is here carried forward continually to the grave. It lies in another world, in a system of things which is beyond and above nature, and so beyond the range and reach also of all merely natural understanding and knowledge. To be known and felt at all then, this supernatural economy must be exhibited to us in the form of a Divine revelation; which we are required to accept simply in this character, in order that we may make full proof of its power. Opinion, speculation, dreamy sentiment, in the case, are not enough. The world in question is not made up of negatives simply and abstractions, but of facts, realities, and actual living relations, which need to be apprehended as they are, that we may be saved by the sense of them from the vanity of our present life; and this precisely is what is accomplished for us by faith. Through the word of God, and especially through this word presented to us bodily in the person of our Lord and Saviour Jesus Christ, it sets us in real communication with things unseen and eternal, and makes it possible for us to have such regard to them as we ought, in working out the fearfully solemn problem of life. It is not the product in any way of reason or logic. These so far as they are concerned with natural things, or with the order only of the present world, have no power to reach the supernatural; and so far as they may be capable of being exercised upon this also, *when* known, have no power ever to originate any such knowledge. Facts here, as always, must go before intelligence and thought; and knowledge consequently must follow faith. We see then the nature of this faculty. It is the power of being firmly

---

21. [Job 28:19 refers to the topaz of Ethiopia. Topaz is a precious stone whose brilliant colors are yellow, green, blue, and red. Topaz supposedly brings joy, generosity, abundance, and good health.]

22. [Prov 3:12–18.]

assured, on the testimony of God who cannot lie, that there is such a world of grace and glory as is set before us by the Gospel, not to be seen by mortal eyes, but yet surrounding us at all points, and continually near at hand, in which, and in which only, is to be accomplished the true object and end of our existence. It is the power of acknowledging the supernatural, the miraculous, the real presence of possibilities, and powers, and actual operations, that go beyond all the resources of nature and surmount all its laws, in a new order of life which is made to be actually at hand in the mystery of the Church, through the death, and resurrection, and glorification of the Son of God. On the necessity and importance of this sublime capacity, this faculty of believing realities which transcend and confound sense, more need not be said. The case speaks for itself. If the true end of our life, and so its universal significance and worth, lie not in the present world but in another; and if all wisdom for us be comprehended in the practical perception and acknowledgment of our proper destination in such view; what terms shall sufficiently express the value of faith, the only power on our side by which it is possible for us to burst the confines of time and sense, so as to communicate with what is beyond in a real and not simply imaginary and notional way. In the nature of the case, it is the gift of God; and well does it deserve the title *precious*, applied to it by St. Peter;[23] for it lies at the foundation of all that wisdom, whose price we have already seen to be above comparison, and is the source, in a certain sense, of every grace and perfection for the human soul. Without faith, it is impossible to please God, and in vain also to think of using life to good purpose in any other way. In such condition, man appears necessarily incomplete always, his nature shorn of its proper glory, his mind looking forth upon us at best in dismal and dim eclipse. Let this thought sink deeply into your hearts. It is something greater really and truly to believe the articles of the Apostles' Creed,[24] every one of which is a mystery transcending the whole order of nature, than to know all that is taught in the best colleges and universities of the land. No literary diploma can ever match in honor that word to Peter: "Blessed art thou, Simon Barjona; for flesh and blood hath not revealed it unto thee, but my Father which is in heaven!"[25] Of the same glorious distinction our Saviour speaks, when he says: "I thank thee Father, Lord of heaven and earth, that thou hast hid these things from the wise and prudent, and hast revealed them unto babes!"[26] Well might that great student of Nature, the late Sir Humphry Davy,[27] tired out with her same everlasting response to all the questionings of science, *It is not*

23. [1 Pet 1:7.]
24. [On faith in the Creed, see Nevin, "The Apostles' Creed," MTSS 8:57–65.]
25. [Matt 16:17.]
26. [Matt 11:25.]
27. [Sir Humphry Davy (1778–1829), British scientist and inventor, indicated at the end of his life, according to two biographies published in the 1830s, his desire for a firm faith. Religious newspapers in England, Ireland, and the United States, after reviewing the biographies, commented on Davy's longing for faith. On this, see for example, "Sir Humphry Davy," *Catholic Herald* (Philadelphia), (August 3, 1837) 242. See also Paris, *Life of Sir Humphry Davy*, and Davy, *Memoires of the Life.*]

in me! It is not with me![28] make the memorable declaration towards the close of his life, that he envied no man any other possession whatever, such as wealth, learning, or worldly distinction, but would cheerfully give all for the one simple privilege of being able to believe firmly and steadily the realities of another world. That indeed is something better than all knowledge, and power, and riches, and glory besides.

[The Aim of Liberal Education]

You need this habitual, practical sense of the supernatural, that you may not walk in darkness and miss the true end of life, regarded as a purely private and personal interest. But you need it no less, in order that you may be able rightly to understand the living world around you, and so be prepared to act a right part in it in your generation. No man is at liberty to live simply and only for himself. Least of all, we may say, is he at liberty to do so, on whom God, in his providence, has been pleased to bestow special gifts and powers, especially in the way of education. You have not been educated for yourselves alone, nor mainly, but for the use and service of others. The very idea of a liberal education forbids the thought of its being devoted merely to selfish purposes and ends, under the low base form particularly which these carry with them for the most part in the present world. It is degraded, profaned, and made grossly vulgar and illiberal, by every association of this sort. But to live for the world really and to purpose, we must have clearly before our minds its true constitution, the actual meaning of it, the fundamental law of its being, its absolute destination and end; just what we need, in one word, in the case of our separate personal life, that it may be ordered wisely and with effect. Self-knowledge here, and the knowledge of the world, condition each other, and go hand in hand together. If we look at the human world simply as a natural organization, a system of existence whose meaning and end hold mainly in the present life, our interest in it, our care for it, our devotion to its service, will assume necessarily a corresponding form. We shall lose our thoughts and calculations altogether in the sense of its temporal relations, and can hardly fail to make all at last of simply material interests. But if this hypothesis be in itself completely false, as we know that it must be in fact if Christianity be more than a dream; if it be certain that the chief end and last destination of the human race, collectively taken, as well of the single man, is *not* in the order of nature at all, but in a strictly supernatural economy which holds above and beyond this; then must all such thinking and acting as are conditioned by that other false and wrong supposition be themselves false also, not according to the actual truth of things, and so of comparatively no worth in the end. We must have firm faith in the invisible and eternal world, in the grand and glorious mysteries of the Christian creed, in order that we may have any firm position, or any

---

28. [The two statements are in response to Job's question (Job 28:12–14) "Where shall wisdom be found?"]

sure and safe judgment, or any power of right speech and action, in our relations to the present world.

And especially may this be regarded as necessary, Young Gentlemen, for the particular period and time, in which you are called to live.

[The Present Age]

We hear much said, in glorification of the present age. It is fashionable in certain quarters, to speak of it as the perfection of all ages, and to magnify the spirit of it as better and greater than the spirit of any other period that has ever yet been known in the world. It is glorified as an age of knowledge, of freedom, of rapidly advancing civilization. It is an age of vast action and talk; an age of astonishing discoveries and inventions; an age in which the arts of peace are everywhere successfully cultivated, giving rise to visions of outward prosperity that never entered formerly into the human mind. It is an age of progress and reform, big with the idea of its own mission to rehabilitate man in the possession of his natural rights, and to bring to an end all sorts of political oppression and abuse. In no part of the world, moreover, may it be said to be more at home, than just here in America. The genius of the age is emphatically the genius of this rising republic. Here it reigns on all sides with a power that seems to carry all before it, and which it is considered for the most part, a privilege to honor and obey. Happy, as the song runs, is the young man, who enters upon life, on American soil, in the middle of the nineteenth century! He has only to yield himself to the genius of the country, and the spirit of the age, that he may live to purpose and do well. Let him only spread out his canvass boldly and broadly to these favoring gales; they will waft his bark happily over the sea of life, and bring it finally to its right end.

Never was there, however, under such plausible form, a more perfect delusion.[29] The age is *not* thus infallible and safe. On the contrary, it is made up, to a terrible extent, beyond most ages that have been, of falsehood and error, sophistry and sham. This becomes evident, just as soon as we bring the strong light of eternity to bear upon it, by making earnest with the thought, that man is formed for a supernatural destiny, and for the accomplishment of this requires a real redemption, that shall deliver him from the power of this present evil world, and engage him to follow after life and immortality in another. The spirit of the age is always at war in reality with the actual truth of things, as we find this exhibited in the Gospel and in the Church; there is a necessary contradiction between this world ('ο αιων του κοσμου τουτουο[30] —the present *seculum*) and the kingdom of God; the course of the world is in and of itself "according to the Prince of the power of the air, the spirit that now worketh in the children of disobedience"[31]—in all those, namely, who do not submit themselves with

---

29. [Compare Nevin's skepticism here to his optimism in document 1 above, "The Year 1848."]
30. [Trans. "the age of this world."]
31. [Eph 2:2.]

the *obedience of Faith* to the mystery of salvation in Christ. But it is peculiar in some measure to our time, that the world in its own order affects to be itself now the very form in which the true ends and purposes of Christianity are to be reached. The spirit of the age, directly or indirectly, seeks to pass itself off as an angel of light, "flying in the midst of heaven, and having the everlasting Gospel to preach unto them that dwell on the earth, to every nation, and kindred, and tongue, and people."[32] In its general character, however, it remains just what the same power has always been over against the true kingdom of Christ. It has no faith in the supernatural; except as this may be brought to resolve itself into some sort of gnostic abstraction or dream; in which form it professes to hold it in high account, taking credit to itself in so doing for its own spirituality. But its spirituality, alas, ends always in mere spiritualism, the working of the simply natural mind pretending to soar above its own sphere of the flesh, but never getting out of it in fact. For the *Spirit*, in the sense of the Gospel, the supernatural under a real form, the mystery of the creed and of the Church, this eminently spiritualistic spirit of the age has no sense or organ whatever. It eschews all that, and holds it in abomination. This notion of the real presence of supernatural powers in the Christian Church for supernatural ends, involving as it does, necessarily, the subordination of the whole order of nature to a higher economy that can be apprehended only by faith, is precisely that which it has no power to endure; and the presence of which, wherever it may come seriously into view, proves always to be for it like the touch of Ithuriel's spear,[33] causing it to start up instantly in its true antichristian shape. However bland, liberal, and sweet, it can show itself towards the Christian profession, so long as this may be content to walk arm in arm with it in the fellowship of merely secular interests and aims, such as useful knowledge, general education, good government, humanitarian philanthropy, and all sorts of moral reform, the whole case is at once changed the moment it is presumed in any quarter to make earnest with realities, which are supposed to reach into another world. Then your bland liberal is at once converted into an intolerant fanatic. If it were Mohammedanism, Mormonism, anything else under the sun, he could bear it and have some patience with it; but to be confronted in such style with what claims to be the actual presence of the supernatural as a real force in the world, having to do with the last and highest destination of men in another life, is more than he finds it possible for a wise man to endure—especially in the middle of the nineteenth century. It is to revive the superstition of the Middle Ages; to turn religion into mechanism and mummery; to open the door for priestcraft and spiritual despotism; to own a power on earth above civil government and the sovereignty of the State, which in this case, moreover, is generally taken to resolve itself

---

32. [Rev 14:6.]

33. [John Milton's *Paradise Lost*, Book 4, lines 810–13. Ithuriel was an angel who found Satan squatting like a toad, close to Eve's ear, and transformed him by a touch of his spear into his proper form. For Nevin, the Gospel is like Ithuriel's spear, transforming falsehood into truth, making those who hear the Gospel aware of who they truly are.]

finally into the sovereignty of the people. It is at once treason thus to the sacred cause of freedom, popular rights, political economy, and modern civilization generally; and so far as it prevails must serve to keep back the millennium of the world's regeneration under this temporal and natural order, God only can tell how long. Does not the spirit of the age do well to be angry with pretensions, which thus stultify its highest wisdom and turn the whole pride of its life into open shame? If there be any truth in these pretensions, it stands convicted of being a wholesale universal lie; and to save itself from this, being secretly conscious in fact of its own falsehood, it has no alternative but to retort the charge on the source from which it proceeds, and then to rage and storm, calumniate and misrepresent, as it best can, for the purpose of giving it effect.

Tried in this way, the spirit of the present period is easily enough found to be predominantly set on natural interests and ends, as the chief purpose of man's life, to the exclusion of such as are supernatural. It is rationalistic, humanitarian, politico-economical. Religion itself is required by it to officiate in the service of the flesh, and eternity is made to stoop obsequiously to the behests of time. For the realities of faith are substituted the spectral phantoms of opinion—or the dismal *irony,* shall we call it, of demoniacal delusions. Materialism bears rampant rule on all sides. The true victory over the world for man, is held to be more and more, not by any such supernatural process of the Spirit as was dreamed of by saints and martyrs of the olden time, but by mastering the elements of nature, multiplying machinery, promoting the facilities of commerce and trade, and making the earth to serve, as widely as possible, the comfort and well-being simply of the present life. Man is held practically, if not in set theory, to be sufficient for his own ends, without the intervention of any higher help than that which is offered to him in his natural constitution. What he is supposed to need, is education, general knowledge, proper room for the exercise of his rights, the benefit especially of republican institutions, and the practice of the natural virtues in the name of religion. Secular ends, temporal interests, the judgments of the merely natural mind in the form of reigning fashion and opinion, are made the standard of truth, and applied as a measure even to the contents of revelation itself. In all directions the most solemn points of faith and duty are settled by principles and maxims, which overthrow the idea altogether of any positive authority in the world that is higher than the world itself. Religion ceases thus to be the daughter of the skies, and loses her holy mission in what must be considered at best, enthusiasm for a simply earthly ideal.[34]

Striking and most truly instructive exemplification of this was presented not long since, when the spirit of the age seemed to find for a moment among us a fit avatar in

---

34. [Increasingly over the next decade, Nevin would pronounce his aversion to contemporary "naturalism" and "humanitarianism," the belief that scientific knowledge and technology would create a better world and remove the sources of human suffering. Nevin, "Jesus and the Resurrection," 151–52 and Nevin, "The Spiritual World," 517-19.]

Document 11: Man's True Destiny.

the form of *Louis Kossuth*,[35] who appeared on our shores as a martyr of the Hungarian rebellion, and a representative of the general cause of revolutionary liberty throughout Europe. It is still but as it were the other day, since the ears of the whole nation were stunned with the noise of his presence, as he passed from one part of the country to another, in a sort of grand triumphal procession, the cynosure, seemingly, of all eyes and the idol of all hearts. Seldom indeed has the delirium of man-worship been carried to a more ridiculous and fulsome extent. His words were received as oracles of wisdom; his oriental bombast was taken for the inspiration of a prophet. To speak against him, or even to be ominously silent in his praise, was held to be little less than blasphemy towards God and treason to the dearest rights and interests of man. For was *he* not the incarnation of the holy cause of freedom, a full living personification of the glorious conception of man's destiny, which forms the very life and soul of the modern revolutionary spirit throughout the world? And did he not invoke besides the authority of the Bible, the genius of Christianity itself, as in full unison with his own mission and cause? Was he not a preacher of righteousness to the nations, and a new Messiah sent forth for their redemption and salvation? Why then should he not be worshipped and glorified, like Diana of the Ephesians, or the colossal image set up by Nebuchadnezzar on the plain of Dura![36] So for a time, as we all know, the furor ran. It was a perfect *stampede*, not of dumb cattle, but of rational and civilized men; which, however, like all stampedes, was doomed soon to come to an end. The practical tact, and sound common sense, of the nation, acted upon by a quick apprehension also, no doubt, of its own material interests, came in due time to its relief, and power to see, finally, that it had been playing the fool. Then its idol was suffered to fall silently into contempt; and before the end of a single year took its departure, under the metamorphosis of "Mr. Alexander Smith," without so much of a *Good bye sirs!* as even to pay its landlady's bill. But after all, the main significance of humbug, regarded as a mirror of the reigning mind of the age, cannot be said to be overthrown by this explosion; for the explosion was not the result properly of any insight into the essential falsehood of the idea which Kossuth represented, but came to pass rather through considerations

---

35. [Louis Kossuth (1802-92), according to Nevin, was perceived by many Americans as an incarnate deity (Hindu avatar). Kossuth was president or governor of Hungary during the revolutionary years 1848-49, but the Hungarian revolution was crushed by the Hapsburg monarchy in 1849 and Kossuth was imprisoned in Turkey. The United States government intervened to free him and have him brought to the United States, where he arrived on December 5, 1849. After several speeches across the country and a successful fund-raising campaign, he departed from New York on July 15, 1852. He was welcomed in the United States as a revolutionary and freedom fighter, but his use of funds for personal and military purposes made him somewhat of a *persona non grata* among those Americans who followed him closely and he was forced to leave the country secretly. See Kossuth and Varady, *Life of Governor Louis Kossuth.*]

36. [Diana (as she is named in the KJV) or Artemis was the goddess of chastity, hunting, wild animals, forests, childbirth, and fertility. On Diana, see Acts 19:24-35. Dura was the name of the plain on which Nebuchadnezzar, king of Babylon, set up a golden image which all his subjects were ordered to worship. See Dan 3:1-6.]

of expediency and interest which were connected with it only in an accidental way. It was Yankee cunning, more than Christian principle, that turned the scale at last in favor of conservatism and common sense. His doctrine of "intervention" was found to be practically impolitic and unsafe; and so it was voted out of good company, and may be considered, for the present, as having gone its way. But the principle of it, the pretended Divine right of rebellion and revolution, the demoniacal idea that the people may upset all governments at their pleasure which do not happen to square with their own notions of liberty, has not been denounced as a general thing even by those who have taken most credit to themselves for opposing the use which it has been attempted to make of it in this way; and what is worst of all, the true relation of the whole affair to Christianity, would seem to remain still as much as ever out of view.

This is indeed deplorable. The political nonsense of the demonstration was as nothing, in comparison with the wrong it did to the religion of Jesus Christ; and until this be generally seen and felt, we have full right to refer to it as a picture, which is still of force to illustrate the subject now in hand—the wrong position, namely, and false spirit of the age, as tried by the supernatural standard of the Gospel.

It will be borne in mind, that a very active disposition was shown, on the part of the Protestant religious press generally and of the so called *evangelical* ministry in our leading cities, to identify the cause and spirit of the Hungarian chief with the very soul of Christianity itself. His notion of liberty was taken to be of one and the same order precisely with the freedom that is preached in the New Testament. "His "brotherhood of nations" and "solidarity of humanity," were allowed to represent in good earnest the last aim of Christianity in the present world, as well as to overshadow completely its higher regards to another. Nothing could be clearer than the fact, that with him all faith in the invisible and eternal was the merest naturalism, and nothing more; that he saw in the Bible at best but a code of high moral maxims, capable of being turned to good account by the natural reason of men for social and particular ends; that socialistic or humanitarian philanthropism made up his whole conception of Christian charity; and that he was of one mind substantially, in his view of man's destiny, and of the problem of the world, with Ledru Rollin, Mazzini,[37] and the leaders generally of the Red Republican movement in Europe.[38] In no one of his speeches, was

---

37. [Alexandre Auguste Ledru-Rollin (1807–74) was a French lawyer, politician and one of the leaders of the French Revolution of 1848. Giuseppe Mazzini (1805–72) was an Italian lawyer, politician, and journalist who spearheaded the Italian revolutionary movement to unify all of Italy under a single government. During the European revolutionary years (1848–49) he went to Rome (in March 1849), where Italian revolutionaries had declared the city a republic. In Rome, he joined the newly established republican government. However, French troops invaded Rome and removed the Italian revolutionaries from power. Mazzini then departed from Rome in July 1849.]

38. It would seem to need only the most ordinary spiritual discernment, to see and feel the truth of this general charge in all his speeches. [On the speeches, see Kossuth and Varady, *Life of Governor Louis Kossuth*.] They are animated throughout by a spirit of Paganism, without the slightest tinge of Christianity. His memorable prayer, at the grave of the Magyar heroes who fell in the battle of Rapoylna, may stand as a fit monument of his mind in this respect. It runs thus:—"Almighty Lord!

Document 11: Man's True Destiny.

there expressed a particle of reverence for the Word made Flesh or for the mystery of the Holy Catholic Church. And yet in spite of all this, nay it might seem on the very strength of it, he was urged and encouraged from all sides to claim for his cause the special sympathy of heaven, and to consider himself a sort of living commentary on the inmost sense of the Gospel, as well as a martyr and confessor for its truth before the eyes of the whole civilized world. A little clap-trap in glorification of the Bible and Private Judgment, some show of respect for the Sabbath, (too thin to wear any time) the compliment of attending church occasionally, (where he was not unlikely to have his ears tickled with something preached or *prayed* in his own praise) all joined with everlasting changes rung on the hackneyed and unmeaning themes of liberty, human rights, universal brotherhood, and the power of the world, if it were only let alone to govern and save itself, was enough, it seemed, and more than enough, to steal away the senses of his undiscerning religious admirers, and to gull them into the belief that he was a sort of hero and saint combined, who had been raised up specially by God to usher in a new era for Protestantism and *Evangelical* Christianity on both sides of the Atlantic. His interpretations of Scripture, generally flat enough, were listened to as though they were felt to drop from the skies. He was able, it appeared, to teach our divines theology, as well as our senators wisdom. Sayings and sentences from his lips on the subject of religion, now happily forgotten, were caught up as apothegms or gnomes pregnant with celestial wisdom, and sent whizzing and blazing like so many fire-balls through the length of the land. It was not enough for the religious papers to praise, laud, and bless his name, from week to week. Pulpits, in many cases, became profane and churches were desecrated, for the same end. Clerical delegations, in New York, Philadelphia, Baltimore, Washington City, Pittsburgh, Cincinnati, press into his presence for the very purpose of flattering his vanity, assuring him of their hearty sympathy, and bidding him God-speed in his revolutionary counsels and designs; and he is allowed, on the other hand, openly to accept these congratulatory addresses, as a formal sanction given in the name of religion, by its supposed authorized exponents,

---

God of the warriors of Arpad! look down from thy starry throne upon thy imploring servant, from whose lips the prayer of millions ascends to thy heaven, praising the unsearchable power of thine Omnipotence. O God, over me shines thy sun, and beneath me repose the relics of my fallen heroic brethren; above my head the sky is blue, and under my feet the earth is dyed red with the holy blood of the children of our ancestors. Let the animating beams of thy sun fall here, that flowers may spring up from the blood, so that these hulls of departed beings may not moulder unadorned. God of our fathers, and God of the nations! hear and bless the voice of our warriors, and let the arm and the soul of brave nations thunder to break the iron hand of tyranny, as it forges its chains. As a freeman I kneel on these fresh graves: by the remains of my brothers. By such a sacrifice as theirs, thy earth would be consecrated, were it all stained with sin. O God! on this holy soil, above these graves, no race of slaves can live. O Father! Father of our fathers! mighty over myriads! Almighty God of the heaven, the earth, and the seas! from these bones springs a glory whose radiance is on the brow of my people. Hallow their dust with thy grace, that the ashes of my fallen heroic brethren may rest in peace! Leave us not, great God of battles! In the holy name of the nations, praised be Thy Omnipotence! Amen." [This prayer was endlessly reprinted by American newspapers and journals. For one example, see "European Affairs," 46.]

to his whole character and mission and doctrine *(intervention* hobby and all) as being in full accordance with the genius of Christianity, and in all respects true to the mind of its glorious and adorable Founder. Doctors of Divinity, and grave Professors of Theology figured, among others, in these demonstrations, and helped as they could, to give them solemnity and eclat.[39] If Kossuth was not convinced of his own title to be regarded as an apostle of the last and deepest sense of Christianity for the men of the Nineteenth Century, it was not the fault, certainly, of those who thus threw themselves as the representatives of American piety in his way. They did all that could be well asked, to help him to this conclusion.

Now the misery of all this is, not just that so vast a blunder should have been committed in the name of religion, but that our religion should have been capable at all of being deceived, to so great an extent, in such gross way—and still more, that there should seem to be, even to this hour, so little sense of the true nature of the mistake. It is with the *ideal* which Kossuth was made for the moment to enshrine, far more than with the passing form of the shrine itself, that we are here concerned; and looking at this, we find occasion enough in the case for the most painful and gloomy reflection. What must we think of a Christianity, arrogating to itself the highest character of evangelical purity and truth, which could so easily and readily find what it took for its own image in the principles and pretensions of such a man! It was bad enough that he should be compared with Washington. But to make him a representative of the doctrine and spirit of Jesus Christ, to accept his rhodomontade[40] about liberty, and philanthropy, and human rights, for the faith and charity which were preached by St. Paul, the lofty morals of St. Peter, or the divine breathings of St. John; to see in the *Gospel according to Kossuth* the likeness, to hear in it the echo of that glorious creed for which the martyrs and confessors suffered in ancient times: how shall we rightly characterize an infatuation so monstrous as this, or how shall we explain it so as to save the honor and credit of the cause that could be carried away by it to so lamentable an extent! Alas, the religious spirit of the age, as it reigns generally in our evangelical sects, could not have been thus egregiously imposed upon by so transparent a falsehood, (the demon of radicalism in such gossamer guise) if it were not itself deeply and sadly infected with the power of the same lie. This is the portentous meaning of the transaction, which it well becomes every thoughtful mind to lay seriously to heart; and it is for the lesson it carries in it under such view, that I have considered it proper to hold it up for contemplation on the present occasion. May you be able to understand it well, and to bear it hereafter properly in recollection.

---

39. [Charles Hodge of Princeton was one of the theologians who supported Kossuth. On February 16, 1852, he wrote his brother and reported: "Kossuth is beyond question one of the greatest men of the age, whatever may be thought of his history and principles. And as to his principles, I do not believe there is one good and sensible man in a hundred who doubts their soundness." Hodge, *The Life of Charles Hodge*, 395.]

40. ["Vain boasting; empty bluster." Webster, *American Dictionary*, 709.]

Document 11: Man's True Destiny.

If you would understand your duty to the world, and be able to live for it to any purpose in your generation, it is necessary, first of all, that you should cultivate a firm and steady faith in the reality of its supernatural relations, and have regard continually to the destiny of man as formed for a higher state of existence. The great error of the age consists just in this, that it is not willing to acknowledge these relations except in a simply nominal way, and is led thus to ascribe to merely natural interests and secular ends, as connected with human life, an importance which does not belong to them in fact. This is done to a great extent in the name of religion itself; which is then always confounded more or less with zeal for such subordinate purposes and aims, while its own proper ends are in the same degree thrown into the shade. But no estimation of interests which belong only to this world, can ever be according to truth, or deserve to be relied upon practically, which is not conditioned by an active regard at the same time to the eternal destiny of men as that which is for them of supreme account. Nay, such lower interests, we may say, thus dissociated in thought from man's chief end, become in fact themselves false, take the form not unfrequently of demoniacal delusions, and are entitled to no enthusiasm whatever. Nothing can be more hollow and fallacious, for this reason, than much of the declamation we hear about education, useful knowledge, liberty, free institutions, and the right of self-government, as though such privileges in the order of nature were to be regarded as in and of themselves the first thing needful for humanity, or might be allowed to rule and control the idea of its destiny in every higher view. Learn to hold all such declamation at its true value. Learn to distinguish well here, between the wisdom which comes from above, and that which is only from beneath. Have courage to see and own the truth. Socialism is not Christianity. It is not the design of the Gospel to subvert thrones and create republics. Secular ends are of just and right force, only as they are held in practical subordination to such as are supernatural and eternal; and they fall over necessarily to the dominion of Satan, the god of this world and the father of lies, wherever this proportion ceases to be observed. The smallest measure of faith is of more value, than any amount of useful knowledge. Education is no blessing, but only a curse to society, if it be not based upon religion, and animated throughout by the sense of its supreme authority in some positive form. Godless schools and colleges, Godless arts and sciences, as well as Godless political and social institutions generally, carrying in them a relation simply to the present world and its wants, and virtually ignoring the claims of another, deserve the abhorrence, and should excite the apprehension and fear of all good men. Not to see and feel all this, is itself a species of infidelity, which opens the way for the very worst disorders and mistakes. It is to set the natural practically above the supernatural; which is to deny in fact the reality of the last altogether. It is to make humanity in and of itself, as it now stands, sufficient for its own ends; which is such a lie as overthrows the whole Gospel, and necessarily turns into caricature all truth besides, by forcing it into false relations and proportions. Hence the universal affinity in which this style of thinking is found to stand with all sorts of rationalistic speculation, sectarian fanaticism, radicalism, socialism, and wild revolutionary republicanism of the most openly anti-christian stamp. Here we have in truth the veritable *Antichrist*[41] of the present age. Learn to know him, and to be aware of his devices. If you are to live wisely for your generation, it will depend much, very much, on this one counsel well kept in mind.

[Seek the Kingdom of God and His Righteousness]

Finally, to return again in conclusion, to what is more directly personal in the application of our theme, let me exhort you all to be true to your own proper destination, by seeking first, each one of you, for himself, the kingdom of God and his righteousness. As it was said once by a distinguished artist, to account for the pains he took with his work, *I paint for eternity;*[42] so let it be your care also, to live seriously and earnestly, not for the world, which is now rapidly passing away, but for that which is to come. Look not at things which are seen and temporal, but at things which are not seen and eternal. Lay yourselves out to know God, to serve Him in the Gospel of his Son Jesus Christ, and to enter at last into the rewards of his heavenly kingdom. Do not count yourselves unworthy of eternal life. Let no man take from you your crown[43]—the crown of glory and immortality to which you are called by the Gospel, and which has been purchased for you by the death and resurrection of the Son of God. Here is an object worthy of your highest ambition and most active zeal, in comparison with which the most dazzling visions of glory in this world are of as little worth as so much dust or chaff. Let it not be to you as a tale only that is told, or as an empty dream. Seek to have firm faith in the grand and glorious mysteries of the Christian Creed, as realities which are to you of infinitely greater account than all events and facts besides. Be not satisfied, in a case of such unutterable consequence, with faint impressions and feeble purposes and aims. Meditate on your own supernatural destiny. Think much of the vanity of the world, the shortness of life, the certainty of death, and the solemn retributions of the world to come.[44] It has been well said, that the thought of eternity, brought home to the soul from day to day, is for every man the thought of all thoughts, which, if it do not make him wise, must show him to be mad. It is a whole volume of wisdom compressed into a single word. Read it much, I charge you, and study it well. Read it especially in the light of the simple, but unspeakably sublime annunciation: "God so loved the world, that he gave his only begotten Son, that whosoever believeth in him

---

41. [Nevin had come to associate "antichrist" with American sectarianism (instead of the older Protestant identification of it with Roman Catholicism). See *Antichrist*, MTSS 5:177–237. He now extends that to the conflation of religion with social and political improvement.]

42. [The saying is attributed to Apelles of Kos (fl. fourth century BCE), the renowned painter of ancient Greece.]

43. [Paraphrase of Rev 3:11.]

44. [Nevin might have been thinking of his own sense of imminent mortality. See Appel, *Life*, 439, 723.]

should not perish, but have everlasting life." Read it through the living commentary of that illustrious cloud of witnesses, apostles, prophets, martyrs, confessors, saints of all ages and climes, whose faith has already received its reward and who now from their heavenly seats look down upon you with unceasing interest, and kindly beckon you to follow them in the path by which they have been themselves conducted to eternal glory. Read it above all at the foot of the Cross, where in the person of Him who is the Truth and the Life, nailed upon it, crowned with thorns, covered with his own blood, and overwhelmed with reproach and contempt, the true sense of this world and the true sense of the next, the nothingness of the one and the infinite importance of the other, are brought into view as they could be by no representative besides. "Consider him that endured such contradiction of sinners" and "arm yourselves likewise with the same mind," that you may run the race of life with faith and patience to its proper goal, and receive at last the victor's palm and crown. "Whatsoever a man soweth, that shall he also reap: for he that soweth to his flesh, shall of the flesh reap corruption; but he that soweth to the Spirit, shall of the Spirit reap life everlasting."[45]

---

45. [Concluding Scriptural texts: John 3:16; Heb 12:3; 1 Pet 4:1; Gal 6:7–8.]

Document 12

"Natural and Supernatural"

Editor's Introduction

Nevin's 1859 review and response to Horace Bushnell's (1802–76) *Nature and the Supernatural* (1858) reflected theological issues that Nevin had been developing within his Pennsylvania German Reformed community since the 1840s.[1] Bushnell's theology came out of a very different Puritan New England context. Bushnell had been educated at Yale, under the tutelage of the Congregationalist minister and theologian Nathaniel William Taylor (1786–1858), who had rejected a Calvinist understanding of inherent depravity and accepted much of the new evangelicalism of the early nineteenth century. After graduating from Yale, Bushnell became pastor of North Church in Hartford, Connecticut, in 1833 and remained as pastor for the next twenty-six years, retiring in 1859 because of poor health. He was a prolific and creative pastoral theologian whose theology led the way in the United States to the liberal Protestant theology at the end of the nineteenth century. In 1847, Nevin called him "one of the most distinguished preachers in New England" when he reviewed Bushnell's *Discourses on Christian Nurture* (1847).[2]

Bushnell grew up in a New England context where the theological battles among Universalists, Unitarians, and Calvinists had been going on for some time. The issues among them, too, were foundational for understanding Christianity: e.g., the doctrines of the Trinity, Christology, grace and human nature, issues that were under attack and were either reasserted in traditional language or were reconceptualized to meet the rise of a modern democratic society. The radical and apparently irreconcilable divisions were complicated in the 1830s by the rise of New England Transcendentalism, Charles Grandison Finney's (1792–1875) revivalism, and the social and moral issues over slavery. In this context, Bushnell tried to reinterpret traditional Calvinist doctrines in light of the criticisms raised by Taylor, Unitarians, and others. He wanted

1. Nevin, "Natural and the Supernatural," 176–210.
2. Bushnell, *Discourses on Christian Nurture*; Nevin, "Educational Religion," MTSS 6:38.

Document 12: "Natural and Supernatural"

to retrieve a sense of the traditional Calvinist doctrines without accepting the language and traditional theological framework in which the doctrines had previously been articulated.

Nevin's review of Bushnell's *Nature* reiterated some of the same themes that he had earlier considered in response to *Christian Nurture*, as was evident in the General Introduction. Nevin praised Bushnell for bringing forth with skill and intelligence the "religious life question of the age" (the relationship between nature and the supernatural), an issue that had been neglected in theological literature in the United States.[3] The Mercersburger concurred with many of Bushnell's major arguments, but he also had significant disagreements. Nevin agreed, for example, with Bushnell that the current tendency to rationalism and naturalism undermined a correct understanding the relationship between nature and the supernatural. Rationalism and naturalism, Nevin asserted, would lead eventually to the destruction of Christianity, make it "purely nominal" or a "baptized Paganism." The current tendency to rationalism was evident to Nevin in attempts to make Christianity conform to nature, or to draw it down to poetry and myth, or to make it easily understandable or acceptable by dressing it up "in evangelical modes of speech," and finally by ignoring "positive Christianity" as a supernatural and authoritative reality.[4]

What was particularly valuable in Bushnell's approach, according to Nevin, was his insistence on the organic relationship between nature and the supernatural and his understanding that the supernatural was based on the centrality of the person of Jesus Christ and the glorious fact of the Incarnation.[5] Bushnell's attempt to link the natural and the supernatural into one system of thought and reality was a particular benefit of his thesis. Christ's life, as an abiding fact, when joined to the general life of the world, united both nature and supernature organically into one system. The divine economy embraces both the natural and the supernatural. That economy is "no product of nature plainly, and yet in such harmony with it, that it shall seem to be at the same time its full outbursting glory and necessary perfection."[6] The supernatural and the natural in history, although united, are distinct one from the other, the one being superior to the other.

Although Nevin and Bushnell shared a common Romantic and Protestant Reformed tradition, they were miles apart in their understandings of these traditions as Nevin made clear in his review. Four major issues separated Nevin from Bushnell: their understandings of what constituted nature and the supernatural; the origin of evil; Christology; and the church. Bushnell had defined nature as that which worked within the chain of cause and effect and the supernatural as the freedom from that chain. The supernatural, Bushnell held, worked on nature from outside that connection

---

3. Nevin, "Natural and the Supernatural," 176–210, quote at 176, 177.
4. Nevin, "Natural and the Supernatural," 178–79.
5. Nevin, "Natural and the Supernatural," 184.
6. Nevin, "Natural and the Supernatural," 189,

and brought about what nature itself could not bring about. Bushnell, according to Nevin, had too restrictive an understanding of both nature and the supernatural. For Nevin, nature was much more than the physical causes and effects; it included the entire moral order of the human condition, with free will and intelligence. In contrast, Bushnell's conception of the supernatural gave it a "most familiar every day character" because it became part of "our own personality" with its intelligence and free will, and did not operate within the physical law of causes and effects. Nevin however held that the supernatural was not just the divine freedom from the course of natural cause and effect, but a power "under an objective form, to perfect" human existence to a higher life.[7]

Nevin also found Bushnell's understanding of the origin of evil defective. Nevin admitted that the origin of evil was indeed a "great mystery," but Bushnell's theory, like that of Calvin's supralapsarianism, ultimately ran into a "Manichean notion of sin with a corresponding Gnostic conception of redemption."[8] In the end, too, Bushnell's interpretation did not agree with the Bible nor with the old doctrine of the church. Although Bushnell made it clear, as traditional Christianity held, that there was no positive ground or cause of sin in human nature and that the Fall was indeed the result of Adam and Eve's free choice, he also asserted that the lapse into sin was certain. For Bushnell sin was a necessary transitional phase because free choice suffered from what he called the privative conditions. "Condition privative" he defined as "a moral state that is only inchoate, or incomplete, lacking something not yet reached, which is necessary to the probable rejection of evil."[9] For Nevin, Bushnell's concept of original sin emerged from the "very constitution of the world itself" or from "natural creation."[10] Consequently, according to Nevin, Bushnell made sin an inevitable condition of the moral order of freedom and deliberation, making it difficult, it seems to me, to understand how such a condition could make humans responsible for sinning and the creator freed from being the author of sin.[11]

According to Nevin, Bushnell's Christology, moreover, was incomplete because it failed to represent the "full significance of the Incarnation in the broad organic view."[12] Bushnell rightfully acknowledged the Christological character of the supernatural in opposition to the contemporary emphases on deceptive "spiritual manifestations."[13]

---

7. Nevin, "Natural and the Supernatural," 196–97.

8. Nevin, "Natural and the Supernatural," 200. For Nevin's understanding of Calvin's supralapsarianism, see "Hodge on the Ephesians," MTSS 7:73 and n27, and p. 90.

9. Bushnell, *Nature*, 109.

10. Nevin, "Natural and the Supernatural," 198, 199.

11. Although Bushnell had in many respects separated himself from some of Nathaniel William Taylor's theology, Bushnell's position on the inevitability of sin and the freedom (power to the contrary) seems to reflect something of Taylor's theology of sin. On Taylor's theology, see Edwards, *Of Singular Genius*, 33–36.

12. Nevin, "Natural and the Supernatural," 204.

13. Nevin, "Natural and the Supernatural," 202.

Document 12: "Natural and Supernatural"

The Incarnation for Bushnell was indeed a new revelation and a new creation in the world that challenged the current false representations of the supernatural. Nonetheless, Nevin charged that Bushnell's view of the supernatural represented a kind of "abstract spiritualism"[14] by which the natural was not allowed to come into any real union with the supernatural and merely floated over the natural in a kind of Gnostic imagination.

Where this "abstract spiritualism" is most evident is in Bushnell's conception of the church. For Bushnell, the church was a community in the Providential ordering of events and was one of the positive institutions of religion that many contemporaries had ceased to value. Bushnell, moreover, attributed the current loss of faith in the church to naturalism. Nonetheless, for Bushnell himself the church was still a natural institution, though guided by Providence through its natural operations. For Nevin, Bushnell's view of the church as a natural institution in which the supernatural floated over its operations was defective because it represented a loss of faith in the church catholic as the organ of the supernatural in history and in Christian life. Bushnell perceived no organic connection between the Incarnation, Christology, and the one, holy, catholic, and apostolic church as that relationship was made manifest in the New Testament and in the creeds of the early church.[15] Like many New England Puritans and many other American Protestants, Bushnell did not perceive the intimate union of the supernatural and the nature in the church and failed to see the church as a means of grace and an object of faith.

---

14. Nevin, "Natural and the Supernatural," 204.

15. For Nevin's more extensive treatment of the biblical and creedal foundations of church, see especially his "Hodge on the Ephesians," MTSS 7:62–125, and Nevin, "The Apostles' Creed," MTSS 8:71–97.

Natural And Supernatural.[1]

Nature and the Supernatural, as together constituting the One System of God. By Horace Bushnell. New York: Charles Scribner. 1858.

A truly interesting work, as may be easily presumed at once in its authorship and title. No subject could well be more important, especially for the present time, than that which is here brought into view; and there are few men better fitted than Dr. Bushnell to discuss any theme of the sort in an earnest, vigorous, and manly way.[2] We welcome the book, with all our heart, as a most valuable accession to the theological literature of the age, and trust that it may exert a large and wide influence in the service of truth. It is no hasty production, but the carefully studied and well digested treatment of a great question, which has been before the mind of the author for years, and on which plainly he has bestowed the whole force of his ripest and best thoughts. The book, therefore, is one which requires study also on the part of the reader. It is not just of the *current* literature sort, formed for the easy entertainment of the passing hour. It grapples with what the writer holds to be the religious life question of the age; its course is everywhere, more or less, through inquiries which are felt to be both intricate and profound. And yet with all this, the work is never either heavy or dull. On the contrary, it may be said to overflow with genial life. Dr. Bushnell has contrived to throw into it the full vivacity and freshness of his own nature. It is rich throughout with thoughts that breathe, and words that glow and burn. A sort of poetical charm

---

1. [*MR* 11 (April 1859) 176–211.]

2. [Horace Bushnell (1802–76), Congregational minister and theologian, was the author of texts that had an impact on theology in the United States, especially on the emergence of the liberal Protestant tradition of the late nineteenth century. Some of the most important among those texts were: *Christian Nurture* (1847, 1860), *God in Christ* (1849), *Christ in Theology* (1851), as well as *Nature and the Supernatural*. Nevin and Bushnell shared some similar views, including an organic and developmental view of Christianity, an opposition to the Protestant sect mentality and revivalism, and an emphasis on the centrality of Christ and the Christological tradition. However, there are particular areas of disagreement, outlined in the document introduction. On Bushnell's and Nevin's debates, see in particular, Edwards, *Of Singular Genius*; Johnson, *Nature and the Supernatural*; Nevin, "Nevin and Bushnell: Christian Nurture," MTSS 6:34–77; Bushnell, *Views*, 100–109; and Layman, "Holistic Supernaturalism," 194–200.]

is made to suffuse the entire progress of its argument, relieving the severity of the discussion, and clothing it oftentimes with graphic interest and. force. Altogether the book is one which deserves to live, and that may be expected to take its place, we think, among the enduring works of the age. It is of an order, in this view, with Hugh Miller's *Testimony of the Rocks*; and as an argument for the truth of the Christian religion, may compare favorably with Reinhard's *Plan of the Founder of Christianity*.[3]

So much we may say, without pretending to endorse in full the course of thought presented in Dr. Bushnell's book. The worth and importance of such a work are not to be measured simply by what may be considered the validity of its opinions at particular points. We may find reason to question many of *its* propositions—we may feel ourselves constrained to pause doubtfully in the presence of much to which it challenges our assent—and yet be fairly and rightly bound, notwithstanding, to own and honor its superiority, as shown in the profound significance of its general thesis, the reigning scope of its discussion, the reach and grasp of its argument taken as a whole. The claim to such respectful homage, in the case before us, is one in regard to which there can be no dispute.

[Bushnell on Rationalism]

We agree fully with Dr. Bushnell, in believing the tendency of the present time to be fearfully strong toward Rationalism—that form of infidelity, which seeks to destroy Christianity, not so much in the way of direct opposition to its claims, as by endeavoring to drag it down from its own proper supernatural sphere into the sphere of mere nature, making it thus to be nothing more in the end than a particular phase simply of natural religion itself. On both sides of the Atlantic, we find a large amount of intelligence enlisted openly in the defence of this view; seeking, with no small measure of learning and ingenuity, to resolve all the higher aspects of the Gospel into poetry and myth, and pretending to bring out the full sense of it at last in the experiences of a purely humanitarian culture. But it would be a most inadequate view of the case, to suppose the evil of such unbelief confined to any formal demonstrations of this sort. As a silent tendency—a power secretly at work to sap the foundations of faith and piety—the rationalistic spirit in question takes in a vastly wider range of action. Multitudes, as Dr. Bushnell observes, are involved in it virtually as a system of thought,

---

3. [Hugh Miller (1802-56), Scottish geologist, argued in his *Testimony of the Rocks* (1857) that geology, rightly understood, does not conflict with revelation and the biblical account of creation. Franz Volkmar Reinhard (1753-1812), Lutheran theologian and professor at the University of Wittenberg, published in 1781 his first edition of *Versuch über den Plan, welchen der Stifter der Christlichen Religion* (translated by Oliver A. Taylor as *Plan of the Founder of Christianity*). Reinhard, assuming the attitude of an unprejudiced inquirer, provided a rational and historical account of the life and character and conduct of Jesus as available in the New Testament. Jesus is presented as divine teacher who excelled all those who preceded and followed him. To some extent, Reinhard anticipated the later quest for the historical Jesus.]

without being themselves aware of the fact. They profess to honor Christianity as a divine revelation, take its language familiarly upon their lips, persuade themselves it may be that they continue strictly loyal to its heavenly authority; and yet all the time they are false in fact to its claims, casting it down from its proper excellency, and substituting for it in their minds another order of thought altogether. In this way, we are surrounded on all sides with a nominal Christianity, which is little better in truth than a sort of baptized Paganism, putting us off continually with heathenish ideas expressed in Christian terms.

Our public life is full of such essential infidelity. It reigns in our politics. It has infected our universal literature. The periodical press floods the land with it every week. It makes a merit generally indeed of being friendly to religion; but it is plain enough to see, that what it takes to be religion is something widely different from the old faith of the Gospel in its strictly supernatural form. It is, when all is done, naturalism only, of the poorest kind, dressed up in evangelical modes of speech. That it should be able to pass current for any thing better—that the public at large, the so called Christian public, should show itself so widely willing to accept any such authority as having any sort of force in matters of religion—is only itself a most painful sign of that general weakening of faith, of which we are now speaking as the great moral malady of the times. Already too the disease has entered deep into our systems of education; and there is but too much reason to fear, that its worst fruit on this ground is yet to come.

[Naturalism and Education]

Our system of public schools is often spoken of, as being the strength of our institutions, the safeguard of our liberties, the crown of our civilization, the distinguishing glory of our truly enlightened age. But we hazard nothing in saying, that it proceeds from beginning to end, not on the believing recognition of the supernatural claims of Christianity, but on their virtual rejection and denial. It does not help the matter in the least, that it offers no formal contradiction to the idea of revealed religion; the burden of the difficulty lies just here, that claiming, as Christianity does, to be a supreme authority for men's minds, it is notwithstanding prohibited by the system from the exercise of any such authority in what is allowed on all hands to be a fundamental interest of our life—that it is politely bowed to the one side, and made to stand out of the way, while another theory of religion altogether is practically introduced into its place. The case is too clear for any controversy. Education, to be Christian, must make earnest with the realities of a higher life in their own true and proper form, subordinating all merely natural and temporal ends to the claims of God and the eternal world, under such explicit and positive view. Under any other character, it must stand condemned at once, as being hostile in fact, and not friendly, to religion. Tried by this rule, our common school system, as it now prevails, loses all title to respect. It ignores positive Christianity, and pretends to educate the young without its help; as though it were possible to fit them for the duties and trials of life, by holding their minds down to the things of the present world only, without any sort of reference to their highest destiny as it is comprehended in the "powers of the world to come."[4]

All such education is in truth "God-less." It reflects honor on the Catholic Church, we think, that she condemns it, and requires her membership to keep clear of it, though it be at the heavy cost of forming and maintaining separate schools for their own use. For what better proof could she furnish, that for *her* at least the truths of religion, in the form in which she holds them, are indeed articles of faith, which as such carry with them supernatural authority, and are not to be set aside, or suspended in their force even for a moment, in favor of any other interest or opinion whatever? If other ecclesiastical communions show themselves more liberal here, and less jealous for the rights of what they hold to be the glorious Gospel of the Blessed God, it is hard to see certainly how it can redound much to the credit of their faith. It would seem to imply rather one or the other of these two things: either that they have no clear apprehension of any positive distinctions in the Christian scheme, or that all such distinctions are with them at last matters of opinion only rather than the power of a living creed. To speak of an extra-ecclesiastical training in the case, that may be allowed to provide for the interest of religion in a general way, handing over its subjects afterwards to the care of the different religious communions, to be completed by them severally in their own way, is only to expose the radical defect of the whole scheme. Every such view proceeds on an assumption, which is found to break down in the end all real distinction, between positive Christianity and the religion of mere nature clothed with its name. Neither is it enough, as some dream, to have the Bible regularly read in such schools; as though that somehow, in and of itself, were positive Christianity, and sufficient in this naked way to meet and satisfy in full the demands of a Christian education. They show a wonderfully poor conception of religion, who think to vindicate its supremacy, and to gain free field for its proper action, in any such easy manner as this. As the use of the Bible falls in readily, we can see everywhere, with the conflicting views of all religious parties and sects, so has it been abundantly shown in our time, that it may be made to suit itself just as readily also to the views and wishes of those who turn all revelation into a mere fable. Infidels and naturalists have shown themselves, in many cases, most zealous for the honor of the Bible in such abstract view, and none commonly are more apparently cordial in crying out for its untrammeled use in the public schools. They are perfectly content to have it thus dignified as a text book of morality, patriotism, and sentimental humanitarianism, if only it be to the exclusion of Christianity in its concrete supernatural form, and in the midst of associations that go always to sink the heavenly sense of it down to the level of their own miserable unbelief. It needs more a great deal than this, we repeat, to redeem our schools from the charge of being against Christ, because they are not with him, and for him, in any direct positive way.

4. [Heb 6:5.]

Part 2: The Church Question and Supernaturalism

The case indeed speaks for itself. If there be anything that may be said specially to distinguish our system of common schools, it would seem to be the intense worldliness of their spirit, as opposed to all practical belief in the existence of things unseen and eternal. They are the agency of the State, directed only toward secular and political ends. The spirit that breathes through their administration is predominantly earthly. Their educational apparatus looks everywhere only to the things of this world. All turns on knowledge—the knowing of things in a simply natural way, for the ends and uses of the present life; as though this, after all, were the "chief end of man,"[5] and the highest good proposed to him this side the grave. No wonder, that in such circumstances the very atmosphere of the school room should come to be impregnated, as it were, with the poison of unbelief, and that the minds of the young, exposed to its daily influence, should grow up cold, hard, materialistic, impassive to heavenly impressions, and ripe at last only for the deeds of the flesh. Is not this result showing itself plainly enough already, for any observing mind? And is there not every reason to fear, that it will come out more terrible still with the progress of time?

Unfortunately the evil answers but too well to the reigning temper of the times. The education of the schools finds no proper corrective in the tone of thought which prevails generally on the outside of the schools. Indeed if that were the case, no such education could be allowed to exist. It argues an eclipse of faith, that so great an interest can be thus passively surrendered, in a Christian land, to the power of unbelief. That must be at best a low sense of what religion is, which can suffer mere intellectual training in any view to be regarded as something of more account than virtue, piety, and holiness. It involves infidelity, to magnify such culture, as is commonly done in our time, at the expense of these higher interests; as though knowledge under any circumstances—and more especially an ability to read, write, and cast up accounts—must needs be a blessing to the possessor of it, and to the community at large; as though the whole problem of individual and social prosperity were to be successfully solved by the art of the schoolmaster, going abroad and letting light into human souls in such style; as though education, in any form like this, might be expected ever to do away with the evils of life, and to beautify it at last into anything like the character designed for it by God. Away with all such abominable glorification of mere naked mind, without any regard whatever to the wants and necessities of the immortal spirit! It is the very cant of infidelity itself. The chief end of man is to glorify God and to enjoy him forever.[6] The "one thing needful"[7] is not to *know* the shadows of this world, but to *be* in the powers of the world to come. The smallest measure of faith, is a higher accomplishment than any amount of learning without faith. Devout ignorance is infinitely better than profane unsanctified science. These are first truths, foundation maxims we may say, in the kingdom of Christ; and not to know them, not to have them

---

5. [A parody of the Westminster Shorter Catechism, quoted in the next paragraph.]
6. [First sentence of the Westminster Shorter Catechism.]
7. [Luke 10:42.]

in mind, not to be spontaneously disposed to fall in with them at once as the only true order of thought and life, is necessarily to have the proper sense and glory of that kingdom obscured to our view, and to be thus to the same extent under the dominion of an opposite antichristian mind. That precisely is the ruling defect of our time. We read of what are called the "ages of faith." Ours, it is plain to see, is no such age. We glory in our intelligence; but it is more earthly in its order than heavenly. We boast of our improvements and arts; but they serve to fix our minds on material interests, far more than on such as are spiritual and divine. We exult in our general civilization, as though it carried in it somehow the promise of the Christian millennium itself, and might be taken for the harbinger of the "new heavens and new earth wherein dwelleth righteousness."[8] But, alas, it is hard to see how it may be shown to be, either the product of those supernatural forces which are revealed to us by the Gospel, or the proper expression of their presence in the world, or a positive momentum in any way bearing them onward to their ultimate destination and end. It is not just the "wisdom and power of God unto salvation,"[9] we apprehend, in the old sense of St. Paul. The angel of St. John flying in the midst of heaven, and having the everlasting gospel to preach to every nation, kindred, and tongue,[10] can hardly be expected to appear in any such form and shape.

[Christ as the Ground of the Supernatural]

We feel the full force of what Dr. Bushnell says on this subject. As an argument for the supernatural truth of Christianity, against the naturalistic tendencies of the age, his book is altogether timely. The evil enters into all spheres and departments of our modern life. It needs to be met in a bold and strong way. "We undertake the argument," says the distinguished author,

> from a solemn conviction of its necessity, and because we see that the more direct arguments and appeals of religion are losing their power over the public mind and conscience. This is true especially of the young, who pass into life under the combined action of so many causes, conspiring to infuse a distrust of whatever is supernatural in religion. Persons farther on in life are out of the reach of these new influences, and, unless their attention is specially called to the fact, have little suspicion of what is going on in the mind of the rising classes of the world—more and more saturated every day with this insidious form of unbelief. And yet we all, with perhaps the exception of a few who are too far on to suffer it, are more or less infected with the same tendency. Like an atmosphere, it begins to envelope the common mind of the world.

---

8. [2 Pet 3:13.]

9. [Nevin's quotation is not exact. See Rom 1:16, "For I am not ashamed of the gospel of Christ; for it is the power of God unto salvation . . . ." Or, perhaps 1 Cor 1:30.]

10. [Rev 14:6.]

We frequently detect its influence in the practical difficulties of the young members of the churches, who do not even suspect the true cause themselves. Indeed, there is nothing more common than to hear arguments advanced, and illustrations offered, by the most evangelical preachers, that have no force or meaning, save what they get from the current naturalism of the day. We have even heard a distinguished and carefully orthodox preacher deliver a discourse, the very doctrine of which was inevitable, unqualified naturalism. Logically taken, and carried out to its proper result, Christianity could have had no ground of standing left—so little did the preacher himself understand the true scope of his doctrine, or the mischief that was beginning to infect his conceptions of the Christian truth.[11]

Dr. Bushnell's argument for the supernatural, is made to rest centrally upon the person of Jesus Christ. This constitutes its main beauty and force. It forms the best distinction, and greatest merit, of the later modern theology generally, so far as it shows itself to be possessed of power and life, that it seeks more and more to make Christ in this way the principle of all faith and knowledge; taking up thus anew, as it were, the grand Christological views of the Nicene age, and laboring to carry them out in full order and harmony to their last results. Great praise is due here to the mighty genius of Schleiermacher;[12] who, however defective his own views of the person of Christ were, may be said to have inaugurated a new era of theology in Germany, by forcing attention to this point as the true beginning of all reality and certainty in religion. Under the inspiration of this thought, all theological studies there might seem to have started again into fresh vigorous life, rising from the tomb into which they had been cast by the melancholy reign of Rationalism in previous times. A new interest was felt to be infused into all the facts and doctrines of revelation, by the light which was shed upon them from the acknowledged centre of the Christian system. They acquired a deeper significance, and became in this way subjects for more earnest inquiry and profound study. Christological thinking—that which, instead of looking primarily to the things taught and done by Christ, fixes its whole gaze at once on the mystery of his person, the glorious fact of the incarnation, and uses this as a commentary and key for the right understanding of all things besides—has come to pervade and rule more or less all spheres of religious science. The method is so plainly founded in the very nature of Christianity, and grows forth so immediately from the apprehension of

11. [Bushnell, *Nature*, 28–29.]

12. [Friedrich Daniel Ernst Schleiermacher (1768–1834), German theologian at the University of Berlin, was, according to Schaff in *What is Church History?*, "the greatest theological genius . . . since the Reformation." Schaff, *Development of the Church*, MTSS 3:285. Nevin and Schaff were both influenced by Schleiermacher and held him in high regard because he placed Christ at the center of his theology, emphasized the idea of communion in religion that opened the way for understanding the incarnational and organic nature of the church, and made religious experience (or Christian consciousness) the fountain of dogmatic knowledge and church life. For Nevin's evaluation of Schleiermacher, see, for example, *Antichrist*, MTSS 6:165–69. On Schleiermacher, see Gerrish, *A Prince of the Church*.]

Document 12: Natural and Supernatural.

its supernatural character, that it must prevail more and more, not only in Germany, but in all other countries also, wherever it may be felt necessary to deal earnestly with the mysteries of religion, over against the growing naturalism of the age. If these are to be upheld successfully as objects of faith, transcending the constitution of nature, it can only be by falling back upon their ultimate ground in Christ, and asserting in the first place the absolute verity of his person, as the principle and source of what is thus to be regarded as a new creation altogether. Not only our systematic divinity, but our homiletic teaching also, needs to be fortified in this way against the downward tendency of the times, by being brought back to what is substantially the method of the old Apostles' Creed[13]—that most simple, but at the same time most grand and sublime confession, into which, as a mould, the faith of the universal Church was cast in the beginning.

Nothing is more certain, than that Christ himself, as the author of the Gospel, claims for his own presence in the world a supernatural character, which is regarded as reaching out to the whole Christian system also from his person. He is not of this world, according to his own declaration—not the efflorescence and perfection simply of its natural life in any view, but the introduction into it really and truly of life and power in a new and higher form. The great men of the heathen world, Pythagoras, Socrates, Plato, and such like, with all the towering superiority of their nature, were nevertheless the historical product always of laws and forces belonging to humanity as it existed before. We may say the same also of such men as Moses, David, Isaiah, and the prophets generally, among the Jews. The supernatural as it appeared in them, and by them, was not properly of themselves, formed no part of their being, but met them, as it were, from abroad, in a sort of outward and transient way. Moses could not say: "I came down from heaven, not to do mine own will, but the will of him that sent me." "I proceed forth and come from God"—"Ye are from beneath; I am from above: ye are of this world; I am not of this world"—"I came forth from the Father, and am come into the world: again I leave the world, and go to the Father"—"And now, O Father, glorify thou me with thine own self, with the glory which I had with thee before the world was."[14] All men would be shocked with language any way approaching this, from his lips. But all is different with Jesus Christ. This exactly is the universal tenor of his language in regard to himself; and with such high assumption agrees in full the whole theory of the Gospel exhibited to us in the New Testament. In no other view is it intelligible. The strictly supernatural origin of Christ and his salvation is everywhere taken for granted, and rested upon silently as a first truth lying at the foundation of all its doctrines and facts; so that it is really one of the strangest things in the world, to find any class of men pretending to accept it as true in connection with any other

---

13. [The "method of the Creed" would seem to correspond to what Nevin (a decade earlier) had identified as "its material structure or organism"—its Christocentric content, and how that generates and binds together its major articles. Nevin, "The Apostles' Creed," MTSS 8:71–88.]

14. [A series of quotations from John: 6:38; 8:42; 8:23; 16:28; 17:5.]

hypothesis—so intimately interwoven this thought, of an order of existence higher than the whole constitution of the world as it stood before, would seem to be with what we may call the self-representation of the evangelical scheme at every point.

The position of Christ, his relations to the world, all the aspects of his character, all his works and all his pretensions, are brought into view everywhere as being in full unison and harmony with his bold claim to a heavenly and divine origin. His birth is by the Holy Ghost; on which account he is called the Son of God. Angels herald his advent into the world. The powers of heaven descend upon him at his baptism. He is no prophet simply among men, closing the Old Testament line, but the bearer of truth and grace in his own person. A new order of existence opens upon the world, in the mystery of his being. In him was life—life in its original, fontal form—and the life became the light of men. It was not his office, therefore, primarily, to publish the truth as something different from himself, to mediate between earth and heaven, man and God, in any mere outward way. His own *being* constituted the deepest and last sense of the Gospel, the burden of its overwhelming mystery. "I am the way," we hear him saying, "the truth, and the life"—not the index simply to these things, but the actual presence and power of the things themselves. "I am the resurrection and the life"—not the promise and pledge only of such glorious boon, but the full realization of it as a fact now actually at hand in my person. For "he that believeth in me, though he were dead, yet shall he live: and whosoever liveth and believeth in me shall never die." Again, "He that believeth on me hath everlasting life—Whoso eateth my flesh and drinketh my blood, hath eternal life; and I will raise him up at the last day."[15] God was in him, reconciling the world unto himself.[16] He is the propitiation for our sins—our righteousness—our peace—the organism of our redemption—the everlasting theatre of our salvation.[17] He stands in the world a vast stupendous miracle—the miracle of a new creation. He is greater than all the powers, higher than all the glories of the natural world. Nay, he is before all things, and by him, and in him, all things consist. His life, therefore, included in itself, from the beginning, even under its human form, the principle of full victory over all the vanity and misery which are in the world through sin; so that when he went down into the grave, and descended into hades, it was only that he might return again, leading captivity captive, and ascend up on high, to inaugurate his kingdom, in its proper spiritual form, as a new immortal constitution, against which the gates of hell should have no power to prevail to the end of time.[18]

So lofty, so wide, so every way large, beyond all the measures of man's merely natural life, or simply human history, are the terms and representations in which the Gospel of our Lord and Saviour Jesus Christ, in wonderful, unfaltering consistency

---

15. [In sequence: John 14:16; 11:25; 11:25–25; a combination of 6:47, 54.]

16. [2 Cor 5:19.]

17. [1 John 2:2; 1 Cor 1:30; Eph 2:14.]

18. [Allusions to Eph 4:8–9; Nevin interprets the "lower parts of the earth" as the descent into hell ("hades"), as confessed in the Apostles' Creed.]

Document 12: Natural and Supernatural.

with itself throughout, bears witness to its own origin, character, and power. If it be not in the fullest sense—first in the person of Christ himself, and then in the outworkings and ongoings of his grace and power in the system of Christianity as a whole—the presence of a new supernatural life in the world, an order of existence which was not in it before, and which is not in it still beyond the reach and range of this fact; if it be not this, we say, and nothing short of this, then must it be denounced at once as being the most daring and wicked imposture ever practiced upon the credulity of the human race.

But let any one pause now, to consider what an amount of peril is involved in so vast and broad a claim, and to what an ordeal Christianity has necessarily subjected itself, in presuming to take this lofty position, and thus binding itself to satisfy in full the terms and conditions of its own world-embracing problem. A consistent fiction is hard in any case, where it has to do with concrete realities under a known form, and is allowed to extend itself at all to specific details; but it becomes of course more and more difficult, and at last is found to be utterly impracticable, in proportion precisely as the points to be met and answered in this way become more and more significant, multitudinous, and complex. Suppose Christianity then to be such an *invention*—a bold hypothesis merely, got up to solve the inmost meaning of the world's life, and to play off in spectral style a supernatural economy of salvation commensurate with all the wants and aspirations of our fallen race and how certainly may it not be expected to break down, by its own incongruities and contradictions, almost immediately at every point. Never did a scheme of religion, surely, offer itself of its own accord to a more searching trial of its merits and claims.

[The Supernatural as Abiding Organic Fact]

For the supernatural here is no transient phenomenon merely, no fantastic avatar, no theophany only in the Old Testament style; much less a doctrine simply, or theosophic speculation. It is made to challenge our faith and homage, as an abiding fact, linking itself organically with the general life of the world, and carrying it out historically to its highest and last sense.[19] It must then be supremely natural, as well as overwhelmingly supernatural; no product of nature plainly, and yet in such harmony with it, that it shall seem to be at the same time its full outbursting glory and necessary perfection. The relation between God's first creation, and that which claims to be in this way God's second creation, may not be conceived of as contradictory, violent, or abrupt. The divine economy which embraces both—proceeding, as it does, from the mind of

---

19. [What Nevin denies here is that the supernatural presence of Christ is momentary or temporary, a magical appearance in the natural world. ("Avatars" again are the "fantastic" appearances of the many Hindu deities.) Rather it is the permanent insertion of a new power into space and time, forever transforming the continuum by its presence and activity, and thus discerned in *history*. Nevin, *Antichrist*, MTSS 5:180, 188; Nevin, "The New Creation in Christ," MTSS 4:39–45; Nevin, "Wilberforce on the Incarnation," MTSS 4:60–76.]

Him to whom all his works are known from the beginning—must be a single system at last, in absolute harmony with itself throughout.

The whole constitution of the world, therefore, both physical and moral, must be found to come to its proper conclusion in Christ, showing him to be in very deed the Alpha and Omega, the beginning and the end, of all God's works.

The physical must show itself every where the mirror of the spiritual and heavenly, as these come out fully at last only in the form of Christianity. Not as having any power to make them known by its own light originally; but as answering to them, in the way of universal parable, when it comes to be shone upon from their higher sphere; even as to the mind of Christ himself, the birds of the air, and the flowers of the field, become types and symbols of righteousness at once, the moment they are needed for any such purpose.

In its whole organization again, the physical, as being plainly a progressive order of things reaching towards the unity of some common end, must put on the character of a ground preparation and prophecy, from first to last, looking continually to the advent of Christ as the only sufficient fulfilment of its sense. This it will be found to do, if it have no power to stop in its own order, or to come to an end in itself, but be forced and driven, as it were, upward and forward always, from one stage and level of existence to another—each lower range foreshadowing still the necessary approach of a higher, till it gains its full summit finally in man; and so transcends itself, if we may use such an expression, in the presence of a new *moral* world, which afterwards again shows itself in its own turn unable in like manner to come to any pause or rest, till it is filled out and made complete by the supernatural grace of the Gospel.

It will be then, more especially, as tried by the actual conditions of this moral world—the circumstances and necessities of our general human life—that the Christian system, in the view now under consideration, must pass through its severest ordeal. Its theory of humanity must be such as to fall in plainly with the actual condition of humanity in the world; while all the lines of history, and all the deeper forces of man's life, shall be found every where struggling toward it, and either consciously or unconsciously bearing witness to its claims.

[The Incarnation and Redemption]

The general fact of man's sin and misery must be such, as to agree with the hypothesis of a strictly supernatural redemption. If the evil were found to be of a superficial character only, neither deeper nor broader in fact than the measure of our life in its ordinary natural form—and in such view capable, accordingly, of being surmounted in some way by the powers and possibilities of this life in its own sphere—the idea of a redemption descending into it from above, in the form of a new creation brought to pass by the mystery of the Incarnation, would be convicted at once of being unreasonable and false. To justify any such mystery, it must appear that sin is a disorder which underlies the universal nature of man as it now stands; that it is itself a sort of supernatural fall or lapse in his life; that the whole present order of his existence is subjected to vanity and death by reason of it; that all other remedial agencies brought to bear upon the case, philosophical, educational, political, socialistic, and such like, have proved themselves thus far, and must prove themselves, utterly inadequate to its demands, coming, as it were, infinitely short of the last ground and seat of the evil; that it can be conquered, therefore, and rolled back in its consequences, if conquered ever at all, only by a force deeper and more comprehensive than the whole order of the world in its natural view, which, as such, shall show itself sufficient at the same time to break through this order altogether, and to rise above it, abolishing death itself, and bringing life and immortality to light. The New Testament doctrine of Christ, involved necessarily a corresponding doctrine of man. No Pelagian Anthropology, denying or slurring over the fact of Original Sin, can move hand in hand, in one and the same line, with a strictly theanthropic[20] Christology.

It must appear still farther, if Christianity be true, that the religious life of the world generally, under what may be denominated its merely natural form, looks toward it, calls for it, reaches after it in all manner of ways, and finds the burden of its dark riddle fully solved at last only in its august presence. Rooted as they are in the same ground, the constitution of human nature itself, all religions must have to some extent a common character, must be concerned with the same problems, must work themselves out into more or less analogous results. The relation then of the absolutely true religion to religions that are false, can not be regarded as one of abrupt and total difference; it should be taken rather to resemble the relation that holds between man in the natural creation, and the manifold forms of animal life in the world below him—which, however far they may fall short of his perfection, carry in themselves, notwithstanding, though it may be in very distorted and fantastic style, some portion still of the idea which is finally disclosed in his person, and thus join in foreshadowing this darkly from all sides as their own last end and only proper meaning. False religions, in such view, should open a wide field of analogical comparison, serving to establish the idea of religion in its true form; not as leading over to it in their own order, not as being on the same plane with it in any sense; but as bringing into view wants, aspirations, questions, problems, soul-mysteries in every shape, which only the true religion at last is able fully to satisfy and solve. Should the grand supernatural facts and doctrines of Christianity seem to be met in this way with dull echoes, and wild visionary caricatures, of their heavenly sense, in the mythologies of the heathen world, the fact would form certainly no ground of objection to its claims, but only a powerful argument in their favor. Heathenism *ought* to be, in such manner, through

20. [Literally, "divine-human." Christ saves men and women by uniting them with his person, who is *holistically* God and man. See Nevin, *Mystical Presence* MTSS 1:140, 157; *Antichrist* MTSS 5:182, 210, 215; for the theological background, see Evans, general introduction to *The Incarnate Word*, MTSS 4:xxvii–xxxi. Here Nevin makes the point that such a salvation also requires a real, radical fall.]

its whole wide empire of darkness and sin, an unconscious prophecy of Him, who proclaims himself the desire of all nations and the light of the world.[21]

[The Incarnation in History]

All History again must come to its proper unity in Christ, if he be indeed what he is made to be in the Gospel. Here, as in the constitution of Nature, God must have a plan in harmony with itself throughout; and this plan can not possibly go aside from his main thought and purpose in the government of the world. It must centre in the Incarnation.

Then after all this, what a range of comparison and trial for the Christian system is presented to us in the general economy of Revelation itself. For this is no single or narrow fact simply; nor yet a multitude of separate, disjointed facts; but a vast and mighty organization of facts rather, involving the most manifold relations, and reaching through long ages back to the very beginning of the world. Religion in this form is exhibited to us under different dispensations, and yet as being always the same, from the first obscure promise in the garden of Eden, down to the fulness of time, when the Word became flesh and tabernacled among men in the person of Jesus Christ. "God," we are told, "who at sundry times and in divers manners spake in time past unto the fathers by the prophets, hath in these last days spoken unto us by his Son, whom he hath appointed heir of all things, by whom also he made the worlds."[22] All these voices of old then—in paradise, before the flood and after the flood, through the patriarchs, in the giving of the law, and by the whole long line of the prophets from Moses down to the ministry of John the Baptist—must come together at last in Christ as their only full sense and necessary end. The correspondence cannot limit itself to a few predictions and types, put forward here and there in an abstract outward way; it must enter into the universal structure of the entire revelation. The Old Testament throughout must be, not only in full harmony with itself, but in full organic union at the same time with the central idea of the New Testament; so that everywhere, in all its oracles, histories, and institutions, it shall be found prefiguring this, reaching toward it, and laboring as it were to find in it its own true rest and glorious consummation.

But by far the most difficult part of the whole problem, it is plain, must be finally to satisfy what we may call the internal conditions and requirements of this New Testament idea itself; by setting it forth in such a form, that it shall appear to be every way worthy of itself, and true throughout to its own constituent terms. Only think, what is involved in an attempt to *construct* a full historical Christ in the manner of the Gospel. Not only to dare so bold a thought as that of the Incarnation, but to dare also beyond

---

21. [Here Nevin anticipated the claim that paganism foreshadows Christianity and points to its truth. A notable advocate of this claim is C. S. Lewis: see Armstrong, "The Pagan Element of Christian Tradition" and "C.S. Lewis on pagan philosophy as a road to Christian faith."]

22. [Heb 1:1–2.]

Document 12: Natural and Supernatural.

this the reduction of such a thought to full artistic representation, in the form of an actual human life; to project and carry out a biography of "God manifest in the flesh,"[23] the Word Incarnate, in whom dwelt the "fulness of the Godhead bodily;"[24] the portraiture of such a character, the picture of such a life, brought down to particulars and details, and exhibited as moving, speaking, acting and working, through a course of years, in the midst of actual human relations—the whole so ordered as to show itself in all its connections, antecedents, and consequents, harmoniously consistent with the grand fundamental thought on which it is made to rest. It is not possible surely to conceive of an ordeal more severe, than that to which Christianity has subjected itself, in coming before the world with its history of Jesus Christ, as we have it briefly outlined in the Apostles' Creed, from his miraculous birth of the Virgin, on to his resurrection from the dead, and his glorious ascension to the right hand of God. For so coming in the flesh, he must have an advent answerable to the glorious mystery of his person; such as shall bring with it the full presence of a new creation, and yet serve to set him really and truly in the bosom of the old creation. He must have a mission commensurate with his nature. He must be at once perfectly human, and yet no less perfectly divine, in all his teachings and doings. He must be in the world, as being all the time above it, and as comprising in himself the power of a life destined to triumph over it at last through all ages. His history may not end in the grave; and just as little may it come to a Gnostic conclusion in the clouds. Such a manifestation in the flesh must justify itself in the spirit; opening the way for a new order of grace among men, that shall be found in fair keeping to the end of time with the vastness of the economy serving thus for its introduction—a thought which leads at once to the idea of the Church, exactly in the order of the Creed, as being the body of Christ, the fulness of him that filleth all in all.

The terms and conditions of the Christian problem being in such general view what we have now seen them to be, the truth of Christianity, it is easy to see, must turn mainly on its power to solve them in a satisfactory way; and in such case, this must be taken always as the first and strongest of all arguments in its favor. Indeed no argument can be of force aside from this. The Christian Evidence thus centres ultimately in Christ himself. He is emphatically the "Light of the world."[25] For the natural cannot reveal, or make certain in any way, the supernatural; but needs this rather to bring out clearly its own sense; and so Christ descending into the world as the fullest and most perfect revelation of the supernatural, must be regarded necessarily as the very principle and source of all real illumination for men. As the absolute truth, he must in the nature of the case prove and authenticate himself.

This, however, does not imply of course that little or no account is to be made of evidences for the truth of Christianity beyond the person of Christ; miracles, for

23. [1 Tim 3:16.]
24. [Col 2:9.]
25. [John 8:12.]

example, prophecies, types, providences, voices of nature and grace conspiring in its favor. It goes only to hold such proofs to their right order and place. Their proper force lies in their organic relation to the presence of Christ himself in the world. They bear witness to him, only by means of the significance and power which they themselves derive from his person. They are the necessary seals of his supernatural mission; which however have force, like all seals, only as they are attached to what they thus serve to authenticate, and not as torn from it, and viewed in any separate and independent way.[26]

[Values and Criticisms of Bushnell's Nature]

The main weight of the argument for the supernatural, in Dr. Bushnell's book, is made to rest on Christ, as being the grand first principle of proof in this order of existence—an order which completes itself fully at last only in the fact of the Incarnation. "The character and doctrine of Jesus," we are told, "are the sun that holds all the minor orbs of revelation to their places, and pours a sovereign self-evidencing light into all religious knowledge."[27] Still, before coming to this, the first part of the work is very properly occupied with the subject under a more general view; the purpose being to show, that the supernatural itself is not something absolutely foreign and strange to the constitution of the world in its natural form, but an order rather which is anticipated and called for by this, and that comes out at last, therefore, in full harmony with its deepest wants, in full explication, we may say, of its inmost meaning and sense.

Here we find a great deal, of course, that is entitled to our admiring interest and attention, as going to establish, in the way of analogical and presumptive reasoning, both the possibility and the necessity of the supernatural, considered as being the proper complement or filling out of the natural—both joining to constitute what the book denominates "the one system of God." The argument, however, as conducted by Dr. Bushnell, is made to involve and assert some things which it seems to us not easy to allow.

[Bushnell on the Relation of Nature to Supernatural]

In the first place, we demur to his line of distinction between the natural and the supernatural. Nature he defines to be the simply physical order of the world, made up

---

26. [Here Nevin attempts to unite his "theanthropic" Christology (a person is saved by being united with Christ's divine-human life) with the usual "evidences" of nineteenth-century evangelical Christianity (that the prophecies and miracles of the Bible verify the truth of Christianity). But now those "evidences" are not external facts (like the facts of science) but internal truths carried in the theanthropic person to which they point. E.g., the miracles of Jesus do not separately verify that Jesus was who he said he was; rather they are miracles because they point to and participate in Christ's theanthropic power, already revealed in his earthly life.]

27. [Bushnell, *Nature*, 365.]

of causes and effects flowing in constant succession, by a necessity that comes from within the scheme itself; in which view, we are told, "that is supernatural, whatever it be, that is either not in the chain of natural cause and effect, or which acts on the chain of cause and effect in nature, from without the chain."[28] In this way, the supernatural is brought to assume at once a most familiar every day character, by entering into the very conception of our own personality; for this, as involving intelligence and will, is not under the law of cause and effect in the manner of the simply physical world, but carries in itself the power of acting on the course of this law from without, in a free self-determining way, so as to produce results, that nature of itself, as here defined, could not bring to pass.

Now it is perfectly fair, to make use of this relation of mind to matter in the world, as an analogical argument for the possibility of an intervention, that shall be found descending into the world miraculously from a higher sphere. But it is pushing the matter too far, we think, to make the first relation of one order, and parallel in full, with the second. That is not the common view of the case certainly; and the interest of the supernatural is likely to lose by it in the end, it strikes us, much more than it may seem at first sight to gain. As distinguished from the supernatural, in the old theological sense—which is at the same time here also the popular sense—the natural includes in its conception a great deal more than the simply material and physical. The term is often used indeed to express the idea of difference from the moral; but never so as to refer this last to the supernatural. When *that* distinction is to be expressed, the moral itself is made to fall at once, along with the physical, into the economy of nature. This includes in its constitution mind as well as matter, self-determining forces or powers as well as simply passive chains of cause and effect. Man belongs primarily to the present world; he is incorporated into it organically from his birth; his relations to it are part of its proper system, quite as much as the conditions and laws of things below him. True, he possesses in himself, at the same time, the capacity of a higher life, original and constitutional relations to an order of existence far more glorious than the present world, the powers of which must be brought to bear upon him in a most real way, if he is to fulfil at last the great purpose of his creation. But this does not of itself lift him out of the order of nature. It shows only how truly he is in it, as needing thus the power of the supernatural, under an objective form, to perfect his existence in that higher view.

[Bushnell on the Origin of Evil]

We are by no means satisfied, in the next place, with Dr. Bushnell's theory of the origin of evil. Sin, if we understand him rightly, is not only a bad possibility in any such world as ours, but a tremendous necessity. He holds indeed that our first parents were

---

28. [Bushnell, *Nature*, 37.]

created in a state of "constituent perfection,"[29] having an inward fitness and disposition for good, that served to carry them toward it spontaneously without or before deliberation. But holiness in such form can have no sufficient strength or security.

> Deliberation, when it comes, as come it must, will be the inevitable fall of it; and then when the side of counsel in them is sufficiently instructed by that fall, and the bitter sorrow it yields, and the holy freedom is restored, it may be or become an eternally enduring principle. Spontaneity in good, without counsel, is weak; counsel and deliberative choice, without spontaneity, are only a character begun; issued in spontaneity, they are the solid reality of everlasting good.[30]

It does not help the case materially, to say that there was no positive ground or cause for sin in man's nature; and that our first parents fell by their own free choice. The difficulty is, that their free choice is supposed here to be so circumstanced, in the way of "privative conditions,"[31] as to be absolutely shut up to this conclusion and no other. "The *certainty* of their sin," we are told, "is originally involved in their spiritual training as powers."[32] Their condition privative was such as to involve "their *certain* lapse into evil."[33]

Sin is made to be thus a necessary transitional stage, in the process of full moral development. The condition of man in Paradise was not, and could not be, a direct onward movement in its own form to confirmed holiness, and so to glory, honor, and eternal life. It was necessary that he should taste evil, in order to become afterwards intelligently and resolutely good. His innocence could be strengthened into its full ripe virtue, only by being required to descend into the rough arena of the world through the fall, for the purpose of needful discipline and probation. This is not a new thought by any means. We recognize in it the familiar face of a speculation, which in one form or another has made itself altogether common in much of the thinking of modern Germany. But we do not consider it for this reason any the less wrong. It agrees not with the old doctrine of the Church on the subject; and the natural sense of the Bible is against it. It turns the Garden of Eden into a mere allegory or myth. It seats the necessity of sin in the very constitution of the world itself; a view, which goes at once to overthrow its character as sin, making it indeed the fruit of man's freedom in form, but so conditioning this freedom, that it is found to be only another name at last for what is in fact inevitable fate.

Dr. Bushnell carries his view of the certainty of man's fall so far, as to hold that the entire natural constitution of the world was ordered and established by God from the

---

29. [Bushnell, *Nature*, 104.]
30. [Bushnell, *Nature*, 104.]
31. [Bushnell, *Nature*, 107. Bushnell defines "condition privative" as "a moral state that is only inchoate, or incomplete, lacking something not yet reached, which is necessary to the probable rejection of evil." *Nature*, 109.]
32. [Bushnell, *Nature*, 107.]
33. [Bushnell, *Nature*, 107, 109.]

Document 12: Natural and Supernatural.

beginning with reference to that terrible fact; which in such view, therefore, could be no doubtful or uncertain contingency in any sense, but must be considered rather as forming from the very start the fixed central pivot and hinge, we may say, on which the whole plan of the world was made to turn. Sin thus has its disordering consequences in the natural creation, not simply as they are found coming *after* it in time; but also, on a much broader scale it would seem, as they have been made in God's plan to go before it, in the form of dispositions and arrangements contrived prospectively to anticipate its advent, and to lead over to it finally as the full interpretation of their own.

Even the long geologic ages, stretching away back of the Adamic creation, are taken to be prelusive[34] throughout in this way of the surely coming fact of sin. "This whole tossing, rending, recomposing process, that we call geology," our author tells us,

> symbolizes evidently, as in highest reason it should, the grand spiritual catastrophe, and Christian new creation, of man; which, both together, comprehend the problem of mind, and so the final causes or last ends of all God's works. What we see, is the beginning conversing with the end, and Eternal Forethought reaching across the tottering mountains and boiling seas, to unite beginning and end together. So that we may hear the grinding layers of the rocks singing harshly:

Of man's first disobedience and the fruit
Of that forbidden tree[35]—

> and all the long eras of desolation, and refitted bloom and beauty, represented in the registers of the world, are but the epic in stone of man's great history, before the time.[36]

On all this, we venture here no particular criticism. The subject, in the hands of Dr. Bushnell, is full of imagination and poetry, while it is made to overflow at the same time with rich suggestive thought. Our great embarrassment with it is, that, by making the universal order of the world dependent centrally upon the fall of man, and the introduction of sin, it makes this no less necessary than the geologic cataclysms, that owe their existence to it anticipatively so many ages before. Calvin's supralapsarianism, and the pantheistic world-progress of Hegel, seem to us always to run out here to the same conclusion, a Manichean notion of sin on the one hand, and as the necessary counterpart of this, a Gnostic conception of redemption on the other.[37]

34. [" . . . indicating that something of a like kind is to follow." Webster, *American Dictionary*, 634.]

35. [Milton, *Paradise Lost*, Book 1, line 1]

36. [Bushnell, *Nature*, 206.]

37. [Nevin periodically criticized what he called Calvin's supralapsarianism—that is, Calvin's view that God predestined both the elect and the reprobate before the Fall of Adam. Like Schaff, Nevin charged Hegel with pantheism because of his identification of the absolute spirit in history. On Schaff's view of Hegel, see *What is Church History?*, MTSS 3:249–50, 284. On Nevin's view, see, for example, *Antichrist*, MTSS 6:166–67, 169. Although both Nevin and Schaff valued much in Hegel's system and accepted particularly his emphasis on the objective spirit developing and coming to realization in history,

Through whatever stages of imperfection and disorder our world may have passed previously to the Mosaic creation, described in the first chapter of Genesis, we know that it was then at least pronounced by God himself to be in all respects "very good."[38] There can be no doubt, too, that this goodness, in the view of the sacred narrative, was held to consist in its full correspondence with the nature of man as he stood before the fall. The world was good, not in the light of a penitentiary prepared beforehand to suit the circumstances of his case in a state of sin, but as a fit theatre for the free harmonious development of his life in a state of innocence. How the fall wrought to disturb this original order, is of course a great mystery. It may have been largely by changes and privations induced upon the nature of man himself, causing the world to be in its relations to him something wholly different from what it would be if he were not thus hurled down from his first estate, and making it impossible for him even to conceive now of what might be comprehended for him in any such normal order. One thing is certain; had he continued sinless, the law of death, as it prevails in nature, could not have extended itself to his person; and how much of superiority this might have involved, in other respects, to the constitutional vanity and misery of the world as we now find it, no one may pretend surely to say.

Dr. Bushnell's idea of the necessity of sin extends logically to all worlds. Even the good angels, spoken of in the Scriptures, he tells us, "for aught that appears, have all been passed through and brought up out of a fall, as the redeemed of mankind will be."[39] The celebrated Christian philosopher, Richard Rothe—one of the profoundest thinkers of the age—adopts the same thought, we remember, in his *Theological Ethics*.[40] We let it pass here without further remark.

[Bushnell on the Personality of Satan]

We have been somewhat surprised to find Dr. Bushnell denying also the proper personality of Satan. He allows the existence of evil spirits; but is not willing to admit the idea of their organization under any single head. Satan, he tells us, is a collective term

---

they criticized the tendency toward pantheism that they considered the implication of the Hegelian system. For Nevin, both Calvin's and Hegel's views led logically into a Manichean dualism, which runs over "continually into the sphere of an equally helpless pantheism; two principles, two kingdoms, that shut out all possibility of a real inward reconciliation, and thus allow no room whatever for the idea of a natural historical salvation, such as it is the object of Christianity to accomplish." *Antichrist*, MTSS 6:194. The Gnostics, according to Nevin, with their denial of the humanity of Christ as the instrument of salvation, made redemption an exclusive spiritual matter. In this Gnostic dualism, redemption had little to do with "the actual presence of the divine heavenly fact itself." *Antichrist*, MTSS 6:192–93.]

38. [Gen 1:31.]

39. [Bushnell, *Nature*, 129.]

40. [Richard Rothe (1799–1867), German Lutheran theologian, opposed rationalism and agnosticism in his day, using a conservative appropriation of Hegel's and Schleiermacher's systems to defend and promote Christian theology. His multi-volume *Theologische Ethik* (1845, 1867) argued for an inseparable relationship between religion and morality.]

Document 12: Natural and Supernatural.

simply, designating "the all or total of bad minds and powers."[41] This is neither biblical, we think, nor ecclesiastical—though it *be* supported, curiously enough, by the authority of *Davenport*,[42] "the ablest theologian of all the New England Fathers."[43] It detracts also seriously, in our opinion, from the objective realness, and full historical significance, of the work of redemption, regarded as an actual supernatural conflict between the powers of light and the powers of darkness. A real personal Satan seems necessary, to bring out in full relief the idea of a real personal Christ. And so far as the danger of any Manichean dualism is concerned, we do not see that we are brought so nigh to it by any means in this way, as by the hypothesis of our respected author himself; which, as we have seen, makes sin to be a necessary thing a fact *sure* to come to pass—in the very constitution of the world itself. It carries indeed to our ear, we must confess, a very Zoroastrish sound,[44] when we are told up and down, that evil is "a bad possibility that environs God from eternity, waiting to become a fact, and certain to become a fact, whenever the opportunity is given;" so that, "the moment God creates a realm of powers, the bad possibility as certainly becomes a bad actuality—an outbreaking evil, or empire of evil, in created spirits, according to their order."[45]

[Bushnell's Christology]

We have said, that the great merit of Dr. Bushnell's book, as a plea for the supernatural, is its Christological character. Its argument centres in Jesus Christ; whose whole personality, as we have it portrayed in the Gospel, is shown with great beauty and force to be an altogether superhuman fact, and such a self-evidencing miracle in its own nature, as may well be considered sufficient to flood with the light of heavenly demonstration the universal *kosmos* of the new creation. And yet we do not feel after all, that enough is made still of the significance in this view of the great "mystery of godliness,"[46] as related to the supernatural on the one side and to the world of nature on the other.

The revelation of the supernatural in and by Christ is not of one kind, with the revelation of it in any other way. Nature in its own order needs the supernatural, reaches after it, and through the human spirit aspires toward it continually as the

---

41. [[Bushnell, *Nature*, 135.]

42. [John Davenport (1597–1670), Puritan theologian and pastor in the New Haven colony, supported a rigorous view of church membership, insisting in his *Catechism* (1659) on a verbal profession of a mature faith for membership.]

43. [Bushnell, *Nature*, 135.]

44. [Bushnell, *Nature*, 134. Zoroaster, an ancient Iranian prophet whose dates are unknown. His disciples promoted the view that two principles existed from eternity, one the cause of good and the other the cause of evil. For Nevin, Bushnell's view seems to resemble such a Manichean or Zoroastrian perspective.]

45. [Bushnell, *Nature*, 135.]

46. [1 Tim 3:16.]

necessary outlet and complement of its last wants. This aspiration, however, is in itself something negative merely, which as such can have no power of course ever to grasp the supernatural or to bring it down to its own sphere; for what nature might so fetch into itself by powers of its own would be no longer *super*-natural; the negative want or nisus here must be met, by a positive self-representation of its object from the other side. In these circumstances, there is room for imaginary or false relations to thrust themselves in as substitutes for the true. Men may invest their own speculative fancies and dreams—the shadowy projections of their spiritual nature itself reaching forth toward the dark void—with a sort of spurious objectivity; thus creating for themselves whole worlds of religion, that shall be found to mimic and caricature the truth in its proper form. Again, the powers of the invisible world may play into the economy of nature in an irregular, abnormal way, through Satanic inlets, offering themselves to the inward craving of the human spirit, as the very presence and sense of the supernatural which it needs for its perfection, and so hurrying it away, by the force of its religious instincts themselves, into a still more gloomy region of horrible unrealities and lies. To this sphere belong the sorcery, magic, and witchcraft of all ages, as well as the oracles and wonders of the heathen world generally, as far as it may be necessary to admit their more than natural character; and we have no hesitation, in referring to it also—as Dr. Bushnell does too—the so called "spiritual manifestations" of our own day, on the supposition of their being what they pretend to be and not mere tricks of jugglery; a question which it is not necessary here to discuss. The world, however, God be praised, has not been left hopelessly to the dominion of these phantoms and lies, growing out of such false relations to the supernatural. The truth has descended into it, under its own proper form. This is the idea of Revelation.

In one view, nature itself is a divine revelation. A supernatural presence underlies it, and works through it, at every point. But still as man now is, he has no power to come by this to any right knowledge of God, and much less to any firm and steady apprehension of a higher order of life in his presence. Hence an actual coming down of God into the world under a wholly new form, becomes the proper full sense of the supernatural as required now to meet our wants. Revelation, so understood, is a single fact; announcing its own advent by heavenly oracles and signs, making room for itself more and more by preliminary heaven-appointed dispensations, from the time of Adam down to the time of John the Baptist; but bursting forth at last, in its whole reality and glory, only in the ever-adorable mystery of the Incarnation. The supernatural in Christ thus is not in one line simply with the supernatural exhibited in previous divine revelations, a fact ranking high and conclusive among other facts of like superhuman order; it is the organic root rather of all true revelation from the beginning of the world; the one absolute truth in this form, which, coming in the fulness of time, makes good finally the sense of all previous oracles and outshinings from behind the veil, disclosing the real ground of them in its own presence. And being so related to what went before in the way of prophetical word and type, with still more certainty must the mystery be organically joined with all that comes after it, in the progressive unfolding of the Christian salvation. The Incarnation constitutes the gospel—being in its very nature a new revelation of God in the world, by which the life of heaven is made to unite itself with the life of earth, in a real abiding way, so as to bring the supernatural home to men in a form fully answerable to their inmost wants. In such view, it is the beginning of a new order of existence, the principle of a new creation, which in the nature of the case must hold under an objective, historical character, as something different from the world in its simply natural constitution, on to the end of time. This is the old Patristic idea of the Holy Catholic Church; and it is not difficult surely to see how, in the light of the subject as thus explained, so much account should have been made of it from the first, as being absolutely necessary for the full carrying out of the Christian mystery to its proper end.[47]

[Bushnell's Understanding of the Church]

We have the feeling, as we have said, that Dr. Bushnell's system of the supernatural, with all its Christological merit, fails somehow after all to lay hold of the full significance of the Incarnation, in the broad organic view now mentioned. In such way, we mean, as to make this, not merely the greatest of all arguments for the supernatural in a general view, but the absolute whole revelation of it, in the only form in which it can ever be truly and steadily objective to faith, and practically efficient for the purposes of redemption; so that all relations to it, all communications with it, on the outside of this great Mystery of Godliness, can never be anything better than relative only, dream-like, apparitional, or it may be absolutely magical, demoniacal, and false. For Rationalism, it should ever be borne in mind, has two sides, two opposite poles of unbelief, that are forever playing into each other with wonderful readiness and ease; an abstract naturalism on the one hand, that owns no reality higher than the present world; and then an abstract spiritualism on the other hand, by which the sense of the supernatural is not allowed to come to any real union with the sense of the natural in the way of faith, but is made to float over it fantastically in the way of mere Gnostic imagination. The one absolute Truth, according to St. John, as against both these antichristian extremes, is the real coming of Christ in the flesh (1 John 4:1–3); in making earnest with which under such view, it is not easy to see how faith should not feel itself constrained to make like earnest also with the old doctrine of the Church.[48]

---

47. [Nevin explained the "old Patristic idea" (in contrast to that of "modern" Puritanism) most fully in "Early Christianity," 538–62. But by the time Nevin wrote the present essay, he knew that it could not be directly retrievable. See his final thoughts on the issue in Nevin, "Thoughts on the Church," MTSS 7. A good overview of the problem is Evans, *Companion*, 82–93.]

48. [Here Nevin summarizes an analysis he had made in *Antichrist*, MTSS 5:177–99.]

This doctrine, we are sorry to say, struggles in vain throughout Dr. Bushnell's book to come to its proper clear and full expression; and the want of it, in our view, is a serious defect in his otherwise admirable Christological argument. He shows indeed at various points the power of churchly ideas—for all profound thinking on the historical significance of Christ's person *must* run more or less that way; he is ready enough too, of course, to acknowledge the existence of the Church in the general New England sense; but the conception of the Church, as it is made to be an article of faith, a first principle or ground element of Christianity, in the Apostles' Creed, and in all the ancient Creeds, has seemingly no place in his system whatever.

Thus the Gospel seems to be regarded by him too commonly, in the light of a constitution or fact qualifying the natural condition of the world generally in a supernatural way, and setting it in new relations to God within its old order of life; in virtue of which, it may be supposed capable then of coming at once, on its own level, within the range and scope of the powers of redemption, flowing around it spiritually at all times like the air of heaven. Whereas the mystery of the new creation in Christ would appear plainly to require, that we should conceive of it, not as any such system of heavenly possibilities added to the world in its general natural character, but as an objective constitution rather, having place in the world under a wholly different form, and carrying in itself relations and powers altogether peculiar, and not to be found anywhere beyond its own limits; an order of supernatural grace, into which men must be introduced first of all (the old ecclesiastical idea of re-birth through the sacrament of baptism) by an outward "obedience of faith,"[49] in order that they may come into the full use afterwards of its quickening and saving help. Any such view must necessarily exclude Dr. Bushnell's suggestion, that a regenerate life may be capable of passing, like the corruption of the race, by natural propagation, "under the well known laws of physiology,"[50] from parents to children; as it demands also a material qualification of a good deal that he says besides, on the subject of Christian experience, the work of the Spirit, and the new creation in Christ Jesus.

It is owing to this want of ecclesiastical feeling, no doubt, that Dr. Bushnell falls in so readily with the stereotyped Puritanic way of thinking in regard to the historical Church of past ages, by which it is made to be from the beginning, a systematic falling away from the proper sense of the Gospel, in all its points of difference from the prevalent spiritualism of modern times. In one of his chapters, we have an argument to show, that "the world is governed supernaturally in the interest of Christianity;"[51] which, carried out in any sort of consistency with itself, would seem to

49. [Rom 1:5; 16:26.]

50. [The exact quotation is not found in Bushnell's *Nature*, but the idea expressed by the quote can be found in Bushnell, *Nature*, 178. Nevin is probably recalling Bushnell's phrasing in the latter's first tract on infant baptism, *Discourses on Christian Nurture*: belief in "natural depravity" is "require[d]" by "the *familiar* laws of physiology" (qtd. in "Nevin and Bushnell: Christian Nurture," MTSS 6:51, emphasis added).]

51. [Bushnell, *Nature*, chapter 13, 405–45.]

Document 12: Natural and Supernatural.

involve necessarily a powerful presumption in favor of the old Catholic Church—the only form, in which, by general acknowledgment now, the truth of Christianity was maintained, through long ages, against all manner of infidelities and heresies seeking its destruction. But our author's theory will not allow the argument in any such way as that—he contrives to find here a wheel within a wheel, an esoteric *under-sense*, by which the outward complexion and first impression of God's providence are made to be one thing, and its hidden ulterior meaning another thing altogether. We are gravely told, accordingly, that Christianity *must* "go into a grand process of corruption at first,"[52] to make room for its own regeneration finally to a higher and better life. And so if the course of events, century after century, fall in concurrently with the march of Christianity in this false shape, verifying apparently in the fortunes of the Catholic Church the symbol of the bush that burned with fire and yet was not consumed, we are not to be moved by it at all as proving anything in favor of the Church, but to read in it on the contrary only a profound ordering of God's providence, designed to open the way for its ultimate confusion and defeat. Need we say that the providential, or historical, argument for Christianity, in any such form as this, is shorn of all force, and turned into a mere arbitrary conceit, which is capable of being used ingeniously with as much effect one way as another?

We have been pleased to find, that Dr. Bushnell does not shrink from confessing the continuation of the power of miracles in the Church, making them to be on fit occasions both possible and actual, from the first century down to the present time. We have long felt, that the popular notion on the subject, which supposes them to have continued for about three centuries after Christ, and then to have ceased entirely, is both against reason and without any sort of proper support in history.[53] The proof for miracles *after* the third century is altogether more full and clear, than the proof for miracles in the second and third centuries themselves. The real possibility of them, moreover, would seem to lie in the very conception of Christianity, considered as an order of supernatural powers enduringly present in the world to the end of time; so that one is at a loss to understand, what kind of faith in it *they* can have, who make a merit of mocking and scouting every miraculous pretension in its name, as being at once, and of itself, the surest evidence of gross imposture or blind superstition. With such irrational and irreligious skepticism our Hartford divine has no sympathy. He believes in the continuation of the power of miracles in the Church, down even to our own day; and more than that, he brings forward quite a number of what he considers well

---

52. [Bushnell, *Nature*, 421.]

53. [On the history of arguments for the end of miracles after the biblical age, see Ruthven, *On the Cessation of the Charismata*. For Nevin, "*faith in miracles*" was one of the criteria that distinguished the early church from "modern Puritanism:" "Early Christianity," 556, emphasis original (*Reformed and Catholic*, 253).]

authenticated examples of the miraculous in modern times, which have fallen in some measure under his own observation. It is curious to read his chapter on this subject.[54]

Here again, however, we are struck with the *unchurchly* spirit of his thinking. The old ecclesiastical miracles are not wholly to his taste; their ecclesiasticism at least seems to be counted a hindrance to their credibility, more than a help. His faith in such things appears to breathe most free, when it passes out of that order, and is allowed to expatiate at large among wonders more or less extra-ecclesiastical in their form and character. We shall not pretend, of course, to enter here into any examination of his cases. We must say, however, that Church miracles in the proper sense—miracles, we mean, as mediated by the idea of the Church in the old Augustinian view—are vastly more respectable, in our eyes, than any such class of examples under a different and more general type. We question, indeed, if it be possible to make earnest with the belief of miracles at all, except in connection with some believing apprehension of the mystery of the Church, in the sense of the Apostles' Creed. Out of that order, the supernatural as related to the present world, would seem to carry with it always, even under its best and most reliable manifestations, a certain character of Gnostic unreality, making it to be no proper object for steady Christian faith. We have been much struck with the frank confession of Dr. Bushnell himself, after all his examples, in regard to this point. "As regards the general truth," he tells us,

> that supernatural facts, such as healings, tongues, and other gifts, may as well be manifested now as at any former time, and that there never has been a formal discontinuance, I am perfectly satisfied. I know no proof to the contrary, that appears to me to have a straw's weight. And yet, when I come to the question of being in such gifts, or of receiving into easy credit those who appear to be, I acknowledge that for some reason, either because of some latent subjection to the conventionalities of philosophy, or to the worse conventionalities of sin, belief does not follow, save in a somewhat faltering and equivocal way.[55]

But so it is, he adds, with many great questions of God and immortality.

> The arguments are good and clear, but for some reason, they do not make faith, and we are still surprised to find, in our practice, that we only doubtfully believe. To believe these supernatural things, in the form of particular facts, is certainly difficult; and how conscious are we, as we set ourselves to the questions, of the weakness of our vacillations! Pardon us, Lord, that when we make so much of mere credibilities and rationalities of opinion, we are yet so slow to believe that what we have shown to be credible and rational, is actually coming to pass."[56]

---

54. [Bushnell, *Nature*, chapter 14, 446–92.]

55. [Bushnell, *Nature*, 491.]

56. [Bushnell, *Nature*, 492. Bushnell's struggle with rational arguments for belief was life-long; see the description of what passed for his "conversion" in Nevin et al., *Born of Water*, MTSS 6:34–35.]

Document 12: Natural and Supernatural.

Verily, it *is* a great thing to have faith, even as a grain of mustard seed; to be able to own and embrace, not merely the thought of the supernatural in a natural way, but the real presence of it in its own order; to hold the proper verity of the Gospel, not in the form of doctrine only, or supposed inward experiences, but in the form of full objective, historical fact. To be able to say the Creed, in its own meaning and sense. To stand before the Man Jesus, and confess, with more than natural knowledge, as Peter did: "*Thou* art the Christ, the Son of the living God."[57] To believe that "Christ is come in the flesh,"[58] with all the necessary antecedents, concomitants, and consequents of such a revelation; his birth of the Virgin, full of grace, and blessed among women; his miracles in the days of his flesh; his resurrection and ascension; his new presence in the world by the Spirit; the supernatural order of the Church, set over against the order of nature, and comprehending in itself the powers of his resurrection life to the end of time. This is the Gospel, as we find it preached everywhere in the Acts of the Apostles—as it underlies all the New Testament Epistles—as it animated the spirit of martyrs and confessors in the first Christian ages; and the power of believing it, we repeat, is indeed so great a thing, that all worldly advantages in comparison, may well seem to be both poor and mean. Such faith, from the very nature of the case, must be itself supernatural—the power of passing beyond nature, so as to lay hold of things heavenly and divine in their own higher order and sphere. It must come into the soul then in and through the constitution of grace itself, under its character of objective distinction from the constitution of man's merely natural life. There may be actings of the organ or faculty, indeed, on the outside of this; but these will be always in a more or less Gnostic and unreal way; forms of believing, we may say, filled as yet with no proper contents of faith; the virtue can come to full exercise in the bosom of the Christian mystery alone. And what now if the standing form of this mystery in the world be still the Church, as it was held to be in the beginning? Could faith do its office, in that case, while denying, despising, ignoring, or overlooking its claims? One use of his argument for the supernatural Dr. Bushnell finds in this, that it provides a place and a plea for the "positive institutions of religion," as he calls them—meaning by these, church organization, the sacraments, the Sabbath, the Bible, the office of the ministry, &c.—which are allowed to be "falling rapidly into disrespect, as if destined finally to be quite lost or sunk in oblivion."[59] This fact itself he ascribes to the growth and pervading influence of naturalism. But may we not reverse the order, and make the loss of belief—we will not say in the positive institutions of Christianity—but in the Christian Church itself, one large cause of the reigning decay of faith in a wider view? To restore the supernatural to its general rights, then, nothing would be needed so much, first of all, as a resuscitation of faith in the Church. Then, also, any argument for the supernatural, any plea

---

57. [Matt 16:16.]
58. [1 John 4:2.]
59. [Bushnell, *Nature*, 509.]

for the Christological in its sound and right form, to be of full force and effect in the end, must be at the same time ecclesiastical also, or, in other words, an argument for the old doctrine of the Church, as it stands enshrined in the early Creeds. Is it too much to hope, that Dr. Bushnell's earnest and active mind may yet be turned to the subject, under this profoundly interesting view?

 Lancaster, Pa.   J. W. N.

Bibliography

Allen, Gay Wilson. *Waldo Emerson: A Biography*. New York: Viking Press, 1981.

Andrews, Reath. *Agency and Autonomy in Kant's Moral Theory*. Oxford: Oxford University Press, 2006.

"The Anglican Crisis." *New York Freeman's Journal* (August 9, 1851), 3, 6.

Appel, Theodore. *The Life and Work of John Williamson Nevin*. Philadelphia: Reformed Church Publication House, 1889. Reprint, New York: Arno, 1969.

———. "A Sketch of Marshall College from 1836 to 1841. Under the Presidency of Dr. Rauch." *MR* 34 (1887) 518–47.

Armstrong, Chris. "C.S. Lewis on pagan philosophy as a road to Christian faith." https://gratefultothedead.com/2013/10/23/c-s-lewis-on-pagan-philosophy-as-a-road-to-christian-faith/.

———. "The Pagan element of Christian tradition: All truth is God's truth." https://gratefultothedead.com/2013/10/22/the-pagan-element-of-christian-tradition-all-truth-is-gods-truth/.

Ashton, Rosemary. *The Life of Samuel Taylor Coleridge: A Critical Biography*. Oxford: Blackwell, 1996.

Aubert, Anne G. *The German Roots of Nineteenth-Century American Theology*. Oxford: Oxford University Press, 2013.

Bains, David R., and Theodore Louis Trost. "Philip Schaff: The Flow of Church History and the Development of Protestantism." *Theology Today* 71, no. 4 (January 2015) 416–28. https://doi.org/10.1177/0040573614552925.

Baird, Charles W. *The Presbyterian Liturgies: Historical Sketches*. M. W. Dodd, 1855. Reprint, Eugene, OR: Wipf & Stock, 2006.

"'Baptismal Grace': A Conversation between Nevin and 'Inquirer' for the Weekly Messenger." In *Born of Water and the Spirit: Essays on the Sacraments and Christian Formation*, edited by David W. Layman, 64–68. By John Williamson Nevin et al. MTSS 6. Eugene, OR: Wipf & Stock, 2016.

Baur, F.C. *History of Christian Dogma (1858)*. Oxford: Oxford University Press, 2014.

Beecher, Lyman. *Plea for the West*. 2nd ed. Cincinnati: Truman & Smith and New York: Leavitt, Lord: 1835.

Beiser, Frederick C. *German Idealism: The Struggle Against Subjectivism, 1781–1801*. Cambridge: Harvard University Press, 2002.

Berk, Stephen E. *Calvinism Versus Democracy: Timothy Dwight and the Origins of American Evangelical Orthodoxy*. Hamden, Connecticut: Archon, 1974.

Beyschlag, Willibald. "Ullmann, Karl." In *A Religious Encyclopædia: or Dictionary of Biblical, Historical, Doctrinal, and Practical Theology*, 3:2415–16. Rev. ed. Edited by Philip Schaff et al. New York: Christian Literature, 1889.

Billington, Ray Allen. *The Protestant Crusade, 1800–1860: A Study in the Origins of American Nativism*. New York: Macmillan, 1938. Reprint, Chicago: Quadrangle Books, 1964.

Binkley, Luther J. *The Mercersburg Theology*. Lancaster, Pennsylvania: Franklin and Marshall College, 1953.

Black, Andrew. "A 'Vast Practical Embarrassment': John W. Nevin, the Mercersburg Theology, and the Church Question." PhD diss., University of Dayton, 2013.

Bonomo, Jonathan G. *Incarnation and Sacrament: The Eucharistic Controversy between Charles Hodge and John Williamson Nevin*. Eugene, OR: Wipf & Stock, 2010.

Book of Common Prayer. New York: The Church Hymnal Corporation, 1945.

Book of Mormon Critical Text. Provo, Utah: Foundation for Ancient Research and Mormon Studies, 1984.

Borneman, Adam S. *Church, Sacrament, and American Democracy: The Social and Political Dimensions of John Williamson Nevin's Theology of Incarnation*. Eugene, OR: Wipf & Stock, 2011.

Bossuet, Jacques. *History of the Variations of the Protestant Churches*. Reprint, Fraser, Michigan: American Council on Economics and Society, 1997.

Bradshaw, Paul. *The Origins of Feasts, Fasts, and Seasons in Early Christianity*. Collegeville, Minnesota: Liturgical, 2011.

Brain, Robert Michael. *The Pulse of Modernism: Physiological Aesthetics in Fin-de-Siècle Europe*. Seattle: University of Washington Press, 2015.

Bratt, James D. "Nevin and the Antebellum Culture Wars." In *Reformed Confessionalism in Nineteenth-Century America: Essays on the Thought of John Williamson Nevin*, edited by Sam Hamstra Jr. and Arie J. Griffioen, 1–21. Lanham: Scarecrow, 1995.

Brown, Stewart J. and Peter Nockles, eds. *The Oxford Movement: Europe and the Wider World, 1830–1930*. Cambridge: Cambridge University Press, 2012.

[Brownson, Orestes A.] "The British Reformation." *BQR* 7 (January 1845) 29–53.

———. The [Orestes A.] Brownson Papers. University of Notre Dame Archives, Notre Dame, Indiana.

———. "Bushnellism: or Orthodoxy and Heresy Identical." *BQR* 11 (October 1849) 495–517; 13 (January 1851) 1–29; (April 1851) 137–64; (July 1851) 318–61.

———. "The Catholic Magazine and Ourselves." *BQR* 7 (April 1845) 258–62.

———. "Christianity or Gentilism?" *BQR* 22 (January 1860) 1–42.

———. "The Church Against No-Church." *BQR* 7 (April 1845) 137–94.

———. "The Church in the Dark Ages." *BQR* 11 (July 1849) 330–57.

———. "Church Organism." *BQR* 20 (January 1858) 103–27.

———. "Civil and Religious Toleration." *BQR* 11 (July 1849) 277–309.

———. "Doctrinal Developments." *BQR* 10 (October 1848) 525–39.

———. "Evangelical Alliance." *BQR* 28 (January 1874) 93–106.

———. "Faith Not Possible Without the Church." *BQR* 8 (January 1846) 1–40.

———. "The Great Question." *BQR* 9 (October 1847) 413–58.

———. "H. M. S. Fields." *BQR* 11 (July 1849) 309–30.

———. "Liberalism and Catholicity." *BQR* 8 (July 1846) 273–327.

———. "Literary and Miscellaneous Notices." *BQR* (January 1847) 128–30.

———. "The Mercersburg Hypothesis." *BQR* 16 (April 1854) 253–65.

———. "The Mercersburg Review." *BQR* 12 (April 1850) 191–228.

———. "The Mercersburg Theology." *BQR* 12 (July 1850) 353–78.

———. "Methodist Quarterly Review." *BQR* 8 (January 1846) 89–107.

———. "Natural and Supernatural." *BQR* 9 (January 1847) 100–16.

———. "Newman's Development of Christian Doctrine." *BQR* 8 (July 1846) 342–68.

———. "Newman's Theory of Christian Doctrine." *BQR* 9 (January 1847) 39–86.

———. "The New Volume." *BQR* 8 (January 1846) 135–36.

———. "Parker's Discourse on Matters Pertaining to Religion." *Boston Quarterly Review* 5 (October 1842) 385–512.

———. "*The Primacy of the Apostolic See vindicated*, by Francis Patrick Kenrick." *BQR* 7 (April 1845) 263–66.

———. "*The Principle of Protestantism*." *BQR* 7 (October 1845) 546–47.

———. "Professor Park Against Catholicity." *BQR* 7 (October 1845) 442–514.

———. "Protestantism Ends in Transcendentalism." *BQR* 8 (July 1846) 369–99.

———. "Recent Publications." *BQR* 9 (April 1847) 216–49.

———. "Religious Novels." *BQR* 9 (January 1847) 128–30.

———. "Reply to the Mercersburg Review." *BQR* 12 (April 1850) 191–228.

———. "The Reunion of All Christians." *BQR* 24 (January 1862) 1–34.

———. "R. W. Emerson's Poems." *BQR* 9 (April 1847) 262–76.

———. "Sermons on the Obedience of Faith." *BQR* 12 (October 1850) 448–65.

———. "Symbolism." *BQR* 1 (July 1844) 408–410.

———. "The Two Brothers; or, Why are you a Protestant?" *BQR* 9 (January 1847) 1–39; (April 1847) 137–63; (July 1847) 277–305; 10 (January 1848) 101–16.

———. "Union with the Church." *Catholic World* 12 (October 1870) 1–16.

———. "We cannot resist." *BQR* 11 (July 1849) 411–12.

Bushman, Richard L. *Joseph Smith and the Beginnings of Mormonism*. Urbana: University of Illinois Press, 1984.

Bushnell, Horace. *Barbarism the First Danger: A Discourse for Home Missions*. New York: American Home Missionary Society, 1847.

———. *Christian Nurture*. New York: Charles Scribner, 1861. Reprint, Grand Rapids, MI: Baker, 1979.

———. *Discourses on Christian Nurture*. Boston: Massachusetts Sabbath School Society, 1847.

———. *Nature and the Supernatural as Together Constituting the One System of God*. New York: C. Scribner, 1858.

———. *Views of Christian Nurture, and of Subjects Adjacent Thereto*. Hartford, CT: Edwin Hunt, 1848.

Calvin, John. *Institutes of the Christian Religion*. Edited by John T. McNeill. Translated by Ford Lewis Battles. 2 vols. Philadelphia: Westminster, 1960.

The Cambridge Companion to Thomas Reid. Edited by Terence Cuneo and René van Woudenberg. Cambridge: Cambridge University Press, 2004.

Canlis, Julie. "Calvin, Osiander and Participation in God." *International Journal of Systematic Theology* 6, no. 2 (April 2004) 169–84.

Carey, Patrick W., ed. *The Early Works of Orestes A. Brownson*. 7 vols. Milwaukee: Marquette University Press, 2000–2007.

———. *An Immigrant Bishop: John England's Adaptation of Irish Catholicism to American Republicanism*. 2nd ed. Washington, DC: The Catholic University of America Press, 2022.

———. *Orestes A. Brownson: American Religious Weathervane.* Grand Rapids, Michigan: William B. Eerdmans, 2004.

Carlen, Claudia, ed. *The Papal Encyclicals 1740–1878.* Raleigh: Pierian, 1990.

Cecil, Anthony C. *The Theological Development of Edwards Amasa Park, Last of the "Consistent Calvinists."* Missoula, Montana: American Academy of Religion, 1974.

Chalybäus, Heinrich Moritz. *Historical Development of Speculative Philosophy from Kant to Hegel.* Translated by Alfred Edersheim. Edinburgh: T. & T. Clark, 1854.

Chambers, Robert. *Vestiges of the Natural History of Creation.* London: John Churchill, 1844.

Cherry, Conrad. *Nature and Religious Imagination: From Edwards to Bushnell.* Philadelphia: Fortress, 1980.

Coakley, Sarah. *God, Sexuality, and the Self.* Cambridge: Cambridge University Press, 2013.

Coleridge, Samuel Taylor. *Aids to Reflection.* London: Taylor and Hessey, 1825.

Collins, Robert E. *Theodore Parker: American Transcendentalist. A Critical Essay and a Collection of his Writings.* Metuchen, New Jersey: Scarecrow, 1973.

Colton, Calvin. *Protestant Jesuitism.* New York: Harper and Brothers, 1836.

Committee of Polish Emigrants in London. *Address to the British Nation.* London: Milton, 1836.

Conforti, J. A. *Samuel Hopkins and the New Divinity Movement: Calvinism, the Congregational Ministry, and Reform in New England Between the Great Awakenings.* Grand Rapids, Michigan: Eerdmans, 1981.

Crossley, John. "Schleiermacher's Christian Ethics in Relation to His Philosophical Ethics." *The Annual of the Society of Christian Ethics* 18 (1998) 93–117.

Crowell, William. *The Church Member's Manual of Ecclesiastical Principles, Doctrine and Discipline.* Boston: Gould and Lincoln, 1852.

Curti, Merle. "Impact of the Revolutions of 1848 on American Thought." *Proceedings of the American Philosophical Society* 93 (June 1949) 209–15.

Davy, John. *Memoires of the Life of Sir Humphry Davy.* Cambridge: Cambridge University Press, 1836.

DeBie, Linden J. *John Williamson Nevin: Evangelical Catholic.* Eugene, Oregon: Pickwick, 2023.

———. *Speculative Theology and Common Sense Religion: Mercersburg and the Conservative Roots of American Religion.* Eugene, OR: Pickwick, 2008.

Descartes, René. *The Philosophical Works of Descartes.* Translated by Elizabeth S. Haldane and G. R. T. Ross. 2 vol. London: Cambridge University Press, 1931.

Dietrich, Donald J., and Michael J. Himes, eds. *The Legacy of the Tubingen School: The Relevance of Nineteenth-Century Theology for the Twenty-First Century.* Freiburg: Herder and Herder, 1997.

Digby, Kenelm Henry. *Catholici Mores, or Ages of Faith.* London: Dolman, 1845.

DiPuccio, William. "The Dynamic Realism of Mercersburg Theology: The Romantic Pursuit of the Ideal in the Actual." PhD diss., Marquette University, 1994.

———. *The Interior Sense of Scripture: The Sacred Hermeneutics of John Williamson Nevin.* Macon, Georgia: Mercer University Press, 1998.

———. "Nevin & Coleridge." *New Mercersburg Review,* no. 17 (1995) 59–63.

Dorner, Isaak August. "Der liturgische Kampf in die deutsch-reformirten Kirche Nord-Amerika's: mit besonderer Beziehung auf die evangelische Principienlehre." In *Jahrbücher für Deutsche Theologie,* 193–250. Dreizehnter Band. Gotha: Rud. Besser, 1868. Translated as *The Liturgical Conflict in the Reformed Church of North America, with Special Reference to Fundamental Evangelical Doctrines*. Philadelphia: Loag, 1868. Reprint, *The Reformed Church Monthly* 1 (1868) 327–81.

Dowe, Dieter, ed. *Europe in 1848: Revolution and Reform*. New York: Berghahn, 2000.

Draper, John William. *History of the Conflict Between Religion and Science*. New York: D. Appleton, 1874.

"Dr. Nevin and Dr. Berg." *New York Freeman's Journal* (June 19, 1852) 5.

"Dr. Nevin on the Theology of St. Cyprian." *New York Freeman's Journal* (August 14, 1852) 6.

Dwight, Timothy. *Theology; Explained and Defended in a Series of Sermons*. New Haven: Clark and Lyman, 1818–19.

Edwards, Mark. *Catholicity and Heresy in the Early Church*. London: Routledge, 2009.

Edwards, Paul, ed. *Encyclopedia of Philosophy*. Vol. 2. New York: Macmillan, 1967.

Edwards, Robert Lansing. *Of Singular Genius, of Singular Grace: A Biography of Horace Bushnell*. Cleveland: Pilgrim, 1992.

Eire, Carlos M. N. *Reformations: The Early Modern World, 1450–1650*. New Haven: Yale University Press, 2016.

"The Election." Reprint, *Western Literary Messenger* 11, no. 4 (December 1848) 190–91.

Ellis, Joseph J. *After the Revolution: Profiles of Early American Culture*. New York: W. W. Norton, 1979.

England, John. "The Republic in Danger." In *The Works of The Right Reverend John England, First Bishop of Charleston*, 4:13–68. 5 vols. Baltimore: John Murphy, 1849.

"European Affairs to Week Ending July 14." *Spirit of the Age* 1, no. 3 (July 21, 1849) 46.

Evans, James H. *We Have Been Believers: An African American Systematic Theology*. 2nd ed. Minneapolis: Fortress, 2012.

Evans, R. J. W. and Hartmut Pogge von Strandmann, eds. *The Revolutions in Europe 1848–1849: From Reform to Reaction*. Oxford, Oxford University Press, 2000.

Evans, William B. *A Companion to the Mercersburg Theology: Evangelical Catholicism in the Mid-Nineteenth Century*. Eugene, OR: Cascade Books, 2019.

———. General Introduction to *The Incarnate Word: Selected Writings on Christology*, by John Williamson Nevin et al., xv–xxxvi. Edited by William B. Evans. MTSS 4. Eugene, OR: Wipf & Stock, 2014.

———. "Twin Sons of Different Mothers: The Remarkable Theological Convergence of John W. Nevin and Thomas F. Torrance." *Haddington House Journal* 11 (2009) 155–173.

Farley, Michael. "The Liturgical Theology of John Williamson Nevin." *Studia Liturgica* 33, no. 2 (September 2003) 204–22.

Faught, C. Brad. *The Oxford Movement: A Thematic History of the Tractarians and Their Times*. University Park: Pennsylvania State University Press, 2003.

Fitzer, Joseph. *Moehler and Baur in Controversy, 1832–38*. Tallahassee, Florida: American Academy of Religion, 1974.

Formal Opening of Franklin and Marshall College, in the City of Lancaster, June 7, 1853 Together with Addresses Delivered on the Occasion. Lancaster, Pennsylvania: Board of Trustees, 1853.

Forster, Michael. "Friedrich Daniel Ernst Schleiermacher." *The Stanford Encyclopedia of Philosophy*. Summer 2022 Edition. https://plato.stanford.edu/archives/sum2022/entries/schleiermacher/.

Fox, Michael Allen. *The Accessible Hegel*. Amherst, N. Y.: Humanity, 2005.

Gerrish, B. A. *A Prince of the Church: Schleiermacher and the Beginning of Modern Theology*. Philadelphia: Fortress, 1984.

Giustiniani, Louis. *Intrigues of Jesuitism in the United States of America*. New York: R. Craighead, 1846.

———. *Papal Rome as it is, by a Roman*. 2nd ed. Baltimore, 1843.

Goen, C. C. *Broken Churches, Broken Nation: Denominational Schisms and the Coming of the American Civil War*. Macon, Georgia: Mercer University Press, 1995.

Gorman, Robert. *Catholic Apologetic Literature in the United States (1784–1858)*. Washington, D. C.: Catholic University Press, 1939.

Guyer, Paul and Rolf-Peter Horstmann. "Idealism." *The Stanford Encyclopedia of Philosophy*. Fall 2022 Edition. https://plato.stanford.edu/archives/fall2022/entries/idealism/.

Haddorff, David. *Dependence and Freedom: The Moral Thought of Horace Bushnell*. Lanham, Maryland: University Press of America, 1994.

Hadley, Arthur Twining. *Baccalaureate Addresses and Other Talks on Kindred Themes*. Reprint, Freeport, New York: Books for Libraries, 1967.

Hamstra, Sam Jr. and Arie J. Griffioen, eds. *Reformed Confessionalism in Nineteenth-Century America: Essays on the Thought of John Williamson Nevin*. Lanham, Md.: American Theological Library Association, 1995.

Harrelson, Walter. "Shekinah." In *New Interpreter's Dictionary of the Bible*, 5:222. Nashville: Abingdon Press, 2009.

Hart, D. G. *John Williamson Nevin: High Church Calvinist*. Phillipsburg, New Jersey: P & R, 2005.

Hatch, Nathan O. *The Democratization of American Christianity*. New Haven: Yale University Press, 1989.

Hegel, G. W. F. *Phenomenology of Spirit*. Translated by A. V. Miller. Oxford: Oxford University Press, 1977.

———. *The Science of Logic*. Translated by George Di Giovanni. Cambridge: Cambridge University Press, 2010.

Hobbes, Thomas. *Leviathan*. Reprint, London: Continuum, 2005.

Hodge, Archibald Alexander. *The Life of Charles Hodge*. Reprint, New York: Arno Press, 1969.

Hodge, Charles. "Critical Notices." *Princeton Review* (October 1845) 626–36.

———. "Doctrine of the Reformed Church on the Lord's Supper." *The Biblical Repertory and the Princeton Review* 20 (April 1848) 227–77. Reprint, *Essays and Reviews*, 341–92. New York: Robert Carter, 1857.

———. "Review of *The Principle of Protestantism* by Philip Schaf." In *The Development of the Church: "The Principle of Protestantism" and other Historical Writings of Philip Schaff*, edited by David R. Bains and Theodore Louis Trost, 213–22. MTSS 3. Eugene, OR: Wipf & Stock, 2016.

———. "Short Notices: *Antichrist; or the Spirit of Sect and Schism* by John W. Nevin." *The Biblical Repertory and the Princeton Review* 20 (October 1848) 627–31.

———. *Systematic Theology*. 3 vols. New York: Charles Scribner, 1872; Scribner, Armstrong, 1873.

———. "What is Christianity?" *Biblical Repertory and Princeton Review* 32 (January 1860) 118–61.

Holifield, E. Brooks. *Theology in America: Christian Thought from the Age of the Puritans to the Civil War*. New Haven, CT: Yale University Press, 2003.

Holmes, Barbara. *Race and the Cosmos*. 2nd ed. Albuquerque, New Mexico: CAC, 2020.

Hopkins, John Henry. *History of the Confessional*. New York: Harper and Brothers, 1850.

———. *The Primitive Church Compared with the Protestant Episcopal Church of the Present Day: Being an Examination of the Ordinary Objections Against the Church in Doctrine, Worship, and Government, Designed for Popular Use: With a Dissertation on Sundry Points of Theology and Practice Connected with the Subject of Episcopacy*. Burlington: Smith and Harrington, 1835.

———. *Sixteen Lectures on the Causes, Principles, and Results, of the British Reformation*. Philadelphia: J. M. Campbell, 1844.

Hopkins, Mark. *The Manifoldness of Man: A Baccalaureate Sermon Delivered at Williamstown, Ms, July 31, 1859*. Boston: T. R. Marvin & Son, 1859.

Hopkins, Samuel. *The System of Doctrines, Contained in Divine Revelation, Explained and Defended*. Boston: Isaiah Thomas and Ebenezer T. Andrews, 1793.

Horky, Philip Sydney. *Plato and Pythagoreanism*. Oxford: Oxford University Press, 2013.

Howe, Daniel Walker. *What Hath God Wrought: The Transformation of America, 1815–1848*. New York: Oxford University Press, 2007.

Hughes, John. *The Decline of Protestantism and Its Cause*. New York: E. Dunigan, 1850.

Hughes, John and John B. Neathery. *The Christian Law of Charity: A Discourse Delivered before the Graduating Class at the University of North Carolina*. Chapel Hill: University Magazine, 1860.

Hulliung, Mark. *The Social Contract in America: From the Revolution to the Present Age*. Lawrence: University of Kansas Press, 2007.

Humboldt, Alexander Von. *Kosmos: Entwurf einer physischen Weltbeschreibung*. 5 vols. Stuttgart: Gotta, 1845–62. Translated as *Cosmos: a Sketch of a Physical Description of the Universe*, by E. C. Otté and W. S. Dallas. 5 vols. London: Henry G. Bohn, 1849–58.

Hume, David. *An Enquiry concerning Human Understanding*. Edited by Tom L. Beauchamp. Oxford: Oxford University Press, 1999.

———. *The History of England: Under the House of Tudor*. Vol. 2. London: Millar, 1759.

Hurter, Friedrich Emmanuel Von. *Geschichte Papst Innocenz des Dritten und seine Zeitgenossen*. 4 Vols. Hamburg: Perthes, 1834–42.

Ives, Levi Silliman, *The Trials of a Mind in its Progress to Catholicism: A Letter to his old Friends*. Boston: P. Donahoe, 1854.

Jackman, Sydney Wayne. *Nicholas Cardinal Wiseman: A Victorian Prelate and His Writings*. Dublin: Five Lamps, 1977.

Jennings, Willie James. *The Christian Imagination: Theology and the Origins of Race*. New Haven: Yale University Press, 2010.

Jenson, Robert W. *Systematic Theology, Volume 1: The Triune God*. New York: Oxford University Press, 1997.

Johnson, Robert and Adam Cureton. "Kant's Moral Philosophy." *The Stanford Encyclopedia of Philosophy*. Fall 2022 Edition. Edward N. Zalta & Uri Nodelman, eds. https://plato.stanford.edu/archives/fall2022/entries/kant-moral/.

Johnson, William A. *Nature and the Supernatural in the Theology of Horace Bushnell*. Lund: C. W. K. Gleerup, 1963.

Joost-Gaugier, Christiane L. *Measuring Heaven: Pythagoras and his Influence on Thought and Art in Antiquity and the Middle Ages*. Ithaca: Cornell University Press, 2006.

Kant, Immanuel. *Critique of Practical Reason*. Edited by Mary J. Gregor. Cambridge Texts in the History of Philosophy. Cambridge: Cambridge University Press, 1997. eBook Collection, EBSCOhost. Accessed October 18, 2022.

———. *Critique of Pure Reason*. Translated by Werner S. Pluhar. Indianapolis: Hackett, 1996.

———. *Groundwork for the Metaphysics of Morals*. Edited by Allen W. Wood. Yale University Press, 2018. ProQuest Ebook Central. Accessed October 18, 2022 and June 27, 2023.

Kenngott, George F. *The Record of a City: A Social Survey of Lowell Massachusetts*. New York: Macmillan, 1912.

Kenrick, Francis Patrick. *The Catholic Doctrine on Justification Explained and Vindicated*. Reprint, Lexington, Kentucky: St. Pius X, 2013.

———. *The Primacy of the Apostolic See, and the Authority of General Councils, Vindicated; in a Series of Letters Addressed to the Right Rev. J. H. Hopkins*. Philadelphia, 1838.

———. *The Primacy of the Holy See Vindicated*. 6th ed. Baltimore: John Murphy, 1867.

———. *Theologia Dogmatica*. 4 vols. Philadelphia, 1834–40.

———. *Theologia Moralis*. 3 vols. Philadelphia, 1841–43.

Ker, Ian. *John Henry Newman: A Biography*. Oxford: Clarendon Press, 1988.

Knox, John. *First Blast of the Trumpet Against the Monstruous Regiment of Women*. In *The Works of John Knox*, 4:365–422. Edited by David Laing. Edinburgh: Johnstone and Hunter, 1855.

Kossuth, Louis and Steven Béla Várady. *The Life of Governor Louis Kossuth with his Public Speeches in the United States, and a Brief History of the Hungarian War of Independence*. Reprint, Budapest: Osiris, 2001.

Krauth, Charles Philip. *Human Life: A Baccalaureate Address Delivered on the Sabbath Before Commencement, September 15, 1850, to the Senior Class of Pennsylvania College*. Gettysburg: H. C. Neinstedt, 1850.

Larson, Wayne A. "Philip Schaff's Idea of Historical Progress & Its Critique of the Church in 19th Century America." http://hornes.org/theologia/wayne-larson/philip-schaffs-idea-of-historical-progress.

Layman, David W. General Editor's Introduction to *One, Holy, Catholic, and Apostolic, Tome 2: Nevin's Writings on Ecclesiology (1851–1858)*, by John Williamson Nevin, 1–6. Edited by Sam Hamstra Jr. MTSS 7. Eugene, OR: Wipf & Stock, 2017.

———. General Introduction to *Born of Water and the Spirit: Essays on the Sacraments and Christian Formation*, by John Williamson Nevin et al., 1–33. Edited by David W. Layman. MTSS 6. Eugene, OR: Wipf & Stock, 2016.

———. "Nevin's Holistic Supernaturalism." In *Reformed Confessionalism in Nineteenth-Century America: Essays on the Thought of John Williamson Nevin*, edited by Sam Hamstra Jr. and Arie J. Griffioen, 193–208. Lanham: Scarecrow, 1995.

———. "The Sources of Nevin's Piety." *New Mercersburg Review*, no. 17 (1995) 4–14.

Lewis, C. S. *The Abolition of Man*. New York: Touchstone, 1996.

Lewis, Tayler. "The Revolutionary Spirit." *The Biblical Repository and Classical Review*, 3rd series 16 (October 1848) 670–98.

———. *The Revolutionary Spirit: A Discourse Delivered Before the Phi Beta Kappa Society of the Wesleyan University*. New York: C. W. Benedict, 1848.

Lilla, S. "Ammonius Saccas." In *Encyclopedia of Ancient Christianity* 1:103–5. Downers Grove, IL: InterVarsity, 2014.

Lindbeck, George A. *The Nature of Doctrine: Religion and Theology in a Postliberal Age*. Philadelphia: Westminster, 1984.

Lindemann, Marty. *Medicine and Society in Early Modern Europe*. Cambridge: Cambridge University Press, 2010.

Littlejohn, W. Bradford. *The Mercersburg Theology and the Quest for Reformed Catholicity*. Eugene, OR: Wipf & Stock, 2009.

———. "Sectarianism and the Search for Visible Catholicity: Lessons from John Nevin and Richard Hooker." *Theology Today* 71 (2015) 404–415.

Livingston, James C. *The Enlightenment and the Nineteenth Century.* Vol. 1 of *Modern Christian Thought.* 2nd ed. Minneapolis: Fortress, 2006.

Livingston, Vanbrugh. *An Inquiry into the Merits of the Reformed Doctrine of Imputation.* New York: Casserly, 1843.

———. *Remarks on "Oxford Theology," in Connection with its Bearing on the Law of Nature, and the Doctrine of Justification by Faith.* New York: J. S. Taylor, 1841.

Lord, Nathan. *Paul a Model: A Baccalaureate Discourse to the Graduating Class of 1860, at Dartmouth College.* Hanover: Dartmouth, 1860.

Lowell, James Russell. *A Fable for Critics.* Reprint, Boston: Ticknor and Fields, 1864.

Loyola, Ignatius. "Rules for Thinking with the Church." In *The Spiritual Exercises of St. Ignatius.* Nos. 352–70, pp. 127–31. Translated by Kevin F. O'Brien. Chicago: Loyola Press, 2020.

Macaulay, Ambrose. "'Strong Views . . . in very strong forms': Paul Cullen, Archbishop of Armagh (1849–52)." In *Cardinal Paul Cullen and his World*, edited by Dáire Keogh and Albert McDonnell, 78–98. Dublin: Four Courts, 2011.

MacCulloch, Diarmaid. *Reformation: Europe's House Divided, 1490–1700.* New York: Penguin, 2004.

Marsden, George M. *Fundamentalism and American Culture: The Shaping of Twentieth-Century Evangelicalism, 1870–1925.* Oxford: Oxford University Press, 1980.

Marvin, Carolyn. *When Old Technologies Were New: Thinking About Electric Communication in the Late Nineteenth Century.* New York: Oxford University Press, 1990.

Maxwell, Jack Martin. *Worship and Reformed Theology: The Liturgical Lessons of Mercersburg.* Pittsburgh Theological Monograph Series, no. 10. Pittsburgh: Pickwick, 1976.

McIlvaine, Charles Pettit. *Oxford Divinity Compared with that of the Romish and Anglican Churches with a Special View to the Illustration of the Doctrine of Justification by Faith.* Philadelphia: Whetham, 1841.

McPherson, James M. *Battle Cry of Freedom: The Civil War Era.* Oxford: Oxford University Press, 1988.

"The Mercersburg Review: July No. Dr. Nevin on Cyprian." *New York Freeman's Journal* (August 21, 1852) 1, 4.

Merriman, John. *A History of Modern Europe: From the French Revolution to the Present.* 4th ed. New York: W. W. Norton, 2019.

Miller, Hugh. *The Testimony of the Rocks: or, Geology in its bearings on the Two Theologies, Natural and Revealed.* New York: Hurst, 1857.

Möhler, Johann Adam. *Der Einheit in der Kirche. Oder das Prinzip des Katholizismus dargestellt im Geiste der Kirchenväter.* Tübingen: Heinrich Laupp, 1825.

———. *Unity in the Church or The Principle of Catholicism.* Edited and Translated by Peter C. Erb. Washington, D.C.: Catholic University of America Press, 1996.

———. *Symbolism: Or, Exposition of the Doctrinal Differences Between Catholics and Protestants, as Evidenced by Their Symbolical Writings.* Translated by James Burton Robertson. New York: Edward Dunigan, 1844.

Monk, Maria. *Awful Disclosures, of the Hotel Dieu Nunnery of Montreal.* Rev. ed. New York, 1836.

Morse, Samuel F. B. *Foreign Conspiracy against the Liberties of the United States.* 4th ed. New York: Van Nostrand & Dwight, 1836.

———. *Imminent Dangers to the Free Institutions of the United States through Foreign Immigration; and the Present State of the Naturalization Laws*. New York: John F. Trow, 1854.

Morus, Iwan Rhys. *Michael Faraday and the Electrical Century*. London: Icon, 2004.

Mulder, John M. Introduction to *Christian Nurture*, by Horace Bushnell, vii–xxx. Reprint, Grand Rapids, Michigan: Baker Book House, 1979.

Mullen, Lincoln A. "The Contours of Conversion to Catholicism in the Nineteenth Century." *U.S. Catholic Historian* 32, no. 2 (Spring 2014) 1–27.

Mullin, Robert Bruce. *Episcopal Vision/American Reality: High Church Theology and Social Thought in Evangelical America*. New Haven: Yale University Press, 1986.

Murray, Nicholas. *The Decline of Popery and its Causes: An Address Delivered in the Broadway Tabernacle on Wednesday Evening, January 15, 1851*. New York: Harper and Brothers, 1851.

Neander. Johann August Wilhelm. *Allgemeine Geschichte der christlichen Religion und Kirche*. 6 Bände. Hamburg: Friedrich Perthes, 1825–45.

———. *General History of the Christian Religion and Church*. Translated by Joseph Torrey. 9 vols. Edinburgh, 1847–55.

Nevin, John Williamson. "The Anglican Crisis." *MR* 3 (July 1851) 359–98.

———. "Answer to Professor Dorner." *MR* 15 (October 1868) 532–646.

———. *Antichrist; or the Spirit of Sect and Schism*. In *One, Holy, Catholic, and Apostolic, Tome 1: Nevin's Writings on Ecclesiology (1844–1849)*, edited by Sam Hamstra Jr., 165–232. MTSS 5. Eugene, OR: Wipf & Stock, 2017.

———. *The Anxious Bench*. 2nd ed. Chambersburg, Pa: M. Kieffer, 1844.

———. *The Anxious Bench*. In *One, Holy, Catholic, and Apostolic, Tome 1: Nevin's Writings on Ecclesiology (1844–1849)*, edited by Sam Hamstra Jr., 27–103. MTSS 5. Eugene, OR: Wipf & Stock, 2017.

———. "The Apostles' Creed." In *The Early Creeds: The Mercersburg Theologians Appropriate the Creedal Heritage*, edited by Charles Yrigoyen Jr. and Lee C. Barrett, 35–97. By John Williamson Nevin et al. MTSS 8. Eugene, OR: Wipf & Stock, 2020.

———. "The Apostles' Creed: II. Its Inward Constitution and Form." *MR* 1 (1849) 201–21.

———. "Bible Anthropology." *MR* 24 (July 1877) 329–65.

———. "The Bread of Life: A Communion Sermon." In *Born of Water and the Spirit: Essays on the Sacraments and Christian Formation*, edited by David W. Layman, 214–44. By John Williamson Nevin et al. MTSS 6. Eugene, OR: Wipf & Stock, 2016.

———. The [Orestes A.] Brownson Papers. University of Notre Dame Archives, Notre Dame, Indiana.

———. "Brownson's Quarterly Review." *MR* 2 (January 1850) 33–80.

———. "Brownson's Review Again." *MR* 2 (May 1850) 307–24.

———. "Catholicism." In *One, Holy, Catholic, and Apostolic, Tome 2: Nevin's Writings on Ecclesiology (1851–1858)*, edited by Sam Hamstra Jr., 11–32. MTSS 7. Eugene, OR: Wipf & Stock, 2017.

———. "Catholic Unity." In *One, Holy, Catholic, and Apostolic, Tome 1: Nevin's Writings on Ecclesiology (1844–1849)*, edited by Sam Hamstra Jr., 112–132. MTSS 5. Eugene, OR: Wipf & Stock, 2017.

———. "Christ and His Spirit." *MR* 19 (1872) 353–93.

———. "Christianity and Humanity." *MR* 20 (October 1873) 469–86.

———. "The Christian Ministry." In *One, Holy, Catholic, and Apostolic, Tome 2: Nevin's Writings on Ecclesiology (1851-1858)*, edited by Sam Hamstra Jr., 35–56. MTSS 7. Eugene, OR: Wipf & Stock, 2017.

———. *The Church*. In *One, Holy, Catholic, and Apostolic, Tome 1: Nevin's Writings on Ecclesiology (1844-1849)*, edited by Sam Hamstra Jr., 138–58. MTSS 5. Eugene, OR: Wipf & Stock, 2017.

———. "The Church Year." *MR* 8 (July 1856) 456–78.

———. "Commencement Address: July 25, 1867." *MR* (October 1867) 485–508.

———. "Cyprian." *MR* 4 (May 1852) 259–77; (July 1852) 335–87; (September 1852) 417–52; (November 1852) 513–63.

———. "The Doctrine of the Reformed Church on the Lord's Supper." In *The Mystical Presence and the Doctrine of the Reformed Church on the Lord's Supper*, edited by Linden J. DeBie, 225–322. MTSS 1. Eugene, OR: Wipf & Stock, 2012.

———. "Early Christianity." *MR* 3 (September 1851) 461–90; (November 1851) 513–62; *MR* 4 (January 1852) 1–54. Reprint in *Catholic and Reformed: Selected Theological Writings of John Williamson Nevin*, edited by Charles Yrigoyen Jr., and George H. Bricker, 177–310. Pittsburgh Original Texts and Translations, no. 3. Pittsburgh: Pickwick, 1978.

———. "'Educational Religion': Discourses on Christian Nurture." In *Born of Water and the Spirit: Essays on the Sacraments and Christian Formation*, edited by David W. Layman, 38–43. By John Williamson Nevin et al. MTSS 6. Eugene, OR: Wipf & Stock, 2016.

———. "Evangelical Radicalism." *MR* 4 (September 1852) 508–512.

———. "Faith, Reverence and Freedom." *MR* 2 (January 1850) 97–116.

———. "*God in Christ*." *MR* 1 (May 1849) 311–12.

———. "Historical Development." *MR* 1 (September 1849) 512–14.

———. "Hodge on the Ephesians." In *One, Holy, Catholic, and Apostolic, Tome 2: Nevin's Writings on Ecclesiology (1851-1858)*, edited by Sam Hamstra Jr., 62–125. MTSS 7. Eugene, OR: Wipf & Stock, 2017.

———. "Human Freedom." *American Review: A Whig Journal Devoted to Politics and Literature*, n.s., 1, no. 4 (1848) 406–18.

———. *Human Freedom, and A Plea for Philosophy: Two Essays*. Mercersburg, PA: P. A. Rice, 1850.

———. "Jesus and the Resurrection." In *The Incarnate Word: Selected Writings on Christology*, edited by William B. Evans, 139–161. By John Williamson Nevin, et al. MTSS 4. Eugene, OR: Wipf & Stock, 2014.

———. "Kirwan's Letters." *MR* 1 (May 1849) 229–63.

———. "The Lutheran Confession." *MR* 1 (July 1849) 468–77.

———. "Man's True Destiny." *MR* 5 (October 1853) 492–521. Reprinted, *Man's True Destiny, A Baccalaureate Address to the Graduating Class of Franklin and Marshall College*. Chambersburg, PA: M. Keiffer, 1853.

———. The [James Alphonsus] McMaster Papers. University of Notre Dame Archives, Notre Dame, Indiana.

———. "The Moral Order of Sex." *MR* 2 (November 1850) 549–73.

———. *My Own Life: The Earlier Years*. Papers of the Eastern Chapter, Historical Society of the Evangelical and Reformed Church, no. 1. Lancaster, PA: Eastern Chapter, Historical Society of the Evangelical and Reformed Church, 1964.

———. *The Mystical Presence and the Doctrine of the Reformed Church on the Lord's Supper.* Edited by Linden J. DeBie and W. Bradford Littlejohn. MTSS 1. Eugene, Oregon: Wipf & Stock, 2012.

———. "Natural and Supernatural." *MR* 11 (April 1859) 176–210.

———. "Nevin and Bushnell: Christian Nurture and Baptism." In *Born of Water and the Spirit: Essays on the Sacraments and Christian Formation*, edited by David W. Layman, 34–77. By John Williamson Nevin et al. MTSS 6. Eugene, OR: Wipf & Stock, 2016.

———. "New Creation in Christ." In *The Incarnate Word: Selected Writings on Christology*, edited by William B. Evans, 32–45. By John Williamson Nevin et al. MTSS 4. Eugene, OR: Wipf & Stock, 2014.

———. "Noel on Baptism." In *Born of Water and the Spirit: Essays on the Sacraments and Christian Formation*, edited by David W. Layman, 78–115. By John Williamson Nevin et al. MTSS 6. Eugene, OR: Wipf & Stock, 2016.

———. "The Old Doctrine of Christian Baptism." In *Born of Water and the Spirit: Essays on the Sacraments and Christian Formation*, edited by David W. Layman, 196–213. By John Williamson Nevin et al. MTSS 6. Eugene, OR: Wipf & Stock, 2016.

———. "Once for All." *MR* 17 (1870) 100–124.

———. *One, Holy, Catholic, and Apostolic, Tome 1: John Nevin's Writings on the Ecclesiology (1844–1849)*. Edited by Sam Hamstra Jr. MTSS 5. Eugene, OR: Wipf & Stock, 2017.

———. "Our Relations To Germany." *MR* 14 (October 1867) 627–32.

———. "Pseudo-Protestantism." *Weekly Messenger of the Reformed Church*. August 13, 20, 27, 1845; September 3, 10, 1845.

———. "Puritanism and the Creed." *MR* 1 (November 1849) 585–607. Reprinted in *The Early Creeds: The Mercersburg Theologians Appropriate the Creedal Heritage*, edited by Charles Yrigoyen Jr. and Lee C. Barrett, 103–21. By John Williamson Nevin et al. MTSS 8. Eugene, OR: Wipf & Stock, 2020.

———. "Reply to 'An Anglican Catholic.'" *MR* 21 (1874) 397–429.

———. *Retrieving Catholicity in American Protestantism: Essays in Church History*. Edited by Michael Stell. MTSS 12. Eugene, OR: Wipf & Stock, forthcoming.

———. "'The Seal of the Spirit': A Sermon, the Substance of Which Was Preached in the Presbyterian Church at Uniontown, Pa. January 21, 1838.* Pittsburgh: William Allinder, 1838.

———. "The Sect System." In *One, Holy, Catholic, and Apostolic, Tome 1: Nevin's Writings on Ecclesiology (1844–1849)*, edited by Sam Hamstra Jr., 238–71. MTSS 5. Eugene, OR: Wipf & Stock, 2017.

———. "Short Notices: *Essays on Various Subjects* by his Eminence Cardinal Wiseman." *MR* 6 (January 1854) 153–56.

———. "The Spirit of Prophecy," *MR* 24 (1877) 181–212.

———. "The Spiritual World." *MR* 23 (1876) 501–27.

———. "The Testimony of Jesus." *MR* 24 (1877) 5–33.

———. "Thoughts on the Church." In *One, Holy, Catholic, and Apostolic, Tome 2: Nevin's Writings on Ecclesiology (1851–1858)*, edited by Sam Hamstra Jr., 131–171. MTSS 7. Eugene, OR: Wipf & Stock, 2017.

———. Translator's Introduction to *The Principle of Protestantism*, by Philip Schaff. In *The Development of the Church: "The Principle of Protestantism" and other Historical Writings of Philip Schaff*, edited by David R. Bains and Theodore Louis Trost, 35–54. MTSS 3. Eugene, OR: Wipf & Stock, 2016.

———. "Undying Life in Christ." In *Tercentenary Monument in Commemoration of the Three Hundredth Anniversary of the Heidelberg Catechism*, 17–43. Chambersburg, PA: M. Kieffer, 1863.

———. *Vindication of the Revised Liturgy*. Philadelphia: Jas. B. Rodgers, 1867. Reprint in *Catholic and Reformed: Selected Theological Writings of John Williamson Nevin*, edited by Charles Yrigoyen Jr. and George H. Bricker, 313–403. Pittsburgh Original Texts and Translations, no. 3. Pittsburgh: Pickwick, 1978.

———. "Wilberforce on the Incarnation." In *The Incarnate Word: Selected Writings on Christology*, edited by William B. Evans, 49–86. By John Williamson Nevin et al. MTSS 4. Eugene, OR: Wipf & Stock, 2014.

———. "The Wonderful Nature of Man." *MR* 11 (1859) 317–37.

———. "The Year 1848." *MR* 1 (1849) 10–44.

Nevin, John Williamson, et al. *Born of Water and the Spirit: Essays on the Sacraments and Christian Formation*. Edited by David W. Layman. MTSS 6. Eugene, OR: Wipf & Stock, 2016.

Nevin, John Williamson, et al. *The Early Creeds: The Mercersburg Theologians Appropriate the Creedal Heritage*. Edited by Charles Yrigoyen Jr. and Lee C. Barrett. MTSS 8. Eugene, OR: Wipf & Stock, 2020.

Newman, John Henry. *Apologia Pro Vita Sua*. Edited by Ian Ker. New York: Penguin Books, 1994.

———. *Certain Difficulties Felt by Anglicans in Catholic Teaching*. 2 vols. Reprint, London: Longmans, Green, 1908, 1914.

———. *An Essay on the Development of Christian Doctrine*. 1845. Reprint, Cambridge: Cambridge University Press, 2010.

Nichols, James Hastings. *Romanticism in American Theology: Nevin and Schaff at Mercersburg*. Chicago: University of Chicago Press, 1961. Reprint, Eugene, OR: Wipf & Stock, 2006.

Nolan, Hugh J. *The Most Reverend Francis Patrick Kenrick, Third Bishop of Philadelphia, 1830–1851*. Philadelphia: American Catholic Historical Society, 1948.

Noll, Mark A. *America's God: From Jonathan Edwards to Abraham Lincoln*. New York: Oxford University Press, 2002.

———. "'Both . . . Pray to the Same God': the Singularity of Lincoln's Faith in the Era of the Civil War." *Journal of the Abraham Lincoln Association* 18, no. 1 (Winter 1997) 1–26.

———. *The Civil War as a Theological Crisis*. Chapel Hill: University of North Carolina Press, 2006.

"'No Pent-up Utica'." *The Living Age* 71, no. 908 (October 26, 1861) 156.

OED Online. "Nisus, n." September 2022. Oxford University Press. https://www-oed-com.ezproxy.ycp.edu:8443/view/Entry/127277.

Owen, John. *The Reason of Faith, or, An Answer unto that Enquiry, Wherefore We Believe the Scriptures to be the Word of God with the Causes and nature of that Faith Wherewith We Do So*. London: Nathaniel Ponder, 1677.

———. *Synesis Pneumatikē: or the Causes, Waies & Means of Understanding the Mind of God as Revealed in his Word, with Assurance Therein*. London: Nathaniel Ponder, 1678.

The Oxford Companion to Philosophy. New Edition. Edited by Ted Honderich. Oxford: Oxford University Press, 2005.

Paley, William. *Natural Theology; or, Evidences of the Existence and Attributes of the Deity, Collected from the Appearances of Nature*. Edited by Matthew D. Eddy and David Knight. Reprint, New York: Oxford University Press, 2006.

Paris, John Ayrton. *The Life of Sir Humphry Davy*. Cambridge: Cambridge University Press, 1831.

Parker, Theodore. *A Discourse on the Transient and the Permanent in Christianity*. Boston, 1841.

Payne, John B. "Nevin on Baptism." In *Reformed Confessionalism in Nineteenth-Century America: Essays on the Thought of John Williamson Nevin*, edited by Sam Hamstra Jr. and Arie J. Griffioen, 125–151. Lanham: Scarecrow, 1995.

———. "Schaff and Nevin, Colleagues at Mercersburg: The Church Question." *Church History* 61, no. 2 (June 1992) 169–90.

Penzel, Klaus. *The German Education of Christian Scholar Philip Schaff: The Formative Years, 1819-1844*. Toronto Studies in Theology, vol. 95. Lewiston, NY: Edwin Mellen, 2004.

Pinkard, Terry. *Hegel's Naturalism: Mind, Nature, and the Final Ends of Life*. New York: Oxford University Press, 2012.

Poetical Works of Joseph Addison, with the Life of the Author. London: C. Cooke, 1796.

Polk, James K. "Fourth Annual Message: Washington, December 5, 1848." In *A Compilation of the Messages and Papers of the Presidents: 1789–1897*, edited by James D. Richardson, 4:629–70. Authority of Congress, 1899.

Rauch, Frederick A. *Psychology; or, A View of the Human Soul*. New York: M. W. Dodd, 1840. 4th ed., 1846.

Reid, Thomas. *An Inquiry into the Human Mind on the Principles of Common Sense*. Edited by Derek R. Brookes. University Park: Pennsylvania State University Press, 1997, 2000.

Reinhard, Franz Volkmar. *Versuch über den Plan, welchen der Stifter der Christlichen Religion zum Besten der Menschen entwarf*. 4th ed. Wittenberg: Samuel Gottfried Zimmermann, 1798. Translated as *Plan of the Founder of Christianity*, by Oliver A. Taylor. New York, G. & C. & H. Carvill, 1831.

"The Republic in Danger." *Southern Religious Telegraph* (July 1, 1831).

Reynolds, Larry. *European Revolutions and the American Literary Renaissance*. New Haven: Yale University Press, 1988.

Richardson, Robert D. Jr. *Emerson: The Mind on Fire, A Biography*. Berkeley: University of California Press, 1995.

Robinson, Marilynne. *Absence of Mind: The Dispelling of Inwardness from the Modern Myth of the Self*. New Haven: Yale University Press, 2010.

Rohr, Richard. *The Universal Christ*. New York: Convergent, 2019.

Ronge, John. *The Holy Coat of Treves, and the New German-Catholic Church*. New York: Harper, 1845.

Rosen, Michael. *The Shadow of God: Kant, Hegel, and the Passage from Heaven to History*. Cambridge, Massachusetts: Belknap Press of Harvard University Press, 2022.

Rothe, Richard. *Theologische Ethik*. 3 vol. Wittenberg: Zimmermann'sche, 1845–48.

Rousseau, Jean-Jacques. *On the Social Contract, with Geneva Manuscript and Political Economy*. Translated by Judith R. Masters. New York: St. Martin's Press, 1978.

Ruthven, Jon Mark. *On the Cessation of the Charismata: The Protestant Polemic on Postbiblical Miracles*. Sheffield, England: Sheffield Academic Press, 1993.

Schaff, Philip. *America: A Sketch of the Political, Social, and Religious Character of the United States of North America*. New York: C. Scribner, 1855.

———. *Amerika: Die politischen, socialen und kirchlich-religiosen Zustande de Vereinigten Staaten von Nordamerica*. Berlin: Wiegandi und Grieben, 1854.

———. *Der Bürgerkrieg und das christliche Leben in Nord-Amerika*. Berlin: Wiegandt und Grieben, 1866.

———. The [Orestes A.] Brownson Papers. University of Notre Dame Archives, Notre Dame, Indiana.

———. *The Confessions and Letters of St. Augustine, with a Sketch of his Life and Work*. Buffalo: Christian Literature Co., 1886.

———. The Philip Schaff Papers. Evangelical and Reformed Historical Society, Lancaster, PA.

———. *The Principle of Protestantism*. In *The Development of the Church: "The Principle of Protestantism" and other Historical Writings of Philip Schaff*, edited by David R. Bains and Theodore Louis Trost, 35–205. Translated by John W. Nevin. MTSS 3. Eugene, OR: Wipf & Stock, 2016.

———. *What is Church History? A Vindication of the Idea of Historical Development*. In *The Development of the Church: "The Principle of Protestantism" and other Historical Writings of Philip Schaff*, edited by David R. Bains and Theodore Louis Trost, 232–316. MTSS 3. Eugene, OR: Wipf & Stock, 2016.

Schiefen, Richard J. *Nicholas Wiseman and the Transformation of English Catholicism*. Shepherdstown, West Virginia: Patmos, 1984.

Schleiermacher, Friedrich. *Lectures on Philosophical Ethics*. Edited by Robert B. Louden. Translated by Louise Adey Huish. Cambridge: Cambridge University Press, 2002.

Senn, Frank. *Christian Liturgy: Catholic and Evangelical*. Minneapolis: Fortress, 1997.

Seymour, Michael Hobart. *Mornings Among the Jesuits at Rome: Being Notes of Conversations held with Certain Jesuits on the Subject of Religion in the City of Rome*. New York: Harper, 1849.

Shaughnessy, Gerald. *Has the Immigrant Kept the Faith? A Study of Immigration and Catholic Church Growth in the United States, 1790–1920*. New York: Macmillan, 1925.

Sherman, S. S. *The Bible a Classic: A Baccalaureate Address, Delivered at the Third Annual Commencement of Howard College, Marian, Ala., July 25th, 1850*. Tuskaloosa: M. D. J. Slade, 1850.

"Sir Humphrey Davy." *Catholic Herald* (Philadelphia). August 3, 1837.

Smith, Timothy L. *Revivalism and Social Reform: American Protestantism on the Eve of the Civil War*. New York: Abingdon, 1957. Reprint, Eugene, Oregon: Wipf & Stock, 2004.

Spinoza. *Theological-Political Treatise*. Translated by Samuel Shirley. Indianapolis: Hackett, 1998.

Stang, Nicholas F. "Kant's Transcendental Idealism." *The Stanford Encyclopedia of Philosophy*. Winter 2022 Edition. https://plato.stanford.edu/archives/win2022/entries/kant-transcendental-idealism/

Stark, Rodney. *The Triumph of Christianity: How the Jesus Movement Became the World's Largest Religion*. New York: HarperOne, 2011.

Stell, Michael J. General Introduction to *Retrieving Catholicity in American Protestantism: Essays in Church History*. MTSS 12. Eugene, Oregon: Wipf & Stock, forthcoming.

Stern, Laurence. *A Sentimental Journey*. In *The Novels of Sterne, Goldsmith, Dr Johnson, Mackenzie, Horace Walpole, and Clara Reeve*, 219–62. London: Hurst, Robinson and Edinburgh: James Ballantyne, 1823.

Stern, Sacha. *Calendar and Community: A History of the Jewish Calendar, 2nd Century BCE to 10th Century CE*. Oxford: Clarendon, 2001.

Stupperich, Robert. *Melanchthon*. Translated by Robert H. Fischer. Philadelphia: Westminster, 1965.

Talley, Thomas. *The Origins of the Liturgical Year*. 2nd ed. Collegeville, Minnesota: Liturgical, 1991.

Thiersch, Heinrich Wilhelm Josias. *Versuch zur Herstellung des historischen Standpuncts für die Kritik der neutestamentlichen Schriften: eine Streitschrift gegen die Kritiker unserer Tage*. Erlangen: Heyder, 1845.

———. *Vorlesungen über Katholicismus und Protestantismus*. 2 Vols. Erlangen: C. Heyder, 1846–48.

Thomas, George M. *Revivalism and Cultural Change: Christianity, Nation Building, and the Market in the Nineteenth-Century United States*. Chicago: University of Chicago Press, 1989.

Tierney, Brian. *The Origins of Papal Infallibility, 1150–1350; A Study on the Concepts of Infallibility, Sovereignty and Tradition in the Middle Ages*. Leiden: E. J. Brill, 1972.

Várady, Steven Béla and Louis Kossuth. *The Life of Governor Louis Kossuth with his Public Speeches in the United States, and a Brief History of the Hungarian War of Independence*. Reprinted, Budapest: Osiris, 2001.

Verplanck, Gulian C. *The Influence of Moral Causes upon Opinion, Science, and Literature: A Discourse Delivered on the Day Preceding the Annual Commencement of Amherst College, August 27th, 1834, at the Request of the Literary Societies of that Institution*. New York: Harper, 1834.

Wagner, Harald. *Die eine Kirche und die viele Kirchen: Ekklesiologie und Symbolik Beim Jungen Möhler*. Munich: Schöningh, 1977.

Wallace, Peter J. "History and Sacrament: John Williamson Nevin and Charles Hodge on the Lord's Supper." *Mid-America Journal of Theology* 11 (2000) 171–201.

Walworth, Clarence E. *The Oxford Movement in America*. New York: Catholic Book Exchange, 1895.

Ward, Wilfrid Philip. *The Life and Times of Cardinal Wiseman*. London: Longmans, Green, 1912.

———. *The Oxford Movement*. London: T. C. & E. C. Jack, 1912.

Wayland, Francis. *Thoughts on the Present Collegiate System in the United States*. Boston: Gould, Kendall & Lincoln, 1842.

Webster, Daniel. *Sketch of the Life of Louis Kossuth, Governor of Hungary Together with the Declaration of Hungarian Independence. Kossuth's Address to the People of the United States, All his Great Speeches in England, and the Letter of Daniel Webster to Chevalier Hulsemann*. New York: Stringer & Townsend, 1851.

Webster, Noah. *An American Dictionary of the English Language*. Revised ed. New York: Harper & Brothers, 1846.

Wentz, Richard E. "John Williamson Nevin and American Nationalism." *Journal of the American Academy of Religion* 58, no. 4 (Winter 1990) 617–32.

———. *John Williamson Nevin: American Theologian*. New York: Oxford University Press, 1997.

White, Andrew Dickson. *History of the Warfare of Science with Theology in Christendom*. New York: D. Appleton, 1897.

Whitney, Asa. *A Project for a Railroad to the Pacific*. New York: George W. Wood, 1849.

Williams, Rowan. "Origen: Between Orthodoxy and Heresy." In *Origeniana Septima Origenes in den Auseinandersetzungen des 4. Jahrhunderts*, edited by W. A Bienert and U. Kühneweg, 3–14. Leuven: Leuven University Press, 1999.

Winebrenner, John, ed. *History of All the Religious Denominations in the United States: Containing Authentic Accounts of the Rise and Progress, Faith and Practice, Localities and Statistics, of the Different Persuasions: Written Expressly for the Work by Fifty-Three Eminent Authors, Belonging to the Respective Denominations.* 2nd ed. Harrisburg: John Winebrenner, 1848.

Wiseman, Nicholas Patrick Stephen. *Essays on Various Subjects.* 3 vols. London: Charles Dolman, 1853.

———. *Lectures on the Principal Doctrines and Practices of the Catholic Church.* Reprinted, Dublin: J. Duffy, 1867.

———. *Twelve Lectures on the Connexion Between Science and Revealed Religion.* New York: Gould and Newman, 1837.

Wolff, George D. "The Mercersburg Movement: An Attempt to Find Ground on Which Protestantism and Catholicity Might Unite." *American Catholic Quarterly Review* 3 (1879) 151–76.

Index

Aids to Reflection (Coleridge), 169n2
Alexander the Great, 332
America, 6–8, 30–45, 47, 49, 90–91, 318
    Catholicism in, 173–74
    Christianity and Christian theology in, viii–ix, 13, 18, 88, 95, 147–48, 169–71, 188–90, 192, 207, 240n92, 294
    as home of progress, 336
American Independence, 69, 158
American Revolution, 51
American Tract Society, 287
Ammonius Saccas, 88
analogia entis (analogy of being), 9
anti–Catholic nativism, *see* nativism
Antichrist, 27, 27n11, 29, 166n18, 281, 312n9, 344n41, 359n19
anthropology, 14–17, 56–59, 98–100, 125–34, 150–52
Anxious Bench (Nevin), vii, 10, 16n50, 18, 148, 193; *see also* Protestantism, pseudo-Protestantism; revivalism
apologetics, 180–82, 189, 220
    and Brownson's "method of authority," 175–76, 179, 185, 215–18
    and evidentiary tradition, 181
Anglicanism, viii, 182–87, 265–306; *see also* Oxford Movement, Puseyism, Tractarianism
Anselm of Canterbury, 279n10, 289
Apostolic succession, 176, 183–84, 266–67, 283–86
Appel, Theodore, 50, 315
Apostles' Creed, 140, 145–46, 166, 169, 181n45, 233, 266, 278, 312n8, 334, 349n15, 357, 363, 372, 374
Aquinas, Thomas, 76, 226n64, 279n10
    aseity, 255
Athanasius of Alexandria, 289n23
Augustine, 279n10, 291, 313

baptism, 173, 183–84, 190–91, 230, 253, 259, 279–85, 311, 358, 372
    and Bushnell on, 190–99
    and faith, 230
    of infants, 190, 259, 279, 280n12, 372n50
    as a sacrament, 279–82
baptismal regeneration, 183–84, 266–67, 280, 289, 297, *see also* regeneration, baptismal
Baptists (church and theology), viii, 171, 190, 267, 272, 280–85, 293, 300, 307–16
    spirit of, 187–88, 303
Baconian method, 84, 93, 169, 179, 317; *see also* Common Sense Realism
Barth, Karl, 4
Basil of Caesarea, 279n10
Benevolent Empire, 7, 12, 49–50
Bible, 13, 46, 90, 117, 124, 143–44, 156, 171, 176, 202, 211, 213, 216, 228, 232, 234, 243, 251, 258, 276, 294–95, 327–28, 331, 339–48, 353, 364n26, 375
    and Baptists, 310–11, 313–14
    and church, 196, 252–53, 278, 285, 307–9, 348, 366
    and private judgment, 187–88, 194, 206, 218–20, 222, 244, 260–61, 272, 285, 293–94, 308–9, 313, 341
    and reason, 313–14
    reading in schools, 353
    as source of Christianity and theology, 13, 90, 179, 196, 211, 213, 227–28, 252–53, 260–61, 285, 307–14
Billington, Ray, 173
Bernard of Clairvaux, 279n10
Bonomo, Jonathan G, 138, 140
Borneman, Adam S., vii–ix, 30, 64, 69, 82, 98, 124
Bossuet, Jacques, 178, 212n30
Bratt, James D, 50, 145

Brownson, Orestes, vii–ix, xiv, 174n20, 175–82, 185–86, 193–264
   arguments against Protestantism, 214–15
   against doctrinal development, 178, 180–83, 187, 194, 203n11, 211–13, 226, 297n36
   dualism of, 181
   on faith and reason, 230–35
   on freedom, neglect of, 220–21
   on history, 211–13, 238–42
   method of authority, 175–76, 185, 195
   and Nevin's criticisms of, 175–82, 193–264
   on no-church theory of, 214–15
   and no salvation outside the church, 207
   on Protestant Reformation, 180, 207, 209–14
   on Puritanism, 207–8
   and revelation, authority of, 224–25
   on separation of nature and supernatural, 188, 227–30
   subject/object separation, 221–25
   as ultramontane, 205
   as unhistorical and authoritarian, 180, 211–13
   as weathercock, 198
Brownson Quarterly Review, 96, 175, 177, 184, 193–94, 198, 245
Buchanan, James, 121, 316
Buddhism, 254, 258
Bushnell, Horace, vii, ix, 174–75, 190–92, 202n9, 203, 259, 346–76
   on baptism, 190–91, 358, 372
   on Christ, as central, 355–59
   Christ in Theology, 350n2
   and Christian nurture, 259n22
   Christian Nurture, 189n80, 347, 350n2
   Discourses on Christian Nurture, 189, 190n83, 346
   God in Christ, 189, 191, 350n2
   Nature and the Supernatural, 189–92, 202n9, 321, 346–76
   nature/supernature relationship, 346–76
   Nevin's criticisms of, 190–92, 346–76
   and rationalism, 351–52

Caesar, Julius, 332
Calvin, John, 5n6, 142, 147, 200, 207, 279–80, 282, 368
   supralapsarianism of, 266, 267n37
Calvinism, 169n2, 170, 203n9, 208n21, 346–48
Canlis, Julie, 5n6
Carlisle, Pennsylvania, vii, 121
Cass, Lewis, 33n21
categorical imperative, 61n13, 65n19, 76n3, 137, 317, 325

Catholicism, vii, viii, 9, 19, 172–74, 185–88, 193–95, 200, 239, 244, 247, 268n10, 271, 275n6, 276n7, 293–94, 304–5; *see also* Popery; Romanism; Roman Catholicism
   and Nevin, 176–82, 185–88, 193, 268n10, 315
   as other extreme of Protestantism (Puritanism), 179–80, 188, 244
Catholicity, 21, 48, 87n23, 103, 148, 177, 194, 208, 21n31, 233–34, 245, 314
Channing, Henry William, 270n3, 290–91
Christ, 4, 11, 14, 12n34, 87, 89, 97, 102n9, 140, 151n3, 151n4, 171, 173, 181, 189, 193, 205n16, 210, 215, 217–18, 226, 229–30, 232–34, 242, 245, 260, 262, 264, 328, 330, 333, 361, 367n37; *see also* Incarnation
   centrality of, 4, 14, 21, 22n3, 35n2, 45, 87–90, 106, 121–22, 156, 192, 347, 355–60, 364, 369–71
   and church, 21, 22n3, 112, 140, 145, 151n4, 176, 183, 188, 193, 234, 245, 250–51, 285, 362–63, 371–76
   and liturgy, 148, 151n3
   and man and woman, 106, 112
   and scripture, 90, 102n9, 171
   as theanthropic, 361, 364n26
Christianity, 3–15, 28, 36, 45, 48, 52, 56, 69–90, 94–95, 102–3, 109–22, 139–45, 147–49, 150, 152–57, 160–61, 163–66, 169, 176–80, 186–87, 191, 193, 195–96, 198, 209–10, 212–14, 218, 250, 252, 282, 305, 308–14, 318–19, 340–43, 347, 362n21, 372–73, 346, 350n2, 351–53, 355–56, 359
   and Anglicans, 267–68, 303–4
   as extrinsic force, 176–80, 215, 220–21, 226, 229, 245, 262
   as life force, 170, 181, 243, 260, 328–35
   restoration of primitive, 182–84
Christology, xiii, 67n30, 170, 191, 250, 346–47, 361, 364n26
   Bushnell on, 191, 348–49, 355–56, 369–71
Chrysostom, John, 183n54, 279n10
Church, vii–ix, 10–16, 21, 37, 48, 69–73, 77–82, 87–88, 96, 103, 110, 112, 124n7, 136, 138–51, 158, 164–66, 169–71, 176–92, 193–97, 199, 204–6, 215, 217–19, 221–28, 230, 232–33, 235–38
   authority of, 177–80, 183–86, 195, 241–45, 252, 260, 283–84, 289, 294, 300, 313
   as association of believers, 192, 308, 311
   Baptist concept of, 307–14
   and Bible, 307–9

Brownson's views of, 178, 198, 206–9, 211–13, 216–17, 225–27, 229n69, 235–38
Bushnell's concept of, 191–92, 349, 371–76
and Creed, 260–61, 349n15, 357
Fathers of, 169, 192, 266, 279n10
as historical (organic), viii, 145, 148, 156–58, 166, 220, 234, 237–39, 314, 368n37, 371, 375
Ideal/actual, *see* ideal and actual
incarnational view of, 169, 184, 193, 196, 201n5 309, 320n2, 356n12
as invisible, 170, 190n86, 266, 287
liberty of, 288–91, 292–93, 293–98
and no-church theory, 214, 218, 266, 268, 278, 280, 282–86, 302
and Oxford Movement, 265–68, 269–83
primitive, 172, 173n12, 176, 182, 184–85, 187, 192, 196, 221–13, 265–66, 269n2, 283, 307, 310, 315
Polity, vii, 7, 10, 63n15, 267, 286–87, 292, 310
and sacraments, 169, 174–75, 287–88
and state, 37, 69, 69n23, 174, 240n92, 246, 260, 265, 270n3, 288–91, 292n28, 293, 295, 337, 354
as supernatural, viii, 278, 286–88, 308, 312
visibility of, 22n3, 170, 184, 201n5, 220, 266, 286, 290
Year, ix, 163–66; *see also*, Year, concept of
see also Catholicism; *ecclesia docens*; Protestantism; and specific denominations
Church history, 212–13, 238n84, 239, 278; *see also* Brownson, on history
Church Member's Manual (Crowell), 307, 310
Church Temporalities Bill, 184–85, 265, 269n2
Church question, vii, 140, 145, 184–85, 266, 270n3, 271–78, 286, 288, 299, 302, 305
Civil War, 12, 20, 173, 189, 192, 308n5, 317, 317n9
Clarke, James Freeman, 270n3
Clay, Henry, 49
Coakley, Sarah, 5
Coleridge, Samuel Taylor, 189–91, 207n20, 233n75
Common Sense Realism, viii, 3, 7–8, 50, 65n18, 84n17, 88n25, 91, 93, 138, 169n2, 176n24, 179, 192–94, 195n10, 312, 317; *see also* Baconian method
condition privative, and Bushnell, 348, 366n31
Congregationalists, ix, 171, 175, 199, 214, 259n22, 272, 275n6, 281–82, 346, 359n2
Conscience, 68n22, 72, 137
and religion, 292–94, 297, 315, 324–26, 355

Cousin, Victor, 175
Creation, 3, 5, 16, 64, 65, 77, 96, 99, 104, 120–25, 128–37, 149, 211, 215–16, 228, 231–32, 250, 253–54, 318, 321–23, 327, 348, 351, 359, 361, 363, 365, 367–68, 371–72
basis of church year, 148–49, 151
fallen, 15, 60n11
parable of spiritual world, 154, 157, 159, 228
see also new creation
Crowell, William, 307, 310n2
Cyprian, 46n40, 182n51, 185–86, 291, 307; *see also* Nevin, and "Cyprian,"

Davenport, John, 369
Davy, Humphry, 334–35
deification, 251
deism, abstract, 251–52, 255
Democratization, 8, 11
Democratization of American Christianity (Hatch), 171
development, theory of, vii, 21n9, 22n3, 80, 100n6, 152n6, 178, 180–81, 184–85, 187, 194, 196, 202n9, 211–13, 219, 226n63, 236n81, 237, 245–47, 255, 266, 297n36, 304–6, 308, 366, 368; *see also* historical development
Digby, Kenelm Henry, 238
Dialectic, Hegelian, 3n1
DiPuccio, William E., 4, 9, 60n11, 64n17, 65n18, 78n9, 87n22, 96, 102n9
Diversity, American theological, 169–75
Doane, George W., 172
donum fidei, 180, 196, 230, 233–35
Dorner, Isaak, 22n3, 139–40, 142–46.
Draper, John William, 317
dualism, 96, 109, 245–48, 251–55, 258, 262, 367n37, 369
Dwight, Timothy, 208n21

ecclesia docens, 178, 196, 217, 218, 225–27
Eccleston, Samuel, 299
education, 179, 189, 190, 200–201, 228, 231, 291n25, 320, 329, 331, 338, 343
aims of, 316–19, 335–36
and naturalism, 352–55
Edwards, Jonathan, 208n21
Emerson, Ralph Waldo, 170, 202–3, 303n49
empiricism, 84, 88n25, 91–93, 317
England, John, 294n30
English Prayer Book, 282
Enlightenment, 7–8, 51, 169, 176n24, 181, 195n10
episcopacy, 173, 184, 199, 201n6, 266–67, 271–72, 282–88, 290n24, 293, 299, 303

397

Episcopalianism, 199, 272, 283–84, 298–300
Epistemology, 3, 17, 76n3, 78n9
Eucharist, 148, 193, 194n5, 266–67, 280
Evangelicalism, 50, 170–72, 174–75, 177, 179, 184–88, 193–94, 227n66, 229, 275n5, 276, 281–82, 284, 256n19, 287, 296, 340–42, 347, 352, 356, 358
   and Nevin, 177, 187, 194
   radical, 187–88, 307–14, 346
Evans, James, 5n6
Evans, William B., 4, 9n18, 17, 46n40, 82n14, 84n17, 138n1, 142n4, 143n8, 361n20, 371n47

Faber, Frederick William, 269n2
Faith, 4, 29, 33, 45, 77, 87, 89, 180, 186, 188, 192, 193–94, 198, 209–11, 218–20, 228, 244, 260, 266, 278, 284, 289, 295, 302, 312, 337–38, 340, 342
   for Brownson, 180, 198–200, 216–17, 230–35, 245
   and Bushnell, 349, 351, 356–57, 359, 371, 373–74
   Catholic doctrine of, 173, 178, 182–83, 187, 195n10
   and the Church, 170–71, 191, 204–6, 213, 218, 222, 234, 245, 266, 279–80, 282, 286–88, 371, 372
   and Nevin, 181, 196, 200, 248, 318, 324, 329, 233n75
   and private judgment, 218–20, 222
   and reason, 92–94, 100, 112, 144–45, 166, 178, 180, 195n10, 196, 199, 215, 228, 230–35, 245, 354
   and revelation, 189, 191, 227, 263, 278, 333–35, 343–45
   subjective appropriation of, 196
   and the supernatural, 189, 191, 227, 230, 262–64, 278, 375
   and testimony, 180, 215–18, 232, 263–64
   and truth, 250–51, 262–64
Family, 8, 16, 64, 73, 96–97, 103–8, 121, 136, 190–91, 246, 259n22, 260, 275
Faught, C. Brad, 265
Fichte, Johann, 3n1, 249
Finney, Charles Grandison, 10, 18n3, 170, 345
Franklin College, vii, 120–21, 188, 315–16
Fitzpatrick, Bishop John Bernard, ix, 175n24, 204n14
Franklin, Benjamin, 315n2
Franklin and Marshall College, vii, 188–89, 315, 316, 320
Freedom, 5, 20–21, 30, 59–74, 98n3, 99, 101, 109, 111, 117, 134–37, 177–78, 180, 183, 188, 223, 225, 242, 245–47, 254–57, 329, 332, 336, 338–40, 347, 366
   and Brownson, 195, 198, 205, 220–22, 261
   of the church, 265–67, 272, 289n23
   religious, 292–93
   divine, 348
Freedom, Ethical, 5, 20–21, 30, 59–74, 98n3, 99, 101, 109, 111, 117, 134–37, 177–78, 180, 188, 196, 198, 220–26, 245–47, 254–57, 261, 329, 332
Freedom of the church, *see* Religious freedom
Froude, James Anthony, 301n44
Froude, Richard Hurrell, 171, 265, 301

German idealism, 9, 51, 76n6, 80n11, 130n15, 138, 144n11, 181, 317; *see also* transcendental idealism
German Reformed Church, vii, 10–11, 18, 19n3, 138, 138n1, 141n4, 143, 147–48, 164n15, 174, 188–90, 263, 315–16, 320n320, 346
Giustiniani, Louis, 275n5
   Papal Rome, 275n5
   Intrigues of Jesuitism, 275n5
Gorham controversy, 182–84, 267, 280, 289, 297n36
Gorham, George Cornelius, 182–83, 280n13
Gregory VII, Pope, 289n23
Gregory of Nazianzus, 279n10
Gregory of Nyssa, 279n10

Hart, Darryl G., 95n1, 120, 145n14, 147n2, 179n39, 317
Hatch, Nathan, 171
Hegel, G. W. F., 3n1, 207n20, 249n4, 367n40
Hegelianism, 3n1, 9–11, 21, 27n11, 58n7, 82n14, 100n7, 105, 141n4, 196, 212, 368n37
historical development, 5–6, 10–18, 22, 46n40, 82–83, 144n12, 178, 185, 304–6; *see also*, development, theory of
history, viii, 3n1, 5–6, 9–17, 18–48, 50–51, 54n2, 56n5, 64, 68–71, 73, 75–78, 80–84, 86–93, 100–103, 128, 134n23, 136, 144–45, 147–51, 155–59, 162–65, 176, 178, 182–83, 192–93, 202n9, 207, 223, 229, 234, 237, 246, 254, 313, 342, 358, 367n37, 373; *see also* Organic
   Brownson's views of, 196, 200, 209–14, 225, 226, 238–42, 255
   as divine thought, 28–30
   implies progress, 211
   and the Incarnation, 3n1, 266, 349, 362–64
History of All the Religious Denominations . . . (Winebrenner), 11, 18, 51n9

History of the Conflict between Religion and Science (Draper), 317
History of the Warfare of Science with Theology (White), 317
Hobbes, Thomas, 207n20
Hodge, Archibald Alexander, 342n39
Hodge, Charles, 12–13, 138–39, 170, 174, 181n42, 194, 194n5, 245n6, 259n22, 342n39; *see also* Princeton theology *and* Mercersburg theology, and Princeton
Holifield, Brooks E., viii, 10, 169n2, 171n6, 172n9, 179n36, 314n15
Holmes, Barbara, 5n6
Holy Spirit, 16, 25, 45, 148, 187, 263n27, 308
  and Bible, 313–14
  and faith, 262–63
Hopkins, John Henry, 172, 214, 222
Hopkins, Samuel, 208n21
Hughes, John, 173n14, 174n20, 176n27, 186n67, 276n7, 296
  Decline of Protestantism and Its Cause, 174n20, 276n7
humanity, 6, 14–16, 21, 43, 45, 56, 78–81, 83, 87n22, 89, 96, 101, 103, 106, 108, 111, 114, 118, 120–22, 148, 193, 212, 226, 229n69, 239, 242, 254, 261, 270, 326, 340, 343, 357, 360, 367n37
Humboldt, Friedrich Wilhelm Heinrich Alexander von, 317, 322, 323n5, 326
Hume, David, 51n9, 92n31, 325
Huntington, Jedediah Vincent, 298n38
Hurter, Friedrich Emmanuel Von, 203n10
Hart, Darryl G., 120, 140n13, 147n2, 317

Ideal, 300, 306
  and actual, 9, 51, 54–55, 54n2, 66–67
idealism, 170, 175n21, 181, 201n5, 317; *see also* German idealism
Ignatius of Antioch, 282, 313
illumination, of Holy Spirit, 216, 308, 313, 331, 363
Immaculate Conception, and development of doctrine, 187, 237, 247
Incarnation, vii, ix, 4, 14, 17, 56n5, 122, 147, 180–81, 184, 192, 201n5, 224, 228–29, 245, 250, 266, 286, 303, 327, 331, 339, 347–49, 356, 359n19, 360–64, 370–71
Individualism, viii, 3–4, 7–10, 18n3, 50, 71, 180, 188, 190, 245, 309
infallibility, of church and pope, 205–6, 212, 225–26, 229, 235–38, 261, 297n36, 313
Infant baptism, *see* baptism, of infants *and* baptismal regeneration
Innocent III, Pope 203n10, 289n23

Irving, Edward, 33n49
Irvingianism, 303–4
Ives, Levi Silliman, 172, 298n38

Jennings, Willie, 5
Jenson, Robert, 4, 5n6

Kant, Immanuel, 9n18, 58n7, 61, 65n19, 76, 89–93, 136–37, 141–44, 170n4, 175n21, 207n20, 249n4, 317, 325–26; *see also* categorical imperative
Keble, John, 171, 265, 269n2
Kenrick, Francis Patrick, 172n10, 173–74, 186, 203n12, 204, 206n17, 236n81
  Catholic Doctrine of Justification, 172n10, 173–74
  Primacy of the Apostolic See Vindicated, 186, 206, 236n81
Kossuth, Louis, 28n13, 318–19, 339–42
Krauth, Charles Philip, 317

Lancaster, Pennsylvania, vii
law, 27–28, 39, 44–45, 51, 82, 84, 86, 97, 100–104, 106n20, 108, 110–14, 116, 118, 124, 130, 135–37, 151–53, 155–57, 159, 162, 204–5, 213, 226, 245–46, 249–50, 258–66, 329, 365
  and Bible, 187–88, 313–14
  and church, 283, 285, 290
  and freedom, 57–74, 196, 220–25, 256–57, 325n8
Layman, David, 46n40, 100n7, 275n5
Lectures on Revivals of Religion (Finney), 171
Ledru-Pollin, Alexandre Auguste, 340
Leibnitz, Gottfried Wilhem, 207n20
Leroux, Pierre, 175
Lewis, C. S., 362n21
Life of Charles Hodge (Hodge), 342n39
Life of Governor Louis Kossuth (Kossuth and Varady), 319n16, 339n35, 340n38
Lindbeck, George, 4
Littlejohn, W. Bradford, xiii, 145
Liturgy, 6, 72n26, 142, 143n10, 147, 149, 280–83, 286–87
  German Reformed, 138n1, 142, 146, 148
  Vindication of the Revised Liturgy (Nevin), 72n26, 139–40
Locke, John, 8, 51, 84, 92
Lowell, James Russell, 175–76
Luther, Martin, 200n4, 207, 209, 279–80, 282
Lutheran, 143, 143n10, 169n2, 177n30, 194n5, 199, 200n4, 275n5, 315n2, 317, 320n2, 351n3, 368n40

Magisterium, and church, 178, 196, 225–27; *see also* ecclesia docens
Malebranche, Nicholas, 253n13
Manifest Destiny, 49
Manning, Henry Edward, 183, 269n2, 280n13, 297
Marshall College, vii, 174, 186, 188–89, 320–21
Materialism, 17, 338–39, 354–55, 365
Mazzini, Giuseppe, 317, 340
McIlvaine, Charles Pettit, 172–73
McMaster, James A., 185–86, 268n10, 298n38
Meade, William, 172
Melanchthon, Philipp, 200
Mercersburg Review, vii, 11, 18–19, 95–96, 185, 188–89, 244, 315
Mercersburg, Pennsylvania, vii, 10, 17, 19, 186, 189, 121, 315, 320
Mercersburg Seminary, 95, 188, 315
Mercersburg theology, vii, viii, 4, 6, 11, 13, 56, 65, 142–43, 148, 174, 185–86, 192, 194, 203
 and Princeton theology, 13, 138–39, 174
Methodists, 171, 282, 293, 308n5
Mexican-American War, 19–20, 31–33, 33n21, 49–50
Middle Ages, 238–40, 273, 279, 294, 337
Milbank, John, 5
Miller, Hugh, 351
miracles, as witness to revelation, 175n24, 195n10, 206, 217, 232, 234, 314n15, 325n10, 362–64, 373–75
Möhler, Johann Adam, 177n29, 201n5
Mores Catholici (Digby), 238
Mormonism, 171, 232, 303–4, 337
Mornings Among the Jesuits of Rome (Seymour), 235–36
Murray, Nicholas, 276n7
 Decline of Popery and Its Causes, 276n7
Mystical Presence, The (Nevin), 193, 194, 308n8, 361n20; *see also* Nevin, John Williamson, and *Mystical Presence*
mystical body, 193n2, 225, 261
mystical union, 119, 177, 184, 193, 279–82, 286

"National Apostasy" (Keble), 171, 265, 269n2
nations, Romantic and Germanic, 240–42
Nativism, 20, 39, 50, 172, 174, 176, 198–99, 202, 272, 275n5, 276n7, 293–99
nature, and the supernatural, ix, 14, 15, 62, 93, 98n3, 145n14, 148, 151n3, 156, 161–63, 189, 246–47, 317–18, 321–27, 347–49, 351, 353, 357, 359, 361–62, 364–65, 369–71, 375; *see also* supernatural *and* supernaturalism

Neander, Johann August W., 10, 175n21, 194, 202–3
new creation, 14n44, 20, 36, 83, 88–89, 106, 151, 181, 235, 250, 260, 314, 347, 357–60, 363–64, 371–72
Nevin, John Williamson, 3–17, 49–52, 95–97, 120–22, 138–40, 147–49, 169–70, 172, 174, 186, 188–89, 195, 244, 315–16, 320–21
 against charges of pantheism and subjectivism, 13, 77, 89, 138–41, 181, 245–47, 249–51, 253–55, 258, 309, 367n37
 assessment of his times, 10–14, 18–21, 30n17, 37n25, 336–44
 on the Anglican Crisis, 182–87, 265–306
 and *Antichrist*, 18, 27n11, 72n26, 139, 166n18, 193, 281, 313n9, 319, 344n41, 356n12, 359n19, 361n20, 367n37, 371n48
 and *Anxious Bench*, *see* Anxious Bench
 on Brownson, 175–82, 193–264
 and Brownson's charge of pantheism and subjectivism, 181
 on Bushnell, 190–92, 346–76
 and "Cyprian," 46n40, 182, 185, 186, 247, 268n10, 303n48, 307
 on development, historical and organic, 54n2, 56n5, 184, 185, 187, 196, 211, 237, 245–47, 266, 268, 297n36, 304–6, 308
 and "Early Christianity," 185–87, 212n32, 247, 268n10, 275n5, 283n17, 294n30, 303n48, 304n41, 307, 371n47, 373n53
 and "Educational Religion," 189n79, 190, 191n89, 90, 346n2
 on "Evangelical Radicalism," 187–88, 307–45
 and "Hodge on the Ephesians," 314n16, 348n8, 349n15
 on "Man's True Destiny," 188–89, 320–45
 and *Mystical Presence*, 11, 18, 72n26, 120, 143n9, 151n4, 193, 194, 308n8, 361n20
 "Natural and Supernatural," 69n1, 189, 192n96, 227n65, 346–49, 350–76
 "New Creation in Christ," 55n3, 106n20, 121n7, 122n9, 308n8
 "Sect System," 68n22, 90n27, 193
 "Thoughts on the Church," 288n213, 71n47
 Vindication of the Revised Liturgy, *see* Liturgy
Newman, Francis William, 301n44
Newman, John Henry, 171–73, 183n54, 186, 194, 202–3, 265
 on development of doctrine, 194, 202n9, 203n11, 211, 269n2, 297

Nichols, James H., 179n39, 182, 265n1
nihilism, 207, 249-51
Nominalism, 8, 51, 54
nurture, Christian, 189-91, 259n11, 280n12

object, as supernatural, 177-80, 257-59, 329; *see also* subject and object
occasionalism, 253
O'Connell, Daniel, 292n27
Onderdonk, Benjamin T., 172
Ontology, 9, 21, 51
Oregon, Boundary Dispute, 31-32, 35n23
Organicism, vii-viii, 5, 9, 12-17, 21-22, 28, 40, 44, 50-51, 56, 64-68, 72, 77-83, 96-102, 104, 106, 115, 117-21, 124-25, 129-30, 135, 144, 148, 153-54, 158, 181, 184, 202n9, 203n11, 206n19, 211, 213, 220, 249-60, 313n11, 350n2, 362, 364, 370
  and church, 169, 176, 190, 307-8, 356n12
  and Incarnation, 192-93, 196, 250, 320n2, 371
  and supernatural, 224-29, 307-8, 347-49, 359-60, 371
  Union (life) in Christ, 148, 151n3, 176
  see also wholeness *and* supernaturalism, as organic fact
Origen, 77, 88
Original sin, and Bushnell, 190, 348, 361, 365-68
Oxford Movement, vii, 170, 182-87, 265-306; *see also* Anglicanism; Puseyism; Tractarianism
  and opposition to, 272-77
  Protestant alternatives to, 303-6
  challenges to Protestantism, 277-79, 300-306

Paganism, 159-61, 362
pantheism, 89, 181, 245-47, 249-51, 253-55, 258, 367n37
Park, Edwards Amasa, 202-3, 208
Parker, Theodore, 170, 194
"Party Spirit" (Nevin), 15, 50, 80n11, 101n8
Paley, William, 84, 93n32, 255n15
Pelagianism, 171, 361
Personality, 52, 56n5, 57-58, 62-63, 97-101, 104-5, 108-19, 133
  in Bushnell, 365, 368-69 (of Satan), 369 (Christ's)
  of God, 258
Phillpotts, Henry, 183, 280n3
Philosophy, 6-8, 44, 47, 52, 75-94, 141, 147, 200; *see also* Baconian method; Common Sense Realism; empiricism; German idealism

Plan of the Founder of Christianity (Reinhard), 351
plastic power, 59
Plato, 75n2, 76, 83, 85, 357
Platonism, 323
Polity, vii, 7, 10, 267, 286-87, 292, 310
Polycarp of Smyrna, 282, 313
popery, 198-99, 202, 224, 240n92, 275n5, 276-77, 290-91, 293, 295
postmillennialism, 12n34
predestination, 170
Presbyterians, 170-71, 175, 199, 213-14, 267, 272n4, 281, 286-87, 294, 300, 303
  of Scotland, 270, 293
Primacy of the Apostolic See Vindicated (Kenrick), 186
Princeton theology, 10, 170-71, 174, 194; *see also* Mercersburg theology, and Princeton theology
Private judgment, 70-72, 187, 194, 206, 218-19, 272, 285, 293-94, 308-9, 313, 341
  and popular Protestantism, 244
  and Romanism, 260-61
The Protestant Crusade (Billington), 173-74, 194n5, 275n5
Protestant Episcopal Church, 171-72, 222n54, 293, *see also* Anglicanism; Oxford Movement
Protestantism, 23, 70, 165, 169-71, 184-85, 188, 266, 268, 280-81, 292, 294, 334, 346, 350n2
  American, 6-9, 11, 35, 95, 147, 169, 170-71
  and Anglicanism, 266, 268, 271-72, 277-79, 300-306
  Brownson on, 202-9, 211-15, 219, 240-42, 244, 248
  and Catholicism, 172n9, 174n9, 179, 182, 185-86, 194, 266, 307n2, 344n41
  pseudo-Protestantism, 176, 196-97, 201, 224, 239, 313n12
  and Romanism, 196, 201-2
  Nevin's views of, 182, 184-88, 315, 318
psychology, 60, 104, 114n30
Puritanism, 10-11, 47, 165-66, 170, 173, 177, 179, 182-83, 188, 190, 194, 201, 207, 219, 240n92, 270-71, 280, 293-94, 298, 300, 305, 312, 313n11, 371n47, 373n53
  Baptistic, 267, 281, 307-8, 313-14
  Brownson as, 201, 205, 208n21
  and Bushnell, 346
  Evangelical, 185, 254, 286n19, 269n2
Pusey, Edward Bouverie, 171, 265, 269n2
Puseyism, 171, 265, 269n2, 272, 274, 277, 288, 290, 301
Pythagoras, 76, 357

401

INDEX

Railroads, *see* Technology, improvements in
rationalism, vii–viii, 179, 219–20, 234, 242–43, 252, 260, 301, 309, 314, 371
 and Baptists, 307–8, 310, 312, 314
 and Brownson, 180, 205, 215n33, 245
 and Bushnell, 347, 351–52, 356
 and Romanism, 196, 198–99, 285
 supernatural, 169, 179, 188–89; *see also* supernaturalism, abstract
 the tendency of the times, 351–52
Rauch, Frederick A., 22n3, 59n10, 80n11, 97n4, 100n7, 142n5
 Psychology, 104n15, 141
reason, 4, 7–8, 11, 27, 34, 37, 46, 50–51, 57–58, 61–63, 82–86, 91–92, 99–101, 104, 132–35, 171, 217, 228, 245, 249, 255, 258–60, 317, 322, 325n10, 333, 340
 and Bible, 219–20, 227n66, 272, 283, 308, 313
 and church authority, 205, 216–17, 222–24
 and faith, 178, 180, 195n10, 196, 199, 215, 230–35
redemption, 327, 336, 339, 348, 358, 360–64, 367, 369, 371–72
Reformation, Protestant, 28n15, 37, 41, 139, 169, 171, 174, 180, 184, 186, 191, 196, 284
Reformed Church, 3, 171, 174, 176n27, 181n42, 188–89, 192–94, 315, 320n2, 347
regeneration, baptismal, 183–84, 266–67, 280n12, 13, 289n23, 297.
Reid, Thomas, 7, 8
Reinhard, Franz Volkmar, 351
religious liberty (freedom), 173, 176, 183, 265–67, 292–98
 and Oxford Movement, 292–98
Republicanism, 32–34, 319, 338, 340, 344
resurrection, 233, 327–28, 334, 338n34, 344, 358, 363, 375
revelation, supernatural, 23–25, 27n9, 54–55, 64, 77, 88, 93, 106, 108, 112–13, 130, 134, 146n16, 156–63, 175n24, 180, 191–92, 194–95, 209, 213, 215, 221, 224, 256, 259, 263n27, 318, 326–29, 362–64
 and Bible, 219, 313, 314n15, 353
 and Brownson, 215n33, 225, 231–34, 250–53, 263, 338, 351n3, 369–70
 and Bushnell, 349
 and church, 195, 218, 261
 and faith, 333–35
 and nature, 191, 227n30, 264, 325–26
revivalism, vii, 3, 7, 9–11, 16, 170–71, 174, 190, 193, 346–47, 350n2
revolutions of 1848, vii–viii, 19–30, 37, 48, 302, 318–19, 339, 340n33, 344

Robinson, Marilynne, 4–5
Rohr, Richard, 5
Roman Catholicism, 177, 202n9, 344n41
Romanism, 48, 95, 172, 174, 176–78, 181–82, 195–203, 206, 208, 211n22, 214–15, 220–21, 223, 227, 244, 248–49, 268, 315; *see also* Catholicism; Popery
 and America, 296, 299
 and Episcopacy, 271–72, 274, 284, 288, 293–99
 as facsimile of primitive Christianity, 212
 and private judgment, 260–61
 and Protestantism, 239, 303, 305
Ronge, Johannes, 198–99
Rothe, Richard, 368
Rousseau, Jean-Jacques, 308
Russell, Lord John, 288, 291

sacraments, 96, 143, 164, 173, 176, 182–84, 190, 193–94, 253n13, 281, 287–88, 300
 as divine acts, 203n11, 209n26, 299n26, 226n64, 267, 279, 398, 312
 and modern Puritanism, 270, 282, 375
Schaff, Philip, viii, 6n9, 9n20, 11–12, 13n38, 17n53, 19, 27n9, 89n11, 138n1, 143n10, 148, 182, 188, 194, 201n5, 202n9, 356n12
 Principle of Protestantism, 194, 201n5, 202n9
 What is Church History?, 11, 194, 198n3, 356n12, 367n37
Schelling, Friedric W. J., 9, 22n3, 76–77, 84n18, 130n15, 144
 and history as divine revelation, 6n9, 11, 27n9, 209n26
Schleiermacher, Friedrich D. E., 102, 105–6, 138–44, 175n21, 356–57
Scottish Common Sense Realism, 169n2, 175n24, 179, 195n10, 317; *see also* Baconian method *and* Common Sense Realism
Scripture, 13, 102n9, 169, 184, 233n75, 263n37, 283, 287, 341; *see also* Bible
Seabury, Samuel, 172
Sect System, 193; *see also* sectarianism
sectarianism, vii, 193, 312n9, 344n41
Seton, Elizabeth Ann, 298n38
Sin, 173, 189, 191–92, 229n69, 236, 256–57, 318, 328–29, 358, 360, 365–69; *see also* Original sin
 Manichean notion of, 348, 367
slavery, 222, 259, 275n6, 303n49, 308, 346
Smith, Joseph, 232, 303n49
Social Contract (Rousseau), 308–11
Socialism, 214, 224, 318–19, 343–44
Social principle, 15–16, 80n11
Spinoza, Baruch, 250, 255

INDEX

State, and church, 69–72, 145n14, 174, 240n92, 246, 260, 265, 270n3, 288–91, 292n28, 293, 295, 337, 354
Stewart, Dugald, 8
subject/object dynamic, 177, 180–81, 195–96
   and Brownson-Nevin debate, 198, 215, 218–19, 221–25, 230, 233–34, 245–47, 249–50, 255, 257–61
   and Bushnell, 364, 367
subjectivism, 181, 245–46, 249
Sumner, John Bird, 280n13, 289n23
supralapsarianism, 367n37
supernatural, 52, 93, 98n3, 161–63, 169, 189, 262–63, 330, 333–38, 340, 343–44; *see also* Church, as supernatural; nature, and the supernatural; supernaturalism
   as fact, 156, 158, 184, 266, 359–60
   destiny, vii, 316–18, 321
   redemption, 145n14, 148, 151n3
supernaturalism, ix, 12n34, 52, 93, 148, 156, 158, 161–63, 178, 179n36, 190n87, 192, 227, 237, 252–53, 259n22, 302, 350n2
   abstract, 178, 227n66, 234, 252–53; *see also* rationalism, supernatural
   in Brownson, 215–35, 245–46, 262
   in Bushnell, 189–96, 347–65, 369–76
   Catholic, 176n24, 177–80
   invisibility of, 220, 231, 263, 326, 335, 370
   in Newman, 212–14
   as organic fact, 17, 98n3, 151n3, 359–60
   as ultimate end, 145n14, 326–29
Swedenborg, Emmanuel, 303n49
Swedenborgianism, 303, 305

Taylor, Nathaniel William, 346, 348n11
Taylor, Zachary, 33n21
Technology, improvements in, 41–44, 338
Telegraph, *see* Technology, improvements in
testimony, and faith, 180, 215–16, 219, 227, 229n68, 232, 263–64, 285, 330, 325–27, 334
Testimony of the Rocks (Miller), 351
Texas, annexation of, 20, 31–32, 35n23, 49
Thiersch, Heinrich Wilhelm Josias, 185, 304, 306
Torrance, T. F., 4
Tractarianism, 171, 265, 269n2
Tracts for the Times (Keble), 265, 269n2
Transcendental idealism, 9n18, 77n6, 130n15, 131n18, 144n11
Transcendentalism, American, 170, 175, 202n9, 207, 214, 215n33, 346

transubstantiation, 194n5, 281
Trinity, the, 77n8, 170, 224, 303, 346
Truth, 7n12, 17, 30, 43, 47, 51, 55–56, 59, 62–64, 69–73, 79–88, 92–93, 100, 105, 113, 116, 125, 128, 130–37, 147, 154–60, 162–66, 178, 195, 206, 212–13, 215, 223–26, 228–29, 238, 250, 257–58, 314n15, 329–32, 336–37, 355–56, 358, 362n21, 363–64, 374
   in extremes, 177, 243, 245, 251–52
   and faith, 180, 218, 220, 227, 230–34, 262–64
   as organic and objective, 180n45, 221–22, 236, 246, 370–71, 259–60

Unitarianism, 170, 175, 177, 180, 194–95, 198–99, 214, 244, 270n3, 346
   and Romanism, 178, 180, 198
Universalism, 170, 175, 346

Vorlesungen über Katholicismus und Protestantismus (Thiersch), 304–6
visible/invisible Church, *see* Church, as invisible *and* Church, visibility of

Ward, William George, 269n2
Wars of the Reformation, 28n15
Wayland, Francis, 311, 316
Webster, Daniel, 319
Weekly Messenger, 190, 279n11
Whig (Party), 33, 49–50, 289
Wholeness, 4–5, 16, 21, 39, 101, 109, 129, 148, 176, 225, 259, 322n5
wisdom, as end of education, 273, 276, 316–19, 325–27, 329–35, 341, 343–44, 355
White, Andrew Dickson, 317
Whittingham, William Rollinson, 299
Will, the, 51, 59n8, 60–61, 65, 68–69, 101–2, 113, 134–37, 332
   and its relationships, 256–57, 259–60, 318, 329
will, absurd as private, 63, 259–60
Windsor Place, Pennsylvania, 121n6
Winebrenner, John, 11, 18, 65n20
Wiseman, Nicholas Patrick, 183n54, 201n6, 288, 290n24, 291
Wolff, George D., 172n9
Wright, Fanny, 175

Year, concept of, 158–59; *see also* Church, year
   Jewish year, 162–63
   Pagan year, 159–61

www.ingramcontent.com/pod-product-compliance
Lightning Source LLC
Chambersburg PA
CBHW081756300426
44116CB00014B/2133